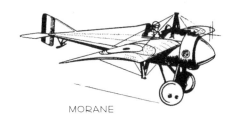

MORANE

NIEUPORT 'SCOUT'
WITH ROCKETS

FOKKER EINDECKER

FARMAN F-40

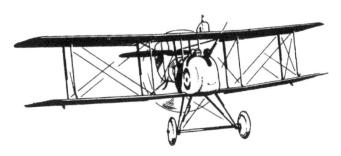

DE HAVILLAND DH2

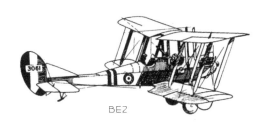

BE2

VICKERS GUN BUS

DE HAVILLAND DHI

LVG

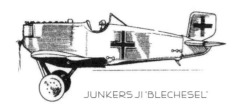

JUNKERS JI 'BLECHESEL'

ALBATROS DIII

HALBERSTADT

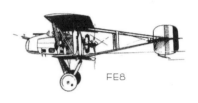

FE8

DE HAVILLAND DH3

ALBATROS C3

ALBATROS DI

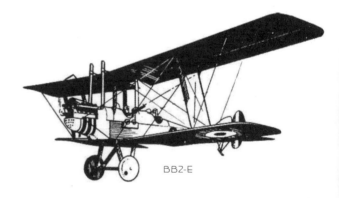

BB2-E

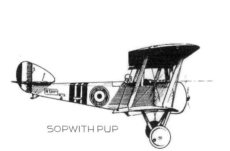

SOPWITH PUP

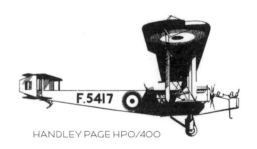

HANDLEY PAGE HPO/400

FEARLESS

For Sandra

FEARLESS

The extraordinary untold story of New Zealand's Great War airmen

ADAM CLAASEN

MASSEY UNIVERSITY PRESS

CONTENTS

INTRODUCTION
6

CHAPTER ONE
THE PIONEERS
1908–1912
12

CHAPTER TWO
FLYING FEVER
1912–1914
36

CHAPTER THREE
LUCKY DEVILS
1914–1915
54

CHAPTER FOUR
ABOVE THE FRAY
1915
74

CHAPTER FIVE
DUST AND DYSENTERY
1915
98

CHAPTER SIX
AIRMEN FOR THE EMPIRE
122

CHAPTER SEVEN
BASHED INTO SHAPE
150

CHAPTER EIGHT
DEATH FROM ABOVE
1916
174

CHAPTER NINE
FIRE IN THE SKY
1916
204

CHAPTER TEN
BLOODY APRIL
1917
232

CHAPTER ELEVEN
THE SUPREME SACRIFICE
1917
260

CHAPTER TWELVE
A BIGGER ENDEAVOUR
1917
286

CHAPTER FIFTEEN
SEA ASSAULT
1918
360

CHAPTER THIRTEEN
**THE 'GREATEST
SHOW EVER SEEN'**
1918
316

CHAPTER SIXTEEN
ONE HUNDRED DAYS
1918
386

CONCLUSION
414

CHAPTER FOURTEEN
SPRING OFFENSIVE
1918
334

ROLL OF HONOUR AND MAPS
428

NOTES
438

SELECT BIBLIOGRAPHY
480

ACKNOWLEDGEMENTS
484

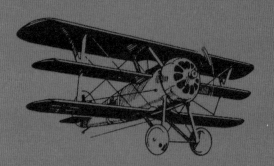

INDEX
488

INTRODUCTION

F earless: The extraordinary untold story of New Zealand's Great War airmen is part of the
First World War Centenary History series of publications, overseen by the Ministry for
Culture and Heritage. One of this project's chief allures is that there is no single book-
length study of New Zealand's contribution to the 1914–18 air war — no official history, no
academic monograph, not even a military aviation enthusiast's pamphlet.[1] Moreover, in the
100 years following the conflict, only one Great War airman, Alfred Kingsford, published his
memoirs.[2] This is incredible, especially when you consider the mountain of books spawned by
New Zealand's Second World War aviation experience.[3]

Only slightly offsetting this dearth of secondary literature are three biographies of
New Zealand airmen which contain chapters covering their Great War flying careers: G. H.
Cunningham tells the story of Malcolm McGregor, and historian Vincent Orange discusses
the wartime work of Keith Park and Arthur Coningham in their respective biographies.[4]
Complementing these are a small number of journal and magazine articles published on
individual airmen, and two university theses that analyse the contributions of Ronald
Bannerman and Leonard Isitt to New Zealand's military aviation history.[5] Elsewhere,
New Zealanders appear in the publications of non-antipodean airmen, but most are short,
incidental entries. Mercifully, a number of families have published collections of letters and
diaries of less well-known aviators.[6]

As I researched this book, a few reference publications were immensely helpful, and seldom
left my side. The first and third volumes of Errol Martyn's *For Your Tomorrow* trilogy were
indispensable.[7] Accurate and exhaustive, they are an invaluable source on New Zealanders
who have died serving in the Allied air services since 1915. For a wider examination of
casualties, Trevor Henshaw's *The Sky Their Battlefield II* is excellent — it chronologically lists
air casualties of British, Commonwealth and United States air services from 1912 to 1919 and,
along the way, offers the best description of the developing air war that you could want in a
single volume.[8]

With few secondary sources and published primary materials available, much of the
research for this book was archival. Some of the personal stories of the airmen were gleaned
from documents held in private collections, but most were gathered from the diaries, letters

and logbooks that are curated by New Zealand libraries and museum archives, including the Canterbury Museum, the Alexander Turnbull Library, the Museum of Transport and Technology and the Auckland War Memorial Museum. Naturally, the largest and most useful collection belongs to the Air Force Museum of New Zealand at Wigram, Christchurch. This is New Zealand's foremost repository for military aviation documents, ephemera and artefacts. In Wellington, Archives New Zealand holds a number of personnel files and other useful material spanning the establishment of the dominion air schools through to papers covering the problems associated with the large number of New Zealand soldiers wanting to transfer to the air service. The National Library of New Zealand's paperspast.natlib.govt.nz website was an invaluable resource for hunting down errant airmen and piecing together their stories. For the operational aspects of the New Zealanders' flying service, the British National Archives at Kew, London, furnished me with everything from personnel files and combat reports to squadron record books and 'inhouse' unit histories.

One of the first things to decide was who to include or exclude from the story. Early in the project I determined to err on the side of generosity rather than parsimony — better to be accused of the former than the latter. The majority of the individuals who populate these pages were either born in New Zealand, served in the New Zealand armed forces, or lived in New Zealand before the war.[9] This last category reflects the fact that New Zealand has always been a nation of immigrants; in 1914, when the war-to-end-all-wars broke out, this was demonstrably so. The last prewar census revealed a diverse population of just over one million, of whom nearly a quarter — 228,779 — were born elsewhere, including in Australia, Europe, Canada and the United States.[10] Many attended New Zealand schools or worked on local farms, in factories, or ran their own businesses in the years predating the Great War. Consequently, the 'New Zealanders' who appear in this book are nearly as varied as the makeup of its population at the commencement of the war.

Having defined a 'New Zealander' for the purposes of this work, it would be nice to say I have a definitive grip on how many this included. I do not — and nor do people who have explored this subject for decades. There were no published Defence Department figures because the New Zealanders who joined the Royal Flying Corps (RFC), the Royal Naval Air Service (RNAS), the Australian Flying Corps (AFC), the Woman's Royal Air Force (WRAF) and the Royal Air Force (RAF) were entering a 'foreign' service. The government did collect some information on New Zealanders who served in this manner but it was not comprehensive. Over the subsequent decades various researchers and writers have suggested the number may be as low as 500 or as high as 1000 individuals.[11] I have gone with the more recent assessments that put the number close to 850.[12] Of these, about a third entered operational units. Most served as pilots, observers or gunners, and a much smaller number of men — and a few women — occupied roles on terra firma as mechanics, fitters, riggers, despatch riders and clerks.

Fearless is not an 'official history'. Official histories are invaluable reference works but seldom hold the attention of even the most motivated reader. Instead, I have attempted to smooth out the narrative in several ways for the general reader. For example, I have kept military ranks to a minimum: since most of the men who populate these pages flew operationally as lieutenants, I have chosen to include an officer's rank only where it deviated from this. Organisational structures make only a brief appearance. In operational matters, this book concentrates on the work undertaken by New Zealanders at the level of the most ubiquitous independent unit in the air war, the squadron. With regard to the 'aces' — airmen with five or more combat claims — I have generally avoided breaking these down into subcategories, such as 'out of control', 'shared' or 'destroyed'. Nor have I felt the need to re-evaluate generally accepted totals for each airman. Readers are directed to *Above the Trenches* by Christopher Shores, Norman Franks and Russell Guest. Although slightly showing its age, it is still *the* starting point for discussion on the war's aces.[13]

I also took the liberty, in general, of not applying the term 'scout' to what modern audiences would call fighter aircraft. In the prewar period scout-type aircraft were lightweight single-seater machines deployed in scouting and reconnaissance operations. When the war commenced these were still unarmed. However, as the air over the Western Front filled with competing machines, scouts were increasingly fitted with armament to engage in air-to-air combat: first, revolvers or rifles and finally forward-firing machine guns. And thus the first single-seater 'fighter' aircraft was born. Nonetheless, the British air service continued to use the term 'scout' for this new class of aircraft, and regularly applied the term 'fighter' to two-seater fighting machines such as the Bristol F2B Fighter. To avoid confusion I have simply called these single-seater, air-to-air combat machines 'fighters'. Some former Great War airmen also adopted this practice years later when they published their memoirs.

One aspect of the air war I could not bend to my stylistic proclivities was the names of the aircraft. As an historian of the Second World War, I was accustomed, at least with regard to RAF aircraft, to the elegant simplicity of names such as Hurricane, Spitfire or Lancaster — but here I was confronted with the bewildering alphabet soup of letters and numbers attached to Great War machines such as the FE2b, DH4, SE5a and FK8. Even the great Sopwith Aviation Company, which gave us the delightfully zoologically themed Pup, Camel and Dolphin, had its own snaggle-toothed offspring, the 1½ Strutter. Who comes up with this stuff? Some machines gained affectionate nicknames, such as the Royal Aircraft Factory 'Harry Tate' RE8, but overall it was a miscellany of letters and model numbers on both sides of the trenches. Of course, the manufacturers did not have my twenty-first-century sensibilities in mind when they named their aircraft, and thanks to the rapid evolution of aircraft over the war, letters and numbers piled up. I'm sure readers will gradually acclimate themselves to this practice, as I had to.

Structurally, *Fearless* is a chronological tale. The book begins (chapters one and two) with an examination of the prewar years and the growing concerns about the place of air power in a future war and what New Zealand's contribution to this might be. At the same time it chronicles the exploits of a string of aviators who were to inspire young New Zealanders to head to the flying services once war broke out. In the war's early years, 1914–15, a small number of New Zealanders were involved in air operations in France, at Gallipoli, and in the Middle East. In chapters three, four and five we follow their exploits, and we see how the fighting on the ground, particularly at Gallipoli, turned the hearts of many young men to the air service. This is followed by a discussion of flight training at New Zealand's two indigenous schools (chapter six) and subsequent military aviation instruction in Britain (chapter seven). The remainder of the book (chapters eight to 16) details the New Zealanders' amazing exploits over the period from 1916 to 1918. Their experiences were often extraordinary — but also, all too frequently, terminally short. This is their story.

Twenty-one-year-old Harold Beamish was typical of the adventure-loving young New Zealanders who yearned to be airmen in the Great War. The son of a Hawke's Bay farmer, he was a pupil at Wanganui Collegiate when war was declared and three years later was flying the celebrated Sopwith Camel over the Western Front, with 3 (Naval) Squadron.

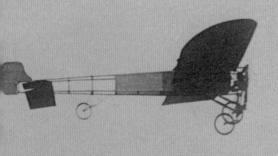

CHAPTER ONE
THE PIONEERS
1908–1912

Miracles were a rare commodity over the Great War's Western Front, and every airman needed at least one. In the late summer of 1918, with only weeks of fighting left in the war, squadron commander Major Keith Caldwell got his miracle. He was flying with a wingman — a Yorkshireman — over territory scarred and cratered by four years of uninterrupted fighting, when he spotted a German aircraft.

Caldwell opened the throttle and the engine growled. He and his biplane were well matched: the New Zealander was a tall and athletic pilot, the product of extensive training and blessed with fighting skills honed over months of vicious dogfights. His weapon, the Royal Aircraft Factory SE5a — the latest-generation fighter — was menacing with its over-long snout, snarling exhausts stretching past the open cockpit, and twin machine guns: it had all the elegance and brutality of a large African cat, an apex predator.

Caldwell and his offsider stalked their prey across the open blue savannah, manoeuvred within striking distance, hunched, then pounced, a final leap to secure their prize. Then it happened: the two Allied airmen collided. In concentrating on their quarry they had converged; the Englishman's undercarriage ploughed into Caldwell's upper left wing at 8000 ft. Like lions competing over their prey, the V8 engines roared at each other, ripping fabric skin and breaking timber bones.

The Yorkshireman came through relatively unscathed, but Caldwell's wing bent and buckled. He wrestled with his quivering, staggering SE5a deep over enemy-occupied territory; his fighter descended rapidly and then entered a flat spin. Death was only moments away. As one squadron member observed, 'Most men — indeed the huge majority — would have become unnerved and paralysed with fear, and resigned themselves to their fate. Not so this tough son of Auckland.' Self-preservation stepped in. Caldwell would not die without a fight. He stood and placed his left foot on the right rudder, leaning as far out as he could. He gained a tenuous equilibrium, his long leather flying coat whipping and cracking against him in the strong wind. Another subordinate had seen his commanding officer's SE5a fall and followed him down; the airman gasped as Caldwell momentarily let go of the joystick and waved to him. The spectator assumed it was a farewell gesture and turned away from the sickening sight of the New Zealander's death plunge.

Caldwell had other ideas. He crossed no-man's land, heading for the Allied trenches.

Heads looked up as he careened over the British troops. It was an impossible sight: Was the pilot flying on the wing? The mud-brown earth beckoned — the grave of innumerable men. He waited for the last moment and, in the heartbeat between flying and crashing, leapt. He hit the ground, somersaulted a few times and, to the surprise of the horrified watching infantry, simply stood up — a bleeding lip and considerable bruising the extent of his injuries — shook off the dirt, and walked to the nearest trench in search of a telephone.

'Very lucky,' he wrote in his flying logbook.[1]

Keith Caldwell was an eight-year-old Auckland schoolboy when the Wright brothers achieved the world's first controlled and sustained powered flight on 17 December 1903. At the time the event barely registered with the world's newspapers, but within the space of six years flying had captured international imagination. Men and women were soon considering how powered flight might be utilised, not only in the delivery of letters, parcels and human passengers but also in matters of warfare. Politicians, generals and futurists wondered how this technological marvel might be applied to defence and war.

In New Zealand, military aviation's most vociferous early advocate was Christchurch businessman turned parliamentarian Henry Wigram. In 1908 Wigram spent a good six months in Britain, a country bewitched by the air craze sweeping the globe and the growing fear that in a future war the home cities of the Empire might be subjected to death from the skies. Newspaper stories of the Wright brothers' increasing haul of aviation records, photographs of the Farman brothers flying around the Eiffel Tower, and reports of Count Zeppelin's vast airships were the staple of European conversation.[1A] The British imagination was captured, too, by futurist H. G. Wells' serialised story of a surprise German assault by airships and large bombers on the American naval fleet and, terrifyingly, on New York City; airships moving down Broadway and clinically bombing and devastating the city. In the unfolding fictional war, London in turn suffered New York's fate.

The story, subsequently published in book form as *The War in the Air*, drew on German advances in airship construction and the rapid development of heavier-than-air machines as pioneered by the Wright brothers in the early 1900s. Why had the Americans and the British been caught so flat-footed by the German attacks

A giant Zeppelin airship glides over Munich in 1909. Widely published images such as these brought home the very real threat air power might pose to Britain.

in *The War in the Air*? The answer lay early in Wells' fictionalised drama, when the British government, failing to recognise the importance of air power, rejected an inventor's plans for an aircraft that would have protected their skies from the German menace. The story was a lesson for governments that dragged their feet in the face of the aerial threat.

Thanks to Wells, fear of destruction-bearing air machines led to numerous false sightings of German airships, not only at the heart of the British Empire but also, improbable as it may seem, in its far-flung South Pacific dominion of New Zealand, where Wells' book had been read by a receptive audience.[2] Some 40 'sightings' were covered in the New Zealand press.[3] While the phantom machines were accounted for by lights at night or fire balloons of various manufacture, many newspapers reasoned that the 'scare' was not altogether unwarranted. The *Waihi Daily Telegraph* reported on British concerns.

> Only a few weeks since a Zeppelin airship not only rode out a gale, but completed a journey of two hundred and fifty miles, and it is assumed that Germany will have an airship fleet capable of excelling this performance . . . It is time for Britain to awaken . . . The only defence against flying machines is to meet them with flying machines, and when other countries are building them Britain cannot afford to be left behind.[4]

'War in the Air' was the byline for the *Wairarapa Age*'s 1909 article on the dangers of air power, and the possibility of Germany not only bombing but also undertaking an aerial invasion of England: in a future Anglo-German war, the difficulties of getting German soldiers past an English Channel patrolled by the Royal Navy would be accomplished by 'aerial transports' conveying 'the German soldiery safe into the doomed country'.[5]

On his return to New Zealand, and in this climate of unease, Henry Wigram addressed the Legislative Council members on 11 June 1909. New Zealand's parliamentary upper house was sitting to discuss naval matters, but Wigram turned the debate towards the promise and threat of air power in a future war. Like most New Zealanders of British extraction, he colloquially referred to the centre of the Empire as 'Home'.

> A few words about the development that is taking place in aerial navigation. I hold that this is a matter that is coming into practical politics. It seems to me there are large possibilities for it in the defence of this Dominion in the near future, and I wish to raise the question as to whether we should consider it. We have always been in the forefront of progress, and I ask whether we should not now take up the matter of aerial navigation. There is an opportunity presented at the present time for the Premier to make inquiries at Home: he might cable Home about it, so that the information may be ready for him on his arrival there. The German nation has awakened to the importance of the subject. I was at Home last year, and the intense excitement created by Count Zeppelin and his machine is fresh in my memory. It was an excitement that passed over the whole of Europe . . . We here, living many thousands of miles from possible hostilities, are not likely to be attacked by airships for many years to come, but in the development that is taking place they might prove a useful defence to us

against hostile ships. The cost is trifling compared to armament — that is to say, big guns and cruisers . . . I should like to see that question taken up at the start, and that we should get expert advice and lead the way.[6]

But Wigram's speech and subsequent public pronouncements had little effect. The members of the Legislative Council made no continuing reference to his speech, and there is no indication that the prime minister raised Wigram's concerns with the imperial government in Britain on his subsequent visit.

One of aviation's biggest hurdles was overcoming recent developments in naval matters. New Zealand could not afford its own naval fleet, but in 1909 the government announced it would 'donate' a large battlecruiser, HMS *New Zealand*, to the Royal Navy as protector of the Empire's sealanes and first line of defence against foreign aggression. Expenditure was calculated at some £2 million over 18 years — to be funded by a loan to the New Zealand government. The idea was popular with the public. With so much committed to HMS *New Zealand* and the dominion's land forces, the Defence Department was naturally wary of any new and as yet untested venture into military aircraft. Still, aviation captured the imagination of the people — and of the military.

On 25 July 1909, within weeks of Wigram's speech, the French aviator and engineer Louis Blériot flew across the English Channel. It was a significant achievement and seemed to vindicate the fears of the aviation prophets. Blériot's Type XI monoplane, powered by a 25-hp three-cylinder engine, had a top speed of 45 mph. Lacking a compass, Blériot took his bearings from the French destroyer *Escopette,* which served as his escort. He arrived in Dover 38 minutes after departing Calais, making a heavy landing in the gusty conditions. The Frenchman collected a £1000 prize and a raft of orders for the machine from numerous countries. The flight made Blériot a prosperous businessman and celebrity.

The implications for military aviation were not lost on observers. The *Daily Express* in England ran the front-page headline: 'Britain is no longer an island'. The English Channel and the Royal Navy could no longer vouchsafe Britain's security: the moat and its vessels could now be leapt by aircraft. The possibilities it opened up were noted by interested parties in the antipodes, too. In October, Henry Wigram revisited the subject of aviation.

> Aerial navigation might be an immense factor in the event of war taking place. It would be perfectly possible for a fleet of these aerial machines to hover over the Thames and set fire to the docks and timber-yards, and pretty well destroy the shipping of the Thames. We are only on the eve of developments that may take place.[7]

In a future war, he argued, Britain might well not be able to render aid to its far-flung dominions in the event of an attack from 'the East'. In saying this Wigram may well have been drawing on the plot of *The War in the Air*, in which the German aggression against America was immediately followed by an aerial assault from Japan. This begged the question: Was New Zealand more vulnerable to attack from this quarter than generally believed? More

William Burn (fourth left, back row) was New Zealand military's earliest trained aviator. His Central Flying School No. 5 Course was full of future air luminaries, including Hugh Trenchard (far right, second row), who did much to shape the early RAF, and Hugh Dowding (fourth left, second row), who led Fighter Command in the Battle of Britain in 1940.

importantly, even if New Zealand did not come under threat from airships — something Wigram admitted was very unlikely — would not a small clutch of defensive machines provide valuable coastal protection against intruding naval vessels?

Not all ears were deaf to the pleas of Wigram and others, and in 1912 the New Zealand Army explored aviation's potential. Captain George Richardson of the New Zealand Staff Corps was despatched to Britain to undertake study at the Staff College at Camberley.[8] During his sojourn in Britain he investigated the place air power might occupy in future New Zealand military priorities.

> If an officer were sent from N.Z. to undergo special Engineer Training he should be given the opportunities for attachment to the Aeroplane Section of the Air Battalion, as I am of the opinion that N.Z. will not be able to afford the maintenance of Air-ships. They are expensive and necessitate huge buildings and workshops as well as a big staff, but Aeroplanes are cheap and do not require the special machinery for air compressors, or a big staff.[9]

Major General Alexander Godley, general officer commanding New Zealand military forces, considered Richardson's assessments.

> The question of aviation has been under the consideration of the General Staff, and preliminary arrangements have been made for the training of certain officers and non-commissioned officers in this important subject; but till next year, when the training is more advanced and our expenditure has become normal, I do not propose to make any definite recommendation or incur any expenditure in connection with the purchase of aeroplanes. We must learn to walk before we attempt to fly.[10]

In other words, fiscal constraints prohibited significant investment in military aviation.

Nevertheless, the army followed through with its plans to send personnel to Britain for training. In late 1913 William Burn was despatched to Upavon, England. A former Christchurch Boys' High School pupil, Burn was to 'receive a general training in aviation . . . and it was intended that he should superintend aviation in New Zealand upon his return'.[11] Aircraft manufacturing at the Royal Aircraft Factory, Farnborough, was Burn's first introduction to this newest of military sciences. He received flight lessons at Hendon, London, and in the New Year he was instructed in a dual-control biplane. At this point he entered what would become the longest-running flying school in history, and the birthplace of many of the great leaders in military aviation: the Central Flying School (CFS), Upavon.

The school was situated on the edge of the Salisbury Plain, with a forest backdrop. The students lived in small wooden huts. Doubtless Burn found the student life agreeable. As his colleague Christopher Draper noted, the food 'in the Officer's Mess was a revelation. Never had I seen such variety or so many rows of hot dishes. We changed into Mess Dress every night except Sunday.'[12] (Draper was later dubbed the 'Mad Major' for his daredevil exploits, notably his penchant for flying under bridges including the Tay rail bridge, Dundee.) Apart from Draper, the student body and instructors included 'five future air marshals of the RAF', among whom were the 'two Hughs': Trenchard and Dowding;[13] the former was instrumental in the establishment of the modern RAF, and the latter was famous for his role in the Battle of Britain. Burn was in good company.

By 24 February 1914 Burn had completed the final requirements for his aviator's certificate, and after nine weeks' instruction he received his pilot's flying badge or 'wings' on completion of the CFS course. Two months later he was headed home to New Zealand, and in all likelihood excited by the opportunity to fly a recently acquired aeronautical gift from Britain.

In February 1913 Britain had offered New Zealand a monoplane. To improve imperial defence, the Imperial Air Fleet Committee — a collection of British businessmen — advocated the establishment of air corps across the Empire's dominions; in this way the advances made by menacing 'foreign powers', Germany and Japan, would be lessened. In all likelihood the presence of former New Zealand Prime Minister Joseph Ward at the Imperial Air Fleet Committee meeting had given New Zealand a 'leg up' on other dominions in receiving a plane.

Minister of Defence James Allen cautiously acknowledged the generosity of the offer but noted that 'until we have men trained to use these machines it would not be of very much service to us'. However, Prime Minister William Massey liked the idea, and the offer was 'gratefully' accepted. The machine was a Blériot monoplane — a military incarnation of the one that had conquered the English Channel, and greatly improved over its 1909 predecessor: it sported a more powerful engine that could pull the unarmed two-seater reconnaissance machine to a top speed of 70 mph in 'calm air'. With over five hours' flying time when fully fuelled and an operational altitude of over 7000 ft, the Blériot was a first-class modern aeroplane in 1913.

Presentation of the machine, officially christened *Britannia*, took place on 22 May at Hendon airfield. Joseph Ward was on hand to receive it. He had never been up in an aircraft, but he was a pushover for new technological advances and took great delight in being the first New Zealander to clamber aboard the Blériot. Newspapermen reported that Ward 'divested himself of silk hat and frock coat, donned a sporting coat and goggles, and went up in the charge of Gustav Hamel', one of the world's leading pilots.

> From the moment the machine started it was impossible to hear oneself speak, especially when going against the breeze, as Britannia did. He was told to keep his cap over the ears,

but it would not go over the ears, and this intensified the sound of the wind, so that no other sound could be heard above the propeller. When the machine righted herself after banking steeply round one of the pylons, Hamel looked round and roared: 'That's all right,' and Sir Joseph replied 'Yes' in his loudest key. The tilt round the corner was a sensational experience, and Sir Joseph for some moments could see the earth straight beneath him.

Caught between joy and white-knuckled terror, Ward hung on for dear life in the steep turn. After several minutes at 700 ft, Hamel gracefully landed *Britannia*. Ward's face was 'wreathed in smiles' as he alighted.[14]

The politicians were happy but the military was still fretting over the implications. It was not that they failed to appreciate aviation's potential; rather, they were all too aware of how the costs of such endeavours could spiral out of control. The machine and any likely supplementary aircraft would require qualified mechanics, riggers, fitters, carpenters and sailmakers for inevitable repairs. The demands of fuel, spare parts and constant maintenance made this aircraft a costly gift. Moreover, who would fly *Britannia*? New Zealand was hardly awash with airmen capable of flying the Blériot. In August, while *Britannia* was on the high seas heading for the Empire's southernmost dominion, a miffed Colonel Alfred Robin, New Zealand's representative on the Imperial Staff, reiterated the now common caution.

> I have in no way been consulted re this machine. In my reports [from London] on aviation I advised holding off purchase of machines, and that the Naval or waterplane would be most suited for New Zealand. Of course we cannot well criticise the gift, but you know monoplanes are not favoured by the War Office. They favour the Biplane as more stable if somewhat slower . . . Had I been consulted in the matter I would have advised that the machine remain here during the time our New Zealand officer was being trained [and] on his return to New Zealand to take it out with him.[15]

Robin had touched on a key impediment to getting the best out of *Britannia*: the 80-hp engine was simply too powerful for training new pilots. The Blériot would need a skilled airman, and at present Burn was still months away from tackling *Britannia*. Into this gap arrived Joseph 'Joe' Hammond, New Zealand's greatest prewar pilot.

Hammond's mild manner belied the irrepressible thirst for adventure that characterised many early aviation aspirants. Born in Feilding, he left home for Australia in 1904 at the age of 18. There he worked briefly on a sheep station, before making his way — with a stopover in Hawai'i — to the gold mines of the Klondike in Canada. Like many fortune-seekers, Hammond found the hastily built Dawson City plagued with fires, high prices and epidemics; the unsanitary conditions assaulted eyes and nose. He had also arrived too late: the mines had reached their peak the year before and general small-scale prospecting was giving way to heavy machinery. He briefly took up animal trapping in Alaska, then for much of the following year he worked on a cattle ranch in Phoenix, Arizona. After an interregnum in New Zealand he returned to the United States in 1908, where he fell in with 'Buffalo Bill' Cody's Wild West show.[16]

Immensely popular at the turn of the century, 'Buffalo Bill' Cody's circus was a fertile playground for Hammond's thrill-seeking. The widely imitated show encapsulated the idealised and romanticised Old West frontier. Performers like Hammond were costumed as fur-skinned trappers, feathered Indians, uniformed rough riders and buckskinned cowboys. Shooting competitions and displays of marksmanship, often from horseback, were staples of the show, but the highlight was the 'historical' scenes, notably the defence of isolated settler cabins and wagon trains and, of course, re-enactments of 'Custer's Last Stand' at the Battle of the Little Bighorn. The Hammond family's Rangitikei farm and their ownership of the Bulls raceway, plus recent ranching work in the United States, had furnished Hammond with obligatory horsemanship for the circus. His old school, St Patrick's in Wellington, later recalled the qualities that Hammond brought to Buffalo Bill's show:

> [H]e never knew what fear was. He had a passionate love for any vocation that held the promise of excitement and danger. It was no uncommon thing for him, when on his vacations, to spring suddenly on to the back of an 'outlaw' and set it at a gate or fence. . . . 'Dare devil Joe' was the name he was known by the School, and his reputation has remained . . . with us for nigh on twenty years . . . his wonderful horsemanship brought him swift renown.[17]

After six months with the circus Hammond departed for Europe, where his passion for flight was ignited by the accomplishments of aviation pioneers. He undertook the study of famous French airmen and by September 1910 was receiving formal instruction at the Sanchez-Besa school in Mourmelon. He was a natural. On 4 October he secured his aviator's certificate (no. 258) from the Aéro-Club de France. Hammond was 'the first Colonial to pass the authorities as a full-fledged aviator', recorded a British newpaper, 'and holds the record for speed in passing the brevet. He has already been inundated with offers of engagement from all parts of the world, some of which he has accepted.'[18] Six weeks later he had his Royal Aero Club certificate (no. 32). As one historian noted, Hammond achieved 'in the space of a few weeks' what had eluded many enthusiasts in New Zealand: he was a 'successful (and qualified) aeroplane pilot'.[19]

Of the 'offers of engagement', Hammond accepted a position with the first British firm to manufacture aircraft on a large scale: the Bristol and Colonial Aeroplane Company, established in February 1910. Its machine was the Bristol Boxkite, a biplane with a 'pusher' engine nestled behind the pilot, who sat open to the elements. A number of early airacraft, including the *Wright Flyer* of 1903, were pushers but others, such as the various Blériot designs, utilised the 'tractor' configuration, with the propeller in front of the engine 'pulling' the machine through the air. The Boxkite's wings and tail were, as its name suggested, similar in shape to a box kite, with a fabric skin thin enough for the sun to reveal the timber skeleton. Bracing the Boxkite was a spider's web of rigging and control wires. The 50-hp French Gnome engine gave the Bristol a

Joe Hammond and
his wife Ethelwyn
with Bristol Boxkites
in England in 1910.
Ethelwyn was a
keen aviatrice and
accompanied Hammond
on a number of flights
in Australia.

top speed in the vicinity of 40 mph. The flimsiness of the prewar machine was evident in the manufacturer's instructions that it could only be flown safely in steady winds not exceeding 30 mph, or gusting winds from 10 to 15 mph.

Hammond would prove more durable than the Bristols, but in many ways he resembled the Boxkite in physical build and temperament. Blue-eyed and fair-haired, he was tall and of spare build, with sharp features. Over his eight years as an aviator he displayed considerable skill and bravery, and he played an important part in the development of military aviation in the Empire — as did the Boxkite itself; it became the mainstay of instruction aircraft in prewar Britain.

With flying certificates in hand, Hammond became one of the company's salesmen and demonstrator pilots. In late 1910 two Bristol company mechanics and a manager embarked for Australia with Hammond, his new bride Ethelwyn and two crated Boxkites. Hammond was about to change Australia's aviation landscape.

Bristol was keen to attract orders for the plane, and on 13 December 1910, the Bristol team disembarked at Fremantle, Western Australia, where they used Perth's Belmont Park racecourse as a base of operations. The Boxkites were assembled ready for flight in the New Year. Australia, like New Zealand, had its share of aviation enthusiasts who had had a modicum of success in heavier-than-air flight, but it was Hammond's Boxkite demonstrations that had the greatest impact on the military authorities.[20] Resplendent in goggles, head gear and garments to protect him from the cold, the New Zealander's initial flight was widely covered in daily print and was of a duration and height yet unseen in Australia. In the early evening of 3 January,

> the machine rising in a distance of about 50 yards, sped through the air with perfect freedom, and with a grace of movement that delighted a small crowd of onlookers who had gathered on the course. The pilot (Mr. Hammond) rose the machine steadily for several hundred feet, and, soaring higher in large spiral movements, he flew the biplane over the [Swan] river and above the recreation ground, at a height of about 1,400 ft. . . . Immediately after ascending, the wind increased in velocity, and the swaying of the machine indicated that Mr. Hammond was having a somewhat difficult passage. After circling, however, for some time, and driving down the wind at a rate estimated at not less than 60 miles an hour, the pilot descended safely and with the greatest of freedom.[21]

This was just the first of many flights the Bristol and Colonial Aeroplane Company hoped would demonstrate the uses of the aeroplane 'for military and commercial purposes'.

After Perth the Bristol team decamped to Melbourne, where Hammond was a sensation. Early on the morning of 2 March, when he flew over Australia's second city, hundreds of thousands of Victorians were about to see an aeroplane for the first time. The New Zealander flew east along the foreshore from Port Melbourne towards Albert Park. Crowds of bathers lifted their heads at the buzzing Gnome engine. They cheered as Hammond turned towards Government House. Australian troopers at the Victoria Barracks let out a rousing cheer as the Boxkite cast its shadow over crowds along St Kilda Road. Tipping his wing, Hammond circled Government House before heading deeper into the city. The flying conditions were almost flawless, and the higher he ascended, to about 5000 ft, the 'stiller' the atmosphere was.

The flyover prompted amusing incidents. Some pyjama-clad workers had almost fallen out of bed at the sound of the propeller; they thought it was the siren for work and that they had somehow overslept. At the Treasury, a sentry observed the mysterious air machine and called out the entire guard. His commanding officer was incredulous. 'Well,' replied the sentry with an injured expression, 'Our orders are to call out the guard if there is a fire or anything unusual, and that aeroplane was unusual enough for me.'

A good number of Melburnians agreed. A little over a week later, at Altona Bay, west of the city, the site of the next Bristol exhibition, a reporter captured the feelings of many who saw Hammond fly in 1911.

> We have all seen the photographs and read the accounts of the deeds of aviators. We know that men fly, but somehow the sight itself gives us a shock of surprise. The great screw revolves in a roar and eddy of furious air-currents, the complicated structure of planes, and wire and wood rolls along the ground for 50 yards; the angle of the planes shifts, and the miracle is accomplished. Almost imperceptibly the earth is abandoned, and the machine moves steadily up an ascending angle into the freedom of the air. There does not seem any reason why it should do so — that is one of the strangest impressions of the performance. There is no appearance of passionate energy, of speed. We know there is 40 or 50 horse power behind the whirl of the screw, and that the machine is flying at a rate of about 30 miles an hour. Yet that does not seem enough. It is an illusion — we cannot believe it afterwards. We expect it to show that it flies, to flap its wings. But it soars above us, the aviator waving his hand, turns and wheels against the white fire of the east, offers towards Sunshine, changes its mind and sweeps back again into the north-west. Its serenity and lack of inherent movement and flexibility do not seem right under the circumstances. Here is a marvel brought about with no fuss beyond the clacking of the screw and the smell of petrol! . . . Not one of the crowd who saw this first public flight but felt the early rising, the tiresome journey, and the expense of 7/6 was well repaid. The sensation of wonder was to be gained in no other way, by reading or by photograph. And a miracle is cheap at that price.[22]

The crowds had been delivered to Altona by special trains laid on for the occasion and were treated to extraordinary feats. Hammond had the Boxkite jumping over fences and appearing to run along a wall. Most thrilling for the crowd were the 'jumps' he made directly over them: 'Coming close to the ground, almost within touch, he charged at the crowd at full speed till within 20 or 30 yards, and then suddenly ascended and came down on the other side. This daring feat was repeated several times, the people falling back like a mob of frightened sheep before a gigantic bird of prey.'[23]

In early April the Bristol team arrived in Sydney, where a temporary hangar was built at Botany Bay and the Boxkite was reassembled. The Ascot Racecourse proved once again the usefulness of racecourses to aviation in a largely pre-airfield era. Duplicating the Melbourne endeavours, there were aerial displays and flights for fee-paying passengers, and Sydney's eastern and northern suburbs were treated to Hammond's skills. Cheering multitudes crowded streets and rooftops to catch a glimpse of the aviator. Over Sydney Harbour, Hammond and his onboard mechanic turned towards the Royal Navy cruiser HMS *Powerful* — which lay at anchor — for a military demonstration. Hammond throttled back the Boxkite and they 'bombed' the vessel with paper balls. The ship sustained no damage and no casualties were reported, but it did highlight the possible 'effectiveness that bomb-dropping could have in a time of war'.[24] It also highlighted the very real business the Bristol Company was hoping to do with the Australian government.

The Bristol sales team were keen to get their Boxkites in front of the defence authorities and had already made a considerable impression on defence minister George Pearce, whose military representatives had attended Hammond's flights in January and February.[25] The most important military demonstration took place in the last weeks of Bristol's sales mission to Australia. On 3 May, Hammond headed west from Botany Bay for Liverpool and a light-cavalry training camp, 20 miles away. Tucked in behind him was the *Sun* newspaper's military reporter, a retired naval captain.[26] The early morning flight drew sleepy-eyed, nightgown-clad New South Wales citizens out from their homes. At Liverpool Hammond's exploits were watched by excited onlookers — cavalrymen, schoolchildren and the Governor-General Lord Dudley; all raucously 'cheered and cheered the plucky aviator again and again'.[27] The New Zealander's most important task, though, was impressing two officers: Major General Joseph Gordon and Lieutenant Colonel John Antill. After breakfast he took the crewcut, square-jawed Antill up for a 15-minute demonstration. As a cavalryman and Boer War veteran who had often been ordered to reconnoitre enemy positions, Antill immediately appreciated the advantage an aircraft-equipped army would have in battle. At 600 ft he picked out various features 'for miles around', including some detached squadrons of the brigade.

> I had doubts about the stability of these machines until Mr. Hammond afforded me the coveted opportunity of trying for myself what a biplane was like . . . From the military point of view I felt that I was able to obtain in a few minutes from my position in the air information that a thousand light horse could not have gathered in such country as we have travelled over in days of complicated operations . . . If we had had aeroplanes with us in South Africa thousands of lives would have been saved during reconnaissance operations.[28]

The flight persuaded Antill that 'aviation is going to be the biggest factor in military operations'.[29] 'I doubt very much,' Gordon concurred, 'whether the science of flying has ever been demonstrated in a more telling and at the same time delightfully thrilling manner . . . all in the camp are now more fully convinced of the part that aviation must necessarily play in the near future as a factor in war.' Hammond nailed this home 24 hours later in a forthright interview with the *Sun*. He laid out the steps Australia should take to avoid catching the aviation wave too late: select a chief instructor, gather a cohort of young officers, build hangars, and acquire half a dozen training machines and a 'good dozen aeroplanes' for operations.[30]

Joe Hammond over Geelong, Victoria, in early 1911. In more than 65 flights the New Zealander introduced practical aviation to Australia, and became a local celebrity.

Joe Hammond and Lieutenant-Colonel John Antill prepare for a reconnaissance flight over a military training camp at Liverpool, New South Wales.

Naturally he hoped Canberra would select the Boxkite as its training machine of choice. Unfortunately the Australian authorities, like their New Zealand counterparts, were reluctant to commit themselves to aviation.

It would be another three years before military aviation was firmly planted in Australian soil, but Hammond had prepared the ground. His efforts in Australia, where he had become a national celebrity, generated a lasting legacy. As one paper glowingly wrote, 'Mr Hammond was an object of worship . . . Men and women ran to clasp his hand, to be seen speaking to him, to implore him to take them up on a trip to the stars. Tiny children were held up in the air that they might join the hero worship.'[31] In all likelihood he was Australia's best-known New Zealander. Across five months he flew over 65 flights. These included a number of 'firsts' for the Australian dominion: the first cross-country flight; the first passenger flights; the first female passenger flight; the first fare-paying passenger flight; the first two-person passenger flight; and the first 'military' flight.[32] When Canberra eventually committed to military aviation, the inaugural flight in March 1914 left from an airfield only a few miles south of Hammond's 1911 Altona base in Sydney; it was made by a Bristol Boxkite popularised by Hammond and flown by men who were inspired by Hammond's dazzling exploits to become airmen.

Over the next two and a half years Hammond devoted the greater part of his time to being the chief instructor at the Eastbourne Flying School in Sussex, England. As well as instruction, he gave public exhibitions and fare-paying passenger flights. The school's aircraft included at least one Boxkite and a few of the popular Blériots. The gift of *Britannia* to his homeland was covered extensively in the British press, and Hammond — now a probationary second lieutenant in the Special Reserve of Officers of the Royal Flying Corps — offered his services to the New Zealand government for the 'tuition of pilots'.[33] Perhaps in expectation of an appointment, the accomplished flyer embarked for his native land.

Surely this would be the boost New Zealand aviation desperately needed. The Wellington *Evening Post* certainly thought so. It was apparent that aviation was 'just beginning to stir again after a period of stagnation' and that 'the little flying that has been done here has been the performance of self-taught aviators, who are going through gingerly and tentatively what America and the Old World saw six or seven years ago'.[34] The editorial's harsh evaluation of local aviation enthusiasts' efforts was not far off the mark. Homemade powered 'flight' had achieved short hops but nothing resembling the 'sustained flying' that included controlled takeoffs and landings, turns and cross-country expeditions.

B y at least one reliable estimate New Zealand's prewar, ragtag amateur aviation community had produced some 30 gliders or air machines and generated more than 70 aeronautical patents.[35] Nevertheless, by the time *Britannia* and Hammond arrived in late 1913, New Zealand aviation had not moved very far from the first attempt at powered flight by Richard Pearse, when he bunny-hopped an uncontrollable homemade machine at Waitohi in late 1909.[36] As encouraging as Pearse's efforts were, they paled in comparison to what was being achieved elsewhere in that same year. In 1909, just six years after the Wright brothers' *Flyer* made its first successful flight near Kitty Hawk, North Carolina, overseas aviators were flying over 100 miles at a time in flights that could exceed three hours.[37] And, of course, Blériot had flown the Channel. The only real advances in New Zealand were made with imported plans, materials, engines and entire machines.

With engineering backgrounds and a backing syndicate of businessmen, two Auckland brothers, Leo and Vivian Walsh, set about procuring the components to build a flying machine. In 1910 they imported the materials and engine for a British Howard Wright biplane: a crate full of rough lengths of Honduras mahogany for the fuselage and wings, ash for the skids, coils of wire for the rigging, and rolls of linen fabric. The only ready-to-install components were the engine and propeller. The £750 rough 'kitset' was unpacked and construction commenced in August in Remuera. Nearly all the components were fashioned by hand.

Shortly after Christmas the completed machine was dismantled and moved to a large marquee at Glenora Park, Papakura. Here the Walsh sisters, Veronica and Doreen, were co-opted into machining 500 yards of fabric for the biplane's 'skin'.[38] To shrink the fabric to the wood skeleton and smooth the surface, sago was boiled to the consistency of a paste and applied with hot brushes. The aircraft emerged, a 'giant grasshopper with the sun glistening on its wings'.[39] To the casual observer the 60-hp biplane shared much of the Boxkite's characteristics, and as such it was only suitable for placid weather conditions and vulnerable to breakage. Nonetheless, the brothers had an aeroplane and an adjacent racecourse for testing. But they were missing a pilot. The elder brother, Leo, was a good manager and planner, but felt he lacked the necessary reaction speed for the task, which fell to Vivian. At 23 years of age, Vivian began his self-taught lessons in their newly completed machine, which the visiting Prime Minister Joseph Ward had christened *Manurewa*, 'soaring bird'.

The early testing of *Manurewa* and the 'training' of Vivian Walsh involved little more than taxiing up and down the field as the pilot felt his way into the task. 'Vivian knew,' recalled his brother, 'that in learning to fly he would have to register each experience and learn from it. There were no printed instructions; no instructors to whom to turn. You felt your way, alone . . . at 60 mph.'[40] Urged on by his siblings and friends, Walsh opened the throttle a little

Leo (at rear) and Vivian Walsh, in *Manurewa*, with their financial backers Alfred Powley (centre) and brothers Charles (left) and Alfred Lester.

Vivian Walsh opens the throttle as the straining *Manurewa* is held back at Glenora Park, Papakura. 'Soaring Bird' was the first aircraft to undertake sustained flight in New Zealand.

and spectators lying on their stomachs were able to gauge the strength of the wheels and undercarriage as the aeroplane made short leaps past them.

The early jumps were not without their perils. In January, on a test run, the biplane's skid caught a mound of earth and tripped up the machine. Walsh and *Manurewa* somersaulted. Vivian crawled out of the wreck with only a minor knee injury, but the aircraft was ruined. 'The engine bolts had all been broken by the impact and the engine had been held above the pilot's head only by a stray wire that had become twisted round the propeller.'[41] The damaged machine was left unattended overnight and calves grazed on the sago-rich fabric. The machine was duly repaired, and on 9 February 1911 Vivian guided *Manurewa* to 20 ft and flew close to 400 yards before gently landing.[42] It was the first sustained, if brief, flight in New Zealand history.

Aside from a notable repetition of the flight over a month later, when *Manurewa* ascended to the unheard-of height of 60 ft, the biplane was bedevilled with minor mishaps. A 22 March exhibition jaunt for the mayor, city councillors and schoolchildren of Papakura ended badly after Vivian took the aeroplane up for a preliminary early-morning run. The engine was turned over and the 'two-bladed propeller was sent revolving at such a speed that left only a blur to be seen,' wrote a reporter from the *New Zealand Herald*. The 'huge flying bird was then started rolling up and down the field, giving the pilot time to get accustomed to his work'. However, at 40 ft the machine was hit by a pocket of wind that lifted the front and lowered the rear: *Manurewa* was almost vertical. It fell to the ground. The damage was not terminal but there would be no exhibition.

In the following months the businessmen investors in the syndicate grew restive about the poor return on their investment. Many hundreds of pounds had been sunk into the venture, but Walsh was yet to attempt turning the aircraft in flight, let alone fly it over Auckland city. The unhappy syndicate members used their majority to wrest *Manurewa* away from Leo and Vivian, thereby temporarily ending their flying aspirations. Aucklanders would have to wait well over a year for a sustained flight that was even close to that being achieved elsewhere in the world.

No 1551.M.

WIZARD

AUG:

CHAPTER TWO
FLYING FEVER
1912–1914

NE'S FLIGHT.

DOMAIN.

PROTD. WAP. 19.4.13.

With the temporary halt to the Walsh brothers' efforts, it was an American who brought the wonders of aviation to a wider New Zealand audience. On 23 April 1913 Arthur 'Wizard' Stone, a motorcycle wall-of-death rider and aviation pilot, made the first practical flights in the nation's history. Mirroring Hammond's earlier achievements in Australia, albeit on a much smaller scale, Stone's flights in his imported Blériot exceeded the duration, altitude and speed of anything previously undertaken in the southernmost dominion. Stone's success was all the more remarkable given that his first 'flight' nearly ended with the destruction of the machine by a mob of disgruntled Aucklanders.

Four days earlier, on 19 April, the Blériot had been wheeled out of its tent on the Auckland Domain. Stone's exhibition had been widely advertised and the local population was eager to watch 'Wizard' take the monoplane through its paces in an inconceivable 20 to 30-minute flight. This was well beyond the short hops other aeronauts had attempted, and nearly a third of the Queen City's 100,000 inhabitants turned out to watch. About 11,000 filed through the turnstiles, surrendering a shilling for the privilege. They overflowed the cricket stand and temporary seating. The greater part of the crowd, unwilling to pay and realising they could get almost as good a view from outside the ground, clambered onto every vantage point of the Domain's perimeter. Throngs also assembled on Mount Hobson and Mount Eden. The demonstration was delayed by nearly an hour because massed Aucklanders had encircled the tent and occupied the 'runway', but the attendees were good-natured and obedient as two mounted police corralled them clear. With the engine running, the huge, dragonfly-like aeroplane,

> began to move along the short crisp grass that curves in a dead level from near the drive towards the grandstand and beyond . . . As the machine moved, there was a moment's tense pause, as waiting thousands thrilled with expectancy. Then the hush of breathless suspense was broken by a cheer — the great white machine skimmed lightly over the broad expanse of green, with pinions outstretched for flight, and lifted gracefully into the air without a quiver. It was a great sight, and Auckland eagerly strained its eyes to follow the aerial flight.[1]

Within seconds, the *New Zealand Herald* reporter realised that the mechanical insect was in trouble. The clapping and cheering gave way to frowns and perplexity. The audience beheld the tilting monoplane dipping drunkenly, wings wobbling; it swayed off course, swinging around to Parnell instead of bearing towards Newmarket.

At the controls, Stone cursed his luck. A little more breeze and he would have cleared the crowd. The 50-hp engine seemed out of sorts.[2] He circled around to lift above the trees and his audience. Unexpectedly a sudden gust of wind, a great heavenly hand, pushed the light frame earthwards and Stone touched the Blériot down with a gentle bump on the slope of a hill outside the grounds. Landing the Blériot was a precaution, but as the American prepared to make a second attempt at flight he was overtaken by events.

The mood of the crowd had quickly turned nasty. They had paid to see New Zealand's first aerial demonstration, promoted as lasting up to 30 minutes. What they had witnessed was a 35-second jump of no more than 400 yards. Indignant, the crowd stampeded onto the ground. They could not reach the defenceless aeroplane and pilot before the non-fee paying Aucklanders. These were colourfully described as 'deadheads' by a journalist.[3] Stone later referred to the local stirrers as 'punks'.[4] Like a swarm of agitated bees they quickly overran the stranded aircraft and its pilot. Stone could do little but watch as the jostling mob pressed against him and his treasured machine. 'They surged around me in hundreds,' he lamented, 'trampled on the machine's tail, doing such damage as to render further flight impossible.' Stone and the Blériot were lost from view until they were rescued by mounted police. The sight was pitiful. 'Like a big wounded bird fluttering down the slope, with the crowd behind supporting its drooping tail it was lifted bodily over the boundary fence, back across the cricket ground, and finally disappeared into its improvised hangar.'

The damaged monoplane and its rider were not entirely free from further assault. As the *Herald* reported, 'there are flights that are flights and flights that are flutters, and Saturday's ascent . . . was distinctly of the latter order'. The formerly amiable and compliant crowd was now a mob of malcontents. Stone had made no attempt to placate the aviation-illiterate gathering with an explanation, and a large and distinctly hostile mob surrounded the tent, hooting and yelling, 'Give us back our money!' and 'Go up again!' The mounted police countered a rush on the tent. A horse became entangled in the tent ropes and came down in the thick of the crowd; mercifully no one was injured and the well-trained animal remained docile until cut free.

Inside the tent, separated from the crush by the all-too-thin canvas, Stone's mechanic feared a sound beating at the hands of the baying rabble. Nervously he set about dismantling the Blériot. Stone appeared remarkably at ease and unconcerned, the calm eye of the hurricane.

The felling of the horse further fanned the crowd and they closed in on their prey. The reporter wrote that 'for a few moments things looked serious'. A police sergeant entered the tent, pleading with the fugitives that unless they gave a satisfactory account to the enraged assembly his officers would not be able to hold them back much longer. Outside, an unidentified but clear-headed peacemaker encouraged a rumour that Stone would in all likelihood make another attempt that day. This placated the most agitated; voices were lowered and the tent siege was slowly lifted. But even if Stone had wanted to get aloft again, the damage inflicted by the crowd made it impossible. The airman quietly assisted his mechanic in disassembling the machine. Over the next hour the 'uproar subsided' and the audience shuffled away.

Stone was not to be beaten by the 'deadheads', and in the backwash of the Auckland Domain fiasco he promised another demonstration, but at a more secure venue where the crowd could be more easily controlled. Over the next few days, as letters to the editor swung from attacking Stone's integrity and flying qualifications to describing the crowd of 18 April as the 'vilest mobs to be found in any part of the world', the aviator, the aeroplane and their entourage were relocated to Alexandra Park.[5] On 23 April Wizard went up three times and 'his flight in the afternoon was witnessed by a crowd, which heartily cheered him as he made his graceful descent after circling Alexandra Park several times at a height over 300 feet'.[6]

In the weeks that followed Stone went on to set further New Zealand records for duration and height — only to have his tour prematurely terminated in Napier a month later. The King's Birthday event was to be witnessed by 1000 townspeople assembled at the Napier Park raceway. When Stone woke he found the morning crisp and wonderfully clear of clouds. However his nemesis, New Zealand's gusty winds, were about to gatecrash the exhibition. There arose a 'nasty wind blowing across the course, coming across the Puketapu hills, full of treachery for the airman'.[7] Stone dispelled speculation of a no-show at four o'clock when he gave orders for the Blériot to make its grand entrance. Boy scouts, honoured with the task, pulled the machine out from the tent and into view. The aeronaut inspected the wires, but was 'eyeing the sky with doubtful looks'. Perhaps Wizard would still cancel. Onlookers and those near the machine had their misgivings.

Stone was having none of it. He turned from the monoplane, shook hands with friends, clambered aboard and the propeller was given a turn. Thirty seconds later he was under way. Almost immediately he had cause to question his decision. Sudden gusts pushed and pulled at the wings; he barely wrestled his first turn before flying near the packed grandstand at 70 ft. Then a stiff squall rolled down the hill, heeling the machine over to one side. Just as 'catastrophe seemed imminent', hope revived. At the end of his run Stone readied to dip his wing to turn by gaining a modicum of height. But the wind would not be denied its prize, resisting Wizard's efforts. The wingtip snagged briefly in the outstretched arms of a willow and, ankle-tapped, horse and rider fell headlong to the earth.

Mockingly, the wind carried the shrieks and gasps of the crowd to Stone, prone on the ground. The detritus of the Blériot was a wood and fabric garland around him. It was almost a complete wreck, with the propeller smashed to 'smithereens'. Shaken, and with a broken collarbone, Stone gathered himself and arose to spectators' cries of 'Well done, Stone.' He noted that the crowd seemed more excited by the crash than by the actual flight. The tour was over, and Stone departed for Australia, judging that perhaps New Zealand was not a 'good place to fly at this time of the year'.

In spite of his recent fall to earth, the daredevil had not only flown further and higher than anyone else in the country, he had also completed a sustained flight that involved turning an aeroplane. In other words, 'practical' aviation had its first airing with Wizard Stone. While he was in Australia, news reached Stone of the gifting of *Britannia*, and in November he offered his services to the New Zealand government. Given the ever-increasing number of accidents he had survived in the two southern dominions it was perhaps unsurprising that the authorities did not take him up on his offer. Besides, New Zealand now had an accomplished pilot on hand.

On 12 November 1913, Joe Hammond arrived in Wellington close on the tail of *Britannia*. Their union seemed fated: surely the best aeroplane in Australasia was going to be united with Australasia's most accomplished pilot. 'The return of Mr. J. J. Hammond, one of the pioneer aviators of the world, to New Zealand is an opportune event,' waxed the *Evening Post*. 'There are probably at least half-a-dozen machines in the dominion today which are capable of flight under the guidance of a properly qualified pilot. It is the pilot so far that has been missing.'[8] The 'pluck and perseverance' of the local aviator-constructors was to be admired, but now New Zealand had a real aviator on the scene. The minister of defence needed to 'seize the opportunity and engage Mr. Hammond to fly the *Britannia* aeroplane'. That Hammond had recently become an officer in the Royal Flying Corps only added to his credentials.[9]

It was envisioned that Hammond would have a role in the formation of an aerial corps in connection with the New Zealand Defence Force. Wigram's 'outlandish' ideas of 1909 were now becoming increasingly widespread, and by 1913 many New Zealanders were firmly persuaded that 'the aeroplane is now a recognised factor in warfare'.[10] This was partly due to the growing numbers of aero clubs across the nation, and the influence of the recently formed New Zealand branch of the Aerial League of the British Empire. The clubs fostered aeronautics, mostly via model-making, ballooning and unpowered glider flights.[11] Among those who played a part in the future of New Zealand military aviation were the youthful George Bolt and his lifelong friend William Angus of the Canterbury (NZ) Aero Club, established in 1911.[12] Their most significant feat was the construction of a glider they flew 380 yards from the Cashmere Hills. Later they went on to design and build an ingenious man-powered, pedal-assisted glider.[13]

The Aerial League's lobby group of important luminaries pushed the argument that New Zealand needed more air-minded individuals and that the country's future security would depend on a strong, Empire-wide aeronautical force. *Britannia* and Hammond were seen

Britannia rules the skies over the Epsom Showgrounds in January 1914.

as the lightning rod around which military aviation in New Zealand could be fostered:

> Here is the means, and here is the man. . . . If Mr Hammond were approached he might be
> persuaded to give a series of exhibition flights on the 'Britannia' throughout the Dominion
> that would furnish funds for the establishment of the First New Zealand Aerial Corps, and
> bring the country reasonably up-to-date in aviation. Here is the means of arousing some
> national feeling with regard to the newest (and in New Zealand non-existent) branch of the
> Service.[14]

Within days of arrival, Hammond was contracted to the Defence Department and was inspecting the military Blériot.[15] He was impressed, though realistic. First, he acknowledged that the machine would need its propeller to function properly. In an extraordinary oversight it had not been included in the consignment, but was languishing in its wooden packing case in Hendon, London; it appeared belatedly two days before Christmas.[16] Second, and more seriously, Hammond noted that the Blériot was unsuitable for training purposes; it was simply too powerful. 'Eighty horse-power is some power,' he said. 'For teaching you want an old coach of 40 or 50 horse-power that only travels at from thirty to forty miles an hour.'[17] The Gnome engine's top speed of 80 mph precluded its use in instructing novices. Nonetheless, it was a pity that such a 'beautiful machine . . . was shut up in a shed month after month'. 'Given fair weather conditions,' Hammond reckoned, 'I could probably drive [Britannia] from Wellington to Christchurch in a couple of hours.' The military, however, wanted to send the machine north to Auckland.

Hammond was keen to fly the monoplane from the capital to Auckland, but cautious authorities sent it by train. The much-heralded duo would, in collaboration with the city's Industrial, Agricultural and Mining Exhibition, held at the Auckland Domain, make its public debut on Auckland Anniversary Day, 29 January. However, a restless Hammond introduced himself and the dominion monoplane to the Auckland public in 'dramatic fashion' nine days earlier.

Only a gaggle of spectators saw Hammond take off from Cornwall Park, but the effect of Britannia flying over New Zealand's biggest city was immediate and dramatic. On 18 January the man and machine that had been endlessly talked about suddenly materialised — a heavenly apparition. 'People were dressing for church . . . when they heard a rhythmic throbbing which set them wondering. They rushed to windows and doorways to investigate the phenomenon, and there, poised gracefully between earth and the blue sky, was the Britannia in rapid flight.' Initially, Hammond had given no thought to his course, but at several hundred feet he purposely turned into Newmarket, rounded the foot of Khyber Pass Road, circled the Exhibition site at the Domain, then wheeled over Symonds Street to the apex of Queen Street.

At one point, to the amazement of the onlookers, he banked Britannia to 90 degrees, 'that is to say he had the wings at right angles to, instead of parallel to the earth'. In the language of airmen, noted the press, this is called 'standing her on her wing tip'. He traced the length of Queen Street to the waterfront. The Waitemata sparkled and the monoplane soared. Britannia sought out the warships HMAS *Psyche* and HMS *Pyramus* at anchor, and daintily 'dipped in her course as a mark of respect to the white ensign'. Having saluted *Pyramus*, the gossamer-winged Blériot wheeled citywards, flying over Mount Eden before coming to rest at the showground. 'Auckland talked of aeroplanes for the rest of the day,' sang the *New Zealand Herald*.

The good work of 18 January was nearly undone the next day when Hammond and the military authorities consented to a passenger flight. A *New Zealand Herald* reporter occupied the seat behind Hammond and eight men held the tail as the pilot increased the throttle and tested the engine. The journalist fidgeted on his leather cushion, staring straight at Hammond's back. The frame of the skilled pilot gave him courage and the deep seat reassured him that he would not simply 'drop out'. Once the engine was opened up, Hammond's hand shot out and the men released the great bird. *Britannia* leapt forward.

Hammond realised something was amiss in the half-second before the machine lifted off: the rudder wires were twisted. Hammond had no control. He cut the engine, but *Britannia*'s speed was such that the monoplane seemed assured of a nasty disagreement with a fence. To the newsman's surprise, flight was aborted and the lanky officer jumped from the cockpit as *Britannia* bounced towards the barrier.[18] In a single bound Hammond reached the rudder and jammed the skid into the ground. *Britannia* pulled up a few yards from the fence and the 'idea of flying for the evening was then abandoned'.[19] A couple of days later, under the tongue-in-cheek subheading 'How it Feels to Fly', the reporter, while lamenting his ill luck, praised the aviator's swift decision-making in preventing damage to man and machine.[20] Hammond had saved *Britannia*.

The day before the long-awaited exhibition display, Hammond invited an Australian actress, Esme McLennan, to accompany him on a flight, and on 28 January she became the first woman to fly over New Zealand. 'I honestly didn't feel the least bit nervous,' demurred the actress. 'We were travelling faster than I have ever travelled in the fastest express trains, but there was not even the slightest vibration.' Breathlessly she told newsmen she felt more elated at the flight than at any time on the stage. At the conclusion of that evening's performance of *Bo-Peep*, Hammond presented McLennan with goggles and flowers in honour of her courage. 'I felt quite the heroine,' she said, 'and never got so much applause in my life.'

Meanwhile, flying fever was about to break out in the deep south as James 'Will' Scotland introduced aviation to Invercargill and the South Island.

Scotland had caught the flying bug while visiting Britain, and his condition worsened when he viewed Wizard Stone's 1913 exploits. The day after Stone's heavily publicised 23 April 1913 flight, Scotland wrote to the minister of defence, declaring his intentions to pursue flying and to tender his services on completion of his training.[21] In reply he was informed that New Zealand already had an airman undergoing instruction and familiarisation; no commitment could be made to Scotland now or in the future.[22] Undeterred, the Pahi-born Scotland left for Britain, where he undertook flying instruction from August to October. Armed with a freshly minted aviation certificate, he purchased a Caudron, a 45-hp, six-cylinder biplane that was a popular prewar machine. The Caudron and pilot arrived in New Zealand in the first week of January 1914. With a single North Island flight under his belt, Scotland, backed by a syndicate, began a tour of the South Island with *Blue Bird*, so dubbed on account of its blue tint.

On 20 February 1914 he flew from Invercargill to Gore. The long daylight hours of high summer in one of the world's southernmost cities easily accommodated a 7 p.m. takeoff. The citizens of Invercargill saw a man flying for the first time: this was no film reel, but rather an actual airman and a flying machine. Crowds gathered as he gained altitude before turning the Caudron northeast, navigating by the railway line. About 30 minutes later he was spotted at the edge of the Gore township. He soared over the Catholic church and the dairy factory before turning towards the school and 'lowered the machine to about thirty feet from the ground, speeding over the post office' towards the showgrounds.[23] Shops emptied at the sound of the six-cylinder engine; eyes darted skyward.

When news of Scotland's improbable achievement reached Invercargill the movie theatre operator interrupted the featured film. Cheers and wild applause erupted.[24] Not only was it the South Island's first flight, it was also the nation's first cross-country aircraft flight and New Zealand's first 'town to town' flight. It was a remarkable achievement for someone who still looked almost adolescent. 'Mr Scotland is surprisingly youthful in appearance,' noted the *Sun*. 'He is only twenty-two years of age but looks even younger and the casual observer would never guess that he is an aviator with considerable experience of the birdman's art.'[25]

Scotland, *Blue Bird* and supporting staff were transported north by rail. The baby-faced birdman wowed the crowds in Dunedin and Timaru. A 'thousand eyes' tracked *Blue Bird* as it flew over Dunedin's sandhills and thence across the rooftops and above gasping inhabitants. 'One wondered if the seagulls homing to their rocky roosts had observed the new, monstrous screaming bird in the quiet heavens,' enthused a local paper. An elderly woman suffered a broken collarbone in a stampede at the Caledonian Ground.[26] Timaru's newspaper of record promised the locals sights of grand proportions:

> Within the last few days an aeroplane has flown over the Sea of Galilee and aeroplanes have been used to locate bands of bloodthirsty brigands in China; today an aeroplane ascent is to be made in Timaru . . . [and] if Scotland carries out his project to fly from Timaru to Christchurch during the present week, whatever feats may be performed by others after him he will have a strong claim to rank as one of the chief pioneers of aviation in New Zealand.[27]

Foul weather cancelled the Timaru exhibition, but on 6 March Scotland set his eyes on Christchurch, about 100 miles distant. He stretched the wings of *Blue Bird* over the town before making a precautionary landing to carry out adjustments in a local paddock, only to be swamped by curious wellwishers. Two hours later at 8.35 a.m. he was on his way, following the rail line north. Temuka received a special gift from Scotland: at 2000 ft over the town he dropped New Zealand's first unofficial piece of airmail — a book for a Temuka garage. Scotland's 'delivery' was picked up by a local and duly handed to the intended recipient. Between the small South Canterbury towns of Winchester and Orari he landed the misfiring

above The crowd presses close to Will Scotland's Caudron *Blue Bird* at Gore during his journey up the South Island of New Zealand.

below A proud Will Scotland with *Blue Bird*. Ill health would bring his military career to a premature end during the Great War.

Caudron. Repairs were made and the flight was resumed, but not before the local school cancelled classes for the day and a hat was passed around the 500 spectators to collect donations for a gift for Scotland.[28] He then embarked on the final leg. His destination was the Addington Showgrounds, where a marquee had been erected for his arrival.

The wind was variable and the Caudron was heavily buffeted. Having ascended at one point to 6000 ft, Scotland was becoming increasingly fatigued and chilled. He overtook a number of trains, and the passengers of one at Rolleston clambered onto the roof of a carriage to get a better view of *Blue Bird* and its intrepid pilot. Progress was monitored in Christchurch by incoming telegrams and a crowd began to gather. Cars and bicycles 'multiplied amazingly' as the arrival drew near. At 5 p.m. the wait was over. Two small lines were spotted, mere scratches on the heavens. These broadened out, and the wings and fuselage came into focus as Scotland approached the venue 'faster than a steam train'. Before long the Anzani motor was making itself known: 'The hum of the engine rapidly growing to become a roar which has been likened to a dozen chaffcutters in angry argument with a quartz-crusher,' said a newspaper the next day. The crowd, which had stood in star-struck silence, now released a full-throated cry as Scotland reduced his height in preparation for landing. Ecstatic Cantabrians rushed *Blue Bird* as it glided to a standstill. They wondered at the marvel of flight and clamoured to get close to this 'god of the air'.

> Mr Scotland was attired in a light tweed overcoat with leather gauntlet gloves. The one thing which betrayed him as an aviator was his leather helmet which takes the place of goggles. It fitted right over his head and the rim came down far enough to cover his eyes and it was only by looking straight up under the rim of the headpiece that the observer could see the twinkle of the birdman's dark eyes. . . . The coldness of the journey up from the south was stamped upon the features of the aviator. They were white, and absolutely bloodless, and even the lips showed up but a very pale pink.[29]

The Timaru-to-Christchurch flight had covered 98 miles in two hours and five minutes. It was a record for travel by air in a single day that stood for five years.

Over the following days Scotland and *Blue Bird* wooed the residents of Christchurch. On 14 March he made for Lancaster Park and an international cricket match; he had been contracted to give the spectators a brief but entertaining flypast.[30] Play stopped as the Canterbury and Australian players peered skyward from under their caps. Scotland approached the ground from height and gradually lowered his altitude in a spiral, dusting the park with a loose halo of yellowish exhaust smoke. To the uninitiated it appeared that he was about to plough into the pitch and players as he dropped to 50 ft. The aviator smiled when the cricketers scurried off the ground and the cheering, thousands-strong crowd rose as one to greet him.[31] It was New Zealand's first aviation display at an international sporting event.

On his last public exhibition in Christchurch he could not help but circle Cathedral Square. It was a Sunday, and the cathedral was full of the faithful, hymnbooks in hand, when the now-familiar bark of *Blue Bird* broke the spiritual mediation. Worshippers abandoned 'God for the devil in the sky' and poured out into the sunlight, to the delight of the mischievous Scotland.[32]

As the Australians had idolised Hammond, so the South Island public fêted Scotland. Vast crowds attended his displays of aeronautical skill and of *Blue Bird*'s considerable attributes. Homes, schools and workplaces were emptied at the sound of the Caudron. Invariably when he alighted after mesmerising an audience, they closed in on him. 'An old man of 98 years of age greeted him and thanked the aviator for allowing him to see the wonder of the age before he died,' recalled an observer. 'Mothers brought up their children to speak to the birdman. And even the policemen seemed to lose their heads.'[33] A flight over Cook Strait was touted, but Scotland was unwilling to test his Caudron over the unpredictable waters; the aeroplane was shipped to the capital for the commencement of the North Island tour.[34]

Wellington's weather, however, was typically temperamental. The claustrophobic confines of Athletic Park, hemmed in by dense housing and embraced by wind-funnelling hills, made it the most demanding of venues. A heavily publicised 21 March display was cancelled, and the disgruntled crowd, whose expectations had been raised by handbills emblazoned with 'Sensational! Exciting! Dipping! Diving!', were equally unhappy the next day when inclement weather again intervened.[35] Reminiscent of the unruly Auckland gathering that had almost rioted after 'Wizard' Stone's aborted flight a year earlier, the Caudron and pilot were surrounded by a mob that included intoxicated louts. One drunken individual became entangled in the rigging and a police sergeant was injured in the jostling press as he tried to liberate him.[36] Only the quick thinking of a local member of Parliament prevented bodily damage to Scotland and *Blue Bird*: he jumped up on a benzine case and hushed the 'barracking' elements in the crowd. Drawing on his own experience as an attendee and passenger at European air exhibitions, he told them it was altogether common for flights to be delayed and cancelled. The risk to man and machine could not be underestimated in the prevailing blustery conditions. Mollified, the crowd slowly dispersed.

The constant postponements affected the tour's schedule, and the unfulfilled commitments to fee-paying crowds were a bitter pill for Scotland. His determination to meet the timetable and crowd demands came to a head on 25 March. Winds gusting between 4 and 20 mph greeted pilot and public. The vagaries of the wind would normally have precluded any flight, but not today: Scotland wanted to fulfil fraying expectations and offered no more excuses. At mid-afternoon he advised that the exhibition would take place. It would be his last flight before the war.

Once airborne, he realised he would have been better off attempting to ride a bucking bronco. The wind turned treacherous as soon as he cleared the shielding bank of Athletic Park. It was as if he had been ambushed. The surrounding hills channelled the wind into 'descending currents, eddies and puffs'. The headwind was sweeping over the hills and down on *Blue Bird*. For the life of him, Scotland could not get the Caudron over 300 ft; *Blue Bird* was more kite than aeroplane in the tempest. It seemed that at any moment the corrugated-iron roofs of the close-packed houses might swallow him. He nearly capsized and sought the relative shelter of hills at the back of Newtown Park. Perhaps he could make an emergency landing. It was to prove a false hope.

Here he ran . . . out of the frying-pan into the fire . . . the hollow in the elbow of the hills about Newtown Park and South Wellington was simply a maelstrom of eddies. He was tossed about in alarming fashion. It was a sensation one would never wish to feel again as one watched Scotland gallantly endeavouring to save his aircraft from the rocks in the fatal abyss underneath.[37]

Then Scotland was hit by a waterfall of downward air that violently buffeted the biplane. He was in a fight for his life. *Blue Bird* dived and sideslipped sharply. He wrestled with the controls, skimming the rooftops by a few feet and telephone wires by mere inches. A boy at the nearby school looked out the window and to his amazement saw Scotland and the 'aeroplane fly past the window'. The teacher dismissed the children and with the class made for the door.[38]

Scotland prepared to clear the park's western-perimeter trees but soon realised this strategy was doomed. The aeroplane dropped another 100 ft. He deliberately nosed the machine down into the main body of the trees, avoiding the tree tops that would likely topple and cartwheel *Blue Bird*. Impact.

Scotland was flung violently forward, his head smacking into the windshield. Dazed, he flicked off the still whirring engine. He and *Blue Bird* were nesting between two pine trees 20 ft in the air. Scotland suffered sprains and bruises but was otherwise intact, saved from serious head injury by his rudimentary helmet.[39] He surveyed the biplane. Much of *Blue Bird* was in one piece but the extremities were smashed and crumpled. The rigging and canvas hung about the crippled wings and littered the ground. By the time he had clambered down, the crowd from Athletic Park had begun to arrive, astonished that he had survived. Out of breath, flooded with adrenalin, many started collecting souvenirs right in front of Scotland. 'Smiling and undismayed,' a remarkably calm Scotland took the crowd in good humour. One friend even thrust a propeller splinter into his hands for an autograph: 'J. W. H. Scotland, 3.10 p.m., 25th March, 1914.'[40] To those in earshot he quipped that he was probably the only person in Wellington to climb down a tree that he had not first climbed up.[41]

With a couple of days to reflect on the near disaster, much of Wellington had the good sense to acknowledge that their lamentable attacks on Scotland's character had been misplaced and had perhaps played a part in the crash: Scotland might not have made such a rash attempt had it not been for the ill-considered assaults on his integrity and courage. 'He has a real grievance against the treatment he has received here at the hands of the public,' wrote the *Dominion*.[42] The behaviour of the crowd at earlier proceedings had been 'unsportsmanlike and unreasonable', and had come from a Wellington element ignorant of the risks involved. Letters to the editor felt the crowd had not wanted to see Scotland killed; rather it 'was evident they had not even considered' the possibility.[43] Criticism was diverted from the now 'courageous' Scotland to the perfidious promoters who, on the days that flights had been cancelled, had continued to take admission fees when weather conditions were clearly going to prevent a flight.

Those who had missed the event could see 'Scotland's Air-flight and Accident' played out over and over again at the King's Theatre.[44] The screenings were well attended. But while money was to be made at the theatre, Scotland was out of pocket for hundreds of pounds. *Blue Bird*'s only salvageable component was the motor, but that had little value without the airframe. Besides, the limited power of the 45-hp Anzani motor had in all probability contributed to the accident.

Scotland was undaunted by the mishap. 'I have not given up on my flying career in New Zealand,' he said. 'I hope to resume aviation on my own account in the near future.'[45] He ordered a replacement Caudron equipped with a 60-hp Le Rhône engine.

In the meantime Walsh, Stone, Hammond and Scotland's efforts had sown the seeds of military aviation in New Zealand. Newspapers were afflicted with flying fever, and called on the government to establish an indigenous aviation service. The *New Zealand Herald* concluded that 'New Zealand should seriously consider the establishment of aviation and the formation of a flying corps.' Notwithstanding Scotland's recent tree-top landing, many now saw flying as an increasingly safe enterprise, thanks to the work of Scotland and his predecessors Stone and Hammond. This view was reinforced by reports that, across Europe, airmen were now looping the loop and others were embarking on flights covering hundreds of miles. According to some premature conjecture, technological advances were about to make 'aeroplaning . . . just as safe, popular, and cheap in 1914 as motor cycling'.[46] Passenger flights and airmail deliveries were increasingly considered to be commercially viable. Scotland's unofficial postal delivery in Timaru was dwarfed by Turkish plans for the establishment of an aerial postal service between Aleppo and Baghdad to replace the camel caravan.[47] Many New Zealanders noted with envy the advances that were being made across the Tasman. 'The [Australian] Federal Government has imported a number of aeroplanes as part of its defence system,' observed the Christchurch *Sun*. New Zealand, though, was 'way off this position'.[48] But, the reporter continued, New Zealand did have the flying 'stock' among its inhabitants. Its list included the 'daring pilot' of Feilding, Joe Hammond; the youthful but 'fine flyer', Will Scotland; and the American, Arthur Stone. The latter, now living in Australia, had his detractors but there was no denying his flying pedigree. Before his departure he had indicated his enthusiasm for a role in creating an aviation school in New Zealand.

As for the location of such a school, Canterbury was the frontrunner. The vast open plains, free of Auckland's volcanic cones and Wellington's treacherous winds, inclined the aviation-minded to the region. The Canterbury initiative called for the acquisition of 60 acres and the construction of two hangars to house an initial three machines.[49] Will Scotland was the focus of a Christchurch businessman's proposal: he was enthusiastic and highly regarded, and had already received numerous requests from military officers for aerial instruction. Perhaps *Britannia* could be co-opted to the task as well? A flying school would enable 'local defence authorities to train officers in this most important branch of military work'. Of course, a successful school would end the need for local men to travel to Britain to undergo training — and there were a good number of men ready and willing to undergo the instruction.

Letters of interest from individuals caught up in the excitement regularly crossed Defence Department desks in Wellington. As one correspondent wrote succinctly: 'To have aeroplanes you want aviators.'[50] Clifford Barclay of Waimate asked for his name to be 'noted as an applicant for instruction in Aviation'.[51] Many of the aspirants were of a mechanical and engineering bent. Raymond Curtis of Greymouth informed the Defence Department he had been 'in the mechanical business for the last six years, repairing motor engines especially'. His other 'qualification' — mentioned by other applicants, too — was that he had 'made a particular study of aviation'.[52] 'I have my mind fully on flying,' wrote Peter Hayward of Milton.[53] Hayward's qualifications: passion and a good understanding of the internal combustion engine.

At least one man tried to ingratiate himself with the authorities through his family connections. A New Zealand-born cousin of Hammond living in Brisbane, Francis Hammond, applied for the yet-to-be-created position of aviator in the nonexistent New Zealand air corps. Alongside his 10-year motoring business experience he recalled the numerous flights he had flown with his cousin in Australia.[54] A Dunedin man, William Lockhead, had been gainfully employed in Britain in the manufacturing of flying machines and now wanted to play his part in his homeland's aviation industry.

Even non-New Zealanders, following Hammond and *Britannia*'s endeavours from afar, saw the Empire's southern dominion as ripe for military flying and submitted themselves for consideration. Notable among these was Frank Cowlin, who claimed to be an aircraft designer with Sopwith Aviation and to have drawn up a number of machines for the British Admiralty and the War Office. He was now seeking work further afield. 'If the New Zealand government are desirous of establishing or extending an aeronautical department,' wrote Cowlin, 'I should be glad to be considered as a candidate for any opening as designing engineer, which might be vacant.'[55] With this much interest, the government had the human resources to create a flying school and a small military aerial service in the dominion.

What the would-be aeronauts and current aeronauts did not know, however, was that the idea of an antipodean air corps was living on borrowed time. Behind the scenes, unforeseen problems with the Blériot and antagonistic forces were moving quickly to bring *Britannia* and Joe Hammond down to earth. His widely publicised first flight for the exhibition in January 1914 had been cancelled because of undercarriage problems; and a scheduled night-time flight also failed to materialise. The nervous exhibition organisers wanted no more embarrassments, and *Britannia* flights were pulled from the programme.[56] More importantly, the military took back control of the machine; Esme McLennan was its last civilian passenger. The honeymoon was over; old fiscal concerns were about to resurface, and although *Britannia* remained on view for the remainder of the exhibition, it was soon dismantled, railroaded back to Wellington and placed in storage in the autumn of 1914.[57]

Hammond could be bullishly, perhaps foolishly, forthright. In the days leading up to the exhibition he had declared that he was 'quite in the dark as to the intentions of the military officials. I suppose they will have an aviation school but where it will be or who will be in charge I do not know. I am at present engaged to give flights . . . and after that my movements are uncertain.' He followed this up with bold pronouncements on suitable venues for an aviation school and its requirements.[58] How this went down with the authorities is not entirely clear, but it may have accounted for the brisk missive he received from Godley on 13 February, thanking him for his 'information and offer of assistance' but proffering no continuing relationship, let alone a role in a military aviation school.[59]

The real issue was fiscal. By 1914, Godley, as general officer commanding New Zealand military forces, was no more disposed to the establishment of an air section than he had been two years earlier. This was despite an interim visit to the Royal Aircraft Factory at Farnborough, where he clambered aboard a BE2 biplane for a joyride. 'The improvements to aircraft are so rapid and incessant that an aeroplane is scarcely built before it is obsolete as a first class instrument of war,' he stated in his annual report. 'Aeroplanes are expensive items.' The military declared publicly that its assessment was a 'waiting policy'.[60] This policy received its stamp of approval from the British inspector-general, Sir Ian Hamilton. In mid-1914, at the conclusion of a five-week visit to the dominion, he touched on aviation in his final report.

> Sooner or later the provision of a service of aviation in New Zealand will become necessary. Military aviation is still today in the experiential stage, and the experiments on the scale that would be financially possible in this country would be unlikely to lead far. Furthermore, the air and landing conditions in the Dominion are not such as to tempt hostile aviators. For these reasons I would recommend a waiting policy for the present.[61]

Even before this, New Zealand's minister of defence had made up his mind; James Allen was reported in the *Otago Daily Times* arguing that the 'cost incidental to the use of the Government aeroplane in experimental flying was excessive in the view of the [meagre] results to be attained. It would be wise,' he considered, 'to leave experimental aviation to other countries better able to afford it.'[62] His only consolation to the nation's downcast flying supporters and prospective aviators was that the New Zealand military would not be completely ignorant in the art of flying given that William Burn was 'now undergoing training in England; and is specialising in aviation, and this officer and others will keep in touch as far as possible with the progress made in aviation abroad'. The New Zealand military and civil government officials were unmoved by the pleas of the press or the offers from the aviators Stone, Scotland and Hammond: the *Britannia* 'experiment' had run its course and it was now time for a dose of realism. Efforts to bring military aviation to New Zealand had failed.

CHAPTER THREE

LUCKY DEVILS

1914–1915

Just as it became clear that the New Zealand Defence Department was not interested in military aviation, the Great War broke out. A Serbian nationalist's assassination of the heir to the Austro-Hungarian throne was the match that lit the accumulated kindling of war. The Balkans was unresolved business in Europe, a quilt of disparate nationalities and small states competing for territorial aggrandisement. In the background, two great empires, Austria-Hungary and Russia, faced off for regional suzerainty. Vienna's deliberately aggresive demands following the assassination were ignored by Belgrade; carrion birds gathered over Europe. On 28 July, with German backing, Austria-Hungary declared war on Serbia. By now the cogs of two alliances — Germany and Austria-Hungary on the one side, and Russia, France and Britain on the other — were interlocking. One country after another duly followed the obligations of their various treaties. Armies massed. The German army, in accordance with the Schlieffen Plan — designed to knock out France in a matter of weeks — advanced through Belgium. London stepped up to protect Belgian neutrality.

On 4 August 1914 the British government declared war. The New Zealand dominion dutifully and eagerly signed up for the European conflict. Familial ties were strong; the greater part of the populace was only a couple of generations removed from their British forebears. Economically, the bulk of the dominion's agricultural produce was consumed in Britain; militarily, New Zealand recognised the importance of the Royal Navy in securing global trade. The rise of German naval power was not to be taken lightly, and although Japan was a British ally in the unfolding conflict, anti-Asian sentiment — fear of the 'yellow peril' — made the public uneasy.

Though it was a distant fragment of the Empire, New Zealand achieved security from these looming threats by dint of its colonial membership, but with this came an obligation that the government and public were only too willing to fulfil. Flags were unfurled, brass bands played and people congregated in town centres at the news of the declaration. Public sentiment was overwhelming that New Zealand would play its part in putting down the Kaiser and his war-mongering generals. The Massey-led government made an initial commitment to despatching an 8000-strong force to support the war effort: the New Zealand Expeditionary Force (NZEF).

Little mention was made of New Zealand's naval commitment, and nothing of its role in an

New Zealand soldiers crowd the deck of the troopship *Athenic* en route to war. Many of the men who would eventually find their way to the air service entered the war this way.

air war. The 1913 Naval Defence Act called for the establishment of a 'unit' of the Royal Navy in New Zealand waters, but the untimely arrival of war torpedoed any hope of its materialisation. Still, the dominion had its battlecruiser, HMS *New Zealand*, which would acquit itself well in the conflict. As for air power, after five years of considering the subject, being gifted a machine and having numerous offers made to lead the charge from individuals as diverse as Wigram and Scotland, little had been achieved. Wigram was still advocating for a local air training school but the government was not biting. As for the prominent airmen, only Joseph Hammond entered the war as an aeronaut. With no contract from the Defence Department, the dominion's best pilot alighted in Liverpool in mid-August and was duly attached to Royal Flying Corps (RFC). Will Scotland was waiting for the arrival of his second, more powerful Caudron. Sadly it was seriously damaged in an early flight:[1] one of the rosewood propeller blades snapped, and the chassis fractured and contorted.[2] Soon after, ill health grounded Scotland, too, and he spent the early months of the war convalescing. And the Defence Department's sole airman, William Burn, was without an aircraft to fly.

With training completed, Burn was shipped out to New Zealand on 24 July 1914. News of the commencement of European hostilities reached them in mid-Atlantic. On his arrival in New Zealand he discovered *Britannia* cloistered away in an army barracks, a static display item. Plucked of its wings, the aircraft rested dejectedly in the corner of the building, as firmly attached to terra firma as he was. His nearly six months of training was redundant in the southern dominion. He would not 'superintend aviation in New Zealand' as originally planned. There was simply no military aviation to superintend; instead he was awkwardly attached to an Auckland infantry regiment. The New Zealand government, meanwhile, offered *Britannia* to the War Office.

Most New Zealanders who aspired to enter the war as pilots or observers would not get the opportunity to do so in 1914. With patriotic fervour running high, they resigned themselves to a role in the land war.

Although the government had done little to prepare for the air war, a few individuals outside the New Zealand military system were involved in the first salvos of the war on the Western Front. Rejected by the Defence Department, Joseph Hammond was in Canada when war was announced. He was recalled by the RFC and he served much of the early war as an instructor, with some brief excursions to France.[3] Unfortunately, almost nothing remains documenting his Western Front experience.[4]

At least one New Zealand-born aviator would see the early war from the air, however: the little-heralded Captain Hugh Reilly. Like many pilots of the era he was smallish and lean, and had considerable strength of character — and flying ability. Like a jockey, an airman of moderate dimensions and weight aided the performance of his mount; oversized and heavy pilots and observers were a stretch for the small cockpits and low-powered machines of the era. When war broke out, the balding and keen-eyed Reilly looked older than his 28 years. He was not only the first New Zealand airman to taste action in the RFC, but he also went on to become the country's first air commander and, less happily, New Zealand's first airman-turned-prisoner of war.[5]

Reilly's parents were born in India, where his father served in the army before leaving the subcontinent for New Zealand. Reilly, who was born in Hawke's Bay, was educated in Britain. As a young man he entered University College School, London, and graduated from Royal Military College, Sandhurst. He then enlisted in the Indian Army, as his father had before him; he saw limited action there in 1908. Four years later his career took an altogether different turn when he was despatched to Britain for lessons in aviation. The War Office was keen to establish a flying corps in India and Reilly was to be an instructor. He had initial training at a Hendon flying school in 1912, where he attained an aviator's certificate within two weeks.[6] After a brief return to India, he was back in Britain undertaking training at the newly established Central Flying School at Upavon, only two intakes ahead of fellow New Zealander William Burn — they were the first two New Zealanders to receive instruction at CFS, and they would meet fatefully over the sands of Mesopotamia two years later. This was followed by further instruction at the Royal Aircraft Factory at Farnborough.

Just after Christmas, Reilly was appointed an instructor at the Indian Central Flying School at Sitapur, in Uttar Pradesh, northern India. On a procurement trip to England in mid-June 1914, he hit a bureaucratic snag. The War Office wanted all the machines he selected to go through a time-consuming and, in the New Zealander's mind, pointless certification. He advised the India Office's military department of his concerns. 'As regards final inspection by the War Office, this will involve great delay, both in placing orders and particularly in the correspondence which will necessarily follow regarding minor alterations . . . It is very desirable that all unnecessary delay should be avoided since the machines are urgently required for the first course at Sitapur in October next.'[7] Reilly was in no doubt that this meddling would inevitably hamper the beginning of the first scheduled course. 'If however these reasons are not considered sufficiently strong,' he concluded, 'I would request the favour of a personal interview before any adverse decision is arrived at.' Unfortunately, the War Office was to be the least of his worries: the Great War was only weeks away.

When war broke out, the establishment of the Indian Central Flying School was abandoned. Reilly, who was living at Farnborough, was promoted to captain and posted to 4 Squadron for immediate action in France. On 13 August he flew his aircraft across the Channel.[8] Hopping from airfield to airfield, he landed at the RFC centre of operations at Maubeuge, five miles south of the Belgian border, four days later. Here his squadron was attached to the British Expeditionary Force (BEF) at Mons.

In August 1914, Reilly and a pitifully small number of RFC airmen faced the German onslaught, the Schlieffen Plan, designed to sidestep France's well-defended border with Germany. The Germans would push through neutral Belgium in a vast flanking manoeuvre and, wheeling behind the French army, they would encircle the enemy in the field. Ultimately Paris itself would be wrapped in a smothering teutonic embrace. The French armies along the eastern border could not be resupplied or reinforced; the French would capitulate — all in the space of six weeks. On 28 July, German forces invaded Belgium and in the latter half of August entered France, clashing with the French army and the smaller BEF and its RFC ancillary.

The RFC was not an independent air service but, rather, the army's aeronautical arm. Its naval equivalent was the Royal Naval Air Service (RNAS). A 'squadron' was the RFC's tactical unit; initially it numbered 14 aircraft, expanding to 18 as the war progressed. Airmen and supporting staff numbered between 100 and 200 and included everyone from pilots and observers to mechanics, fitters, riggers, sailmakers, carpenters, cooks, orderlies and clerks. Organisationally, squadrons would eventually be paired under the command of a wing; two wings constituted a brigade. Each BEF army received a brigade. In 1914, these structures were still in embryonic form and the numbers of squadrons was insufficient for the task at hand. At the outbreak of the war the RFC had only four squadrons ready for France. Yet in spite of their minuscule numbers, the presence of aeroplanes was immediately felt.

At the commencement of hostilities, combatants were still trying to determine what tasks their nascent air services could be utilised for, but they were in agreement that at the very least they offered the opportunity to 'see over the hill'. As Hammond had clearly demonstrated to Australian officers in 1913, and as prewar European military manoeuvres had confirmed to many commanders in Britain, France and Germany, a man aloft could see much further than a man astride a horse. One of the observers on an early sortie had been told that he might expect to see a few odd German troops; instead, as he reported, 'I saw the whole area covered with hordes of field grey uniforms — advancing infantry, cavalry, transport and guns. In fact it looked as though the place was alive with grey German ants. My pilot and I were astonished because it was not a *little* more than we'd been looking for — it was *infinitely* more.'[9] Nonetheless, traditions die hard, and some officers laid less weight on RFC intelligence than they might have — including, on this occasion, the BEF commander in chief, Field Marshal Sir John French. Horrified by the sheer numbers of Germans amassing, the airmen were rushed to a château well behind the lines. The room was full of elderly officers dripping in gold braid.

> All of these senior generals, it was Sir John French's own personal conference that was going on. Somebody announced us and he said, 'Well here's a boy from the Flying Corps, come here and sit down.' I was put to sit next to him then he said, 'Now, where have you been? Have you been flying? What have you been doing?' . . . I showed him a map [I had] all marked out. He said, 'Have you been over that area?' and I said, 'Yes, Sir!' I explained what I had seen and they were enormously interested. Then they began reading the figures that I had estimated, whereupon I feel that their interest faded — they seemed to look at each other and shrug their shoulders . . . [French] looked at me and said, 'Yes, this is very interesting, what you've got, but you know *our* information — which of course is correct — proves that I don't think you could have seen as much as you think! Well, of course, I quite understand that you may have imagined that you have, but it's not the case.'[10]

Young observers in the first months of the war were often poorly trained in military observation and sometimes mistakes were made, but French's officers could not easily dismiss a flood of corroborating RFC reports confirming the size and disposition of the German force bearing down on their men; and BEF strategy became increasingly dependent on the RFC reconnaissance reports. In 1914, it was in good part aviation-derived intelligence that led to the BEF's retreat 100 miles south to the Marne, thereby saving it from being flanked and overwhelmed by the numerically superior German infantry.[11]

Reilly's squadron was forced to jump from aerodrome to aerodrome in the face of the onslaught. It was a precarious game of hopscotch in which there was no guarantee that the airfield he and his fellow airmen had taken off from would still be open to them upon completion of their sortie.[12] Across three hectic weeks the squadron utilised a dozen airfields and men slept in a school, a hotel and even under a hedge.[13] The first casualty was incurred by the RFC on 22 August, when German small-arms fire hit an RFC sergeant-major. The infantry took great delight in opening up on aircraft; it was grouse shooting on a large scale. Enthusiastic young men fired indiscriminately at anything that took to the air, even their own machines. An airman with one of Reilly's sister squadrons rued the arrival of the British troops near the airfield.

> We were rather sorry they had come because up till that moment we had only been fired on by the French whenever we flew. Now we were fired on by the French *and* the English . . . To this day I can remember the roar of musketry that greeted two of our machines as they left the aerodrome and crossed the main Maubeuge–Mons road, along which a British column was proceeding.[14]

Union Jacks were hastily painted on the undersides of the machines. As for aerial combat, Reilly had little to worry about: it was not until October that the first air-to-air kill was confirmed.

What consideration that had been given to defending aircraft from enemy machines had led to individual airmen loading their machines with rifles or revolvers. More incredibly, some were advocating flying above enemy machines and bombing them. An overcoat, goggles, helmet, gauntlets, roaring engine and the buffeting windstream made it very difficult for an observer in an exposed cockpit to hit an enemy airman in his bobbing machine, no matter how good a marksman he was. When determined airmen attempted to deploy machine guns in late 1914, they found the added weight exceeded the ability of the poorly powered aircraft to reach their airborne targets. It would not be until the spring of 1915 that aircraft and engines had developed sufficiently for air-to-air fighting to become practical.

The aircraft that Reilly's squadron were using were largely unarmed and performed only marginally better than the machines with which Hammond and Scotland had dazzled New Zealand crowds over the summer of 1913–14. Only two of the squadrons, one of which was Reilly's 4 Squadron, were equipped with a single model, the Royal Aircraft Factory BE2; the two other squadrons made do with at least five other types. The BE2 was a two-seat 'tractor' biplane that proved a stable platform for reconnaissance duties but was vulnerable to enemy aircraft as the war progressed. However, it was competitive in the early months of the war and, on 25 August, 4 Squadron forced down a Taube — a German monoplane with giant pigeon-like wings and no rudder.

above A German Taube prepares for flight in 1914. The Taube was the first mass-produced German machine of the war, but was quickly superseded by better aircraft.

below The Bristol Scout served well in the war's early months, but by late 1915 was increasingly vulnerable to enemy fighters. These early models bore Union Jacks rather than the roundels of later machines.

By late August the Germans had reached the outskirts of Paris, only to be met by counterattacking French armies and the BEF along the Marne River on 5 September. Over the next seven days the Germans were shunted back in the decisive battle. In the aftermath of the First Battle of the Marne, both sides endeavoured to outflank the other. Reilly appears to have viewed this as an observer rather than as a pilot throughout September. He had a 'beastly "recce"' on 17 September and seven days later was again an observer on an intelligence-gathering flight.[15] He left Fère-en-Tardenois around midday and headed north, where he recorded sighting 'columns of artillery, horse transport, infantry and cavalry up to a mile long'.[16] The German movements were part of an attempt to outflank the Allies. The Franco-British armies in turn attempted to outflank the Germans. The result was an ever-lengthening front line, dubbed the 'race to the sea'. Over the next three weeks the front line marched headlong toward the coast, and in October reached the watery terminus of the North Sea. Neither side had gained a decisive victory. Stalemate. The Allies and Germans dug in, and the horrors of four years of trench warfare commenced.

October 1914 was a significant month for Reilly and his southern hemisphere countrymen. The New Zealander and another airman in the squadron were withdrawn to England. 'Lucky devils,' wrote one of those who remained in France.[17] How 'lucky' Reilly would be was yet to be revealed; but his return to England did allow him the opportunity to marry his sweetheart Alice on the last day of the month in London. As Reilly celebrated his nuptials the NZEF was already en route to war.

The NZEF troops arrived in Egypt and Britain by way of the Main Body embarkation in October 1914 and then subsequent reinforcement embarkations running through until October 1918. In the war's opening stanzas these future airmen made their way westward from New Zealand to Egypt via the Suez Canal. After the termination of the Gallipoli campaign and the NZEF's removal to the battlefields of France and Belgium, subsequent New Zealand embarkations swung around the Cape of Good Hope. Only after the United States entered the war did troopships strike out eastward through the Panama Canal, cutting precious time from their journey.

On board the *Arawa*, the conversion of passenger and merchant ships to military troopships was for the sole purpose of accommodating as many men and horses as possible — with the result that the comfort of man and beast was minimal. With over 8000 men and 3800 horses, the 10 troopships of the Main Body embarkation held the population of a good-sized rural New Zealand town. The ships had their own cooks, orderlies, doctors, dentists and chaplains.

The men were unaware that the graceful *Britannia*, which had won many of their hearts, was travelling with them. The War Office had accepted Wellington's offer and the dismantled Blériot was stowed, in its original packing with an extra coating of waterproof canvas for the journey, among the cargo on the deck.[18]

The largest vessel, the *Athenic* — designed to accommodate 688 individuals in its prewar guise as a passenger and cargo steamship — now shoehorned 1300 men and 354 horses into a

Hugh Reilly and his wife
Alice just after their
marriage in October
1914. A year later Reilly
was captured and
imprisoned by the
Turks. Alice would not
see him for three years.

500-ft by 63-ft hull. The human and animal cargo sat atop a large and volatile mix of munitions, an ever-present reminder of the deadly task ahead. The men descended below decks with great care, negotiating a route devised for a mountain goat with 'roughly improvised', steep stairs. The claustrophobic sleeping quarters were bunks 'in three tiers, packed as close as they could go'.[19] Jack Skinner found his accommodation too small for even a cat.[20] 'For washing etc the arrangements are very bad,' wrote another New Zealander, noting that 'the ship is in an insanitary state already. You have to wait your turn for a wash for about twenty minutes in the morning, and shaving is an awful nuisance.'[21] The officers enjoyed only marginally better accommodation. One recorded that agitated horses on the deck above were a constant impediment to a good night's sleep; he resolved the issue by laying a thick coir doormat beneath the hooves of one particularly distressed animal to dull the incessant banging.[22]

Most of the men were enthusiastic seafarers until heavy seas made them green about the gills. Journeys that began with waving crowds in placid dockside waters turned ugly only days from port, when seasickness gripped their stomachs. 'I can assure you I am in no mood for writing,' penned Melville White to his family, 'no more than you would be if you had been the colour of grass.'[23] On the *Maunganui* the voyage had begun well enough in blazing autumn sunshine on millpond-like waters; off the Wellington coast, White and his mates looked wistfully at the spots where they had enjoyed picnicking and shooting. But when the ships began to roll the mood took a darker turn. To put them out of their misery, 'Most of us wished the Germans would "ram" us with some torpedoes' — an overwrought sentiment that took a full three bedridden days to overcome.

White never did find his sealegs. The 22-year-old — who would eventually be posted to the RFC's first single-seat fighter squadron — survived on biscuits a family member had handed him just before his departure; they were the only thing he could keep down. Very few men made an appearance at mealtimes — a stark testament to the conditions, given the healthy appetites evident in camp ashore only a week earlier. And when the men did manage to wobble their way to the galley they were sorely disappointed. On one vessel the result was palpable after a lunch of 'barrelled beef that was inedible on account of its saltiness and toughness, potatoes, mostly bad, bread that was sour and doughy'. Even the tepid water was tainted. The hungry throng called for the officers to hear their grievances. 'Our spokesman said that our stew was not fit for dogs and its appearance on our tables was far too frequent, and the dinner today was not edible, and it must be remedied for the men would not stand for such treatment.'[24] In 1915 Cantabrian Robert Sloss wrote to his brother James, a future RFC pilot, that his ship, the *Waitemata*, had better 'tucker' than most, something he put down to superior cooks. Nevertheless, the canteen was popular, but it had sold out of most items within days of departure. Shaving brushes remained, as did the ever-popular soft drinks and tinned fish. 'Half a dozen of us buy tinned fish [and] soft drinks and put all the fish on one plate then we all get around it with forks, the man with the biggest fork gets the most.'[25]

By the time the vessel had departed Albany on the west coast of Australia, even the soft drinks and tinned fish were gone. Rumours of hungry, mutinous troopers were too numerous to be ignored. The matter of poor food was never fully resolved during the war years; it even received parliamentary attention. The disagreeable cuisine at sea, and later in the trenches, was to prove a compelling reason why young men were looking to join the infant air services, where a better quality of fare was available.

Aside from the challenging meals, what most men on the troopships recalled of their voyage was the boredom that set in only days after departure. The usual routine was a physical drill at 6.15 a.m., and parades at 9 a.m. and in the early afternoon. In between they were assigned various duties. 'It is pretty tedious,' wrote Robert Sloss, 'having to do the same drill day after day but I suppose it is necessary to keep us fit, old Len is getting terrible lazy on it, he can't stand drill and [as] he always argues with the NCOs it is a miracle he hasn't got into trouble before this.'[26] To relieve the boredom White played card games and listened to music in one of the emergency boats perched over the boat-deck:

> [S]omeone brought the Gramophone up and we had that going merrily in the boat a crowd of us were in, for a couple of hours, one minute a hymn would be put on, next minute a Rag-time in order to suit everyone. After tea the Sergeants held a meeting as regards the 'mess', but most of the time was spent arguing about the Gramophone until one wit suggested it should be thrown overboard which ended the discussion.[27]

In the hotter climes men went barefooted and in various states of dishevelment. Troopers lay around sleeping, reading, playing cards or gambling. Organised sports brought some relief. 'The Maoris are great fellows for boxing,' noted Sloss, 'which is about the only sport we have.' A hastily roped-off ring and gloves were always at hand. The fights were eagerly watched and critiqued by the mob, while the combatants vented their frustrations on each other.

Thievery was an unorganised but widespread diversion. Food was, of course, a popular target, but clothing and bedding entered a merry-go-round of preloved clothing. Men went to sleep with blankets and clothing items close at hand, only to arise propertyless. If a man's trousers were stolen the solution was pilfering someone else's. As long as the men turned out in uniform officers were little concerned with suppressing the widespread practice. One New Zealander who had turned up to parade hatless avoided censure the next time around when one of his mates took him to his bunk and produced six hats from under his mattress. 'The way things were shaping up,' he reasoned, 'I had better get in a good supply.'[28] Items of importance were particular targets of pranksters, observed White:

> A young man cleaned a very nice pair of canvas shoes he possessed and placed them on a wind-scoop jutting out from a port-hole, to dry in the sun. A practical joker grabbed one and hid it so the owner would think that one had fallen overboard and he wanted him to 'hold-forth'. The owner came along in due course and gave a terrible gasp when he only saw one shoe there, he picked it up and in a *very* mild language bade it chase the other . . . so he hurled it out of the port-hole — which was in my cabin — together with a volley of *gentle* words. When the practical joker heard this he thought the only thing to do was to throw the one that *did not go* overboard after the other and keep quiet.[29]

Relieving the boredom of the journey to war, men enjoy the 'line-crossing' ceremony on board *Athenic*.

One opportunity to break the tedium was Neptune's Court, the equator 'line-crossing' ceremony. Ronald Bannerman, a flying cadet from Otago, oversaw the proceedings from the safety of an upper deck, camera in hand.[30] The 'guests' — those who had never crossed the equator — were seized, none too gently, knelt before a bath, had their heads shaven and then were 'unceremoniously tipped head-over-heels into the pool'; at this point attendants of the court could further plunge the initiates in a playful fashion. The ritual was a briefly democratising, if sometimes cruel event: officers were brought down to earth by the power of the court and dunked alongside the soldiers. The victims were frequently 'quite pathetic', observed White, 'dragged to court, with their arms waving like lunatics and legs kicking frantically. One could almost imagine that they were going to be executed. Some of them could not have made more fuss if they were.'

Proceedings could quickly take a turn for the worse: freshly initiated and drenched, several men rushed the king and queen to pitch the royals into the bath. In the ensuing riot 'poor old Neptune had his crown crooked to one side on his head' and Mrs Neptune's hair came off to reveal a convict-like haircut. The royal robes were torn asunder.[31] At least one of the king's courtiers was knocked to the deck and received a black eye inflicted by a trooper's well-placed foot. White spotted bubbles coming from under the bathwater and 'naturally concluded that one victim was "enjoying" his last moments, caused through another person standing on him'. On this occasion the dunking was not terminal, but onboard another vessel an inductee received fatal injuries. In an attempt to avoid being forcibly pushed in, a lieutenant who was a doctor and well liked, dove into the bath, struck the bottom and dislocated his neck; he died four days later.[32]

Brief stopovers in coastal ports broke up the daily regime. On the westward voyages this might include less exotic places like Hobart, Tasmania, or Albany, Western Australia, but other ports were nothing like their English-styled home towns. For good reason the troops were not always granted leave, given the ever-present prospect of men absconding. General shore leave was not granted when the Main Body embarkation stopped in at Hobart, but they did hold a route march through the city. White was corralled into a 'picket' under the charge of a captain. Their task: scouring the town for deserters or men without leave. 'The captain had a pair of field glasses,' he wrote, 'and if when levelling these he saw Khaki in the distance he would despatch a couple of men to find out their business for being ashore, some of them were caught who had "sloped ashore".'[33] The picket was only partially successful and 11 men remained at large when the convoy set sail.

It was not until Colombo in Ceylon (Sri Lanka) that the men got shore leave. For most New Zealanders this was the first unfamiliar city they had laid eyes on, and it did not disappoint. A natural port that had seen 2000 years of traders, Colombo was an attractive stopover on the way to war. White and others headed to the 'native' quarter.

> This is the most fascinating part of Colombo as it gives one a glimpse of real Indian life. Here are narrow smelly streets lined with typical native shops that open right out on to the street, natives swarming the streets like flies and robed in all the colours of the rainbow, though I

wouldn't vouch for the cleanliness of their garments however gorgeous they might be . . . Every time the rickshaw halted when the crowd got too dense I was surrounded by hordes of natives, some pressing me to buy articles at extortionate prices, and others gazing idly on, while little children begged for coins, pitching a long tale of woe as an excuse . . . all the misfortunes that could be possibly inflicted on him. The remarkable part of all was that they were so plump and sturdy, and by no means looked uncared for.[34]

However, as the Main Body drew closer to Africa events elsewhere were conspiring to deliver the New Zealanders to the sands of the Middle East. Originally the Main Body had been making for Britain and then straight on to France. Everything changed when Ottoman naval forces opened fire on Russian ports and vessels in the Black Sea in October 1914. The Ottoman Turks had entered the war on the side of the Central Powers: the German and Austro-Hungarian empires. This new combatant threatened the strategically significant Suez Canal. The half-century-old waterway linked south Asian produce and raw materials with European markets and factories without shipping having to navigate around Africa. 'We suddenly learned that our trip to England was cancelled,' wrote Melville White, and 'that we had to winter in Egypt'. On 30 November, the redirected NZEF landed in Egypt via the canal. Two days later, at 2 a.m., the rattle of winches awoke Arthur Skinner at the canal's northern entrance.

I looked round to find that we were just getting tied up in Port Said. Even at that early hour the natives were ready to load us with coal. When I got up at daylight a beautiful scene met my vision. We were surrounded by boats, some of them our fleet. There were three French warships . . . one British battleship and one cruiser, also three torpedo boats, destroyers and our escort the *Hampshire* . . . Everyone was busy, motorboats, rowing boats many about in hundreds. At 9 pm we steamed slowly through a great line of ships passing the three French warships on our right. They gave us some very hearty cheers and lifted their hats when our band played the 'Marseillaise'. We passed about 20 Australian boats. I was absolutely hoarse with returning their cheers. It was a great sight, one not easily forgotten.[35]

At Port Said, Skinner also spotted evidence that his compatriot Hugh Reilly had preceded them; among the magnificent collection of vessels of war was a collection of fragile flying machines, including 'several French Hydroplanes' and some men 'fitting an Aeroplane up on the wharf'.

Shortly after his marriage Reilly had been posted to Egypt; he arrived just days before the NZEF. Reilly was one of the leading officers in RFC Egypt Detachment, a small force of three machines that would eventually grow into 30 Squadron.[36] At the time of its inception the detachment possessed Maurice and Henri Farman's biplanes, which shared a superficial resemblance to the Boxkites flown by Hammond in the prewar era but were larger, stronger and capable of carrying a pilot and an observer. When war started they were already unsuited to the demands of the Western Front; nonetheless, it was believed they could satisfactorily carry out useful reconnaissance duties in the less crowded skies in the Middle East. The Farmans were augmented by the arrival of a French seaplane flight that Skinner had spotted at Port Said.

As a theatre of war, the Middle East was particularly demanding on man and machine, but aviation was the best means of gathering intelligence on enemy strength and disposition. The main base of operations was near Ismailia, halfway along the canal. The detachment also operated from forward bases, including one at Qantara on the eastern side of the canal. These advance positions enabled longer sorties. The very first flight indicated the detachment's worth when a pilot reported that at 4000 ft over Ismailia he could observe Port Said and Suez in one sweeping vista. Reilly and his men made some of the first flights seen in the region.

As in France, the New Zealander was at the forefront of delivering aviation to the front line, in this case over Egypt and Palestine. Gone for Reilly were the green, rolling landscapes of France; in their place was an expanse of sand, broken by rocky outcrops, stretching to the horizon. To cover the distances involved, the machines were fitted with some of the earliest long-range fuel tanks. In flights that ventured as far north as Palestine, Reilly gathered invaluable intelligence. It was exhausting flying but the open landscape made it difficult for enemy forces to conceal their strength and movements.

Reilly and his observer were the first airmen of RFC Egypt Detachment to be fired on. On 17 January 1915 the pair located a large force of 720 infantrymen and units of cavalry closing in on one of the advance air bases.[37] The retort of gunfire alerted the New Zealander to the fact they were coming under ground fire. The fabric of the Farman was pierced but no great damage was done. Reilly's report was soon substantiated and augmented by further reconnaissance missions that indicated the Ottomans were readying for an assault on the canal, with troops concentrated in and around Beersheba, barely 100 miles from the canal.

On 25 January a series of sorties by the detachment spotted over 6000 infantry and 600-strong cavalry, some less than six miles east of Qantara.[38] Many more would have been located but weather over the Sinai was demanding: in the morning, mists pushed back flight times; and flying was often impossible in the afternoon thanks to strong northwest winds and the occasional sandstorm. Because of this they flew only 25 sorties over January.[39] Yet Reilly and the detachment officers, with only three operational machines, had done a remarkable job: their observations meant the defending forces were ready when the attack came on the central sector of the Suez Canal. The aircraft would continue to be the 'eyes' of the Canal Defence Force, which included elements of the NZEF, during the battle.

On 3 February the Ottomans launched their assault on the New Zealand positions.[40] In the pre-dawn hours, 10 miles south of Ismailia at Serapeum, the Turks attempted to cross the canal and secure positions on the western bank. The Canterbury Battalion was dug in, though none too comfortably, as Turkish artillery homed in on their location. 'I don't mind saying I was horribly frightened,' said Cecil Malthus, 'and dug in to the sand like a rabbit.'[41] Reilly was observing proceedings from on high. Peering through their flying goggles, pilots and observers saw the western side occupied by 30,000 British Empire soldiers and on the eastern bank attacking elements of a force that numbered around 20,000 Ottoman Empire men.

The RFC kept the commanding officer of the Canal Defence Force informed of enemy movements. On the day of the attack, airmen undertook over five hours of reconnaissance. The next day it was 14 hours.[42] Thanks to Allied preparedness and strength along the water channel, the Turks were repulsed with considerable losses: the Ottomans suffered 2000 casualties to the Allies' 200. Reilly saw the enemy withdrawal, and Skinner from his frontline trench noted that 'aeroplanes [were] over us all day'.[43] General Sir John Maxwell, commanding the British troops in Egypt, asked the detachment's commanding officer to pass on 'my appreciation of the hard and good work they have done with inferior machines. I do not know what we should have done without them.'[44] Further praise followed from one of Maxwell's immediate subordinates, General Alexander Wilson:

> I desire to express my high appreciation of the valuable work done by the pilots and observers of the French hydroplane squadron and the detachment of the Royal Flying Corps in the numerous reconnaissances carried out by them previous to and during the advance of the enemy. They were constantly under shrapnel and rifle fire and carried out their difficult and dangerous duties with . . . resourcefulness and courage.[45]

Over the following month 23 flights were undertaken, including one marathon sortie by Reilly. Their plane fitted with an extra-large fuel tank, Reilly and his observer flew for El Murra in Palestine. Departing Ismailia and flying alone in clear skies, they crossed the blue ribbon of the canal and headed deep into the Sinai. Flanked by the distant Mediterranean Sea in the north and Mount Sinai in the south, Reilly pushed into the Negev Desert and their destination. With 170 miles behind them they spotted in the distance white flecks: tents, hundreds of tents. They had discovered a substantial Ottoman encampment. The airmen dropped small and rudimentary bombs on the camp and were in turn recipients of ground fire before they wheeled for home. The four-hour flight was the longest undertaken by the detachment.[46]

The sortie was one of Reilly's last in Egypt: in April he was transferred to Mesopotamia, where he joined a small air contingent assembled to support a British advance up the Tigris River at the eastern extremity of the Ottoman Empire. His posting coincided with the departure of the NZEF for action nearer the heart of the Ottoman Empire, in the Dardanelles and Gallipoli. It was here, on the dirty, stubbled ridges of Gallipoli, that many men first encountered combat. Their experiences at Gallipoli would lead a number of them to request a transfer to the fledgling RFC and RNAS.

CHAPTER FOUR
ABOVE THE FRAY
1915

The British hoped to use the Gallipoli campaign to knock out the Central Powers' weakest link: the Ottoman Empire. When the Anglo-French naval advance on the Ottoman Turk capital of Constantinople was thwarted by strong defences in the narrows of the Dardanelles, it fell to an invasion of the Gallipoli Peninsula to clear the way for a renewed attempt by the fleet. Based on recent dismal performances in the Balkan Wars, it was assumed that the Turks would prove a pushover. 'There will be no Turkey — as we know it now — in a few months' was Melville White's assessment as he surveyed the 'gigantic fleet' at anchor between the green hills of Mudros harbour, Lemnos.[1] A sergeant attached to the NZEF headquarters, White had an excellent vantage point from which to view the campaign — but his prediction, and those of others, proved wildly at variance with subsequent events. As the staging post for the invasion, just 40 miles from the Dardanelles, Mudros was filled with transports and ships of war, including a great five-funnelled Russian warship and the mighty dreadnought battleship HMS *Queen Elizabeth*. A veritable armada. How could it possibly fail against the 'sick man of Europe', the arthritic and rheumy-eyed Ottoman Empire?

The New Zealanders were combined with their trans-Tasman cousins into the Australian and New Zealand Army Corps (ANZAC). The Anzacs were only one part of a force that included substantial British and French elements. Two days out from the landings, the assembled forces received a circular from General Ian Hamilton, commander in chief of the Mediterranean Expeditionary Force:

> Before us lies an adventure unprecedented in modern warfare. Together with our comrades of the Fleet we are about to force a landing upon an open beach in the face of positions which have been vaunted by our enemies as impregnable . . . the positions will be stormed, and the war brought one step nearer to a glorious close. . . . the whole world will be watching our progress. Let us prove ourselves worthy of the great feat of arms entrusted to us.

On the eve of the battle White accurately predicted that the 'first fight with the Turks . . . may prove one of the hottest of the campaign'.

On 25 April 1915 the initial landings were made. On board the fleet, New Zealanders woke to the sound of shellfire: the heavy guns of the warships were bombarding the Turks. Guns flashed continually across the large fleet in the early morning darkness. It was a 'wondrous sight', Arthur Skinner wrote in his diary as he waited in a boat ready to deliver him to the beach. 'Looking out of the port we can see the troops landing,' he scrawled in the gentle see-sawing of the vessel. It was not until midday that he landed and the 'wondrous sight' was dispelled. Following in the footsteps of the Australian assault, they scrambled off the beach for the steep hills.

> On our way we passed a terrible number of dead and wounded Australians and Turks and everything looked in a most deplorable state. We had orders to reinforce the firing line straight away and we had to scale steep cliffs with snipers trying to pick us off. When we got to the firing line there was a perfect hail of shrapnel and rifle fire to say nothing about the machine gun. It took me nearly a day to get on the firing line and when I did arrive there was no cover except that which our fellows had been able to build under very heavy fire.[2]

White watched the grim assault from his ship's railing. Some inbound troopers abandoned their boats before they grounded and leapt in the water fully equipped, then 'waded ashore amidst hails of lead, and like their Australian brothers charged valiantly up the steep hill, driving the Turks before them at the point of a bayonet'. The steep range that rose from the beach proved the downfall of many Anzacs as entrenched Turks poured down a 'murderous stream' of fire. 'Meanwhile the battleships were heaving their shells thick and fast into the Turks slaughtering them wholesale,' wrote White, 'smashing up the big batteries in the hills.'

> The constant rapid cracking of machine guns, the unceasing reports of rifle fire, the flashing, booming, and shrieking of immense shells and the thundering reverberations amongst the hills all occurring simultaneously made a mighty tumult never to be forgotten. Though wonderful it was awful, for it needed no imagination to know that our brave troops were falling every minute, and that all this fearful execution of mankind on a bright and lovely day . . .[3]

Onshore, Skinner and his fellow troopers occupied captured Turkish trenches.

> We laid there all afternoon and replied to the enemy's fire. All the next day we remained in the trenches keeping up a heavy fire and it was an absolute hell on earth and few of us expected to get out alive. Very heavy casualties, fellows were falling all around me, getting their heads blown off . . .[4]

By nightfall little more than a toehold had been established.

At 11 that night, Clarence Umbers was onboard a warship when boats carrying casualties drew up alongside. 'I shall not forget the cries of the wounded as they were hoisted aboard,' Umbers wrote to his father in Dunedin. The initial batch of men were Australians who had borne the brunt of the fighting on the first day; the following day, badly shot-up New Zealanders arrived. Umbers was put in charge of the wounded and dead men's belongings. He and the others cared for some 500 poor souls: 'There is not much sleep for us at night, as the moaning of the suffering is so loud.' Umbers was subsequently transferred to the RFC and flew with distinction in Salonika.[5]

Over the next two days the New Zealanders and Australians struggled to consolidate their position, and by 28 April the Anzacs and Ottomans had fought themselves to a standstill. The Allied forces here and at the British landing at the southern tip of the peninsula, Cape Helles, failed to attain their objectives, but the Turks had also failed to repel the invaders. Stalemate. Further attempts to break out in the south brought heavy casualties for no gain. Then the Ottoman commanders attempted to wipe out Anzac Cove. Wave upon wave of Arab and Turkish infantry made frontal assaults on the two square miles of Anzac-occupied territory. The successful defence yielded a terrible 3000 casualties for the Ottoman force. The field of battle was so befouled that, for the one and only time, both sides agreed to a single-day truce to allow the removal of dead and wounded from the battlefield. In spite of this, and a lull in the fighting, the conditions at Anzac Cove were appalling.

The location yielded no natural fresh water and all provisions had to be landed by boat. Rations were sufficient but troops subsisted on a limited fare: 'Bully beef, hard biscuits and jam and cheese and dried vegetables and a little bacon,' was the daily menu as described by future airman Charles Mills to his mother in New Zealand.[6]

Then there was the accommodation: up to 25,000 men were living in slum-like conditions.[7] 'We are at present living in "dug outs" cut into the sides of the gullies and present rather a remarkable appearance I'm sure,' wrote Mills; 'we manage to make ourselves fairly comfortable anyway and that is the chief thing.' The officers on hand were similarly housed in dugouts. Added to this was the poor sanitation. As fast as latrines were dug, they were filled. Lice and flies proliferated; men accustomed to cleanliness were demoralised by an onslaught of the crawling and flying tormentors. Under the Mediterranean sun the flies, feasting on the waste accumulating at the latrines and the battlefield's rotting dead, swarmed in biblical proportions. Preparing meals under such conditions was stomach-churning. It was little wonder that the men were stricken with all manner of ailments, especially skin rashes and dysentery. Thanks to dysentery, Wellingtonian Arthur Browne, who would fly as an observer at Cambrai in late 1917, and landed at Gallipoli weighing 11 stone 7 lbs, was barely 8 stone when he left the peninsula.[8] Mills had only just been delivered to Anzac Cove when he was struck with typhoid, a disease caused by the consumption of food or water contaminated with human waste. He was transferred back to Egypt and hospital.

The campaign dragged on for a full eight months. In between the offensives, Anzac Cove was regularly shelled. In May 1915 Melville White, who had returned from a brief visit to Alexandria with his headquarters colonel, noted that the cove 'presented a much different appearance . . . being stacked with cases of ammunition [and] food . . . which troops were busy stacking and issuing, and strings of mules were being led along the beach by Indians loaded with provisions for the boys in the trenches'.[9] Nonetheless, the beach was not free from danger. Not long after his arrival a shell burst among the mules, killing about 30 and wounding many more. The Turks habitually saved their heaviest bombardments for mealtimes. Not a day went by without a man being killed and others wounded on the beach.[10] A few were even killed while they enjoyed one of the few pleasures of Anzac Cove: swimming in the cool, clear waters of the bay. It is remarkable that more did not die in this manner, given how exposed they were to enemy artillery.

For those among the forward elements of the Anzac effort it was even worse. A former West Coast clerk, Henry Rasmussen, was involved in securing the New Zealand left flank early after the landing. As a trooper he was ordered to dig trenches over ground that had already seen action. 'I was driving my pick into the ground,' he recalled in a postwar interview, 'I drove it in and pulled out the head of a body that had been buried some time during the hour when this area had been fought back and forth over. There were bodies all through that ground.'[11] A little later he occupied a tract where a strong Turkish attack had been repulsed, 'leaving the ground . . . littered with dead Turks. You could hardly throw a stone over it without hitting somebody.' Over the next three weeks the corpses expanded and deflated in the hot sun. Then the Turk artillery began lobbing shells on the corpses.

> They would explode amongst these bodies and over would come pieces of clothing, pieces of dead bodies while you stood on the fire step and watched out. That was hideous and terrible. They used to get on fire and the wind always seemed to blow from them towards us and you would get this smoke of burning bodies which is a revolting thing. It causes a violent headache for one thing but there is nothing else to breathe so you had to breathe it.[12]

Unsurprisingly Rasmussen became very ill and was evacuated, and soon thereafter applied for a transfer to the RFC.

Offensives in August were brutal, and ripped the heart out of the New Zealand effort. In November the faltering Allied strength and the ever-increasing Ottoman numbers led to an evacuation order being given. In the days leading up to their departure they made a large bombardment on the Turkish positions. 'The shells landed with beautiful accuracy in the Turkish trenches and generally played havoc,' wrote White. 'As each missile landed and ploughed into the hill side up went a column of earth, from which rose clouds of yellowish smoke, preceded by a long drawn whine which an imaginative person might deem to be the sighing of lost souls (Huns and Turks) while making their exit from earth to Hades.'[12A]

The New Zealanders began embarking on 15 December. In their final gasping moments on Anzac Cove, equipment was destroyed in order to leave nothing of use for the enemy. White burned documents, papers and maps. A huge supply depot was opened to the troops. 'It was amusing to see,' the New Zealander observed,

> an Australian walking away with half a dozen pairs of gumboots round his neck and a huge grin spreading over his face; also a Punjab strutting around like a peacock, wearing a British warmer [coat] and a shiny pair of smart leggings. The troops were at liberty to help

themselves to thousands of pounds worth of beautiful winter clothing which could not be shipped away. Many of us did not bother to participate in the scramble, as we were quite content to get away with nothing more than a whole skin.[13]

In 1915 the skies above the Sinai and Gallipoli had not exactly been swarming with machines but there were enough to catch the attention of the entrenched men. Between February 1915 and January 1916 the RNAS flew over 2300 flights in the region; of these, nearly two-thirds were either reconnaissance or spotting sorties.[14] Airmen carried out a limited number of bombing, experimental and anti-submarine flights, too. This meant the RNAS was engaged in flights and fighting that incorporated much of what was occurring on the Western Front, with the notable exception of anti-aircraft patrols. The Central Powers had no more than four machines in the early part of the campaign, and fewer than 10 for much of the second half of 1915.[15] This was, of course, nothing like the great numbers of machines that would populate the skies of the Western Front in subsequent years; nonetheless it was an indication of the increasing importance of air power, and it captured the imagination of some on the ground.

Prior to Gallipoli, Lieutenant Colonel W. G. Malone, who rose to prominence on Chunuk Bair, was swatting away flies on the Suez when he saw two aeroplanes flying overhead; one very likely piloted by Reilly. He conveyed the sentiment of his terrestrially bound countrymen when he wrote wistfully in his diary: 'I would like a flight in one. It must be lovely.' Melville White arrived at the same opinion a few months later at Gallipoli:

> I turn and face the sea, and observe an aeroplane soaring tranquilly but mysteriously with wings outspread, like some wondrous bird of higher regions, towards the setting sun which was sinking slowly and majestically behind Imbros and Sarathrace into the mythical waters of the Aegean Sea, throwing a crimson shaft to the shores of Gallipoli, symbolic of the path man must tread until the ideas of humanity in the great world struggle have been attained.
>
> The mechanical bird soars higher and farther into space until lost in the folds of the golden cloud. With it my thoughts go, even still further to the homes of relatives and friends in Maoriland, somewhat at the end of the world.[16]

In 1915, aside from Reilly and Hammond, few New Zealanders had managed to escape the snares of earth for the sky. One soldier who did was prewar aviation enthusiast and glider constructor William Angus. As a trooper at Gallipoli, Angus soon learned that although airmen were subject to great dangers, they also had distinct advantages over their soldier counterparts — and not just when in flight high above the fray. Airmen simply lived better. The Allied aeroplanes that criss-crossed the peninsula did so from bases at arm's length from the enemy: the islands of Imbros or Tenedos, both some 20 miles from the front line. At Imbros, which New Zealand troops visited during their tenure at Gallipoli, Angus could not help but notice that most Allied airmen were housed either in the tents adjacent to General Hamilton's general headquarters or onboard HMS *Ark Royal*, the world's first aircraft carrier — accommodation that was a world away from the deprivations of Anzac Cove.[17] The airmen were well beyond the range of Ottoman shells when on land or at anchor off Imbros. They could sleep easy, far from the roar of the artillery, and carry out their daytime pre-flight and post-flight duties safe in the knowledge they would not experience the terrifying effects of a stray artillery shell. Ordered rows of tents and well-planned and maintained sanitation offered living conditions of which troopers and officers at Anzac Cove could only dream. Charles 'Sammy' Samson, a pioneer of naval aviation who was commanding the RNAS forces supporting the land and sea campaign in the Dardanelles, described the respectable conditions of his airmen at Imbros: 'We soon settled down at the aerodrome. Some of us lived in the Greek owner's house, the rest in tents, and we used a large marquee we had obtained in some mysterious way as a mess tent. The men made splendid homes for themselves in the aeroplane packing cases.'[18]

In October 1915 Angus, now a driver with the NZEF, was pleased to learn he was being transferred to the RNAS.[19] As one of the early members of the Canterbury (NZ) Aero Club and an experienced mechanic, he was an ideal colonial addition to Samson's unit, which numbered over 100 men and some 18 officers.[20] Angus worked on the aircraft but also flew as an observer when required. In this latter role he may well have watched the final weeks of fighting and the evacuation of Anzac Cove.

At Imbros, Angus found the food to be a step up from the fare served on the peninsula. Imbros airmen had real beef on the hoof, not out of a can, and fresh local produce. By the time he arrived the officers' mess tent had been upgraded to a solid stone-and-tile structure where meals could be eaten in a civilised manner and without the swarming flies of Gallipoli.[21] With tents, hot water for ablutions and mess orderlies catering to the officers' needs, it was a decidedly more genteel existence.

The considerable advantages of being an airman were well known to the men in the trenches of Anzac Cove, and the contrast was felt even more keenly by those who, having trudged through the squalor of Gallipoli, then went on to the filth of the Western Front. 'For the first time in my life I found I was covered with lice. It was that that really made me think that trench warfare was not for me!' wrote one veteran of the Western Front. 'I used to look up with great envy at these aircraft flying round about. So I immediately put in an application to join the Royal Flying Corps.'[22] James Dennistoun of Peel Forest, Timaru, got scabies when he was on the Western Front and had to see a doctor. 'I was so ashamed. I must have got them in the trenches I think . . . Ough!'[23]

The prospect of sleeping between clean sheets in a tent or being put up in homes well behind the front lines, often in the vicinity of local drinking establishments and female distractions, were amongst the considerable attractions of being an airman.

As Arthur Coningham later attested, the decision to join the RFC simply came down to the fact that he preferred 'sleeping in bed to the incredible discomfort of a trench'.[24] Keith Park of Thames, who landed at Gallipoli and then endured the mud and wretchedness of the Somme, concurred: 'I can tell you after two and a half years at the front with the artillery on various theatres in summer and winter we were incomparably better off [in the RFC]'.[25] When stories

William Angus was
seconded to the RNAS
as a mechanic and also
flew as an observer.
Here he is in the front
seat of a Henri Farman
of 3 Wing on Imbros.

of frontline deprivations reached New Zealand, some discerning parents recognised that their offspring would be better suited to the air service. Malcolm 'Mac' McGregor of Hunterville wanted to become a soldier at the age of 17. His parents refused as they believed he was ill suited to the rigours of the trenches, but when he suggested the RFC they agreed. McGregor went on to become an ace and flight commander.[26]

Other men sought to follow in Angus's footsteps, not just to escape the trenches but also because the possibility of a commission in the flying corps meant higher pay and greater social mobility. While William Coates was languishing with the NZEF at the Zeitoun Camp, Egypt, awaiting his turn at Gallipoli, he wrote home to his family in the Kaipara for additional funds because his pay was insufficient to see him through the week. 'I hope you were not alarmed to get a cable from me to send some money. It is only because I have been very short of money, that is not sufficient to last between paydays and there are several things I want to get as soon as I can get the money.'[27] Upon receiving their wings, officers in the flying service received an additional 12s 6d per day, a substantial bonus on the 7s 6d basic income of an officer in the infantry.[28] Consequently, an airman could pull in nearly twice as much income. Alongside financial advantages, the RFC, RNAS and subsequent RAF facilitated a freedom rare elsewhere in British military service.

Initially, public (i.e. private) school and university types dominated the flying service, but as the war progressed and the RFC and RNAS expanded, a broader class of men won admittance to officer positions. Moreover, officers in the air services operated in a culture where social conventions were blurred. As one historian observed:

> The pilots of the Great War were able to claim a level of pay, a responsibility for complex machinery and a latitude in the interpretation of orders which in the ground war belonged only to Dominion brigadiers or British corps commanders. Little wonder then that recruiting officers of the RFC and RAF were never short of applicants even during the bloodiest days of April 1917.[29]

The middle-class sons of New Zealand doctors, lawyers, engineers, accountants and farmers wanted positions commensurate with their perceived social status, and the flying corps offered this. The son of a prominent Kaipara landholder, Coates had more reason than most to aspire to ascend the ranks: he had a remarkable older brother of considerable social standing. Gordon Coates had served as chairman of the Otamatea County Council, was a highly regarded commander of the local mounted rifles volunteers and, in 1911, entered Parliament as the member for Kaipara. Gordon wanted to enlist when war broke out but was dissuaded by Prime Minister William Massey. With such a high-profile brother, William was not keen on remaining a soldier; he wanted to get ahead but felt that his chances within the NZEF were poor. In 1915 he found promotions hard to come by in the confines of Zeitoun Camp; in his own estimation he was more likely to get demoted to trooper than to climb the ranks.[30] He toyed with the idea of transferring out to a British regiment: 'I don't altogether like the idea of deserting the New Zealanders . . . but they won't give me a chance here, whereas in the imperial army there are no end of opportunities.' But his colonel stood in his way: he had given orders not to allow any transfers.

(If William hoped to gain some parity with his brother, he was to be disappointed. Gordon won a Military Cross and bar on the Western Front, served as a cabinet minister in the postwar government and eventually held the highest office in the land: prime minister.)

Many men in the colonial NZEF tried to obtain advancement via prestigious British regiments. But there were two things these foreign regiments could not offer that the flying services could: the chance to fight the war while working with engines and airframes; and the heart-pumping adventure and glamour of aviation.

Men with engineering or motoring backgrounds like William Angus gravitated to the RFC and RNAS because military aviation was a technical and mechanical undertaking. The wood and fabric frames, complex rigging, machine guns, bombing apparatus, flight instrumentation and engines of the aircraft needed carpenters, riggers, armourers and mechanics. New Zealand pilots, observers and gunners often demonstrated a strong mechanical bent.

Wesley Spragg of Mount Albert, Auckland, for example, had a 'marked talent for mechanics'. He was a fine swimmer and rider — his horse Jacko was a champion jumper — but from a young age he gravitated towards making 'engines and things'. He undertook formal engineering training and had just became partner in Haydock & Spragg, motor engineers, when the war began.[31] 'He made what for him was a natural selection,' recalled a family friend, 'the Royal Flying Corps — as his branch of service.'[32] Shy and reserved by nature, Spragg was also quietly determined. He shipped out for Britain and the RFC in October 1915. By the end of 1917 he had flown in night defensive operations and had served in France and in Egypt.

Eric Croll came from a family of engineers and was obsessed with mechanical technology. His grandfather was the first inspector of machinery with the Maritime Department, Canterbury; his father served his apprenticeship at Anderson's foundry in Christchurch, and his older brother Cecil eventually became chief engineer with Farmers produce stores in Christchurch. Fifteen years and a relocation to Wellington later, Eric's father came home and asked if any of his sons wanted 'a trip to England'. The New Zealand Shipping Company commonly took two engineer's apprentices on their voyages to Britain — usually the sons of middle-class families. One of the boys selected had fallen ill and Eric's father, who now managed an engineering firm in Wellington, was asked if one of his sons wanted a 'free' trip.

Within 24 hours Eric was at sea, working his passage as a greaser. His aim was to arrive in Britain and turn his mechanical interests to becoming a pilot in the fledgling RFC. But in Britain there were no vacancies for 'stray New Zealanders', especially one without appropriate references or the requisite family connections. In desperation he joined the RFC as a despatch rider and mechanic with 8 Kite Balloon Section and was sent to France. Aside from keeping frontline elements of the unit supplied with rum, he had more than enough to keep his mechanical hands busy.

> Yes there were plenty of engines with us — the winch of the balloon and the blowers and
> the workshop light plant and the transport with 25 ton Leylands and two Crossley tenders,

two motor cycle sidecars and most important of all our two solo cycles, Phelon & Moore 3.5 H.P. chain drive fixed inclined engine — nice machines but not robust enough for the work. I believe mine fell apart when I left.[33]

Eric's persistence eventually saw him in the air as an observer-gunner and then as a pilot.

Former Nelson College pupil Donald Harkness loved taking things apart, tinkering and reengineering them to function better than before. 'He understood not just *how* things worked,' his family recalled, 'but *why* they worked, and read avidly about new advances in technology that seemed to be everywhere — everywhere except New Zealand.'[34] He enrolled to study engineering at Canterbury College, University of New Zealand. Writing to his father, Harkness expressed a view common among the motoring and engineering fraternities: 'I reckon it would be first rate if … I could go Home to the aviation school, as I would give anything to be able to use an aeroplane, especially at the present time when they are all-important to both the Army and Navy.'[35]

For some men, though, adventure called them to flying during the war. It was exciting and dangerous; men who had watched and admired Stone, Hammond and Scotland were gripped by the desire to emulate the flying pioneers, and experience the thrill of powered flight. It became readily apparent to young New Zealanders that the RFC and RNAS offered almost limitless opportunities to fly. Some exceptional adventurers gravitated to the air service.

Anthony Wilding was a good example of a New Zealander who combined motor mechanics and a hunger for flight. An avid motorcyclist and adventurer at large, Wilding was also the world's leading tennis player of his day, and one of the early twentieth century's sporting celebrities.[36] He was born in Christchurch, but is now largely forgotten in his native land; in Europe and the United States, however, he was widely known and admired as the tall, handsome and goodnatured athlete who, by the age of 31, had won eight Wimbledon finals and a clutch of Davis Cup titles. He also loved the internal combustion engine, especially when fitted to a motorcycle frame, and he ploughed the money he made on the tennis circuit into his motorbike, a 412-cc Phelon & Moore two-speed, which he rode the length and breadth of Europe. In 1908 he rode in an 876-mile reliability trial from Land's End, Cornwall, to John o' Groats, Scotland. He won the gold medal — just over half of the three-score machines entered made it in one piece. In 1910 he piloted his motorcycle 3000 miles on a remarkable grand tour that departed London, crossed the Channel, passed through Belgium, the Netherlands, Germany and Switzerland and finally returned to Britain. In that same year he flirted with the latest craze: aviation.

In France he wangled a flight at a leading airfield: Mourmelon-le-Grand, in northeast France. Four aircraft were already aloft with pupils under instruction when he arrived late morning.

I was soon up in a machine, seated with the head pilot-instructor, a very jovial man. His only words of English were 'Goad-bye,' and these he always hurled at me with an accompanying dig in the back when he took a corner at an angle calculated to cause alarm, or made a 'Vol Plane' [controlled downward flight, often with the engine off]. All went well for a bit, and we flew round the course several times, when my friend said 'Goad-bye,' and shot off over a plantation of trees, sending the machine higher and higher. Suddenly the wretched engine began to misfire. I knew a misfire well by the sight and sound, but at this moment it was more significant than ever before. My friend behind me said 'Goad-bye,' and off we went at a great pace toward earth. But just as we looked like making a hole in it, the elevating planes seemed to be raised up a bit, and we glided up, and then went along beautifully on fairly smooth ground. The sensation was very fine, and I hope to have many more 'Vol Planes'; but when the engine stopped dead of its own accord, I really thought my last moment had come. [37]

Aside from this close brush with death, Wilding greatly enjoyed the sensation of flying: 'When high up the wind seems to shake the frail craft, and its general behaviour is very similar to a light boat on water slightly ruffled by the wind.' His mother was less than impressed with her son's flight, which was widely reported in New Zealand with a touch of sensationalism that awoke her maternal instincts; perhaps Anthony was risking his life needlessly in such a new and perilous endeavour. He assured her that he had taken no undue risk and that flying was not going to supplant tennis and his motorbiking.[38] 'I am so *very* thankful,' his mother wrote in her diary.[39]

In the end, when war broke out Wilding attached himself to the Royal Marines, where he worked with Charles Samson as a driver with a newly conceived force of transport assistance and reconnaissance armoured cars, thus combining his love of freedom and action and the automotive world. Horses were more or less useless, he concluded; this was a 'motor war'.[40]

When Samson left for the Mediterranean, Wilding continued his work on the Western Front. He named his pet dog 'Samson' after his commander and good friend. 'The main job is roughly this,' he told his 'dearest Mother' — 'go out about 5.30 am and motor as near to the German lines as possible and report this and all other information to headquarters.'[41] When winter arrived the soldiers dug in and stalemate ensued — 'when two armies are practically stationary and strongly entrenched armoured motors are very little use,' he informed his family.[42] As he noted, this only served to emphasise that the armoured cars were 'a side show'; the 'flying show' was the primary business of the RNAS. His thoughts once again turned skyward.[43] At Dunkirk, he went on flights with naval airmen hunting submarines, and on the odd reconnaissance above enemy trenches.[44]

On 9 May 1915 Wilding was killed when a shell struck the dugout in which he was sheltering. He lost his life very close to the place he had first taken to the air at Mourmelon-le-Grand. Such was his fame that not only was his death widely reported globally, but his dog, Samson, was also shipped back to Britain and eventually despatched to New Zealand and his family in the South Island. No doubt inspired by Anthony's flying adventures, his younger brother Edwyn joined the RFC.

Another airman with New Zealand parentage and a fascination with motoring and flying was killed in action only days before Wilding. William Rhodes-Moorhouse was the son of Mary Ann Rhodes, a member of the Ngāti Tama, Ngāti Ruanui and Te Ātiawa Māori iwi of Taranaki. His maternal grandfather, dubbed 'the Millionaire of Wellington', was a former whaling captain

William Rhodes-Moorhouse typified the mechanically-minded and adventurous men who sought a place in the air war. He was the RFC's first Victoria Cross recipient.

who had turned his hand successfully to business and politics. Born in London, Rhodes-Moorhouse was a motoring devotee who, in the spirit of Arthur 'Wizard' Stone, applied his daredevil tendencies to the combustion engine — with tragic consequences when he was involved in an accident while on a visit to his ancestral homeland.[45]

On 22 March 1907, while practising on New Brighton Beach for a motorcycle race, Rhodes-Moorhouse hit a seven-year-old boy, knocking him up to 25 ft away; the boy's injuries were fatal.[46] At the coroner's inquest Rhodes-Moorhouse admitted he had probably been tearing over the sand at close to 60 mph. Supported by numerous witnesses, he told the authorities he had tried to avoid the boy but the boy had become confused and had run towards the machine. Two months later he appeared before the Supreme Court in Christchurch, alongside a line-up of men accused of abduction, indecent acts, assault and robbery.[47] It was an ignominious 'homecoming'. Rhodes-Moorhouse was fortunate not to face civil proceedings from the boy's parents, who accepted a cheque for £250 from the family.[48] Nonetheless, he faced two courts and widespread press coverage before he secured an acquittal on a charge of manslaughter in August.[49] He slipped quietly out of New Zealand and returned to England, where he entered Cambridge University before turning his hand to flying.

Rhodes-Moorhouse was an above-average pilot. Reportedly he learnt to fly a year before he obtained his flying certificate in 1911.[50] The following year he came in second at the Aerial Derby around London, beaten by the aviation pioneer Gustav Hamel. In 1912 he also became the first person to carry two passengers across the Channel, one of whom was his new bride, Linda Morritt; and in 1913 he participated in the Monte Carlo Rally.[51] When war broke out he joined the RFC and was soon occupying the cockpit of a BE2 with one of the early squadrons that had accompanied Reilly into France. Here, in 1915, he flew frequently with Sholto Douglas, the future marshal of the Royal Air Force, who described Rhodes-Moorhouse as a 'small, slight, sandy haired man of extraordinary vitality' and 'one of the pioneers of flying in England'.[52] During the Second Battle of Ypres (April–May 1915) their squadron was flying bombing operations against German communication lines, bridges, roads and railway junctions. Four days into the battle Rhodes-Moorhouse found himself in the thick of the fighting.

On 26 April 1915, the day after the New Zealanders came ashore at Gallipoli, Rhodes-Moorhouse left Merville in northern France to attack the Courtrai railway station in Belgium. The 40-mile flight took him over the Ypres Salient and the enemy trenches. Rhodes-Moorhouse was flying alone in the two-seater because he thought an observer would compromise the mission: the delivery of a single 100-lb bomb. Douglas had argued for his inclusion on the mission but Rhodes-Moorhouse was adamant he would go alone.[53] With little thought for his safety he attacked the Courtrai station at 300 ft, which exposed him to murderous rifle and machine-gun fire, some emanating from the church belfry. He had released the bomb and wheeled for home when he was hit in the abdomen, thigh and hand. Badly wounded, he dropped the plane to 200 ft and skimmed over the ground, nursing the riddled BE2 to Merville.

Sholto Douglas was shocked by his friend's injuries and noted that the observer's seat, where he would have been sitting, had 'half a dozen bullet holes'. Rhodes-Moorhouse insisted on completing his after-action report before being taken to hospital, where he died the next day.

He was awarded the Victoria Cross for his bravery — a first for an airman in the war.[54] Douglas summed up the feelings of many in his autobiography: 'Although born in England, Rhodes-Moorhouse had strong family ties with New Zealand, and the view was expressed recently by Linda Rhodes-Moorhouse, his widow, that his "courage and endurance" were possibly the result of an infusion of the blood of the vigorous fighters of that country.'[55] Wilding and Rhodes-Moorhouse epitomised the kind of individual who were attracted to military aviation; young men who joined the RNAS or RFC were not looking for a quiet war.

Merely being tired of the trenches, seeking social advancement, wanting to potter with engines or hoping for a more exciting life was not going to get you into the flying corps, however. For one thing there simply were not enough vacancies to meet the demand. Even during the worst of Allied air losses in 'Bloody April' 1917, men were clamouring for admittance to the air service. The number of applicants always exceeded the number of cockpits available. Moreover, most men already in uniform had to make an application to transfer to the RFC or RNAS, and their commanders were naturally reluctant to lose some of their best and brightest to the flying service.

The NZEF was no different in this regard. In 1915 General Godley, now the commander of the NZEF, found that he had men on active service in the Middle East and troopers injured at Gallipoli who were seeking to move up the ranks. As soon as the latter group began turning up in British military hospitals, individuals began seeking commissions outside of the NZEF. Although some did so in order to enter highly regarded British regiments, a growing number desired to join the new flying services. This was also true of men who had yet to serve. In New Zealand it was feared that large numbers of 'the very best class of men' might want to leave the dominion to 'attempt to obtain commissions either in Australia or the United Kingdom'.[56]

But even those with real aviation credentials failed to procure entry into the air service. Seaforth McKenzie came from a Rangitikei motoring family. He already had some useful flying experience as a result of his pioneering work with his much older brother Hector: as early as 1909, at the age of 13, Seaforth was assisting his elder sibling with the design and construction of an aeroplane — a tractor biplane that the brothers never completed because of Hector's ill health and problems with storing the machine.[57] The McKenzie brothers' efforts were resurrected in 1913, at the time of the Stone and Scotland flights, but with an imported American machine. The crated Hamilton Aero Manufacturing Company machine arrived in August and was assembled by the two brothers in their time off from working at their father's garage. Seaforth gained extensive experience from the work as well as technical knowledge from reading the numerous aviation magazines to which his brother subscribed: *The Aero, Flight, Aeronautics* and *Aero & Hydro*.[58]

Once the machine was completed in September, they began making short hops and then 500-yard flights at 20 ft.[59] Seaforth was the smaller of the two and was more adept at the art of flying; he undertook the bulk of the flights. At 16 he was already a local celebrity. 'Most gracefully the aeroplane rose, and for 700 yards the young aviator flew the paddock at a speed of between 40 and 50 miles an hour,' reported the *Wanganui Chronicle* of one of his flights. 'Several were following in motor-cars, but they were left hopelessly in the rear . . . the descent was made without any trouble whatever, and Mr Seaforth McKenzie, who handled the machine with great skill, was warmly congratulated.'[60] Despite a series of mishaps: striking the brow of a hill, crashing into a swamp, and a 'pancaked' landing — largely a result of being self-taught and the low power of the 50-hp motor — the brothers' flying endeavours were relatively successful. By the standards of the time Seaforth McKenzie was an accomplished homegrown pilot; when war came he was ready to try his hand at military aviation.

McKenzie applied to enter the RFC as early as June 1915, when he made an application with the support of his local commanding officer in the Wellington district for an appointment as an aviation mechanic. He was 18 but lied about his age, asserting he was 20 years old. Unfortunately the chief of general staff, Colonel Gibbon, was familiar with McKenzie and declined the request. The only crumb he offered McKenzie was that his name would be 'noted for future reference'.[61] McKenzie, however, was tenacious and the following year made his case more strongly to an infantry instructor at Featherston Military Camp.

> I have the honour to submit this my application for a transfer to the Royal Flying Corps. The qualifications for such a transfer are as follows:—
>
> (a) Practical experience of flying, in as much as I made about two dozen perfectly successful flights on my brother's machine. With the exception of two or three times my brother went up, I have never seen a machine in the air. The fact of my being entirely self-taught, I think speaks for itself.
>
> (b) Theoretical knowledge. I have gone fairly deeply into the theory of flight and could do more so.
>
> (c) I have a commission in the New Zealand Forces.
>
> (e) [*sic*] I have had nearly five years experience of motors in my father's garage.[62]

The request was sent up the command chain to Defence Headquarters in Wellington and landed on Gibbon's desk. The chief of general staff was again unpersuaded and 'regretted permission could not be given'. 'Officers are brought into camp and trained to fill certain positions with Reinforcement Drafts,' he continued, 'and they cannot be replaced once their training has commenced.'[63] Frustratingly, there was no recognition of the need for airmen overseas, nor of McKenzie's unique flying experience. It would take a full year before he was able to secure a secondment to the RFC.

For those already serving it was equally frustrating. In July 1915 Major General Godley received a telegram from New Zealand's high commissioner in London, Thomas Mackenzie, regarding the eager and 'numerous' applicants for commissions in imperial forces, including the RFC and RNAS.[64] This was an unforeseen development, but Godley quickly moved to stifle a potential avalanche of requests. 'Convalescent men . . . should be ordered to return to duty immediately they are fit for duty,' he shot back, and applications for 'Commissions Imperial Forces should be refused on the grounds that they have opportunity of promotion in New

Zealand Expeditionary Force, if deserving.'[65] What Godley did not appreciate was that there were plenty of 'deserving' men who could not get commissions in the NZEF and that the lack of opportunities was only going to get worse throughout 1915 and into the following year.

A number of NZEF troopers felt that there were not enough spaces in the officer ranks for advancement. The soldiers who fought at Gallipoli argued that later reinforcements were arriving fully and unfairly 'officered' up.

> Members of the main body and of the second and third reinforcements have expressed their discontent of the later reinforcement contingents from New Zealand being fully officered, thereby affording no opportunity for those men of the main body and the two succeeding contingents who bore a large measure of the fighting, and who had actual experience in battle to obtain commissions in the fresh contingents, but were superseded by men from the training camps.[66]

Godley argued strongly that this was not the case, but this did not stop the men thwarted from commission believing it was so.[67] Mackenzie acted on Godley's 'strong protest against losing any of his men' in this manner and refused to assist individuals who appeared at the High Commission. But if Godley hoped his directive would simply be accepted by these men he was very much mistaken. Some of the soldiers were 'very indignant at not being permitted to apply', Mackenzie wrote to Godley in October 1915.[68] Matters were made worse by a number of approvals that were made in contradiction of the sanction and which therefore smelt of favouritism.[69]

The 1915 Christmas card delivered to the men from General William Birdwood, the NZEF commander in the field, was poorly received in some quarters thanks to Godley's policy. Birdwood's card warmly encouraged his charges to be of 'Good cheer, boys, from all old comrades in the firing line. Return soon and we'll see this through together.'[70] Appended to the card was a missive from Mackenzie in London; with only the dimmest comprehension of the difficulties at hand, he regaled the troopers with 'Heartiest Season's Greetings to the tried and true Sons of the Bull Dog Breed from Maoriland.' Although the men thought highly of Birdwood, some had already made it clear they wanted a shift sideways to the rising air service. They were all in favour of seeing it 'through together' but not necessarily in a trench, and Mackenzie was becoming a lightning rod for disaffection thanks to Godley's orders.

The hospitalised Charles Mills made it clear he wanted to transfer out of the 'Bull Dog Breed from Maoriland' to the 'Fighting Falcon Breed' of the RFC, a different species altogether. 'The time passes so slowly here as there is nothing else to do and we get no news or anything and we are not allowed off the balcony,' Mills wrote to his mother from Alexandria. '[It] is a month now since I was admitted to hospital and I am beginning to get a bit tired of it.'[71] When Birdwood's Christmas salutation arrived, Mills had only just learnt that his attempt to escape the boredom of Egypt and the confines of the NZEF for the RFC had been rebuffed. The letter was from the high commissioner. 'Definite instructions' had been given, recorded Mills, 'that no transfers may be sanctioned from the New Zealand Expeditionary Force to the Imperial Army.'[72]

In the Sinai, Coates wrote home regarding his failed attempt to get into the flying service:

Awfully sick about being turned down for the RFC by our own people after promising me a thumbs-up. I found out afterwards that I had been the first to have applied for flying in the Brigade and Div[ision] turned it down. Could not be spared as an expense. I certainly cannot understand it when there are so many officers playing about . . . However, they say it is temporary owing to a shortage of officers and the present situation here and that when this is cleaned up the transfer will be granted.[73]

Back in London, Mackenzie was fielding requests from men who turned up at his door and via letters in the post. He pleaded with Godley to 'kindly direct' him in 'what is to be done in this connection'.

In conjunction with the War Office, Godley had his staff draw up a workable policy that would create a release valve but not bleed him dry. A quota of five men a month was proposed, and that number increased to eight a month until the last year of the war.[74] Those in the Middle East had to attend the Cadet School in Egypt and those in Britain could apply directly to the War Office. In every case the applicants had to go through the 'proper channels' and correct paperwork had to be completed.[75] Of course only a relatively small number of these were applicants to the flying service; many were to British regiments. It was not much, but it was a start. 'I think this is very fortunate that this decision had been made,' said Mackenzie, 'because great dissatisfaction existed amongst the men' because of the arbitrary nature of the system.[76]

For the applicants the process was frustratingly slow. Mills and Coates were eventually successful but it was not until the first half of 1917 that they were seconded to the RFC.[77] Even with personal intervention it was rarely a quick journey from the trenches to the airfield. Ninian Hyslop of Hastings had General Andrew Russell personally put his name forward and was duly nominated by Godley for one of the five monthly openings. He even had a perfect background as a motor mechanic and had held the New Zealand speed championship for two years in succession.[78] In spite of all this he was not attached to the RFC for training until October 1916 and received his wings seven months later. Other New Zealanders transferred into the RFC from British regiments that they had entered at the beginning of the war. Albert Holden of Clyde, Central Otago, took an even more convoluted route to the flying service.[79] When war was declared he was gold dredging in the Philippine islands and tried to join the New Zealand soldiers when he arrived in London in 1915. He was unable to do so and joined a British regiment before finally getting into the RFC.

Not all men were discouraged from moving into the air service. In Egypt, Trevor White, a veteran of both the Samoa Advance Force and Gallipoli, was approached by a superior. In October 1916, Brigade Commander General Edward Chaytor told the British-born New Zealander: 'The Royal Flying Corps is looking for lightweights! Would you like to go?' At 5 ft 3 in, 'Tiny' White was an ideal candidate for the RFC; not only was he diminutive, he had also been interested in flying since the airborne arrival of the dashing T. E. Lawrence near Bir el Abd. The famous leader of the Arabs arrived by aircraft, only to mount a racing camel and vanish into the haze with his Arab escort.

This incident created wide interest throughout the Brigade. Small drafts of men each month commenced leaving for the Royal Flying Corps in England. Men from the Mounted Regiments were being sought because they had the same natural characteristics that made for a good pilot; a light hand and a good sense of balance.[80]

With the Mounted Rifles in Egypt, White rode an 'ugly, hardy, cunning, bob-tailed Australian chestnut brumby . . . I loved him,' he admitted. But the offer of flight was too great; it was 'a new and exciting future . . . I bid my brumby a fond and sad farewell and reported to the Royal Flying Corps Depot at Heliopolis . . . A few days later the cable from my father arrived, "DON'T BE A FOOL! COME HOME."'

One dangerous, indirect way to avoid the bottleneck in the NZEF system was to become unfit for service in the army through serious illness or injury. Once discharged from the NZEF, or any other force, it was possible to make application directly to the RFC or RNAS without permission from New Zealand or British authorities.

In August 1914 Arthur Coningham, a Wellington university student, answered the call to arms. Four weeks later he landed with an advance force in German Samoa — New Zealand's first foray in the war. When he returned to New Zealand in April 1915 he had only seven hours' leave before departing for the Middle East. The fly- and lice-ridden Anzac Cove got the better of the New Zealander. His health had been ravaged by tropical disease in Samoa, and at Gallipoli he crumbled under an onslaught of sunstroke, dysentery and typhoid.[81] Doctors believed that Coningham, after being repeatedly cut down, had very little prospect of a full recovery in Egypt and he was shipped home in September. On 1 April 1916 in Wellington, he was discharged, deemed unfit even for home duty and recommended a pension.

Within a few weeks, and against medical advice, he embarked for Britain with two other New Zealanders, Robert Livingstone and Leslie Macfarlane.[82] Like Coningham they had been invalided back to New Zealand from Gallipoli; one with a gunshot wound and the other with a leg injury. All three men were unwilling to allow the decision of a New Zealand medical board to prevent them from further wartime service. 'We risked the journey, sparing no expense,' recalled Coningham. Almost immediately they were picked up for military service. 'I was in London Tuesday and in the Flying Corps on

Like a number of New Zealanders, Leonard Isitt (back row, second from left) came to the RFC after serious illness forced him out of the army.

Friday, a second lieutenant,' said Macfarlane, 'and I could not fly a thing.'[83] Within three weeks Coningham was part of the RFC machine, while Livingstone entered the British Army.[84]

Some New Zealanders were wounded on the Western Front and entered the air war from a hospital bed in Britain. They included two men who, alongside Coningham, were destined for great things in the Second World War: Leonard Isitt and Keith Park. Both had sustained injuries at the Battle of Somme in 1916. Isitt, a veteran of action in Egypt, was part of the New Zealand Division's 15 September attack, the Battle of Flers–Courcelette,[85] during which the leading companies came under intense machine-gun fire and Isitt was hit in the head.[86] The scalp wound had him shipped to Britain and he was discharged from the NZEF in March 1917. That month he became a flying cadet.

There is little indication that Coningham, Macfarlane or Isitt had given much thought to flying before they were injured, but Keith Park, even as an artilleryman, had paid the matter considerable attention. It was in Egypt as a corporal in a howitzer battery, preparing for the ill-fated Dardanelles campaign, that Park first spied an aircraft. It captured his interest and that of his comrades. A more regular acquaintance, albeit at a distance, followed when he landed on Gallipoli's western coast from where he would have seen the flights undertaken regularly over the peninsula. From early September 1915, when he transferred to the British Royal Horse and Field Artillery, much of his time was spent closer to the peninsula's southern airfield.[87] After his deployment to the Western Front in March 1916, it soon became apparent to Park that air power was unparalleled in its ability to locate targets and range in artillery. He had previously requested to go up in an aircraft to assess its effectiveness in an observational role, but had been told that this was unnecessary and that the idea of using such machines in reconnaissance was nonsense.[88]

Park soon had a chance to satisfy his growing interest in aviation. On the Somme his brigade commander ignored warnings that their position required greater concealment until aircraft-directed shelling fell accurately on them. Park was despatched to the nearest squadron for a flyover. He reported that the furrows created by the movement of machinery and the long shadows cast by the artillery emplacements clearly gave away their location to any airborne observer.[89] Only then were rudimentary adjustments carried out to camouflage their position. Park's excursion indicated his affinity for flight and his appreciation of its considerable military potential.

An injury Park sustained on 21 October 1916 on the Somme led to his career in flying. While he was attempting to remove a damaged artillery piece, an enemy shell landed directly beneath his horse: his mount was killed and Park was injured. Within days he was convalescing in England.[90] Although he was hobbled by a chest wound and racked by nightmares, he later considered the injury a fortuitous turning point.[91] Time away from the front offered him the opportunity to advance his flying aspirations. His previous attempts had been blocked by superiors who were reluctant to release him to this precocious service: they dismissed the RFC as a 'ragtime show', or unfairly accused Park of displaying war weariness.[92] When he was eventually deemed unfit for duty he saw his chance and took it.

Edwyn Wilding

Vincent Toulmin

Wesley Spragg

Arthur Skinner

Edmund Reeves

Ross Brodie

Owen Warnock

Geoffrey Callender

Herbert Drewitt

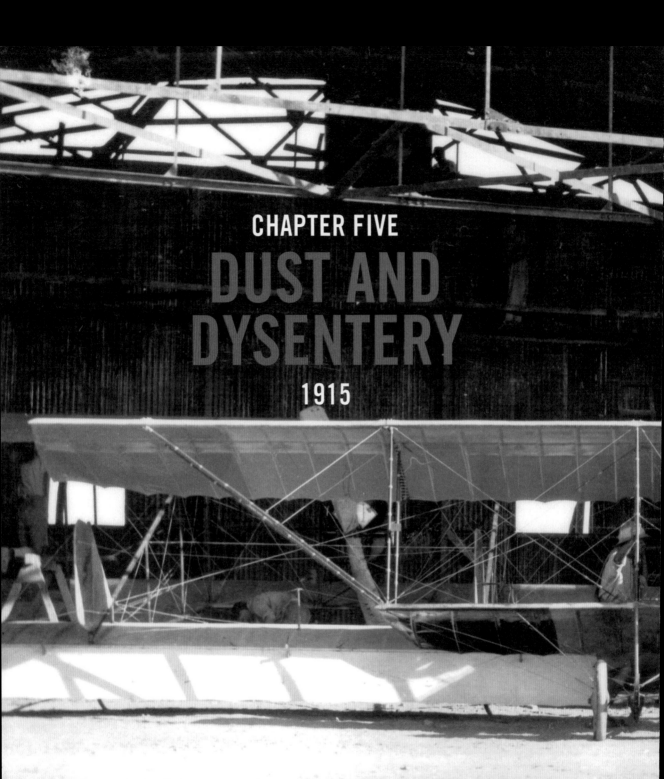

CHAPTER FIVE
DUST AND DYSENTERY
1915

n the meantime, some of the New Zealanders who were already flying were being tested in extreme conditions further east. After his Suez adventures, Hugh Reilly was despatched to Mesopotamia. In early February 1915 the Canberra government received a request from the Viceroy of India for an aviation contribution in preparation for a campaign against the Turks at the very extremities of their empire in the Tigris Valley. The aircraft would be the eyes of the offensive. This Australian component was small; it was coined 'Half Flight' because it approximated half a squadron's flight strength in 1915 — that is, five machines with attendant airmen and mechanics, plus Indian infantry deployed in erecting sheds and guard duty. By June it numbered no fewer than 65 personnel.[1] Supporting the operations were a small number of lorries — some of the first in Mesopotamia — and various waterborne transports such as tugs, lighters, barges and motor launches for ferrying men and materiel along the waterways of the region. The Australian contingent under the leadership of Captain Henry Petre was in turn absorbed into Reilly's Indian Army Flight. In the combined Mesopotamia Flight, Reilly had operational command of the force, which had a distinct Anzac feel to it, with the core Australian component supplemented over time by at least six New Zealanders: airmen Reilly, William Burn and Will Scotland, and air mechanics including Francis Adams, Stanley Brewster and Laurence Pitcher.[2]

Burn, the nation's sole New Zealand Defence Department pilot, had been left flightless with the return of *Britannia* in 1914 and was cooling his heels in a desk job in Auckland. Following a request from India he was happily seconded to the RFC, and in May 1915 found himself with Mesopotamia Flight in Basra, alongside Reilly.

Scotland was a civilian in July 1914; and his second Caudron was severely damaged in an accident in September, soon after it arrived in New Zealand. To make things worse, he was struck by diphtheria and isolated at Christchurch Hospital for three months. From the infirmary his further attempts to get the New Zealand government to fund a flying school proved predictably fruitless and in early 1915 he sought a commission in the RFC. 'I will be put through a course of military schooling, be taught the proper use of the compass and how to drop bombs,' he announced to the New Zealand press. 'I have learnt all of the flying part and what is to come will be purely from the military point of view.'[3] Scotland never made it to Britain: he was scooped up with the other airmen for the Arabian Gulf and Mesopotamia.[4]

The three air mechanics were part of a small but important number of New Zealand men who contributed to the war effort with their maintenance work on the aero engines. Francis Adams was an early New Zealand member of the Australian Flying Corps. Born in Christchurch, he was a carpenter with the New Zealand Railways Maintenance Department before he left for Australia.[5] He was studying architecture in Sydney when the Kaiser attacked France. He joined the Australian Army and was attached to the fledgling AFC. Robert Brewster and Laurie Pitcher were motorcycle mechanics from Levin and Masterton, respectively.[6] Within weeks of their departure for the Gulf of Arabia they were working with Adams and other mechanics on Mesopotamia Flight's aircraft.[7] They found themselves rubbing shoulders with an eclectic group of men, maintaining and repairing engines, rigging, airframes and fabric. Australian pilot Thomas White wrote that the English, Australian and New Zealand mechanics

> worked side by side with Musselman [Muslim], Hindu and Christian Indians, a stray Persian or two, and Arabs wielding tools of trade such as Noah used. A motley collection of Arab labourers and long-legged Sepoy guards were interesting supernumeraries, while a cola-black Baluchi, blessed with as many tongues as wives, performed the manifold duties of interpreter, castigator and general factotum.[8]

The aviators imported for Mesopotamia Flight were generally youthful airmen who were well suited to the task, but the machines that India provided — one Maurice Farman Shorthorn and two Maurice Farman Longhorns — were decidedly knock-kneed and care-worn. Considered too vulnerable for frontline action in Europe, the Farmans were shipped to Mesopotamia in November 1914.[9] Over the course of the campaign they were supplemented by equally inadequate Caudrons and Martinsydes. The Farman and Caudron engines were susceptible to overheating, and the Martinsyde's undercarriage was so delicate it required a 'croquet lawn' to land on.[10] Only with the arrival of BE2s in late 1915 did the Mesopotamian air corps have a military aircraft worthy of the name. The general principle was that anything, no matter how decrepit, was good enough for Mesopotamia.[11] The only saving grace was that the enemy did not as yet have opposing aircraft to threaten these museum pieces.

Given his experience, it was hardly surprising that Reilly was charged with commanding this ragtag collection of men and machines. He had flown in some of the earliest sorties of the Western Front and over the wastes of the Sinai and, in the latter skirmish, had flown machines of similar antiquity under comparable conditions. He came from a family with strong colonial connections to India and its army and had been trained in British military tradition; he was therefore the ideal man to lead the airmen as they scouted ahead of an army.

The most common opinion expressed by the antipodeans was that southern Mesopotamia looked nothing like the site of Adam and Eve's garden of their Sunday school lessons. 'We are quite near the Garden of Eden, which is supposed to be at the junction of the Tigris and the Euphrates,' wrote Scotland, but there 'is practically nothing except desert here'.[12] The sole consolation was the picturesque Shatt-al-Arab River — the confluence of the Euphrates and the Tigris that opens out into the Arabian Gulf. The riverbanks were studded with date palms laden with fruit that Arab men were harvesting for market. It was an idyllic vista. Less calm but no less alluring were the streets and bazaars of Basra which, in Scotland's opinion, were 'very weird and Oriental'.[13] Established soon after the birth of Islam, Basra was a trading entrepôt for the region and the starting point for colonial adventures in the Persian and Arab Middle East. The dusty, ancient streets were populated with

> itinerant carpet sellers, vendors of highly coloured sherbets, noisy water carriers bending under the weight of dripping goat skins, clamorous shopkeepers, haggling buyers, whining beggars and yelping mongrels [who] make a babel of noise and medley of colour that is never associated with an Easter bazaar. Scribes with reed pen, ink and sand, still squat on the ground writing love-letters at the direction of amorous illiterates. Under ragged awnings that shade crate-like benches along the Basra Creek, the wiseacres and indolents of the town sit cross-legged, sipping coffee and puffing many stemmed *narquiles*, just as their eighth-century prototypes did. . . . In the pageant of Eastern modes that crowd the bazaars, the khaki-clad Britishers appear strangely incongruous.[14]

In Basra resourceful New Zealanders could procure all manner of oriental artefacts at bargain prices. Air mechanic Laurie Pitcher acquired a taste for Persian and Arab militaria for which he haggled in the streets of Basra and shipped off to Masterton where, the *Wairarapa Daily Times* reported, they became display items in his father's store:

> There is now on view in the window of the Reliable Cycle Depot in Queen Street, an interesting exhibit of Turkish armour. The armour was sent from Mesopotamia by Mr L. Pitcher, one of the proprietors of the firm, who is now operating as an aviator with the British Flying Corps. The exhibit includes two helmets, two fighting shields, and two sword-arm protectors. The armour had evidently been made many years ago, and consists of steel with figures worked in of beaten wire.[15]

The canals of Basra were plied by 'gondolas of this Eastern Venice, flitting swiftly from point to point, ferrying veiled Arab women or gaily clad Chaldean girls'. They were also a Petri dish of malaria and dysentery; the very air of Basra seemed malarial and its waters choleric.[16] And then there was the climate. Temperatures commonly reached 45 degrees in the shade, and climbed as high as 50 degrees when it had a mind to torture visitors. Dehydration, sunstroke and all manner of waterborne and mosquito-borne diseases plagued Mesopotamia Flight. On one occasion nearly two-thirds of the 32 aviation mechanics sent out from England were out of action within just three days of arrival.[17] The imperial forces only just held the malarial onslaught at bay with doses of quinine taken every two days. Robert Brewster sent a postcard home that eloquently illustrated the local conditions.[18] It sported the corps' freshly drafted coat-of-arms depicting an alligator, a tortoise, flies and mosquitoes, all hanging from a date palm alongside a thermometer registering 55 degrees in the shade.

A Maurice Farman Shorthorn two-seat reconnaissance and light bomber biplane in Mesopotamia. Too antiquated for the Western Front, the Farmans found useful work in Mesopotamia in 1915.

The novelty and the exotic locale soon palled under the constant assault of insects and unescapable heat. 'There is a certain charm about the place for a while,' observed Scotland, 'but it soon wears off.'[19] The 'novelty of the scene, the colour, and the strange primitive old-worldliness of vegetation, villages and people, live long in the remembrance,' White wrote later, 'even though hardship amid such surroundings and a surfeit of similar views, may subsequently detract from the original glamour.'[20] Perhaps appropriately, the airfield and airpark were laid out in a cemetery near the small village of Tanumah, opposite Basra on the left bank of the Shatt-al-Arab. Built on the highest ground available in order to avoid the annual floods, the cemetery was the only location from which Mesopotamia Flight could operate under all conditions. Even so they laboured to complete a mud dyke that would ensure that machines and men were safe from unseasonably high flooding; the maintenance of the dyke was a never-ending burden.

The Farmans were assembled within four days, and the Flights' base of operations at Basra remained home to the greater part of the unit's personnel throughout the campaign. As the British and Indian force advanced up the Tigris, elements of Mesopotamia Flight would leapfrog forward to rough-and-ready advanced aerodromes.

General Sir John Nixon, commander of the mixed British and Indian force, was charged with securing British oil interests that lay just outside Turkish-held territory around Abadan Island on the Shatt-al-Arab. Nixon was of the opinion that it would prove highly advantageous if, rather than merely establishing a strong defensive position here, he could also defuse the Turkish threat by advancing up the Tigris and Euphrates and assaulting Baghdad; its capture would severely dent Ottoman prestige.

The first objective was Amara on the Tigris River. Nixon's commander in the field was Major General Charles Townshend, commanding the 6th Division. Of the New Zealand airmen, Reilly as Mesopotamia Flight's commanding officer and Burn as an observer were immediately seen in action. On 31 May 1915 Burn was an observer on one of the first reconnaissance flights of the campaign. With no enemy aircraft to contend with in the region, the airmen's greatest foes were their antiquated machines and the climate. The 70-hp Farmans were underpowered; just days before, in the first ever flight over Mesopotamia, Reilly estimated he had barely clocked 55 mph.[21] In addition to their poor performance, when the strong seasonal northwesterly wind — the dust-laden 'Shamal' — pressed

The ancient ruins of
Ctesiphon, 22 miles
southeast of Baghdad.
The great archway was
a prominent marker
for the long-distance
reconnaissance flights
of Hugh Reilly's airmen.

above Hugh Reilly's
photograph of Kut
al Amara. The small
desolate town became
the site of one of the
British Empire's worst
defeats.

below Australian
members of
Mesopotamia Flight.
From left: Henry Petre,
Thomas White —
who chronicled the
deprivations he and
others experienced as
prisoners of war of the
Turks — unidentified
and George Merz.

against the Farmans they were essentially flying backwards:[22] it took two hours to fly just 50 miles upriver.[23] Nonetheless, the two sorties were useful and the observers were able to correct important details on the division's maps.[24]

The next day, south of Amara, White and Reilly observed Turks abandoning their positions. This was confirmed on 2 June when a dawn sortie by Petre and Burn reported a 'few barges in Amara' but 'no other sign of the enemy'.[25] The aerial reconnaissance encouraged Townshend to press forward with a small advance force, and the following day Amara fell. When the main force arrived they discovered 41 sailors and marines in control of the town, having netted 1200 Turkish soldiers in the process. There were more sorties to determine the vulnerability of the Allied positions in Amara. One of these was undertaken by Reilly and Burn.

Stretching the capacity of the Farmans and their own confidence, the two airmen made a trip of 123 miles to the town of Kut al Amara.[26] 'The wind on this day was so strong that it was necessary to fly within a few feet of the ground wherever possible, in order to accomplish the distance in time,' recorded Reilly.[27] The two men were able to prepare a map of an uncharted region of the Tigris hinterlands that would prove very useful in an upcoming advance on Kut, and they scouted out a refuelling point at Ali Gharbi. This flight and additional reconnaissance informed Townshend that the Turks had retired and were unlikely to counterattack. Reilly's combined Anzac force had helped deliver the first major objective on the path to Baghdad.

Reilly, however, was uneasy about the toll the relatively small number of sorties was taking on Mesopotamia Flight. The unit was struggling to meet the demands of the ground force. The taking of Amara had tested his force to the limit and had exposed a number of shortcomings. One machine was out of action for four days because they only had one spare engine and a single barge to deliver it to the forward base. The supplies reaching him at Amara were 'very inadequate'. He fretted over the lack of oil and airframe fabric required to maintain the operational capacity of the aircraft.[28] The logistics of running Farmans so far from the Basra base was proving a nightmare. Even when supplies were on hand the men could only work a few hours a day in the incapacitating heat, and when malaria and gastritis knocked out a good number of the mechanics, work proceeded at a snail's pace.[29] On 13 June an air mechanic died from 'effects of climate'.[30]

Establishing buildings at the Basra airpark, and tents and structures at forward airfields, to protect the fragile aircraft was fraught with difficulties. Delays meant machines, engines and spare parts were susceptible to rapid deterioration in the heat and the dust-laden winds. Reilly's concerns were heeded and General Nixon's headquarters requested more men, machines and equipment.

Nixon's attention now shifted west to the Euphrates, which he wanted cleared by the other force under his command: Major General George Gorringe's 12th Division. Once this western flank was secured he would have a free hand to take Baghdad. Gorringe's principal objective was the capture of Nasiriyah. On 22 June, Mesopotamia Flight prepared the way with a reconnaissance mission by two Farmans. Petre and his observer, Burn, located solid ground for a landing by Gorringe's planned amphibious advance and corrected errors in Nixon's maps.

In spite of the successful preparatory work, Reilly was cautious. He was only too aware that the aviation engines were prone to failure in the heat and that with so few aircraft it would be difficult to maintain continuous coverage of the advance.[31] This was demonstrated in the opening push up the Euphrates, when engine failure meant that Gorringe was temporarily without aerial reconnaissance. On this occasion a forced landing by one of Reilly's airmen had been trouble-free, but this was a hit-or-miss affair, especially as it was almost impossible to tell whether those occupying the area were well or ill disposed to the British effort. For Reilly's airmen an engine failure meant a forced landing.

Unlike the Western Front, where friendly and hostile zones were demarcated by a clearly defined trench system, with Allied armies to the west and Central Powers armies to the east, the Mesopotamian theatre was characterised by a narrow sliding front that ran north and south, up and down the Tigris and Euphrates rivers, with the surrounding countryside a swirling amorphous collection of Arab tribes of uncertain allegiance. 'It was a feature particular to the Mesopotamian front at the time,' wrote one of Reilly's pilots,

> that one is only safe, except from Arab snipers, within the precincts of one's own camp. The conquered territory in the rear of the most advanced fighting troops right back to the base was practically a no-man's land roamed over by ruthless and merciless Arabs, while the towns on the line-of-communication were held by meagre garrisons . . . in blockhouses and entrenched camps. When a battle was pending, the marsh Arabs and Bedouin tribes in the vicinity would gather and camp on either flanks and in the rear of the contending armies, so as to be conveniently placed to cut off small parties and stragglers, so as to snipe ships bringing up reinforcements and supplies, and on the day of battle fall upon the beaten side, kill and loot the wounded, and anticipate the victors in the fruits of victory. . . . these treacherous marauders hovered round the camps like jackals and spared neither Britisher, Indian nor hapless Turk who fell into their hands.[32]

Consequently, even if one of Reilly's airmen made a forced landing south of Nixon's front line there was no guarantee that they would find themselves among Arabs who were favourable to the British–Indian mission in Mesopotamia.

Thomas White discovered this for himself when, a little later in the campaign, he was despatched on a perilous mission. Reilly had been reluctant to assign men to the task because the target lay close to Baghdad and thus well behind the Ottoman front line. He asked for volunteers, and two Australians put their hands up. Their mission: to land their antiquated machines in enemy-held territory in a hit-and-run demolition raid on Ottoman communications. It was 60 miles to the target and White and his observer, Francis Yeats-Brown, were forced to carry additional fuel and oil because of the headwind on the outward leg.

Within sight of Baghdad's 'gold cupolas and minarets' White spotted a clear piece of land crossed by telegraph lines. Rapidity of action was uppermost in his mind, with roaming Arabs his biggest concern. He brought the machine down with what should have been ample space to turn in front of the telegraph poles on which they intended to lay the gun-cotton charges. Unfortunately a contrary wind pushed White further than anticipated and, as he wheeled around, 'I saw to my dismay the lower plane strike one of the telegraph posts, smashing longeron and ribs to matchwood.' The crash tore the struts off the lower wings. Yeats-Brown dismounted and ran to the poles to wrap them with the charges.[33]

Arabs who had witnessed the landing gathered like vultures around the stranded plane and its two-man crew. At 300 yards they opened fire, kicking up dust around the Mesopotamia Flight airmen. With the sound of rifle reports and shouting ringing in his ears, White knelt in the observer's seat and fired on the closest scavengers. An explosion from the charges reduced a pole to matchwood and temporarily dented the enthusiasm of the assault. White refuelled the aircraft under fire, which had grown in intensity with the arrival of a small but well-armed detachment of Turkish cavalry. The airmen were now in a crossfire. The second charge successfully brought down another pole but the severed wires whipped back and ensnared the aircraft. On one previous occasion White and Yeats-Brown had come down behind enemy positions and were able to taxi the aircraft ingeniously, like a motorcar, 15 miles past Turkish positions all the way back to the nearest friendly camp.[34] That would not be the case here.

The first assailant to approach White was a 'hideous black Arab, with shaggy hair, who was stark naked but for two broad bandoliers of cartridges across his chest'. White reached for his revolver as the man rushed him with a 'massive' rifle. Other attackers rained blows on him with their rifle butts and smashed his pith helmet. He was viciously struck again on the head with the discarded fuel can and then with an adze: the three-inch cut opened up his head and blood ran thickly over his face and clothes.

White and Yeats-Brown would surely have been killed had it not been for the intervention of the Turks, who wanted to take them prisoner. As it was, the Arabs struck and spat on them as they were being led away. A final cruelty was delivered by a 'bull-necked ruffian' who offered the bridle of his horse to Yeats-Brown in feigned aid; when the Australian reached up to take it, the man stabbed him with a concealed dagger.

Both men spent the rest of the war in harsh captivity in Anatolia. They survived; others were not so fortunate.

In July 1915, the plans for taking Nasiriyah were hampered by the demands placed on such a small number of machines. In addition to waiting for more infantry, Gorringe called for more aircraft; he needed to know what lay ahead of him before committing to the attack. The two Caudrons arrived on 14 July and five days later took off for the advance airfield at Asani. Reilly's machine overheated and was forced to land. It took three days to reach Asani. Both the Farmans and the Caudrons were plagued with overheating problems in Mesopotamia: Scotland put it down to the rotary engines failing in the extreme heat.[35] 'It is not really surprising considering that they are air cooled,' reported Reilly, 'and the air from 500 to 3000 feet is often like a blast furnace.'[36] In the meantime, the remaining Caudron made its first reconnaissance of the enemy positions on 22 July and added more detail to maps prepared by cavalry officers.[37] Although they failed to spot a large contingent of Turkish troops concealed in a large date farm, the airman and observer 'located the enemy's dispositions and obtained topographical information of value, clearing up the situation' before the battle.[38]

The assault began on 24 July and within hours the Turks were abandoning their positions, with Nasiriyah taken the following day. Once again Reilly's airmen were able to confirm that there were no threats to the newly acquired Allied position on the Euphrates. Even with the engine problems and only two machines, Reilly felt Mesopotamia Flight had been 'distinctly useful'. One of his few laments was that they had not been able to carry out any offensive actions with bombs or range in artillery on enemy positions. It was 'a pity', he noted, that they were hampered by the poor technology at hand; in particular, a 'wireless' would have proven highly beneficial in directing artillery fire. A camera had recently been introduced to Mesopotamia Flight, but the airmen needed more experience in its use and intelligence officers more training in deciphering what they saw in the photographic material produced.[39]

On 30 July, with Nasiriyah in Allied control, the two aircraft set off for Basra. The pilots had agreed to stay in visual contact but soon after ascending they became separated.[40] Although the engines had just been overhauled, both Caudrons were forced down with overheating problems. Reilly was fortunate to land among amenable Arab tribesmen and, following repairs, was able to reach the advance airfield for refuelling.[41] Burn was not so fortunate: he and his pilot, Australian George Merz, found themselves caught in the wilderness of Mesopotamia among murderous marsh Arabs, in not too dissimilar a situation to that in which White and Yeats-Brown had found themselves on their demolition sortie.

While Burn and Merz were attempting repairs they were set upon by a 15-strong force. They faced off this well-armed attack with revolvers. For four miles across shelterless, sunbaked marshlands they fought a defensive battle, retreating towards the refuelling station beyond the horizon.[42] One of the airmen was wounded and they made their last stand, shoulder to shoulder, as the Arabs closed in.

Reilly waited for Burn and Merz to appear and as the hours passed, Mesopotamia Flight in Basra hoped that the Anzac airmen had been taken prisoner. A few days later Reilly and Petre carried out a search and located the Caudron 25 miles south of Abu Salabikh.[43] Burn and Merz's bodies were nowhere to be found but the aircraft was slashed and hacked about. Rumour circulated that the men had been captured and were alive and with Arabs.[44] Arabs who had observed the atrocity confirmed their worst fears, however: both Burn and Merz were lost. 'A fight took place and the English were killed,' reported an Arab witness, 'but first they defended themselves with their revolvers and killed one of our men and wounded two.'[45] It was subsequently reported that the 'principal murderers' were from a village on the right bank of the Shatt-al-Arab and had the lost officers' kit in their possession, but this could not be confirmed.[46] Burn was New Zealand's first military airman to be killed and Merz was Australia's first. Burn's brother, Robert, was killed in action only seven days later at Gallipoli.

William Burn was New Zealand's first army officer to obtain his Royal Aero Club certificate and also the first New Zealand airman to be killed in the war, when his Caudron force-landed and he and his Australian pilot, George Merz, were attacked by hostile Arab tribesmen.

The loss of the New Zealander and the Australian was a blow to the small, close-knit Mesopotamia Flight. Reilly was down two popular airmen and a third of his flying strength. He was, however, relieved to hear that Nixon had successfully persuaded the War Office to strengthen the aviation capacity of his Mesopotamian force; Reilly's old Egypt-based detachment was to join Mesopotamia Flight. In the process, Mesopotamia Flight was absorbed into the RFC and its airmen all became recipients of British commissions, effective 5 August 1915. The Egyptian detachment had recently been renamed 30 Squadron, suggesting Reilly might soon command a proper, fully fledged force. In reality a complete squadron was still 12 months away, and the two-flight 30 Squadron was never going to fully meet the requirements of Nixon's force thanks to operational losses and the inadequacies of the machines at Reilly's disposal. The sole consolation was the arrival on 5 September, by barge at Amarah, of additional aircraft in the form of Martinsyde G100s.[47] Nicknamed 'Elephant', they unfortunately lacked manoeuvrability and did not perform well on the uneven airfields of Mesopotamia.[48]

Reilly was informed that the next objective was Baghdad, the Ottoman Empire's 'second capital'. The only impediment: the town of Kut, over 100 miles south of Baghdad. Reilly's flight was sent north to Townshend's advance camp at Ali Gharbi and from there they flew reconnaissance missions in support of the advance. Over the first two weeks of September Townshend was heavily reliant on aerial observations for his progress.[49] The greater part of these were undertaken by Reilly, as a result of the recent loss of officers and illness among the remaining pilots.

One of the ill airmen was Will Scotland, who was a relatively recent arrival and had yet to fly operationally. For much of his time at Basra he was 'engaged in testing and fitting up aeroplanes'.[50] Before long, however, he was out of any action after he smashed up one of the original Farmans. It became clear to his superiors that he had unfortunately not 'entirely recovered from the effects of diphtheria which he had had in New Zealand'.[51] By late November the air pioneer had been invalided to India with an aggravated throat condition.[52] 'The climate of Mesopotamia did not agree with him at all,' wrote his air mechanic Laurie Pitcher. Although Pitcher and Stan Brewster, working out of the airpark in Basra, were in better health, Pitcher informed his relatives back home that he was 'sick' of Mesopotamia and 'he would be glad if he could get to France or any European country'.[53] Petre and White were sent north to aid Reilly.[54]

With no other pilots immediately on hand, Reilly was forced to undertake a 'single handed reconnaissance over Turkish positions'. 'Major Reilly carried out the reconnaissance I had asked for excellently well,' wrote Townshend, 'he brought back a very fine piece of work — a map and detailed information.'[55] Reilly's map showed tents indicating reinforcements and, on both sides of the river, earthworks, entrenchments and redoubts. Importantly, he had confirmed suspicions that the Turks had established a 13-mile line blocking the Tigris advance on Kut, and that the town was more 'extensive and more strongly entrenched' than had been anticipated.[56]

On 28 September, after the arrival of reinforcements, Townshend launched his attack. It involved a diversionary frontal assault, with the main effort — based on aerial reconnaissance

— a flanking manoeuvre on the northern line of the defences. During the action the RFC machines were too few in number to significantly influence the outcome; Reilly had only two aeroplanes on hand. Supplementary work for Townshend was undertaken by a pair of RNAS seaplanes working from downriver. The next day, Nixon received aerial reconnaissance reports that the Turks were retreating north along the Tigris.[57] The doorway to Baghdad now appeared to be open. In the tragic events that were soon to follow, Hugh Reilly was to unexpectedly play an important and fateful part.

On 3 October 1915, Reilly flew up the Tigris towards Baghdad. Twenty-two miles south of the great city, his attention was drawn towards major earthworks: the Turks were digging in at Ctesiphon. Townshend's divisional diary noted that Reilly's report had stated that the position 'was strongly held'.[58] The report was forwarded on to Nixon's headquarters with Townshend advising: 'You will see the chance of breaking up the retreating Turkish forces . . . no longer exists . . . The position is astride the Baghdad Road and the Tigris is estimated to be six miles of entrenchments. They have probably been reinforced from Baghdad.' [58A]

Townshend was urging caution. He was now operating with an ever-weakening force 200 miles from Basra, while the enemy was growing stronger, with Ctesiphon only a few short miles southeast of Baghdad. As the water of the Tigris reached its low point, reinforcing and replenishing his forces was becoming increasingly difficult. He informed Nixon that he would need at least another division, with additional forces deployed along the watery logistics and communications line of the Tigris.[59] In the meantime he advised retiring to Kut.

Nixon ignored Townshend's recommendation — and thus Reilly's report, on which it was based. In spite of evidence showing that Nixon's headquarters received the original communication, it appears he chose to replace Townshend's assessment of Reilly's reconnaissance report with one of his own.[60] The Turkish positions went from being 'strongly held' to merely 'partly prepared'. Aerial reconnaissance was being ignored in the interests of personal glory and a War Office back home eager to counter the negative news from Gallipoli. In wilful denial of Townshend's cable, Nixon argued that the Turkish force at Ctesiphon was inferior in numbers, and ordered his subordinate to continue as planned.

Reilly's initial reconnaissance had been accurate: the Turks had dug a double defensive line and had some 16,000 to 18,000 troops on hand, with others in reserve. In all, it appears that in Mesopotamia the Turkish commander had over 36,000 men; significantly larger than the 11,000 to 13,000 estimated by various British–Indian intelligence branches. Townshend, for his part, had 14,000 isolated and weary troops. For the first time in Mesopotamia, the enemy had superior numbers.

With further aerial reconnaissance supporting Reilly's initial appraisal, Townshend made one last appeal to be allowed to retire south to Kut. But his political and military superiors were decided, perhaps influenced by a smattering of reconnaissance reports which noted that Baghdad was relatively free of troops — a fact mostly likely attributable to the enemy moving under the cover of darkness directly to the front, without the need for garrisoning in Baghdad itself.[61] In London, the War Committee, under the misapprehension that Townshend had superior numbers, and adequate shipping to support the operation, authorised the capture of Baghdad.[62]

eilly had one more part to play in the proceedings before he was bustled from the stage. Doubt was gnawing at Townshend, and on the eve of the assault he despatched two reconnaissance flights. The early sortie was destined for Ctesiphon; the later mission headed for Baghdad. Reilly took the Baghdad mission, and he had plenty to report. On the outward flight he flew four miles east of Ctesiphon; here he observed that the Turkish positions had been considerably bolstered by additional men. More importantly, he noted there was a substantial reserve of men on hand. He abandoned the Baghdad reconnaissance in order to get a closer look, tipping his wing and pushing the Martinsyde's nose down. At 1000 ft, disaster struck: his machine was hit by ground fire. At this most vital juncture of the entire campaign shrapnel took out the engine, knocking out the only airman and machine that could have confirmed Townshend's fears and perhaps prevented the disaster that was to come.

Reilly glided as far from the enemy positions as possible, then set out on foot to reach Townshend's advanced elements.[63] Ever watchful Arabs saw the powerless machine land and chased Reilly down. He was captured. The airman was unable to destroy the documents hidden in his uniform. At first flush, 'Reilly's greatest gift to us was a sketch showing the course of the Tigris from Diyala to Aziziya,' recorded the Turkish account of the campaign. Fortunately, the map also featured 'hills and canals' that were unknown and consequently unlocatable by Ottoman intelligence, rendering 'Major Reilly's sketch' less than useful.

With Reilly 'in the bag', Townshend was dependent on the earlier reconnaissance of Ctesiphon, which did not indicate any of the strengthening of the Turkish positions noted by Reilly. The first sortie had been flown by an airman newly arrived at the front, with minimal practical knowledge in aerial observation. His lack of experience stood in stark contrast to Reilly's, the squadron's most accomplished airman. On numerous occasions Reilly had demonstrated his keen eye for locating enemy dispositions and estimating enemy strength. With the head of the squadron captured, 'it was a pity,' lamented the RAF's official history, 'that the fate of thousands' depended on what this inexperienced subordinate saw.[64]

> Had Major Reilly been the officer who returned, Major-General Townshend would have known that his troops, on the morrow, would be called upon to face far superior enemy forces in well-prepared positions. It is possible that a withdrawal could not have been made without fighting, but it is reasonable to suppose that . . . Townshend would never have persisted in his offensive had Major Reilly got back with his report and the consequence of such a decision would have been far-reaching; there might have been no siege of Kut.[65]

But Reilly did not make it back, and there would be a siege.

n 22 November 1915 Townshend's men ran straight into the Turkish defensive positions and took the first line, but at a high cost: Townshend lost a third of his officers in the fighting and total casualties ran to 42 per cent. With only marginal logistical support up

above A wingless
Martinsyde S1 on
an RFC barge on
the Tigris River.

below Hugh Reilly's
Martinsyde in Turkish
hands after being
brought down by
groundfire. Reilly's
capture deprived the
British of valuable
intelligence.

the shallow Tigris, he realised that Baghdad, only 18 miles distant, was beyond his reach. He hastily retreated to Kut. The division arrived on 3 December. With exhausted men, Townshend judged it unwise to strike further south towards Basra; he would hold the line at Kut. Semi-enclosed in a horseshoe bend in the river, the town occupied a natural defensive position for Townshend's 12,000 men. Among the British and Indian force was a sizeable element of the RFC's Mesopotamian contingent, as only four airmen had managed to fly out. The officers and their supporting 'rank and file' personnel could only look forlornly at the three unserviceable aircraft resting at the Kut airfield.[66]

Among the 30 Squadron mechanics was New Zealander Francis Adams. He observed that Kut, population 7000, was an assault on all the senses. As a colleague noted, 'the whole place is indescribably filthy, owning to the unsanitary inhabitants and to the accumulation of refuse and filth on the thoroughfares, the river banks and the immediate confines of town'. The arrival of Townshend's men overwhelmed the rudimentary infrastructure of Kut. Adams doubtless agreed with the 6th Division's chief medical officer, who cheerfully described Kut as the 'most unsanitary place we occupied in Mesopotamia'.[67]

The Turks arrived four days later and proceeded to lay siege to the town by establishing a defensive line south of Kut on the Tigris. Townshend was cut off from waterborne reinforcement and resupply. It was the beginning of the longest siege in British military history. After a month Townshend wanted to attempt a breakout and retreat but was ordered to hold his position for a relief operation. The battles to reach Kut from Basra ran from January through to April 1916 and were ultimately unsuccessful: the combined British and Indian casualties rose to 23,000, more than twice as many as the 10,000 Turks killed or wounded. The inhabitants of Kut could only watch in despair as the relief operations failed. As the siege progressed, food became 'an acute problem'.[68] By February Adams and the besieged thousands were each subsisting on 12 ounces of bread and eight ounces of meat.

> Tobacco was first out, and we were smoking anything that would smoke, green leaves (dried over a fire), tea leaves and sawdust mixed . . . . Milk and sugar had given out long ago, likewise mutton, and all the bully beef was gone with the exception of two days' emergency rations which were kept back until the very last.[69]

Of the original 3000 horses and mules available to eat at the beginning of the siege, many had already been slaughtered and those that remained were underfed; some resorted to eating their blankets and 'even their own hair'.[70] Eggs and tinned milk were solely for the infirm. The results were widespread scurvy and dysentery.

On 13 February German aircraft appeared over the town, part of a 10-strong German–Turkish squadron. Fortunately the limited number of bombs could do little damage; the greater fear was that the infantry would waste their ammunition taking potshots at the machines. In March, however, a raid by three German aircraft resulted in women and children being killed and the hospital being hit.[71] 'It is pitiful to go to the Hospital,' wrote one of 30 Squadron, 'as they are all bad cases and helpless and in a good many instances their nerve is gone.' The stranded airmen were powerless, and Townshend recorded the general anger towards the German airmen: 'If any of the German pilots had fallen into the hands of any of my troops he would have been torn to pieces.' Townshend requested aerial countermeasures but the RFC machines at Basra were no match for the new arrivals, especially for the four Pfalz monoplanes.

By March the ration was reduced to 10 ounces of barley and less than two ounces of horse meat for British soldiers. Some of the 'ravenous' British Tommies raided the offal pit for horse livers and hearts, until an anthrax outbreak among the horses temporarily forced the authorities to stop the practice.[72] Indian soldiers suffered even more harshly as they refused to eat horse meat on religious grounds. Men started shooting starlings, and made fruitless attempts to stun fish in the Tigris using explosives.[73] After flooding, flies in their millions fell on Kut, and armies of frogs appeared to feast on them. Disgusted with standing on the fly-filled frogs in the trenches, men cut steps for them to escape, but many tumbled back into the filth.[74]

The besieged men's brief, and poor, prospect of hope was the first air supply operation in the history of aviation: in April Reilly's old unit began dropping food and ammunition. Townshend was of the opinion that they needed 5000 lbs of supplies daily. Observers were discarded to enable the aircraft to carry greater amounts of supply bags. Adams saw laden aircraft drop supplies overhead and must have known that his fellow airmen were undertaking an impossible task. There simply were not enough machines, and those on hand were so underpowered that the maximum load they could take on any given sortie was only 250 lbs. On their best day, 30 Squadron dropped 3350 lbs, a remarkable but unsustainable level, and well shy of Townshend's requirements.[75] The 140 food-delivery flights in April delivered 19,000 lbs, some of which landed in the Tigris and others on enemy positions — an unavoidable outcome at 6000 ft with rudimentary release gear and skittish pilots wanting to avoid the prowling German–Turkish squadron. Kut was doomed.

The final throw of the dice was a secret attempt to pay the Turks for the emancipation of the garrison. Lord Kitchener, secretary of state for war, approved a mission by two officers, one of whom was T. E. Lawrence. It failed, and further initiatives by Townshend were unfruitful. On 29 April the garrison surrendered: they had endured 147 days. The soldiers, all 12,000 of them, were marched off to Anatolia and captivity — 700 miles distant. Their journey and imprisonment would prove unforgiving: over 4000 would not see the end of the war. Of the 47 RFC men captured, eight were mechanics; one of these was Francis Adams.[76]

With the surrender of Kut, only two of the original New Zealanders in Mesopotamia Flight remained: mechanics Robert Brewster and Laurie Pitcher. But even their robust constitutions were no match for the conditions in Mesopotamia. The climate and pestilence of the Basra airpark in the so-called 'Garden of Eden' took its toll. In April Pitcher was struck down with heatstroke and heart trouble, and Brewster succumbed to enteric and malarial fever soon after. Brewster spent 14 weeks in an Alexandria hospital before being sent to a military camp in England. 'This [camp] is a convalescent home compared to the one I knew in the Garden of Eden,' he wrote to his friends in Levin, 'yet some growl because the porridge is served without milk.' The veteran of the deprivations of Mesopotamia added that it was 'easy to spot the rookies'.[77]

The war was over for Hugh Reilly and Francis Adams — but not the suffering. Reilly's capture and imprisonment in Anatolia was far from pleasant; but the treatment of the men who survived Kut was truly inhumane. Those who had made it through the siege were now a pitiful, emaciated collection of skin and bones. Initially, thanks to the British down the river, their food situation briefly improved. Men had their first small helping of vegetables in months and portions of bully beef and mouldy rice. This played havoc with the men and there were 12 to 15 deaths a day. The British provisions were soon gone, and when Adams began his forced march to Baghdad on 6 March he was allotted a daily ration of three Turkish biscuits (nicknamed 'paving stones' on account of their toughness), three ounces of jam and a few dates.

On the second day they were forced to cover 18 miles in the heat of the day — close to 40 degrees Celsius in the shade. In one column 'three Europeans and eighteen natives' died and up to 500 became ill, observed one of Adams' fellow mechanics.[78] Adding to the torment, the Indian men periodically broke into vicious fighting among themselves as various castes warred with each other. The Turkish officers showed the men no mercy, marching them through the hottest part of the day, and by six days into their ordeal there were not even 'paving stones' to eat. Adams had a short reprieve in Baghdad before the leg to Mosul, 200 miles north.

Some of the men were taken by train, but others marched. Their only consolation was that this leg was done largely at night, but some of the marches ran from 6 p.m. to 9.30 a.m. the next day, and the men were so exhausted they did not have the strength to rig up even a blanket as a shelter from the relentless sun. Poor rations and the shingle-covered terrain sapped their pitiful reserves of strength. Even when they took short breaks, such as at Takrit, the prisoners were not free from torment: 'Sick men and men with sore feet came slowly in till the evening. We were placed in the hospital (so called) but were attacked and stoned by the Arab women and children of the town.'[79] When they finally arrived in Mosul by way of Kirkuk, two Mesopotamia Flight officers were on hand to meet them: Thomas White and Francis Yeats-Brown. Yeats-Brown recorded the arrival of the walking dead:

> I saw a party of twenty English soldiers, who had been marched from Kirkuk across the mountains, arriving moribund on the barrack square of Mosul. They were literally skeletons alive, and they brought with them three skeletons dead. One of the living men kept making piteous signs to his mouth with the stump of an arm in which maggots crawled. Presently he died in a fit.[80]

'Then there was the saddest tea-party at which I have ever assisted,' said Yeats-Brown. The two Australians bribed a sentry to get some bread and buffalo cream to feed their guests. After telling their story, one of the travellers fainted. Starving as they were, the food was 'too rich', one of the men explained. White picked up the waif-like invalid and carried him to their cellar and looked after him for as long as he could, 'But it was to no avail. When he returned, his clothes were swarming with vermin, for lice leave the dead.'[81]

From Mosul, the men were marched west into Anatolia. Some considered this the worst stretch of their journey to captivity, in particular the 250 miles from Mosul to Ras-el-Ain: 'Each man was allowed a quart of water for the two days' march across one waterless stretch; and as many of the men could not restrain the desire to drink on account of the intense heat a great number died.'[82] Many were clubbed to death by sentries and stripped naked. Some men simply fell by the wayside, their lifeless bodies consigned to the barren wastes. Those who made Ras-el-Ain were then crammed into railway trucks — 40 to 50 a truck — bound for western Anatolia. Another mechanic reported on their suffering:

> Most of the day and all of the night the doors of these closed trucks were kept locked, and as almost every man was suffering from fever, dysentery and diarrhoea, the state of affairs can be imagined . . . After three days and nights . . . five men in my wagon were found to be dead when the doors were opened, and some other wagons were just as bad as ours.[83]

The entire journey consumed up to three-quarters of those captured at Kut.

Francis Adams somehow survived the horrors and was imprisoned in Anatolia in the spring of 1916. Sometime in the second half of the year he sent a postcard to his mother that revealed that he was a prisoner of war in a camp north of Constantinople. 'Am pleased to say I am still alive and kicking,' he informed his parents. Then, silence. Doubts grew, and his father, Francis Adams senior of Addington, began a heart-rending, three-year letter-writing campaign to military officials. Desperate, he corresponded with the officer in charge of Base Records in Melbourne. That officer informed the father that since the postcard, 'I have not received any news regarding your son' — despite the officer having written to the Turkish authorities 'every week' in Constantinople.

It was not until August of 1917 that Adams senior was informed that his son was likely a prisoner at Afion Kara Hissar camp in western Anatolia. He contacted the office of Base Records, Melbourne, to thank them for this crumb of information, and added, 'I shall be very thankful for any item of news.'[84] When that news finally arrived it was not good. Correspondence via Thomas White informed the family that their son was dead.

It was not until after the war that a court of inquiry found that he had most likely died between August and November 1916; that is, soon after he had sent his one and only postcard. Adams' father struggled with the loss of his son and the bitterness he felt towards those who treated him and other Kut survivors so appallingly. In 1919, in his last letter to the military authorities, he asked, 'Can you tell me if any action is to be taken in regard to the inhuman treatment these men received as I consider they were murdered.'[85]

Will Scotland returned to New Zealand just before the fall of Kut. Unlike Reilly and Adams he had escaped Mesopotamia, although not unscathed: the climate and pestilence had taken their toll on his health. Nonetheless, thanks to his military foray and as one of New Zealand's pioneering aviators, he was keen to resurrect plans for training airmen.[86] The war was not about to end any time soon, and New Zealand could still play its part in preparing men for the air war.

AIRMEN FOR THE EMPIRE

When Will Scotland returned to New Zealand he discovered that, in his absence, a flying school had sprung up in east Auckland. Vivian and Leo Walsh, in association with an American engineer and Cadillac car dealer, Reuben Dexter, were already admitting students to their newly established New Zealand Flying School. New Zealand's most famous aviation pioneers had set about rectifying the embarrassing fact that by mid-1915 not a single airman had been trained in New Zealand and sent to aid the Empire in war. In rectifying this the Walsh brothers produced some of New Zealand's best Great War airmen.

The Walsh school was founded on seaplanes. Having lost control of *Manurewa*, the two men turned their minds to what type of aircraft would best suit Auckland. The volcanic cones of the city presented land-based aircraft with violent gusts and swirling eddies, but the watery environs seemed perfectly designed for a machine that could alight from and land on the Waitemata Harbour. Vivian and Leo had researched the latest developments in naval aviation, and they were impressed with the work of American aircraft designer Glenn Curtiss, who had developed two types of seaplane: those that replaced traditional undercarriage with pontoons, known as floatplanes; and those that used the fuselage like a ship's hull, known as flying boats.

When the brothers chose the flying boat it was the beginning of a 15-month project in a garden shed. Aside from a 10-cylinder, 80-hp Anzani engine purchased by Dexter, the craft was made largely from New Zealand materials. The machine was no great beauty — if anything, it resembled a wooden clog with wings stuck to its heel — but the brothers' careful design kept the completed weight as low as anything being produced elsewhere in the world at the time. In all, it was a remarkable achievement for two self-taught men far from the centres of aviation expertise.

When the last brushstroke of lacquer on the hull had dried they dismantled the craft. It was carried in pieces under cover of darkness along the 'notorious mile-long concrete sewer crossing Hobson Bay, and over a hill, ending at Bastion Point, Orakei, to the foreshore'.[1] The hull was towed there. The reassembled machine was dipped into the water with the aid of local soldiers.

The flying boat flew on New Year's Day 1915: the southern hemisphere's first seaplane, designed, constructed and flown by New Zealanders.[2] A yachting publication reported on the harbour's newest arrival:

For some time past there have been rumours of a strange craft which has been seen on the lower end of the harbour, and last Sunday was seen manoeuvring around when many of our yachts and launches were returning from their cruise. This strange craft, which was said to do over 50 miles per hour, turned out to be a flying boat.[3]

Over a year into the war, the implications of this development in New Zealand aviation were not lost on the local newspapers. Critics were initially cautious about the Walsh brothers' ugly duckling, but in the months that followed it proved its worth in experimental and passenger flights. This was proof that the machine was 'not a toy', said the reporters. Here was an aircraft and team that would enable the antipodes to play its part. Many young men agreed and began writing to the brothers.

The failures of the past, the lack of military interest and a major world war had not damped interest in flying; if anything it had fanned it. Vivian and Leo Walsh were inundated with letters. 'With the big demand now existing for qualified pilots,' said Leo, 'it is only natural that New Zealanders, soldiers and intending recruits alike, should feel sore that no facilities are granted them to join the Flying Corps, if they take the trouble to qualify here.'[4] Mac McGregor of Hunterville wrote breathlessly to the adjutant-general of the New Zealand Defence Force:

> As I am only 19½ years of age and my parents will not allow me to go to the trenches till I am 21, I am anxious to serve my country, and my ambition is to join the Flying Corps. Could you please supply me with full particulars of which course to follow. Is it necessary for me to apply to the Flying School, Auckland, or through the Defence Recruiting Officer? . . . Please pay this matter your most urgent attention as I am anxious to join the Flying Corps straight away.[5]

The only fly in the ointment for the Walsh brothers and men like McGregor was the government. McGregor was informed that the Defence Department was in no position to assist.

Just as local interest had not diminished in the hearts of would-be aviators, so Wellington authorities were no less convinced of the need to concentrate on the land war. The faltering Gallipoli campaign was not shaking the Defence Department's resolve in this matter; rather, it strengthened it. Additional men and materials would be gathered and funnelled into the NZEF and its continuing efforts in the Middle East and, in the future, the Western Front. The Allied cause would be won or lost there, on the ground, and distractions and diversions were to be avoided at all cost. The government met the two aeronaut brothers but was unpersuaded. Nonetheless, Defence Department officials were not about to quash a private endeavour and it was true that the War Office was asking for qualified airmen. There would be no funding, but the Walsh brothers secured the government's blessing for the school, and with that came limited cooperation. As good as its word, the Defence Department sent a telegram to the imperial government seeking approval for the Walsh brothers' efforts and for a system for guiding New Zealand-trained men into the Royal Flying Corps.

above Student tents behind the hangars of the New Zealand Flying School at Kohimarama, today's Mission Bay. The Walsh brothers located their headquarters in the old Melanesian Mission building.

below Students Malcolm McGregor, Herbert Robson and Frederic Sharland in front of their tent lodgings. Both McGregor and Sharland became specialists in deadly ground strafing work on the Western Front.

The school took in its first students in October 1915, a handful of hopefuls that included Keith Caldwell and Geoffrey Callender. They were interviewed and accepted and paid their flying fees. The school now had pupils, one self-taught instructor and a home-built machine. Operations originally based at Orakei were soon transferred to Kohimarama, now known as Mission Bay. The site there looked more like a laid-back New Zealand camping ground than a flight training school — grassy, tree-hemmed, home to baches and visited by wandering cows. The students lived in tents on the shoreline, falling asleep and rising to the sound of lapping waves. It was an idyllic setting, and probably one of the most picturesque training schools of its day.

On fair-weather days students launched the flying boat by 4 a.m. to take advantage of the dawn hours' calm waters and low winds. In the dual-control trainer, students would sit side by side with Vivian on the bench seat. Turning the engine over was by heavy crank, not an easy task in choppy seas, as the student had to do this standing on the seat. The motor was also prone to oil fouling the spark plug; after failed attempts to start the engine, the bedraggled crew would have to be towed back to shore by the brothers' launch. Taxiing acquainted Caldwell and Callender with the controls, and the slow and sluggish flying boat was forgiving in their hands. In a spartan cockpit that lacked even the most basic instrumentation, shouting and hand signals substituted for a non-existent intercom. A fluttering tape indicated wind direction.

On 28 November Caldwell and Callender undertook their solo flights without mishap. Not long after, a second machine was added: Scotland's second damaged Caudron had been purchased, repaired and fitted with floats. By mid-December Vivian Walsh and students were flying the Caudron floatplane. Caldwell and Callender never completed their Royal Aero Club final tests at Kohimarama because inclement weather intervened. Nonetheless, in the New Year they departed New Zealand, confident that letters from the Walsh brothers attesting to their competency would gain them RFC admission.[6]

On 21 February 1916 the school was granted imperial recognition. Officials in England were keen to take up the offer of New Zealand-trained airmen. The New Zealand Defence Department had indicated that 25 'gentlemen' from the Walsh school might be wanting commissions, but the imperial flying service was 'willing to accept a further hundred'[7] — in other words, as many as New Zealand could produce. Commissions would be granted to graduates of the Walsh school who qualified with a Royal Aero Club certificate.[8] The Royal Aero Club, in turn, agreed to grant certificates to the New Zealand trainees — under the age of 25 and in good health — but required the qualifying flight to be witnessed by military officers appointed by the New Zealand government.[9] The final flight required the cadets to fly a figure-eight course over three miles and at a height of at least 300 ft, and then land with the engine cut off.

Once they had graduated, the cadets would be given their fare to England and paid at the rate of a second lieutenant with effect from embarkation.[10] 'On arrival in London they will be posted to a school of preliminary [ground] instruction,' the War Office advised, and they would be credited a £50 'outfit allowance'. On their successful completion of the preliminary ground school they would be transferred to a flying training school. Those men who proved

Aviation pioneer George Bolt working on a Walsh brothers' flying boat. He learnt to fly at the school and after the war set a number of New Zealand aviation records.

above Trainees at
the Walsh brothers'
flying school enjoy
the sunshine while
work is carried out on
the school's Caudron
floatplane. The rails
carried it from the sheds
to the sea.

below The Caudron
suffered heavy damage
when it stalled on a
flight and side-slipped
into the Waitemata.

their worth would get about three-quarters of their New Zealand training costs reimbursed.[11] At the completion of their full service, their return passage to New Zealand would be covered by the War Office, along with a gratuity of £150 for each completed year of continuous service.

The War Office had offered a clear path and attractive inducements to young New Zealand men wanting to enter the flying war. The news spread quickly through the dominion. Kaiapoi-born Hugh Blackwell wrote a pleading letter to his mother in March 1916: his uncle had been keeping him abreast of developments at the Walsh brothers' flying school.

> Uncle Ralph says they put you through the course for £100 at the end of which time they grant a pilot's certificate. With this certificate you rank as a Lieutenant with 12/6 a day and keep. Then you go to England for four months training and from there to the front. I hope pecuniary matters wont [sic] stop me. If you lend me £100 I will pay you back at 6% after the war. I would like to start before next month, as the territorial camp commences 3rd April, so please do your best for me.[12]

Apart from the age and medical restrictions, the £100 fee was one of the few impediments to entering the course. It was a not insubstantial fee — nearly an average yearly wage. The New Zealand authorities also stipulated that applicants should not be current members of the NZEF. 'It has been laid down,' wrote the minister of defence, 'that no man will be transferred from the New Zealand Expeditionary Force to an Aviation School, unless there are exceptional circumstances in connection with his case.'[13]

By this time Kohimarama was now home to an array of ramshackle buildings, including hangars with rails leading down to the shore for the seaplanes, a fitting shed and a collection of workshops.[14] The hangars were constructed from old motorcar packing cases from Dexter's business. The students still lived in tents, but these were now lined up behind the hangars. At the heart of the school were stone buildings that had once held missionaries bound for Melanesia; these were converted to the school's headquarters, a dining hall and accommodation for the staff.

The haphazard teaching that Caldwell and Callender received gave way to systematised instruction in 'the mechanism of aeroplanes and their engines and other technical knowledge', reported the *Dominion*.[15] Over time, more aircraft, instructors and mechanics were added to the staff, including the New Zealand aviation pioneer George Bolt. By June 1916 they had three aircraft on hand.

Training began in the early hours and, depending on the machines available, included four 15-minute flights. After lunch there were lectures on the theory of flight, and instruction in Morse code.[16] In blustery conditions and heavy seas the aircraft remained in the hangars and the students adjourned to the workshops for instruction with the mechanics. Eventually, drill was added to the daily routine, giving the training a more martial air. These daily marches and exercises were overseen by two great Norfolk pines, planted five decades earlier by Bishops Selwyn and Patteson of the Melanesian Mission. 'Where these Christian ministers established their first school and taught the gospel of peace,' a visitor waxed lyrical, 'New Zealand airmen now learn to fly, and get their first lessons in the most modern and deadly methods of warfare.'[17]

The school was hampered, however, by the low-powered engines that struggled when encumbered with both the pilot and a student; sometimes they used the wake of passing boats to bounce the seaplane aloft. In addition, the engines required a complete overhaul after every 20 to 50 hours of flying time.[18] At least one machine was out of action at any time. In August, a solo flight was abruptly terminated when the Caudron, 70 ft in the air, sideslipped into the harbour. The airman was unharmed but the aircraft was badly buckled, struts were broken and the engine waterlogged. A newly imported Curtiss seaplane proved unsuited to the conditions and the hull had to be substantially rebuilt. The financial strain nearly broke the school and it was saved only by the backing of prominent citizens and donors.

The cumulative result of all this was that in 1916 it took, on average, six months for pupils to reach the proficiency required to obtain their ticket. McGregor secured his Royal Aero Club certificate in five months, but Ronald Bannerman of Gore entered the course in March and did not attain his until December, nine months later;[19] he had only four hours' flying time in his logbook.[20] Only 18 students graduated that year.[21]

In 1917, when Hugh Blackwell entered the school, the period of training was reduced to four months. He greatly enjoyed his training there but felt he never quite had enough time in the air. 'I was up at 4.30 this morning and flying started a little before five. It was a beautiful morning,' he wrote from Kohimarama. 'I can tell you it is a great sight watching the machine 200 ft up, all flooded with sunlight . . . had a perfect flight.'[22] His only criticism was that it lasted barely eight minutes, which he estimated was about average for the students. After Vivian Walsh told the young men they would learn more from short rather than long flights, Blackwell reasoned that he had better get as many of these as possible. He spurned social gatherings with friends in Auckland when flying weather prevailed. Walsh told Blackwell he would need seven hours' flying time, which, at eight minutes a flight, meant over 50 flights. Blackwell qualified for his certificate in May — one of the 23 students who had graduated since the school came into existence. This figure climbed slowly to 48 in October 1917 and 83 by the Armistice.[23]

Henry Wigram watched the rise of the Auckland school from Christchurch. The Walsh brothers were providing airmen for the Empire, if at a slow rate. Wigram had lost none of his determination to create a fully fledged flying school for national defence, and advances in Australia convinced him that New Zealand could do so much better.

In May 1916, nearly a full seven years after his first address to the Legislative Council on the subject, Wigram once again asked the government to establish 'a school or schools of flying in preparation for the foundation of an aviation corps for the purposes of national defence'.[24] He argued that aviation was no longer a matter of experimentation and impractical daydreaming but was now a mature technology that was being widely used in battle. Aircraft in 1908, he told the council, travelled at 39 mph and could climb to 400 ft; now aircraft were travelling at 126 mph and could reach an altitude of 25,000 ft. There was support for Wigram inside and outside of the council, though some thought it was a waste of time to 'fiddle about with aeroplanes' in the midst of war.[25] For his part, Minister of Defence Allen was unmovable; he stated that the government had no intention of establishing such a school in the South Island. He did, however, privately inform Wigram — echoing sentiments made to the Walsh brothers in 1915 — that neither he nor the government objected to private enterprise undertaking the task.[26]

Provocatively, Wigram published the government's response to his pleas in the *Lyttelton Times*, and argued forcefully for a private initiative in Canterbury. While he applauded Allen's efforts in the land war, Wigram noted that the government had displayed 'a strange want of initiative and imagination', and should now 'lay the foundation' for New Zealand's aerial defence of the future.[27] Riding the crest of his self-manufactured publicity wave, Wigram met influential Christchurch citizens, a representative of the Walsh brothers' flying school and aviation experts such as Scotland, who was still convalescing. In July 1916 he ordered two Caudron biplanes from England, a risky £1700 investment that rested on his own personal funds. On 22 August, at a meeting of 40 representative citizens, Wigram laid out his plan to train aviators for war, promote aviation for national defence and encourage commercial aviation.[28] The Canterbury (NZ) Aviation Company was founded with a proposed capital of £20,000. The next step was the location of the school, which Wigram saw as New Zealand's 'Hendon' — a southern hemisphere incarnation of one of England's finest airfields.

With advice from Scotland, farmland just six miles west of Christchurch was selected. Roads, trams, rail and power lines all ran close to the Sockburn site, which was far enough from the Port Hills to avoid 'atmospheric disturbance'.[29] The initial 100-acre purchase, added to over time, was adjacent to the Canterbury Park Trotting Club raceway, a handy emergency landing ground if required. Existing sod cottages and poplars were removed in December, and considerable work had been completed by April 1917.

> The flying ground has undergone a transformation in the last week or so. It is a vast expanse of short-cropped green grass sloping almost as evenly as Brighton beach at an ideal landing slope in front of the hangars. Possibly nowhere in Canterbury could better flying ground be found. It is longer than Hendon [Britain] and more favoured, being an open, sunny acreage, clear of local wind currents with a clear landing in any direction . . . The hedges that once intersected the area have disappeared, except one corner, where 24 acres are under potatoes.[30]

Scotland was Wigram's first choice for instructor.[31] In August 1916 Wigram attempted to secure him, but Allen reminded Wigram that the airman was under orders, if and when he recovered, to return to England;[32] therefore it was not possible to discharge him to Wigram.[33] Wigram still held out hope when, in October, Scotland was deemed permanently unfit for further military service — the throat complaint was proving impossible to shrug.[34] The after-effects of the Mesopotamian deployment lingered; hospitalisation in India, convalescence in New Zealand, and still he was unwell. Wigram had waited for Scotland's anticipated recovery, but the disappointed airman was eventually forced to decline the position.[35]

Wigram turned to the New Zealand high commissioner in London, who recommended

Cecil Hill, the chief instructor at the Hall Flying School, Hendon.[36] The local newspapers alerted readers to the arrival of the 28-year-old and his wife and child in May 1917:

> Mr. Hill has trained some of the most brilliant of fliers at the front, he describes the progress of aviation since the war began as extraordinary. When the war broke out the ordinary machine was able to fly from 40 to 65 miles per hour, with a relatively low capacity for keeping in the air and could not 'hover' or fly slowly. The latest British machines are so stable that they will fly without any hand on the control. Air pockets are no longer a terror to them, and wind of little consideration. They can keep in the air for eight hours, in which they can do their 800 miles. A new British machine had a 250 hp Rolls-Royce engine, and can fly as slowly as 25 miles an hour and as fast as 120 miles . . . now Britain has thousands of pilots and machines, so much so that it is ever so much more difficult to get into the Flying Corps than it was . . . only gifted fliers . . . get through, for it is more than ever recognised that though practically anyone may be taught to fly, the fighting flier had to be born as well as made.[37]

Sockburn was much to Hill's liking. The site allowed for future expansion and the hangars — unlike the Kohimarama motorcar packing-case hangars — were well made and able to house several machines. He was full of praise for Wigram's efforts and, on 7 May, took up the recently arrived 60-hp dual-control Caudron.

Because of red tape and the demands of war, it had taken nine months since the first machine was ordered before it flew above Sockburn. On its arrival, Hill soon discovered the Caudron engine needed repairs. The second overseas Caudron would not appear until October. With only one flyable machine on hand, the ever ingenious mechanic John Mackie, recently transferred from the Auckland school, built an aircraft for the engine salvaged from the machine Scotland had crashed in 1914.[38] The school also had an old Blériot monoplane that had been imported years ago. This served as Sockburn's non-flying trainer, enabling students to taxi around the airfield and familiarise themselves with the cockpit controls.[39]

In the meantime, prospective students had been lining up as soon as Wigram's plans had been made public months earlier. At the beginning of the year, 40 students were already on the books, with a further 30 applications pending. The first six students were

Henry Wigram and his wife, Agnes, surrounded by Canterbury (NZ) Aviation Company trainees and staff, including Cecil Hill, at the right of Mrs Wigram.

Sockburn students, instructors and ground crew hamming it up for the camera, with a Caudron in the background. Wigram's school was more efficient in producing flying cadets, but its late establishment meant that far fewer of its students would fly in frontline squadrons by the time the war ended in 1918.

very happy with the living conditions. Accommodation was a sun-drenched, north-facing, 12-bedroom barrack block still smelling of fresh timber and paint. Wigram was famous for his love of inventions and innovation, and the barracks were fitted out with electric lighting. Students had to provide their own linen and blankets, but the Canterbury Aviation Company provided the beds and mattresses. The young men had hot baths and showers on tap. A weekly fee of £1 per student covered the cost of food and a cook.[40] Recreation was accounted for at Sockburn, and Hill considered that:

> It was very essential that pupils should keep themselves fit and probably some gymnastic appliances will be provided. The present pupils have laid out a golf course, rather deficient perhaps in bunkers, which are not encouraged on the flying ground, and there is a grass tennis court which should come into use as summer comes on. It is proposed to gradually form a library of books on aviation and allied subjects.[41]

On 19 June the students watched the first flight of the dual-control Caudron: the Canterbury Aviation Company was open for business. Hill's first passengers were Mr and Mrs Wigram. All six students were then taken up in what became a school tradition: new trainees were taken on a joyride as their introduction to the course. On this day, Edwyn Wilding took to the air with Hill. Edwyn was relaxed: the machine was flying at peak performance and he was carried to 80 ft for three or four circuits of the airfield. 'No sensation at all,' he pencilled in his diary, 'other than riding in a very comfortable motor car. I fooled with the joy stick for a bit.' At the bottom of the page he logged his air time at 10 minutes then hastily amended it to 11; he was on his way to becoming pilot and there was not a minute to lose.[42]

James Sloss from Cheviot, North Canterbury, arrived in October, and his joyride with Hill was considerably longer and higher: 'we went to about 1000 ft up and it was a lovely sensation only devilishly windy — one has to wear an aviator's helmet and goggles or he would get his hair blown off him . . . It is great to look down on houses and paddocks . . . the houses look like boxes . . . I could see Lake Ellesmere, the Waimak and all the country for miles and miles.'[43] Most new cadets agreed with Ross Brodie's estimation: 'it was exhilarating . . . but it was far too short'.[44]

Within six days Wilding had accumulated 41 minutes and felt he was getting better: 'Hill didn't swear so much.' The crisp and clear mornings of a Canterbury winter were ideal for flying. The pupils started with 'straights' — level flights designed to familiarise the arrivals with the machine, basic principles of flight and the all-important landings — followed by the use of the rudder, and they then progressed to circuits. Accidents were mercifully few, sometimes caused by the uneven patches in the airfield. Once the 'old bus wouldn't switch off and ended up in a fence', and on another occasion Wilding was on a flight when a shock absorber broke on the Caudron.[45] He was quick to point out that the bumpy airfield was to blame rather than himself. Hill may have been unconvinced, and for the better part of three days Wilding was assigned 'a bit of [airfield] levelling . . . with a horse and cart . . . plough and scoop'.[46] Wilding's most serious accident occurred on 17 July when the engine was playing up and, without sufficient height, he sideslipped in a turn. Hill was not hurt but the 'bus was smashed up a bit [and] I dislocated my hip'.[47] He was out of action for 17 days, but made good on his first day back with a full 30 minutes' flying. On 5 August he made his first solo flight. 'Feel quite at home on her now,' he recorded.

The great day arrived for the Royal Aero Club certificate test on 24 August. On hand were the two military observers, including Major James Sleeman, who had overseen early examination flights at Kohimarama.[48] He had no practical experience in flying but was New Zealand's director of military training and had visited flying schools in England and France. Wigram's long-held dream was about to be fulfilled. This was an event of 'Imperial as well as local significance', wrote an attendant reporter. The aircraft constructed by Mackie and students, dubbed *White Wings*, was brought out into the sunlight. Hill oversaw his charges and spoke a few kindly words of instruction to each man. Wilding was the first pupil in the air.

> He rose gently and made steady flights across the ground, the machine throwing a huge shadow like a cloud that coursed over the ground and leaped the gorse hedges as the aeroplane droned its way along at sixty miles an hour. The sky was fleckless, and only a few mists hung close to the hills . . . The young aviator was master of his machine and knew it.

Ross Brodie, one of the new entrants at the school, was among the audience. The test was the same as those in Auckland, with three flights including figure-eights, landing 'within 60 yards' of a given mark in the centre of the 'drome', wrote the impressed Brodie. On the ground, barking, was Edwyn's brother Anthony's dog, which had been shipped all the way back to New Zealand after Captain Wilding's death on the Western Front. It was a touching moment, felt by the small gathering. Every time Wilding flew past, Samson 'made frantic attempts to get off the chain'.[49] On his final flight, Wilding climbed above 350 ft, shut the engine off 'and swooped down in the dangerous dropping volplane, only to recover with a twist of the tail, and come hopping along gaily to the mark'. Wilding was overly critical of his own performance — 'I was pretty rotten, don't know why' — but full of praise for the aircraft: 'Little bus went like a hero.'[50] When he alighted, Hill was there to shake his hand.

All six candidates passed: the Sockburn instructor was delighted, and judged their efforts as good as anything he had seen in England. Wigram had his Hendon.

Each of the half-dozen students passed with under four hours' flying time. More importantly, it had taken only eight weeks for the Canterbury aviation students to complete their course, and Hill reckoned it could have been much shorter. Some of the students had been ready a fortnight earlier but the military observers were not available. The *Press* reported that 'their actual training has lasted only a little over a month'.[51] The great Sockburn pilot-producing machine was up and running. As the six graduating students moved quickly to complete their final medical examination in preparation for shipping out to England, Hill carried on with the next intake, whose completion was equally expeditious.

On 16 July Ross Brodie of Rangitata had entered the school as part of the second course. He had just escaped the clutches of the NZEF. Only weeks before, he had been drawn in the ballot for army service. Like most of the students at New Zealand's flying schools he had to appeal. Brodie had had his name down with the Canterbury Aviation Company since Christmas of 1916, had paid a deposit a month later and was determined not to miss his place. 'I have been accepted as a pupil for the Aviation School at Christchurch,' he wrote on his appeal form. 'I have passed the medical test . . . and expect to enter there in a month.'[52] His request, with a supporting letter from the school, was granted.[53] Brodie's relief was short-lived: he had a final hurdle to surmount.

His greatest fear was 26 September 1917 — his twenty-fifth birthday.[54] If he failed to secure his ticket by then, he could say goodbye to a place in the RFC. Hill took him up for 27 minutes the day he received this Defence Department missive, and the next day he did 32 straights. Hill set the young man a demanding schedule of flights; the only significant interruption was a hugely successful Sockburn open day on 5 September. Over 5000 people attended the midweek event. 'Hill gave a wonderful exhibition of flying,' Brodie said glowingly. 'His greatest feat was to loop the loop . . . this was the first time this . . . had been performed in NZ and done on a locally built machine.'[55] On 15 September, nearly a fortnight before his deadline, Brodie flew before an examining officer. 'This completed my flying at the Canterbury flying school,' he proudly wrote in his diary.

But of far more interest to the press reporters was Brodie's compatriot that day: Ernest Taniwha Sutherland. The Turakina-born student was one of a few Māori airmen in the Great War. 'Mr Sutherland the next candidate was regarded with the greatest interest, insomuch as he was creating a record, and possibility a world's record,' wrote the *Christchurch Star*, 'in being the first Maori to enter the Flying Corps.'[56] Of Ngāti Apa and Ngā Wairiki ancestry, Sutherland was a mechanic and farmer before joining Wigram's school. His ethnicity became a topic of interest to officialdom and the public. Apparently the imperial government had made 'purity' of European descent a factor in entering the flying service — a restriction that had not hindered Rhodes-Moorhouse from flying and winning a VC in the process in 1915. Nonetheless, communication with the War Office smoothed the way for 'any candidate with Maori blood, provided he was not a full-blooded Maori'. Sutherland obviously met this arbitrary precondition and was deemed 'qualified for service, greatly to the satisfaction of his friends, among whom he has long been known as a capable motorist, and a very keen follower of flying'.[57]

Sutherland qualified very comfortably against a bumpy rising wind. If he was ruffled by the

Ernest Taniwha
Sutherland was the
first Māori graduate
to gain a Royal Aero
Club certificate in New
Zealand. Sutherland
went on to serve in a
coastal patrol squadron
in the Great War.

focus on his ethnicity he did not say so publicly; if anything he seemed uplifted by it. Later, while training in England, he wrote to his uncle.

> Personally, I am at present doing fine, and in another six weeks or so from now . . . should find me trying conclusions with the Huns. Some weeks ago I was seriously ill owing to an accident I had in South Surrey, and then I contracted tonsillitis; however, now I'm A1 and can hold my own any day. We are leaving there this week for our final course of instruction in aeronautics. Undoubtably this is the service d'elite of the Empire, especially when you have got your wings up; but of course you have all the risks, but that's all in the game. I am quite proud of myself as an airman, especially being the first representative of the race.[58]

In 1918 at Kohimarama, Charles Barton was the second Māori to obtain a Royal Aero Club ticket at a New Zealand flying school. Race made no difference to either man's ability to fly but was of concern to the authorities in London, and by the end of the war the Defence Department was having second thoughts. It instructed Wellington that the educational standard of Māori students 'should be higher than that for the European candidate'.[59]

The 15 September test once again demonstrated the efficiency of the Sockburn school. Brodie and Sutherland, like Wilding before, had completed their course in less than two months. It was a grand achievement: Sockburn training took only a third of the time to complete compared to Kohimarama in 1916, and half of that of 1917. Both schools got their men up to Royal Aero Club certificate standard with sometimes as little as four hours of flight time, but the land-based instruction and superior aircraft at Sockburn were telling factors. The Waitemata Harbour was a fickle training venue that added weeks to the schedule of the Auckland-based students. The seaplanes were homemade and heavy, while the Caudrons were lighter and more easily maintained.

It took the Auckland school 17 months to graduate 75 students; the Canterbury school achieved this in nine months.[60] Moreover, Vivian Walsh, for all his enthusiasm and industry, was self-taught and had nothing like the instructional experience of Hill. Even though it had started a year and half later than the Walsh brothers' New Zealand Flying School, Wigram's Canterbury Aviation Company had pushed through more students by the time the war ended in November 1918: when the Armistice arrived, Sockburn had graduated 170 airmen and Kohimarama 83.[61]

In spite of all this, the Kohimarama school had a major advantage over Sockburn: its students were far more likely to fly operationally in the Great War. The late establishment of the Canterbury Aviation Company, caused by delays in aircraft procurement, precluded the greater part of its students from participating in the war. For example, Sutherland, one of the first nine graduates at Sockburn, saw very limited action. He arrived in Britain in late 1917 and progressed to observer training. He did not receive his commission until 4 October 1918. From Mullion, Cornwall, he flew on anti-submarine patrols until the end of the war, only 38 days later. And Wilding, who was the first person to gain his flying ticket at Sockburn and who had been commissioned into the air service a day before Sutherland, was still under instruction in Egypt when the Armistice was signed.[62] He was one hour shy of completing his time in one of the war's leading air combat machines when the 'flying war washed out'.[63]

By contrast, many of the Kohimarama pupils were actively engaged in reconnaissance, bombing and scouting sorties in Europe. 'No fewer than fifty pupils have obtained certificates and gone into active service,' Vivian Walsh said proudly in an interview in January 1918.[64] Among these 50 pupils were some of New Zealand's most exceptional airmen of the war: Keith Caldwell, Geoffrey Callender, Malcolm McGregor, Ronald Bannerman, William Cook and Herbert Dewitt.

But their New Zealand training mattered very little when they were required to undertake extensive instruction in Britain. At best it briefly reduced their time in flying training.[65] The months required to get a Royal Aero Club ticket were hardly worth the few hours' flying time saved in England, something the New Zealand authorities had realised by 1918. In a letter to the Dunedin district headquarters, Sleeman noted that although the Sockburn school now incorporated a drill centre where the men gained instruction in map-reading and machine guns, 'nothing that is taught in New Zealand shortens the period of training in England'.[66]

In fact some New Zealanders were wary of entering the local schools because of the waiting lists that added further delays, and the time taken to gain flying proficiency. Sockburn had 21 men on its waiting list in mid-1918.[67] Arthur Coningham, for example, decided against a position at Kohimarama and made the journey to Britain with no guarantee of placement there. His reasoning was simple and to the point: 'The teaching was so slow' in New Zealand, he wrote in 1916, that 'it would have entailed the loss of eight or ten months'.[68] Coningham was joined by numerous New Zealanders who felt they could get into the air war faster by undertaking training directly in England.

The establishment of the New Zealand Flying School and later the Canterbury Aviation Company was a public acknowledgement of the need for more airmen to serve in the war. That the schools ran with the moral support and cooperation of the Defence Department and encouragement from the War Office in Britain was undeniable proof that flying was now a respected avenue for young men wanting to play their part in the war. In early 1916, just after Callender and Caldwell departed from Kohimarama, the Department of Internal Affairs reported it had received many applications from 'young men who . . . wished to proceed to the United Kingdom in order to join the Royal Flying Corps'.[69] Given the British government's endorsement of such initiatives, Internal Affairs wished them well and instructed them to report to the high commissioner in London, where they would be required to make a declaration that 'if they were not required for the flying Corps they would join some other branch of the imperial service'.

The local flying school students departed New Zealand shores under similar stipulations. Although they were officers in training, they were technically members of the NZEF. Their enrolment in the NZEF was a precautionary measure. Prospective New Zealand-trained graduates who failed to secure a position in the air services became members of the New Zealand army: in this way those who did not become airmen could not avoid military service.[70]

U nlike the greater bulk of the New Zealanders who went to war as soldiers, the graduates from the two schools went as flying cadets, and those who sought direct entrance did so as private citizens. Generally, both groups journeyed to Britain in conditions that were a world removed from their trooper counterparts. The Main Body and subsequent reinforcements had dismal sea voyages with poor sleeping conditions and less than satisfactory food. Any shore leave the soldiers had was heavily regulated and tightly controlled. It was a largely joyless experience. The flying cadets and those going independently were well favoured in their passages to England.

James Sloss, younger brother of Robert Sloss, left for Britain as the war entered its last year, and was in no doubt he had made the right decision to try out for flying. The cadets shared the ship with the latest round of reinforcements. 'I'm far better going the way I am,' he told his sisters, 'than going as a private. We lead the life of gentlemen compared with the way the troopers are treated.' The shipboard conditions of a flying cadet were much improved over those his brother had endured as infantryman.

> We have a grand little deck to ourselves right away from the troops where we can sit and read or scrap in the fresh air and sun. There are nine of us — Templeton, Grant, MacDonald, Laurenson, Chapman, Dalwood (Percy), Adams and a chap Smith from the Auckland school so you see I have all my flying mates. Grant, MacDonald and I occupy one cabin between us. Grant brought a lot of tucker on board with him and we have afternoon tea and supper every day. He brought a lot of tinned fruit which is very acceptable [in] this hot weather. There is a dry canteen on board where one can buy almost anything that he wants, but Grant's supply meets our requirements; it is grand to have pals. I often feel glad that I came because it would have been much harder and more unpleasant to have come away with strangers and we have great fun sometimes. Every night after it is too dark to stay on deck we join the Sergeant Majors in the mess room and have some music (good music too), smoke, play draughts, cards, read or write letters.[71]

One thing he was certain of from his vantage point on the 'grand little deck': 'I reckon I have taken on the best job of all. I can't bear to think that relations and friends of mine had to put up with the life of a private.'[72] In the tropics the soldiers melted in the heat; and in winter, especially in the southern and northern extremities of their voyages, they froze. Sloss explored the lower reaches of the 'tub' and found the accommodation sorely wanting. Even though he was having trouble sleeping in the tropical heat, he pitied 'the poor privates sleeping in their hammocks down in the hold — they're packed in like sardines'.

When they hit the cold northern Atlantic it was even worse. 'It takes the poor beggars all their time to keep warm,' Sloss wrote to his mother.[73]

Hugh Blackwell, a Kohimarama student, went with a clutch of fellow cadets in May 1917 and they were very happy with travelling arrangements on *Iconic*:

'A bath this morning, Sir?'

'Yes, I think I'll go down this morning steward. Everything ready?'

'Yes Sir.'

So down we nobles go and enjoy a warm bath, make as much mess as we can and leave the steward to clean up. We often indulge in a free water fight over the partition. Breakfast at 8.30 am. Fruit to start with. The milk is not good so we cut out the porridge. Fish is next to be followed by bacon and eggs, and 6 slices of toast. We wind up the meal with coffee and cheese. We read or play games until 11 am when the steward brings up iced oranges. They are very acceptable I can assure you and if the steward turns his back we invariably get two. At 1.30 pm we have lunch. It generally consists of soup, 3 or 4 meats, 2 kinds of puddings and fruit. We mess round until 4 pm when tea arrives. About 6.20 we go to our cabins, and find our hot water waiting and a clean towel. We generally have a busy half hour getting ready for dinner. At 7 pm the bugle blows and in we all troop. The spread is on the same lines as lunch only more elaborate, and finishes with ice cream. After dinner we proceed to the library, and generally start a pillow fight, Gould and I against Fouby and George. The odds are against us but we give them a good run for their money.

Sandwiches arrive about 9.30 pm after which we have a lemon squash each and get to bed about 11.00 pm. You know we are beginning to tire of this sort of thing after doing it for nearly three weeks.[74]

Aside from the NZEF and flying cadets, a number of young men made their way to the war in the air as private individuals, either working their passage or as general passengers. Nelson-born Donald Harkness worked his passage one year into the war. Although his vessel, the *Paparoa*, was no White Star luxury liner, it was a floating palace compared to the dilapidated vessels the troopers were crammed into. Harkness's engineering experience and family connections saw him appointed a 'fitter', maintaining the machinery essential to the vessel.[75] On his first night at sea he got a good night's sleep and his roommates and near-neighbours were a civilised crowd. As well as the luxury of arising to face the new day much later than his soldier compatriots, Harkness was also engaged in useful and rewarding labour across civilised hours. NZEF troopers' concerns over their woeful food paled in comparison to Harkness's gastronomic deprivations.

Arose at 8.30 for porridge, bacon and eggs, curry and rice, and mutton. Set to work soon after and fooled round with connecting rod and brasses of one of the pumps. Dined on soup, chicken, kidneys on toast, cutlets and vegetables, plum pudding and jam tarts. Afternoon worked for about two hours when an adjournment was made for eatables, consisting of fried fish, Welsh rabbit, haricot mutton and beef. Played bridge with two others . . .[76]

The Montgomerie brothers, Oswald and Seton, travelled to Britain in June 1916. Both would be pilots before the war concluded. Unusually, they travelled with their family: two siblings and their father and mother, Roger and Annie. Annie had decided that if her sons were to fight she wanted to be as close to them as possible. In mid-1916 the family left their Waitaki farm in the hands of a manager and boarded the *Remuera*. As paying passengers in second-class cabins, they had a freedom of movement and degree of luxury not found on the crowded troopships or even those working their passage. 'Our daily routine,' wrote Annie in her diary,

> is early tea, then soon afterwards a stewardess announces bath is ready. On going to the
> bathroom one finds the water run (salt) and basin with hot fresh water also ready. Then dress
> leisurely for 8.30 breakfast. After that lying in deckchair talking, reading or sleeping whiles
> the hours away or an occasional walk thrown in.[77]

Breakfast in bed, glasses of stout, choir practice, deck billiards and lunch with the captain were all added into the mix.

The troopship passengers had greater restrictions on their excursions than those working passage, and considerably less than those paying their own way by passenger liner. Montevideo, Uruguay, welcomed Harkness with a dazzling midnight tropical thunderstorm that transformed darkness into daylight with lightning 'sometimes colouring the whole sky a rich purple or red, and always leaving tree and fern formations over nearly all the heavens'. The city was a collection of pretty squares and streets threaded by odd little trams fitted with cane-backed seats. These 'wobbled about from side to side in a very alarming manner and blundered along the streets; the rails never running in a straight line or on the same level for half a yard at a time'.[78] Most striking, however, were the inhabitants. 'Tiny little fellows, never more than 5 ft, 6 in' was how Harkness described the well-turned-out police officers of Montevideo, their shiny boots and huge helmets outdone only by the long sword on one hip and 'terrifying' great revolver holstered on the other. After barely three hours of sightseeing in Montevideo, Harkness and his fellow tourists found they were laden with Spanish coins surplus to requirements. Dockside fruit vendors ambushed the embarking men in a mutually advantageous exchange.

> The parson went aboard with his pockets full of peanuts; the doctor had bananas bulging from
> the pockets of both coat and overcoat, while Newbrook seemed to prefer oranges. I succeeded
> in getting rid of the thirty cents I had left, and as I found myself once more on the ocean wave,
> saw that all my available pockets had their full share of peanuts, oranges and bananas.[79]

Raucous vendors and street urchins were grudgingly accepted as part of the landscape, but New Zealanders raised with ordered shops and a more gentrified form of retail found that the chaotic, loud and insistent cry of locals plying their wares wore their patience thin.

On the final stretch to Britain, Harold Butterworth's ship briefly called in to Tenerife, the largest and most populous island of the Canary Island archipelago. Butterworth was a 'pantryman', working his passage in 1915 on the *Karamea*. His main role was ensuring the cooks were supplied with ingredients. Handily for him, the ship carried not only flax and wool but also a cargo of 8000 sheep carcasses. Off west Africa the kitchen ran short of meat,

> so I dressed up in a suit like Captain Scott went to the pole in and went from the freezing chamber through the snow boxes to the hold and got 4 sheep up. It was quite an experience to go through a tunnel lined with snow and see thousands of carcasses of mutton all frozen and covered with snow at the end.[80]

At Tenerife, where the ship picked up 4000 boxes of tomatoes, he did not set foot on the island, but he did have dealings with the vendors who pulled up alongside the ship in small boats, selling fruit and vegetables. To his mind the main city was 'very picturesque . . . situated between high hills which are very rugged. The houses are either white, pink, or yellow, and with grey rocky hills well to the back, and green market gardens laid out in squares close behind the houses it is a lovely sight.' Nevertheless, 'although this town is so beautiful to look at', he concluded — doubtless after getting on the losing side of negotiations for provisions — 'the inhabitants are a very low immoral lot. Although I would have liked to have gone ashore very much to see the town, I saw all I ever want to see of its people.'[81]

As for those who traversed the Panama Canal, it was a trip not to be forgotten. From the ship's deck at Panama City, Oswald and Seton Montgomerie's mother painted an excited picture as she laid eyes on a woman who looked as if she had stepped out of a Mark Twain novel: 'A Negro woman standing on the wharf with a tray of fruit on her head was one of our first artistic sensations, a real old Aunt Chloe.' At dockside their ship was the 'thing of the moment. Crowds of blacks and whites were staring at us and we at them.' The young Montgomerie brothers and family procured a car to take in the sights. Unlike the sedate streets of small New Zealand towns, Panama was crowded with 'funny little fruit stalls, the queer foreign tropical look everywhere caught our eyes, funny little donkey carts with black men driving, plenty of motor cars, buses and vehicles of all descriptions with mules in harness, steam rollers even, all in a conglomeration on every narrow street'.[82]

Back on board two hours later, the Montgomerie family slowly traversed the freshly dug 'eighth wonder of the modern world': the Panama Canal. Thirty years in the making, the most significant manmade waterway in history was opened a mere three weeks after the start of the greatest conflict to date. Soon after its opening, at least 1000 ships annually were criss-crossing the canal, cutting weeks off the hazardous Cape Horn route. The huge machines, dredges and connected locks that lifted vessels some 90 ft, were nothing like anything the New Zealanders — or the rest of the world — had seen. The Montgomerie matriarch, born and reared in Dunedin, found the humid, verdant New World wilderness captivating. 'A tropical picture, every outlook is beautiful. I hated having to go down for my dinner. The sunset tints on township and on foliage of the hills around will remain a memory for all time, just beautiful.'[83] The scenery and peace was broken only by the loss of a man overboard. Dubbed a

Henry Hugh Blackwell

James Sloss

Oswald Montgomerie

Francis Adams

Charles Roderick Carr

Edgar Garland

Herbert Russell

George Aimer

Trevor Alderton

religious maniac by passengers, it appeared that he was simply having a swim before breakfast. The captain was unhappy with the risks his rescuing crew were exposed to, and the arrival of sharks soon after they had plucked the man from the canal only confirmed his concerns. One of the passengers noted that at least the man 'was ready to visit his maker', to which another quipped, 'His maker was evidently not ready to meet him and sent him back.'[84]

The first cohort of seven flying cadets from Sockburn and two Kohimarama graduates, sailing on the *Arawa*, were favoured with a final stopover at Newport News, Virginia. The men, particularly those trained on seaplanes at the Auckland school, wanted to see the city's famous Curtiss Flying School. From their ship at anchor, they enjoyed watching a pilot stunting, looping and nosediving. They wangled their way ashore past local police by flashing their flying badges. Brodie wrote that a 'one-legged man' drove them to the flying school's base of operations.

> This was a private school, run by the Curtiss company, where pupils take their first course in Aviation. The machines we saw were all land planes of the Curtiss type fitted with Curtiss 90HP engines. These busses were vastly superior to anything we had seen, both in size and strength as the instructor proved to us in the way he turned it about in the air, looping the loop 6 times without a stop and doing a spinning nose dive which we always understood was a most dangerous thing to get into, but he came out of it without the least difficulty. At the school they go in for passenger flying, for ten dollars they will take you up for ten minutes loop the loop several times and do a tail spin, as we call the spinning nose dive. If you are not content with a short trip, they will see you up to New York . . . Sutherland was very keen to be the first Maori to loop the loop so paid his 10 dollars and was taken up for 10 minutes in which time he did 12 loops and a tail spin and quite near the ground too. These pilots seem to have no fear of an engine failure as they will loop when only about 150 ft off the ground.[85]

From 1915 onwards, concerns over onboard conditions, the adventure, camaraderie and new sights were pushed into the background as the troopships neared their destinations. The waters lapping the British Isles and the Mediterranean coast had increasingly become a theatre of war owing to the threat of German U-boats. During the Great War these vessels sank a staggering number of merchant ships — nearly 5000 in all. On the final leg of Butterworth's journey, word came through of the 'sinking of the *Lusitania* and the loss of many lives'.[86] In an attempt to blockade Britain, the Germans had declared British waters a war zone: in effect, Allied ships could be sunk without warning. The *Lusitania*, a British luxury ocean liner, was torpedoed on 7 May 1915. One of the era's great ships, it was struck beneath the wheelhouse and a second great explosion followed almost immediately after. Of the 1962 passengers, 1191 were lost, most as a result of hypothermia in the bone-numbing Atlantic. This shocking news put Butterworth on edge; *Karamea* observed a strict blackout and lookouts were increased.

Nine days later, off the English coast, in broad daylight and within sight of the Thames, a submarine suddenly arose 200 yards off the starboard bow and advanced on *Karamea*. Butterworth thought his flying career was about to end at sea long before it had begun in the air. As he looked for the tell-tale signs of an incoming torpedo, he heard gunfire. A Royal Navy ship had appeared, but the shells were landing 20 yards astern of the menacing attacker. Butterworth anticipated the submarine would submerge in the face of this onslaught, but to his surprise it turned towards the *Karamea*'s 'defender', pulling alongside. This was no surrender. It dawned on Butterworth that he had been watching a British submarine at manoeuvres, with other vessels undertaking gunnery practice, all under the watchful eye of an airship circling the mouth of the Thames. Sheepishly he realised that he would make landfall after all.[87]

The U-boat scourge increased, and the threat remained until the war's end. One of the later reinforcements from New Zealand carried 17 New Zealand flying cadets aboard the troopship *Mokoia*. Although by this time the Allied authorities had a comprehensive convoy system in place that greatly reduced the effectiveness of the German submarines, it did not stop the Imperial German Navy's attempts to strike at the transports. Christ's College old boy Edmund Reeves was one of the small group of aviation hopefuls on the *Mokoia*. The crew were in a high state of alert; only days earlier, two German submarines had been destroyed by mines near Dover. The 20-strong convoy entered the English Channel, and on the first day received over a dozen U-boat reports and five alarms. Reeves was part of a three-man gun crew that stood a four-hour watch. When one of the convoy ran up the sign 'chased by a submarine' all hell broke loose as the six escorting destroyers swung into action. The intruder was spotted and depth charges deployed, causing the *Mokoia* to 'shudder through and through'.

> Our captain, thinking he had been hit, stopped his engines and ordered the lowering away of the boats. Gordon Rich and myself were on duty at the gun. We cleared our gun for action, put on our lifebelts, and then had nothing to do but watch the excitement. All this took place in about two minutes. Within that time the destroyers from all round the convoy tore at full speed to the scene of the action, circled round the place where the submarine was spotted, and dropped more bombs. There was no sign of panic whatever, although one or two went a bit pale. I myself was conscious of a feeling of excitement, and a sorrow at leaving the old '____' [*Mokoia*], and at parting with my belongings.[88]

With the threat seen off, Reeves took a few photographs as mementos of the heart-stopping but ultimately non-fatal action.

James Sloss, only days out from Britain, had a fright when 'we saw what we thought [was] a German submarine coming towards us but luckily it was nothing worse than a dead whale floating on the surface. It gave everybody a great scare.'[89] On 23 June 1917 Hugh Blackwell wrote to his mother: 'England at last. We sighted the Land's End lighthouses last night at 11 pm.' On his last three days at sea, Blackwell realised that he was closer to his goal but also closer to danger. His ship had been 'zigzagging to avoid subs'. The English coast was a sight he would not forget as the ship passed many motor patrol boats and minesweepers and two airships and an aircraft on the hunt for the enemy U-boats. 'Everything we see impresses war on us.'[90] With their arrival in England, the New Zealanders were entering the final stage of their journey to the air war.

CHAPTER SEVEN

BASHED INTO SHAPE

A four- to six-week course at the School of Military Aeronautics, typically at Reading or Oxford, was the New Zealanders' first taste of military aviation instruction. Despite its name, the students were entering a 'ground' school — there was no flying and the closest they got to aircraft were static airframes and engines designed to increase the young men's understanding of design, construction and repair. Essentially they were entering a concentrated university programme. Unlike a university, however, the schools were run on 'military lines', Hugh Blackwell noted at the Reading school, 'and we cannot go out without leave'.[1] Students were knocked into shape with parade-ground discipline and the cadets had to salute all instructors, even when the cadet's probationary rank was above the instructor's. The military nature of the course was highlighted by rising at 6.15 a.m. for physical drill, breakfast and morning lectures. Lunch was followed by more lectures, with dinner at 7.30 p.m.[2] Kohimarama graduate Mac McGregor recalled the weeks crammed with lectures and practical instruction:

> Courses of Instruction, most intensive and comprehensive, were commenced immediately. Each pilot was required to learn the structural details of eight types of engines, even to the firing order of the cylinders and periods at which inlet and exhaust valves opened; bombing and bomb sighting; theory of flight, rigging, aerial and artillery observation; meteorology; map reading; wireless signalling; structure and operation of the Lewis, Vickers and Maxim machine guns; and photography.[3]

Blackwell's diary reveals a demanding regime. In his initial week at Reading he had six lectures on the Lewis machine gun, five on wireless, four on the theory of flight, one on bombs ('how they work, etc.'), and a 'lantern lecture' on different types of machines. The course mixed theory with practical work. Blackwell had been there only a couple of days before his class was dismantling and reassembling a BE2c and learning the correct way to patch a wing.[4] The only unpleasantness was the two rounds of inoculations that made students 'thick-headed' and hindered their copious note-taking in class.[5] They have 'crammed a lot about aeroplanes into our heads', wrote Blackwell as he was about to start a week or two on engines.[6]

Many of the young men were not enamoured with the ground school: after all, they had joined the flying corps to fly, not to sit through lectures they considered overly complicated, theoretical and, in many cases, irrelevant to the actual business of flying. They learnt the necessary operational intricacies of wireless telegraphy and the all-important aerial observation theory and practice, but also how some engine parts were manufactured and the componentry of aneroid barometers. Students filled notebooks with tightly written script that would never be referred to again. Some cadets were taught how to remove a broken Lewis bolt, in spite of the fact that this was impossible while flying and that nowhere on the aircraft was there a spare machine-gun bolt. While subjects like mess etiquette appeared early in the curriculum, the theory and mechanics of flight were not introduced until 1917.[7]

At Oxford, Melville White had the tedium of a lecture broken by the commanding officer hunting for volunteers: 'My two friends and myself stepped out and we were amused when he told us to clean all the windows in the front of the building.' White had not left NZEF headquarters, London, to wash windows, even if they were lead-paned and attached to a venerable 700-year-old university. But he had volunteered, and wash he did. His efforts were interrupted by the sudden arrival of a cavalcade. It was George V, King and Emperor of India. 'We felt rather flattered to think that we had been appointed window cleaners to the King. Quite a high position in fact considering we could only reach the windows by fire escape ladders.'[8]

After only two weeks at Reading, Blackwell had had enough. He was wistfully anticipating the day when he would exit the classroom for the airfield. 'I won't be sorry when we do,' he told his mother.[9] In his fourth week the novelty had well and truly worn off, and a bored Blackwell jotted in his diary that they 'had a lecture on military law by Col. somebody'.

The mind-numbing proliferation of facts and diagrams and the creeping boredom that plagued trainees at Reading and Oxford were inflicted on those in Egypt, too. Schools were established there to facilitate the rapid expansion of the air effort in the Middle East. Ross Brodie shipped out from England to Egypt for his final training; with him were Edwyn Wilding, Herbert Hawker and Eric Orr from the Canterbury Aviation Company and James Woods of the Auckland New Zealand Flying School.[10] Brodie commenced his training after a month-long battle with measles.[11]

In addition to square-bashing and military training, days were spent filling up notebooks and evenings swotting. Wilding was wilting under a daily monotony that closely resembled that of his counterparts in Britain: a 6.15 a.m. start of invigorating physical training, an uninspiring breakfast, an hour of drill, two hours of deadening lectures, a lunch break to recharge, an afternoon of more stupefying lectures, another hour of drill just in case the previous hour of drill had been forgotten, the main meal of the day — dinner — and an hour of study before laying their heads to rest at 10 p.m. with the knowledge that tomorrow offered them more of the same.[12] This went on for weeks in which they were peppered with tests on squad drill, judging outside distances and even a 'written musketry exam'.[13]

The heat and dust in Egypt were not to the students' liking. This, combined with the tedium, meant that pathetically small mercies were richly savoured. 'Loafing about all day. Had weekly bath,' recorded Wilding. 'We have changed into shorts and shirt sleeves. Splendid.' Even the loathed sandstorms proved a blessing under the school's drawn-out schedule: 'Had a pretty good sand storm today. We got into our tents and battened everything down. Missed most of the work for the day through it.'[14]

When the formal School of Military Aeronautics commenced, it was a further month and a half of classes. Wilding initially found them more interesting, given that they directly related to the business of flying.[15] Nonetheless, after months of study the students simply wanted it all to end. 'Work as usual, the jolly course seems to have been increased into 7 weeks, very fed up,' wrote Wilding.[16] The Egyptian programme was under-resourced and not on the same demanding schedule as its British counterpart — as was made evident by the length of time it took to complete. Excluding a month convalescing, Brodie had nearly six months of ground training compared to Blackwell's two. One of the few consolations was the wonderland of places to visit and sights to see when on leave.

While they were training in Egypt or Britain, the New Zealanders spent much of their downtime as tourists in countries they knew only from schoolbooks. War offered the chance of a lifetime, and many of them grabbed it with both hands. The world of the ancient pharaohs and the monarchs of Britain filled many an airman's photograph album.

The day he left hospital, Brodie embarked on a serious sightseeing adventure. His first jaunt, with Orr in tow, was to a little bit of Europe in Egypt — and pure escapism: Heliopolis Luna Park. It was Africa's first Western-style amusement park, but more recently it had been colonised by the Anzac authorities for much-needed medical space. The ice-skating rink and the haunted house had been covered in beds to accommodate Gallipoli wounded, and the ticketing station had been converted to an operating theatre. Still, enough of the original entertainment survived the closure of the hospital in 1916 and the two New Zealanders enjoyed the water chute, maze, laughing gallery and scenic railway. It was a 'wonderland and a jolly good time', wrote Brodie.[17] Six days later, 'all we NZ boys decided to spend the afternoon at the Pyramids'. Fortified with tea and bread, they clambered aboard camels to traverse the sands to see some of Egypt's best-known sights. At the great Pyramid of Khufu (Giza), they climbed 50 ft up one corner to view the countryside and then plunged down a small passage barely four feet high. 'At the bottom of this we go up another long passage still crouching, an Arab leading with a candle,' Brodie wrote. '[This] passage leads up to the King's Tomb . . . [Everything is] as solid as the day they were built 6000 years ago.'[18]

Egypt's population was as intriguing as it was frustrating to the visitors. On the one hand, the locals fulfilled the New Zealanders' romantic images of Middle Eastern Arabs as they made jars and water bottles from the Nile's mud; or at the end of Ramadan when 'they have flags flying everywhere and are holding festivals in all the parks; like the Maoris they go in greatly for colour and the children are dressed in all the colours of the rainbow'.[19] Nothing was more pleasant than spending an evening in lovely gardens on the banks of the Nile, watching the locals gliding by in their sailboats. On the other hand, the sellers and guides that proliferated in the bazaars and at the tourist attractions irritated many New Zealanders. As one trainee airman noted when he visited Egypt's most popular spot:

Our car pulled up at the foot of the Giza Pyramids. Sure enough even at this early hour we were plagued with one of the everlasting 'guides', who although listening calmly to my varied vocabulary of uncomplimentary Arabic epithets showed not the slightest sign of skedaddling. His rasping voice continually drowning out our conversation with innumerable boring details concerning the pyramids ... He did not want our money — oh no — he merely wanted to enlighten us for he loved us. Nevertheless he loved us for what he could get ... baksheesh ... The best guide I remember was the one our party had at Assouan [Aswan] who remained as silent as the Sphinx (we paid him extra for this concession!!!!).[20]

Of course, when longer excursions were not possible there was always Cairo, then a city of 800,000 inhabitants. After a lunchtime parade, Brodie and the others scampered off to the city's bleached-brown Citadel. Saladin's medieval fortress had originally been designed to fend off crusaders, but for Brodie it offered the twin pleasures of a light breeze and an unimpeded view of the city's buildings and houses tumbling off into the distance. On their way down into the city they entered the Blue Mosque. Brodie admired the blue and green tiles with floral motifs. From there they went to a well-known bazaar, 'where you can buy any kind of Egyptian article. Saw some very fine silk and lace, it was really well worth a look through.'[21] Over the weeks that followed, leave was filled with trolley rides along the Delta Barrage spanning the Nile, touring the ancient capital of Memphis, strolling through the Zoological Gardens, investigating the tombs of the Mamelukes, and appraising the artefacts at the Museum of Egyptian Antiquities.[22]

Having nothing doing today, and the Egyptian Museum only being open in the mornings we decided to pay it a visit, and were well repaid for the trouble. It was full of Egyptian Antiquities ... mostly from 1 to 2 thousand years BC. There you will see the mummies of the ancient Egyptian kings, the wrapping having been taken off and on the brow are still to be seen the wrinkles of old age ... there are also granite statues of the kings which stand 10 and 13 ft high, the greater the power of the king the larger the statue, any statue with a beard shows that that person belonged to the royal family. The great many beautiful statues carved out of pure alabaster, and the work is as fine as anything that could possibly be done today.[23]

Sacred embalmed rams, crocodiles, bulls and cats, and the jewels of the long-dead kings and queens all fascinated the visitors. New Zealand's budding aviators had turned amateur Egyptologists.

Rhoda Island in central Cairo reminded them of their Christian heritage and bible school lessons in New Zealand.

Rhoda Isla ... is the garden of Moses, in which are date palms, fig trees and all kinds of Egyptian shrubs. The guide paid ... to get us in. In this garden is Moses' well and it was alongside this well that he was supposed to be found in a basket among the bulrushes ... Next visited the oldest Coptic Church built in 950 AD, it has some lovely carved woodwork inlaid with carved ivory. It was in a cave under this church where Mary and Joseph took refuge with our saviour when he was a baby ... when they fled to Egypt.[24]

Air and ground crew
took full advantage
of their time in Egypt
visiting historical sights.
This photograph of
the famous pyramids
at Giza was taken by a
New Zealand airman.

Mementos of their visits emptied their wallets. Shopping expeditions collected 'gold inlaid vases done in Egyptian work' and shawls that were packaged and sent home to New Zealand.[25]

London proved less exotic to cadets but no less alluring. Most of the New Zealanders saw London not as a foreign city but as the administrative, economic, cultural and military centre of their Empire. After all, nearly all were sons of Britons and subjects of the king. Britain was 'Home' and London its hearth.

Donald Harkness was one of many New Zealanders who wasted no time in warming himself in its glow: London Zoo, the Tower of London, Buckingham Palace, the Houses of Parliament, Kew's botanical gardens, and Westminster Abbey. At Madame Tussaud's the figures 'looked so life like', wrote Harkness — so much so that he embarrassingly mistook one for a woman selling catalogues. He observed another male visitor fall for the same ploy. Later he spotted this same 'chap' examining a police figure: 'He proceeded to pull its belt around and inspect a medal it was wearing when he discovered to his horror that this figure was not made of wax at all!'

At Christopher Wren's St Paul's Cathedral, Harkness 'blew in with the crowd'. 'The altar is a beautiful piece of work, as [were] also the mosaics on the ceilings and the woodwork of the choir. The organ is one of the best in the world, and the bell at the top of the clock tower, 17 tons in weight, the largest in England. In the crypt below are graves, tablets and memorials to Wellington, Nelson . . . the great painters.' Like all colonials before and since he stood at one side of the Whispering Gallery running round the inside of the great painted dome as a church caretaker at the other side, 100 feet distant, spoke in a very low voice and Harkness 'heard every word he said almost as if he yelled it'.[26]

Then there were the delights of the stage. Harold Butterworth made for the theatre whenever he was in London. Over Christmas and New Year 1915–16 he feasted on *Romeo and Juliet*, *Madama Butterfly* and *Il Trovatore*; the latter was simply 'lovely right through and the music and scenery magnificent'.[27] Most of the men, however, had a less refined palate: they preferred London's popular West End theatres to Shakespeare and the opera. The shows were hardly classics of the stage but they were just the light and uplifting distractions wartime audiences craved. Many were marvellously staged and performed, and outshone anything the bedazzled Kiwis had ever seen in their home towns. 'Holborn Theatre is a most beautiful place inside,' wrote Harkness, 'while the acting, and stage scenery and lighting was something one never sees in NZ. The entertainment was a kind of vaudeville, but of a very fine kind such as I had never dreamed of before.'[28] Ronald Bannerman wasted no time in consuming West End shows while he was in London. In addition to numerous films, he took in 11 stage shows, including *Wanted: A Husband*, *The Cinema Star*, *Arlette*, *A Bit of Fluff*, and *Chu Chin Chow*, the box-office behemoth of its day.

A musical comedy, *Chu Chin Chow* was a loose adaption of *Ali Baba and the 40 Thieves* and starred the milky-skinned, dark-haired Lily Brayton as the female lead, along with a large supporting cast and a collection of animals, including chickens, snakes and a donkey. New Zealand airmen competed for tickets to the show with soldiers on leave from the Western Front. Bannerman's ticket was one of 2.8 million sold, many to repeat attendees. The musical's chief allure rested on the manufactured 'Eastern atmosphere' and a bevy of scantily clad slave

NEW DRESSES FOR "CHU CHIN CHOW"
Very Suitable to the Sultry Climate of Old Bagdad.

Photographs by F. W. Burford

THE COSTUMES OF SOME LOVELY HOURIS WHICH WERE INTRODUCED UPON THE
ANNIVERSARY OF THE FAMOUS PLAY AT HIS MAJESTY'S

New Zealanders adored London's West End shows. *Chu Chin Chow*, with its mock Arabian harem, was the highlight of many an airman's stay; several were repeat attendees.

girls. The harem attire was, according to *Tatler*, 'very suitable to the sultry climate of old Baghdad'.[29] Not everyone approved, and the Lord Chamberlain, acting in the capacity of the British theatre censor, ordered 'this naughtiness' to be ended. Bannerman avoided this very temporary setback, and after seeing the production in all its finery declared it a 'most joyous show'.[30] 'Excellent, the best show I have seen yet,' agreed Wilding, just before he was shipped off to Egypt.[31]

The other theatrical production Bannerman considered a 'must see' for the New Zealanders was Chung Ling Soo's magic show. William Robinson adopted this Chinese stage name and affectations in the prewar era and became one of the most popular performers of the Great War. He shaved his head and crafted an elaborate back story that cast him as the son of a Scottish missionary and a Cantonese woman. On stage he spoke no English, and in front of reporters he used an interpreter. The illusion was so complete that when he died the public was surprised to learn that he was not in fact Chinese.

Bannerman and the crowds loved the production, which had as its highpoint the famous bullet trick set to the backdrop of the historical Boxer Rebellion. In the act called 'Condemned to Death by the Boxers', Soo was captured and a 'Boxer' would call on members of the audience to inspect marked bullets. These were loaded into muskets and fired at Soo, who would appear to catch the bullets and drop them on a plate in front of him. 'He was good,' wrote Bannerman, who along with vast numbers of attendees made Robinson one of the wealthiest vaudeville performers of his day. His show ended with his death in March 1918, when the gun malfunctioned and he was shot in the lung, at which point he spoke, for the first and last time on the stage, uttering: 'Oh my God. Something's happened. Lower the curtain.'[32]

T he only thing that trumped the theatre in the minds of the New Zealanders was their flight training. Having been bashed into shape at various camps and learnt something of flying technology, men now passed on to the aviation schools, where they finally got their hands on the controls of an actual aircraft. The quality of their instruction depended largely on the date on which they entered the system. Those who commenced their training in the first three years of the war had a very different experience to those who entered from the autumn of 1917 onwards. From 1914 to September 1917 the flying training the New Zealanders received was decidedly rough-hewn and often dangerous, with poor instruction and inadequate aircraft.

The airmen's first forays duplicated much of what the New Zealand cadets had experienced at Kohimarama and Sockburn: taxiing, takeoffs, straights, landings, turns, volplaning and a modicum of extended flying — essentially, just enough to secure a Royal Aero Club ticket. It was here that airmen were winnowed out of contention. By one estimate, about 45 per cent of all initial inductees were 'deemed unsuitable'.[33] Butterworth, who had completed his own training and was instructing in late October 1915, would not have been surprised: it was clear to him that not all pupils were up to the task. Some men were a menace to themselves and their instructors. In early 1916 he took up an officer with no experience at all. 'It was very funny the machine instantly started turning & also dropped her wing, I corrected the machine several times but whenever I gave over the controls she started doing the same thing & all the officer did was to hold the controls tight & just let her go where she wanted.'[34] The following day he took up an observer known for boasting about what he would do if given the opportunity to control the aircraft.

> The machine got a slight upward bump on the tail so he pushed the stick forward (too much) & then he started seesawing backwards & forwards until at last he got out of step with the machine or forgot which way the controls worked or something & put the nose down when he should have brought it up with the consequence that we nose dived after him only having control ¼ of a minute. I set the machine straight again and after giving him a short flight landed with much of his former confidence in himself shaken.[35]

A number of New Zealanders fell by the wayside in this manner. Sometimes it was a simple physical impairment that had escaped the medical authorities. James Dinneen, an Auckland Grammar School dux, completed his training at Brooklands in Surrey and received a probationary commission in the RFC, only to be rejected at the final hurdle because of a minor eye defect.[36] Thus in June 1915, through no fault of his own, he had the 'dubious distinction' of being one of the first New Zealand airmen to leave the flying service.[37] Dinneen joined the land war, only to be killed the following year.

Others lacked the psychological wherewithal for military flying — this even included men with a background in early New Zealand aviation. In the prewar period, as a student at Auckland Technical College, Lister Briffault built one of the city's first gliders. 'The machine had cane skids and was carried by the operator by shoulder straps with his arms resting on side pieces . . . and with the three helpers he ran down an incline and was launched into the air, flying about 150 yards,' the *New Zealand Herald* reported of its first flight.[38] In England he received his flying ticket, but was found 'unsuitable in every [way]' to be an officer in the RNAS'.[39] 'He is very willing,' wrote his assessor, 'but makes very little progress and seems to lose his head at the least opportunity.' Briffault stayed with the air service as a mechanic, where he served with considerable distinction.[40]

Those who remained with the flying service noticed a number of differences between their training in New Zealand and that in Britain in the early years. First, the slow and steady approach evident in New Zealand was not replicated in England. The New Zealand schools' limited collection of aircraft meant the Walsh brothers and Wigram had a vested interest in conserving their resources. The loss of a single machine to an accident could add weeks to the training of a class and push back the next student intake. New or replacement machines were difficult and costly to procure in wartime and took months to arrive; consequently, the New Zealand schools were forced to produce their own homegrown machines. The RFC and RNAS schools, on the other hand, had in their backyard a whole industry producing large numbers of new aircraft. Harkness highlighted the embarrassment of riches in Britain during his 1915 preliminary flight training at RNAS Eastchurch, Kent.

The Maurice Farman
Shorthorn was the
ubiquitous training
machine of the RFC
and many New Zealand
pilots flew it during
their instruction period.
The aircraft's low speed
made stalling an ever-
present threat.

At any rate there is no disputing the fact that there is any amount of flying to be had here, and the flying on all kinds of machines practically whenever you like. There is no paying for breakages or smash-ups, full pay if temporarily laid up through accident, all of which is more than a millionaire could afford in ordinary peacetimes.[41]

A second major point of difference was that the chief instructors at both Kohimarama and Sockburn were cautious by nature. Vivian Walsh's unwillingness to take risks and preference for incremental advances was well known and acknowledged, as was Cecil Hill's extensive experience in England and his concern for his students. In addition, the schools' aircraft, while dull and mediocre, were also generally safe machines. As a result there was not a single flying fatality in New Zealand over the course of the war.

In the RFC and RNAS, war losses and increasing demand for airmen meant hasty and truncated training. While the New Zealand and British students passed out of the initial flight training in about the same amount of time, the advanced war flying training in Britain greatly added to the possibility of accidents. And more time flying increased the odds of something going wrong. Advanced training demanded much more of the airmen and their machines; flying was tricky enough without adding lessons on bomb-making or photography.

The instructors were often either newly qualified airmen themselves or survivors of the early fighting in France. None had a specialised education in how to teach flying; there were as yet no instructor schools. Kohimarama graduate Trevor Alderton was appointed as an instructor a day after completing his training in England. He was 24 years old. As the best flyer his own instructor had ever put through, Alderton was given charge of incoming students.[42] Barely one day later, while in a formation flight and with a pupil on board, the machine stalled on turning back to the airfield. The aircraft sideslipped into the ground. His pupil survived but Alderton was killed.

The novice instructors and the 'old hands' from France had one thing in common: a fear of their pupils that ranged from latent caution to pathological terror. Many instructors were wary of allowing the inductees to take full control of the aircraft in their dual-control flights. Greenhorn instructors with relatively low flying hours under their belts remembered their own all-too-recent close calls and were reluctant to risk their lives by easing their hands off the joystick.[43] Similarly, those veterans who had barely escaped France with their lives were not about to now throw them away on a petrified student. Pupils were sometimes called 'Huns', to be feared every bit as much as the German pilots. Even good instructors were wary of their young charges. One young student observed that his 'instructor was a chap whom I'm quite certain had had a bad shaking up and thoroughly lost his nerve because I never touched the controls when I was supposed to be having dual. With the result that when I did go solo I got off the ground all right but I did a mighty bounce on landing and squashed the undercarriage.'[44] Well-regarded Welshman Ira Jones noted that 'some were too hasty tempered, intimidating the trainees when they should have been encouraging them . . . or rushed their pupils into going solo to claim credit for having trained the highest number of pilots in a given period'.[45] Whether they were afraid of students, or simply wanted to increase their turnover of trainees, instructors often sent students to their first solo with only a couple of hours of dual-control under their belts.

Another cause of injury or death was the rudimentary aircraft available in the early years of the war. The workhorses of the schools were machines like the Maurice Farman pushers of the prewar era. Students often started on the Longhorn and then graduated to the Shorthorn. (The Shorthorn lacked the Longhorn's front-mounted elevator and the elongated skids from which it derived its name.) Sitting in an open cockpit, trainees were unable to hear what the instructor was yelling above the hammering engine. With no intercom, it was possible to throttle the engine back for a second or two and shout instructions, but most instructors were reduced to writing notes or communicating with kicks and slaps to the body of the student in front of them.

The Farman Shorthorn was a fabric-and-wire machine that looked more like a Wright brothers *Flyer* than a modern aircraft. More fragile insect than bird of prey, its great weakness was its low speed. Flight is dependent on airflow over the wings, which produces lift: insufficient airflow and the machine stalls, the aircraft falls from the sky and, as a wing dips, the body rolls, entering a spin from which the untrained airman has little hope of escaping. The trouble with the Farmans and other early trainers was that their airspeed was perilously close to their stalling speed. Even with rudimentary airspeed indicators, the margin between flight and non-flight was very small, particularly when turning. Hence, when struck by engine failure on takeoff — a common problem throughout the war — trainee pilots often fatally attempted to turn back, the result of which was stall, spin, death.

The aircraft were also unforgiving and skittish. 'These machines [the Farmans] are the most dangerous of all to fly, as they have no natural stability, and you dare not let the controls go for a second,' cautioned Wellingtonian Edgar Garland.[46] He calculated that Farmans killed five people in the nine weeks he was at flying school.

The early engines were also decidedly touchy and prone to misbehaviour. Even the more advanced machines in the training schools were not entirely trustworthy. One of New Zealand's earliest military pilots of the Great War, Alfred de Bathe Brandon, began his military flying career with Shorthorns before moving on to the famous Avro 504, a machine that was inherently stable and was still in use as a trainer in 1918.[47] As the war progressed they received improved engines, but in 1915 they were fitted with a less than trustworthy power source. 'The Avro was a beautiful machine,' noted Brandon,

> but it had a tricky Gnome engine which hadn't got a throttle. The petrol went in direct through what was called a fine engine adjustment. If you gave it too much or too little the engine would conk out. You then cut the petrol off and if the engine picked up, you had been giving it too much, but if it didn't, too little. You were usually about to land when this would come about and it wasn't very pleasant at first.[48]

The final piece of the puzzle was the weather conditions in Britain. Fog, clouds and rain claimed more than their fair share of young victims. Brandon was especially wary of low clouds after a pilot and passenger were 'badly bumped about in a cloud and without knowing it when they came out they were upside down'.[49] Harkness's first solo attempt was nearly his last. He had strayed away from the airfield to avoid other machines taking off and was soon lost.

> I was then caught in a thick fog and had . . . climbed to 600 feet and could see no ground whatsoever. I can tell you it is not over pleasant to an absolute beginner to be tearing through the air at about sixty miles an hour, an 80 horsepower engine whirring away in front, the propeller spinning . . . and nothing to be seen in front, behind, above or below . . . The trouble is when one is quite close to the ground, when not being able to see anything in front he may at any minute find himself precipitated into a brick wall, a house, tree or fence.

He gingerly lowered his altitude to see whether he could spot landmarks to guide him home: nothing. And it started to rain — not heavily, but enough for the splatters and streams of water on his goggles to blind him. He could not take his goggles off, however, because the propeller was waterblasting his face. It was 20 minutes before he could see clearly. Harkness eventually found a farmer's field to land in: he glided, touched down, rolled up a grassy slope and came to rest atop a small hill. The other trainees could not believe he had not smashed up the aircraft; they put it down to luck, more than anything else, that 'I landed without mishap', Harkness wrote.[50] As he noted, when good flying conditions prevailed, the English 'made a terrific song and dance about the beautiful weather . . . [but] it was only such as one gets in Nelson almost every day'.[51]

The combination of inadequate and haphazard instruction, aircraft with prickly handling characteristics and unreliable engines, and the poor British weather resulted in accidents, injury and loss of life on training fields. Approximately a fifth of all flying service losses were incurred during instruction, and among those lost were New Zealand trainees.[52]

One of the first confirmed New Zealand training fatalities occurred on 20 June 1916. With a fresh Royal Aero Club ticket in his pocket, George Aimer was an early direct entrant into the RFC. The Northlander was flying a Martinsyde solo at Northolt, Middlesex, when the accident took place. At the inquest into his death a witness described what happened.

Deceased [Aimer] was 4000 ft up, and all at once he seemed in trouble. The machine began to descend rapidly. It went head downwards about as vertical as it is possible to get a machine, and was spinning very slowly to the right . . . Deceased had lost control of the machine, and witness did not think that he ever regained control.[53]

Given his experience at a Hendon civilian school and the amount of time he had accumulated at RFC Northolt, Aimer was considered by his instructor to be one of the best students he had. The machine had been tested and Aimer had flown at least twice that morning before the fatal flight. The Martinsyde was not a machine for a novice, but the New Zealander had at least three hours on it.

A doctor rushed to the scene and spoke to the mangled Aimer, who had a fracture at the base of his skull, a fracture to his shoulder and internal haemorrhaging. The 30-year-old could speak and wanted to assure the doctor that the crash was not his fault. 'But his actual words showed me that he had no idea how it happened,' reported the doctor. Aimer died hours later. The inquest was unable to determine the cause but concluded that Aimer must have 'committed some small error of judgement, possibly when turning.'[54] Aimer's death demonstrated that even those with a good degree of flying skill had no guarantee of a long flying career.

On 15 September 1916, Horokiwi farmer Victor Abbott was on his third solo flight when it all unravelled. At Netheravon, Wiltshire, he was approaching the airfield for a landing when his Farman Shorthorn nosedived at 100 ft.[55] His father had only days before received a letter from Victor in which the 23-year-old told him that he had attained the dream of many young men, a place in the RFC. Mr Abbott was devastated at losing his only son. The local tennis club wrote that it seemed such a brief journey for the 'sturdy, thick-set, yet small lad, who had had some difficulty in wielding his large racket' but who had 'won the singles event from allcomers . . . by sheer pluck', to being an airman 'Killed in action'.[56] The steps from childhood to manhood to death seemed shorter for those in the flying corps.

A month later, the flying schools took the life of another New Zealand trainee. Arthur Greenwell, a Brick and Fireclay Company employee from Huntly, gained a place with the RNAS in May 1916. Five months later he was at Cranwell, Lincolnshire, for his flight training. Three minutes into the 19 October flight, at barely 200 ft, the Royal Aircraft Factory BE2c turned right sharply and nosedived

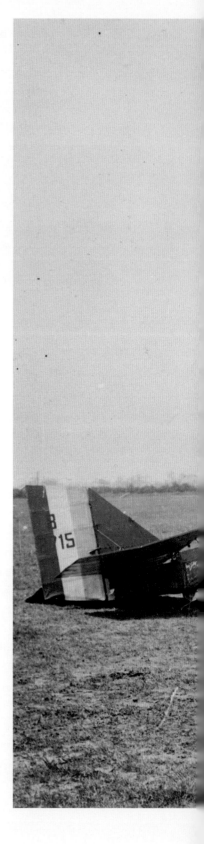

Two training aircraft — a Royal Aircraft Factory BE2c and an Airco DH6 — collided in the middle of Duxford airfield. Instructors were leery of trainees, and often referred to them as 'Huns' because of their proclivity to crash and kill themselves and their mentors.

into the ground. Greenwell sustained fractures of the thigh, arm and skull, and never regained consciousness. He had completed six weeks of training and was about to pass out of the school. 'It was the sort of accident that could happen to anyone,' was the inquest's unsatisfactory conclusion. It was a double blow for the Greenwell family; Arthur's brother George had been killed only weeks earlier on the Somme.[57] Another brother, Nicholas, was with the RFC.[58] As a result of an injury he was afflicted with 'neurasthenia' — a form of nervous stress. While hospitalised he was given the option of staying in England as a mechanic or returning to New Zealand. He chose the latter, arguing that his father had already lost two sons and he was needed at home.[59]

Many survived through simple good fortune. Eric Croll made it through flight training but not without mishap. He was forced to make an emergency landing in a farmer's field, only to misjudge the attempt and, much to the farmer's amusement, perch the machine on a hedge. A fellow pilot bested Croll by landing his aircraft on the base hangar, from where it could only be extricated by being tugged down like a daddy longlegs having its legs pulled off.[60] 'First solos are generally a nightmare to pupils,' wrote Melville White, 'and crashes on these occasions frequently occur.'

> My first solo proved very disastrous, and I regretted that there was not enough of the propeller to make a cane as a memento, which is the usual thing to do. I should imagine that, following this rule, some fellows have quite a collection of canes!! My second attempt was more successful, only it was very disconcerting to notice several crashes on the plain beneath me, the work of other budding pilots, nor did I feel reassured when I spotted the camp sargt-major conscientiously instructing a number of men in the funeral step, also a motor ambulance standing by, for the benefit of unfortunate youths who descend much quicker than they ascend.[61]

One of New Zealand's best airmen was nearly killed in a freak accident in his early training in England. Ronald Bannerman was sitting in his aircraft when another machine landed on top of him. 'My Avro was matchwood,' he wrote in his diary, 'very lucky to get out alive.' The offending pilot claimed he never saw Bannerman or his biplane.[62] As photographs of the incident reveal, it was a miracle Bannerman walked away from the event.

Henry Rasmussen was badly injured in his second solo flight in Egypt. He took off without mishap and climbed to a good altitude before it registered that he was straying from the airfield: 'I thought, my God, I want to find my way back.'[63] His eyes darted to the dashboard clock: it had frozen. He had been flying for longer than he had thought and was now much higher than any novice airman should be. He tipped the wing to descend and entered a terrific spin. 'One thing flashed back through my mind,' he recalled. 'We had been discussing amongst our pupils [what you should do] if you are in a spin. One fellow said, I would let everything go. Hands and feet off. So I did just that and the crate came out of the spin.' He was too close to the ground, though, and crashed heavily, obliterating the aircraft.

I woke up staggering around. I was going to blast my batman for letting me sleep in because the sun was shining. We always got up in the dark but this is not my quarters. There are no white washed walls . . . Then a little feeling of [un]ease started creeping through me about there. Wasn't I in trouble some time this morning and then I saw the mechanics. There were about 20 mechanics coming haring out and I said, 'well that is what happened and there was a crash.' There couldn't be, there was no wreck. There is always a wreck when there is a crash isn't there. Finally they told me that I was twettering around like a fellow who had been knocked out in boxing.[64]

Rasmussen had been struck by the controls and his left eye was completely closed; his right eyeball was hanging from its socket. His cheekbone had been 'smashed to pulp' and the eyeball had narrowly escaped being squashed. It took a long recovery and a lot of persuading the authorities, but eventually he was able to return to flying training.

Sometimes the airmen were favoured by having good — and in some cases exceptional — instructors. A handful of these, like Butterworth, were from New Zealand. 'I was fortunate to have a young New Zealander, Carr by name, as my chief instructor,' recalled Englishman John Poole. The Wellington College old boy Charles Roderick Carr had flown with the RNAS before being posted to a training squadron in Vendôme, France.[65]

My first solo flight was in a Caudron, a very old fashioned bus . . . an ideal machine for the novice or ham-fisted pilot as it could be dropped on the ground from some feet above without any resulting damage. In a modern plane this would mean sheer destruction, but Caudrons would only bounce up lightly and settle gently again like brooding hens. When the great moment arrived, Carr impressed on me that I had to have flying speed before taking off. 'Keep her nose well down; there's plenty of room on these downs.' Keep her nose down I certainly did, careering over the aerodrome until I heard some sort of explosion and came to a standstill. I had shoved the propeller into the ground somehow, and it was smashed to pieces. A long walk back to the hangars to face Carr. He'd had a bad morning; another of his pupils had taxied into the officer's mess at breakfast time. However, he took it very well and at once sent me off in another machine. Evidently I was not the first offender to pass through his hands.[66]

In his memoirs, Alfred de Bathe Brandon noted that he had been privileged to get instruction from Cecil Hill, before Hill joined the Canterbury Aviation Company. 'A very good fellow,' was Brandon's estimation, and his recommendation played a part in Hill's appointment in New Zealand.[67] On another occasion Brandon was given some sage advice by fellow Wellington College old boy, the legendary Joe Hammond. When he chanced upon Brandon in 1915, Hammond was the country's longest-serving military pilot, with long hours of flying time and experience behind him. He had been observing his compatriot and asked him if he wanted some advice. 'Nothing would please me more,' replied Brandon. Hammond felt his young charge's weakness was his landings; he encouraged him to practise them more than the sharp turns he and an Irishman called Porter had been vying to better each other with. 'I followed Hammond's advice and did landings,' recalled Brandon. 'A few weeks later Porter crashed and was killed.'[68]

Others were similarly impressed by Hammond. London-born Charles Blayney, who went on to become an accomplished bomber pilot, was mentored by the New Zealander.

> 'Joe', as he was popularly styled, was an instructor, and when he was not instructing, he was filling in spare moments showing 'Huns' (i.e., young officers who had not obtained their pilot wings, and probably so called for the awful things they did in the air without receiving terrible punishment) how to stunt. He knew no fear, and in the writer's opinion he was the best pilot England possessed at the time. It was a pleasure to see the way he handled a machine in the air, never putting an undue strain upon it, and always landing in such a way that it was difficult to see really when he actually touched the ground — all the movements were so graceful . . . Joe was so far above us all in skill as a pilot that we looked upon him almost as a wizard, and paid due respect to everything he said. Everything that fell from his lips was retailed over and over again in the anteroom.[69]

Unlike many instructors, Hammond went out of his way to aid young and inexperienced airmen. 'Hence in this way,' noted Blayney, 'Joe was very popular.'

A number of the New Zealanders who survived the hit-or-miss methods did so in part because of their Kohimarama training. The four hours or so they had had in New Zealand was just enough to spare them a premature death at the hands of RFC and RNAS schools. The men trained by the Walsh brothers came to the military aviation schools with at least a modicum of experience. 'I have been getting on pretty well with flying the instructor told me,' wrote Hugh Blackwell. 'I haven't let on about the New Zealand flying.'[70] As for the Sockburn students, they were lucky enough to arrive at the overseas institutions after a major overhaul of the British training system in late 1917, prompted by the high number of casualties on the training fields and the unacceptably heavy losses of newly trained men over the trenches.

Robert Smith-Barry, an eccentric Irishman of aristocratic descent, was shocked at the poor skill levels of the airmen being sent to his squadron in France and wanted to establish a more scientific and uniform method of training. The RFC listened, and Smith-Barry developed his techniques and systematised training at Gosport, Hampshire, where he became the 'patron saint of flying instruction'.[71] In the latter part of 1917 he ushered in a revolution in air training: instructors would be taught how to instruct at specialised schools. Pupils who had previously sat behind instructors were moved to the front seat, from where they would eventually take their first solo flight. Speaking tubes — dubbed 'Gosport tubes' — were introduced to facilitate clear communication between instructor and student in flight. This significantly lowered the likelihood of a loss of life in the preliminary training. Smith-Barry also standardised much of the first stage of the training around the generally reliable Avro 504. The new training methods became known as the 'Gosport System'.

Once airmen had survived their initial brush with aviation, they were despatched for further training to increase their flying hours, work with more powerful aircraft and undertake specialist instruction in the role for which they would eventually be deployed. Familiarity with flying is the bedrock of a competent pilot, and it played a big part in an airman's ability to survive in his first weeks above the trenches. Before Smith-Barry, airmen were routinely posted to frontline squadrons with as little as 30 hours recorded in their logbooks. Early pilots like Clive Collett and Brandon completed their training with just over 20 hours' solo flying. New Zealanders Keith Caldwell and Francis Crawford arrived in France with 27 and 22 hours respectively.[72] After tabulating his meagre flying time before being sent to France, Crawford scribbled incredulously at the bottom of the logbook page: 'Am now supposed to be a Pilot.'

Being diverted first to instruction duties before operations could be a decided benefit. Notwithstanding the fear under which some novice instructors operated, many others, in spite of having no formal instruction training, were more than up to the task. Keith Park had only 35 hours to his name on the completion of advanced training, but by the time he entered the war proper he had 135 hours' flying time, thanks to a lengthy period as a flight instructor. This was a considerable advantage in the white-hot fighting over the Western Front. Although by 1918 average hours had increased markedly, it was still not uncommon for pilots to have accumulated no more than 50 hours.

Unlike in the Second World War, where a few tried and tested aircraft predominated, the Great War was a menagerie of different manufacturers and machines, some indigenous and others exotic. In addition to two-winged biplanes, there were monoplanes and triplanes. While it was more common for the engines to be placed in the front of the machine, 'pushers' were still flying operationally at the cessation of hostilities. Inline water-cooled engines had different characteristics to the air-cooled rotary ones. Airmen needed to be acquainted with the aircraft they were likely to encounter in an active squadron. 'I am now on my third machine,' wrote West Coaster John Martin to his sisters, 'and I have two more still to learn.'[73]

Like many airmen, Ronald Bannerman's flight training was a progression from relatively tame machines to seriously high-powered weapons of war. He commenced with the staid — but potentially troublesome — Farman Shorthorn before moving on to the safer Avro 504 as his first 'advanced' machine at 6 Training Squadron, Catterick, Yorkshire. After conquering the Avro he in turn mastered the Bristol Scout, the Sopwith Pup, the Spad SVII, the Sopwith Dolphin and finally the Royal Aircraft Factory SE5a.[74] Over 16 weeks of training he had advanced from the 80-hp Shorthorn, which coasted along at 70 mph and had a service ceiling of 12,400 ft, to the 200-hp SE5a, with a top speed of 118 mph and the ability to perform comfortably at 17,000 ft.

From the summer of 1917 onwards the air students were taught every manoeuvre a pilot might need in the air, such as stalling and recovering from a spin. Where previously young men had been dissuaded from 'stunting', Smith-Barry encouraged flying an aircraft to its limits. This was especially true for the fighter pilots. As Mac McGregor's biographer noted:

> Only the finest type of pilots were employed by the fighter squadrons. They had to be keen
> of eye, quick in thought and action, and above all to possess that cold nerve which makes

one hazard fighting alone or against the odds. Then, too, they were required to be adept at handling their aeroplanes, and in the use of machine guns.[75]

Former Dunedin motorcar salesman Clarence Umbers was at the Central Flying School, Upavon, where he was nominated for air combat. 'My training is different from that of other pilots,' he wrote home. '[They] train for bombing, observation, directing artillery fire etc., but we train for fighting. Therefore, we have to be absolutely "stunt" pilots and gunnery experts. We have to "loop" our machines, to "stall", to dive, to "spin", to side-slip, to bank vertically, to fly upside down, and, in fact to do anything at all in the air.'[76] Like lion cubs they tested themselves against each other in mock air battles. 'We practise fighting by means of camera guns,' wrote Umbers, 'which, on being fired, take a photo of the part of the other machine that would have been hit had it been a real gun used.'

With a high-powered machine at their disposal and with growing confidence, their stunting sometimes devolved into activities that were in no way sanctioned by officialdom. On one occasion Bannerman flew his light Bristol Scout along a beach just two feet above the sand before breaking into a series of low stunts, diving at the people on the ground at 100 mph. He swooped to within a few feet of the crowd, putting the 'wind up them properly'. He then proceeded to 'attack' a fishing fleet off the coast. It was a rather 'risky business but jolly good fun', he concluded.[77] A few weeks later he was at it again when he 'chased some people off the road for fun'.[78]

The fun was tempered by the potential for mishap, however. Eric Croll's most serious crisis occurred when the belt in the empty seat of his machine wrapped itself around the joystick at the top of the loop. His only option was to accelerate and loop again. Losing altitude rapidly, the belt unwrapped itself and he was able to land safely, but not without an earful from the instructor. Bannerman suffered a similar scare when looping a machine that stayed on its back; he hung between heaven and earth with only his safety belt preventing him from falling out. As blood rushed to his head, he wiggled round in the belt and stretched out his leg. He pulled back on the joystick with his foot and 'got her right'.[79] 'There were lots of crashes,' said Croll, 'an average of one pupil per week while I was there.'

'They were much harder than they look,' was Ross Brodie's summation after being introduced to the half-roll under dual control. The New Zealander prudently climbed to 6000 ft before he pulled the machine over. The result was a completely unexpected spin: 'Straight her nose went down and she spun like a top.' Brodie wrestled with the controls but nothing worked as centrifugal forces pinned him to one side of the cockpit. 'I began to think she would never come out and all sorts of things flashed through my brain when suddenly she took a great swoop and came out and what a relief it was. I shall never forget the experience of my first half rolls as I had spun for 3400 ft.'[80] He nearly died the next day when attempting the same manoeuvre, dropping a further 2000 ft. Upon inspection it was discovered that the rigging was faulty, and 24 hours later he mastered the half-roll in a new 'bus'.[81]

In spite of the inherent danger, aerobatics was a vital confidence-builder and ensured that airmen understood the capabilities of their machines and themselves, thereby giving them a fighting chance in their first fateful encounters with a determined and experienced enemy.

above Ronald
Bannerman (left),
pictured here with
fellow Kohimarama
graduate Herbert
Drewitt, arrived on
the front lines in
early 1918 with over
50 hours' flying time,
considerably more than
most New Zealanders.
He became one of
New Zealand's most
successful fighter pilots.

below While training in
England, Bannerman
only just survived when
another aircraft landed
on top of him. 'Very
lucky to be alive,' he
wrote in his logbook.

CHAPTER EIGHT
DEATH FROM ABOVE
1916

By 1916, increasing numbers of freshly trained New Zealand airmen were appearing in active squadrons. Among them was former Wellington solicitor Alfred de Bathe Brandon. Like all early pilots, he was thrown into action almost as soon as he had sewn his wings to his jacket. He was commissioned as a second lieutenant in January 1916, and by March had been assigned to home defence duties with one of the squadrons shielding London from the giant German airships known as Zeppelins.[1] His two spectacular attacks on these rigid airships would make him New Zealand's most famous airman of the war.

When the first airships dropped their bombs on Britain in January of 1915, it was as if H. G. Wells' fictional *The War in the Air* had leapt from the page onto the streets of London. The English Channel, Britain's great defensive moat, had been jumped. The loss of life and material damage fell well short of Wells' apocalyptic carnage: the first raid killed four and injured 16 and inflicted £7740 worth of damage — insignificant losses when compared to the great swathe of men cut down on the Western Front in the same year.[2] Nonetheless, it was a psychological blow to the British public. D. H. Lawrence described the scene:

> Then we saw the Zeppelin above us, just ahead, amid the gleaming clouds . . . high up, like a bright golden finger, quite small . . . Then there were flashes near the ground — and the shaking noise. It was like Milton [*Paradise Lost*] — then there was war in heaven . . . I cannot get over it, that the moon is not Queen of the sky by night, and stars the lesser lights. It seems the Zeppelin is in the zenith of the night, golden like the moon, having taken control of the sky; and the bursting shells are the lesser lights.[3]

The impossible had happened: the war had been delivered to London's doorstep.

> I had just got into bed when I heard a terrible rushing of wind and shouts of 'fire' and 'The Germans are here.' I jumped out of bed and carried my four children into the basement and then went out to the street door and saw the house next door was on fire . . . The father was burnt and the daughter, who my daughter used to play with, had met her death . . . We later found the poor little dear had crawled under the bed to get away from the flames.

For young New Zealand airmen in training, the early Zeppelin raids initially had all the flavour of a play writ large across London. Those who had not yet tasted war sought a glimpse of the aerial action as eagerly as they queued for tickets to the West End: it was simply another London experience. In the early hours of a Sunday, only four weeks into their 1916 London adventure, the Montgomerie family were rocked from their sleep. Gunfire. 'Those d____ Zeps are here,' cried Seton's father. To those untested in war it sounded for all the world as if they themselves were the target, but the bombs were in fact falling some distance off. In their dressing-gowns, the whole family peered through an upstairs window, the glass glowing in the reflection of explosions and fire. A Zeppelin was caught in a powerful searchlight.[4]

The actual theatre was not immune from the air war. Seton Montgomerie had booked tickets for a comic romance, *Trelawny of the Wells*. As the Montgomerie family entered the theatre they heard bombs dropping: a German raid. To Seton's mother's surprise no one seemed the least bit interested and they took their seats with the rest of the audience. The stage manager told the attendees that the show would proceed; the audience could stay or leave as they saw fit. 'We sat still, very few walked out, but it was pretty tough work sitting there and trying to take an interest in the play with the sound of bombs and gunfire all around us,' wrote the Montgomerie matriarch in her diary. 'Seton was very practical and calm all the time.'[5]

Later in the war, the Germans added twin-engine bombers and even four- and six-engine machines in their attempts to terrorise Britain. Hugh Blackwell and his Canterbury Aviation Company friends were returning from a London jaunt when they discovered they had escaped the city barely half an hour before a raid by 20 to 30 machines. 'Unfortunately,' he lamented, 'we just missed it.'[6] The horror of the raids, however, was brought home to young New Zealanders when they were caught among the falling bombs.

Before casting off for Cairo, Ross Brodie and fellow cadets were walking to the Strand Palace when thunderous gunfire broke the calm; then 'down flopped a bomb with a thud that shook the whole place'. They dived for cover under a storm of explosions, some barely 20 yards from where they had stood. A nearby building was an inferno and mangled bodies were being brought out. They retreated to their hotel. The next day they returned to the wreckage, where a policeman told them that over 90 people had been killed. 'It had been a raid shelter and the bomb had cut off the escape and the building took fire, it was an awful affair,' wrote Brodie. 'We had no more wish to see another raid.'[7]

The Germans argued that the attacks were purely military in nature, but given that all the raids were at night, using the most rudimentary and ineffectual aiming devices, the chances of intentionally hitting any military target were very low. The civilian deaths caused outrage and the Germans were dubbed 'baby killers'. The Kaiser lauded and decorated the Zeppelin crews, further fuelling British and imperial anger.[8] Speeches in Parliament condemned the Germans but also questioned the seemingly fruitless attempts being made to deal with the 'Zep' threat. By the end of 1915, 181 people had been killed and 455 injured in 20 raids. Sir Charles Wakefield, the lord mayor of London, offered a £500 reward to anyone who brought a 'terror-ship' down.[9]

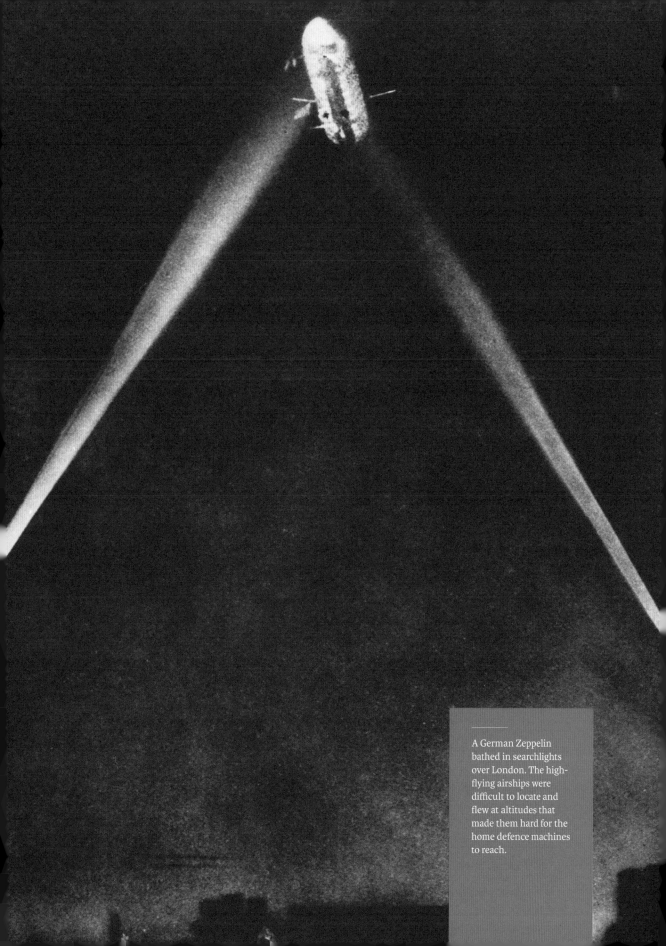

A German Zeppelin bathed in searchlights over London. The high-flying airships were difficult to locate and flew at altitudes that made them hard for the home defence machines to reach.

The early raids demonstrated that Britain was woefully ill-equipped to meet this kind of attack. The RNAS had established a series of seaplane bases along the southeast coast of Britain as a weak shield from incoming airborne assaults; but in behind this forward line London lay open to attack. The first pilot assigned with the task of defending the capital recalled his commanding officer asking him: 'Can you fly a Caudron?'

> I said, 'No!'
> He said, 'Well you've got to it's the only one we've got! Do you know the way to Hendon?'
> I said, 'No!'
> 'Well at dawn tomorrow you will fly in a Caudron to Hendon!'
> I went straight to the Admiralty after I landed and the fellow in charge of aeroplanes there said, 'Now, you are the air defence of London — the only one!'
> I said, 'But I've got no guns or observer or anything, what sort of protection can I give against the Germans?'
> He said, 'I'll leave that to you!'
> So I hoped the Zeppelins wouldn't come over![10]

By the time Brandon arrived in early 1916, the home-based defences had brought down only a single Zeppelin, and that by anti-aircraft gunfire. Brandon was under no illusion that tackling a Zeppelin was going to be easy. The first challenge was night flying, for which he had received only the most rudimentary instruction. On 29 February he commenced a night flying familiarisation sortie at dusk, with flares guiding him in to land.[11] At 6.30 the following evening he carried out his second 'night' excursion. Other than these twin dusk flights, totalling no more than 20 minutes, he had received no formal training in night flying. This was inadequate even by the poor standards of the day. 'At the time not much was known about night flying,' he noted. 'The Higher Command and some of the pilots . . . took a dim view of night flying practice, the former because machines were hard to come by, and the latter while they didn't mind crashing in a raid, they had no desire to do so on night flying practice.'

When he arrived at Hainault Farm airfield in Essex, Brandon encountered his second challenge: his aircraft. The Royal Aircraft Factory BE2c was the pioneer night fighter of the British defence system. Unlike its daytime two-seater counterpart, the night fighter was flown as a single-seater biplane, with the observer's accommodation occupied by a supplementary fuel tank with a temporary fabric covering. The machine was stable but not particularly manoeuvrable. Its top speed was frustratingly close to the Zeppelin's 70 mph.

The biggest problem for the defenders was the altitude of the incoming airships. By the time Brandon was stationed outside London, the airships were operating at over 11,000 ft. It took the BE2c over an hour to reach this height. Timing was critical if an interception was to be made. Brandon would need plenty of warning to get anywhere near a Zeppelin. And once in the general vicinity of an airship, he still had to find it.

In spite of their considerable dimensions, Zeppelins were difficult to locate in the night sky. While the incoming Germans were able to find London by following the thin, silver thread of the

River Thames, the defending anti-aircraft gun crews and airmen discovered that the airships — operating under a stringent blackout regime — offered no such natural illumination.[12] The defenders were forced to assemble large searchlight arrays. These formed two concentric haloes within London. Even so, it was a hit-or-miss affair, as a single searchlight could hold an airship within its beam for only a short period of time.[13] Brandon's best hope of spotting and attacking an airship was when it was continually illuminated by multiple searchlights.

However, even should this unlikely event occur, his options for attack were not confidence-building: the weaponry on the BE2c was pitiful. None of the Royal Aircraft Factory machines was equipped with a forward-firing gun because those fitted with synchronised or interrupter gear were destined for France. The home defence aircraft that were armed with a machine gun had it mounted with the muzzle pointing upward to strike at airships from below. In theory this appeared to be a reasonable solution, but in practice it was seldom successful. While the Zeppelins were bigger than the proverbial 'barn door', and loaded with volatile hydrogen, their construction made them difficult to shoot down. Underneath the outer fabric layer of a P-class Zeppelin was a framework of 16 compartments, each encasing a gas cell.[14] If a bullet pierced the outer skin and punctured a cell, it did not ignite the hydrogen; at best it caused a leak, reducing the chances of the airship reaching home.

The best form of anti-Zeppelin ammunition was explosive bullets. One of its early inventors of explosive bullets was John Pomeroy of Invercargill.[15] British authorities knew about his bullets as early as 1909, but it was not until April 1916 that the RFC tested them, and in May of that year it ordered a batch of 500,000 rounds.[16] This was too late for Brandon's early defensive flights, but the bullets proved invaluable in the months that followed. In the meantime, Brandon would have to make do with bombs and aerial darts. The authorities generally felt that dropping projectiles onto a Zeppelin had the most potential to destroy it. The Rankin dart — a 13-inch metal and wood dart with three spring-loaded arms — was specially designed for engagement with the rigid airships. In the launch tube the arms were closed, but on release they opened and locked, acting as a grapple when the dart penetrated the Zeppelin fabric, at which point the high explosive was ignited. Aside from the difficulty of getting above a high-flying airship, dropping the darts from a small bobbing aircraft onto a Zeppelin while being fired upon was not particularly appealing. The odds were decidedly against the newly graduated 32-year-old Brandon being in the right place and the right time, latching onto a Zeppelin, making a successful attack, and then landing without injury to himself.

Brandon had been on duty for only a week at Hainault when, on 31 March 1916, an early warning that Zeppelins were on their way to England 'and that some of them might be coming to London' came through. An agitated Brandon did not believe there was much chance of seeing any Zeppelins, but he did think that a more likely and unappealing prospect was a crash and premature death. A month before, at his old Northolt airfield, his commanding officer had been killed in a night-time test flight. The replacement commander promptly crashed and was killed in an actual raid. At Hainault, the lieutenant in charge of Brandon's flight station was still recovering from a night crash into a haystack. And, Brandon grimly reflected, the only reason he was the 'next cab off the rank' was the fact that he was filling the boots of a young man who only days before had taken his father up for spin and promptly crashed the machine, killing his father. With all of this in the back of his mind, and the 'inexperience of under 30 hours flying, the night ahead suggested something unpleasant,' he wrote.[17]

Nightfall, and still no word of Zeppelins. The hours of inaction kneaded out the tension in the New Zealander's shoulders. Perhaps he would not be required. 'At about 9 o'clock we were rather hungry, rather bored and without a care in the world, and then the telephone rang' — loud and insistent. Brandon sensed this was no ordinary call. A strained voice: 'Zeppelins approaching London, standby.' Orders were given for aircraft to be brought out of their hangars and prepared for imminent action. Ground crew marked off the airfield with flares — oil drums filled with fuel and waste. A chasing telephone call had Brandon donning the night airman's garb. He prepared for the bitter cold at altitude by pulling an extra sweater over his uniform and buttoning up a British Warm — a heavy double-breasted woollen overcoat — before wrapping himself in a long leather greatcoat: his insulation was at least four layers deep. The dreaded final call came through, and he ran headlong down the stairs and then the 200 yards to the airfield. It was a moonless but clear night. Mechanics parted for Brandon. His BE2c sat ready. He clambered into the cockpit 'panting and apprehensive', he checked for 'revs' and waved the chocks away. The V8 engine roared as he opened the throttle. There was no chance for a countermand order: he was under way.

The Royal Aircraft Factory machine left the ground and plunged into the darkness. Veering off to port over the flares, Brandon straightened and steered by a bright star, 'hoping to God that the engine won't cut out'. At Northolt another airman was scrambled and immediately killed as he clipped a hangar in the darkness. Fortunately, Brandon's engine was running perfectly; the BE2c climbed slow and steady to 6000 ft. At around 10 p.m. he spotted the enemy off to his right: a Zeppelin caught in the blinding glare of searchlights. Cruising at 8000 ft, the distant Zeppelin was a 'small cigar' with shells bursting just below it.

His quarry was part of a 10-strong armada with its sights on London and East Anglia. Mechanical problems and inclement weather had thinned the fleet to five. Of these, only one breached the defensive perimeter of the capital: L15, a P-class Zeppelin, an enormous vessel at 536 ft in length and 61 ft in diameter: Brandon's 27-ft-long and 37-ft-wingspan BE2c was a gnat attacking an elephant.

Kapitänleutnant Joachim Breithaupt occupied the forward of the Zeppelin's twin gondolas, with a crew of 18.[18] In spite of the vessel's size, Breithaupt had few instruments at his disposal: an altimeter, an airspeed indicator, a thermometer and a liquid compass that was prone to freezing at high altitude.[19] The four Maybach HSLu engines were loud and often funnelled noxious fumes into the cold, spartan gondolas. Twenty-one hours and 30 minutes into the flight, he struck the River Thames and turned westward. The searchlights groped for L15, the roving beams bathing the crew in an eerie glow. Then more searchlights ensnared it, blinding Breithaupt.[20] Guns across London opened fire. Two shots hit L15 astern, rupturing gas cells and damaging the steering gear. As the crew restored order, Breithaupt released 44 bombs. Another shell hit amidships, failing to ignite the hydrogen but bursting open more cells. L15 began to sink gradually as it swayed drunkenly for home.

Brandon turned towards the Zeppelin, slowly reeling it in. Another airman, Claude Ridley from Joyce Green airfield, optimistically opened fire from maximum range but lost the airship when it eluded searchlights. Soon after, *L15* was again captured in a beam and Brandon closed in alone. 'It was getting larger and larger as we approached each other and finally passed over my head 6 or 700 feet above me. I turned and followed and was underneath it. She looked magnificent against the stars.' The German behemoth distracted Brandon; his aircraft wallowed, close to stalling. He pushed the stick forward and regained flying speed. He pressed ahead of the Zeppelin, gaining altitude in a long languid loop until he was flying directly at the oncoming airship.

L15 had at least four machine guns, one each in the forward and aft gondolas and two on the 'roof' of the airship.[21] The latter were accessed by men from the forward gondola, who would climb up a ladder through the hull, surrounded by volatile hydrogen cells. Breithaupt ordered the machine guns manned. The BE2c was an incoming 'white cloud', said one German machine gunner, who was waiting for the New Zealander to get within range.[22]

Brandon was now face to face with his foe. It was suddenly an 'enormous size'. At only 300–400 ft above the Zeppelin, he reached over the side of the BE2c to release three exploding Rankin darts. The German gunner opened fire. Above the thumping engine and the crack of the machine gun Brandon heard 'three reports'. 'Exploding Rankin darts causing a large rent on the port side,' he judged.

Still *L15* lumbered on, losing altitude. Brandon turned to attack from the stern. The Germans in the hindmost gondola shouted '*Flieger*' (aviator) in alarm.[23] 'Approaching, they got a machine gun cracking well.' It was only as Brandon was flying along the spine of the beast that it dawned on him why the machine gunners were able to easily pick him out of the moonless sky — a novice mistake:

> I was halfway past when I realised I had forgotten to put my lights out, the red and green wingtip and white tail and the instrument lights. I have never done anything more quickly than get those lights off, and with them off the shooting stopped. My stupidity didn't help to improve my self possession.[24]

He turned for another run but his layered clothing — uniform, jersey, British Warm and leather greatcoat — proved a frustrating impediment.

> I was even more rattled. I had intended to pass along the top of the Z[eppelin] at 300 feet but found myself much higher. I now throttled down and the plane was volplaning towards a point on the Z about a quarter of the way from the stern. I got out an incendiary bomb to put into the tube but it wouldn't go in. I now had to take my eye off the Z and get well forward in the cockpit. In the darkness I felt the runner on the bomb and the groove in the tube, but the bomb wouldn't go down. I found out later that it was the extra clothing that prevented my getting forward. And now very rattled and to see where I was I gave a quick look outside, and to my consternation and despair I saw that I had nearly passed beyond the Z. In desperation

at bungling a golden opportunity and letting London down, I flung the bomb into my lap and let off 6 more darts but heard nothing. The Z was now out of sight . . . [25]

He flew around for an hour more, but the fight was over.

Brandon had one final task, a night landing. He had no idea where he was. He flew north and then west, exhausting his fuel, intending to use parachute flares if necessary to facilitate a rough emergency landing. The first flare would be dropped at 3000 ft to find an open field, the second at 1000 ft to aid the landing. As he contemplated his prospects, Brandon saw lights twinkling in the far distance: Farningham airfield. 'I could not believe it. They looked like flares about an inch long.' On any other occasion the prospect of a night landing would be a 'grim business' but after his ordeal it was a 'haven of refuge'. He glided to the flare-lined runway and by 'the Grace of God landed with only minor damage to the plane. I couldn't believe it.'

During the 105-minute sortie, Brandon had proved something of a surprise, even to himself.[26] The New Zealander, with no practical training in night flying, in an aircraft devoid of adequate weaponry, had attacked a Zeppelin while under heavy fire and had landed to tell the tale. Three bullet holes in the BE2c were testament to the accuracy of the German gunners and to Brandon's bravery.

Unbeknown to Brandon, the Zeppelin was in its death throes. Breithaupt was throwing everything overboard to lighten the load, in a vain attempt to reach the Belgian coast. The remaining bombs and surplus fuel were jettisoned, and his men set about throwing the machine guns off the side.[27] They then ditched mechanical spare parts and motor covers from the gondolas. Still the stricken airship sank. There was no hope of a safe landfall on the other side of the North Sea. A brief distress signal was transmitted before the wireless was dumped over the side. Breithaupt's best hope was a soft sea-landing and the destruction of the Zeppelin, keeping it from the prying eyes of British scientists.

At only 1000 ft above the waves he ordered the crew up on top of the long hull. At about 11.15 p.m., *L15*'s structure collapsed in two places and it dropped rapidly. The control gondola was pushed underwater by the weight of the superstructure. 'Tossed around like a cork in the masses of water,' the semi-conscious commander escaped with one of the helmsmen, dragged onto the unsubmerged bow by surviving men.[28] The remaining helmsman drowned — the sole *L15* fatality. The Royal Navy scooped up the Germans for interrogation and imprisonment. The waterlogged Zeppelin was towed to shore near Margate, but much of it was lost in the process.[29] What did make it to shore was quickly dismantled and the leftovers were scavenged by local souvenir hunters.

The crew was interrogated. They were of the opinion that the fatal blows to their airship had been inflicted by the early anti-aircraft fire. The first official report of the attack noted that Brandon's assault 'may have obtained a hit', although the writer was not unequivocal on this.[30] In the end, Brandon shared the 'kill' with another pilot and anti-aircraft crews across the capital. Lord Mayor Wakefield realised that it was impossible to make a significant financial award to all the claimants so he had 300 medals stamped. Brandon was issued with his eight-carat Sir Charles Wakefield Medal — Zeppelin *L15*. Other honours were soon to follow.

Alfred de Bathe Brandon attacks Zeppelin *L15* in his Royal Aircraft Factory BE2c, using bombs and darts. This newspaper illustration captures some of the perils facing the airmen charged with attacking the large airships.

Brandon was the toast of London and Wellington. The newspapers could not get enough of the New Zealander. The *Daily Sketch*, a British tabloid with a print run of over a million copies, ran a photograph of 'Lieut. Brandon, the hero of Friday's Zeppelin raid' front and centre on its Monday edition under the banner: 'The Man Who Dropped the Bombs on a Zeppelin'.[31] Flanking him were pictures of a little girl, a young boy and a woman, just three of the 48 killed and 64 injured by the airship raid. The British public was informed that Brandon had given up 'a good position in New Zealand to come to the Motherland to "do his bit"'. Brandon had received his wings just a few weeks earlier and it was well known among his associates that he had 'only one desire . . . to have a "smack at the Zepps"'.

In New Zealand, the newspapers were proud of 'Gallant Brandon'. The bylines in the days that followed included 'Lieutenant Brandon's Brilliant Feat' and 'New Zealander's Daring Exploit'.[32] Brandon was the 'young Wellington flying man who just leapt into fame by attacking and winging a German Zeppelin'.[33] The Christchurch *Press* sent its London correspondent to the Hall School of Aviation at Hendon, where its instructor noted that they had also taught the New Zealander Will Scotland, but that it was Brandon 'who has come so prominently before the public'.[34] Brandon flew five more sorties before taking some well-earned leave. He was later awarded a Military Cross for his exemplary gallantry in active operations.[35]

While Brandon was making a name for himself in Britain, other New Zealanders were testing their wings in France. By far the greater number of recent flying graduates were being posted to the Western Front.

The failure of the Gallipoli campaign demonstrated that the war was going to be won not at the fringes of the conflict in the Middle East but at its very heart, in Europe. The European land battles of the previous year had been relatively localised affairs that had proven indecisive: bombardment followed by infantry advance across limited sectors of the front had met with negligible success. Germany simply had too great a reserve of men. Any time a breakthrough threatened, the German high command was able to amass sufficient resources to contain the British and French initiatives. If the smaller battles had failed to bring a resolution to the war, then perhaps it was simply a matter of scale. The solution, in the eyes of both sides, was confrontations without parallel in the history of warfare.

By early 1916 the Allied side of the Western Front was watched over by large French, British and Belgian armies. The British and much smaller Belgian forces were responsible for the northernmost quarter of the front abutting the Channel. While the Germans proposed to bleed the French 'white' with a long struggle at Verdun, Britain and France proposed a great breakthrough battle on the Somme. The German offensive began in February and ran through until the end of the year, but the Somme offensive was set for the second half of 1916. In preparation for this latter attack, massive numbers of men and large quantities of materiel were funnelled to the British First, Second, Third, Fourth and Fifth armies in northern France. To support the ever-growing armies a much larger air presence was required.

Overseeing the air effort was Brigadier General Hugh Trenchard, who, in the summer of the

Alfred de Bathe Brandon, resplendent in his great leather overcoat. On two occasions in 1916 he assisted in bringing down 'baby-killer' Zeppelins.

previous year, had been appointed officer commanding the RFC in the field. In 1916 Trenchard bolstered the RFC on the Western Front with 15 new squadrons.[36] Moreover, as the year progressed all squadrons, including RNAS units, would increase incrementally in strength from 12 to 18 machines. To more efficiently utilise these units the air service was organised into brigades, one to each army. A brigade consisted of two wings; the number of squadrons in each wing varied. One wing carried out artillery work and close reconnaissance work with the army corps and was designated the corps wing; the other, which operated directly under army headquarters and carried out work such as fighting and reconnaissance, was designated the army wing. With the Somme build-up there was a substantial increase in the numbers of New Zealanders involved in the air war.

At 30 years of age Clive Collett, as with Alfred de Bathe Brandon, was one of the older New Zealanders to enter the air war when he arrived on the Western Front in March 1916. He was just one of hundreds of RFC men being assembled for the great Somme Offensive. The Blenheim-born airman had worked his passage to Britain as an engineer on SS *Limerick* as part of the 1914 Main Body convoy. Unlike his Gallipoli-bound compatriots, however, he did not disembark at Suez but carried on to England and one of the many private flying schools at Hendon. A little over a year later, with civilian and military training under his belt, he was despatched to the Western Front.

The first port of call for many airmen was the base depot at Saint-Omer, tucked in the far northwest corner of France. Here men cooled their heels waiting in the RFC 'pool' before they were called upon to replace those removed from the battlefield.

After disembarking in France, the newly trained Michael Gordon of Hastings was squeezed into an overcrowded train for Saint-Omer. He arrived at 5 a.m. and was unable retrieve kit or find lodgings, so slept in a hut, propped up in a chair by the fire.[37] At dawn he found the small airfield was crammed with machines; after lunch he went into the township. Many were unimpressed with their new surroundings. 'I must say, I think France is a bit of a hole,' wrote one airman.

> We are now at the best hotel in town but except for the food and a comfortable bed, it isn't in it with a comfortable inn at home. It is purely an eating house, nasty and untidy. Kitchen chairs and tables lie about in a mucky looking room with funny looking wash basins in the corner. The streets are dirty and the people have a habit of throwing refuse out into the streets to be taken away. The women are very slovenly and the whole place seems asleep.[38]

Although Gordon found Saint-Omer devoid of any noteworthy features, the serious nature of the task ahead was brought home to him when a hospital train pulled into the town. 'It took ages to clear,' he penned in his diary. 'Most of the men were just out of the trenches that day and the mud was still on them.' In spite of their cheerful demeanor, 'many of the poor devils were shaking and shivering with the cold'.[38A] A few days later his posting finally came through and he was transferred to a frontline squadron. He joined a throng of infantry, guns, armoured cars and cavalry headed into the maws of war.

Clive Collett's destination was 18 Squadron. Aucklander and former flying instructor Harold Butterworth was already with the unit; he had arrived in early February. The two New Zealanders found themselves in a squadron dedicated to army cooperation at Auchel airfield, near Béthune.

Collett was billetted at a farmhouse close to an airfield. Other New Zealand airmen across the Western Front were housed in tents or in purpose-built huts. The New Zealand airmen in 60 Squadron in Filescamp Farm, west of Arras, felt particularly lucky. Their base was near a picturesque house, 'half farm and half chateau, and the airfield's purpose-built corrugated-iron hangars, together with Nissen huts for the officers and NCOs and good accommodation for the men . . . were all built by the sappers'.[39] 'The contrast between our quarters and those occupied by the infantry and gunners in the line was striking,' noted a Christchurch-born airman. 'We had cream with every meal, and a hot bath — made by digging an oblong hole in the turf and lining it with a waterproof sheet — whenever we felt inclined.'[40] Many men slept two or more to a tent or hut and made them as homely as possible. 'My room is looking quite ship shape, with rug, gramophone, pictures and Harrison Fisher girls on the wall,' wrote Hugh Blackwell. '[There] is only one thing for perfection and that is the removal of the whole some 12,000 miles to a spot in NZ called Kaiapoi.'[41]

Their living quarters were kept in order by their batmen, or orderlies. The New Zealanders, who were unaccustomed to servants, readily accommodated themselves to their new status as 'temporary gentlemen' whose batmen waited on them as butlers. Nelson pilot Alfred Kingsford's batman was simply know as 'Minns':

> It was Minns who brought the drinks, Minns who waited the table, Minns who brought the breakfast in bed and collected the half franc for bringing it, Minns, who cleaned the boots, made the beds, in fact Minns did this and Minns did that, and there was nothing Minns didn't do. It was also Minns who led the crowd to the dug-out, at the double too, when the alarms went, yet through it all his ruddy face was always beaming.[42]

Many batmen were older men who were only too happy to avoid the squalor and dangers of the trenches for what was considered a 'plum' position with the flying service.[43]

When they were not in the air, Collett and Butterworth spent much of their time in the officers' mess, the central gathering point for the men. In the depths of winter, one New Zealander freshly posted to France entered his squadron officers' mess for the first time.

> It looked comfy enough. In the middle of the ante-room was a brazier, a big open-work basket of wrought iron holding a huge, cheery wood fire. On a corner table was a phonograph, apparently suffering badly with asthma, judging by the wheezing noise it made, the walls were adorned with cuttings from illustrated papers, while over the far corner stood a piano, minus one caster, judging by its tilt. Two or three of the fellows were reading round the fire, while at a couple of small tables card games were in progress.[44]

Invariably the mess was also the venue for the squadron's parties, where alcohol flowed and singing and general merriment could rapidly devolve into violent and destructive rampages.[45] Victories and losses were commemorated in the mess. In some squadrons, a promotion or an officer being sent on leave was cause enough to launch a wild evening of carousing. Some squadron commanders believed that the drinking bouts enabled the airmen to let off steam, though they had to be carefully managed to avoid injury.

One of the few gripes was the variable European weather, especially the bone-chilling winters. Nissen huts and tents only just kept the rain and wind at bay, but the extreme cold seeped past all defences. 'I haven't described the cold in France, for really it is beyond description,' wrote one aviator from Wellington.

> The ink in my office was always frozen, and if you melted it to a liquid and tried to write it froze on the pen before you could get it to the paper. Reports written with boiling ink and a hot pen required no blotting, but when they were taken into a hot room the ink melted and ran. This is no exaggeration at all — it actually happened. Trouble with the engines was awful, because the carburettor would freeze up just as you left the ground, probably meaning a landing in a field, where they would be thawed out with hot cloths. The milk in the mess used to be frozen, despite the huge fires.[46]

Another Wellingtonian, Roy Kean, found the winters so cold he requested a transfer to a warmer climate, perhaps Egypt, India or even Mesopotamia. 'Prior to the war he lived always in New Zealand,' wrote his commanding officer; 'in winter he suffers constantly from ill health.'[47] Kean's efforts were unsuccessful.

Fortunately Collett's arrival at 18 Squadron coincided with early spring and an upswing in operations. He and Butterworth were flying the unit's Vickers FB5 'Gunbus', the first British fighter aircraft. A two-crew pusher biplane, the FB5 was designed for air-to-air combat. The Gunbus pilot sat with his back to the engine and propeller, with the observer-gunner in front of the protruding nacelle — the timber and fabric housing of the cockpit. This got the pusher round the problem of forward firing through the propeller. Its great disadvantage, however, was its slow rate of climb and low speed, a severe drawback exposed in mid-1915 by the arrival of the Fokker Eindecker. The meeting of the German purpose-built fighter and the British purpose-built fighter

The Fokker Eindecker monoplane was one of the most feared machines of the early air war. The synchronised machine gun could fire through the arc of the spinning propeller, and revolutionised air-to-air combat. This captured Eindecker is being inspected by French troops.

was a very lopsided affair. The single-seater Eindecker monoplane not only used its higher speed and rate of climb to great advantage, but it also had an all-important gun synchroniser which allowed the pilot to fire through the arc of the propeller. Pilots could now 'point' their machine at the enemy and fire. It was an unequal battle, and the Gunbus, alongside the widely deployed and infamously outclassed BE2c reconnaissance aircraft, became known as 'Fokker fodder'.

The 'Fokker Scourge' increasingly called for machines suited to the task of protecting Allied aircraft in their reconnaissance and artillery patrolling duties, and preventing German machines from seeing 'over the hill' and ranging in bombardments. This gave rise to the formation flying that would characterise operations for the rest of the war. Although frontline squadrons were gradually being re-equipped with new machines, Collett and Butterworth's unit was still languishing with the FB5, which was now well outclassed in air combat. The squadron generally avoided mixing it up with enemy machines and was assigned a miscellany of tasks. 'I am quite an old hand now and do my daily spell over the German lines causing as much annoyance as possible,' wrote Collett — a four-week 'veteran' of the front — to his brother in March 1916.

> I am still flying my old fighting machine [an FB5 biplane] but find she is too slow to catch the majority of the Hun machines. Perhaps an outline of our duties may interest you. I am with a fighting Squadron and we all fly the same type of machine, our work consists of patrolling the lines and driving off any Hun machines which may attempt to cross. We also do a lot of photography from the air of the trenches and keep a lookout for the position of enemy artillery. For all these duties you can guess we are pretty heavily loaded, our equipment consisting of machine-gun and ammunition, camera and plates, also wireless installation for instructing our artillery about targets etc. This lot with the pilot and observer brings our weight up to 2000 lbs, which is some weight to get up to 10,000 feet or so.[48]

In spite of the Gunbus's vulnerabilities, Collett was up for a fight, even when outnumbered. 'As the German machines are faster than ours we keep climbing all the time,' he told his brother, 'and then dive onto them when we do see them about.' One Sunday in March he spotted a trio of intruders. He used his height to dive on them. The FB5 protested, and the nine-cylinder Gnome engine began to disintegrate as the propeller revolutions increased in the sharp descent. A valve blew under the strain and he passed through the enemy and landed behind his own lines. On another occasion Collett noticed a biplane being fired on by Allied anti-aircraft batteries and closed in, his observer firing off a couple of bursts with the Vickers machine gun. When the 'enemy' machine turned, Collett and his observer thought they spotted RFC markings and broke off the attack.

Collett's flying regime was commonplace on the Western Front. From 11 March to 16 April he undertook around 30 flights with a string of different observers — nearly a sortie a day, some of which were over three hours in duration.[49] The missions were intense, and he force-landed on five occasions during that time.[50] Collett was only withdrawn from action because he required surgery for a long-standing injury he had sustained the previous year.

Sketchy records seem to suggest the incident occurred on 6 July 1915. Collett was test-flying an aircraft destined for France. The engine had performed satisfactorily on the ground but in the climb it failed. 'I tried to get round to clear a lot of obstacles but had no speed so, of course, fell,' he wrote, the 'result a broken leg, a broken nose, and a sprained ankle.'[51] Scar lines cross-hatching his cheeks and a misshapen nose served as a reminder of the seriousness of the accident. Twelve months later his nose still needed corrective work; he was in hospital three days after leaving 18 Squadron. When he was finally declared fit for flying in June 1916 — sporting a moustache, perhaps to cover some of the worst damage to his upper lip — it was not to a frontline squadron but as a specialist test and evaluation pilot with the temporary rank of captain.

In the meantime Butterworth continued his work with 18 Squadron, but now in the FE2b. Superficially the FE2b bore a passing resemblance to its predecessor, but the new machine was a considerable improvement. The 160-hp engine could propel the machine to a maximum speed of 90 mph and carry the airframe and crew to an operational service ceiling of 11,000 ft. It carried two Lewis guns. The observer's gun, with an enormous field of view, was supplemented by a second gun between the observer and the pilot; in theory, the pilot could fire this over the observer. In practice, the observer often stood and utilised the pilot's gun to fire backwards over the upper wing. It was a precarious position, standing high and leaning back over the front of the cockpit, but it did offer some protection from rear attack.

One of the New Zealanders to get the better of an enemy machine in the FE2b was Whanganui's 'Fighting Parson' Cuthbert Maclean. Before the outbreak of war, Maclean was a missionary engaged in work among Māori in the Bay of Islands, before becoming a curate at Newington, in south London.[52] In late 1914 he had served with the Royal Fusiliers, and was awarded a Military Cross for action at Ypres. Having exchanged his curate's vestments for an army uniform, he then swapped this for a flying badge when he was seconded to the RFC the following year. In January 1916 he was given command of 25 Squadron's 'C' Flight. Squadrons were usually divided into three flights, 'A', 'B', and 'C', consisting of up to six machines each. The flight commanders were generally the most experienced active airmen in the squadron, and the performance of the unit and longevity of their charges was in large part determined by the quality of these men.

Maclean's squadron was assigned reconnaissance and escort duties.[53] As the squadron's official postwar history recorded:

> The daily patrols [were] designed to prevent enemy aircraft from interfering with the artillery work and photography of the corps squadron's machines working in the neighbourhood of the line and prevent hostile aeroplanes from doing artillery work and photography over our trenches.[54]

The squadron had a number of successes, including shooting down Baron von Saalfeld, son of the prince of Saxony.[55] In May it was cooperating with Butterworth's squadron, and in June the squadron was part of the preliminary preparations for the Somme attack.

above Clive Collett, seated here in his FB5 Gunbus, was one of New Zealand's most accomplished airmen. His letters from the front paint a vivid picture of the air fighting in 1916.

right After securing his 'wings' Harold Butterworth served as an instructor in England before his posting to 18 Squadron, where he served with Clive Collett.

Maclean led patrols with the squadron and, on 22 June, with an observer, he scored his only air combat success of the war. Flying at 11,000 ft, they spotted a Roland and attacked. The German two-seater biplane had a monocoque plywood fuselage: it was sleeker and offered less drag than the box-shaped, fabric-covered British FE2b. It was expensive to build, however — and not particularly fast. Maclean pounced on the Roland 1000 ft below. The German dived and the 'Fighting Parson' followed, his observer firing two drums at close range. Tracer bullets punched through the plywood body. At 5000 ft the Roland entered a vertical dive and the FE2b overshot. By the time Maclean had wheeled round the German machine was on the ground.[56]

As the Somme Offensive drew near, more New Zealanders appeared in frontline units. Squadrons were instructed to shield preparations from prying eyes, including the German observation balloons, and to disrupt German movements, reinforcement and resupply by bombing targets behind enemy lines.[57] Pilots Rainsford Balcombe-Brown and Herbert Russell and observer James Dennistoun were ordered to carry out balloon-busting and bombing sorties leading up to the July offensive.

Rainsford Balcombe-Brown, of Wellington, arrived in the RFC via the Royal Field Artillery. Before the war the dominion airman, who was proficient in five languages, had been a student at Oriel College, Oxford.[58] In 1916, he was flying with 1 Squadron. The core of the formation was its reconnaissance aircraft, supplemented by a trio of newly arrived French Nieuport 16s. The Nieuport was one of the first true single-seater fighters of the Great War, and was lethal in the hands of airmen like Canadian Albert Ball. Light and nimble, it was blessed with an excellent rate of climb: 10,000 ft in just under 11 minutes. In conjunction with the FE2b, the Nieuport 16 helped secure temporary ascendency over the trenches, ending the Fokker Scourge. The squadron's Nieuports were generally deployed as escorts to protect the vulnerable reconnaissance machines. However, in the last week of June orders came through for them to strike a line of German observation balloons ranging in artillery on British positions. Balloon obervers on both sides used telephones to communicate with their repective artillery batteries well behind the lines, informing them of how close their shells were landing to the intended target, incrementally ranging them in until shells were falling right on the enemy. Because of injuries, the squadron had only two airmen available who had trained on the Nieuports; Balcombe-Brown, a Nieuport virgin, volunteered to take up the third.[59]

Balcombe-Brown set about familiarising himself with the French aircraft. It was nothing like the unit's plodding Avro 504s or the lethargic machines that home defence airmen like Brandon were flying. At dawn he took the Nieuport up for a test flight and fired off some rockets. The Le Prieur rockets had entered the airmen's arsenal only months before, at the Battle of Verdun. They were cardboard tubes filled with black powder and with spear-like tips, attached to long rods fitted into launch tubes. Usually four such rockets were attached on the two struts, which had the unfortunate effect of lowering the Nieuport's performance — as Herbert Cooper had discovered only five days earlier.

Cooper, the son of a Supreme Court judge and an old boy of King's College, Auckland, had

above The French-designed Nieuport 16 helped bring an end to the 'Fokker Scourge' in 1916. As well as the Lewis machine gun attached to the upper wing, this particular Nieuport has air-to-air Le Prieur rockets fitted to its 'vee-struts' between the upper and lower wings.

below The sliding rail of the Foster Gun Mounting enabled the pilot to pull the machine gun all the way back in a single, smooth movement. This permitted the airman to clear stoppages, swap out ammunition drums and to fire directly upward at an enemy machine.

learnt to fly at Hendon before the war. By October 1914 he was an instructor at Farnborough, and was one of the first New Zealanders to enter the air war.[60] He joined 11 Squadron in the summer of the following year, where he scored the squadron's first 'Hun machine' with his observer, Algernon Insall.[61] The experienced Insall considered Cooper, whom he dubbed his 'Maori pilot', one of the squadron's best airmen.[62] When the unit received a clutch of Nieuports as escorts for the squadron's two-seater machines, Cooper was selected to fly one operationally. The choice of Cooper was to have far-reaching consequences.

Because the Nieuport 16 lacked synchronisation gear for firing through the propeller, the standard machine gun on the aircraft was a Lewis gun mounted on a pillar above the upper wing. Changing drums was done by way of a quick-release device that allowed it to be tilted back. 'Although ingenious,' Insall recalled, 'the device could not be operated by a pilot of short stature.'[63] Cooper, who was only 5 ft 2 in., requested an alternative mechanism to allow him to change the drum. The result was a curved rail, developed by a young sergeant, Ralph Foster, which allowed the Lewis to be slid all the way down and then quickly snapped back into place. Moreover, what came to be known as the Foster Gun Mounting could be fixed to fire at any angle the pilot desired. This innovation was later exploited by many other pilots, including Ball, and was fitted to other machines, including the mighty SE5a.

By mid-1916 Cooper was a captain commanding one of the squadron's flights. On 21 June he took off for Rouvrel to practise with Le Prieur rockets when things went terribly wrong. His Nieuport 16 had banked sharply on takeoff and then sideslipped into the airfield. He died within minutes of the accident.[64] The fighter was unarmed at the time but the squadron's commander laid the blame on empty rocket strut fittings and tubes, which he felt had considerably increased weight and drag on the light fighter.[65] Cooper was a very experienced pilot, making it all the more surprising that he was killed on what should have been a routine flight.

The squadron's commanding officer informed Cooper's family that in spite of a scarcity of labour and wood, which meant men were routinely buried without a coffin, two non-commissioned officers and a mechanic — 'all skilled woodworkers' — had given up their night's rest to ensure this would not be their son's fate.[66] Fifteen brother officers and 80 non-commissioned officers and a firing party followed Cooper's body to the graveyard. 'On a brass plate, screwed to the lid, the following inscription was punched, as we had no materials for engraving,' wrote Cooper's commander, '"Captain H. A. Cooper, R.F.C., S.R. Killed on active service. 21.6.16. Honoured and respected by all."'

In addition to degrading the single-seater's performance, the electrically fired rockets were famously inaccurate. A pilot was required to close to within 120 yards at an angle of 45 degrees before launching them; as a result, attacking a balloon was no easy task. Many pilots considered it more hazardous than aircraft-on-aircraft combat. Located a few miles behind their own front, German balloons were well defended by a palisade of machine guns and heavier anti-aircraft guns, as well as their own marauding aircraft. It was not unknown for an observational balloon to be surrounded by barrage balloons, tethered to the ground with cables capable of slicing the wings off an aircraft.

All of this meant Balcombe-Brown would be flying an unfamiliar machine on a mission armed with performance-hampering, short-range rockets that would require him to swoop in close to the German observer hanging in his wicker basket, while all the time being pelted with enemy gunfire. Despite all this, on 26 June Balcombe-Brown shot a balloon down in flames.[67] 'At dawn he commenced to learn the machine,' reported the *Otago Daily Times*, 'and the same evening brought down the kite [balloon],'[68] one of nine destroyed over a two-day period.[69]

The following week Balcombe-Brown crossed enemy lines near Grévillers and began diving on another balloon, when all hell broke loose.

> When at about 4000 ft suddenly about 50 shells burst around the balloon I was aiming for, forming a white halo about 200 yrds in diameter. This white cloud was on exactly the same level as the kite balloon. Then a few seconds later I noticed two streams of balls of fire coming in a continuous stream as though from a hose, one at each end of a wood 300 yds to the side of the balloon. The fireballs were about five yards distant from each other. One of these streams was some distance from me, but the other exactly crossed my line of flight down towards the balloon. I carried on the same course for a few more seconds, then seeing that I was going straight through the spray, I pulled the elevators [*sic*] back and passed straight over it. This caused me to lose sight of the balloon and on putting the nose down practically vertical again, I found I was very close to the balloon and slightly to one side of it. I tried to twist round and fired my torpedoes [rockets] which passed to the side. My height was 1200 ft when my engine finally picked up. At first the engine would not pick up as soon as it usually does. After passing the balloon I was in the surrounding halo for about 2 seconds. On emerging from that another spray of fire started at me, and as I turned it followed the machine round in a semi-circle about 40 yards behind the tail. Each spray seemed to last about 15–20 seconds. On the way back to the lines A.A. [anti-aircraft] guns were very active.[70]

Balcombe-Brown survived the two attacks and was later awarded a Military Cross.[71]

On the day of Balcombe-Brown's first balloon-busting success, New Zealanders Herbert Russell and James Dennistoun took to the air, but with a decidedly different outcome. The two men were cousins. Russell, a former Wanganui Collegiate pupil, had advanced from observer to pilot the previous year and had joined 23 Squadron in February 1916.[72] Dennistoun, of Peel Forest, South Canterbury, was an accomplished climber and adventurer. The mountains of the Southern Alps and Southland were his playground as a boy: at the age of 12 he had stood atop Little Mount Peel, at 14 he had conquered Big Mount Peel, and at 16 Ben Lomond.[73] He climbed Mount Cook and was the first to reach the summit of Mount D'Archiac. His most famous effort, though, was on Mitre Peak.

Mitre Peak, although less than half the height of Mount Cook, was long considered unscalable because of its near vertical rise from the waters of Milford Sound to the 5560-ft summit. Shaped like a bishop's mitre, the mountain is a notoriously difficult climb, and few attempt it even today. In the nineteenth century it was beyond the reach even of Fiordland's most noteworthy and rugged pioneer, Donald Sutherland, who had failed in his 1883 attempt. The peak had remained unconquered for nearly two decades when Dennistoun, with Milford assistant guide Joseph Beaglehole in tow, made his attempt.[74] Beaglehole panicked on the steep face of the mountain, leaving Dennistoun to clamber up the peak. On the rough granite, Dennistoun swapped his climbing boots for thin-soled tennis shoes and the final assault.[75] In the early afternoon of 13 March 1911, resting at the summit overlooking the waters of Milford Sound, he collected rocks for a cairn to which he secured his handkerchief, a surety of his success.[76] Sutherland scoffed at Dennistoun's improbable claim, and it remained in doubt until three years later, when the handkerchief was found by the next successful ascendant.[77]

In 1911 Dennistoun joined Captain Robert Falcon Scott's Antarctic expedition. A Royal Navy officer responsible for provisioning Scott's expedition out of Lyttelton had visited the Dennistoun farm at Peel Forest, and the sniff of adventure had enticed Dennistoun to apply to look after the expedition's seven Himalayan mules — an unpaid position.[78] Scott's *Terra Nova* was to act as the transportation and resupply vessel for the British Antarctic Expedition of 1910. The scientific staff in biology, geology, glaciology, meteorology and geophysics made important observations during the expedition, but the attempt to become the first to reach the South Pole failed by only 33 days — Norwegian Roald Amundsen's flag was already there — and the harrowing return leg claimed all five lives of the small party. For his part in tending the doomed expedition's animals, Dennistoun was awarded the King's Antarctic Medal and the Medal of the Royal Geographical Society.

When the Great War arrived, Dennistoun travelled to Britain. He entered the conflict in the North Irish Horse before being seconded to the RFC. He joined the squadron in early June 1916 and Russell immediately requested 'Jim' as his observer, 'knowing what a stout fellow he was and thinking that after a little training he would turn out the best observer in the squadron'.[79] Russell took his cousin out on a few practice runs on their own side of the lines until he felt his cousin was ready for a short bombing raid into enemy territory.

The 26 June 1916 sortie was a bombing mission against the Biache railway junction. The biggest threat was the Fokker Eindeckers, which liked to 'wait for a machine to either lose his formation or lay behind . . . and mob a solitary machine'. Russell reasoned that although Dennistoun was inexperienced the mission included four other FE2bs — more than a deterrent to the opportunistic Fokkers. The pair climbed in the biplane, Russell seated slightly higher in the rear pilot's seat and Dennistoun in the front cockpit. They were armed with bombs and the two Lewis guns. The rendezvous was over Arras at 7000 ft; from here all five machines would push on to the target only five miles to the east. Nowhere on the Western Front was entirely safe for airmen in mid-1916, but it was hoped this would be a relatively quick hit-and-run operation.

The New Zealanders 'got off the floor' first but a valve rocker arm broke, a cylinder failed and revs fell. Russell glided the faltering bird to the 'drome' as the others flew on. 'I was secretly rather pleased as I hated bomb-raids on which one has to fly (for bombing purposes) too straight for comfort, with Archie [anti-aircraft fire] potting at you from below,' recalled Russell. Moreover, it was a 'beast of a day with low clouds and the devil of a wind blowing towards Hunland: not ideal by any means'. His commanding officer was not so pleased; he rushed out to see why they had returned and, much to Russell's surprise, demanded another machine be brought out for them. There was no hope of catching the other FE2bs: the New Zealanders would be arriving alone, flying into a hornet's nest of anti-aircraft fire. When the plane was wheeled out Russell's heart sank further.

> It had no bomb-racks or bomb-sights fitted, so we had not much hope of hitting the target. I pointed this out to the C.O. [commanding officer], who replied, 'Never mind, let Dennistoun take them up in his arms and throw them over when you think you are about right. You've had enough experience by now, to tell more or less.' It is true that I had been in a good many raids, but you cannot hope to hit things without the necessary implements. However, not more could be said, so off we went.[80]

The cloud layer had sunk lower, and they crossed the lines at 6200 ft through a barrage of anti-aircraft fire. They were 2800 ft lower than he would have liked, but Russell was comforted by the clouds, which offered a bolthole if Fokkers materialised. At the target, Dennistoun 'chucked the bombs over'. They spun down and exploded surprisingly close to the rail junction. Not a bad effort, thought Russell, given the drama involved in getting there and the lack of bombsights. He banked the FE2b sharply and was heading for home when he spotted a lone Fokker in the distance.

He made some fast calculations: the Eindecker was low and would not be able to climb rapidly enough to catch them before they hit the enemy trenches; but if the German did intercept, Russell reckoned he would be able to glide the FE2b over their own lines and, if the enemy did pursue them, they had a fighting chance, 'even in our old machine'. His projections seemed about right until his cousin, who was scanning the heavens for fighters, shouted at him. Russell pivoted in his seat, craning his neck. A Fokker with two flanking companions had snuck up behind them. The New Zealanders were well short of the German front line, let alone their own.

The Fokker lined them up and started firing. They were in a vast blue lake of open sky, the shoreline of clouds and safety beyond reach. 'Jim got our rear gun into action very promptly but as he was standing up firing his first burst he was hit low down in the stomach and collapsed in the front seat.' Russell's only hope was to evade the Fokker. He threw the biplane 'all over the place' but the much quicker single-seater 'stuck like a leech'. Then, disaster: the main petrol tank was hit with tracer fire and the machine became a fiery torch. The sole consolation was that the pusher engine was behind them and the flames were blown back, saving them from immolation during the descent.

> He [the enemy] continued to fire and finally hit me just under the right shoulder blade in the lung and after 2 or 3 minutes I, like a fool, fainted and, in consequence the machine

The observer on a Royal Aircraft Factory FE2 was required to stand, turn and lean out to fire the machine gun over the head of the pilot. It was in this precarious position that James Dennistoun was shot by the pilot of a Fokker Eindecker in June 1916.

nose dived. The cold air blowing on my face just brought me round as we were close to the ground, and I succeeded in flattening her out enough to prevent her actually nosing into the ground.[81]

Trailing flames and ribbons of dirty smoke, the wounded airmen flew low and level towards the trenches. Dennistoun was unable to stand to fire the rear gun and his cousin yelled: Could he manage to fire the front Vickers to at least give an appearance of 'fighting power'? Incredibly, Dennistoun fired just as Russell momentarily passed out again. When he 'came to', he thought he saw Dennistoun's machine gun spitting up dirt, inflicting damage on the German second-line trenches; a softening-up for a hard landing. It was these trenches they struck.

The aircraft belted into the ground at 75 mph and the crew was flung into the air. 'A lot of burning petrol was thrown over me as the machine jerked over on to her back and I got pretty severely burnt,' said Russell, 'but Jim having fallen rather to my left just escaped it.' German soldiers piled out of the trench and covered the burning Russell in a blanket, rolling him until the fire was extinguished. The pair was carried from the smoldering FE2b carcass to a large dugout. Anxious officers crowded around them as a doctor administered rudimentary first aid and dressed their wounds. When the Germans realised the pilot and observer were in no fit state to answer questions, the New Zealanders were driven by motor ambulance to Biache — 'the very place we had been bombing', Russell wrote later.

Dennistoun was eventually taken on to Hamblain, four miles away, and Russell was informed that in all probability Jim might 'die in the next 48 hours'. Dennistoun was unable to write but was befriended by an English-speaking Bavarian nurse, Lili Eidau. 'She seemed so very nice and kind hearted,' recalled Russell, 'and spoke very encouragingly to Jim.'[82] She wrote to Dennistoun's mother, Emily: 'He has been shot in the stomach . . . there is a danger for this life but we hope sincerely to bring him over it.'[83] Dennistoun underwent two major operations and appeared to come through them remarkably well. 'Mr. Dennistoun is a great deal better,' wrote his nurse three days later, 'He still feels uncomfy, but — after having been so gravely wounded it cannot be otherwise — the danger is less and we hope from day to day more that he will recover.' The two cousins were reunited in Biache, where they shared a room and managed 'to keep one another quite cheerful'.[84] On 5 August they were transferred to the Ohrdruf prisoner of war camp in Thüringen, central Germany, 500 miles away.

Dennistoun seemed to travel well, and they were both placed in the prisoner of war hospital. Russell's only complaint was that he did not think his cousin's bandages were being changed regularly enough. On 9 August Russell, who was still recovering from his burns, awoke to a commotion. One of Dennistoun's bedside neighbours — another 23 Squadron airman — said that Dennistoun was feeling faint and looked very white. The doctor arrived and rushed the New Zealander into surgery. Russell intercepted his cousin and asked if he going to have another operation. Dennistoun said 'Yes'; he believed it was essential if he was to get well more quickly. After the procedure, approaching midday, the German doctor informed Russell that Dennistoun had had to 'undergo a very severe operation, that they had done the best for him, and that he had come round from the anaesthetic'. The young man from Peel Forest felt 'rotten', but the doctor was astonished at the success of the procedure. 'Jim talked quite cheerfully' to the German doctor, recalled Russell.

It was a false dawn: 'At about noon he became suddenly weak and died very peacefully and with no pain at 5 minutes past 12.'[85] Grief-stricken, Russell wrote to his mother.

> Jim died this morning . . . It came as a great shock to me and is of course to you: but oh I am sorry for the family . . . Poor Aunt Emily and Uncle George. I am afraid it will be a great shock to them and I am not one of those skilled in breaking these things gently. God help me to do so in this matter at any rate.[86]

Later that day he wrote the letter to his aunt and uncle. After recounting the final hours of their son's life, he wrote of how much he savoured their time together.

> Of course I feel his loss a very great deal. It was nice having a relation who knows our own family intimately to talk to. We were always talking together about our respective families and his doings at Peel Farm, the family . . . and all sorts of things. He was so nice and at all times good to me. Words fail me to express my sympathy with you and Uncle George and Barbara in your great loss and really I cannot attempt it as I can hardly realise it myself yet. But I really and truly am very sorry for you my dear Aunt Emily and please excuse this blundering letter. Your affectionate nephew, Herbie Russell.[87]

Still the war went on, and Russell had to face it without Jim. 'At present I am rather feeling things,' he confessed to this mother. 'However, I must get over that soon, for after all it is war and so many many people have seen their relations and friends killed beside them in trenches and elsewhere.'[88]

CHAPTER NINE
FIRE IN THE SKY
1916

As preparations for the Somme progressed on the Western Front, a small number of New Zealanders arrived in one of the war's more demanding theatres: East Africa. Conditions here rivalled those that had tormented the New Zealand airmen and mechanics of Mesopotamia Flight. The German Empire's master plan for Africa was the creation of Deutsch-Mittelafrika (German Central Africa), a vast sub-Saharan territory that would link its dispersed possessions in east, west and southwestern Africa. Most of the envisaged territorial gains would be at the expense of the Belgian colonial possessions in the Congo. If successful, Germany would be the most powerful colonial power on the continent. Fortunately for the Allies, Berlin's ambitions greatly exceeded its resources in the field. Almost all of its European and African soldiers were concentrated in East Africa — modern-day Burundi, Rwanda and Tanzania — where the numerically inferior Germans were forced into defensive operations with the limited aim of tying up as many British and Allied troops as possible.

German East Africa's defence was in the capable hands of General Paul von Lettow-Vorbeck. His primary strategy was to threaten the important British Uganda Railway but never to directly engage in a decisive battle; rather he would use his limited resources in guerrilla warfare — continual attacks designed to frustrate the much larger British force. The Germans would set up concealed rifle pits and machine-gun emplacements on a road used by the British forces, ambush them and then, in the confusion, retreat into the bush.[1] On many occasions the enemy was never actually seen during an entire engagement. The arrival of a squadron of aircraft on the British side offered the possibility of bringing the Germans to a decisive battle or, at the very least, of monitoring the itinerant enemy.

By early 1916, 26 (South African) Squadron was operating from its chief base at Mbuyuni, Tanganyika. During the squadron's work in East Africa a handful of New Zealanders came and went, among them the Fijian-born New Zealander Charles Hathaway and recent immigrant and Pohonui farmer Vincent Toulmin. Hathaway, who had been with the RFC since October 1915, began service with the unit on 9 May 1916.[2] The aircraft under his care were principally BE2cs and a small number of Farmans that had been flying in West Africa.[3] It was a ragtag collection of outdated hand-me-downs. The Farmans were poorly maintained and the humid conditions had had their way with them, warping the wings and rotting the fabric. When the

BE2cs were unpacked and assembled a startling omission was revealed: the propellers were not those designed for the BE2c. The modifications the mechanics had to make affected the performance of the already underpowered machines.[4]

In addition to this, the lumbering aircraft had to negotiate the topography of the region, most notably Kilimanjaro and the ochre-cliffed Pare Mountains, a barrier to direct action against the German-operated railway. Observational sorties had to contend with low, cloaking mists until they burnt off at around 9 a.m., only to find themselves facing dense bush, which made concealment relatively easy for the enemy. The Germans lacked their own aircraft to combat British reconnaissance and bombing sorties, but they had unwitting allies in the large flocks of locusts that on occasion forced sorties to be abandoned.[5]

On the ground, Hathaway and the others were confronted with insects and animals. When the squadron first arrived, strange creatures beset them in the night. A large thorn barricade enclosed the camping ground. After the crew set out their beds under the stars, a roaring fire was set to cook the evening meal and they then prepared to retire for the night. The fire, however, had been laid near a large anthill, out of which emerged an overheated 10-ft-long snake. The cook let out a bloodcurdling scream and bolted as 'though the devil himself had suddenly appeared', wrote an observer.[6] He hurled himself through piles of glasses, bottles, pots and pans, one of which poured its contents onto the fire. Complete darkness engulfed the camp. 'Each of us thought he could feel it crawling about his legs, and never in my life have I seen a more utterly panic-stricken crowd of grown up people.'

Calm was restored with a week's worth of rum rations, and the men were just reaching a stage where 'one begins to tell others what a darned good joke it had been' when a piercing howl from the direction of the servants' quarters 'fairly made our hair stand on end'. They gathered weapons and advanced timorously on the threat. They found the head servant, a Cockney, who had been getting into bed when he put his hand right on the snake. As the others stood in a semi-circle with spades and bayonets at the ready, a reluctant volunteer mustered the courage to gingerly lift the blanket.[7] 'There, nestling comfortably underneath was — an empty bottle!'

> As the night dragged on we had ample opportunity for studying the zoological and nocturnal wonders of East Africa. The whole place swarmed with ants . . . one never felt certain that it was not a centipede or a scorpion crawling across one's chest. The buzzing of the beetles and the chirping of countless crickets was almost deafening, and loud above their unmelodious din came the occasional roar of a lion, and the more frequent wail of a hyæna. Jackals, frogs, grasshoppers, and various smaller fry each contributed to this wild and primitive concert, which, strange to say, quickly lulled me off into a deep and dreamless sleep.[8]

Hathaway found that the greatest immediate threat was not the Germans but the insects. On one occasion the feasting termites collapsed a hangar. Before working on the cockpit of a BE2c or a Farman, mechanics would turn over both seats to ensure that no dangerous creatures were lying in wait. The engines offered numerous nooks and crannies for the curious, and sometimes dangerous, crawling and slithering invaders.

Vincent Toulmin arrived in East Africa a full year after Hathaway. Discharged from the NZEF early in 1917, he had flying training in Egypt before shipping out for East Africa in June to establish advanced airfields in the fluid East Africa theatre. The work was demanding and could only be completed with local assistance. It could take a month to clear the bush, 'stomp' the airfield flat and erect the hangar.[9] It was here, away from the relative safety of Mbuyuni, that the New Zealanders encountered even larger threats.

In the area dubbed 'Daniel's Den' on account of the large numbers of lions, the roaring allowed little sleep. One night a lion passed between two beds not 10 ft apart; the terrified men built up the fire and 'spent the remainder of the night huddling in their blankets before the fire'.[10] Once, a machine was forced to land in Daniel's Den on account of poor light. The airman sank low in the cockpit as a dozen of the big cats languidly circled the machine and its petrified occupant throughout the night. He was rescued by mechanics the next day. On another occasion a pilot with engine trouble was forced to land in a swamp. After four days of aimless wandering in the jungle without food, he was discovered, physically and psychologically exhausted. He was naked except for his helmet, a vest and boots: baboons had stolen his pants, shirt and revolver when he was bathing.[11] He also barely escaped the jaws of a crocodile and spent one sleepless night up a tree, trapped by a prowling leopard below.[12]

Not that the African wildlife had it all its own way: Toulmin was a keen hunter and, when he was not turning a rough piece of African countryside into an airfield, he could be found in the bush enjoying his surroundings and stalking game. In one of his typically cursory diary entries he recalled his day's activities: 'Left Songea, lunch at Ingaha, shot baboon, arrived Leluhi, had swim in Lake Nyasa [Lake Malawi].'[13] It was an idyllic spot: the lake is one of the Rift Valley's great waterways, filled with brightly coloured fish swimming in remarkably clear water. It was an all too brief respite from high temperatures and unrelenting humidity.

At the airfields, Hathaway found the humidity played havoc with the squadron's bombs. Airmen reported the failure of numerous bombs to explode; the fuses were perishing in the conditions. By early 1917, of the 1600 bombs in the munitions dump, only a couple of hundred were unaffected.[14] One of Hathaway's mechanic colleagues found an ingenious chemical solution and began returning the faulty bombs to service. One month later, in his workman's hut surrounded by explosives, there was a sudden blast. The mechanic was killed.

Few of Hathaway and Toulmin's 26 Squadron colleagues were lost in operations, but many succumbed to the various pestilences pervasive in sub-Saharan Africa.[15] 'Tsetse flies, mosquitoes, maggot flies, malaria, dysentery, and few other diseases' were just as big a threat as machine guns, wrote Englishman Leo Walmsley.[16] Tsetse flies flocked to livestock and humans. Drill jackets and shorts were no impediment to their sharp proboscis that stabbed painfully into human flesh.[17] The nasty wound could quickly lead to septicaemia. In 1917, a crew crash-landed in the bush and was lost for three days with dwindling water and food. They were mercilessly attacked by swarms of tsetse flies. When they were finally found, their 'face and arms were swollen beyond recognition'.[18]

As in Mesopotamia, the great plague was malaria. Men succumbed in droves, often without access to medicine when operating from a forward base: 'For aspirin — an essential remedy in the treatment of the malaria — we had to depend on private stocks, which were soon exhausted, and a man with a temperature of 105 degrees had to go without this merciful drug and suffer untold agonies.'[19] The previous month, the heavy rains had arrived and illness cut a swathe through 26 Squadron. The temperature was not particularly high, but the humidity was debilitating. On one occasion, 75 per cent of the mechanics were struck down with malaria.[20] Those mechanics left standing had to work 12 hours continuously in order to have at least some of the machines airworthy. At one point the squadron considered itself fortunate to have two machines ready for operations.

In the first 12 months the unit had been in East Africa, it had had a total strength of 346 NCOs and other men. But in April only 125 were at effective strength; of the rest, eight had died, 33 were hospitalised and the remaining 180 were 'discharged for medical reasons or invalided to South Africa'.[21] Hathaway was among this latter cohort. He was struck down with malaria at least twice in 1916, and by the second half of the following year he was unable to continue his duties. He was transferred south, and left Africa via Cape Town for New Zealand.[22] 'A contingent of sick and wounded soldiers arrived in Auckland yesterday,' reported the *New Zealand Herald* on 25 September 1917. 'The invalided draft included three officers, two nursing sisters, and 240 other ranks, also one air mechanic.'[23] The paper made mention of Hathaway's 18 months of service in East Africa, but now he had 'received his discharge'. Six months into his posting, Toulmin was seeking medical assistance: 'Got tonic from Doctor. Went for a walk in bazaar . . . bought [walking] stick.'[24] The climate, topography and pestilence had taken its toll on the 33-year-old; he was posted to Egypt in the New Year.

The struggle in East Africa spluttered on without the two New Zealanders until the end of the war. Rampant disease was the leading cause of military casualties on both sides, while conscripted worker and civilian losses were even higher, thanks to drought and war-related food shortages.

On 1 July 1916, after seven days of preparatory artillery bombardment at the Somme, during which over a million shells were thrown at the Germans, the British infantry left their trenches and advanced on the German defensive line. The results were horrific. Far from incapacitating the German defenders, the British artillery had forewarned the Germans of the impending attack and facilitated the reinforcement of the Somme sector. Moreover, during the barrage the German troops had simply lain in wait, safely under cover, emerging largely unscathed and ready to face the onslaught. It was a bloodbath: the opening day saw nearly 60,000 British casualties. It was the beginning of one of the costliest battles in the history of warfare.

In the air, the RFC's leader, Hugh Trenchard, gave his air units six tasks in order of priority: aerial reconnaissance, aerial photography, observation and direction of artillery, tactical bombing, contact patrols, and offensive sorties against German intruders. With 167 machines compared to the Germans' 129 aircraft, the British had superior numbers. Even more telling, they had twice as many fighters. The recently arrived FB2b and Nieuport 16s were an advance on the German machines available at the time. As a consequence, early losses were lighter than might have been anticipated. Nonetheless, Trenchard insistenced on a continuous air offensive. The commander of the RFC believed that superiority in the air was best achieved by taking the battle to the Germans rather than allowing them to dictate the conduct of the air war; a lesson he had learnt from French offensive air operations at Verdun. As a result, the Somme produced a steady stream of casualties.[25]

While Dennistoun was fighting for his life in hospital, three other New Zealanders were killed in operations. They included another observer, John Reid, who was 22 and, like Dennistoun, had only just arrived at his unit, 22 Squadron. The 15 July attack on enemy infantry in the vicinity of Hébuterne, southwest of Arras, attracted groundfire and Reid was struck.[26] Soon after, the engine was knocked out and the pilot made a forced landing, fortunately behind British lines. The crippled machine attracted artillery fire and was destroyed. The pilot survived, but Reid died the following day — the same day Harold Butterworth was killed.

In the week before Butterworth's death the squadron had seen heavy action, flying three artillery patrols and a night bombing raid.[27] On 16 July, just after midnight, Butterworth took off on another night-time bombing raid. He was returning from the operation an hour later when his propeller sustained damage from an enemy machine at 1000 ft. Butterworth valiantly attempted to glide to the Allied side of the lines but fell short by 50 yards.[28] The FE2b hit the rear of the forward-most German trench. The heavy jolt bounced the machine over the entrenched Germans and into the barbed wire of no-man's land. His observer, Captain John McEwen, was violently thrown from the machine. In the dark, both sides opened fire on the wrecked FE2b and its crewmen. Butterworth was shot as the machine crashed. He scrambled with McEwen into an enemy trench.[29] Three days later, uncertain of his aircrew's fate, the squadron commander sent a letter to Butterworth's father in New Zealand.

> I am awfully sorry to break the news to you that your son is a prisoner, but, I think, probably all right. He was one of our most gallant pilots, and has the heart of a lion — the loss to the squadron is enormous. He is full of initiation and enterprise and does not know what fear is. You can realise how we value him. The work he has done has been continuously good ever since he joined me, and I hoped he would shortly be going home for a rest as Flight Commander.[30]

McEwen was captured, but Butterworth's father would never see his son again: Harold had died from his wounds almost immediately after he gained the trench. The Germans dropped a message over Allied lines informing them of the New Zealander's fate. He was already buried and at rest by the time his father received the squadron commander's letter of false hope.

While Herbert Russell made a long and painful recovery from his burns as a POW in Germany, his two siblings were serving with the RFC. His older brother Francis was retraining as a pilot after sustaining injuries with 7 Squadron earlier in the year as an observer, and his younger brother Lawrence had arrived at the front in late July and had just landed in the same squadron as a pilot. Lawrence was 18 years old but looked barely 13 — a schoolboy in a man's uniform. In preparation for the Battle of the Somme the squadron had been moved to Warloy, France.[31] Most of its duties revolved around reconnaissance and artillery cooperation.

'I have now been over Hun-land four times,' Lawrence wrote in August, 'each time on an "artillery shoot."'[31A] Many pilots found artillery work a dangerous grind, but to Lawrence it was grimly satisfying. In the second week he strapped himself in for a 'shoot', laid out his map on his knees and instructed the mechanic to swing the propeller. Once they were in the air he signalled the observer to crank up the wireless and sent a test message to the airfield's wireless station. He looked down and saw the men on the ground laying out an answering letter. The wireless was working. He headed for the lines, only five miles distant. Soon they were over the trenches, then no-man's land. The ground was lost in shell holes and British guns were flashing behind him.

As one of Lawrence's fellow former Wanganui Collegiate School pupils John Canning discovered, Allied guns were not without risk to RFC airmen. The massive displacement of air when the shells were shot was unfriendly to the light wood-and-fabric aircraft of the day. Canning was flying too close to a British battery when its 15-inch guns went off. 'My machine was bodily lifted through the air for nearly 100 feet and then bumped me almost over,' said Canning; 'I always keep well away from them now.' [31B]

Well clear of the British artillery, Lawrence and his observer settled into their task. They were cruising between the Allied and German trenches at 5000 ft looking for flashes from the enemy artillery. Half an hour into the operation they spotted a 'big fellow firing pretty often'. The gun was noted on their map and they flew back to a 12-inch howitzer. The observer called up the artillerymen wirelessly with the exact position of the gun. Lawrence waited two minutes for the howitzer to load, then returned to observe the results. 'We flew steadily on with our eyes fixed on the target, a mere black mark on the ground, and then suddenly a jet of earth and smoke rose slowly into the air with an enormous flash 25 yards to the right.' Lawrence returned and the observer relayed the correction. They resumed their patrol over no-man's land to see the result. It took three attempts, but the last was a direct hit: 'No more flashes from that spot!' Their next target was even more spectacular; they hit a gun and its ammunition. Lawrence marvelled at the terrific violence and enormous flames stretching skyward. 'Earth was flying everywhere at once. I bounded about in my seat and sang with delight, making the machine swerve and rock, and doing terrific turns right over on one wing.' He was only too happy to knock out German guns that had been pasting Allied infantrymen, including his own countrymen. 'You can't think how delightful it is to do this when you see some of their big shells landing right in our trenches.'[31C]

On 26 August Lawrence and his observer took off for artillery observation over Contalmaison, one of the Somme Offensive's objectives. Their greatest threat was the ever-present anti-aircraft fire. Clive Collett gave a vivid description of the threat of 'Archie' in 1916:

> I have had the usual close shaves but have to take them as they come for it is all in a day's work. The German anti-aircraft guns are very much better than ours as their gunners are more methodical and get more practice, for it is the usual thing for us to go over the lines, they seldom venture over ours and then only at such a height that they are almost out of range. They usually start shelling you by firing a series with fuses set for different altitudes

Lawrence Russell
was on an artillery
observation sortie when
his plane was hit by
anti-aircraft fire. His
observer was killed,
and Russell died of his
wounds a week later. In
early 1917 his brother
Francis was killed when
his machine was struck
by flak and crashed.

FRIGHTFULNESS IN RUINS.

Ruins of the Zeppelin brought down near Enfield on Sept. 3rd, 1916.

Skeleton of one of the Zeppelins brought down in Essex on Sept. 24th, 1916.

Wreckage of one of the Zeppelins brought down in Essex on Sept. 24th, 1916.

The wrecked Zeppelin L15, brought down at the mouth of the Thames on March 31st, 1916.

Where the Zeppelins have been brought down
(N.B.—This map does not include losses subsequent to Sept. 3rd, 1916).

Zeppelin L20, wrecked off the coast of Norway on May 3rd, 1916.

Wreckage of the Zeppelin brought down at Salonica on May 5th, 1916.

Wreckage of the Zeppelin brought down at Salonica on May 5th, 1916.

THE ALLIES' TOLL OF GERMANY'S ZEPPELIN FLEET.

Germany's war on children—funeral leaving the church.

After a German air-raid: funeral of some of the victims.

British propaganda attempted to reassure citizens that the Zeppelins were not winning the battle. The 'bird's eye' map showed where Zeppelins had been brought down by September 1916.

thus picking up the range, then get them hot and strong, the machine sometimes being jumped about like a sheet of paper. They use both shrapnel and high explosives and after a strenuous time we nearly always find some holes through the wings, etc. Just lately when out on patrol I had a high explosive burst very close underneath my machine, we got three big rents in our wings and had a control cable cut clean through, we were nearly 11,000 feet up at the time and partially lost control so that we started falling, however, I managed to check and correct the machine and though it was mightily unpleasant flying we succeeded in finishing our patrol in proper order.[32]

Lawrence was not so lucky; his BE2d was hit by flak at 11 a.m. A shell exploded beneath them: the observer was killed and the pilot's legs were shredded. Unlike his brother, Lawrence was able to crash the machine on the Allied side of the battlefield, but he did not survive his wounds and died seven days later. He was New Zealand's youngest airman to die in operations.

It might have been thought that the Russell family had already paid its dues to the Great War. As the parents fretted over the health of Herbert and grieved over the loss of Lawrence, the oldest Russell brother was returning to active duty as a pilot. Four months after the death of Lawrence, Francis was flying out of Bertangles, piloting a single-seater BE12 biplane. He was on early afternoon defensive patrol, about 16 miles south of Arras, when the BE12 was hit by flak and plummeted to the ground. In the space of six months the Russell family had lost a nephew and two sons to the war. Herbert was sent to Switzerland in late 1917 as part of an exchange of severely wounded prisoners.

As the Battle of the Somme opened, the first two New Zealand-trained airmen arrived on the scene. Keith Caldwell and Geoffrey Callender were posted to their frontline squadrons in August, but the Kohimarama boys were given no time to acquaint themselves with the battlefield. Caldwell joined 8 Squadron, and with only three days of test flights he was thrown in at the deep end on bombing runs and artillery patrols. With 22 operational sorties over 28 days alongside practice flights, August was hectic. Flying a BE2, Caldwell quickly overhauled his pre-combat flying hours; in his first month of operations alone he accumulated 47 additional hours.[33] Across his four months with the squadron he engaged the enemy on at least seven occasions. His sole victory was achieved on 18 September, flying in the region of Grévillers–Bucquoy at 4500 ft on artillery work.[34] He had encountered two enemy aircraft and the observer fired three drums. In spite of the machine gun jamming on four occasions, they hit one of the Rolands. The German went down trailing smoke, while the other ran for home.[35] It was not a particularly spectacular result considering the numerous contacts Caldwell had had with the enemy, but he had survived his first months unscathed. This period of 'finding his feet' would set him up to become one of New Zealand's highest-scoring pilots of the Great War.

The exploits of the New Zealand students were not lost on the founders of the Auckland flying school. A reporter asked Vivian Walsh about his fledglings, now fighting on the other side of the world. Walsh proudly identified Callender, who had been 'decorated for conspicuous bravery'. He recounted how, on 20 October 1916, Callender had won his Italian Silver Medal of Military Valour: 'He was flying over the German lines in France, at a height of several thousand feet, and whilst engaged in combat he was shot, one bullet passing through his cheek and another through his arm.'[36] Callender's FE2d engine was knocked out, and as he glided down he was met by another enemy machine. His observer 'put half a drum into him at about 200 yards'. The hostile machine was last seen in a steep dive. Callender's wounds were not life-threatening, and he later re-entered the war as an instructor.

As the battle raged over the trenches, Donald Harkness joined Alfred de Bathe Brandon in anti-Zeppelin work — not in defensive operations over England but in offensive attacks against the airships and their sheds in Belgium. In the early hours of 1 April 1916 Harkness was with the RNAS and witnessed the backwash of the Zeppelin raid in which Brandon had attacked L15. As the remaining airships headed back to Belgium and their hangars, one had dropped bombs on Dunkirk, where Harkness's squadron was based, killing two civilians and wounding four others. 'Everyone has evinced sighs of intense satisfaction on learning of the Zep having been brought down on the Kentish Coast,' wrote Harkness in reference to the efforts of London's anti-aircraft gunners and the RFC's Brandon. The initial defensive operations against the airships were undertaken by the RNAS in England but, as Brandon's success revealed, the RFC was now taking a serious role in aerial defence. The two air arms soon tussled with one another to impede and, if possible, destroy the airship menace.

Harkness was keen to strike a blow against the 'baby killers'. Earlier in his career, while under instruction in England, he had witnessed the great 8–9 September 1915 raid on London. The assault resulted in 120 casualties, including 26 deaths.[37] It crystallised his ambition to defend England from the air. On that day only one of the four Zeppelins made it to the city on the Thames, but its bombs were well placed. Under the command of Kapitänleutnant Heinrich Mathy, the most celebrated German airship commander, L13 was carrying a full load that included the first 660-lb bomb to be dropped over England. Near 10.30 p.m. the deadly cargo was released. Harkness was about a mile and a half from their landfall.

> There came a terrific crash, like a resounding peal of thunder, which shook the house as if it had been an earthquake. Then another crash a few seconds later, followed by a third, a fourth and several more. Someone in the street called out 'a Zeppelin' and an indescribable hubbub ensued: the women ran down to the basement and started to weep; people were calling out and bells were going; motor cars were flying up and down; horns, whistles, explosions in rapid succession.[38]

Harkness took to his heels to find the source of the pandemonium. 'On looking up I saw a sight which I shall never forget,' he recorded in his diary. 'The night was clear and starlit, and there, far up amongst the stars, was a Zeppelin, looking like a tiny silver pencil under the blinding glare of London's searchlights.' The bombs fell in a line from Euston to Liverpool Street, destroying buildings and rattling the windows in a great series of blasts that spread out like ripples on a vast city-wide pond, shaking the city's foundations. 'We would hear first the crash

Having witnessed the effects of Zeppelin raids on London first hand, Donald Harkness, shown here in front of a Sopwith 1½ Strutter, was keen to hit back at the great airships. He was awarded the Distinguished Service Cross for his attack on Zeppelin sheds in Belgium in 1916.

from the gun, then the piercing scream of the shell as it tore upwards on its mission of revenge, and a few seconds later see a tiny flash as it exploded, sometimes right below the Zep.' In the aftermath, the New Zealander spied a glow behind the rooftops in the distance, and joined the crowds heading in its direction. He found 'an indescribable scene of destruction'.

> The grunting horns of the motor ambulances as they sped along the road carrying away the injured; the jangling of the bells on the fire engines as they cut their way through the crowds; the rattling of broken glass on the streets where shop front windows had been torn out by the force of the concussion and hurled across the road; the shouts and cries of people who were collecting their families or their property from burning buildings, the flames leaping out of the windows and licking the walls of the houses opposite; — they all formed details of a picture which would be hard to forget. . . . Though it was now past twelve, thousands of people had congregated; people from all classes and all places; gentlemen in dress suits and silk hats mixing with beggars in rags; poor costers [fruit-cart sellers], paper sellers and street urchins; all moved to a common sympathy with sufferers and vowing vengeance on the devils in the sky.[39]

Eleven months later Harkness would be a deliverer of that vengeance. In the late summer of 1916, he was posted to a specialist bombing force at Coudekerque in France's northernmost Nord-Pas-de-Calais region. Coudekerque lay within sight of Dover and Belgium. The unit — named 5 (Naval) Squadron in December — was home to 18 machines. Strategic bombing was in its infancy, and this was reflected in the poor machines at the crew's disposal: Caudron G4s, Breguet Bre.4s and Sopwith 1½ Strutters.[40] None was particularly powerful, and they carried very limited payloads. Harkness's aircraft of choice was the Sopwith, the light bomber version that eliminated the observer's seat and allowed more fuel and 12 bombs to be carried. Playful and outgoing, Harkness had painted a kiwi on the Sopwith's fabric flanks. As his diaries and letters demonstrate, he possessed a great sense of humour and a keen eye for a good story. When he took off on 9 August 1916, he was about to compose a significant chapter in New Zealand military aviation history.

The mission was a bombing raid on the airship sheds of Brussels, some 80 miles distant. The hangars were huge, some of the largest free-standing buildings in Europe. If Harkness were lucky he would catch a Zeppelin tucked in bed, and destroy the shed and its sleeper. If not, the sheds alone were an extremely valuable target. He was one of two airmen selected for the task; his wingman was an Indian-born Englishman, Ralph Collet. The sortie began just before daybreak.

As light glowed on the eastern horizon, the two machines flew only yards apart out over the North Sea, striking northeast, parallel with the Belgian coast. Harkness hoped to catch the Germans still with sleep in their eyes. The aircraft steadily gained altitude to 14,000 ft. They tipped their wings and clipped the southern tip of the Netherlands as they headed southeast into Belgium. Zeebrugge, Bruges and Ghent dropped away to their right. 'The sun rose . . . it gave me my first glimpse of Antwerp, lying amongst the bright haze far away to the east.'[41] On a slow descent, the two Sopwiths followed the silvery thread of the Scheldt River inland until Brussels was in sight. The sheds were soon in view, forming a triangle around the small town of Evere on the Belgium capital's northeastern fringes. They looked huge even from 10,000 ft, and Harkness eyed them eagerly.

His reverie was broken by the sight of 'anti-aircraft shells bursting very low down and just above around the shed'. Collet was no longer at his side; he was diving into flashes of gunfire and cross-hatching grey smoke above the hangar. The Englishman's bombs hit the target and the eastward end of the roof peeled back, a long column of black smoke snaking heavenward. Soon the other end was belching smoke; the belly of the vast cavern was ablaze. Harkness dived. At 4000 ft he rushed headlong into the fully awake and angry anti-aircraft fire.

> [F]lying diagonally across the shed I released eight of my twelve bombs in quick succession, and putting on the engine again circled round once or twice over the flying ground waiting for the result. The shells were getting thick and close . . . At last I saw something happen on the ground: a short line of explosions passed slantwise directly over the center of the shed. I saw bombs burst just on each side of the shed, and almost at once the quantity of smoke coming from the ends of the shed increased three or four times.[42]

The building was doomed. He swung the biplane across the town to the next shed at Berchem-Sainte-Agathe; it too stood out against the tiny houses and miniature trees.

It was now a perfect morning and the town was as pretty as could be with its great central cathedral and adjacent Palais de Justice towering over the 'surrounding buildings like giants among pigmies; and the whole, intermingled with beautiful parks and winding paths and bathed in the early morning sunlight, was not a sight to be forgotten' — not the least for the backdrop of billowing grey-black smoke and the chasing anti-aircraft shells exploding at Harkness's heels, a bucolic and apocalyptic vista. Every gun was now trained on him, but the Germans were off their game and shooting was wide of the mark.

The next airship shed was more fortunate: the New Zealander's bombs fell across the shed but were too widely spread to hit it. Harkness glanced towards Evere, the Zeppelin shed wreathed in smoke. He climbed away to the coast and the safety of 18,000 ft; the 'old brown Sopwith, number 9420, with the kiwi on either side, did her run well, and arrived back without a hitch at Coudekerque after a flight of 3¼ hours'.

The success of the two airmen was celebrated across the RNAS and was widely covered by the newpapers. A bubbly Harkness wrote home to his mother, noting that a recent RFC attempt, with considerably more aircraft, had achieved nothing, missing with all their bombs. Harkness and Collet's effort was in marked contrast. 'Everyone here is very tickled at the idea of two unprotected machines having enough "cheek" to get off like that and "do in" a Zep shed — if not a Zep as well.' Both buildings were in fact empty, but the damage was considerable. The massive destroyed shed and its equipment was worth approximately £100,000 — of greater monetary value than the airship it had housed. It was a considerable achievement for two lone airmen and a few bombs.

A few days later in the officers' mess a memorandum from the admiralty was waved in Harkness's direction. It declared that His Majesty the King was pleased to confer upon 'Flight Sub-Lieutenant Donald Harkness and Flight Sub-Lieutenant Ralph Collet the Distinguished Service Cross in connection with their recent operations on the Zeppelin sheds at Evere and Berchem-Saint-Agathe'. Harkness bought the obligatory drinks for everyone and made an impromptu speech. To his mother he simply wrote, 'I am sure there are many others who have done more and got nothing for it, but I am glad that I have helped to advertise No. 5 Wing.'[43] However, Harkness's war was about to take an unexpected turn during another bombing raid over German-occupied Belgium.

On 17 September 1916, Harkness led a sortie of 11 Sopwiths — nine bombers and two escorts. It was his first stint commanding a flight. The airfield of Saint-Denis, Westrem, a couple of miles south of Ghent, was their target. After an uneventful inbound flight he spiralled down from 14,000 ft above the target and turned the nose of the Sopwith to cross the line of buildings, dropping the bombs in a neat row. Anti-aircraft fire came in thick and fast, like 'fireballs . . . whirling up to me at a terrific pace'. He was surrounded by columns of fire and turbulence punching past him. He pulled back on the joystick and climbed out and away from the forest of death. In clear air Harkness peered over the side, watching his men dropping their 'pills', but the haze obscured the target and he could not tell whether anything had been hit.

With the mission completed, he wheeled towards Zeebrugge and the coast. A persistent squeak coming from the engine began to gnaw at his confidence; something was wrong. He lost power, revs fell, the engine stopped. Harkness managed to restart the aeroplane by diving, only to have it falter again. The machine spluttered towards the Dutch island of Zeeland. Gunfire found it, and a shell exploded below the Sopwith. 'The machine rocked and pitched frightfully and seemed . . . on the point of collapse,' wrote Harkness. Fragments ripped the fabric. One tore through the cockpit floor; the small piece of shrapnel cut through his trousers, slightly injuring his legs. Crossing the coast he passed over a dyke, seeking a secluded spot to land and destroy his aircraft. He had less control than he hoped, and as the Sopwith lost flying speed he 'pancaked into a mass of about twenty telegraph wires and a fence'. It broke his fall, and he and the aircraft were suspended in a wire hammock, a few fenceposts puncturing the wings. Zeeland had ensnared the New Zealander: Harkness was interned in the Netherlands for the remainder of the war.

A week later, Brandon picked up the challenge of the Zeppelins from Harkness. Just before midnight on 23 September 1916, he was ordered up from Hainault. Forty minutes later he saw a Zeppelin caught in searchlights and he turned the nose of his BE2c for the German airship. His target was *L33*, one of 12 Zeppelins attacking Britain that night. The older airships were given the task of attacking the Midlands, but four recent additions to the German fleet — the so-called super Zeppelins — were destined for London. At 644 ft in length and 78 ft in diameter, and with a volume of nearly two million cubic feet, these R-class Zeppelins were considerably bigger than the Zeppelin Brandon had helped bring down six months earlier.

Significantly, their defensive armaments had been boosted to 10 machine guns. When the Zeppelin escaped the searchlight he pushed on, estimating its course and hoping for the best. He had guessed correctly: when it was recaptured in the defensive lights Brandon reached down to gather a drum of ammunition.

Brandon's weaponry had also been upgraded. In addition to Rankin darts, his BE2c of 39 (Home Defence) Squadron had a machine gun with explosive bullets and Le Prieur rockets. Explosive bullets had proven their worth only three weeks earlier when he was flying with a fellow squadron member, Leefe Robinson. The Englishman knocked out an airship firing a drum of mixed explosive bullets, half of which were New Zealand Pomeroy-designed and manufactured. Robinson saw a red glow blossom inside the belly of the airship, setting it ablaze.[44]

He received a Victoria Cross as the first pilot to destroy an airship over Britain. The now proven explosive bullet was distributed to all the defensive squadrons. Rockets had been useful against observation balloons, and it was hoped they would also be effective against the large airships.

Brandon was no longer the 'greenhorn' of only a few months earlier; he was now one of Britain's most experienced night-fighting pilots. His famous baptism of fire with *L15* had been followed by a Zeppelin chase in April and a string of sorties over the summer of 1916. By September he was closing in on 80 hours' flying time.[45] The BE2c machine gun was positioned at an upward angle that allowed the pilot to fly under the airship and rake its belly with bullets.[46] Brandon's drums were loaded with explosive bullets including Pomeroys.[47]

Fully armed, Brandon closed in on *L33*. After bombing London, the airship had been holed by a direct anti-aircraft hit and was losing vast amounts of gas. The senior officer, Kapitänleutnant Alois Böcker, had ordered the gondola machine guns overboard as he struggled to maintain altitude.[48] Brandon planned to open up with two drums at long range and then deliver the killing blow with another couple of drums at close range. Immediately his scheme went awry: the fuel pump failed and he had difficulty in cocking the gun as he had to work the hand pump.[49] Then, as he pulled the machine gun up to shoot, 'it jerked out of the mounting and as it fell I dragged it across the nacelle'.[50] Brandon wrestled with the loaded Lewis, contemplating abandoning it to the British countryside 11,500 ft below. He decided to give it another try. He stood up. The chill midnight air buffeted him as he reattached the gun to its mount; but by the time he had the Lewis in place, sat down and strapped himself in, he had overshot the Zeppelin.

> I did an about turn and there was the Z coming towards me. I raised the gun to shoot but we passed each other too quickly . . . Again I did an about turn and came up from behind. This time I fired a whole drum, most of it into the vulnerable stern and the rest all along as I passed. It was impossible to miss it fore and aft and its breadth made it an easy target sideways. I remember being astonished at my poor shooting. The tracers were going from side to side, but she must have been hit by all or nearly all shots except those that burnt out before they reached it. I turned, put on a new drum and again came up from the stern. This time after about 10 shots the gun jammed. Owing to the danger of fire from incendiary bullets we had been instructed not to try and correct a jam, but I gave one jerk on the cocking handle but no result.[51]

Brandon prepared to fire the rockets, which were attached to the struts on either side of the fuselage, but the moment was lost. He had been fortunate to locate *L33* on at least five occasions during the attack, but now his luck ran out: the Zeppelin was nowhere to be seen. 'Either it was invisible against the grey band between the lower stars and the earth or it had turned,' he reasoned. After recovering from engine failure he continued to patrol until he saw another Zeppelin, *L32*. He made for it, and five minutes later saw it come under a 'stream of tracer bullets'. Another squadron pilot was hosing the machine with explosive ammunition. It caught fire 2500 ft above him. He turned the BE2c to get out of the way of the falling Zeppelin. Nearly three hours after taking off, Brandon landed at Hainault.

Böcker was unable to keep *L33* in the air, and attempted a forced landing at Little Wigborough, Essex. The final descent was uncontrolled and fast. During their subsequent interrogation the crew stated that 'immediately before striking the ground' an explosion lit a fire aft. The crew scrambled free, barely escaping with their lives as the fire billowed along the ship. Other reports suggested the crew had set the dying vessel alight.[52] Either way, the burnt-out hulk was a rich source of intelligence on the latest Zeppelin design.[53]

Brandon had once again been instrumental in bringing down a Zeppelin. He was wretchedly unfortunate not to have delivered the coup de grâce. *L33* was found to have a collection of bullet holes through its fuel tanks, and if Brandon's machine gun had not jammed at close range it is hard to see how he could not have destroyed it. As with *L15*, he shared victory with the London anti-aircraft gunners. In October, Brandon visited the king at Buckingham Place and was decorated with a Distinguished Service Order (DSO) for meritorious service under fire.[54] With a Military Cross already to his credit, the DSO made him New Zealand's most highly decorated airman to that point. In the years that followed, he rose steadily through the ranks, ending the war as a major commanding a home defence squadron.

The destruction of the sister vessels *L32* and *L33* was an important turning point in the defence of Britain from the Zeppelin menace. The loss of an airship earlier that month to Leefe Robinson could be written off as a singular event, but the loss of the much bigger and highly regarded 'giant Zeppelins' so soon after was an altogether different matter. The confidence of the raiders was dented, and never fully recovered. As Brandon, his fellow airmen and the anti-aircraft gunners had demonstrated, Britain was no longer defenceless against the 'baby killers'.[55]

Airship *L33* was attacked by Alfred de Bathe Brandon. Thanks to the work of the New Zealander and anti-aircraft gun crews, all that remained of the Zeppelin after it crashed and burnt was the metal skeleton and scorched engines.

While Harkness and Brandon had been battling the Zeppelins, the Somme Offensive raged on. For three months the British RFC held sway over the battlefield, but this slowly yielded to changes on the German side of the lines. To counter British numerical superiority, the German Imperial Air Service began using its machines in force rather than in isolation, and newer models were introduced to the battlefield.

Callender's face wound was one of a series of New Zealand casualties in the last month of the offensive. Within a week of this there were two deaths: Norman Brain and Forrest Parsons. Onehunga-born Brain arrived as a mechanic with 11 Squadron soon after the death of fellow New Zealand pilot Herbert Cooper. Equipped with the FE2b, the unit was heavily involved in reconnaissance, photography work and, less effectively, offensive patrols.[56] In this latter role Brain received fatal wounds. In the early afternoon of 22 October, he was flying east of Gommecourt as an observer-gunner with pilot Arthur Shepherd. They were last seen in combat with an enemy aircraft low over the lines.[57] They failed to return, and were listed as missing. The machine had come down on the German side of the lines. Brain had sustained a serious gunshot injury and died that day. His pilot, also badly wounded in the fracas, subsequently died.

Soon afterwards, Forrest Parsons was engaged in an artillery observation sortie over Mametz Wood–Miraumont. At 34 years of age, he was 10 years older than Brain. As such he was one of New Zealand's older airmen, and had previously served in the Boer War with his father.[58] Formerly employed on a Kaikoura farm, he entered the Great War with 7 Squadron at Warloy, France, in the last week of September. Like Brain's unit, Parsons' squadron was involved in corps support work, with additional bombing raids thrown in as required.[59] On the 26 October sortie, he and his observer were lost, possibly in combat.[60] The two airmen's bodies were never located. Parsons had been killed less than a month after joining the squadron. That short transition between arriving with a frontline unit and dying was to be repeated by others on many occasions to come. Three weeks later, the Somme Offensive was concluded. The last New Zealander to lose his life that year demonstrated that the battlefield and the training airfield were not the only threats. In Napier, George Powell had been a car enthusiast and member of the local motorcycle club. Like so many others, he worked his passage to fly in the war. In the first week of December 1916, as a trainee pilot, Powell was pushing a cycle along Euston Road in London when he was struck from behind by a motorcyclist.[61]

During 1916 the New Zealanders Joe Hammond and Clive Collett had been involved in testing machines and experimental work. In December of the previous year Hammond was transferred from instructional duties to evaluation flying with the Aeronautical Inspection Department. In mid-1916 he was posted to Lincoln. Since Lincolnshire was home to a large number of aircraft designers and manufacturers, the RFC established a couple of testing airfields within sight of the famous Lincoln Cathedral. It was, of course, an ideal fit for the accomplished airman and exposed him to a wonderful collection of machines. His friend Charles Blayney called in to see the New Zealander, and Hammond took him up on a joyride in a new Sopwith.

> We shot up to 3000 feet in three minutes . . . and then made for Lincoln Cathedral with its
> two tall towers on the hill, and coming down to about a thousand above them he 'threw

a couple', to use his own words, meaning that we looped twice. This on top of 'spinning' down gave me quite enough for the time being, and I was quite glad to see him head for the aerodrome and after some close spirals we landed, or again to quote Joe, we 'perched'.[62]

One of Hammond's most challenging test aircraft was the Robey-Peters Gun-Carrier. Only two prototypes were constructed, possibly in part due to Hammond's less than positive evaluations of them. Although the gun-carrier was a single-engine biplane, its resemblance to contemporary machines stopped there. With a wingspan of 52 ft, it was about twice the size of most single-engine aircraft in 1916. Moreover it had two gunner gondolas perched on the upper wing; one gunner would be armed with the innovative recoilless Davis gun against Zeppelins or in anti-submarine work, while the other brandished a standard Lewis machine gun to fend off enemy fighters. The pilot was seated well behind the gunners, just ahead of the tail section — making landing the gun-carrier a challenge. It was a Frankenstein design that met the demands of the RNAS in home defence work, but was unwieldy in flight and plagued with problems.

Although Hammond's solo maiden flight went off without a hitch, his 16 September flight three days later ended badly. On his return path to Lincoln the large V12 engine caught fire. Flames licked at the fabric and soon the wings were ablaze. The overheating engine began to disintegrate, flinging parts over Lincolnshire. Hammond was not going to make the airfield two miles south of the city, and crash-landed on the local lunatic asylum. What was left of the machine was consumed in the flames. The onlookers sought the pilot but he was nowhere to be found; some assumed the machine was his fiery coffin. Hammond had in fact survived the conflagration — as had the substantial brick institution — but he was nowhere to be seen. Conflicting stories arose about his escape. Blayney had his own version:

> Joe climbed . . . down the drain spout of the roof into the asylum, thence out at the back and made his way to town. Meantime the spectators and helpers had arrived and were all saying 'poor old Joe, this is the end of him!' However, they could find no trace of him, till sometime later someone in Lincoln found him in a barber's shop enjoying a comfortable shave and listening to the people waiting their turn to discuss his awful crash.[63]

When the second prototype was wheeled out the following year, Hammond was on hand to put it through its paces. In spite of several improvements, the gun-carrier stalled on takeoff, crash-landed and flipped; Hammond was saved by the large tail section behind the cockpit. The gun-carrier was not put into production.

One hundred and twenty miles southeast of Lincolnshire, Clive Collett was employed in test flights at the RFC's Experimental Station, Orfordness.[64] A massive shingle spit on the Suffolk coast, the isolated and barren Orfordness was for much of the twentieth century synonymous with clandestine defence work, including Cold War-era nuclear tests. During the Great War it was used by the RFC for trialling and evaluating aviation weapons and equipment such as bombs and armaments. The New Zealander arrived in August, having recovered from his operation in April. Stocky and rugged, and with his misshapen nose and facial scars from his accident, Collett looked every bit the test pilot. Promoted to temporary captain, he commanded one of the three flights at the airfield.

Flying was, however, not his sole love interest at Orfordness. While he was occupied in experimental work he wrote numerous romantic letters to a young woman who had stolen his heart in 1916. When Collett met Margaret Cumming she was a 16-year-old dancehall entertainer, working under the stage name Peggy Reid.[65] Collett was 29, and smitten. In spite of the age difference, Peggy seems to have more than held her own in the relationship and 'Jack', as he preferred to be known, was on occasion forced to plead with her not to speak so harshly to him, and begged her to write to him. 'You were not a bit nice that morning I saw you last,' said Jack. 'What made you say those nasty things in the taxi?' Nonetheless, Collett was not about to let a little lovers' tiff get in the way of his strong feelings towards her. In the same letter he informed her of his successful medical and subsequent posting to Orfordness, as well as the terrible weather for flying and his attempts to fill the time by 'playing cards and telling yarns'. More importantly, he ended the letter by wishing very much that he 'could come round in the little car' and take her for 'another joy ride'.[66]

Collett seems to have been constantly waiting for her letters, which Peggy may well have delayed sending to play on his nerves. 'You are a real naughty girl to forget me so soon,' he wrote in an undated letter. 'You must be having an awfully good time at Brighton, or you would find a few minutes to drop me a line.'[67] On another occasion, he remonstrated with her over his treatment at her hands the last time they had been together and the privileged place her kittens had at her London residence. 'I am looking forward to my next trip to town as you have to be extra nice to make up for last time,' he wrote. 'I envy those kittens of yours cuddling up to you in bed, it is not right for cats to have all those good things, besides I am sure they do not half appreciate you, and you know I do.'[68] 'I miss our cuddles ever so much,' he wrote.[69]

Orfordness was, in the words of Collett, 'very tame', and in the evenings he and other officers generally just went for a walk until dark.[70] Unfortunately, because he found his weekends were much busier than his weekdays and the airmen at Orfordness were watchful of the Zeppelins threatening the area, he could not get to London as much as he liked. Collett suggested that he could smuggle Peggy onto the base by disguising her in boy's clothes. 'You would make a fine boy,' he wrote playfully, 'and then you can come down to Orford and look after me' — not a novel idea for the couple, it seems, since Collett appears to have disguised himself at least once on a visit to her in order to avoid censorious eyes.[71]

Collett was in his element in the Orfordness experimental work. His prewar training as an electrical engineer in Wellington at William Cable & Co., his flying expertise and his devil-may-care attitude placed him in high demand. Collett tested bombing sights and flew exotic machines including the Armstrong Whitworth FK10, a novel British quadruplane.[72] The four wings produced lift but impeded performance; only eight of the planes were built, and none saw service. In one major project Collett brought together a war-changing technology and one of the latest aircraft designs: the Constantinesco synchronised gun system and the prototype Bristol Fighter. In August 1916, inventor George Constantinesco patented his hydraulic-driven synchonisation gear, a system superior to existing mechanical methods. The following month the British and Colonial Aeroplane Company's Bristol Fighter prototype took off on its inaugural flight. Collett's task in January 1917 was to fit and test the forward-firing synchronising system. The result was the powerfully armed two-man Bristol Fighter that appeared on the front line in April with 48 Squadron. There the Bristol Fighter was joined by Keith Park, who ably took advantage of Collett's efforts.

Collett's undeniable courage and proclivity for taking risks were exemplified when he carried out an unofficial structural test of a FE2b by looping it. 'It is hardly possible to imagine an aeroplane less suited to looping,' wrote a Collett acolyte, 'but Captain Clive Collett . . . held the view that a great many things could be done in the air if one really tried.'[73] The New Zealander did not want to risk an observer falling out of the machine, so he balanced the aircraft by lashing ballast to the front cockpit. After a slow climb, he pushed the lumbering biplane into an impressive dive. Using all his skill and strength, he pulled it up into something resembling less a loop than a 'circle or even an ellipse'.

The Royal Aircraft Factory machine looped, but only just. In the process the ballast dislodged itself. Collett released his belt and stood up to reseat his wayward 'passenger'; leaving the aircraft to fly itself, he clambered from the rear cockpit to the front and wrestled the ballast into place. He then resumed his seat behind the joystick and looped it again for good measure. Those who witnessed the loop were suitably impressed. As one noted, 'Whether this manouevre was done by other FE pilots I do not know. None of those from the squadron in which I served attempted it or knew of anyone who did.'[74]

Collett's most famous exploit, however, was a series of experimental parachute jumps from RFC aircraft. Parachutes offered the possibility of saving an airman's life over the front; without one, aircrew had no way of escaping a doomed machine in flight. Canadian Captain Robert Ferrie, for example, was caught in a dogfight when his plane began to disintegrate. 'His right wing suddenly folded back, then the other, and the wreck plunged vertically down . . . The others went down after him.' His appalled squadron colleagues could see Ferrie wrestling with the harness and then standing up in the plummeting machine.

> It was horrible to watch him trying to decide whether to jump. He didn't and the machine and he were smashed to nothingness. I can't believe it. Little Ferrie, with his cheerful grin, one of the finest chaps in the squadron. God, imagine his last moments, seeing the ground rushing up at him, knowing he was a dead man, unable to move, unable to do anything but wait for it. A parachute could have saved him, there's no doubt about it.[75]

For many, fire was the other great fear. A wood-framed machine with its engine and fuel tank encased in doped fabric was a potential flying torch. Being burnt alive was the stuff of nightmares. The service revolver that airmen carried was of no use in air-to-air combat and of limited value if a pilot was forced down in enemy territory, but it offered a crude escape from the flames. When a newly arrived pilot asked why they were issued with handguns, Caldwell, a squadron commander by that time, told the greenhorn to use his own 'bloody imagination'.[76] British airmen were familiar with Edward 'Mick' Mannock's thoughts on using the Webley

Wrecks of Allied
machines littered
the Western Front.
Without parachutes,
airmen who found
themselves caught high
above the trenches in
burning machines could
either die a painful
death, jump or shoot
themselves.

sidearm to bring things to a quick end. 'The other fellows all laugh at me for carrying a revolver,' he told a friend. 'They think I'm doing a bit of play-acting in going to shoot a machine down with it, but they're wrong — the reason I bought it was to finish myself as soon as I see the first signs of flames. They'll never burn me.'[77] Those who had seen a man writhing amid the tongues of fire did not doubt the reasonableness of this.

> Suddenly there was a blaze in the sky nearby. I looked. It was [Hamilton] Begbie's S.E. A sudden feeling of sickness, of vomiting, overcame me . . . A Hun was still at him, pouring more bullets into his machine. He was making sure of him, the dirty dog . . . One by one the Huns left the fight . . . I flew towards Begbie's machine, which was floating enveloped in flames. It was a terrible sight. I hope he followed Mannock's advice and blew his brains out . . .[78]

The lack of parachutes seemed inexplicable to many, especially since it was common knowledge that observational balloonists deployed them to avoid being engulfed in flames when their hydrogen-filled perches were under attack. And when, in 1918, German airmen were seen exiting doomed machines by parachute, this added to the ire of Allied airmen.

Parachutes were in use well before the Great War, but almost universally by balloonists, not heavier-than-air aircraft. In the prewar years, New Zealand had its own share of domestic parachute descents in the form of aeronautical exhibitions that were popular worldwide. Visiting troupes of aeronaut performers would amaze audiences with 'triple-treat' descents and parachute races. In September 1910 the *New Zealand Motor & Cycle Journal* chronicled the so-called triple-jump act undertaken by an aeronaut of the American-led Beebe Balloon Company. The exhibition was viewed by at least 4000 Aucklanders at the Dominion cricket ground:

> Up, up went the Balloon, and when it had reached a certain height the spectators were startled by seeing the aeronaut go through a series of acrobatic feats upon the trapeze, and at one time hanging from it by his feet . . . Taking his parachute[s] with him he leapt into space, and fell like a stone for 100 feet or more, when the uppermost parachute streamed out, and, quickly filling with air, spread umbrella-shaped, and arrested the falling man's progress. This was only for a second or two, as the aeronaut cut himself away, and dropped another space, when his second parachute opened to the rush of air, and held the adventurous voyager once more suspended . . . [79]

The balloonist cut this second parachute away before floating down safely over Epsom on his third. In the parachute race, twin parachutists leapt from a balloon and 'raced' to earth.

The technology for jumping from balloons was well understood by the time the Great War arrived, and during the conflict parachutes were issued to Empire airship and balloonist aircrew. However, the parachutes were attached directly to the observation baskets and not carried on the backs of the crew members. When the occupant 'bailed out', a line attaching the balloonist to the parachute would pull the chute out of its container — in other words, a static line jump. The result was generally successful and many balloonists' lives were saved. But these parachutes were not designed for jumping out of fast-moving aeroplanes, and their weight and bulk were difficult to accommodate in military machines. Another solution would be needed.

Englishman Everard Calthrop carried out conceptual and experimental work with parachutes for deployment in aircraft. Principally a railway engineer, Calthrop had taken up parachute development in the prewar era when his good friend Charles Rolls, of the Rolls-Royce motor company, had been killed after losing control of his aircraft. This and a non-fatal aviation accident involving his son convinced Calthrop of the need for a reliable parachute that was suited to aircraft. His invention, marketed as the 'Guardian Angel', was lighter than those used by balloonists and technically more advanced.[81] The silk chute was packed between twin metal discs in a canvas bag affixed to the aircraft's underfuselage.[81] The airman's harness was attached to this by a cord. When the airman jumped free from the aircraft and the potentially entangling tail section, the parachute was pulled free and the airman floated to earth.

It was this device that Clive Collett was going to test. In the days preceding his 'live' jump, he watched a series of airborne dummy loads being cast overboard to approximate his own upcoming effort. On 13 January 1917 the big day arrived, and the New Zealander took the rear seat in a staid and stable BE2c. The pilot, Captain Robin Rowell, eased the aircraft down the runway before climbing to 600 ft. Looking down, the laconic Collett spied the station ambulance and fire tender conspicuously in attendance — vultures gathered in anticipation of a meal. 'Much good they'll be if my 'chute doesn't open, but anyway it pleases the authorities,' Collett yelled to Rowell. On the ground, a camera was tilted and running. It captured Collett awkwardly exiting the cockpit and easing himself out onto the port wing. Exposed to the elements, with the roar of the wind and the V8 engine assaulting his ears, Collett paused, then launched himself headfirst into thin air. He felt the jerk of the line as it snapped tight and the parachute was pulled from the base of the fuselage. Within seconds he had made landfall. The Guardian Angel had worked as advertised, and Collett became the first man to make a parachute descent from a RFC machine. He made a second, equally successful and drama-free jump on 21 January.

In spite of Collett's achievements, the British authorities never really took to the idea of parachutes. Further experimentations and vocal remonstrations from Calthrop were unsuccessful in persuading military aviation boards and committees to adopt the lifesaving parachute that Collett had so ably tested. Calthrop's parachute was too heavy and cumbersome for use in the battlefield of the sky; however, it did offer the possibility of further development, had the authorities been fully persuaded of its necessity. Empire airmen could only watch and ponder in mid-1918 as German pilots escaped certain death to gently float groundwards. Where, they wondered, were *their* silk angels?[82]

One of the few people in England to actually get a parachute was Collett's sweetheart Peggy. He gave her two Guardian Angels; the luxurious creamy-white silk was intended for her wedding dress.[83] When Peggy unfurled them they were sprinkled with sand from the beaches of Orfordness. She was already close to seven months pregnant with their child.

Clive Collett's parachute jumps from a Royal Aircraft Factory BE2c were the first from an RFC machine. In spite of his success, British military authorities never developed the parachute for frontline use in aeroplanes.

CHAPTER TEN
BLOODY APRIL
1917

With the winding down of the Somme and the arrival of winter, the exhausted combatants held back from any major military encroachments over Christmas and New Year. The British offensive had advanced barely five miles, none of the strategic objectives had been secured — all for the cost of over 600,000 British and French casualties. On the other hand, the enemy's 450,000 dead and wounded across Verdun and the Somme sapped the German capacity for offensive operations.

The German high command decided that 1917 would be the year of hunkering down and holding the line. In February they fell back and filled up new defensive trenches — the Hindenburg Line — thereby shortening their front by 30 miles. With some justification the British argued that the German retreat was a result of the casualties inflicted at Verdun and the Somme. Consequently, despite suffering the greater losses, the British would continue their aggressive operations on the ground in 1917, notably offensives at Arras in April–May, Messines in June, Ypres in July–November, and Cambrai in November. Once again the flying services were heavily involved in operations over German lines in preparation for the attacks. The greatest threat to the RFC and RNAS was another swing in the technological war in favour of the German air service.

In concert with the slackening of the ground war, there was a marked decline in aerial operations in the winter of 1916–17. This lull in air fighting hid the true strength of German improvements in tactics and machines. The old Imperial Air Service was reorganised into the German Air Force (Deutsche Luftstreitkräfte), a reordering that hastened a move to specialist formations that had begun during the Somme. German strategic bombing and close air support squadrons appeared and — fatefully for the Allies — the Germans copied the RFC's year-old deployment of specialist fighter squadrons with their own Jagdstaffeln or Jastas. With time, the Germans combined several Jastas into even larger wings (Jagdgeschwaders or JG). The most famous, JG1, under the command of Manfred von Richthofen, known as the 'Red Baron', totalled no fewer than four Jastas. Because of its size and its gaudily painted machines it was dubbed the 'Flying Circus'.

Over the winter the Germans replaced their older assorted fighters with the Albatros D-series machines. The pick of the bunch was the Albatros DIII, a compact single-seater biplane with a plywood-skinned fuselage. Its propeller nose-cone flared gracefully into the streamlined body of the machine and ended with an elliptical tail section. The 170-hp Mercedes engine and the wing configuration gave the fighter a top speed of 108 mph. It was manouevrable and had a rapid rate of climb. Earlier German fighters like the Eindecker had been armed with a single machine gun, but the Albatros-series aircraft were furnished with twin forward-firing weapons. In the hands of an average German pilot the DIII was a formidable adversary; handled by airmen like Richthofen, Ernst Udet and Kurt Wolff it was lethal. Supporting the Albatros were a variety of older machines including the Halberstadt Scout, a fighter with a good air fighting reputation among Allied airmen who faced it, but which was slowly being superseded by the Albatros.[1]

Unfortunately for the New Zealanders, older machines continued to dominate the Empire's flying services' inventories. Incredibly, older 'Fokker fodder' aircraft were still flying in some frontline squadrons, including the weak BE2c. The FE2b, DH2, Sopwith 1½ Strutter and early Nieuport Scouts that had contained the Fokker Scourge six months earlier were now quickly slipping into obsolescence. New and more powerful machines that men such as Hammond and Collett were evaluating would not filter into operational squadrons until mid-1917.

Compounding this technological mismatch was Trenchard's insistence on maintaining an offensive stance against the Germans. In the wake of the successes of the Somme, the commander of the RFC published his 'Future Policy in the Air':

> From accounts of prisoners [captured during the Somme] we gather that the enemy's aeroplanes have received orders not to cross the lines over the French or British front unless the day is cloudy and a surprise attack can be made, presumably in order to avoid unnecessary casualties. On the other hand, British aviation has been guided by a policy of relentless and incessant offensive. Our machines have continually attacked the enemy on his side of the line, bombed his aerodromes, besides carrying out attacks on places of importance far behind the lines. It would seem probable that this has had the effect so far on the enemy of compelling him to keep back or to detail portions of his forces in the air for defensive purposes.[2]

Consequently, aggressive offensive operations were the order of the day for British units and remained so until the end of the war.

Manfred von Richthofen, the commander of Jasta 11, his fellow pilots and dog, Moritz. From left: Sebastian Festner, Karl Emil Schäfer, Manfred von Richthofen, Lothar von Richthofen and Kurt Wolff.

Meanwhile, the German Jastas generally operated on their side of the lines in order to conserve their resources and meet the RFC on favourable terms where possible. Trenchard's policy had proven successful over the Somme but in the face of superior enemy machines it would be tested to breaking point.

The one-million-strong Allied operation set for April 1917 — the Nivelle Offensive — was designed to punch through German lines in a 48-hour attack. In the north, the British Expeditionary Force would draw away German troops from the southern French front by securing high ground above the plain of Douai. The Germans would be forced into a defensive posture in Cambrai. This would prepare the way for a French thrust, bisecting Oise and Reims. Once that was breached, the plan called for a reconstitution of manoeuvre warfare, exploiting German numerical inferiority. In this way, it was hoped, they would avoid a repeat of the drawn-out bloodletting of the Somme.

The air services once again provided valuable intelligence in the pre-battle phase. Squadrons dedicated to photographic reconnaissance were in high demand. They were also the main target of the German air units. Early in 1917, General Fritz von Below, German General Staff, issued a memorandum prioritising the air effort: 'The main objective of fighting in the air is to enable our photographic registration and photographic reconnaissance to be carried out, and at the same time prevent that of the enemy. All other tasks . . . must be secondary to this main object.'[3] The Allied desire for vital pre-offensive intelligence on enemy strength, disposition of forces and defensive entrenchments, and the German determination to thwart this, led to considerable losses leading up to the Battle of Arras. Among those drawn into the dangerous observational work were William Shirtcliffe, Roderick Munro and George Masters.[4]

The observer was vital to reconnaissance missions. Pilots were certainly more than mere chauffeurs, but in photographic work the observer was undeniably king. As well as a strong constitution when wielding a defensive machine gun at an incoming hostile enemy spitting bullets, the observer had to have the technical skills to carry out intricate photographic work. In the opinion of the time, the observer should be 'a steady, philosophical and physically tough type. In vertical map making he needed all these qualities, for despite shaking from Archie bursts he had to fly an undeviated course, exposing plates at finely calculated intervals so that they could overlap precisely to form a mosaic.'[5] It was also a distinct advantage if the observer had knowledge of military practice on the battlefield, 'because in reconnaissance of this nature, an untrained person cannot interpret the military significance of what he sees'.[6] The work could be tedious, but many came to enjoy it. 'There was something hugely satisfying,' said an observer, to 'go over the lines and look vertically down on the enemy's most treasured and private property, and know that you had it in your power to bring about his destruction or capture, that was in truth a job worth doing.'[7]

The early cameras were a traditional folding apparatus with delicate bellows; but robust purpose-built units soon followed. The 'A Camera' revolutionised aerial photography. Made largely of wood, it had the plate-changing mechanism at the top and the lens, completely protected in a tapered box enclosure, at the bottom. For the unwary operator the camera was a handful. In the air, leaning over the side of the aircraft, the novice could be caught out by its weight, the tugging of the wind and sudden lurches of the aircraft. 'I nearly lost my balance as I leant over the side with my two gauntleted hands firmly clamped in the weighty affair's straps,' wrote an early practitioner. 'Therefore I made sure my feet were firmly braced before indulging in any similar exercises. I had always been told that you don't bounce if you fall out of an aeroplane at 8000–9000 feet.'[8] Cameras progressively improved. Eventually they were attached to the fuselage by a bracket; and later still they were mounted internally, with a small aperture in the base of the fuselage.

Over the Somme, British airmen had taken over 19,000 photographs from which nearly half a million prints were produced.[9] The incredibily detailed images of trenches and enemy dispositions were pored over at headquarters all along the Western Front. A single photograph, often covering 10 square miles of the battlefield, yielded intelligence that could not be obtained in any other manner. By 1917, the time it took for a photograph to be taken over the front lines and the processed and printed image handed to an intelligence officer could be as little as 40 minutes.[10] As both sides realised the importance of acquiring photographic material for themselves — and denying it to the enemy — the information-gathering operations became increasingly dangerous.

William Shirtcliffe of Wellington was heavily engaged in aerial reconnaissance duties with various observers, although it was for an unusual bombing incident a few months earlier that he had risen to minor fame in 25 Squadron. On 10 November 1916, during the course of an offensive patrol, enemy machines were spotted leaving Douai aerodrome.[11] Shirtcliffe roamed over the machines as they took off and, at 11,000 ft, dropped a 40-lb phosphorus bomb. Freakishly, the bomb exploded immediately over one of the hostile aircraft as it was taking off from the runway, sending it crashing to the ground. Thanks to the mysterious white phosphorus blast, the remainder of the enemy formation thought better of their mission and swung back to land at base.

But it was a 29 January 1917 photographic reconnaissance mission that really demonstrated the challenges and peril that Shirtcliffe's observer Alfred Blenkiron faced. The Birmingham-born airman was perched at the front of the FE2b pusher surrounded by machine-gun drums and photographic paraphernalia. Shirtcliffe wrote home to his family, recalling the grim proceedings.

> I had some photographs to take about seven miles over the lines, and with a protecting escort of five of our machines and two scouts the job looked fairly simple except for the ever-present 'Archie' (anti-aircraft fire), and for about half an hour or so things went well, although 'Archie' was rather too accurate to be at all pleasant. We had just about finished up, and my observer (Blenkiron) was looking rather pleased with himself, when I observed nine Hun machines tackling our escort, who were about a quarter of a mile away and a bit higher. I waved to the observer to snap off the last two plates, intending to join in the fight, but a few seconds later I heard the noise of a machine-gun just behind me, and the smack of bullets hitting the engine behind me. I turned suddenly and found five Huns diving on our machine.[12]

Shirtcliffe expected to hear the barking of the FE2b Lewis gun in reply, but discovered Blenkiron 'curled up in the bottom of the machine': the observer had been struck in the thigh. Then the engine spluttered and stopped; the propeller was motionless. With no one manning the machine gun and the engine dead Shirtcliffe pushed the stick forward and began a steep gliding dive, 'dodging and twisting to put the Huns off their aim'. His goal: the Allied trenches. When the Germans realised that no counterfire was issuing from the FE2b they fell on the defenceless machine, closing to within about 10 ft of its tail; close enough for Shirtcliffe to see the 'whites of their eyes'.

Badly wounded, Blenkiron emerged Lazarus-like from his faint and, in considerable pain, stood up. Sighting the machine gun on the impossibly close enemy, he let him have it, firing at point-blank range over the back of the FE2b. Machine-gun lead tore chunks from the German Halberstadt. It burst into flame. Down it plunged, columns of oily-black smoke signalling its imminent fate. Blenkiron swung the machine gun on the next enemy, and tracer fire arced towards him. Either the German pilot was wounded or his machine was damaged: he retired from the battle and attempted a forced landing, only to overturn his machine. 'The other three decided that attacking us was unhealthy, so off they went,' recounted Shirtcliffe.

The New Zealander coaxed the engine back into life using the reserve fuel tank. A cylinder had been shot through and the radiator was dry, but it worked after a fashion and he 'scraped' home. Blenkiron was immediately taken to the local hospital. The Englishman was subsequently awarded the Military Cross — 'richly deserved', according to a thankful Shirtcliffe — for his remarkable resilience and bravery while wounded and under fire. His actions had saved his own life and Shirtcliffe's.

Despite the attack by a dozen Halberstadts, the 25 Squadron formation had returned with no loss of lives.[13] However, Shirtcliffe's aircraft was nearly wrecked and another machine, flown by the squadron's other New Zealander, Robert Munro, was 'rather knocked about'. 'My poor machine was a sight — nearly wrecked,' said Munro.[14] Their two aeroplanes had taken most of the damage but they had got their photographs.

Shirtcliffe was soon moved on to other duties, but Munro remained and was engaged in heavy work leading up to Arras. Munro's squadron was kept active in bombing sorties, offensive patrols and the all-important photographic reconnaissance.[15] In over 60 operational flights with the squadron Munro and his observers dropped no fewer than 90 bombs and survived numerous brushes with death.[16] All the reconnaissance missions that Munro's squadron undertook were hit by between two and 20 enemy aircraft. Many of the attackers were Halberstadt fighters, but increasingly Albatros DIIIs were being reported. Consequently, the squadron's FE2s progressively needed protection in the form of single-seater fighters.

On 16 March, Munro and his observer undertook a bombing sortie combined with offensive patrol work. The FE2bs were accompanied by six Sopwith Pups from a neighbouring squadron. The operation started badly as Munro watched four Pups retire with engine trouble: two-thirds of the escort had evaporated before crossing the line. On the way in, this did not seem to matter: clear skies, no threatening specks on the horizon. Then, having dropped four bombs on a munitions dump, they were met by 16 hostiles. At 10,000 ft 'a very stiff fight ensued'. The

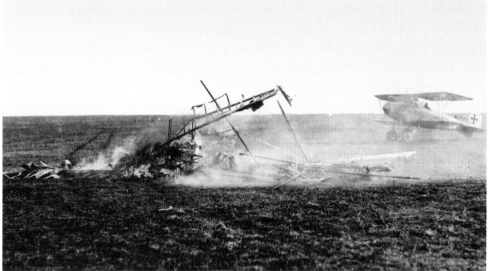

above Over the winter of 1916–1917 the Germans replaced their older fighters with Albatros D-series machines. The pick of the bunch was the Albatros DIII, a single-seater with a top speed of 108 mph. This particular plane was shot down in Palestine and repaired by AFC mechanics.

below A British plane brought down in flames behind German lines. An Albatros DIII is in the background.

FE2bs bore the brunt of the assault. One was caught between two enemy fighters; the engine was punctured by machine-gun fire and the pilot and observer were wounded. Another had its petrol tank shot through; the observer was assumed killed. A third machine's radiator was holed. Munro and his observer drove an aircraft down — believed crashed — but were set upon by the enemy. Machine-gun bullets smashed into the cockpit, riddling the instrumentation. Wings were shredded, the fuel tank perforated. Blood ran down Munro's right leg from two wounds.[17] He nursed the FE2b home; his luck held, barely. Over half the FE2bs were struck but miraculously none was lost. 'Sent home to Blighty on the 31st March,' Munro scrawled in his logbook.

In the weeks prior to the launch of the Arras offensive, two New Zealand-born airmen were thrust into command positions: Alan 'Jack' Scott and Cuthbert Maclean, the nation's first squadron commanders on the Western Front. Both airmen were in their thirties and had strong personalities. They were just two of a dozen or so New Zealand airmen who would eventually command squadrons in the Great War.[18]

The rough-round-the-edges, devil-may-care Scott was given 60 Squadron. Born in Christchurch, he had spent most of his life in England. An Oxford law graduate, he was a barrister in London where he was friends with numerous well-known Englishmen, including Lord Birkenhead, a heavy drinker and the most highly paid barrister in prewar Britain. Scott also had a close friend in Winston Churchill, with whom he went on to fly after the war.[19] 'Always cheerful and imperturbable, and charming in his manner towards everyone,' was Englishman Sholto Douglas's assessment of Scott when he served with him in France. 'At first I felt rather awkward giving orders to this thirty-five-year-old who was obviously a man of the world,' said Douglas.

> I felt that such orders coming from a whipper-snapper of only just twenty-three years of age might be resented; but Jack Scott was to teach me a very good lesson both in balance of maturity and the handling of men. Such was his charm and good humour that neither of us ever knew in our relationship anything approaching a difficult moment, and even though, up to that time, Scott had not done any operational flying at the front, he soon proved that he was a splendid leader of men.[20]

Yet, as Douglas also noted, Scott was a 'ham-fisted' pilot. The former barrister had broken both his legs in a nasty training crash early in the war and was forced to walk with canes for the rest of his life. But Scott was tenacious. When he arrived in Douglas's squadron, he persuaded the commanding officer to provide assistance for him so he could clamber in and out of his machine. His perseverance and good humour in the face of difficulties won him the admiration of his peers. In combat Scott was determined to the point of recklessness; he developed a reputation for returning from missions with his machine 'riddled from end to end'.[21] When he took over 60 Squadron on 10 March 1917 he had lost none of this fighting spirit. He was the only New Zealand squadron commander of the war to accumulate all his victories *after*

Alan Scott was the first New Zealand-born officer to command a squadron on the Western Front. Sixty Squadron flourished under his careful if somewhat eccentric leadership.

Michael Gordon

Charles Barton

James Robert Dennistoun

Roderick (Robert) Munro

Charles Mills

Albert William Gordon

Frederic Sharland

Hubert Solomon

Gordon Pettigrew

receiving command of a squadron.[22] He was one of the few squadron leaders to fly regularly with his subordinates and to engage in combat.

Scott's squadron was hammered during the 1916 Battle of the Somme. It was then rebuilt around Nieuport Scouts and a collection of outstanding pilots, including the Canadian Billy Bishop and New Zealander Keith Caldwell. Caldwell was posted to 60 Squadron in late 1916 and was already a well-established pilot by the time Scott arrived.

Like many airmen, Caldwell had had his share of amusing incidents. On 11 December 1916, an offensive patrol of six was being led by Englishman Eustace Grenfell when they chanced on a lone hostile Albatros two-seater over Dainville.[23] All the pilots had fired bursts at the cornered enemy, and the 'Hun hurriedly landed' on the British side of the lines. Grenfell wanted to claim the prize — one of the new Albatros designs, which offered the potential for valuable intelligence. He attempted a landing, stalled the aircraft and crashed. He emerged from his crippled Nieuport with a broken leg and a bloodied gash across his forehead.[24]

The remainder of the patrol, including Caldwell, landed with a view to assisting, only for three of them to crash, too. None of the pilots was hurt but their aircraft were inoperable without repairs. In the meantime the 'Boche observer' set light to his machine before the 60 Squadron airmen could intervene. The aircraft exploded, seriously injuring the observer and a number of soldiers who had been attracted to the spectacle. Caldwell could only look on with dismay: the smouldering enemy machine and its wounded observer were 'guarded' by a sorry collection of RFC airmen, one bloodied and dragging a broken leg, half a dozen Nieuports, of which three were stranded, and a number of singed infantryman[25] — not the unit's finest hour.

Scott's command, however, kicked off the squadron's most successful period of the Great War.[26] Meanwhile he had lost none of his eccentricities. When a brigadier general from headquarters arrived with his staff for a surprise pre-breakfast inspection of 60 Squadron's Filescamp airfield, located between Arras and Saint-Pol, he watched an early-morning patrol of Nieuports arrive and was startled to see an airman being lifted from a machine and handed two walking canes. It was Scott, hobbling towards him in pyjamas and flowing dressing gown.[27]

As many of his subordinates noted when they entered his office, Scott loved to collect trophies — not, as one might expect, from aircraft he had destroyed but rather the damaged parts of his own maltreated machines. And he would have plenty of opportunities to get knocked about in the air. He kicked off his command with a victory on 31 March on a photographic flight. Scott spotted a lone Albatros; he attacked from above and fired a burst, whereupon the enemy stalled and dived with Scott in pursuit. A whole drum was emptied into the Albatros — which was also hit by another squadron airman — and it went down steeply before force-landing. Scott's Lewis gun refused to fire once a new drum was fitted, so he resumed his photography.[28]

The day before Scott's success, Cuthbert Maclean took command of 11 Squadron.[29] Maclean began the war as a second lieutenant and by the time he stepped into his squadron commander's office on 30 March 1917 he was Major Maclean. His squadron FE2bs principally reconnoitred enemy trenches and gun emplacements, but, unlike Scott, Maclean was comfortable commanding his men from their Le Hameau airfield, near Savy, rather than taking part in operations.[30]

In the final countdown to the Nivelle Offensive, Maclean despatched his airmen to collect photographic intelligence on enemy dispositions and the effects of the massive 'softening up' barrages.[31] On the afternoon of 3 April he ordered a reconnaissance patrol. George Masters, of Hastings, was one of the mission's observers.[32]

Masters was a Gallipoli veteran, who had been mentioned in dispatches.[33] He was also the brother of the well-known New Zealand back-country hunter and author Lester Masters. Before the war the siblings regularly hunted in the dense Ruahine Ranges. George's abilities in the bush were complemented by his kind-heartedness and his Christian faith. Masters was in England as a divinity student when war came. In 1914 while he was in camp near Salisbury, waiting for transfer to the NZEF in Egypt, he met some wounded Belgian soldiers who had barely escaped the ferocious German invasion of their country. One infantryman recounted the nature of the foe Masters would soon face. 'Some of the German atrocities were awful,' Masters wrote later in his diary.

> For instance he told me of one Belgium village where they locked up the whole population of the Church, giving them no food or water for three days, and then shot them! This is a fair example of a German . . . No wonder the poor Belgians are very bitter towards these German barbarians. They wanted me to kill as many as I possibly could.

The German barbarism had to be stopped. Masters had written to his Sunday school students before the war that to be 'truly manly' they needed to 'stand up for what is right' and to cultivate selflessness — putting others first and 'yourself last' — a quality he himself demonstrated as a soldier.

Masters, who was also a trained accountant, was regularly marked out for a military desk job. This was something he repeatedly attempted to avoid: he reasoned that 'after the war, one will feel that he had taken no active . . . part that others have gone and borne the brunt of things, and I have been right out of it'.[34] He served in Gallipoli and seems to have fully escaped clerical work when he arrived in France the following year. On the front lines in September, as a member of the New Zealand Pioneer (Maori) Battalion, his unit came under heavy shelling. The company's commanding officer was killed and all other officers were wounded. Lieutenant Masters 'by his coolness and personal example was the means of keeping the men of his Platoon working on the digging of a most important communication trench to one of the captured trenches'.[35] It was to be his last major act on the ground. Masters had seen notices for the RFC, and was fascinated by aviation. His knowledge of weapons from long hours of hunting with Lester and his ability to act independently without immediate oversight were no doubt contributing factors to his acceptance as an observer on probation with the RFC in October 1916.[36]

With only six days until the launch of the great offensive in 1917, Masters was airborne, perched in the front of an FE2b. Two and a half hours into the flight, the FE2b came under

above Nicknamed the 'Flying Parson' by New Zealand newspapers, Cuthbert Maclean was an Anglican minister before he joined the RFC. By the end of the war he was New Zealand's highest-ranked airman.

The accomplished Bavarian ace Max von Müller with his Albatros DIII. This machine was the pre-eminent German fighter during 'Bloody April' in 1917.

fire and suffered a catastrophic direct hit.[37] Witnesses on the ground saw the aircraft and its crew plummet into the Scarpe River. Masters was declared missing, then presumed dead.[38] His death was confirmed by a note dropped by German airmen over British trenches. His body and that of his South African pilot were never recovered. After soldiering through the horrors of Gallipoli, Masters had written a poem on Christmas Eve 1915. Its last stanza captured the young New Zealander's eternal hope.

Let Christmas Day bring you within
Remembrance sweet that Jesus came.
Yes, came and lived a human life
Resigned for us, his throne on high
Gave up so much, that knowing death
Have we but Faith, We need not die![39]

Masters' death was just the first of many over the month of April as German superiority took a heavy toll on the Allied men and machines. While the ground assault would not be launched until 9 April, the air assault began the day after Masters' death. In the British Arras sector, 25 squadrons, with over 365 aircraft, were gathered in readiness. Trenchard and his staff were unwavering in their adherence to offensive operations, and intense fighting was anticipated. Some squadrons with advanced models held them back, waiting for the right moment to strike.

Against them were 195 machines of the Luftstreitkräfte, with more anticipated to arrive once the British intentions were known.[40] Numerically outnumbered, the Germans could take considerable solace in the fact that their aircraft were generally superior to most British models in the field: morale was high among their aircrews.

The intensity of the fighting was evident in the British losses incurred in March; they proved to be greater than all of those for the entire year of 1915. More than 80 per cent were attributable to air combat and, in the first four days of April, 60 per cent of losses were suffered by units engaged in reconnaissance.[41] When the offensive was launched the British airmen faced their biggest challenge since the start of the war. Two units — 48 and 59 Squadrons — were quickly gutted. On 11 April 48 Squadron lost 10 crewmen, and two days later 59 Squadron, equipped with two-seater reconnaissance machines, failed to meet up with its planned escort.[42] The result was the loss of six 59 Squadron machines, many falling in flames.

Alan Scott's 60 Squadron was pulled right into the heaviest of the operations. He temporarily lost one of his New Zealanders, the well-regarded Caldwell, to illness, but another antipodean arrived just in time for the main event: Nelsonian John Cock.[43] Wounded on the Western Front halfway through the previous year, he had transferred to the RFC and arrived with the squadron on 11 April 1917 with a pilot's badge freshly sewn to his uniform.[44] His baptism of fire was going to be brutal, and he would be one of the squadron's 20 casualties in April. Scott had his men in reconnaissance duties over Douai, escorting photographic aircraft, undertaking balloon attacks at Vis-en-Artois and engaging in numerous offensive patrols hunting down enemy reconnaissance machines.

On 14 April, Scott sent Cock with four others in their Nieuports on an offensive patrol. Their aim: to cover a photographic mission by Maclean's squadron. But the five-strong patrol was not well balanced, in part because of losses sustained in the previous month. Novice airmen outnumbered the experienced by four to one. Australian Alan Binnie was the only pilot with any extensive fighting time with the squadron; the others had only a single sortie to their name except Cock, who had none. It was a disaster waiting to happen.

At 9.15 a.m. the patrol spotted a pair of German two-seaters and attacked. Binnie dived on the enemy with his clutch of greenhorns in tow.[45] Unfortunately the reconnaissance machines were not unattended and the assault was countered by six hostiles, pilots from Richthofen's Jasta 11. Only through dumb luck did one 60 Squadron airman return; his shots had gone wide of the mark, the gun had jammed and his Nieuport had fallen into a spin.[46] When he eventually flattened out, the patrol was nowhere to be seen. In the meantime, Binnie was hit in the shoulder protecting two of his pilots. 'Blood from his wound spurted all over the nacelle, obscuring the instruments,' recalled Scott.[47] The machine then caught fire. Binnie put out the fire, only to faint soon thereafter. The Nieuport fell into a glide. When he revived he was startled to discover himself on the ground in enemy territory: the aircraft had miraculously landed itself with no further injury to its pilot. Binnie was taken prisoner and lost his arm in surgery. Two others also force-landed and entered prisoner of war camps; one died of his wounds days later.[48] Cock was killed outright in the fighting, just 11 days after he had received his pilot's badge; his death was confirmed in the same German letter dropped over British lines that had listed Masters as killed in action.[49]

For Scott, 14 April and the two days that followed were part of a nightmare weekend, a blur of men killed, wounded or taken into captivity. The loss of Cock and four others in A Flight on the Saturday was followed on the Sunday with two more from B Flight, and then, on Monday, only a single man returned from C Flight.[50] Only a sliver of the squadron survived 'Bloody April' and the Nivelle Offensive. Over eight weeks of fighting, Scott calculated nearly 35 officers lost; that is, nearly twice the squadron's establishment of 18 men.

During the tumult, the squadron entered a vicious cycle of fresh replacements followed by more losses. It did not help that not only were the men hastily trained but that, also, their introduction to the squadron was also often their introduction to an aircraft foreign to all of them, the Nieuport. Lost men 'had to be replaced from England by officers who had never flown this particular type of machine, because there were none in England,' wrote Scott.[51]

The intensity of the fighting also winnowed out those untouched by physical injury but nonetheless ill-suited for the work in single-seater scouts. In spite of the losses, Scott could not afford to maintain men who were clearly falling short of the mark. Even over the weekend of heavy casualties he was forced to write to his superiors about a pilot whom he wanted transferred out: 'On 4th April he lost formation and on several occasions between the 5th and the 10th he either failed to start with the patrol, being unable to start his engine (once), or, having started came back because he had lost his leader.' On the day Cock was killed, the wayward pilot completely lost the patrol and was never seen again on the mission over Arras, only to return 'by accident about the same time as the patrol'. The squadron had spent more time on him than on any other airman in training, but to no avail. Scott was generous and concluded that 'he is not a bad pilot' but recommended him to a two-seater squadron, where an observer would keep him on track.

Some men realised their own inability to sustain the intensity required. One pilot admitted that he had lost all confidence in himself during April and May. 'He is tremulous and jumpy and is at present unfit to fly,' concurred a Royal Army Medical Corps report. The doctor doubted the pilot's 'nerves will ever stand any prolonged term of flying under service conditions'.[52] Scott was blunt: the airman would never make 'a real scout pilot and I think he is wise to make this application [for a transfer], which was not suggested by me'.[53] He tempered his comments by recommending the nervous pilot be diverted to a squadron with bigger and inherently more stable machines than the skittish Nieuports.

'He is a good pilot, exceptionally resolute, but, as can be seen from his appearance, is delicate and highly strung,' Scott noted of another airman who had been with the squadron only since March. The pilot had not been sleeping well and was therefore unable to fly.[54] In nearly all the cases he dealt with, Scott was careful to not completely undermine the airman in question. In this case he concluded his letter with: 'I should be extremely grateful if this application could be granted, as in my opinion to keep him working would seriously impair the efficiency of an exceptionally useful officer.'

Added to his woes, Scott had to deal with less than satisfactory replacement aircraft. The airmen had initially been excited about the fresh machines arriving from Paris, but soon discovered all was not well with the Nieuports.

> Some of these new machines were not well built, and began — to add to our troubles — to break up in the air. Lieut. Grandin's fell to bits while diving on a hostile two-seater, though this may have been due to injury from machine-gun fire. Cafffyn's and Brackenbury's collapsed when practising firing at ground targets on the aerodrome, and the former was killed; while Ross's wings folded upwards when pulling out of a dive after firing a burst; he was badly injured, but has since recovered.[55]

On one occasion an officer had to call off an assault on a hostile aircraft. After landing he reported to Scott: 'My lower plane [wing] came off, so I thought I had better land. Sorry I left the patrol.' Eventually it was discovered that the wood had been badly seasoned and the fault was fixed.

The loss of so many men and machines, and the rigours of command, did not deter Scott from continuing to fly with the squadron. Over April and May he returned at least a dozen combat reports and secured two victories. In the third week of April he concocted a plan to deal with the enemy scourge. Near Vis-en-Artois he flew his Nieuport on what appeared to be a lone photographic sortie. In fact he was 'bait' for the prowling enemy. At 2500 ft above him and half a mile to his east was Billy Bishop, leading a flight. At 11.20 a.m. the trap was sprung when five Fokker biplanes swarmed Scott. He fired a burst at the two leading hostiles, while another attempted to manoeuvre behind him. He fired off a few rounds but was overwhelmed. The bait was almost eaten. The other waiting airmen flew to the rescue of their commanding officer, ambushing and driving off the Fokkers. Although the wing headquarters noted the patrol with 'bait (in the shape of Major Scott photographing) which worked very well', it was not repeated. Perhaps Scott realised that this was excessive foolhardiness, even by his own standards.[56]

The day after Scott's cunning trap had nearly backfired, another New Zealander — Melville White — was in the air. On completing his training White had requested a posting to Palestine or Mesopotamia: he detested the cold climate of Britain and the Continent. The Picton-born pilot was duly posted to France on 11 April 1917. He found himself in 24 Squadron, a unit equipped with the Airco DH2, a one-man pusher with more than a passing resemblance to the ubiquitous two-seater FE2b. As with its lookalike, the DH2 was no match for the new-generation fighters such as the Albatros DIII. Twenty-four Squadron was one of the last to be flying the DH2.[57] Based at Flez, the formation utilised its DH2s in line patrols on the front of the Fourth Army, flying at between 2000 and 4000 ft on their side of the lines.[58]

White was a thoughtful officer. On the day before he collected his wings he reflected on the brutal fighting he had witnessed on the Gallipoli Peninsula and was about to revisit in France. In a reference to a prewar science-fiction film in which a Martian spies on earth, he mused:[59]

> I wonder what thoughts would pass through the mind of a 'Messenger from Mars' if he should descend to our earth from the peaceful starry heights and see millions of human beings fiercely struggling with each other in a gigantic murderous conflict? If he were an enlightened Being he would sympathetically realise that the *civilised* inhabitants were bravely struggling to rid the fair earth of the brute beasts . . .[60]

About the leader of the beasts he was forthright:

> The Huns said they would preserve . . . [Westminster] Abbey and Buckingham Place when they took London, so that they could use the former to crown the Kaiser in and the latter as his residence. I think the Kaiser stands a better chance of taking his residence in the Tower of London, and it would be a good opportunity to make use of those fiendish instruments of torture collected there, which our forefathers delighted to use in the 'Good old days'.[61]

On 20 April White sent a letter to his sister, and in his postscript he added instructions regarding the lengthy correspondence sent home covering his experiences from Anzac Cove to the Western Front — 30 months at war. 'My dear Alice . . . Don't forget my request to save all copies sent to you, as I will want them someday, I am still optimistic about being in NZ for Xmas.'[62]

On 23 April he took off at 6.30 p.m. with three others for early-evening sentry duty over the trenches. Forty minutes later they were on the patrol line with four FE2s from another squadron when they were attacked by four hostiles; it was Jasta 5. Kurt Schneider, an Iron Cross holder, dispatched an FE2b in flames. He turned on another of the two-seaters and shot

above A small number
of the New Zealanders
found themselves
in RNAS squadrons
equipped with the
Sopwith Triplane; it
was one of the few
Allied machines in the
first half of 1917 able to
outfly the Albatros DIII.

below A rare air-to-air
photograph showing a
Royal Aircraft Factory
BE2c in flight over
trench lines in the
Grand Bois area.

the pilot through the head. The out-of-control FE2b collided with White's DH2. The squadron circling below observed the aftermath: an aircraft spinning earthward minus its wings, then bits of wood and other 'remainders of a wing' surreally 'floating about in the air'.[63] With a single bullet Schneider had knocked out two machines. White, surrounded by the remnants of his aircraft, fell 7000 ft.[64] Melville White had only been with the squadron a dozen days. 'It was the most awful bit of bad luck that could possibly happen,' the squadron's commanding officer wrote to White's family. 'We are all very sorry to have lost him and everyone had a splendid opinion of his abilities, although we had only known him a short time.'

A few weeks before his death White had expressed his hope of a joyous and not-too-distant homecoming. After an especially stunning springtime scenic flight over the English countryside replete with billowing clouds and a molten setting sun, he wrote:

> I can already see the fern-clad hills of a little country known as 'God's own' rising majestically out of the sea at the far end of the earth. I believe that the day is not far distant when this mental picture will materialise, and my good comrades and I will be back again in 'God's own country' which name has now a far deeper significance than in pre-war days. Kia Ora, Yours affectionately . . .[65]

April 1917 was a period of losses, but for accomplished airmen blessed with a modicum of luck, and flying one of the few modern machines, it was also a period of accumulating victories. Among these was Thomas Culling. Born in Dunedin and educated at King's College, Auckland, he volunteered for the New Zealand Samoa Expeditionary Force at the outbreak of the war. Only three months into his eighteenth year he was keen to see action, but his father, Thomas Shepherd Culling — businessman and local politician — was not impressed. He wrote to his daughter:

> Our Tom is among the first to be called off to duty, he is in Wellington in camp. I have protested against him leaving New Zealand, being only 18 years, whereas the government promised that they would take none under 20 years. I am trying to get him back to Auckland. If he got away, the probability is we would never see him again, and if he did come back, he might be ruined for work, like many of the members of the contingents who returned from the Boer War.[66]

On the day of his Wellington departure, an excited Culling selected his bunk and stowed his gear onboard the *Monowai*: his dreams of war were soon to be realised. However, only hours from departure for Apia, his father's efforts were successful and the authorities instructed him to disembark. But the young Culling was not to be denied the war, and in August he sailed for Britain and the RNAS. Perhaps the young man left without his father's consent, or perhaps the senior Culling believed that the lengthy training period for flying would mean his son would not see any action. After all, many believed the war would be over by Christmas. However, the war did extend beyond the Christmas of 1914 and was hitting its stride in destruction and carnage when the young aviator was posted to 1 (Naval) Squadron in September 1916.[67]

Aside from utilising aircraft and airships in maritime work, the RNAS deployed a number of crack squadrons on the Western Front, and Culling's unit was one of these. The squadron had an enviable reputation as one of the oldest military air units in Britain. On its roll of honour was an early Victoria Cross recipient, the late Reginald Warneford, who had shot down a Zeppelin in mid-1915. The squadron included at least three other New Zealanders: Aucklander John 'Jack' Carr, Waiuku-born Forster Maynard, and former Whanganui resident Kenneth Millward. Occasionally this meant that patrols were dominated by New Zealand-born airmen.[68] However, it was an Australian who was to play the greater part in Culling's success as an airman. When he arrived at the squadron he met one of the Great War's exceptional pilots, his flight commander Roderic Dallas DSC.

Six years Culling's senior, Dallas was already a seasoned pilot, and over the summer of 1916 the Queenslander had accumulated five victories and was well on the way to becoming one of Australia's highest-scoring pilots. 'Fighting in the air had developed into a science and every ruse and trick imaginable is employed to trap your opponent,' wrote Dallas. 'A scout [fighter] pilot of today must be able to do almost anything at all with his machine. Looping, diving, spinning, and such stunts are necessary and are often employed in fighting.'[69]

Culling was fortunate to find himself in such good company. Tall and exuding confidence, Dallas had a well-deserved reputation for easing new arrivals into the business of aerial combat. The New Zealander became a fixture of Dallas's flights, and was essentially his wingman. It was a fruitful combination. Dallas had his most successful period of combat with Culling; while Culling, under the Australian's tutelage, became New Zealand's leading fighter pilot by mid-1917. Culling not only had the benefit of a master aviator as his flight commander, he also had a superb fighting aircraft: his posting coincided with the re-equipping of the unit with the Sopwith Triplane, affectionately dubbed the 'Tripehound' or simply the 'Tripe'.

Because RNAS had an exclusive contract with the Sopwith company — a source of interservice rivalry with the RFC — Culling's squadron was the first to fly the triplane operationally. Fewer than 160 of these three-winged machines were manufactured, but they immediately made themselves known. The plane was very agile, possessed a great climb rate, and had an impressive service ceiling. Dallas tested an early model and considered it an 'excellent' machine.[70] Millward, who had been flying obsolescent Bristol Scouts and slowly ageing Nieuports, clambered into a Tripe for the first time in late February. 'Practice flight,' he wrote in his logbook, 'like the machine very well.'[71] Best of all, it outclassed its principal adversary, the Albatros DIII. Nonetheless, the Tripe's operational history would be relatively short thanks to the arrival of even better aircraft, including its stablemate, the Sopwith Camel. In the meantime, the Tripe proved more than a match for the enemy machines in the hands of 1 (Naval) Squadron in April–May.

On 6 April 1917, after a number of close calls with the enemy, Culling bagged his first victim when he flew out from Chipilly, northern France. His combat report was brief and to the point:

At about 11.50 a.m. about 4 miles N.E. of St. Quentin I dived on to a H.A. [Hostile Aircraft] at 12,000 feet, and fired about 100 rounds into it at very short range. I saw the H.A. stall and get into a spin, and could see it falling from about 11,000 feet until it fell, still spinning, through the low clouds which were at 2000. It appeared to be totally out of control throughout its fall.[72]

Culling was on his way.

The squadron's record book reveals that Dallas and Culling were usually accompanied by New Zealander Jack Carr. Originally with the New Zealand Samoa Expeditionary Force, Carr later sailed with his mother Ada to Britain in order to put his mechanical and motor engineering knowledge to better use.[73] Unlike Culling's starring role in the squadron combat reports, it appears Carr played a part as supporting cast member in the trio's aerial operations. He was nonetheless a good airman, and during April he flew in more than 20 patrols; in fact, he was only weeks away from leaving the squadron and embarking on coastal patrols over British home waters, searching for U-boats, for which he would receive a Distinguished Service Cross later in the year.[74] Meanwhile the fruitful Dallas–Culling show was about to receive some prominent recognition.

The pair's biggest test came on two consecutive days: 22 and 23 April. On the first day, a late afternoon patrol became one of the Great War's classic air battles. Dallas was accompanied by Culling and Carr, until mechanical problems forced the latter to return to Bellevue. The two remaining Anzacs took up their offensive patrol positions before encountering at least 14 enemy aircraft with wild colour schemes.[75] The German formation was comprised of single-seater and two-seater machines working in tandem; in all likelihood fighters escorting observation aircraft. Dallas and Culling were determined not to let them penetrate the Allied lines, and they dived on the enemy flock. Outnumbered, the flight commander and his wingman struck from above, unleashing measured bursts of fire; then, utilising the triplane's excellent rate of climb, they entered turns to regain height over the Germans. Like wasps, they delivered attack after stinging attack — over 20 in all. Each smarting blow prodded the enemy back away from the front line.

The assault had begun at 16,000 ft but, over the course of an energy-sapping three-quarters of an hour, the Germans were pushed lower and lower. Culling got the first victory at 5.30 p.m., over Arleux. Diving on an Albatros DIII, he opened fire at close range. Fifty rounds of bullets sent the enemy falling 7000 ft, completely out of control. This action brought up his second victory. It might have been his last, as another enemy fighter bore down on the preoccupied New Zealander. Dallas made a sharp climbing turn and dived on the threatening Albatros, sending it smashing into the ground. Moments later he took out another. Demoralised and bloody-nosed, the hostile survivors stumbled eastward at low altitude. 'Big scrap,' summarised Dallas. 'Met the Travelling Circus, and Culling — my valuable comrade in the air — went with me into a formation of 14 of them. We revved around and counter attacked.'[76] Both men were singled out in the British official history of the air war for their tactical nous and astute use of the triplane's 'superior speed and climbing power' to overcome their numerical inferiority.[77] It was a master class.

Thomas Culling was
New Zealand's first and
youngest ace of the war.

Barely 15 hours later, Culling was in the air again. The early-morning patrol was led by Dallas and included two additional squadron airmen. An attempted German incursion was spotted: nine enemy fighters and two-seaters. It was a 20-minute affair and all the patrolling RNAS squadron pilots hit something, but only two were able to make decisive claims: Dallas and Culling. Culling attacked a mottled-green, two-man machine, chasing it down over 7000 ft. Filling the gunsight with the enemy he fired; it stalled, sideslipped and plummeted through the clouds. Having already destroyed another two-seater, Dallas now watched Culling's efforts and confirmed the details to the squadron's intelligence officer.[78] Both men were recognised for their combat successes: Culling received a Distinguished Service Cross and Dallas a bar to his existing medal.[79]

One of the squadron's other New Zealanders, Forster Maynard, added to Culling's efforts. The son of a Church of England clergyman, Maynard was a future air vice-marshal in the making, but in April 1917 the 24-year-old had only recently arrived in the squadron via Oxford University, the Royal Naval Air Station Eastchurch, a brief period as an instructor, and operations with home defence units. He is easily identified in squadron photographs by his piercing eyes, strong nose and thin, slightly lopsided smile. On 29 April, he experienced his most intensive contact with enemy to date.

The day began with a late-morning offensive patrol. His flight of six was hotly engaged by up to 12 enemy fighters. An audience of enemy airmen and ground crew watched from the airfield at Épinoy below. Out of the sun, the flight commander dived first, engaging at point-blank range. The hostile spun seemingly out of control, only to flatten out and land on the airfield. Maynard peppered a machine with bullets; tracers entered the central fuselage and it dived out of sight. It was an inconclusive result and Maynard returned to the airfield.[80] Eight hours later, on his second sortie of the day he secured a confirmed combat victory. At 7 p.m. his five-strong flight was attacked by enemy machines. Skirmishing was indecisive in the initial contact but 55 minutes into the mission he fired 50 of the Sopwith's 500 rounds into an Albatros. The aircraft turned on its side, falling straight out of control into a spiralling plunge.[81] It would be the first of six sole and shared claims Maynard made during the war.

The next day Maynard found himself with Dallas, Culling and Millward and an Englishman escorting six Bristol Fighters on reconnaissance.[82] The two-seater Bristols were set upon by a large German formation of about 20 machines.[83] The naval squadron intercepted. Dallas and Culling were in the thick of it; Dallas fought with at least seven individual aeroplanes. The battle raged for 20 minutes. The odds were against them, and Dallas signalled to his wingman to break away and escort the Bristols back over the lines. Culling kept the numerous pursuers off the two-seaters, bringing them home safely. With that, the New Zealander had seen out the month with three confirmed victories against his name. Over the month of May he would add three more.

On 5 May there was another large dogfight: 20 Allied and hostile machines swirling above the front lines. The combat report noted at least 26 engagements.[84] The flight commander and his wingman fought together. Dallas was forced into a steep dive with his triplane's wings 'bent downwards like a bow' while Culling closed in and attacked. Dallas regained level flight to observe the New Zealander's efforts: a machine with black crosses falling thousands of feet, the enemy pilot trapped, helpless in the plunge. On 19 May, the squadron was hit with two losses, but Culling and Millward knocked out an enemy machine apiece.[85] Millward was particularly plucky: he had taken on five aircraft and survived to tell the tale. Culling's effort brought up his fifth victory and the newly promoted flight lieutenant became New Zealand's first 'ace' of the Great War. The next day he added another, his sixth. Culling was the first of 15 New Zealand Great War aces.

CHAPTER ELEVEN
THE SUPREME SACRIFICE
1917

When the French failed to bring the Germans to a strategically decisive battle, the southern Nivelle Offensive devolved into another attritional quagmire as the Germans flooded the battlefield with reinforcements. The French were forced into a defensive and rebuilding phase and the weight of the Allied effort shifted north for the upcoming British effort at Ypres. Success here would consolidate the Allied position in the northern sector of the Western Front, preparing the ground for the impending arrival of the Americans the following year.

In June 1917, preliminary to the main attack, British forces would assault the German stronghold at Messines Ridge south of Ypres. Messines, with its complex network of trenches and barbed wire, gave the Germans a commanding view across the British sector. Its seizure was essential for success at Ypres. The Messines assault would be launched by one of the biggest chains of explosions in the history of warfare. The British had been digging tunnels under the German position for nearly two years, and had jammed them full of close to a million pounds of explosives. Once that was detonated, the Second Army, with over 200,000 men — including the New Zealand Division — would assault the ridge.

In preparation for Messines, air units once again gathered valuable intelligence. While most of this work was undertaken by aircraft, static lighter-than-air balloons were also utilised. Carrel Fidler was deployed as a balloon observer near Messines, one of a number of New Zealanders who were engaged in lighter-than-air balloon work in the Great War. Others, such as Newtown tram conductor Percival White, crewed with the non-rigid airships of the RNAS over home waters. These airships, sometimes called blimps, lacked the solid internal structure of their much bigger German counterparts, the Zeppelins, but thanks to their gondola-mounted engines and rudders they could actively patrol large maritime areas off the British Isles. Fidler and White's training for unpowered and powered lighter-than-air observation work could be as dangerous as their compatriots' in heavier-than-air machines.

Roderick Carr, who subsequently switched to aircraft, began his aviation career with RNAS balloons.[1] In the second year of the war, Carr and five others were on a training flight they never forgot. It was a perfectly calm and sunny day when they ascended in their untethered balloon from the exclusive Hurlingham Polo Club, London. 'I was piloting for practice, and we rose to about 5000 ft and passed over London in line with Piccadilly Circus and the Tower Bridge,' he wrote to his parents.[2] They crossed over the capital and were searching for a place to land when an upward current seized the balloon and basket and carried it to an uncomfortably high altitude before a thunderstorm pushed them down at an equally disconcerting speed toward Romford, on London's northeastern fringes. They levelled out at 200 ft, and the six men were then propelled at over 50 mph, skimming a railway station and train before snagging in telephone wires. Trailing cables, the basket successfully crashed through a brick wall, then a wooden fence, before it met its match: a brick house. This brought the show to a 'standstill'. The town's shops and homes emptied to see the spectacle. The men were battered and bruised: one suffered a broken leg, and several had sprained ankles and wrists. One side of Carr's face had been sandblasted, but he thought he would be right in a week. 'It was a most exciting experience,' he concluded, 'I would not have missed it for anything.'

Percival White went on to serve with Submarine Scout (SS) class airships. These vessels were 143 ft in length and 32 ft in diameter, and were used to protect British shipping. White was trained to operate with a five-man crew on *SSZ 64*, an airship powered by a single 75-hp Rolls-Royce engine.[3] Equipped with a machine gun and bombs, the Submarine Scout Zero (SSZ) series of airships were able to attack sea mines and U-boats. During the final months of the war, White took part in patrolling and escort operations with Submarine Scouts off the Yorkshire coast in missions that sometimes exceeded 12 hours.[4] His only 'combat' action was an attack with a 100-lb bomb on suspicious 'oil bubbles' while protecting a convoy of 45 ships.[5]

As challenging as White's airship career was, and as dangerous as Carr's London escapade had been, they were nothing like the terrors facing RFC balloonists suspended above the Western Front — something Carr himself found out when he spotted for artillery in the 1915 Battle of Loos.[6] Unlike their unstable spherical balloon siblings, military kite balloons were elongated and sported an air-filled stern fin that stabilised the craft. Although the shape of the kite balloon meant it could fly in almost all conditions, in rough weather it was nausea-inducing for any crew who did not have their 'sea-legs'.[7] From the balloon's wicker basket, observers recorded enemy movements and spotted for artillery. As with the German balloons that had come under attack from Balcombe-Brown in 1916, British balloonists were protected by anti-aircraft guns and had powerful winches that lowered them as soon as the observers had exited the basket by parachute. Nonetheless, they were extremely exposed and vulnerable to enemy aircraft and artillery.

A New Zealand artilleryman at Messines, Cyril Spear, noted that the Germans liked to attack the balloons at dusk.[8] One evening he heard anti-aircraft fire and 'on looking up saw a Hun close to a balloon; as he passed he fired a volley . . . turned & came close again'. The German made three passes, setting the balloon alight before turning for home amid a torrent of shells and machine-gun fire. A few days later a 'Hun suddenly appeared, and commenced spitting bullets' at a balloon. The observers bailed out and made it to safety amid the cheering soldiers.

Enemy aircraft were not the only threat to the lives of balloonists, as Fidler found out during an artillery barrage. The Auckland-born serviceman entered the war with the Canadian Expeditionary Force, only to transfer to a British regiment and finally be attached to the RFC as a balloonist observer in early 1916. Fourteen months later, in May 1917, he was on the front

An Allied observation balloon at Ypres in 1917. The stationary tethered balloons were no place for the faint-hearted, as they were attractive targets for enemy aircraft and artillery.

line with a fellow observer, Englishman Goderic Hodges. Hodges was instructed to prepare the way for an attack on trenches along the Messines salient. The offensive was imminent. This required relocating the balloon for observing the enemy and surveying the 'lie-of-the-land'. He called upon Fidler — 'a very neat worker with a mapping pen' — to assist.[9] It was a beautiful early summer's day as they strode across the fields and entered 'a lovely meadow', an unreal setting on the fringes of hell.

> The sun threw the shadows of the trees across the grass. It was a heavenly May morning. Here there was no noise of war. Frogs were croaking round a pond. To the north the jagged outlines of what was left of Neuve Eglise stood up not far away. In this bright sunlight with the fresh green of the trees about them, they looked not at all suggestive of war, death, suffering. They looked like some romantic folly in a park or even a stage-setting. It was etherealised.

The two men were in no hurry, and Fidler plotted the course for the balloon in detail across fields and around ponds. By midday Hodges was ready to return and visit the battery commander for whom they would be observing that afternoon. 'You'd better come with me,' he said to Fidler. 'You don't know these people I'm going to see. You'll be sure to be observing for them before long.' They walked together across a field to the heavy howitzers and then the battery headquarters, a little farmhouse with 'thatched roof and lilacs all around it, all in blossom'. The commander stood at the map table with his subaltern; in all, the room was filled with seven individuals, including Hodges and Fidler. Hodges was leaning across the table clasping a photograph of the trenches in question — when suddenly their world was obliterated.

> The photograph had gone. So had the Battery Commander. I could see nothing, hear nothing. I could feel nothing under my feet. I thought, 'Well I suppose I must be dead' . . . I seemed to be floating in space. Then I realised I was not dead, and it gave me no pleasure at all. . . . [B]eams, chimneys, God knows what broken things were falling, and falling on me. When things stopped falling I could hear groans. I found that if I kept quite flat and stretching my arms forwards, dug my fingertips into the cracks between the bricks, I could pull myself forwards. The violent explosion had squashed me like a concertina. I was gasping, but taking in not air but fumes. I must get to the door, get some air into my lungs and then go and help those who were groaning. I stood up and fell against the wall . . . I could see the insides of my left foot.[10]

The headquarters had been hit by a fluke first ranging shot from German artillery. Hodges' foot was hanging by a thread of flesh. Fidler was nowhere to be seen, but another New Zealander appeared and carried Hodges three-quarters of a mile, some of it under shelling, to the newly arrived New Zealand Field Ambulance. A surgeon removed his leg without anaesthetic. Hodges later discovered that Fidler's legs had been blasted away and he had died from the horrific injuries.[11] Fidler's Observer's Badge was sent to his mother. For years afterwards, Hodges hated the 'sight of lilacs'.[12]

n the air, over 300 aircraft were collected for Messines, including a number of RNAS formations. As at the Battle of Arras, these units would primarily be employed as escorts for reconnaissance machines and to prevent enemy incursions on the hunt for British artillery emplacements. Nearly all the German gun batteries were beyond the sight of British artillery and the aircraft offered the only way to gain meaningful intelligence.[13]

Thomas Culling, Forster Maynard and Kenneth Millward in 1 (Naval) Squadron were supplemented by Fabian Pember Reeves in 6 (Naval) Squadron. Reeves was the only son of Hon. William Pember Reeves, a former cabinet minister in New Zealand's Liberal government and, during the war, director of the London School of Economics. The day before the Messines assault, 6 June 1917,[14] Fabian Reeves was on an offensive sortie when his patrol of Nieuports encountered the enemy. The commanding officer wrote to Fabian's father:

> Your son took part in a big fight between 20 and 30 machines each side, from which he did not return. Flight-Sub-Lieut. Redpath stated that he saw a Nieuport . . . going down out of control near Havrincourt Wood but he was not absolutely certain, as he was some distance away. And to a pilot of your son's capabilities it would be a normal tactical manoeuvre to spin and twist and roll. This is all we know, and it is so little. To us, excepting for the late C.O. only, it was the biggest loss the Squadron sustained. One of the very best and cheeriest of comrades, with his quaint quiet humour, we all loved him. As an Officer his natural qualities endeared him not only to the men of his Flight, but to all in the Squadron. As a Pilot he had no superior in either of the air Services for Cross Country work, and for long trips on new machines in foul weather his record was unique. The wishes of every Officer and man in the Squadron are with you, in this, your time of anxiety.

The squadron commander offered the family a sliver of hope, but it was emotional torture. The oft-repeated phrases 'did not return' and 'missing in action' could cripple a family. The Reeves were locked in a dark netherworld where everything was grey and dim. Was Fabian alive? A prisoner? Wounded? For two months the uncertainty and rumours unravelled William Reeves, whose nerves were already frayed from a serious air accident that Fabian had survived the previous year. News arrived, cruelly spread, over the remainder of the year. It was three months before they knew for certain that Fabian was dead, and another two before the Red Cross offered information on how he had died — in his Nieuport, shot down in a large fight over Driencourt.[15]

Reeves senior sank into depression at the final slamming of the door. His work at the London School of Economics foundered and he eschewed public appearances. Suffering continual malaises, he could often be found 'wrapped in rugs in his room'.[16] Fabian's mother Maud, a woman of prodigious political talent and stamina, never completely reconciled herself to the loss. In the postwar era she was ensnared — like many in Britain who were deprived of their sons — in fraudulent spiritualist séances; she listened to 'Fabian's' vague and disjointed messages from beyond the grave.[17] Reeves' death was not a good start for the New Zealand airmen in the campaign.

Submarine Scout airships scoured British coastal waters on the lookout for mines and enemy submarines. As New Zealander Percival White discovered, patrols could last for up to 12 hours.

On 7 June at 3.10 a.m. Messines shook and staggered like a drunk man. The great joint explosion upended German positions, and artillery cleared the way for the advancing ground troops. Aerial formations monitored and supported the advance up the ridge. By the end of the day it had been an almost overwhelming success. The following 24 hours were spent consolidating the ground taken. Culling's squadron was at the forefront of operations.

Roderic Dallas went on leave in the second half of May. Within days, Culling was leading flights.[18] On 8 June a special mission was despatched to locate a reported 'Hun aircraft' intruder. New Zealanders Culling and Millward made up half of the four-man flight that encountered the seven-strong enemy southwest of Ypres.[19] The dogfight was indecisive — and Culling did not return. Millward could only wait for news of his countryman. Culling's father was notified that his son was missing. Culling never returned and his body was never recovered. Three years after his 'Tom' had attempted to join the war, his father's fears had been realised. New Zealand's first ace had fallen. Millward was not far behind.

In early July Millward gave a guided tour of the base facilities and Sopwiths to New Zealanders encamped nearby. Among these was one of his old Wanganui Collegiate schoolmates, Corporal Godfrey Payne.[20] When he was forced to abandon the tour for a sortie the New Zealand soldiers begged him to fly over their village of tents and give them a display of what a fighter pilot could do.

Later, after their evening meal, the infantry heard machine guns blazing — a sure sign of a scrap — and they piled out of their tents. It was the Tripes 'coming back from Fritz's side for their lives'. Payne counted 20 'Hun' planes hot in pursuit of the 'jolly little triplanes'. A wall of anti-aircraft fire turned the enemy home. Millward passed over the camp then tipped his wing and swung back to the tents at 3000 ft. He fired off a few rounds to announce his arrival. 'Then he started to give us the most marvellous exhibition of flying that any of us had seen,' enthused Payne.

By Jove, he has nerve! He literally tumbled down like a wounded pigeon, rolling sideways, looping the loop, threading the bootlace, and all the rest of it, till he was about 100 feet off the ground. Then he flew round and round the camp in small circles at about 120 miles an hour; this is no exaggeration — they can do 140. As he got to know the country and saw there were no trees, etc., in the way, he got lower and lower, till he was just skimming the tents.

By Jove, it was great! We waved a paper, and he waved his hand over the side as he roared past within a few feet of us. His final stunt was to frighten us; he climbed at an angle of about 50 degrees till he was 400 or 500 feet up. Then he did a straight nosedive at us. We thought he would never pull up in time, and scattered to get out of the way, but it wasn't necessary; he came down to within 20 feet of the ground, and then jumped almost straight up again and made a dive for home, firing a green flare as he went to show he was all right, and was out of sight in a moment.[21]

As one chap remarked, 'The bally birds ought to be ashamed of themselves!'[22]

A few days later, on the morning of 7 July, with some 80 operational flights to his name, the 20-year-old was escorting a photographic reconnaissance sortie.[23] Millward's flight of triplanes ran into 15 enemy aircraft of Jasta 11 and Pomeranian ace Kurt Wolff. The unit was the most feared German Jasta, and Wolff was one of its most lethal practitioners. The Jasta had claimed an incredible 89 victories during Bloody April, twice as many as any other; and of these, 22 had fallen to Wolff's red-and-green-coloured Albatros DIII. One of Manfred von Richthofen's adjutants described Wolff:

At first glance, you could only say 'delicate little flower'. A slender, thin little figure, a very young face, whose entire manner is one of extreme shyness. He looks as if you could tip him backwards with one harsh word. But below this friendly schoolboy's face dangles the order Pour le Mérite [Blue Max]. And so far, these modest looking eyes have taken 30 enemy airplanes from the sky over the sights of his machine guns, set them afire, and made them smash to pieces on the ground.[24]

With Wolff at the height of his powers and possessing at least a three-to-one numerical advantage, the Jasta dove on the 1 (Naval) Squadron flight.

The Sopwith Triplanes dropped below 150 ft and fled west. German ground observers ducked for cover as machine-gun bullets struck their observation post. When they finally emerged they saw triplanes strewn over the countryside near Comines, northeast of Armentières. They rushed to the smouldering wrecks and saw one of the German pilots standing next to his prize, his Albatros at rest nearby. A ground observer recognised the officer: 'I knew him well — little Wolff with the "Pour le Mérite".'[25] In the July heat, a perspiring Wolff was 'endeavouring to prise the riveted number-plate off the engine . . . for he collected such souvenirs'. With prize in hand Wolff paused to view the dead bodies: Millward lay near his machine adjacent to a railway line. 'It was he or I,' said Wolff, 'and I prefer it to be him.' Millward was his last victim; Wolff was killed the following month.

At 1 (Naval) Squadron it was noted that Millward had 'failed to return'.[26] His family was inundated with letters from the New Zealand soldiers encamped nearby. The squadron's commanding officer, Roderic Dallas, extolled the virtues of their son and suggested that he might still be alive.[27] Not long after, the Germans confirmed Millward had been killed. 'It was a sad but glorious end to a young life, and to the promise of a brilliant career,' said Payne.

above The wreck of Kenneth Millward's machine on 7 July 1917. The New Zealander was German ace Kurt Wolff's thirty-third victim.

below A German anti-aircraft crew poses for a propaganda photograph. Many New Zealanders were killed, brought down or wounded by accurate German 'Archie.'

A German Gotha GIV in flight. The three-man Gothas joined the Zeppelins in their raids on England. Later in the war the heavy bombers were turned to attacking Allied airfields on the Western Front.

Millward's death was the last of an unusual confluence of New Zealand losses in mid-1917: all three Great War RNAS operational deaths — Reeves, Culling and Millward — occurred over just 32 days.

The Germans continued to launch Zeppelin raids until the end of the war, but a far more potent weapon entered the strategic bombing campaign in 1917: the twin-engine heavy bomber, the Gotha GIV. With a six-hour endurance, the three-crew Gothas were ideal for raiding Britain's southeastern cities from German-occupied Belgium. With a cruising speed close to 80 mph and a service ceiling of over 21,000 ft, they were also difficult to intercept. Their 78-ft wings made them easy to locate, but they also carried up to three defensive machine guns. When 21 Gothas made their first daylight raid in the fourth week of May the results were sobering: 95 people killed and a further 195 injured.

On 13 June the Gothas reached London for the first time. The result: 162 deaths and 432 injuries. It was the deadliest aerial attack of the war. The daylight incursion was a surprise, and the height from which each machine dropped its ordnance of up to 1000 lbs meant that not a single Gotha was lost. None of the 94 British sorties was able to bring down an enemy machine. The home defence squadrons simply did not have aircraft capable of reaching the Gothas in time; their best machines were at the Western Front.

The defensive failures forced a change of plan. A unit of Sopwith Pups was transferred to Calais and a squadron of frontline fighters was brought home. When authorities were notified of Gothas departing on a raid, the Calais airmen would patrol in front of the Thames Estuary. At the conclusion of the patrol they would land at Manston airfield, Kent, before returning to Calais for the next raid. The England-based fighters would meet the enemy over London.

The Calais unit was 66 Squadron. Across its Great War service the unit had at least three New Zealand pilots: Ralph Stedman, John Warnock and Edgar Garland. Stedman and Warnock were former Christ's College and Nelson College pupils respectively, and both were recent arrivals to the squadron: Stedman was involved in offensive patrolling sorties at Messines, and Warnock, a Kohimarama flying school graduate, was undertaking his inaugural operational flight in the first week of June. Both men were now on patrolling duties with the squadron's single-seater Sopwith Pups.

Light and manoeuvrable, the Pup was well liked by its pilots, but by mid-1917 it was rapidly being surpassed in speed and firepower by the newest German fighters. Nonetheless, the Pups did have the requisite service ceiling and speed to reach and overhaul a Gotha.[28] Catching the high-flying Gothas between the Belgian and English coasts required early notification of a raid, good communication between the various home defence elements, and more than a modicum of luck. It is hardly surprising, then, that when the next raid came the results were poor.

On 4 July, 25 Gothas left for England and an attack on Harwich and Felixstowe. These targets meant a northern route for the attackers, a route that was less well monitored than that taken to get to London. The Germans felt that this would greatly reduce the likelihood of British action until late in the mission. It was a good assessment. The first indication that something was up was the sound of heavy engines reported at Orfordness, just before 7 a.m. Bombs were dropped 20 minutes later on the Harwich naval installations and Felixstowe RNAS station. It was only as the bombs dropped that the order for the England-based squadron was given: the delay was perhaps the result of a mistaken belief that London was the real target.

An hour later 66 Squadron was ordered into the air to catch the raiders on their return run. Stedman and Garland took off.[29] Half the squadron was despatched to run picket on a line between Dunkirk and the North Hinder (Noord Hinder) lightship and the rest would scour the waters to the west. Stedman flew for an hour and 20 minutes and Garland two hours and 20 minutes. After fruitless searching, the New Zealanders landed in England. The Gothas had passed within easy striking distance but because of 'some unexplained disorganisation in communication' the opportunity had been squandered.[30] The entire 103 defensive sorties failed to bring down a single Gotha.

One of the few New Zealanders to get close to the Gothas in their daylight raids was 21-year-old Harold Beamish. He was farming his father's Whanawhana hill-country station near Hastings when war was announced. A former Royal Navy uncle furnished Beamish with a letter of introduction to an admiral, and he found a home in the RNAS. In 1917 he was flying with the Canadian-dominated 3 (Naval) Squadron, who nicknamed him 'Kiwi'. 'When we first went to France, we were not experienced; that was something that you had to learn,' he later noted. 'If you could see out the first month or so without being killed, you had a reasonable chance of staying alive for quite a long time.' This fact was something he gleaned from the squadron's swelling losses and his own early brushes with death. On one occasion he arrived home with his machine pockmarked with a dozen puncture wounds, and he later discovered a bullet hole in one of his boots; he had been saved only by the intervention of two experienced pilots. 'That was the only time that I got caught unawares,' he wrote. 'I was never again jumped after that.'[31] On another sortie he was returning from escorting bombers over the lines when he got lost in low cloud. Puzzled, he landed to get directions — only to find himself surrounded by Germans. To his relief he soon discovered they were prisoners, and they were put to work extracting Beamish's machine from the mud. Like Culling before him, he successfully negotiated 'Bloody April', adding two victories over April and May to one he had collected in February.[32]

In July the squadron's Pups were replaced by the famous Sopwith Camel — so called because of the metal fairing that hunched over the twin machine guns. Beamish's squadron

above An airman from Harold Beamish's squadron leaps from his Sopwith Camel. Beamish adored his machine for its manoeuvrability and twin machine guns.

below Beamish relaxes in his hut at Dunkirk. From here the New Zealander's RNAS squadron was responsible for intercepting Gothas bound for Britiain.

was one of the first three naval units to receive the Camel. It was an aircraft to Beamish's liking. 'The Camel was a different plane altogether from the Pup,' he explained. 'It had nearly twice as much power . . . The Camels that we flew had 150 hp Bentley rotary engines and the Pups only about 80 hp . . . They weren't faster than the enemy but they were more manoeuverable, we could turn quicker.'[33] He figured the twin machine guns, as opposed to the Pup's sole gun, doubled the chances of hitting something.

The Camel was not without its vices. The rotary engine's strong torque could catch the unwary off guard, and pilots had to actively counteract its tendency to pull the machine over. But it was a supremely versatile machine, and well suited to home defence, night fighting, seaborne sorties, ground attack and, of course, air-to-air combat. In the latter role the Camel proved the nemesis of the German Albatros DIII and DVs. Because of its challenging handling but excellent manoeuvrability, the Camel was said to offer airmen the choice between 'a wooden cross, the Red Cross, or a Victoria Cross'.[34]

Based at Dunkirk, Beamish's squadron was given the role not only of shielding Allied naval vessels from German aircraft, but also of keeping an eye out for the Gothas. On 12 August, at the end of a long patrol, Beamish spied a flock of nine Gothas heading towards England. The fuel gauge was low but he calculated they might just have enough to reach the Germans and return to base. 'Timing was critical,' he noted. The Camels overhauled the Gothas at the limit of their endurance. Beamish fired off a few bursts, then his 'engine conked'. It was then that he noticed that the chase had taken them close to the English coast.

> We had an emergency tank, which gave us another quarter of an hour's running and I switched over, but she wouldn't pick up. I had a look over the side and I had picked out a ship to try to land alongside, when all of a sudden, the engine came alive again, so I set off to try and get to land, which I did. I didn't like what I saw beneath me — it looked to be all mud flats and God knows whatnot, but in the end, I spied an aerodrome. Just in time I got to it, I ran out of petrol but made a landing there. The other four all reached England safely and landed in different places. We spent just over four and a half hours in the air, which is pretty good for a Camel.[35]

While Beamish and his flight did not secure any noticeable damage on the Gothas, other defenders did; and by the time the Germans had scampered home they had lost one heavy bomber and a further three crashed on landing, perhaps as a result of damage inflicted by defensive machines.

This signalled the beginning of the end of daylight raids. Better-coordinated heavy anti-aircraft guns and home defence squadrons were now inflicting unacceptable casualties. The Germans turned to night raids in September, supplementing the Gothas with the Zeppelin-Staaken Riesenflugzeug (giant aircraft) — the true aerial behemoths of the Great War, sporting up to six engines and a 138-ft wingspan.

On 14 June the well-planned Messines assault came to an end. It had been a tactical success: the ridge was captured. The British now prepared for the main event, set to commence on the last day of July. Over the weeks in between, New Zealand pilot Arthur Coningham would lay the foundation of a glittering military aviation career that would see him — a quarter of a century later in the Second World War — commanding the Desert Air Force in North Africa against Erwin Rommel, for which he would receive wide acclaim and his picture on the cover of *Time* magazine.[36]

When he burst on the scene in July 1917, Coningham was a 22-year-old with an unusual nickname: 'Mary'. At least three theories explain how he acquired this name. The first, and most common, is that it was a corruption of 'Māori' — a reference to his adopted homeland of New Zealand. Born in Brisbane, Coningham sailed to New Zealand in 1901 with his family; his father was fleeing blackmail and conspiracy proceedings. Coningham's parents had conspired to blackmail a priest who was secretary to the archbishop of Sydney for the sum of £5000. The pair concocted a sordid tale that included the priest sleeping with Mrs Coningham and fathering a child. The case went through two trials that drew thousands of spectators and were widely reported in Australian and New Zealand newspapers. Eventually, the conspirators' case fell apart and they attempted to start a new life in Westport, New Zealand. The father was soon imprisoned in Hokitika for fraud.[37]

The saving grace for Arthur was that in his teenage years he gained a place at Wellington College, where he was free from his father's misdeeds. He was not particularly academic, perhaps because of the turmoil of his family still swirling around him, but he demonstrated that he was an excellent shot when the college team won the national shooting championships. When war arrived in Europe he had been living in New Zealand for 13 years.

The second theory was that the nickname referred to his fair complexion, which consigned him to female roles in amateur theatre. The third theory was that the name stemmed from a romantic interest. Fellow RFC pilot Christopher Musgrave believed the name 'Mary' came after Coningham was wounded at Gallipoli.

> He landed at Suez, caught typhoid and was sent to the hospital for infectious diseases, just east of the Egyptian 'City of the Dead,' and was placed in the bed next to mine. We became great friends . . . He fell for the charms of nurse Mary Steele of Auckland, and for four nights running when Mary came on duty, 'Connie' disappeared apparently to go to the lavatory. One of the lads got suspicious, looked into Mary's office and found them not only sharing a cup of cocoa, but kisses. When 'Connie' returned to his bed, there was a chorus of 'Connie loves Mary,' over and over again and he became 'Mary' for the rest of his life![38]

Regardless of the origins, 'Mary' stuck with him throughout his starred military life.

Unlike Culling and Millward, who were blessed with the Sopwith Triplane, Coningham flew 32 Squadron's Airco DH5. Vacant and at rest on an airfield, the DH5 cut a pleasant silhouette, but put a pilot in the cockpit and it was immediately evident that something was not quite right. The de Havilland machine had an unusual staggered-wing arrangement whereby the pilot sat directly under the leading edge of the top wing. The pilot was 'pushed' forward against the engine, his face looking directly along the cowling with its synchronised Lewis machine gun, and the propeller mere feet away. This forward position afforded the pilot an excellent view but it also created a massive blindspot behind and above; pilots turning to see if there were any hostiles on their tail found themselves staring at the fabric-covered upper wing. Many DH5 pilots perished because of this design flaw. Moreover, although the DH5 was manoeuvrable it performed poorly above 10,000 ft and, as a consequence, it was vulnerable to attack from above. All in all, it was not well suited to its role as a fighter, and in many ways it performed worse than some of the previous generations of aircraft, such as the Sopwith Pup. The very good forward view and the DH5's preference for low-altitude flying meant it would serve with distinction in ground attacks but it never gained the confidence of pilots in air-to-air combat.

Coningham seems to have been undeterred by the failings of the DH5. In the months prior to July he had accumulated a couple of victories, but the three-week lead-up to Ypres was his most fruitful period of the war. Coningham was involved in 60 air combats, culminating in a string of successes.[39] On 11 and 12 July he bagged an enemy machine each day.[40] Eight days later he had his busiest morning of the war when he shot down three aircraft. At 9.50 a.m. he and an Australian, George Wells, ganged up on a two-seater; then at 10.15 a.m., at 11,000 ft, the New Zealander dispatched an Albatros — it half-looped and then spun down, escorted by an entourage of three forlorn circling enemy machines; and finally at 11.05 a.m. he attacked another Albatros at close range and followed it down to 2500 ft, its left wing folded back in a death plummet.[41] It was a remarkable morning's work for the New Zealander, flying an aircraft not really suited to the hurly-burly of a dogfight. Coningham was recommended for a Military Cross, which came through a week later, in recognition of his 'conspicuous gallantry and devotion to duty in attacking enemy aircraft'.

His run was not over, however. On 27 May, north of Polygon Wood, he spied an enemy two-seater reconnaissance machine under heavy escort. His patrol attacked; Coningham hit the observer and the machine fell, trailing smoke from a damaged engine. It crashed near Zonnebeke. That afternoon he had another success east of Houthulst Forest.[42] He was again recommended for a commendation.

It was his last sortie on the eve of Ypres that caught the attention of the New Zealand public. On 30 July Coningham was only hours away from taking some well-deserved leave when he went up on a patrol with two of his squadron mates — Wells and the newly arrived Aucklander Albert Gordon. The Anzac trio were planning a leisurely early evening flight at the end of a day in which cloudy weather had precluded much in the way of enemy activity in the air. Gordon had yet to be baptised in aerial combat: the sortie was not expected to meet trouble, and it would give him another opportunity to get acquainted with the DH5.

All was going according to plan until, at 6000 ft, Coningham spotted five aircraft emerging from clouds just 1000 ft below: red machines with black crosses.[43] It was a gaggle of Kurt Wolff's famous Jasta 11, the Luftstreitkräfte's most accomplished squadron of the war. Coningham dived, with Gordon and Wells at his heels. Gordon was under the misapprehension that the machines below were 'friendlies', and that they were merely taking a look at another set of

above Although the Airco DH5 was one of the earliest British machines to feature an improved gun synchroniser, it also had a 'back-staggered' wing configuration that impeded the pilot's vision behind and above.

left In spite of the DH5's limitations, Arthur 'Mary' Coningham was credited with nine victories with it in 1917.

above The flying
officers of Manfred von
Richthofen's Jasta 11.
Richthofen is seated in
an Albatros DIII.

right William Coates
was the younger brother
of future New Zealand
Prime Minster Gordon
Coates. He was posted
to Coningham's 32
Squadron in July 1917.
Here he wears both his
old army insignia and
his new RFC wings.

British aircraft. It was a short-lived mistake. Gordon heard the angry *rat-tat-tat* of his captain's Vickers gun as Coningham removed an Albatros from the sky. Wells' gun jammed and he pulled away. The unsuspecting Gordon came under fire. Coningham attempted to protect him; within hours the newcomer would be in hospital with two broken legs, thanks to a nasty crash landing.[44]

Coningham was now alone with four machines seeking to get above and behind him, right into the DH5's blindspot. They were successful, and a gaudily painted Albatros fired. Coningham ducked; two bullets grazed his head. He slumped forward on the joystick, pushing the machine down. Unconscious, Coningham dropped from 5000 to 2500 ft; the dirt of the Western Front was beckoning. He revived to find himself still under attack, but the enemy craft overshot and Coningham latched onto its tail, firing the Lewis.[45] In the heat of the dogfight Coningham's nerves had vanished, replaced with a sense of humour. 'Nerves,' he said later, 'there wouldn't be any if the flying men would only try to see the funny side. For even the most exciting fight possesses amusing incidents. I was laughing nearly all the time I had four Germans tackling me, and popping at me from all directions.' With blood running down his back and still laughing, he knocked out another German then drove off the remaining fighters. Thirty minutes after taking off, the wounded Coningham landed back at base with Wells.

Coningham and Gordon were sent to the New Zealand hospital at Hazebrouck. Gordon died of 'wounds received in action' a fortnight after his first and only foray in the air.[46] His mother was notified of her son's death, only to then receive a misleading telegram from him that read, 'Hope to be London on 6th Aug.' Gordon had died only days after drafting the wire. His mother wrote to the minister of defence, James Allen: perhaps her Albert was alive and there had been a terrible mix-up? But there was no mistake. The family placed a memorial notice on the *Thames Star*'s front page:

> What happy hours we once enjoyed
> How sweet his memory still,
> But death has left a vacant place
> This world can never fill.
> We often think of days gone by
> When we were all together
> A Shadow o'er our life is cast
> Our boy is gone for ever.[47]

Gordon was the first New Zealand flying school-trained pilot to die in action, and had been with the squadron only three weeks. He was not the only New Zealander to find the squadron a temporary lodging house between life and death.

In July Coningham welcomed William Coates of Kaipara to his flight. Coates was now free of the encumbrances of the NZEF and was extremely happy to be in the RFC. He was asked to stay in England as an instructor but, in spite of the great temptation, he 'felt frightfully keen to go on service again'. 'Settled down to the work which is intensely interesting and exciting,' he wrote to his mother Eleanor. '[In] many ways it reminds me of the old days wild bull hunting . . . though much more sporting . . . I am thoroughly enjoying myself and ever so much happier than I was in Egypt.'[48] Coates felt in his element. He had overcome earlier trepidations.

> When I first started to fly I felt I would never be any good at it and couldn't honestly say I liked it, but since coming to England I improved immensely and absolutely surprised myself with the confidence I gained. Once you have intentionally put a machine into all the dangerous positions it is possible to get into such as 'a spinning nose dive' (for about 2000 ft), 'a side slip,' a stall and a loop and can take her out [of it] successfully there is nothing more to fear and you are master of the machine . . .

Coates was caught between the reality of the situation on the Western Front and the need to allay his mother's fears. Yes, it was true that as a rule 'a pilot's life out here is a short one', he wrote, but 'the risks are really no greater than in any other part of the service'.[49]

> I trust you don't worry about me. I am in better health and spirit than I have ever been before and am happy as the day is long because I have got the chance of my life time, a chance beyond all dreams and taking part in the most glorious game in the world.[50]

In these letters home Coates barely touched on his deepest fears, and he never mentioned the heavy losses the squadron was taking. Over July, 32 Squadron had 13 officer casualties; over two-thirds of its establishment was lost as a result of death, wounds or capture.[51] The unit suffered one serious casualty nearly every two days. It was obvious to Coates that regardless of how glorious being an airman was, it was also very perilous and an uncommonly short-lived avenue of military service.

As the squadron's losses piled up, Coates welcomed the distraction of the local New Zealand military hospital and its nurses. There he regularly met New Zealand nurse and family friend Mary Hovey of Kaipara.[52] Coates was overjoyed to hear from Hovey that his brother, Captain Gordon Coates, was encamped near the airfield. The squadron's commanding officer generously offered Coates the airfield tender to go and pick Gordon up. He found his brother in a tumbledown cottage not far behind the lines — 'he was amazed to see me thinking I was miles away'. William brought his brother back to the airfield for a decent meal and a proper bed.

When they arrived at 10.30 p.m., William introduced his brother to the commanding officer and the squadron's pilots. The two Kaipara men were a study in contrast. Gordon was nine years William's senior and, with his heavy moustache and careworn face, looked almost old enough to be his father; William affectionately referred to him as 'old Gordon'. The senior Coates was already a well-known parliamentarian. He was a charismatic officer with a sense of humour, and was appreciated by his men. The two brothers talked late into the night, sharing tales of their adventures at war.[53] The next morning they arose early and William, resplendent in his new airman's uniform and RFC wings, showed his older brother around the airfield and sheds. They called in on William's own DH5 and Gordon quietly noted the numerous bullet holes and damage. It confirmed Gordon's assessment of flying. He and his fellow New Zealand soldiers liked nothing more than to see a 'Boche airman' running for 'dear life' with one of 'our airmen after him', but they all knew it was a 'very risky game'.[54]

Five days into his posting, William Coates tenderly wrote to his mother, telling her that in all likelihood he was due some considerable backpay and that he wanted her to withdraw the funds she had deposited in his account for his upkeep. He wanted Eleanor to treat herself.

> Don't whatever you do . . . put it by for me as I want you to be comfortable . . . After all there is nothing in this world a son could give his mother to repay her for what she has been to him. I fear [it is] the only gift I am in a position to offer at present . . . I am sure there may be more opportunities days later on when this ghastly war is over, and I am looking forward to many happy days in my little mother's company.[55]

He told her that he had pledged not to marry until he was assured she was comfortably looked after, unless of course he should have the good fortune to find a loving *and* wealthy bride — something he considered possible, 'especially as a flying officer'. For the time being, he wrote, he could count many female friends whom he thought 'a lot of', but none had taken his heart.

On 21 July he visited Mary Hovey. Coates was cheery, and Hovey considered him not a bit changed from the boy she had known years ago at Ruatuna. Yet Coates was also unsettled. He spoke to her of the uncertainty of an airman's life and the probability of an early death. He was not thinking so much of himself, but rather of the grief of those he would leave behind, especially his mother and sisters. He asked Hovey to write to his mother after a short time, should he die. Seven days later he was dead.

When Gordon received news that his brother was missing he rushed off to find the source of the story. The local field ambulance directed him to a nearby hospital, but all he uncovered were wild rumours, including a story that 'Bill' had crashed his machine on landing. Gordon did not believe it; he had seen that William was an accomplished pilot, a fact his flight commander, Coningham, had confirmed. It did not make sense; if William had had a spark of life in him he would have been able to land his machine. Gordon failed to secure further information and the 'wretched suspense' worried him day and night. In the end his enquiries revealed the horrible truth: 'Bill had crashed behind Bosch lines.' He wrote home, 'Mother dear, I am afraid there is going to be bad news for you long before this letter reaches you. Poor old Bill has been reported Killed.' There would be no one on earth 'happier than I if I can deny the wretched news,' Gordon wrote as he waited for verification of his brother's fate. The sliver of hope was extinguished when an eyewitness confirmed William's death.

On 22 July William Coates had embarked on an offensive patrol with another member of Coningham's flight, Englishman St Cyprian Tayler. The pair crossed the enemy lines after midday and Tayler attacked a German observation balloon. The balloon was hastily winched down. As they headed home Coates was hit by enemy anti-aircraft fire at 1.15 p.m. The out-of-control DH5 crashed near the enemy's second line. German infantry converged on the mangled machine and airman, only to be scattered by a strafing Tayler.[56]

Even with Tayler's report on the action, the lack of a body ate at Eleanor. Perhaps her dear son was still alive? Gordon undertook further investigations. But phone calls and letters to Coningham and the squadron commander Major Thomas Cairnes all pointed to the same conclusion: William had been killed in the vicinity of Gheluvelt.[57] 'I very much fear,' Cairnes informed the family, 'there is little hope of his having survived.' Hovey kept her promise to William, and after a short duration wrote to his mother.

> I hope you will forgive me if, by writing, I intrude on a sacred grief, but I thought you might like to know that I had the privilege of seeing Willie shortly before his sad but glorious ending . . . He was with us all evening the day before he went out into the Great Beyond . . . I have seen several of his brother officers and his end was quick and must have been painless and I am sure he would have chosen it so, to living on possibly as a helpless wreck, as so many fine men have had to do. Everyone had spoken very highly of him, and though one cannot help grieving, it must help to know that your son lived and died a brave, honourable man, a son to be proud of indeed. I shall always feel proud that I knew him and met him in France . . . I trust that you and y[ou]r family are all well and pray that y[ou]r other son may be spared to come home to you.[58]

Eleanor was devastated. Her sister in England, with whom William had spent many hours when training and on leave in England, sent her deepest condolences.

> Oh my dear. Words cannot say how I feel *with* you, and all your dear girls . . . one can think of nothing but the sorrow, and the awful heart ache, but presently by God's grace we shall see beyond the cloud, and we shall realise that all is well . . . he is safe forevermore. You dear, must be thankful and proud to have such a son — a strong, true, noble man and a brave and gallant Christian soldier.[59]

In the great battle that was about to commence in Flanders, Gordon held the memory of his brother close. When a determined enemy raid was made on his company's sector early in the 1917 Ypres offensive, he exacted some revenge for the death of his brother. In the face of the onslaught and with great 'coolness and presence of mind', Gordon regathered his men to safety, thereby preventing heavy losses. He then reinforced his front line and re-established two forward posts. Finally, he led a raid on the enemy which, in the words of his Military Cross citation, 'was largely responsible for the success of the entire operation'. Through it all, Captain Coates was mindful of the previous month's events and his family's loss. 'Bill was constantly before me,' he penned to his mother, 'and he was more than avenged . . . many a Hun went under.'[60]

In the meantime Coningham was invalided to England, although he was well enough to receive his Military Cross and Distinguished Service Order at Buckingham Palace in late August 1917. 'I am prouder of being spared to keep the reputation of the College and of New Zealand than anything else,' he wrote to his former high school. 'It is a treat to have one's efforts recognised, but at the same time very saddening to think of all the other top-notchers not so fortunate.'[61] The squadron had lost three New Zealanders in July — Coningham to wounds and Gordon and Coates killed. The latter two losses were testament to the rapidity in which newly trained men entered the air war and were spat out. They had both been with the squadron for less than a fortnight.[62]

Two other losses of note were Captains Wyndham Fitzherbert and Melville Johnstone. Fitzherbert, an observer, failed to return from a bombing raid on Ramegnies-Chin airfield. The Lower Hutt-born Fitzherbert and his pilot were last seen gliding over Lille with the propeller stopped.[63] It was the second loss for the family — his brother Harold had died storming a trench on the Somme.[64] On 16 July 1917 Melville Johnstone was also on a bombing sortie when things went terribly wrong. Flying a Martinsyde G100 'Elephant', a single-seater of large and ungainly proportions, Johnstone was returning from a bombing mission with 27 Squadron when he noticed that the undercarriage had snagged one of his bombs. It would appear that the Hawke's Bay pilot was fearful of the ordnance exploding on landing and decided to ditch in Lake Arques. He drowned in the attempt. His father Robert and mother Anastasia, of Waipukurau, were promptly informed of their son's death.[65] 'Captain Melville Johnstone, of the Royal Flying Corps, has paid the supreme sacrifice in the Empire's cause,' wrote the *Hastings Standard*.[66] The newspaper reminded their readers that all the family's five sons had enlisted and were giving their service in the 'great struggle'.[67] At the time of Melville's death the youngest brother, Godfrey, was only weeks away from getting his pilot's badge in England. Six months later the Johnstones received news that Godfrey had been killed on the Western Front on an offensive patrol.[68]

A little over a month later Arthur Skinner arrived as replacement for 27 Squadron losses, which included Johnstone. Skinner had come a long way from his grim experiences at Gallipoli and had finally fulfilled his dreams of flight, although he quickly discovered that the squadron's work was no less perilous than his life as a soldier. The squadron was regularly crossing the lines above the cloud cover and then descending to bomb airfields, encampments and railway junctions. As the Martinsydes emerged from the clouds they were pelted with anti-aircraft fire. On 16 August, in a particularly hair-raising mission, Skinner was struck in the head by shrapnel from an exploding shell. He momentarily lost consciousness at 5000 ft.[69] When he came round, the New Zealander found the controls had been damaged and the machine was on fire. He was unable to rein in the 'Elephant', which inelegantly crashed into a tree on the German side of the lines. Skinner was captured; after only a handful of sorties his fighting war was over.[70] For reasons unknown, the Germans did not remove a small piece of shrapnel from his head, but it mattered little given that the wound did not bother him and he soon returned to full health.[71]

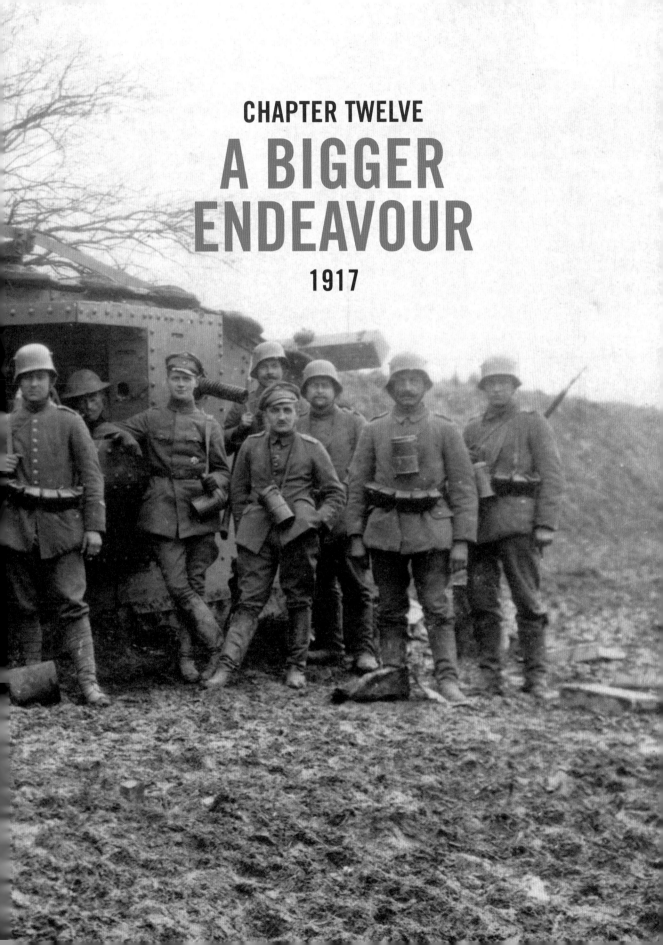

CHAPTER TWELVE
A BIGGER
ENDEAVOUR
1917

The loss of men in July was only the preamble to a much bigger endeavour set before the New Zealand pilots and observers. The Flanders offensive was designed to secure territory east and northeast of Ypres; the capstone of the assault would be the capture of Passchendaele Ridge. On 31 July, 100,000 men and 136 tanks advanced over no-man's land. Into this offensive the Royal Flying Corps and the Royal Naval Air Service inserted close to 750 machines, of which 330 were fighters. Opposing them were some 600 enemy machines. For the first time in many months, British aircraft were eclipsing the German Albatros DIII and DV. The new Sopwith Camel that Harold Beamish was already enjoying was just one aircraft of a trio of formidable machines pointed directly at the Luftstreitkräfte. Also in the air were the Royal Aircraft Factory SE5a and the Bristol Fighter.

While the snub-nosed Camel bore the delicate lines of its Sopwith antecedents, the SE5a was muscular, almost brutal in appearance. Its V8 engine projected menacingly forward of the pilot, and the elongated exhausts running down past the cockpit accentuated its aggressive look. The SE5a sported twin machine guns: a Vickers firing through the propeller arc and a single Foster rail-mounted Lewis on the upper wing. Unlike the Camel and SE5a, the Bristol Fighter was a twin-seat machine. It was agile and versatile, able to perform equally well in reconnaissance and offensive fighter operations. The Rolls-Royce Falcon engine gave the Bristol a maximum speed of 113 mph and lifted the airframe and crew to 20,000 ft. Armament was provided by one forward-firing Vickers and a Lewis for the observer. The Bristol more than held its own against nearly all German adversaries.

To counter this qualitative mismatch the Germans concentrated their best resources into powerful wings (Geschwader) — a conglomeration of several squadrons. Most important was the establishment of Jagdgeschwader 1 (JG1), a German fighter wing, commanded by Manfred von Richthofen, that incorporated some of the Luftstreitkräfte's best squadrons: Jastas 4, 6, 10 and 11. It was hoped that this intensification of firepower would offset the RFC and RNAS's growing numerical and technical ascendency, and would offer the best prospects of attaining aerial superiority at crucial moments over the battlefield. The result of the British and German advances and tactics were periodic massive aerial battles of a scale hitherto unseen over the Western Front — clashes attracting more than 60 machines at a time.

Aside from these very large dogfights, Ypres saw the systematic use of aircraft in close support of advancing infantry. Over 1915–16, low-flying airmen had raked enemy positions with machine-gun fire and bombs, but in 1917 this was formally adopted as an effective means of supporting ground forces that were advancing beyond the range of British artillery.

Into this strode two outstanding New Zealand airmen: Keith Park, an experienced fighter in the ground war, and Clive Collett, New Zealand's most skilled airman of the war. Park and Collett came to the battlefield in mid-1917 better equipped for the rigours of the air war than many of their countrymen. William Coates had turned down his opportunity to instruct in England before being posted to the Western Front, but Park's decision to serve as an instructor meant he had at least four times more flying hours than most men posted to frontline squadrons in 1917.[1] Collett was, of course, a seasoned airman of the first order; he had been flying since January 1915 and was a veteran of the air. After his experimental parachute flights he requested a posting to the Western Front. In France, Park and Collett would fly the new generation of fighters.

Three weeks before Ypres, Park took up residence with the unit with which he would spend the rest of the war, first as a pilot and then as its commander: 48 Squadron. It was the only unit on the Western Front equipped with the new Bristol Fighter. To Park's mind, the Bray-Dunes airfield on the French coast was small and dingy, but the men all seemed in good spirits and the mechanics were tireless in maintaining the machines.[2] Park quickly spotted areas ripe for improvement. He was critical of how poorly the new arrivals were prepared for air fighting. The usual practice was to send these airmen up in one of the squadron's old machines for an informal test to gauge their abilities. A few weeks might pass before the pilot flew his first mission. In the period between the initial 'test' and the baptismal sortie — in some cases several weeks — the lack of machines for practice flying often precluded the novice combat pilots undertaking many familiarisation flights. Moreover, when they were inserted into the fight the newcomers were often left to 'sink or swim': formation flying and tactics were rarely discussed, let alone practised in a squadron. The more experienced airmen seemed to concentrate solely on the next offensive patrol, with little interest in the new postings.

The old hands argued, 'I had to buy my experience over the lines, so why shouldn't these new hands do the same,' Park recalled. It was a recipe for disaster, and it was little wonder that the rookies, who had flown on only a couple of occasions in the preceding weeks and had no idea about what was expected of them in the air, died in such vast numbers in 1917.

As to the intention of the leader, if E.A. [Enemy Aircraft] were met above, below, east, on the same level, in larger, or even smaller numbers — all was left to the spur of the moment. The result was we seldom fought in any formation, but immediately became split up and fought a 'Dog Fight'. This haphazard method of fighting worked excellently as long as most members of the patrol could handle their machines and guns aggressively. The inexperienced invariably went down followed by E.A., who in turn were often shot down by the experienced pilots. Unintentionally the poorer and newer pilots acted as good bait for the enemy scouts.[3]

Thunie
1928

above Thames-born Keith Park standing in front of a Bristol F2B Fighter. His 48 Squadron was the first to receive this excellent machine.

left Park met his future wife Dorothy 'Dol' Paris while delivering the personal effects of a deceased airman to his family in London.

Bristol Fighters at first blush looked for all the world like the Airco DH4 bomber. Overconfident Central Power pilots misidentified the Bristols and attacked them eagerly, unaware of their impressive performance statistics. It was not uncommon for a single German fighter to boldly assault a collection of the DH4s, only to discover their costly mistake. The enemy scouts were slow to learn the difference, and it took some eight weeks for the Germans to realise that a new machine had entered the conflict and that care was required when engaging it in combat. Park took full advantage of this breathing space.

During his initial period with 48 Squadron, Park became an exceptional military pilot. Over August and September he was the unit's highest-scoring airman — a position he still occupied at the Armistice. Of course he did not do this alone but rather in conjunction with a collection of observers. The seasoned observer-gunners were often the Bristol's first line of defence, and they saved many a novice pilot. Park had no fewer than 11 different observers throughout late summer. Among these was Englishman Arthur Noss, with whom Park secured seven victories in August. Their single best day occurred three weeks into Ypres.

Flying patrol on 17 August, the pair spotted a Sopwith Camel cornered by a trio of Albatros DIIIs. Park and Noss managed to drive off the enemy, only to discover two additional Albatros attached to their own tail. Noss fired first and an Albatros overshot the Bristol, allowing Park to open up with the Vickers. The out-of-control machine fell from the sky and was soon followed by another fatally wounded Albatros crashing to the ground. Three additional enemy machines jumped the pair, but Noss removed one from the formation's inventory. The final action involved defending another Camel under attack. Park closed to 50 yards of the assailant and unloaded 100 rounds; the enemy tumbled into an uncontrolled spin.[4] It was a quadruple victory for the pair, for which they were each subsequently awarded the Military Cross.[5] By war's end, Park's tally sheet totalled 20.

High summer was also a happy hunting ground for Collett in this target-rich corner of France. The former combat and test pilot, with a logbook chronicling a staggering 1000 hours' flying time, was now fighting with 70 Squadron southwest of Park's position. Unlike Park's coastal location, however, the Estrée-Blanche airfield was set in bucolic countryside, with a sixteenth-century church and a substantial château. It was a very busy ground, home to three additional squadrons besides Collett's: 19, 56 and 66. With the squadrons came a collection of colourful aviation notables, including Richard Maybery, Arthur Rhys-Davids and the mercurial James McCudden. Collett was not the sole New Zealander at Estrée-Blanche: John Warnock and Ralph Stedman with 66 Squadron and Frederick Horrell with 56 Squadron were just a few of his fellow countrymen. A sheep farmer from Rangiora, Horrell had been with his squadron only a short time but was fortunate to be flying the SE5a.

Collett was well known across the three other squadrons and was held in high regard by his men. Once the pilots got past his facial disfigurement, which gave him an aggressive and somewhat arrogant air, they found him extremely generous and paternal. Cedric Jones flew with Collett in France:

above In the months before his posting to France, Clive Collett extensively flew this Sopwith Pup. On his arrival on the Western Front he took the controls of the Pup's replacement, the Sopwith Camel.

below This overturned Sopwith Camel is testament to its tricky handling attributes. It was one of the war's most celebrated aircraft, but it was not for the faint-hearted.

Clive Collett was my Flight Commander in 70 Sqn., so of course I got to know him better than most . . . he was one of the very best pilots and I owe [to] him practically everything I learnt about aerial fighting. The front line was very active at this time, and I had only two days practice before I went over the line. I had complete confidence in Collett, and Collett had complete confidence in himself. If I thought any of his patrol were in trouble he would be round in a flash to rescue, and he never failed to remedy the situation.[6]

Flying the squadron's newly arrived Camels, Collett's first aerial victory came in one of the big battles on the eve of Ypres. It was a classic 'bait-and-ambush' operation. Twenty Albatros attacked eight 'defenceless' FE2ds. Over Polygon Wood they were met by the Estrée-Blanche squadrons. The ensuing battle sucked in all the Allied and enemy machines in the vicinity. Triplanes, Camels, SE5s, Spads, Nieuports and German Albatros were spread from 10,000 to 18,000 ft. 'It must have been a fantastic sight from the ground,' wrote one of the participants, 'this great fleet of flights invading German air . . . nothing like this mass attack had been seen before.'[7]

The New Zealanders Collett, Horrell and Coningham — the latter on one of his last sorties before his injury — were in the thick of it. From 7.45 p.m., aircraft from both sides engaged in an hour-long battle ranging across Flanders. In addition to Coningham's success, Horrell took on a trio of hostile fighters and got three good bursts into one of them.[8] Collett was caught in a tussle with no fewer than six of the newer Albatros DVs. He attacked and found himself being circled by the others, which took turns to dive on his Camel. He managed to get beneath one and fired into the fuselage; its propeller fluttered, the nose dipped and it glided down. Both of Collett's guns jammed. He dropped in altitude to gain time and clear the weapons. With one of the guns cleared, he carried out a climbing turn and fired under the pilot's seat of an Albatros. It immediately fell into a vertical dive. The surviving gun-shy Germans would not close with Collett; they fired ineffectually from 500 ft before abandoning the chase when the New Zealander crossed the line at 800 ft.[9]

The Albatros DV become a feature of the German effort during Ypres, and appeared prominently in Collett's combat reports. The machine supported the Central Powers' attempt to claw back some of the ground taken by the Camels, SE5s, Spads and Bristols, but while it gained something in appearance, with an aesthetically pleasing fully elliptical fuselage, it offered nothing materially to offset the new generation of Allied fighters.[10]

Over the next six weeks 70 Squadron was involved in almost continual offensive patrols, with low-level ground attacks carried out when required.[11] Collett accumulated more victories over the DVs; by the second week of September he had eight successes and a Military Cross, and was about to have his most fruitful day over the front.

On 9 September, patrolling between Gheluvelt and Houthulst Forest, Collett's flight attacked a couple of small two-seater formations.[12] At 5.10 p.m. he shot one down with the aid of another pilot, and 15 minutes later he accounted for another; the aircraft trailed a rope of black smoke as it ploughed into the ground. He watched it crash — an almost fatal mistake. The barking of an enemy machine gun broke his post-victory revelry and he craned his neck to find himself facing some top-flight opposition. It was almost his undoing.

The rest of the unit was under assault, and an Albatros was spitting at him. It was Karl Hammes of Jasta 35, an Austrian with four combat victories.[13] Yet Collett easily outmatched him. The New Zealander manoeuvred the Camel behind his assailant and fired. Hammes' machine started to fall, but not entirely out of control. Collett's suspicions were confirmed when the Albatros attempted to make a forced landing. The New Zealander shut off his engine — silent death — and dived on the unsuspecting Hammes. Flying 'straight at him', Collett put in a long, purposeful strafing burst. The helpless machine burst into flames. Hammes survived the terror but did not fly in combat for the remainder of the war. The Austrian was Collett's third victory in the space of 40 minutes.

However, the strafing run had dropped him to a very low altitude and more Germans arrived, determined to balance the ledger. Over Houthulst Forest, tracer bullets arced towards Collett's tail from three Albatros. In all likelihood one of the pilots was the highly regarded Max Ritter von Müller, the highest-scoring Bavarian of the Great War and a Pour le Mérite ('Blue Max') recipient.[14] Müller's DV sported a red spinner, yellow tail, and a fiery black comet sweeping along the red fuselage. The pale blue undersides to the lower wing were festooned with twin large black 'M' letters to aid ground observers in the confirmation of his kills.[15] Collett set his face westward, skimming 30 ft above the forest, throwing the Camel all over the place. If he could only prevent them getting a clear shot. In the eternity it took to clear the line he was hit in the hand. 'I crossed the trenches at 40 feet and returned home,' he reported. He made it, albeit with a bloodied hand — just another disfigurement in a catalogue of scars.

James McCudden, the most highly decorated British airman of the war, was impressed with Collett's ability and courage and befriended the New Zealander. McCudden noted that Collett's Camel was 'shot to ribbons nearly every time he went out'.[16] Perhaps he recognised a kindred spirit in Collett; certainly he was impressed by his unrelenting assault on Hammes and made a point of mentioning it in his autobiography published posthumously after the war. Making sure of the kill by low-level strafing spoke to the Englishman's heart. 'Collett was always for downing the Hun,' he wrote, 'whenever and wherever he could find them.' The authorities agreed, and Collett was awarded a bar to his Military Cross. Fortunately for the enemy, Collett's injury forced his withdrawal from active service with 70 Squadron.

On the same day and at the same time as Collett was injured, Park was also in the air, attacking six Albatros.[17] Park and his observer shot down a single machine near Middelkerke-Slijpe. The Thames-born airman was nearing the conclusion of a six-victory run over a dozen days.[18] It ended on 14 September with a double success that highlighted the combined efforts of the pilot and gunner in the work of the Bristol Fighters, and which showed that Park was just as determined and ruthless as Collett in ensuring the enemy went down and stayed down.

> While leading evening patrol rear machines [were] dived on and attacked by three E.A. of [a] formation of 10. Doubling back under our machines gave my observer good shooting at one

Keith Park's sterling work in 1917, when he and his observers between them accumulated 16 victories in the Bristol Fighter, saw him promoted to Major Park, commanding 48 Squadron in 1918.

E.A. which was attacking our rear machines. We fired one complete drum at E.A. which dived steeply. I then got on his tail and followed diving and fired 500 rounds at about 100 yards range. Hostile machine dived more steeply, slide-slipped and was last seen going down out of control.[19]

With that, Park 'zoomed' to the aid of another Bristol under attack. He drove off the hostile, firing until he saw the pilot slump forward in his seat. Park closed to within 25 yards — the machine completely filled his field of vision — and fired continually until the DV burst into flames. It crashed just 'our side of the lines' south of Dixmude.

In spite of Park's flying successes, the morale of the squadron deteriorated over September as it was given a series of new tasks. In conjunction with offensive patrols, they were now expected to escort other machines, undertake photographic reconnaissance and, finally, prepare for night flying, with a view to intercepting nocturnal bombers. This last demand was a most unwelcome addition to the unrelenting offensive duties of 48 Squadron.

The compact Bray-Dunes coastal airfield was not suited to this latter enterprise: the west of the base was skirted by low sandhills topped with ensnaring barbed wire running all the way down to the airfield, while along the eastern boundary an unbroken stand of tall trees could pluck the unwary from the sky. Completing the picture on the northern and southern perimeters was a series of narrow but surprisingly deep canals.

The Bristols shared the airfield with a squadron of triplanes, adding to the potential for mishap. 'In the daylight,' wrote Park after commencement of the night-flying training, 'Bristols and Sopwith triplanes were not infrequently seen standing on their noses in one or other of the three canals.'[20] The night flying, the intensity of the sorties and the fact that leave was being withheld from the squadron's airmen because of the demands of the ground offensive meant that even experienced fliers were being culled from the unit. In August there were eight casualties, and there were 14 more in September.[21] Park himself escaped joining these losses only by a hair's breadth on a number of occasions.[22] He calculated that by the time winter arrived the only experienced airmen left would be the flight commanders.

The squadron was then moved down to the Arras sector, away from the action. It was now essentially a new squadron, and Park set to the task of training his flight in preparation for reinsertion into the battle. In the meantime, the squadron was shifted westward closer to Dunkirk and on to less dangerous tasks. The shift saw a rapid decline in losses; only three airmen were killed in October. One of those was Park's good friend, Captain John Milne.

Park was given the unenviable job of gathering Milne's personal effects, boxing them up and delivering them to his grieving wife, Janie. Before his death, Milne had furnished Park with his home address so the New Zealander would have somewhere to visit in London while on leave. In October, with the small collection of Milne's piloting possessions under his arm, Park arrived at the newly widowed Janie's front door. It was here, under uncomfortable circumstances, that Park would meet his future wife.

Among those comforting Janie was her cousin Dorothy 'Dol' Paris, a 24-year-old London hospital nurse from a wealthy family. Dorothy's family connections, great beauty and sense of humour ensured that she had a prominent position in London society. Park was captivated. His biographer, historian Vincent Orange, captured the moment.

> Perhaps it was not surprising that she and Keith should promptly fall in love, for each found the other not only physically attractive, but also quite unlike anyone else they had ever met. Then twenty-five, he was very tall (at least a foot taller than Dol) and strikingly handsome. Three years of active service in notoriously dangerous campaigns had given an edge to a naturally masterful character. He was grave and serious, she light-hearted and cheerful; they seem to have responded instantly to each other . . . She had had many admirers, but none of Park's distinction, and he had never met anyone like her. He would give a sense of purpose to her life and she would bring humanity to his.[23]

Though Park and Dol had an 'understanding', they decided against a wartime marriage. Park had seen so many losses at 48 Squadron, and he realised that the possibility of his own death could not be discounted. Did they want a marriage that would end with another member of his squadron delivering his personal effects to his new wife? Their love for one another would have to deepen through letters and time together as leave allowed.

The Zeppelin raids continued in 1917, but they were now attacking at between 16,000 and 20,000 ft in order to avoid the ongoing improvements in the home defence squadrons, which had grown to 12 in number. Among this force was a small but growing clutch of New Zealanders. Joining the hero of the previous year, Alfred de Bathe Brandon, were Alfred Kingsford and Hubert Solomon — both serving with 33 (Home Defence) Squadron. Kingsford was a Nelson photographer from the New Zealand Medical Corps who had joined the unit in mid-1917. Solomon was a former Wellington engine salesperson. Like many New Zealanders, Solomon was appalled by the early reports of German atrocities in 1914. Over that Christmas he organised a street collection and sale in Christchurch for Christmas gifts for the children of German-occupied Belgium.[24] New Zealand papers reported that he had originally turned down a commission in New Zealand to more quickly enter the war in the air.[25] Once in England he was selected, along with Kingsford, for night-flying duties in home defence.

Both men found it to be one of the more challenging avenues of flying. Kingsford wrote of the general course of events during the night of a Zeppelin raid.

> The Huns' Zepp Base was at Heligoland, due east of Spurn Head. His course was due west until he struck Spurn Head, where he would pick up the lights of Hull, invariably turning south and passing right over our aerodrome, then picking up Lincoln and apparently following the Northern Railway down to London. He always came in what we called the dark period, when there was no moon, and during this time we were not allowed to leave the aerodrome after dark, operational pilots standing by all the time, with machines ready and ears pricked up every time the telephone bell rang. We always hoped it would be orders to

take to the air, our first intimation usually being from the Navy, 'Zepps sighted forty miles east of Spurn Head, proceeding west,' later, 'Zepps still proceeding west, now twenty miles from the coast.' At this stage, the first operational pilot would be ordered up with certain instructions, the remaining two at ten-minute intervals. Our patrol was for three hours, and we took our turn in being first.[26]

Of course, being on patrol was no guarantee of meeting the quarry, and the airships, if successfully located, always seemed just beyond their grasp — as both men soon discovered.

On the night of 21–22 August 1917 the New Zealanders were scrambled from Scampton. It was Kingsford's first foray against the Zeppelins. The night was clear but cold as Kingsford and his observer, E. G. 'Robie' Roberts, took off into star-laden heavens at 11 p.m. Flying north, they reached 10,000 ft as they crossed over the Humber River. They spotted searchlights over Hull and Kingsford turned the nose of the FE2b. 'I don't know what Robie's eyes were like but mine seemed to be nearly out of my head by this time,' wrote Kingsford.[27] Beams of light lacing the sky and shellfire seemed to indicate an enemy airship nearby, but they found nothing.[28] 'We groped around for another two hours,' he wrote, 'realising that we'd been pretty near, and still not wishing to give up all hope, saw the remaining hour out and then, with benzine being low, we were obliged to land.'

Only two airmen saw anything of the Zeppelins that night: Solomon and a Canadian. At 8000 ft the Canadian spied a distant Zeppelin caught briefly in a searchlight. He gave chase but after nearly four hours of fruitless casting about in the darkness above northern England, returned to base. On patrol at 15,000 ft, Solomon saw *L41* surrounded by a thicket of anti-aircraft bursts near Beverley.[29] He was flying the lacklustre BE12a, a single-seater version of the BE2a. Just after midnight he gave chase. The fleeing airship was commanded by Hauptmann Kuno Manger. A longstanding airship commander, Manger looked the part with his undercut hair slicked back and a carefully groomed toothbrush moustache. This would not be the last time a New Zealander would attempt to bring him down.

Manger's airship was at 20,000 ft and Solomon moved in, but was only able to fire at extreme range. There was no result, but he continued his pursuit. Frustratingly, he could keep up with the Zeppelin only if he stayed on level flight; as soon as he attempted to climb the enemy inched further away. He stalked the airship for 20 minutes out to sea but was unable to make any headway, and with the fuel gauge dipping desperately low he retreated. Although the defenders had little to show for their efforts, the Germans had fared no better. Strong headwinds and the inadequacies of the rudimentary oxygen equipment at 20,000 ft diminished the effectiveness of the intruders.[30] They managed to bomb a Methodist chapel and injured a man at Hedon, Yorkshire.

Kingsford realised that because of the height at which the airships were entering Britain in 1917, it would be much harder to repeat the efforts of his friend Brandon the previous year. The FE2bs had a service ceiling of only 15,000 ft, a full 5000 ft shy of the Zeppelins. Kingsford made it his personal mission to try to reach a Zeppelin, and set about modifying his FB2b for the task. He reduced the weight of the machine by doing away with the observer and mounting the machine gun so he could fire it from the rear cockpit. To streamline the craft he placed a cowling over the now vacated observer's forward seat. It was a failed experiment. He staggered to 16,000 ft, 'but at that height, I almost froze in the process, so I didn't try that again. Frost-bitten nose is quite painful, believe me.'[31]

The weeks between the raids were occupied with night flying, without much incident for Kingsford, except for one fatality, 'for which I was responsible'.[32] He and his observer were practising forced landings when a dropped parachute flare failed to ignite. Days later a local farmer presented him with a bill: the flare had hit and killed his horse, and Kingsford — or, more correctly, the RFC — owed him £25. It was Kingsford's sole equine casualty of the war.

Kingsford hated home defence work, in large part because many of the unit's patrols were over the North Sea, which was plagued with foul weather, making it something of a 'personal enemy'. Sudden fogs reduced visibility to nothing and hid potential hazards. The flights were long, tedious and cold, and brought few tangible results. And of course there was always the danger of engine failure and a watery grave. It was the great fear over home waters: an inability to find an airfield in pea-soup fog and being forced to ditch in the icy North Sea.

Not that night operations over land were a walk in the park either, as Kingsford well knew. He was on a Humber to Lincoln defensive patrol when the entire coast became shrouded in dense fog. After two hours in the air he lowered the machine, but this only made matters worse; he could not even see his observer's head directly in front of him. He was flying blind with only the 'bubble' keeping him level. After half an hour Kingsford was faced with the harsh reality of having to land. He dropped to 300 ft, but feared he was 'out at sea'. The observer excitedly pointed to dim lights: the squadron's commander had made a number of telephone calls and emergency landing sites were listening for the drone of the machine. The New Zealander dropped a parachute flare but that only made matters worse, lighting up the immediate fog and obscuring what little they could see. 'Waiting for it to burn out,' said Kingsford, 'I decided I'd have to land without lights.'[33] It was an extremely dangerous but unavoidable decision.

Kingsford had no idea how close he was to the ground. He thought he had 50-odd ft as he turned and throttled back. He was wrong. The FE2b slammed into a field and Kingsford's observer was catapulted from his seat, somersaulting through the foggy darkness. Kingsford hit the dashboard, knocking out some of his teeth. The undercarriage splayed, and the FE2b's rear end stuck up in the air, signalling surrender. The shaken observer brushed himself off and demanded a cigarette from the concerned mechanic who found him.

The incident highlighted the dangers of night operations. When he finally arrived back at his base, Kingsford discovered that another squadron pair had also crash-landed, and that another pilot and observer were missing; a trawler found the wreckage of their plane days later in the North Sea. In a single fortnight, 33 Squadron lost six airmen and three machines.[34] 'All transpired to make it a frightful job, no matter how often our Senior Officers reminded us of the importance of the job,' said Kingsford. He had had enough. 'This Zepp strafing job wasn't much good, so . . . I decided to put in a request to be transferred overseas.'[35]

William Cook of 75 (Home Defence) Squadron was the only New Zealander to actually hit a Zeppelin in 1917. Formerly from Palmerston North, Cook was ordered aloft from Farnborough to intercept a raid of 10 Zeppelins on the night of 24–25 September. Only five actually crossed the coast, and adverse wind and low cloud frustrated the German attempts to attack industrial centres and airfields. In the early morning, rising through the clouds in his BE2e, Cook turned northeast towards *L55*, the airship ensnared by a number of searchlights. It was 1.45 a.m. when he arrived well below the prey. His quarry was a further 4000 ft higher at 16,000 ft, beyond his immediate reach and above the bursting anti-aircraft shells. He began the climb to meet *L55*, but it soon evaded the searchlights. The great airship scattered its bombs well wide of its industrial targets at Skinningrove.

It was futile to continue his hunt, so Cook took his place on the patrol line at 14,000 ft before deciding to go out to sea; perhaps he could waylay a Zeppelin on its homeward run. In the faint light of the early morning a long white cylinder could be seen. It was Manger and *L41*, the German commander and Zeppelin that had escaped Solomon in August. Aided by a strong tailwind, Cook slowly reeled in the Zeppelin and gained altitude. At 800 yards he poured four drums into the rear of the fleeing airship. Tracers scuttled hypnotically across the dark night sky towards the looming Zeppelin. The great hull was struck. Cook waited. Nothing. It was frustrating. When the German ground crew inspected the airship on its return they found two bullets had pierced a gas cell.[36] Cook had come close, but Manger had denied his airship to another New Zealander.

Four hours in, and Cook was very low on fuel. Sixty miles out to sea, he dipped a wing and set a westerly course for Farnborough. The 60-mph wind that assisted his outward flight now fought his return. It was 75 nail-biting minutes before he spied land and managed to make landfall in a field only 400 yards from the lapping waves of the North Sea. It had been a five-and-a-half-hour sortie.[37] Cook was rewarded with a Military Cross for his skill and determination.[38]

On the night of 19–20 October, one of the war's biggest Zeppelin raids — a major attack by 11 airships on the industrial centres of northern England — was launched and Solomon was thrown into the action.[39] The Zeppelins faced extremely difficult conditions, including freezing temperatures and a strong headwind that reduced their ground speed to no more than 15 mph off the Farnborough Heads. The contrary winds and poor navigation spread the Zeppelins over England, from Birmingham to London. However, the bombs still fell. In what would be dubbed the 'Silent Raid', inhabitants heard nothing as the atmospheric conditions carried the noise of the Zeppelins' engines away. 'The fall of the bombs caused the utmost surprise' in London, and the effects of the bombs were 'freakish'. A crowded and well-lit factory survived five bombs unscathed; but a single bomb wiped out three houses, in one of which eight people were killed — a mother, two boys, four girls and a baby.[40] Seventy-eight defensive sorties were launched but few airmen saw an airship, and only a couple made weak attacks. The meteorological conditions were more punishing, however: some Zeppelins were blown east over France and five were eventually lost.[41] It was a massive blow. The costly raid brought an end to the Zeppelin raids for 1917.

Solomon's effort began at 7.55 p.m. and ended not long after. He took off from the squadron's headquarters at Gainsborough, Lincolnshire, in an FE2b to engage the northernmost Zeppelins. Ground crew saw the aircraft rise to 200 ft and then inexplicably dive steeply to the right. The machine crashed, flipped on its back with the engine still running. The traumatised observer was thrown clear. Men rushed to assist Solomon but found him already dead, tightly secured in the cockpit.[42] The aeroplane then burst into flames. An inquiry into the New Zealander's death was inconclusive, but the squadron commander thought that perhaps Solomon's 'clumsy, thigh-length fug boots' had somehow fouled the controls.[43]

One of Solomon's brothers, a sergeant in the Canadian forces, attended the Gainsborough funeral and a clergyman who was officiating to the Jewish troops took the service. The *Press* recorded:

> One can only give the best that he possesses, more is impossible. Bert Solomon was another of those who have offered up their lives on the altar of patriotism. Gifted with the fine qualities that commanded the respect of everyone who was fortunate enough to come into contact with him, friendship and affection were ever his. Like all really brave soldiers, he had a quiet unassuming nature; a man full of ability and promise, he gave his life in defence of the Mother country. There will often come to the many of those who cherish the memory of this fine young New Zealander a sweet recollection of everything that was good and noble in man.[44]

Solomon was killed on his thirty-fourth birthday. He was mourned by his widowed mother and his fiancée.

I n Belgium, Ypres was a vast quagmire. The heavy rain and the intensive shelling had turned the Flemish countryside into a series of ponds, burst rivers and swamps, surrounded by mud. During the seven weeks of fighting the British forces had advanced no more than a few miles. Rather than cut their losses they made one final, intensified push. The substantial initial objectives of the campaign were now a distant memory, and in an attempt to gain some advantage for the coming year they proposed the capture of Menin Road Ridge in the Ypres salient. The air service would carry out its traditional role of reconnaissance and artillery spotting and offensive patrols, but it would also increase 'disruption of enemy forces by low patrolling'.[45] This included fitting bombs to the single-seater fighters.

At the same time, Frederick Horrell's 56 Squadron kept up its usual role of deterring enemy incursions and escorting bombers to their objectives. By the evening of 29 September, 56 Squadron had accumulated over 198 victories, and there was considerable competition among the men as to who would bag number 200. When it came up the following day, the commanding officer assembled the entire squadron in front of the sheds and they each fired off red, white and green flares, known as Very lights, in celebration. In the course of six months the squadron had become one of the RFC's premier fighter units. However, not all the squadron's airmen were rejoicing. The cost had been considerable, not just in men killed or physically injured but also in psychological strain.

Horrell had flown many patrols with the squadron and had acquitted himself well, but on the

Gordon Pettigrew devoted a full page of his photograph album to crashed machines, including this dramatic image of a 65 Squadron Camel going up in flames at Wye, Kent, in September 1917.

night of the squadron's big celebration his endurance faltered. Horrell was no timorous pilot seeking a quick trip back to Blighty; he had served eight years in the New Zealand Volunteers before the war and had entered the conflict with the NZEF in Egypt, the Sinai Peninsula and Gallipoli.[46] At Gallipoli he had been in the thick of the fighting and had suffered a gunshot wound. After that he had pursued a flying commission. He had undertaken preliminary flying instruction in Egypt and, at the time of his last flight with 56 Squadron, he had accumulated some 160 hours' flying. During the heavy air fighting of Ypres he completed no fewer than six combat reports.[47] As is evident in a mid-September fight south of Houthulst Forest, he was not afraid to engage with the enemy.

> Crossed the lines at 11,000 ft above thick clouds and dived upon eight E.A. in opening in clouds, East of Ypres. I got on one's tail and fired a drum of Lewis and about forty Vickers into it at 60 to 80 yards. E.A. went down out of control. After changing Lewis drum, I saw an SE.5 diving on E.A. and firing slightly above me. I also turned on E.A. and fired until E.A. went down in a steep nose dive and from that zoomed, and fell sideways. I think the pilot was shot.[48]

Nonetheless, the demands of never-ending sorties and the threat of imminent death seem to have overwhelmed him. Like so many others, he crumpled under the pressure. His October medical report described his nervous condition:

> About a month ago he began to suffer from sleeplessness and nervousness, and lost confidence in himself, this gradually got worse and he reported sick . . . and was then sent down to Base and England. He still has sleeplessness and headaches and his heart condition is not strong.[49]

Horrell left the unit on 29 September 1917.[50] By February 1918 he was much improved, only 'very slightly tremulous' and was sleeping better, with no headaches or bad dreams. His sole medication seems to have been self-prescribed: 12 cigarettes a day and three pipes of tobacco.[51] It is testament to his courage that he re-entered the RFC in the same month with a home defence squadron, albeit with limited flying duties.[52]

September 1917 was not a good month for the New Zealanders. Just a few days earlier, Gordon Pettigrew was admitted to hospital. At Bruay airfield, 11 miles behind the trenches, Pettigrew had been flying with 40 Squadron, whose Nieuports regularly flew a patrol line between Armentières and the Scarpe River, preventing hostiles from molesting RFC artillery cooperation machines. The Wanganui Collegiate old boy was also employed in balloon attacks, but could easily be distracted by the enemy milling around behind the German trenches, and on at least one occasion 'had spotted a company of cyclists riding along a road . . . and had scattered them with a burst from his machine-gun'.[53] Petttigrew was a well-thought-of airman and an engaging character, always at the centre of the mess poker games. On one occasion he was dining at a hotel with squadron colleagues, including Mick Mannock and the wing's brigadier, when the meal turned into a 'battle royal' with food being thrown around the room. A lobster claw missed its target and flew out the window and struck a major. Only Mannock's quick thinking and the presence of the brigadier prevented further bloodshed; the bald-headed major was bleeding profusely.[53A]

In spite of the hijinks and squadron's relaxed atmosphere, the demanding nature of the operations wore Pettigrew down, and after four months in France he suffered a nervous breakdown — exacerbated by ill health. The medical board proceedings revealed he had lost two stone, was smoking 20 cigarettes a day, had difficulty sleeping and was 'tremulous'. The official report simply stated 'neurasthenia' caused by 'stressing service'.[54] Pettigrew fully recovered and in 1918 served as a flying instructor.

In the same month, Charles Mills arrived at 65 Squadron. The unit, based at Wye, Kent, had been newly equipped with Sopwith Camels and was preparing for its transfer to the Western Front. It lacked experienced officers, however, and only the squadron commander and a flight commander had seen action in France. Moreover, the light and manoeuverable Sopwiths proved a handful for the young pilots. There were two collisions between the Camels, and Mills filled his photograph album with snapshots of crashed and up-turned machines. The former Auckland accountant had only flown four hours with the squadron when he himself was involved in a life-threatening crash. The result was crippling. Mills had been unwell before the accident — back pain and a lengthy battle with dysentery, in all likelihood stemming from his service with the NZEF in Gallipoli and Egypt — but now he was beset with insomnia, nightmares and loss of memory. He had 'difficulty in finding words to express himself' and when he spoke he stammered.[54A] By the middle of the following year he was described as suffering from shell-shock and was advised that he should return to New Zealand for a well-deserved and prolonged rest. Horrell, Pettigrew and Mills were just three of a large number of airmen who suffered under the stress of the air war.

The use of ground attacks was ably demonstrated by the Spad SVIIs of 23 Squadron. A French fighter, the Spad was a sturdy machine with a good rate of climb and diving ability. Its primary weakness was that it had only a single machine gun. In the first week of August, two squadron airmen delivered low-level assaults: one on enemy infantry heading to Menin, and another on a diverse series of targets. The pilot involved in the latter assault was one of the unit's many New Zealanders in 1917, the strapping Frank Bullock-Webster. Like Joseph Hammond before him, Bullock-Webster was an adventurer. Born in Hamilton, he was well known in the hunting circles of the Waikato, where he not only shot a good deal of game but also put his sketching talents to work capturing New Zealand flora and fauna in his diaries. At seventeen he had left New Zealand to work for the 300-year-old Canadian fur-trading business, the Hudson's Bay Company, before trying his hand at gold prospecting. He entered the war with the Canadian Forces as an officer in the machine-gun corps. Trench fever in France led to his transfer to the RFC and 23 Squadron.

Flying his Spad, Bullock-Webster pushed the nose down and opened fire on a train at

Staden Station, before attacking a wagon and horses and two lorries on the Roulers–Torhout road.[55] Nine days later he was on an evening sortie against enemy aerodromes with another pilot. His colleague was to attack Rumbeke airfield, but molestation by hostile aircraft forced him to drop his bombs over Passchendaele in order to deal with his assailants. The New Zealander's intended target was the Abeele aerodrome but darkness prevented him from locating it; he simply dropped his bombs on the 'biggest building in the town and fired at lighted windows'.[56] Abeele straddled the Franco-Belgian border, with one side of the main street in France and the other in Belgium, so the New Zealander was effectively peppering walls and smashing the windows of two different countries. It is unclear why he did this, but perhaps it was frustration after a close call earlier that day. In the morning he had survived a large dogfight: eight Spads against 48 enemy fighters and two-seaters. During the arm wrestle, the outnumbered New Zealander engaged no fewer than eight hostiles and sent one into a vertical spin.[57]

Over 20–21 September the squadron almost exclusively engaged in hunting down ground targets. Bullock-Webster was joined by more New Zealanders — Herbert Drewitt of Christchurch and Frederic Sharland of Auckland — in the aggressive, low-level attacks. On the morning of the first day, Drewitt made four raking runs on a large gun east of Houthulst, spraying it with 300 Vickers rounds. He then fell on an active battery in the throes of shelling British positions.[58] The big guns were firing and generating a good deal of air turbulence when he pushed the Spad low, exhausting his ammunition and scattering artillerymen. Nearby, northeast of Langemarck, Germans dived for their dugouts as Sharland and another pilot shot up their battery. The big guns were silenced, if only temporarily.

Drewitt and Sharland were Kohimarama graduates. Drewitt had been a shepherd at Stonyhurst Station in North Canterbury when he applied for the Walsh brothers' flying school.[59] Sharland was a pharmacist and a keen golfer.[60] If he looked older than his 28 years when he applied for the RFC, he was: the Aucklander lied about his age when entering the Kohimarama flying school and on his registration with the RFC. He somehow 'forgot' he had been born in 1882, not 1887 — a repeated lapse of memory brought on by aviation contagion, perhaps. Both men had arrived with the squadron on the same day.[61]

Just after midday they continued their low-flying violence. Sharland struck first. Enemy troops were moving through a crossroads when they heard the drone of a Spad's V8 engine followed by the barking of the Vickers. Men ran for cover as bullets struck the road, kicking up clods of dirt. Sharland then flew along the Poelcappelle–Westrozebeke road, picking off isolated parties of men and sending them fleeing for roadside cover. Drewitt also attacked men on local roads and assaulted a gun emplacement.

The operations were dangerous and not for the faint-hearted. Fighter pilot Mac McGregor elaborated on the joys and challenges of the low-level operations.

> [O]nce you find the lines (and you do that by flying east until you are shot at), it is wonderful
> the good that can be done by helping the infantry, knocking out machine guns, shooting up
> troops and transport etc. It bucks up the troops to see aeroplanes flying about in front of

them as they advance, as for one thing the fact of us being shot at and shooting back, gives a very good idea as to where the Hun is, and how strongly he holds the position.

Whenever an aeroplane flies low over hostile troops, it seems to be the craze for anyone with anything that will shoot to let blaze, and they are getting pretty good at it too — as you perhaps would have thought had you been able to see my machine yesterday, and the hole in my pal's leg from an explosive bullet. Plucky little beggar, after being hit he turned back into Hunland and dropped his bombs on the people that fired at him, all on one of the worst days an aeroplane had flown.[62]

Performing risky attacks in conjunction with Bullock-Webster's squadron was another Spad unit, 19 Squadron. 'The heavy mists that prevail make low flying essential for good work, and machine guns, field guns, Archies, Flaming Onions — that is, phosphorus balls — and rifle fire all try hard to render our work impossible,' wrote Harold Dawson of Christchurch to his family on 3 October 1917.[63] The keen hockey player and Baptist was himself the recipient of the enemy's venom. He calculated that on one particularly heavy day, four of his machines were so 'shot to pieces' that they were temporarily retired from the battle. The squadron had taken a beating in the demanding sorties. 'Really it is great sport,' enthused Dawson, but he confessed, 'We have been rather unfortunate lately, as ten out of eighteen in our squadron have "gone west" during the last nine days.' He felt the losses were unusual, but then again, the former Somme despatch rider had only been with the squadron four weeks when he wrote this letter and he was clearly excited with his new role as fighter pilot. He told his St Albans family that although his Spad had been riddled with bullets on many occasions, he himself was yet to receive so much as a scratch. He died in action the next day.

In 23 Squadron the ground attacks continued apace, and at a high cost. The first New Zealander to make his mark in the squadron was the first to go. Bullock-Webster survived a crash in August but was killed the next month. On 20 September the 33-year-old was hit on an offensive patrol. Badly wounded, he force-landed, smashing the Spad to pieces in a shell hole. Bullock-Webster was extracted from the wreckage but died of his injuries hours later.

In October the squadron restored its number of resident New Zealanders to three with the arrival of James Hewett. The Wanganui Collegiate old boy had failed in his attempt to join the army and navy, so applied for the RFC. All three New Zealanders came together on an 18 October offensive patrol near Zonnebeke. It was a variation of the squadron's recent activities but one for which it was well suited. The trio were part of a flight of five Spads when, at 2.20 p.m., they spied a large formation at 13,000 ft: about 22 enemy machines, a dozen of which were twin-engined bombers, and the balance newly arrived Fokker DrI triplanes.[64]

The Fokker imitated the three-wing structure of the successful Sopwith Triplane. Like its British equivalent, the Fokker made up for its lack of straight-out speed with a very good climb rate and agility in combat. It was favoured by Manfred von Richthofen, Werner Voss and a string of successful pilots with the Central Powers. In all likelihood the bombers were a collection of AEG GIV and Friedrichshafen GIII machines, three-man aircraft that were the mainstay of German bombing operations on the Western Front. For the New Zealanders the most important consideration was the German defensive armament in the form of a Parabellum free-firing machine gun manned at the forward and rear cockpits of each aircraft. Twelve of these bombers in formation were an impressive and daunting prospect. The Friedrichshafen, in particular, was of similar proportions to the infamous Gotha, with a 77-ft wingspan — three times that of the Spad.

The New Zealanders' solution was simple: a head-on attack. With the Spads rapidly closing in, the leading bomber thought better of a face-to-face confrontation and peeled away slowly, the straining six-cylinder Mercedes engines vibrating through the machine's skeleton in protest. The Spad flight commander let loose 100 rounds on its rear, only pulling away because of the threat posed by the Fokkers. The retreat of the forward German machine led the other bombers to wheel round in a lumbering ballet, 12 overweight dancers waddling off stage. The Spads pounced. Herbert Drewitt launched himself from below, avoiding the defending guns as best as possible. The underbelly presented a tempting target, and the Vickers leapt in its mechanism. From 150 yards he raked the cross-marked bomber. He closed to 50 yards with another, the great airframe hanging overhead. How could he miss? He then swung away and continued attacking from above and the flanks. Helmeted and goggled German airmen fired, spitting machine-gun fire from forward and aft. Simultaneously Hewett and Sharland struck. Hewett fired three bursts at a turning bomber and then, following Drewitt's lead, homed in on a second one from below. He pulled the Spad up, stalling it beneath the vulnerable behemoth. Hanging there, caught between heaven and earth, he pelted the underside. Sharland made a flank and rear attack on another. Bullets flowed from fighter to bomber. The escorting enemy triplanes intervened. Sharland fired on one, looking directly down his Aldis gunsight. He thought he had made a hit.

And then, as quickly as it had started, the battle was over. Incredibly, all the bombers had scraped through the fight, their large bodies and twin engines absorbing the withering fire. The 23 Squadron flight and its three New Zealanders returned to base, somewhat incredulous that their prey had escaped. The after-action combat report ended with just two words: 'All indecisive.'[65]

Only days later, one of the New Zealanders was killed on an offensive patrol in the vicinity of Zonnebeke. Sharland's machine was found wrecked but, because of its proximity to the fighting, neither he nor the broken airframe could be recovered. By the time the battle had passed, his remains were nowhere to be seen.[66] On the eve of Sharland's departure for England in 1916, the Northern Pharmaceutical Association had gathered in Auckland to present him with a farewell gift: a purse of sovereigns.[67] With these gold coins Sharland had purchased his flying officer's outfit. Less than a year later, the uniform and Sharland were swallowed by the mud and devastation of Flanders.

The remaining New Zealanders continued their support of the ground forces. Hewett was flying alongside Drewitt on 26 October. The squadron's mission: locate the enemy's likely reinforcement routes. Hourly reconnaissance flights at 2000 ft were to be carried out and, although hostile troops were to be attacked when spotted, the primary objective was the speedy

above The Fokker DrI triplane was an impressive machine and a favourite of many German aces, including Manfred von Richthofen.

below This captured Spad SVII was brought down by anti-aircraft fire while carrying out an early-morning offensive patrol.

accumulation of information on enemy movements.[68] Both men gathered intelligence and fired on advancing troops. Drewitt's low-level assaults were only one part of his impressive military aviation skillset: he was also a very aggressive air-to-air combat pilot. For these efforts and later instructional work back in England, Drewitt received the Military Cross and Air Force Cross.[69]

In his Walsh brothers' flying school portrait, the blue-eyed and dark-haired Drewitt looked every bit the easy-go-lucky North Canterbury shepherd in training. Yet his combat reports are full of forceful language and reveal an airman determined to get results, even at considerable risk to himself. Apart from the low-level attacks in 1917, he met a number of enemy aircraft at altitude across his RFC career. In October he saw a lone Albatros: 'I at once turned out of formation and got on his tail.'[70] Drewitt closed to within 10 yards, almost near enough to reach out and grab the Albatros by the tail. 'At times I thought I was going to ram him.' Instead he let the Vickers have its say, delivering 200 rounds at almost point-blank range. The Albatros went belly-up, the underside fuselage and wings facing the sun, the cockpit and pilot earthward.

On another occasion, a two-seater spotted him and sought to evade the New Zealander by dropping into a downward spin. Drewitt was not fooled, and followed. The Spad closed to 20 yards as he fired. 'I was afraid he might flatten out,' he told the squadron's intelligence officer, so 'I followed him down to about 200 ft.' He saw the aircraft and its two occupants crash, 'smashed to atoms on the ground'.[71]

His method was simple: gain an advantageous position and then press in as close as possible to the enemy. It was, of course, not without its perils, as Drewitt discovered the following year when he spotted an enemy reconnaissance machine flying towards his squadron's aerodrome. He dived from above, 'firing over him and turning, zoomed under his tail and only pulled out when about to collide with him'. Collision avoided, the already smoking enemy machine burst into flames.[72] On another occasion he manoeuvred directly behind a two-seater and fired. Suddenly flames sprang up just behind the enemy cockpit. 'I had to pull out then to avoid the burning pieces which were flying back.'[73]

General Douglas Haig belatedly brought Ypres to an end on 10 November. The fighting had become bogged down in the mud of Passchendaele and his forces were sustaining heavy losses for very little gain. The appalling weather and shelling of the battlefield made infantry advances slow and treacherous. The conditions favoured the Germans' defensive posture; they gave as little ground as possible, while inflicting as many casualties as possible. In the end only four to five miles was actually taken.[74] The airmen were given a 10-day respite before the last British offensive of the year: the great tank assault on Cambrai.

Unlike the vast Ypres offensive, Cambrai involved a much narrower front. It was an exploratory attempt to break the deadlock of trench warfare with a combined arms assault, notably through the inclusion of tanks in large numbers. Situated at the centre of the Hindenburg Line, the firm and high ground of Cambrai was an ideal point for a breakthrough with massed tanks. To overcome the deep German defences, the tanks would flatten a path through the obstacles that shielded the trenches. In the air, the concentration of

British air squadrons meant the RFC would start Cambrai with nearly a four-to-one advantage over its German counterparts.

One of the units heavily involved in supporting the tanks was 8 Squadron. Among its airmen was Wellingtonian Arthur 'Brownie' Browne. At the age of 13, Browne had attempted to join the Boer War as a bugle boy until his father intervened, and so when the Great War arrived he was not about to miss the adventure of a lifetime. After serving at Gallipoli, where he witnessed firsthand the courage of New Zealand's only Gallipoli Victoria Cross winner, Cyril Bassett, he then fought on the Somme.[75] The following year he was serving in the RFC at Mons-en-Chaussée airfield, and flew throughout Cambrai. Browne was an observer in the two-seater general-purpose Armstrong Whitworth FK8. Nicknamed the 'Big Ack', the FK8 was a reliable machine in army support duties. Browne was engaged in artillery observation and photographic reconnaissance.[76] During the Cambrai offensive he followed the advance at close quarters in contact patrols designed to keep headquarters well appraised of developments right at the cutting edge of the assault. Browne flew low enough to follow the advancing troops, before turning back and dropping the vital intelligence at the local command centre.

On 20 November, after a bombardment from over 1000 guns, the ground assault was spearheaded by more than 400 tanks. In the air, however, flying conditions were extremely hazardous. One Camel squadron suffered eight casualties in a raid on a German airfield, many to low-lying mist. A pilot from another Camel unit described the challenges.

> A few casualties occurred through pilots flying into the ground, but the majority were from ground fire. Those of us that did survive did so, I consider, because we flew very close to the ground until our objective was reached. I recollect, on our first 'show' on the morning of the 20th, having to rise to pass over tanks moving through the thick haze of smoke towards the German defences. One retains vivid pictures of little groups of infantry behind each tank, trudging forward with cigarettes alight, of flames leaping from disabled tanks with small helpless groups of infantry standing around, of the ludicrous expressions of amazement on the upturned faces of German troops as we passed a few feet above their trenches.[77]

At times the Big Acks were forced below 300 ft in the valuable contact patrols. Larger, and lacking the nimbleness of the Camels, the FK8s were groundfire magnets. An 8 Squadron machine's fuel tank was punctured, forcing it down. At 7 a.m., Browne and his pilot were also struck by machine-gun fire, and the pilot was injured in the forced landing.[78]

The tank-led ground forces advanced rapidly, in fact faster than at any other time during the war. By nightfall the British forward elements had covered nearly five miles. However, over the following week the Germans moved in ground and aerial reinforcements, slowing the advance. Ten days into the offensive, the Germans launched a surprise counterattack. Using the ground-strafing and low bombing tactics perfected by the RFC and RNAS, the Luftsreitkräfte aggressively attacked British infantry. 'The aeroplanes came over in considerable numbers at the time of the assault,' noted a contemporary report on Cambrai, 'and flew at altitudes which have been described by witnesses as being lower than 100 ft, firing their machine guns into our infantry. The ... effect of this was very great and no doubt tended to facilitate the enemy's success.'[79] Aerial casualties also rose.

Because of a sinking cloud base, the Big Acks were once again forced to fly lower than was good for them: an 8 Squadron machine was hit by machine-gun fire and the observer was killed in action. Near midday, Browne was flying with a fresh pilot on a contact patrol. With low cloud blanketing the battlefield, they pushed right into the onslaught of infantry-supporting German aircraft. They were set upon by no fewer than half a dozen enemy machines. Browne fired his Lewis on an enemy aeroplane with a 'draughtboard pattern' marking on the top wing.[80] The FK8 was shot up and Browne suffered a wound to his hand. The elevator controls on one side were shot, but he succeeded in beating off the enemy machines and delivered 'very valuable information'.[81]

On the ground the Germans were advancing rapidly, although they encountered strong resistance at Bourlon Ridge. German successes elsewhere threatened the British position on the ridge, however, and in the end it was abandoned, with tank carcasses littering the battlefield. When the battle closed on 7 December, the British could argue that manpower and territorial losses and gains at Cambrai were equally shared by the combatants, but the Germans had ended the year with a morale-boosting victory. Browne survived the offensive but another New Zealander was killed only days later.

Having fully recovered from the wounds he had sustained in September, Clive Collett had been posted to Martlesham Heath Airfield in Suffolk near his old stalking ground at Orfordness. Here he tested new British designs and evaluated captured enemy machines. Ironically, the machine Collett flew commonly in this capacity was the very aircraft type he had been so intent on shooting down only weeks before: the Albatros DV. It must have been a strange feeling sitting in the Albatros, when so many times before he had viewed the DV down the sights of his Camel's twin machine guns.

Collett took the captured aircraft on a national south–north tour through Britain's training and reserve squadrons, familiarising airmen under instruction with the foe they would all too soon face over the Western Front. On 5 November at Hendon he met one of his old colleagues from France: James McCudden. The Englishman took Collett's DV up for a spin. He was not impressed; he wondered 'how the German pilots could manoeuvre so well, for they were certainly not easy to handle'. Afterwards, Collett chauffeured McCudden in a two-seater DH4 to Martlesham. The British ace, relaxing in the assured hands of Collett, spent the trip imagining himself an observer-gunner, contemplating the disadvantages under which they operated. Later that day the two pilots travelled to London by train, and spent the evening reminiscing over their shared Estrée-Blanche escapades. They must have looked quite the pair: the prematurely aged and crumple-faced 31-year-old Collett and the baby-faced 22-year-old McCudden musing over aircraft flown and battles fought.

In late December, Collett arrived at Turnhouse, Scotland. Two days before Christmas, he took the DV up. What the Albatros had failed to do over France in combat, it achieved over

While at Orfordness in January 1917, Clive Collett undertook extensive work with the prototype Bristol F2 Fighter seen here. After a period of active squadron work later in the year, injury once again forced him to return to evaluative testing in Britain, including flying German aircraft.

home waters in a routine demonstration: the New Zealander and the Albatros were seen to plunge into the cold waters off Turnhouse. There were conflicting reports about the sodden wreckage and the recovered body. Officially it was argued that the pilot, who had over 1200 hours in his logbook and three years' military service, had made a simple mistake over the Firth of Forth: Collett had misjudged his height and failed to pull out of a spin before striking the water and drowning.[82] Others believed that the exhaust manifold had worked its way loose and had violently struck Collett, stunning him.

'As gallant a pilot as ever lived,' eulogised McCudden. Collett was one of the few New Zealand pilots to receive a lengthy tribute in the *London Times*, from his former squadron commander in France, Major Michael Nethersole. 'This officer invariably displayed a determination and gallantry beyond all praise, and the example he set was invaluable to the whole squadron . . . Had not an unfortunate wound sent him back to England, it is certain that he would have made an unrivalled name for himself.' Nethersole's assessments were not the bromides of a senior officer comforting his readers. While at Estrée-Blanche, Collett had knocked out 12 machines. Over the same period, from the same airfield, McCudden had accounted for four, Maybery seven and Rhys-Davids five.[83] In his own unit, 70 Squadron, Collett was not only the highest-scoring airman of 1917, he was also the highest since its formation in April 1916, one year and eight months earlier. He had accomplished all this in the course of a mere six weeks of sorties. He received a full military funeral and was buried in Edinburgh.

Peggy was devastated. In a letter, perhaps written in the second half of 1916, Collett had reminded her of the demands of war: 'I don't know when I shall be up in town now, in fact they may send me to France anytime but if they do I shall try to arrange so I can see you before I go. We should have an evening together for in these times you never know when it will be your last, so may as well make the best of life in case it is short.'[84] At the time of Collett's death their child, Marion Renée Collett Cumming, was nine months old. Jack and Peggy had never married and the parachutes were not transformed into Peggy's silk wedding dress. After Collett's death, Peggy visited the extended Collett family in London to seek assistance, but there was no reference to her or Marion in Collett's will.[85] Over time, Peggy, a 'very accomplished dressmaker', made the Guardian Angels into pretty garments for Marion and other family members.[86] The last photographic link between Peggy and Collett and his airman's exploits is a photograph taken of a 10-year-old Marion holding a violin. The dress she is wearing appears to be made from one of her father's famous silk parachutes.

Ten-year-old Marion Renée Collett Cumming. She was nine months old when her father was killed.

CHAPTER THIRTEEN

THE 'GREATEST
SHOW EVER SEEN'

1918

At the end of 1917, the Allies looked back on a year with little to recommend it. Their efforts on the Western Front had failed to bring about the much sought-after breakthrough, and had ended in the quagmire of Passchendaele and the burnt-out tank carcasses of Cambrai. An extravagant number of British and Empire men and materiel had been consumed at Arras, Messines, Ypres and Cambrai: close to half a million casualties were the cost of the four offensives.

The losses seriously depleted the Allied capacity for offensive warfare in 1918. The British and Empire forces on the Western Front were reduced to 75 per cent of their 1917 establishment.[1] Internal problems with the French army exacerbated the grim Allied position, and the British were forced to extend their thinning resources further south along the line. Their only consolation was that the United States had entered the war and, by January 1918, had four divisions in France. This was only a fraction of the Allied presence on the front lines, but more were on the way, promising to tip the balance in the high summer of that year. But that was six months away.

On the other side of the trenches the Central Powers still hoped to force the war in their favour, but Germany needed to act before the Americans arrived in greater numbers and the British and French made good their casualties. German losses in the previous year had also been heavy, but over the winter of 1917–18 they transferred over a million troops, plus aeroplanes and equipment, from the Eastern Front, thanks to the successful conclusion of the Russian campaign. The German high command was eager to launch an attack, and used the cover of winter to cloak the build-up of resources for their biggest offensive of the war: Operation Michael, slated for spring. The British were all too aware of this possibility and began to prepare defences to face the assault when it came.

The German army was boosted by a strengthening German air force. Significantly, it had doubled the size of its fighter squadrons and increased training to meet demand. Organisationally, and on the back of the success of JG1 the previous year, the Luftstreitkräfte created two more Jagdgeschwader of four Jasta each: JG2 and JG3. The Luftstreitkräfte was increasingly being augmented with the Pfalz DIII, a sturdy, workmanlike machine, and more Albatros DVs — the final iteration of the D series. A few airmen clung to the Fokker DrI triplane for its impressive dogfighting abilities. There was only one new offering of note in 1918, but it was impressive: the Fokker DVII. Squarish and homely-looking, the Fokker DVII was nonetheless the best German fighter of the war and the pilots adored it. It was easy to fly but also agile and, by one assessment, it had the ability to 'make a good pilot out of mediocre material'.[2] With twin Spandau machine guns and a top speed of 116 mph, it was a good match for the SE5a and the Camel, without the difficult handling qualities of the latter machine.

Initially, Allied reaction to the plane's arrival in the skies was indifferent — the new Fokker did not have the killer looks — but once it made its presence felt even the best Allied pilots thought twice about tussling with the aeroplanes with the box-shaped wings. Fortunately for the Allied airmen, the first Fokker DVIIs would not arrive until late April and it would take weeks for German Jastas to be fully re-equipped with the new aircraft.

The British air service had recovered from its losses in Bloody April and, with the introduction of the single-seater SE5a and Camels and the two-seater Bristol Fighter and DH4, it still held the ascendency into 1918. In line with developments in Germany, the British were now producing machines and airmen in greater numbers than ever before. Although newer models were in development, the aircraft from the second half of 1917 were more than able to hold their own in 1918. The sole new machine of note entering the frontline ranks was the Sopwith Dolphin, an aeroplane that compared favourably to the Fokker DVII and was flown to great effect by one of New Zealand's most outstanding pilots of the war: Ronald Bannerman. The advent of schools of instruction to train the instructors, the gradual increase in pre-operational flying hours, and Smith-Barry's overhaul of the way in which airmen were trained meant that there was a general improvement in the calibre of airmen arriving at the squadrons.

Organisationally, the most profound change would be the merging of the RFC and RNAS on 1 April 1918 into a single service: the Royal Air Force. It was felt that the RNAS machines and men were underutilised on the Western Front, and that a unified air force would bring an end to inefficient competition between the RFC and RNAS over aeroplane procurement. The result was a new service on an equal footing with the army and navy.

From January until March of 1918, the RFC and RNAS were kept busy in three principal activities: gathering intelligence, disrupting German preparations and keeping the enemy air service on the back foot.[3] Reconnaissance and photographic aircrew were to assemble as much information as possible about the accumulation of men and equipment on the other side of the lines. The Allies needed to know when and where the assault would fall. To interfere with enemy preparations for the offensive, British bombers would attack railway junctions and sidings, ammunition dumps and enemy camps. In order to degrade the Luftstreitkräfte, assaults would be made on German airfields, and British single-engine fighters would continue direct engagement with the German fighters beyond British lines. In other words, the offensive operations of the previous year were to continue.

The intelligence and interference were well executed over the three months, but British efforts to weaken the German air units were ineffectual; in preparation for the big offensive, the Germans had wisely marshalled and shielded their still considerable air strength well away from the front.

Among the British strategies to impede German preparations was the deployment of the RFC night bombers, and key to this were 100 and 101 Squadrons flying FE2bs and an assortment of similar machines. The FE2bs were equipped with night-flying paraphernalia: the pilot's flying instruments were coated with a luminous paint or lit up by small electric lamps; for map-reading, the observer used a torch or a fixed lamp; and the machine was outfitted with navigation lights, a recognition light, parachute flares and wingtip landing flares.[4] To aid navigation for night operations, inland lighthouses, numbered A, B, C and so on, were established along the front line at 10-mile intervals. Their flashing individual Morse letter could be seen from at least 25 miles away and enabled crews to gauge their positions along the front. Adjacent to the lighthouses were emergency airfields for damaged machines and wounded men.

When 100 Squadron arrived in France it struck a threatening pose: its FE2bs were painted in a dull black from wingtip to wingtip, with a dark grey fuselage and black tailplane and rudder. Even on moonlit nights they were virtually invisible, and searchlights found them frustratingly difficult to latch on to. They were informally nicknamed the 'All Blacks'.[5]

Appropriately, the squadron counted some New Zealanders among its ranks: pilots Hugh Chambers of Havelock North and Alfred Kingsford of Nelson. Like most of the early night-bombing aircrews they were transferees from the 'nursery of night-flying' — the home defence squadrons.[6] Chambers was one of the squadron's 'old hands' in night bombing, having seen extensive operations in September of the previous year with its sister 101 Squadron.[7] Kingsford was pleased to see another New Zealander when he walked into the officers' mess in early 1918. Chambers looked his full 30 years and then some: a weathered face, battered by his prewar mountaineering and etched with the strain of recent night-flying sorties. Chambers was quiet, although Kingsford got enough out of him to discover that he 'liked climbing mountains better than flying'. Kingsford was more outgoing by nature and when he was allotted his FE2b he promptly marred the black livery with paint. He had dubbed his machine 'Peps' in honour of his wife Charlotte, but without a brush on hand he simply used a stick to scrawl her name inelegantly on the side of his bus. 'Does not look so bad,' he remarked.[8]

'Reggie' Kingsford had married Charlotte 'Peps' Pepperdine the previous year, just as he was beginning his duties as a home defence Zeppelin hunter. They were both married in their uniforms, Reggie proud in his brand-new airman's garb and Peps in her nursing 'whites'. During the early months of their marriage Reggie was able to spend a good deal of time with his bride, but home defence flying was not to his liking. After three months of this 'monotonous and soul-destroying work' he put in the paperwork for a transfer to an operational squadron in France.

In early January notification came through that Reggie was going to get his overseas posting. 'I am rather unhappy today as I have to part with Reggie,' Peps wrote in her diary, 'we both feel it is best to do this, but life together had been so happy . . . I am going to have to try to be brave.'[9] In the fortnight before her husband's departure she filled her days with business and with reading Reggie's letters regularly sent from his base at Scampton, but Reggie's imminent departure cast a gloomy pall. 'I feel depressed and miss my husband very much,' she wrote.

A few days before his departure for France, Reggie arrived in London, looking tired. 'He is all I have in life. Oh how I fear he will not come back. I cried myself to sleep . . . thinking of him going into such danger,'[10] Peps wrote. When the day of departure arrived they caught a taxi to Victoria Station. The couple stood on the platform surrounded by friends: it was a rushed goodbye. At 7.35 a.m. the train departed for Folkestone, from where Reggie would journey by boat to France. His only consolation was that he was travelling with a good friend and fellow airman; they were in full expectation of being sent to the same squadron. But it was not to be: on the other side of the Channel they found out they were destined for different units. At the hotel 'we drank to drown our sorrows and I wrote to my dear wife'.[11]

Reggie and Peps began an intensive letter-writing communication over the last year of the war. They also kept individual diaries for each other. In his, Reggie recalled standing at Gare de Paris-Est in preparation for the final leg of his journey. He watched the French wives, mothers and sweethearts farewelling husbands, sons and boyfriends on their way to the front. The train began to move, but two girls held their father steadfast. 'He kissed them both dozens of times on both cheeks and both girls' eyes were filled with tears. I felt so sorry for them, having just gone through the same thing.' The young women had seen Reggie watching them, and kindly waited at the station for him to leave on his own train. They 'waved to me, being absolutely alone I appreciated it, it seemed to me as though "fate" had sent them to wave me farewell as my dear wife would.'[12]

In London, Peps decided to put her best foot forward and return to nursing: 'I feel I must work, or I shall go just mad with worry for my loved one.'[13] She got her uniform in order. Within days she was nursing — work that was incredibly demanding and which, combined with the sleep-depriving air raids and worry about her Reggie, contributed to her health slowly declining over the weeks that followed. She seemed continually fatigued and plagued by minor illnesses. She was relieved to hear that Reggie's new squadron included a number of his old colleagues from England. Her intermittent joys were his letters, and she loved writing to him. It pleased her no end that he had named his 'bus' 'Peps'.[14]

Kingsford appears to have shielded her from the worst of the war and the perils he faced as bomber pilot. The sole incident he relayed to her was an accident he had when he was riding on a tender: it had crashed and rolled down an embankment, pinning his foot.[15] Peps's diaries gave no indication that she knew of the squadron's losses and horrific crashes. It was two months of letter-writing and diary entries before they would see each other.

Reggie Kingsford and Hugh Chambers' squadron operated from Ochey, on the far south end of the British line, hard against the French sector, and the base was also home to a French squadron. At one side of the field was the small town with its scattering of no more than 40 homes. The airfield lay atop a rise, and although it was exposed it was free of encumbrances other than the hangars. Its only limitation was the airfield's immediate environs; the undulating and forested countryside would make forced landings perilous.[16] It was a pretty home for such dangerous endeavours.

The newly wed Alfred
'Reggie' and Charlotte
'Peps' Kingsford in
their RFC and nursing
uniforms.

100 Squadron undertook periodic special operations by single aeroplanes, but generally the unit was deployed en masse. Flying close formation was precluded by the likelihood of collision in the darkness, so individual machines were despatched two to three minutes apart, on a prearranged setting. To keep everyone on track, flight leaders would fire Very lights over prominent landmarks, towns and rivers — a chain of fiery breadcrumbs that meant most of the aircraft arrived at their targets most of the time. Once over the objective, the lead machines would drop phosphorus bombs in addition to their standard ordnance. These burned incandescently, sending flames high into the night air and illuminating the target zone — a deadly beacon that could be seen for 20 miles on a clear night.[17]

The squadron had been largely inactive over November and December of the previous year, but in January flights were resumed with a vengeance. Kingsford's first big operation arrived on 9 February: an attack east of Metz on the Courcelles railway station. He took off with his Welsh observer Huw Edwardes-Evans and two 25-lb and two 112-lb bombs; the squadron would drop close to a ton that night. Forty minutes into the flight they crossed the line at 3000 ft. They were now in enemy territory.

> 'Keep your eyes skinned,' my observer leant over and yelled at me.
>
> 'Can't see a damned thing,' I replied, and there was not a light to be seen anywhere, just blank, impenetrable darkness, broken only by the red glare of the exhaust and the glow of the dashboard.
>
> Keeping her nose N.N.W. for twenty minutes, I peered over the side to try and distinguish something that might serve to assure us that we were on the right course, but the density of the night gave no sign, except the whistling of the wind as we sped by. The drone of the engine kept us company, purr, purr, it was running perfectly. We were doing seventy miles an hour at twelve hundred revolutions . . . In spite of warm clothing and the usual thigh boots, I was getting cold, and the bitter stinging of the keen wind making my face tingle. My observer was well hidden in his seat, the only part showing occasionally being his head popping up above the nacelle.[18]

The creeping cold was suddenly forgotten when they were caught by a searchlight. It was a shock: the darkness had abandoned them and they were being tracked in a cone of light. Edwardes-Evans emerged from his bolthole and pointed earthward as he prepared the machine gun. Kingsford kicked the rudder, 'pulling the joy stick over . . . and dived straight down the beam'. Edwardes-Evans pulled the trigger, spitting bullets. Undaunted, the searchlight glared. Kingsford sideslipped out of the beam at 1800 ft, only to be caught a second time. In they plunged, and Edwardes-Evans fired off a string of bursts. The light winked out; the Germans had had enough. Kingsford levelled off and reset his course. Ten minutes passed before they spotted the leader's phosphorus bomb lighting up the target.

It must have been seen for miles, and we immediately swung around and made for it. Approaching and keyed up with excitement as we were, we saw another burst, then three in quick succession and only a few yards apart. It was good bombing and the five made an excellent group. The first had caused a fire and we flew round once to have a look, discerning a group of buildings. Guiding the plane over them, [Edwardes-]Evans let two go and the bursts were quite visible, close together. Looking down to watch the effect, another searchlight caught us, and realising that the place was well protected against aircraft raids, I turned to dodge him, and instinctively looking over the side, I noticed a whole string of machine gun fire making directly for us. Like a procession of glow-worms these phosphorous bullets approached, and I immediately turned the plane in the opposite direction, dodging one searchlight but running into another line of machine gun fire. We'd dropped all our bombs, so I turned her nose down and beat it. We ended up at eight hundred feet and headed for C Lighthouse. We'd stirred up a hornet's nest and we felt that some of the machines to come after us would have a pretty hot time.[18A]

On the return flight all was still dark and the lighthouse had disappeared. Their world was black. Kingsford's only guide was his instruments: the bubble that indicated level flight, the altimeter registering their height and the compass their course. As the adrenalin dropped, cold seeped back into their bones. There was still no lighthouse to be seen and he was certain they had drifted, so he turned a modicum south, closing his aching eyes momentarily to ease the strain. When he opened them he spied a pinprick of light. He bore down on it, their 'hearts full of hope'. It flashed a signal and Edwardes-Evans leant over, held out his hand and shouted, '"That's it all right — put it here," we shook hands away up at three thousand feet.' They said nothing more, both relieved they had crossed onto their side of the lines, Kingsford wrote; 'in twenty minutes or so, my first raid over Hunland would be over. We'd been lucky.'[19]

Two hundred miles northwest, at the other end of the British front line near the Calais coast, Seaforth McKenzie was one of the unlucky ones. McKenzie's aviation pioneering work in prewar New Zealand had done little to speed his entry into the RFC, but in the second week of August 1917 he was seconded as an observer under training: he had finally entered his preferred service, albeit not as a pilot. He was posted to 101 Squadron, and secured his observer's badge on 13 January 1918. The squadron was equipped with FE2bs and was flying from Clairmarais near Saint-Omer. Its principal bombing objectives were airfields and railway stations.[20]

On the night of 25–26 January the squadron attacked two airfields in German-occupied Belgium: Gontrode and Scheldewindeke.[21] The former was bombed successfully at dusk, but Scheldewindeke would be attacked after midnight. At 1 a.m., McKenzie took off from Clairmarais with his pilot, Welshman Robert Lovell, in a flight of four machines.[22]

Perched at the front of the FE2b the New Zealander was initially greeted by clear skies, but a ground mist arose quickly, reducing visibility to 30 yards. The pilots and observers persevered, and at least two crews found the target. The airmen released their bombs over Scheldewindeke. Returning was a nightmare: a thick fog now coated the French countryside and landing would be a lottery. Even though Very lights and additional flares were deployed, the two-man crews would need every ounce of experience they possessed to land without pranging their machines. One of the aeroplanes flew over the aerodrome but could not actually see the field. It flew along the coast in search of clear air but in the end was forced to return and make a scary, almost blind landing. Another machine never appeared — McKenzie and Lovell's.

The after-action report simply stated: 'One machine missing (Pilot — 2/Lt. R. C. Lovell — General List & R.F.C. Observer — Lieut. W. S. McKenzie, N.Z. Division.)'[23] It was only later that the mangled FE2b and the dead bodies were found, five miles short of their home base.[24] The machine had clipped a tree and crashed in the dense mist. It had taken McKenzie over two years of requests and cajoling to secure his RFC secondment, but only two months in an active squadron to be killed.

Some of the bravest acts of the war occurred in February and March 1918, and they were carried out by mechanics. Thomas Nicoll, a Scottish immigrant to New Zealand, was working on the 'All Black' FE2bs for Chambers and Kingsford's 100 Squadron. A dentist, Nicoll had failed his medical for the NZEF but was accepted as a mechanic in the RFC and by 1918 was a flight sergeant.[25] The keen footballer and cyclist from Edendale, Southland, had his hands full on the night of 26 February. The squadron was preparing for a major operation against the Frescaty aerodrome.[26] Officers, observers and mechanics were milling among the FE2s when tragedy struck: two bombs exploded beneath an aircraft. There was carnage. Two men were burnt to death right in front of Kingsford.[27] In all, five men were killed and others wounded. Nicoll's senses were assaulted by the sight of the dead men, the cries of the wounded and the smell of cordite and acrid fumes. As heavy as the casualties were, it seemed certain there would be more. Ignited by the blast, a phosphorus bomb had caught fire underneath an adjacent machine. It glowed in its rack, threatening to set off the machine's other bombs.

Nicoll saw the danger. The mechanic moved towards the burning bomb, unhooked it and released it from the rack. He carried the lit ordnance to safety, burning his hands in the process.[28] His actions were in total disregard for his own safety and displayed a great presence of mind; he undoubtedly saved another machine from destruction and prevented further loss of life. King George later presented the Southlander with the Albert Medal at Buckingham Palace.[29] Nicoll was one of only three New Zealanders to receive the award, which had as its principal criterion that the probability of the recipient's death exceeded their chance of survival.[30]

Although mechanics were generally not close to the front line, there were occasions when they became embroiled in the shooting war. One of these was Lister Briffault, who had 'washed out' as a pilot due to his propensity to 'lose his head at the least opportunity'. Lister was the son of prominent Dunedin-trained surgeon Dr Robert Briffault. Both father and son went to war in 1915, and both were awarded medals for strikingly similar acts of bravery.

Robert Briffault, who had lied about his age to get into the Royal Army Medical Corps — he was 51, not 49 — worked at a clearing station on the beach at Suvla Bay in the Dardanelles before taking charge of the hospital ship *Scotian* in England, followed by service in France.[31] In 1918, he secured a bar to the Military Cross he had been awarded late the previous year when he went forward under shellfire to wounded men sheltering in craters. Medical personnel came forward to relieve him, but instead of returning to the lines he went beyond the forward post in search of an officer.[32] It was an act of considerable bravery.

Lister was cut from the same cloth as his father. Undeterred by his failure to become an airman, he became a mechanic in the RFC.[33] It was in this capacity with 41 Squadron on the Western Front that he demonstrated that he *could* keep his head under the severest duress. In March 1918 he was advised that two of the unit's SE5s had landed at an advanced aerodrome between the lines. The fighters were in need of urgent repairs before they could be flown to safety. The 21-year-old mechanic gathered his tools and led a two-man party to the stranded and exposed fighters. Arriving on foot, Lister closed in on the machines under shelling; the aircraft were just too attractive a target for the German artillery to ignore. Exploding ordnance rocked the base, tearing great chunks out of the field. Hot shrapnel laced the SE5s. They carried out repairs under heavy fire and the aircraft escaped largely intact, 'a result entirely due to these airmen's splendid devotion to duty'.[34] As a non-commissioned mechanic Lister Briffault was awarded the non-commissioned equivalent to his father's Military Cross: the Military Medal.

New Zealand's most highly decorated mechanic of the war was Sydney Anderson of Napier. His former workmates described Anderson as a bit of a 'character'.[35] In February 1916 he paid his own way to England, where he was soon wearing an RNAS uniform. Much of his service was undertaken on the east coast at RNAS Felixstowe, Suffolk.[36] From here he regularly flew as part of the four-man crew on board Curtiss or Felixstowe long-range flying boats on anti-submarine and anti-Zeppelin operations. The aircraft were large, with a wingspan of over 90 ft and a full loaded weight in excess of 10,000 lbs. Anderson's principal responsibility was the twin 12-cylinder Rolls-Royce Eagle engines, but if enemy aeroplanes were on hand he manned one of the machine guns. The patrols often stretched to six hours over an area known as the Spider Web — 4000 square miles of the North Sea.

Anderson's first commendation followed a rescue. On 29 May 1917, while on routine patrol, the flying-boat crew spotted something in the water. The aircraft descended, and two men were discovered bobbing in the North Sea, hanging on to an upturned seaplane float.

Five days earlier, this pilot and wireless operator had completed a few hours on patrol and turned for home when, almost immediately, the engine began missing; revolutions fell, it stopped, and the aeroplane landed on the water. They found themselves in the midst of an extensive minefield with an unrepairable engine — just the sort of place that potential rescuing vessels avoided. As they drifted deeper into the minefield, the likelihood of a chance discovery by a ship faded further. To lighten the floatplane, the bombs were released and the tank cocks opened, pouring the fuel into the sea.

Once a damaged aeroplane lands on terra firma an airman's troubles are generally over, but at sea it is often just the beginning of the trial.[37] The motion of the waves and the buffeting of the wind 'possess a malevolent cunning, whereby they search out any weak spot'.[38] The waves grew higher and the wind picked up to such a strength that eventually the tail float was worked loose; it broke off and sank into the depths. The elements now began pulling the machine apart, limb from limb, until the pilot and wireless operator were left clinging — half in and half out of the water — to an upturned float. Their make-do raft rode high and because of its shape rolled in the heavy seas whenever they attempted to pull themselves atop it. They coped well enough the first day and the fog-shrouded next day, but on the third day the sun came out and a deep thirst arrived. Mercifully, calmer conditions allowed them to rest on the float, and they swam to keep cool. The next day their swollen feet ached and the sun licked up the moisture in their bodies; they were tormented by the purgatorial thirst. Abrasions and cuts sustained in the wreckage flared up in the salt water. On the fifth day they began to sip the seawater: 'This was the beginning of the end.'[39]

Only a chance break in the fog and their keen eyes allowed Anderson's flying boat to spot the waterlogged men from 1200 ft. The aircraft banked and descended to 600 ft, confirmed the sighting, and flew directly over the pair at 60 ft. It would be a risky rescue in strong winds and heavy seas. They landed, taxied close and managed to haul the grateful airmen aboard. The pilot attempted to take off but the additional weight was against them and the machine was damaged in the process. The tailplane took a hammering and the starboard wingtip float was torn away. Leaks appeared with the loosening of its joints. They were stranded.

To make matters worse the heavy seas were threatening to swamp them — waves were breaking over the bow and the tail.[40] A crew member was placed on the bilge pump and another worked the fuel-feed pump, as the air-driven pump was impotent on the sea.[41] With no prospect of flying home the pilot steered the machine for Felixstowe, attempting to taxi the 25 miles in the face of a headwind and thumping waves. The tail filled with water and, without its float, the starboard wing continually dug into the sea before wrenching loose, only to repeat the cycle. Nearly four hours later they emerged from the thick fogbank into the shipping channel. The flying boat was towed to shore by a passing vessel that had spotted the distress flares.

For risking their lives, Anderson and the crew were awarded the Sea Gallantry Medal.[42] In July Anderson received a Distinguished Service Medal and was then mentioned in despatches for anti-submarine work. His third gallantry award came in early spring of the following year.

A Felixstowe long-range flying boat similar to the machine to which Sydney Anderson made repairs while in flight over the North Sea.

On 19 March 1918 Anderson was part of a three-aircraft-strong long-range reconnaissance over the Heligoland Bight, photographing ships and noting their locations. Forty miles west of Wilhelmshaven, Germany, the trio was intercepted by two enemy seaplanes. Anderson manned the aft machine gun.[43] One of the two-seater German aircraft was hit in the fighting. 'It burst into flames, nose-dived into the water, and a pennant of black smoke, ever increasing in volume, trailed off down wind.'[44] It was a costly victory: the 'Hun' had extracted his pound of flesh by riddling the flying boat with machine-gun fire, damaging the fuel tanks, 'fortunately above the line of the liquid'. The New Zealander made the necessary repairs but noticed that the coolant in the starboard engine was violently boiling: over half the water had been lost.[45]

Anderson yelled to the pilot, requesting he drop airspeed as low as he dared. The starboard engine was stopped and the other throttled back. Anderson peeled off his flying jacket, gathered his tools and stuck his head out of the cockpit. His ears were assaulted by the port engine's 12-cylinder cacophony, its four-blade propeller — taller than Anderson — thrashing and whirling, and the wind whistling loudly through the spars and the rigging. He clambered out and was immediately hit by a 90-mph wind, gusts whipping and snapping his shirt and trousers against his arms and legs. It was hard to move. Spider-like, he edged to the starboard engine, located just below the upper wing; at 5 ft 6 in, Anderson had to stretch to reach it. His concentration was total. As he worked on the engine he had to stop the wind from wrenching his tools and materials away. If he lost his footing he would be blown overboard in a 5000-ft death plunge. The repair took him over an hour, and the pilot was then able to restart the engine.

It was surely one of the most astonishing acts of bravery by a New Zealander in the Great War. Anderson had saved the crew and the machine. For his efforts he was awarded the Conspicuous Gallantry Medal.[46]

Alongside the RFC night bombing raids of Chambers, Kingsford and McKenzie, the RNAS was also involved in daylight bombing operations. Among this force was Euan Dickson in 5 (Naval) Squadron. Born in Sheffield, England, Dickson emigrated to New Zealand and was a foreman in an engineering company in Thames at the start of the Great War.[47] In 1916, when he discovered that the Walsh brothers' Kohimarama flying school was oversubscribed, he sailed to Britain for immediate training. After disembarking he lied about his age and secured a spot in the RNAS. By 1918 he was already an accomplished airman with an extensive bombing résumé. Among the long list of sorties he'd flown in 1917 were two that had particular significance for the pilot with the keen eyes and charismatic personality.

On 26 October, 5 Squadron's DH4s were grounded. The weather was abysmal: strong winds, squalls, low cloud cover. The airmen sought other distractions and the aircraft were tucked away against the storm. The sheltering two-seater DH4s were the mainstay of the daylight bombing campaign and usually carried two 230-lb or four 112-lb bombs. The biplane was powered by a Rolls-Royce Eagle engine and armed with twin forward-firing Vickers for the pilot and a Lewis machine gun for the observer. The powerful armament meant that the

DH4 was sometimes used as a 'fighting escort' to other bombers. It was a robust and strong-performing machine, well liked by aircrew. One of its few drawbacks was the placement of the fuel tank between the pilot and observer, which created a fire risk and, more importantly, made communication difficult.

In spite of the poor weather, an order was given for a two-aircraft mission: a bombing raid on Torhout railway station. The squadron's commanding officer asked Dickson and a fellow pilot if they were willing to undertake the task. Given the 'overcast sky with storms and squalls about and a strong wind', members of the squadron were surprised at the request.[48]

It was a hellish operation, and the two machines became separated soon after takeoff. Dickson arrived over Torhout alone and delivered his bombs in the face of determined anti-aircraft fire. He landed just before nightfall. The other machine become lost, bombed another target, but made it home. Both men received a special telegram of thanks for their 'stout effort' and a Distinguished Service Cross.[49]

Six weeks later Dickson had his first confirmed victory. At midday on 8 December he and his air gunner, Ralph Saw, were part of a force of four machines escorting six bombers that were attacking an airfield. After sustaining damage from anti-aircraft fire, the force turned for home, shadowed by Albatros DVs. When they crossed their own lines the Germans flew parallel with the trenches but would not follow. At this point in a sortie the pilot usually counts his blessings and makes for home, safe in the knowledge that he is free from pursuit, but Dickson had other ideas.

Five miles east of Dixmude at 10,000 ft he turned back over the lines into enemy territory to face the foe.[50] He picked out one with wings and fuselage festooned with black crosses in red circles and an engine cowl featuring a garish red circle. Dickson fired a 70-round burst. Soon seven more Albatros fighters were in on the punch-up. Although keen for the fight, Dickson was not naive. He wheeled the DH4 around and opened the throttle; the Rolls-Royce engine bellowed as he made for the British trenches. He heard Saw fire a 40-round burst and craned his neck to see an enemy machine drop into a dive that devolved into a spin, puncturing the clouds below.

Both these incidents were indicative of Dickson's approach to flying: a calculated determination to see through an operation and a willingness to pursue the enemy. Dickson undertook more bombing sorties than any other airman in the Great War, and he went on to become one of the two most successful bomber pilots in aerial combat.[51]

Over February and March it became clear that the German effort would focus on the British armies in the south, adjacent to the Cambrai salient, which had seen so much attention in the latter part of the previous year. Aerial reconnaissance reported the massing German forces. In addition, airmen spotted improvements to the rail system, supply dumps being assembled, and new airfields being established and older ones enlarged.[52] Nonetheless, very few aerial elements were shifted south from the Calais region in response because the British were determined to maintain a strong presence near the vital French ports. One of the very few concessions made was posting Dickson's naval squadron south to Villers-Bretonneux to augment the work of the night and daytime bombers in attacks on airfields and dumps.

They wasted no time. Dickson arrived before 10 a.m. and was up 'learning the country' by mid-afternoon on 6 March.[53] For the next nine days the squadron alternated between bombing and fighting escort duties. Their efforts, however, were increasingly hampered by the arrival of German aerial forces in the region in preparation for the upcoming offensive. Manfred von Richthofen's JG1 had recently appeared and over two days, 12 and 13 March, cut a swathe through a squadron of Bristol Fighters, removing six machines. The RFC wanted revenge and decided to bloody the Germans' nose. The plan involved using Dickson's squadron as bait for 85 Squadron's SE5s.

Ten DH4s crossed the lines on 16 March and bombed Busigny munitions dump and airfield.[54] Enemy machines were scrambled and headed to intercept. The 5 (Naval) Squadron flight commander gathered his brood of DH4s into a wide circling formation above the fires breaking out in the dump below. The bait was set, with enemy fighters converging on the scene. Unfortunately, the SE5a fighters 'never came', wrote Dickson.[55] They were alone and outnumbered four to one as some 40 enemy fighters fell on the bombers. A large sprawling dogfight broke out, with the DH4s edging towards their lines. Dickson's observer, Walter Scott, was whipping the Lewis gun around firing bursts at several machines. He downed an Albatros. Two DH4s were lost.

On the return journey a weakened machine was separated from the herd by 12 unchallenged enemy aircraft. It was helpless: an exhausted deer surrounded by hungry wolves. Dickson saw the danger and kicked his rudder and 'though he had no ammunition left whatever', wrote his squadron commander, flew into the heart of the enemy formation to break it up.[56] Other reports said that Dickson had exhausted his ammunition in the ensuing fight and that Scott's machine guns repeatedly jammed.[57] In the confusion Dickson drew a number of the enemy away, enabling the straggler to make it home, although the observer had been hit and the pilot wounded in the cheek.

In saving their comrades, Dickson and Scott were lucky not to be killed as they evaded fire from a triplane and three biplanes. Once safely on the ground they looked over their DH4 and discovered that the tail was shot through, the petrol tank pierced, a tyre punctured, and there were numerous bullet holes in the wings and fuselage.[58] They themselves were remarkably free of even a scratch. Dickson, who had now completed 68 daylight bombing raids, was awarded a bar to his Distinguished Service Cross. Given the losses it was a surprise that the squadron was used again in the same manner two days later.

This time the RFC bolstered the fighter presence by adding 54 Squadron Camels to 84 Squadron SE5s. The DH4s would still be the bait, but it was hoped that this time the fighters would actually make good their promises and pounce on the enemy. Dickson and Scott were carrying four 25-lb bombs and were vulnerable to attack. As they approached, small specks became a mass of enemy machines. 'The sky ahead was literally full of aircraft,' gasped one airman.[59] Late in the morning of 18 March the German fighters waded into the DH4s even before some had reached Busigny. The German force included elements of Richthofen's Circus, flying brightly coloured Fokker triplanes and Albatros. Fortunately for Dickson, the SE5s and Camels appeared and a massive dogfight ensued — up to 60 enemy and nearly 40 British machines in all. It was one of the largest dogfights of the Great War. Later Dickson wrote simply in his logbook: 'greatest show ever seen'.[60]

As they fought, the agitated mass of men and machines drifted eastward to Le Cateau. The DH4s were in mortal danger, and the flight commander waved his men off: retreat and leave the battle to the fighter boys. It was not so easy. A DH4 fell, trailing a long banner of inky smoke. The squadron's observers laced the sky with their Lewis machine guns as they turned for home. One airman sawed the tail off an Albatros. Dickson's observer, Scott, knocked out a red enemy machine. They in turn were struck and their bomber's two tail-elevator controls shot away. It was a nasty affair and both sides were badly knocked about. The British claimed to have destroyed four enemy machines and driven eight out of control, but they lost five Camels and two SE5s. Dickson made it home damaged but essentially in one piece; two other DH4s were less lucky. That evening Dickson's commanding officer telephoned through to the Camel squadron's leader to discuss the bloody fight. The Camel pilot was unnerved by the whole thing and kept repeating, 'frightful affair, frightful affair . . .'[61] It was the last major dogfight before the German offensive two days later.

In the meantime Kingsford was granted some long-awaited leave in England. On the day of his arrival in London Peps received a telegram: Reggie would be at Victoria Station at 3.50 p.m. She met him on the platform and they went to a hotel. In the morning they had a cup of tea in bed and a leisurely breakfast, then spent the day shopping at Selfridges, visiting friends and, in the evening, attending a show at the London Coliseum. 'So lovely to wake up and know that Reggie was safe in England with me,' Peps wrote.[62]

They went to Peps's parents' home in Surrey, where they walked in the garden, sat by the river watching the boats and attended the Palm Sunday service. The day rolled around to supper and bed; 'a lovely moonlight-night and no fear of air raids'.[63] With Reggie at her side Peps enjoyed unbroken and 'glorious sleep'. 'I was so happy,' she wrote.

For some 'unknown reason', seven days into the leave they both began to feel depressed. Peps could not shake a gnawing premonition; and after a nice dinner, to her 'sorrow a telegram came recalling Reggie to duty in France'. His leave had been cut short by the demands of the Western Front.[64]

Peps was heartbroken. 'I had a ghastly night, awoke with the porter's knock on the door. I knew we must part in a few hours . . . I in a dream dressed, and went out to the platform of the station . . . The whistle blew and we parted, oh, if I could just think he would come back, I love him so much, I want him so much.'[65] The next day she was no better: 'I am feeling so lost and heartsick, the battle raging and my own husband gone into it.' She went to stay with a friend but was unable to ignore reports of the battles raging in France: 'War news very black.'[66]

The long-awaited attack was under way.

CHAPTER FOURTEEN

SPRING OFFENSIVE

1918

On 21 March 1918, only minutes before 5 a.m., the great guns of German artillery announced the first phase of the Spring Offensive: Operation Michael. Shells filled the heavens and shook the earth. Dickson's squadron was one of the first to 'enjoy' the day's proceedings. A flight commander recorded the event.

> Awakened . . . by terrific drum fire and the bursting of shells all around us. They came screaming over about every 60 seconds and some were too close for comfort. Being a former German aerodrome, the gunners know our range exactly, though firing blind due to the thick fog which blanketed everything. While several of us were in the Mess doorway one screamed over our heads and burst by Dickson's cabin some 50 yards away, throwing up a volcano of earth and stones which fell around us . . . An amusing incident while we were being bombarded was a telephone call from HQ instructing our CO to take steps for growing vegetables on the station![1]

Dickson survived the destruction of his accommodation, and over the next five hours the Fifth and Third Armies' leading positions were pummelled by more than a million shells. Then the massed German infantry arose and swarmed across the battlefield — 62 strengthened divisions, with reserves at hand, against barely 30 weakened British divisions. Not only did the Germans have superior numbers on the ground, they had them in the air, too. The Luftstreitkräfte had assembled 730 machines for the offensive, of which 326 were single-engine fighters. The British, continuing their policy of maintaining considerable strength evenly along their front all the way to the French coast, had only 579 serviceable machines on hand, including 261 single-engine fighters. 'For the first and only time,' wrote Trevor Henshaw, 'the German air concentration assembled for the battle on the Western Front would exceed that of the Royal Flying Corps.'[2]

The early German assault was aided on the ground and in the air by a dense, impenetrable fog. When he took off at 11.15 a.m. to test the flying conditions, Major Rainsford Balcombe-Brown was one of the first New Zealanders into the air. He had been 56 Squadron's commanding officer since the autumn of the previous year.[3] He had difficult flying boots to fill: his predecessor

Richard Blomfield had been extremely popular and congenial. Balcombe-Brown was more regimented in running the squadron and was a stickler for proper procedures. This was an approach he had demonstrated at a young age: as a six-year-old student at Pipitea Preparatory School, Wellington, he had won an award for 'good conduct, neatness and punctuality'.[4] Now, as a 23-year-old on the Western Front, he was always correctly attired, his uniform perfectly starched and pressed.

Balcombe-Brown required forms to be filled out correctly and all claims for victories to be verified. The squadron's historian described him delicately as 'somewhat of a martinet in these matters'.[5] His own combat reports are exemplars of exactitude. In one he noted that his Lewis 'after firing very slowly for about 4 rounds stopped with a No. 1 and Vickers immediately stopped with a No. 3'.[6] The detailed reference to the specific numbered stoppages was just the sort of attention to detail at which Balcombe-Brown excelled. Most airmen reported just a 'stoppage' or 'guns jammed'. Balcombe-Brown was a diligent and conscientious leader under whose direction the squadron maintained its stellar fighting record.

Unlike his predecessor, who avoided flying, Balcombe-Brown was also a highly regarded pilot. He seemed to take pleasure in assessing weather conditions with early morning flights and carrying out various test flights, during which he was easily drawn into chasing intruders he spotted. A few weeks into the campaign Balcombe-Brown was undertaking a routine test flight when, nearing the lines at 6000 ft, he saw at great height an enemy two-seater being lit up by puffs of anti-aircraft fire. It was a Rumpler C.IV.[7] He opened the throttle and pulled back on the joystick. The Viper engine kicked into life and he began to pull the reconnaissance aircraft in. He inserted himself between the hostile and the German lines. At 18,800 ft, he was at the very edge of the SE5a's service ceiling and just below his prey. He snuck 'up very close under his tail without being seen'.

As soon as he opened fire Balcombe-Brown realised he was in trouble. The cold had thickened the lubricants on the Lewis machine gun and it was firing very slowly; after only four rounds it stopped entirely. He tried the Vickers but it also failed to operate. As his numbed fingers fumbled their way to clearing the jams, the Rumpler's rear gunner started sending bullets his way. The New Zealander made one last attempt but another stoppage and the unreliability of the Lewis gun forced him to let the enemy slip away east. It was just the sort of flight that earned him the respect of his men — but it would lead to his downfall a month later.

The squadron had an enviable reputation as one of the Great War's prestigious units — it was home to Victoria Cross winners Albert Ball and James McCudden. The latter had recently left the unit for a period of home service. In the weeks preceding the German offensive the squadron was operating from the spacious Baizieux airfield, and Balcombe-Brown's men were heavily involved in the effort to degrade German preparations. They had claimed 16 victories, including six by the squadron's rising star, Maurice Mealing.

On the opening day of Operation Michael, Balcombe-Brown reported that a mist lay over much of the Third Army's front, but he despatched two flights of SE5s. The air over the battlefield was thick with aircraft, and Balcombe-Brown's men were soon embroiled in a dogfight with over 20 hostiles. Mealing heard the bark of a machine gun and turned to look:

'I saw a Triplane firing at an SE5 about 20 yards above me with his wheels close to my centre section. I pulled down my Lewis and fired half a drum of ammunition right into his fuselage, just below the pilot's seat. He immediately went down out of control, but I then had to turn and engage another EA.' It was the helter-skelter combat for which the squadron was well known.

A haze delayed action in the morning of the next day but Balcombe-Brown gave the all-clear after a midday flight above Baizieux. Again, more successes. A couple of Fokker triplanes latched onto Canadian Wilson Porter, but he eluded them. A triplane crossed his nose in a climbing turn and, as it almost stalled, Porter fired and tracers bore into the Fokker. It fell into a vertical nose-over-tail cartwheel. Over 48 hours Balcombe-Brown's men knocked out eight enemy machines.

Nonetheless, losses across British squadrons soared. Only the difficult flying weather — a feature of March and April 1918 — prevented more losses. Balcombe-Brown recorded four casualties, including Porter and Mealing.

As the commanding officer it fell to the New Zealander to write to next of kin with the bad news. By March he had written numerous letters informing families that airmen were missing in action, imprisoned or dead, and composing them never got any easier. As a grief-stricken mother told him, 'I could never thank you enough for your letter, certainly it comforted me enormously. What a colossal task is yours!'[8]

Just before the offensive began, he received a letter from the mother of one of the squadron's deceased airmen: her son, the highly decorated Arthur Rhys-Davids, had been killed in late October 1917. Initially, Caroline Rhys-Davids was informed that the fate of her son was uncertain but that in all likelihood he had been killed in action. She wrote back immediately to Balcombe-Brown's predecessor, Blomfield, wanting to know why he had allowed her son to stay beyond his six months' frontline duty, and arguing that he should have compelled Arthur to return to relative safety in England — after all, 'he was all we had!' Blomfield informed her that there was no 'fixed period for a pilot to serve overseas' but he had nonetheless offered Arthur the opportunity to return home to serve in England. Arthur had refused, preferring to stay with fellow airmen over the front line. As time passed without firm confirmation of her son's fate, Caroline Rhys-Davids' hopes lifted; perhaps he was a prisoner of war after all. But it was not to be: she received news that her son's name had appeared on a casualty list in a Berlin newspaper. Her grief and anger were evident in a letter to Balcombe-Brown in March.

Concerning the fate of my only and utterly beloved son . . . late of your squadron, we have received, since early in November *absolutely no news* . . . no burial place, no relics save the CO's and WO's [War Office's] messages. Not a soul of those who knew him and were on patrol with him that day . . . have sent us a single word, either of what they saw of him, or of sympathy to us or of tribute to their comrade!! Is this usual in the RFC? . . . *Think what we have suffered for over four months* — the blind darkness, the silence — has no one in 56 the least imagination what it has all cost us? . . . It makes me think that he must in some way, after his swiftly earned fame, have disgraced the squadron at the end. What am I to think?[9]

Balcombe-Brown wrote back that he sympathised with her loss and frustration. 'I am sorry that none of the officers on that ill fated patrol wrote. The commanding officer's letter is usually written on behalf of the squadron and that letter should supply all the available details as it is the CO's job, in my opinion, to question all the officers and find out whatever he can about the fight.' He pointed out that they had all been in the dark, and still were, concerning the exact circumstances of her son's death. Moreover, by the time Arthur's death was confirmed, the airmen in the unit who might have written to her had themselves been killed in action. Balcombe-Brown reassured her that her son had not somehow shamed the squadron or died ingloriously. He said that given what he personally knew of Arthur, and given his widely acknowledged courage — bordering on recklessness — this was a 'non-existent' possibility. He gently noted that 'all of us have lost brothers and close relatives in the war so we can imagine slightly what it is like'. Balcombe-Brown's own 23-year-old brother had been killed by shellfire on the Western Front in 1915, and doubtless this loss coloured all his correspondence to grieving families, but it was still no easy task.[10]

The correspondence highlighted the difficult job squadron commanders faced in meeting the expectations of family who had recently lost a son, husband, fiancé or brother. What people desperately wanted were the details surrounding the death. 'What is the full information you have so far? Was he flying with an observer or was he alone? Did his machine go out alone or in a flight?' asked one supplicant.[11] Families were grateful for any scrap that might help frame their lost one's last moments. Some family and friends just wanted the unvarnished facts, good or bad. The military brother of a dead airman told Balcombe-Brown, 'You need not spare me any horrible details as I have been through the beastly business.'[12]

In cases where airmen had failed to return from sorties and none of their colleagues in the flight were able to shed any light on the absent airman's fate, commanders were in the very difficult situation of informing families that the airman was missing: they might be dead but equally they might be prisoners of war. In such cases Balcombe-Brown had to temper the hope that they had been captured with the very real possibility they had been killed in action.

Porter and Mealing had failed to return from their afternoon sorties. Mealing had taken off in a formation of nine SE5s Balcombe-Brown had despatched to strafe rapidly advancing German infantry. With the British line holding on by a thread, the greater part of the Allied air effort was thrust into attacking ground forces. Air units were required to fill in the gaps that British artillery was unable to cover in the quickly changing battlefield. It was a costly affair for both sides. Balcombe-Brown's pilots spotted German cavalry who dismounted and bounded for cover. Skimming low, the SE5a must have been terrifying to man and beast as they machine-gunned troops and horses.

Mealing and another pilot did not take part in the strafing; they were distracted by a couple of German two-seater machines that they promptly attacked. Mealing's wingman abandoned the fight after constant gun jams. He last saw Mealing attacking the two-seaters. Another airman much later recalled that he was sure he had later seen Mealing on the ground, waving next to his SE5a — perhaps he had suffered engine failure or been hit.

After gleaning what few facts were known, Balcombe-Brown wrote his obligatory letters and

Rainsford Balcombe-Brown (left) and Richard Blomfield outside the office of 56 Squadron in late October 1917, when Blomfield handed over command to Balcombe-Brown.

received replies. Of course the recipients gravitated to the possibility that their family member was alive, although likely a prisoner of war. 'I am exceedingly sorry to hear that Wilson Porter is missing, but as you seem to think he is likely to be a prisoner, I feel hopeful that this is the case,' a woman wrote to Balcombe-Brown in April.[13] In the end it was discovered that Porter had been killed and the wreckage of his SE5a dispersed over the battlefield.[14] Mealing's father corresponded in neat longhand with Balcombe-Brown on the uncertain fate of his son: 'We are very grateful to you for giving us the best information you had available about him and also his work since he had been with the squadron. Of course we feel it very acutely that something has happened to him and the suspense will be a great trial for us, but we shall still hope for good news of him.'[15] But it would not be good news: Mealing was eventually listed as missing, his ultimate end unknown. It is possible that the ace was killed by German infantry in an act of revenge for the strafing of their lines by his fellow 56 Squadron pilots only minutes before.[16]

When the fate of the victim was confirmed, the airman's belongings were assembled and catalogued. Naturally, families were eager to receive their lost one's personal effects. Balcombe-Brown received a letter from the brother-in-law of an airman killed in action. 'My wife brought up her young brother who was left motherless . . . With regards to this boy's effects . . . you will understand we are very anxious to have some little souvenir.'[17] Balcombe-Brown promised a cap and glove. 'I crave for all his small possessions,' replied the grateful sister seven days later.[18] And most of the possessions *were* small: unremarkable items of daily life — towels, pillowslips, a comb; or personal items imbued with the spirit of the man — letters, photographs, an engraved cigarette case; and the flying he loved — goggles, gloves, a logbook.[19] It was a pitiful legacy of a man's life but it meant everything to the surviving family.

As the Allied losses piled up the Germans were making large gains on the ground. In the first week they overran as much territory as the Allies had taken in a full six months in 1916.[20] But it could not last; the Allies, by the narrowest of margins, held on in fierce defensive fighting. By the last week of March both sides had fought themselves to exhaustion. The vigour of the initial German offensive had dissipated. It would not be the last German offensive for the year, but they had already made their biggest gains of 1918.

On 1 April 1918 the RFC and RNAS were amalgamated into a single unified and independent air service, the Royal Air Force. The army and admiralty relinquished control of their units to the newly created Air Ministry. The momentous change was the result of recommendations made by South African Jan Smuts in a report on British air power, which argued that a single force on equal footing with the army and navy would avoid duplication and the divisive rivalry for air resources. Old RFC squadron numbers were retained, and the RNAS units were renumbered in the 200s: for example, Euan Dickson's 5 (Naval) Squadron was redesignated 205 Squadron. The RAF was now the world's largest air force, with over 100,000 personnel.

With the creation of the Women's Royal Air Force (WRAF), increasing numbers of women were drawn to the colours. A small number of New Zealand women served with the WRAF, including Madeline Ranken from Stewart Island and Harriet Simeon of Dunedin. Unlike many women who gravitated towards more conventional positions as clerks or cooks within the WRAF, Ranken was a motorcycle despatch rider at Biggin Hill airfield, Kent. Clad in knee-high boots and breeches, the female despatch riders were a novelty in an age when women who wore trousers were regarded as 'fast'.[21] A motorcycle offered a degree of freedom and glamour not found in other WRAF trades, and despatch rider positions were oversubscribed. 'It was an exciting life,' Ranken told a reporter, 'no two days were alike.'[22] The 20-year-old travelled across England on her motorcycle accompanied by a mascot, her mustard-coloured teddy bear 'Ginger Mick'. Ranken could be sent anywhere at a moment's notice:

> Perhaps to the Air Ministry in London — 40 miles there and back — or to some big R.A.F. stores, or perhaps to some other aerodrome. I had to keep my bike clean and beautiful and do all the road repairs, such as punctures etc. The weather was of no account. The dust was my only worry in the summer. But in the winter I generally had to go about all day with wet feet, and mud from head to foot. But I was very suitably clad — mostly in leather and fur. People on the streets often took me for a lady aviator because of my uniform, and I was asked very funny questions sometimes, and I had many nicknames.[23]

Her worst moment came when she was carrying a passenger in her sidecar and the axle broke while they were going down a steep hill. Both the passenger and Ranken were thrown from the bike and landed on their heads. Neither was injured but they were very shaken.

Although she had very little leave and often worked Sundays, there were considerable advantages to the job. Aside from the motorcycle riding, which she adored, Ranken had a small but close group of friends on the base, including the five other WRAF drivers. 'We sometimes had little impromptu tea parties in our little W.R.A.F. hut, to which a few cheery pilots were invited — though it was not really allowed,' she confessed. They attended local social events and dances at Biggin Hill, where there was a very good jazz band. 'We needed all the fun we could get to keep our spirits up when we were cold, wet, and tired.' The other advantage to being a WRAF at a large airfield was the ample opportunities to fly: airmen were only too happy to take the young women up and show them the skies. Having flown on a number of occasions, Ranken concluded, 'the more you go up the more you want to go on going up — so long as they keep on stunting you'.

Simeon served in the Great War with her husband Major George Simeon, an officer in the New Zealand Rifle Brigade.[24] At 42 she was a couple of decades older than Ranken, and it was perhaps on account of this that the New Zealand authorities were unwilling to offer her a position in 1915. Undeterred, the lean and sharp-featured Simeon paid her own way to England. At first she took up night duty in a munitions canteen at Enfield. From there she secured a position in the British Nursing Service in Egypt, before she returned to work in Wales and then finally in France in May 1917.[25] There, at an infectious diseases hospital, she served four months' duty in a cerebromeningitis ward where her own health deteriorated under the very demanding working conditions.

Harriet Simeon was
New Zealand's highest
ranking woman in the
Women's Royal Air
Force.

After two months' leave, Simeon requested a discharge from the army nursing service, and in 1918 she became a quartermistress in the WRAF. Her initial posting was to the 1st Area Depot. Here, women were 'clothed, trained and thoroughly drilled in their duties before being sent out to various aerodromes'.[26] As well as training in traditional domestic and secretarial skills such as cooking, tailoring, shorthand and typing, Simeon's charges also learnt distinctly aviation-directed skills such as aero engine fitting, carpentry, acetylene welding, wireless telegraphy and meteorological recording. 'They were a splendid body of women,' said Simeon, 'keen on their work and amenable to discipline. I can tell you there was no slackness with my girls. I had them clicking their heels — as fine, sturdy, able, sensible [a] lot of young women as you could wish to see.'[27]

In September, thanks to her success in England, Simeon was despatched to Scotland to establish another depot. She had to start from scratch. In the evenings she travelled through Glasgow recruiting by car, encouraging 'young women to do their bit'. For her efforts she was promoted to major — New Zealand's highest-ranking WRAF of the war. By the time she left military service she was a deputy assistant commandant with 300 officers and over 5000 women under her command.[28] Not a bad effort for someone who started the war working in a canteen.

The first German offensive of the year came to an end on 5 April. As both sides caught their breath, and as the Germans girded themselves for their next onslaught, some RAF airmen were granted short leave. Among them was Seton Montgomerie. He had arrived from New Zealand with his family in 1915 and was now an accomplished pilot with one of the RAF's founding units: 2 Squadron.[29] Over the first three months of 1918 he had flown more than 30 reconnaissance, aerial photography and artillery cooperation sorties. His mother Annie was euphoric when she learnt he was due a few days' leave back in England in early April. 'It was a joy to see him again,' she wrote in her diary, 'so we are all under one roof, which is a great comfort.'[30] They attended the theatre and Seton visited his brother Oswald, who was still undergoing RAF training.

News of the German offensive cast a pall over their time together, although Annie was grateful her son had made it to England before all leave had been cancelled. One of Seton's friends, an observer from the squadron, called in and Annie was pleased to hear that her son was 'the best pilot in their flight'. They had a pleasant few days and Seton was looking better for the break, but Annie confessed that she was 'sore, sore, sore' at having to let him go. She was under no illusions about the threats to her son's life — and was not above prying into correspondence arriving from Seton for his brother.

> Two letters from Seton, one for me and one for Oswald. I opened his letter and found that Seton's 'low flying' that he told me about had been quite dangerous and his machine had been hit. He had been lost in the mist over Hunland and only his common sense had helped get safely back. Of course I have always known his work was dangerous each day, but it seemed appalling to read the dear kid's letter. Of course I was not supposed to read it.[31]

The day before his departure, 'My darling boy gave me a lovely RFC brooch' made with gold and diamonds, reported his mother. It was a tender gift but did nothing to assuage her fears and the pain of separation the next day: 'God knows it's hard . . . my baby boy set off again for France.'[32] Seton arrived just in time for the next German offensive.

With the movement of British forces south to defend Amiens, the Germans believed the time was ripe to once again push in the north for the French coast and the ports supplying the British effort. Success in Flanders with the capture of Ypres would make the British position untenable. Operation Georgette commenced on 9 April, and immediately broke through on a portion of the front manned by a weary and casualty-stricken Portuguese division. Montgomerie wrote to this mother, 'This nasty war has started today to the north of us.' He told her not to worry about him. 'If we fall back I shall be quite safe as we don't have a panic like the ground people . . . [it] does not take long to move.'

Montgomerie's assessment was overly confident. Yes, most squadrons did escape the rapidly advancing Germans — but not all. A Camel unit, 208 Squadron, was fogbound in the face of the German onslaught and the commander was forced to gather all the machines in the middle of the airfield and set them alight before evacuating.[33]

Mist and cloud cover not only trapped this unit, it also hid enemy efforts from the RAF's prying eyes. '"Dud" all day,' wrote a grounded Montgomerie in his diary. 'Huns start an offensive north of the La Bassée canal and advance at almost six thousand yards.'[34] The next day he was up at 9 a.m. on patrol from the squadron's Hesdigneul-lès-Béthune airfield, but the weather was still rotten and he got lost. To add insult to injury, heavy anti-aircraft fire holed his machine.[35] The squadron's two-seater biplanes, the FK8s, were very reliable and stable machines, although vulnerable to German fighters. The following day was washed out, and it was not until 12 April that he was able to get any real work completed. He and his observer exposed 12 plates in a photographic sortie.[36] The photographs revealed that the Germans had made prodigious gains: within two days they had advanced five miles and, by 13 April, 10 miles.

The next day Montgomerie was up with his observer at 3.10 p.m. After a successful shoot on a battery he dropped a bomb on the enemy, but was wounded in the process. 'It was a machine gun bullet that got me, the only one that entered the machine — some luck, eh! It hit me just under my right knee from the right side and came out about an inch and a half from where it entered.'[37] He continued the shoot and dropped another bomb before landing at an emergency airfield.[38] His wound was examined: the bullet was protruding from his skin. A medical orderly cut it out and handed it to Seton as a memento of his brush with death. The squadron had been very successful, with airmen reported to have 'sent down 8 area calls with good results and firing 800 rounds into enemy batteries which were silenced'.[39] Montgomerie's knee wound made him one of the squadron's six airmen casualties over two days of intensive action.[40]

The New Zealander wrote to his mother that he might be getting a 'Blighty' — that is, being shipped off to England for medical care and recuperation. He had been wounded in France on a Sunday and was in London by the following Thursday. The next day Annie got a telegram: Seton was at the RAF hospital at Eaton Square. Through snow and sleet she arrived at her son's bedside: 'Found Seton asleep and looking quite bonny in his smart blue pyjama suit.' He recovered quickly but did not resume duties overseas; he was posted to a training squadron as an instructor in July.

In France the German advance continued apace, and intensive air operations were carried out to slow the German breakthrough. On hand was 4 Squadron, Australian Flying Corps. Equipped with Sopwith Camels, the unit was the premier Australian fighter squadron and at the war's end led AFC tally sheets with nearly 200 enemy machines claimed. In the opening weeks of the Spring Offensive it was engaged in extensive strafing and bombing operations in line with instructions from the commander of the Allied forces in France, General Ferdinand Foch: 'at the present time the first duty of fighting aeroplanes is to assist troops on the ground by incessant attacks . . . Air fighting is not to be sought except in so far as it is necessary for the fulfilment of this duty.'[41] A Camel could be fitted with four 25-lb bombs. During Operation Michael, the squadron fired more than 67,000 rounds and dropped three tons of bombs in low-level operations.[42]

Among the squadron's members were a handful of New Zealanders. Onehunga-born fitter and turner John Classon Courtney had arrived with the squadron in France in December of the previous year. By March of 1918 he was a flight commander and leading strafing assaults. In that same month he led a 10-strong formation against the German-occupied village of Vaux.[43] Piloting one of the machines was another New Zealander, Herbert Watson. Born in Otago, he was the son of a reverend and had worked as a clerk in Sydney.[44]

Vaux and its approaching roads were clogged with enemy men and trucks. Courtney dived on them and, from 200 ft, fired 550 rounds into groups of troops; he 'saw many fall and the remainder scatter in all directions'. His Camel's oil tank was holed and the engine seized but he made British lines. Watson's aircraft was also struck by machine-gun fire but he made it back to base. Fifteen days later Courtney was killed on another low-level assault. Close to midday on 7 April he was seen near Illies descending in flames, apparently hit by anti-aircraft fire.[45] His body was recovered and he was buried near Marquillies but the grave's location was subsequently lost. Watson carried on the fight with the squadron.

On good flying days Watson's unit was dropping between 20 and 80 bombs on artillery batteries, transports and troops. The low-level work was costly, however, and he witnessed many men vanishing from the squadron's mess. From the beginning of Operation Michael until the end of April the squadron had to replace all its aircraft; the majority were lost to ground fire.[46]

While the squadron was supporting ground operations there was still the opportunity to engage enemy aircraft when required. Watson had his first success on 19 April. At midday, after dropping his bombs, he saw two enemy two-seaters flying low at 2000 ft and he dived on them, only to find himself face-to-face with a bright yellow Albatros as it emerged from a cloud right in front of him. Watson fired 50 rounds at very close range; bullets penetrated the hostile and it fell from the sky in an uncontrolled spin.[47] It was the beginning of a streak of successes. By the time he finished the war Watson would have amassed 14 victories, including three balloons, and he ended the war as the highest-scoring New Zealand pilot in the AFC.

Part of Watson's success was attributable to flying with one of the Great War's leading airmen, Australian Harry Cobby. Square-jawed and dimpled-chinned, Cobby was the quintessential flying ace with his movie star looks and flying brashness. He was a high-spirited character, known for decorating his machines with aluminium cutouts of the comedian Charlie Chaplin.[48] Watson often flew in Cobby's flight and the Australian confirmed most of his victories.

In mid-June they were together for Watson's best day of the war. He and Cobby climbed into their Camels in the early evening of 17 June.[49] They flew east of Laventie, where they encountered enemy machines. 'Whilst on Offensive Patrol with Capt. Cobby,' Watson wrote, 'we saw a formation of 5 enemy Scouts.' The two Anzacs dived on the four Pfalz and single Albatros. At 4000 ft they both struck the rearmost hostiles; Cobby took the one on the right and Watson the one on the left. The New Zealander closed in to within just 20 yards, right on the tail of the black-and-white Pfalz. He fired 70 rounds, including Buckingham incendiaries. The exploding bullets had an immediate effect: the enemy aircraft 'burst into flames and crashed'.[50] Cobby's target half-rolled under fire and went down with its starboard wings torn off.[51] Watson and Cobby moved up to the next two machines and Watson's twin Vickers barked loudly, but with little effect. He climbed above and made sure at very close range. The Pfalz was despatched, and crashed alongside Cubby's second for the day. The Anzacs had two apiece.

Although the German effort was waning there was considerable concern on the ground. 'The Hun push is going badly against us,' wrote Reggie Kingsford. On 20 April, the day after Watson's first kill, Kingsford was involved in a very close call — a frightening incident that he deliberately left out of his letters to his wife Peps.

When the push against the British position looked bad for the Allies, 100 Squadron was ordered to bomb Chaulnes railway junction, some 75 miles northwest of Villeseneux and in the vicinity of some of the heaviest fighting near Amiens. To reach this target they would cross a French airfield near the German-occupied town of Soissons. They made the landing in good time but the takeoff was not so well executed.

> I might explain here that the French used for night flying, a large
> lamp on a pylon about 20 feet high, principally as a landing aid,
> and rarely in use for takeoffs. I had just cleared the ground and

An aerial photo taken north of the Somme in March 1918. The interpreter has drawn indications in pen of new German communication wires and entrenchments showing a build-up of activities ahead of Operation Michael.

thought that all was well when — BANG!! — I wondered what on earth had happened. All seemed well for a moment but then the left wing began to drop. I immediately looked over, and by the glow of the navigation lights, made out a gaping hole in the lower plane. It was ripped to blazes and the centre strut was waving about in the breeze. I realised that I must have hit one of the landing light pylons, and was almost out of control, too close to the ground to release my bomb load, and damned worried about the whole thing. Straight ahead of me was a stream, bordered by high poplar trees, so I was in a nice old pickle. I kicked over a boot full of rudder, throttled back and just waited. It did not take long. The machine curled around in a left spiral and — CRASH!! — It was all over, though neither of us was hurt, we were both badly shaken. And the poor old machine lay smashed to pieces. Why the bomb load did not explode I cannot explain. I guess our luck was in. But our FE.2c, the last of the Squadron's complement of six, was well and truly finished. I was more than a little sad, for she had carried us home safely so many times. And to top it all off the show was a failure due to the appalling weather. Most of the squadron simply came back, while only a few went roaming on in the murk trying to find the target. Very few did.[52]

Eight days later the Germans — overextended, with exposed flanks and a thinning logistical support — wound down Operation Georgette. Both sides had lost close to 110,000 men, but the Central Powers had failed to overrun Hazebrouck. The German offensive was halted for four weeks. General Haig lauded the airmen.

> The work of the Royal Air Force under the Command of Major-General J. M. Salmond, in co-operation with other arms has been brilliant. Throughout the period of active operations our airmen have established and maintained a superiority over the enemy's air forces without parallel since the days of the 1st Somme battle. Not content with destroying the enemy in the air they have vigorously attacked his infantry, guns, and transport with bombs and machine gun fire and in the fighting S. of the Somme in particular gave invaluable assistance to the infantry by these means on numerous occasions. In addition the usual work of reconnaissance, photography, artillery co-operation and bombing has been carried out vigorously and with remarkable results.[53]

In the second quarter of 1918 Balcombe-Brown was joined on the Western Front by Keith Caldwell and Keith Park as squadron commanders. They were the most recent additions to a growing cohort of New Zealand airmen leading squadrons. In the autumn of 1917 Alan Scott and Cuthbert Maclean had been joined by Alfred de Bathe Brandon, 50 (Home Defence) Squadron, and Keith Murray, 10 Squadron. Murray was a founding member and secretary of the Aero Club of New Zealand (1910) and a keen glider designer. He took over his squadron, an artillery cooperation unit, on the Western Front in September 1917 and was still at the helm at the cessation of hostilities.[54] 'He is a corker,' reckoned a former 10 Squadron airman, 'I have never met a fellow with personality more prominently written all over him. When you look at him, you cannot resist saying: There goes a *man* . . . he is worshipped by his squadron [flight] commanders.'[55] In all likelihood Murray was New Zealand's longest-serving squadron commander of the war. Other men had much shorter commands. Maurice Lee, a former Indian Army officer and early RFC trainee, led 27 Squadron in bombing and photographic reconnaissance operations for only the first 11 weeks of 1918.[56]

In February 1918, Caldwell was given command of 74 Squadron, equipped with SE5s. Ira 'Taffy' Jones recorded his arrival in the squadron.

> The new C.O. was Major Keith Caldwell, M.C., a New Zealander from Waikato, near Auckland. He was a big man, with jet black hair, swarthy complexion, deep-set eyes and a prominent chin which was a good indication of a determined character. It was not necessary to speak with him to realise that he possessed an outstanding personality. He was already famous throughout the Royal Flying Corps as a great fighter and a dashing patrol leader. I had heard much about him when he was serving in Jack Scott's crack 60 Squadron. . . . Jack Scott once said that, in his opinion, 'Grid' Caldwell (he got his nickname because he called all aircraft 'grids') had engaged in more fights for the number of times he had been in the air than any other pilot. When one remembers Scott's vast knowledge of air fighters, that was no mean tribute.[57]

At the first opportunity Caldwell gathered the airmen to outline what he required of them. 'His manner of speaking was straight and to the point,' Jones recalled. The New Zealander let them know that they were going to be fighting with the best fighters over the Western Front and that they were blessed with some of the best flight commanders the RAF had to offer. He wanted everyone to 'fight like hell' and, regardless of the odds, he required all men serving with him to go to the aid of a fellow pilot in trouble. He also let them know that he liked his men to be punctual, and that the squadron would never take off late.

The squadron's famous flight commander Edward 'Mick' Mannock informed the unit what to expect from Caldwell: 'Our C.O. is the bravest man in the air force and he'll frighten the hell out of you when he leads the patrols.'[58] Caldwell had nine victories to his name by the time the squadron arrived on the front lines and was widely recognised as an outstanding fighter pilot. By his own admission he was not the best shot in the game, and he might well have accounted for more aircraft had he possessed a keener eye. Others were less convinced. 'Remarks on Caldwell being such a bad shot I think are wrong,' wrote one airman, 'it was his absolute honesty . . . he would never make a claim unless absolutely certain of the result.'[59] Caldwell may well have been influenced by the silliness surrounding some extravagant and unsupported claims made by his squadron colleague Billy Bishop in the previous year, and decided that certainty and verification were overriding criteria in such matters. Nonetheless he would end the war in impressive style as New Zealand's highest-scoring pilot and among the top five per cent of the Great War's airmen.

As a commanding officer Caldwell presented a relaxed but determined face to his subordinates. He had a knack for cajoling his men without the need for a regimented and

Keith Caldwell was an extremely competent airman and was the best-known New Zealand squadron commander in France in 1918.

overly ceremonious command. In marked contrast to many commanders of the era he had an informality about him, not dissimilar to his old New Zealand commander Alan Scott, but without the latter's eccentricities. Outsiders were wary of the squadron's apparently lax discipline. While men from other units acknowledged that 74 Squadron had a 'cracker of a C.O.' in Caldwell, they also voiced concern that the unit lacked the requisite military order; it was a 'ragtime show'. Caldwell's men would not hear of it. 'Certainly we cut out as much as possible the empty but deceptive type of discipline — "Yes, sir," "No, sir." "Three bags full, sir,"' Jones noted, but 'One word from Grid, and the thing was as good as done.'[60] He could make serious demands on his men in a light-hearted way that pulled them along rather than drove them. At the beginning of their campaign he let it be known that he would not forgive anyone who dived away from the enemy; he promised to kick any shirker's 'backside all round the aerodrome'. And, as one airman joked, 'Grid, like most Aucklanders, has big feet!'[61]

He aimed to create a family that worked together. He also had a knack for smoothing over potential troubles. On one occasion at the local watering hole in France a couple of the young pilots were picked out for being teetotallers. One of them was Jones. He tried to fit in by drinking beverages that resembled wine, but others clearly thought he and his fellow abstainer were letting the side down. Caldwell deftly and casually moved the conversation on. 'Caldwell says it is a good show that we don't [drink],' wrote Jones, 'which is typical of him. He is a great leader of men. I would do anything or go anywhere for him.'[62]

Jones was not the only one to adore Caldwell. Pilot Leonard Richards flew on numerous sorties with his commanding officer. According to Richards, 'Grid Caldwell has got to be the finest C.O. ever in France or any other country. He is "one of the boys" and more interested in our welfare than making a name for himself. I'd go west before I'd let Grid down.'[63]

Caldwell's mercurial flight leader Mick Mannock had accumulated 16 victories by the time he joined Caldwell's crew and would not only add victories to the squadron's tally sheet but also greatly improve the survivability and success of Caldwell's young charges. Mannock could be loud and opinionated but his opinions were well worth heeding.

> You'll be flying SE 5s when you get your fights. The Huns have produced a good triplane fighter — a Fokker triplane . . . don't ever attempt to fight a triplane on anything like equal terms in altitude. He'll get on your tail and stay there until he shoots you down. Take my advice, if you ever get into such an unfortunate position, put your aircraft into a vertical bank, hold the stick into your belly, keep your engine full on — and pray hard. When the Hun has got tired of trying to shoot you down from one position, he'll try another. Here's your chance, and you'll have to snap into it with alacrity. As soon as your opponent starts to manoeuvre for the next position, put on full bottom rudder, do one and a half turns of a spin, and then run like hell for home, kicking your rudder hard from side to side, so as to make the shooting more difficult for the enemy. And keep praying.[64]

On the other hand, a German firing long bursts at you meant he was invariably a novice and windy: 'Fight him like hell — he should be easy meat.'[65] He told young airmen that showboating was a waste of time; quick turns, not stunting, were the order of the day. 'Mannock was not a stunt pilot,' Caldwell noted. 'I never saw him looping or wasting energy or engine power in this manner, nor was he better than the average pilot.' Mannock's commander put the Englishman's success down to 'his tactical approach to a fight' and his precise deflection shooting. Mannock always sought out a positional advantage and seldom engaged until he had procured it. His axiom was: 'Always above; seldom on the same level; never underneath.' Finally, Mannock despised Germans with a passion and that added an edge to his ruthlessness.

Caldwell saw this firsthand in operations with the Englishman. On one patrol with Mannock and Henry Dolan, British anti-aircraft fire signalled the presence of an intruder — a two-seater 'beetling' back to his own lines. It was hunted down by the faster SE5s. The intruder crashed under a hail of bullets. 'Most people would have been content with this — but not Mick Mannock,' observed Caldwell. Mannock dived repeatedly on the stricken machine, strafing the terrified crew. Caldwell flew alongside the Englishman, yelling at him at the top of his voice to stop. It was pointless, Mannock had his blood up and the wind swallowed the shouts. When Caldwell asked him back at base to account for his wild behaviour, Mannock replied, 'The swines are better dead — no prisoners for me!'[66] 'He really hated Germans — there was absolutely no chivalry with him and the only good Hun was a dead one,' concluded Caldwell. Mannock dubbed Germans caught in airborne fires 'Flamerinos'. It was not pretty, but Mannock had seen his share of Germans shooting down his colleagues, and by 1918 the air war was as brutal as anywhere else on the battlefield — kill or be killed. In a way it was an essential grim motivation for getting some men to carry out their duties. 'I am afraid we rather fostered this blood-thirsty attitude in 74 Squadron,' noted Caldwell, 'because it helped to keep a war-going atmosphere which is essential for the less tough types.'[67]

Offsetting Mannock's hatred of the enemy was his concern for his subordinates and his willingness to risk all in the defence of a brother airman in perilous straits — an attribute that would ultimately lead to his downfall.

Caldwell's squadron arrived late to the war in April 1918, but quickly made up for lost time. With the Allied position poised on a knife edge, 74 Squadron had its first major sortie from its base at Clairmarais. After breakfast on 12 April Caldwell addressed the men with General Haig's powerful message:

> Three weeks ago today the enemy began his terrific attacks against us on a fifty mile front. His objects are to separate us from the French, to take the Channel ports, and destroy the British army . . . Many in our ranks now are tired. To those I would say that victory will belong to the side which holds out the longest. The French Army is moving rapidly and in great force to our support. There is no other course to us but to fight it out. Every position must be held to the last man; there must be no retirement. With our backs to the wall, and believing in the justice of our cause, each of us must fight on to the end. The safety of our homes and the freedom of mankind depend alike upon the conduct of each one of us at this critical moment.[68]

Caldwell had barely got the last sentence out when Mannock leapt to his feet. 'They're going to

above Bertangles
airfield near Amiens
was home to Keith
Park's 48 Squadron
when it was attacked by
Gothas in August 1918.

below New Zealander
Herbert Watson (front
row, centre) with his
fellow officers of B
Flight, 4 Squadron,
Australian Flying
Corps (AFC), at their
aerodrome near
Clairmarais in June 1918.

RAF officers at the burial of Manfred von Richthofen in April 1918, at Keith Park's Bertangles airfield. Known as the 'ace-of-aces', the Red Baron's 80 combat victories and dashing persona made him the most feared and revered airman of the Great War.

get it now — and they won't have more than half an hour to wait for it! Come on "A" Flight. We take off at eight twenty-five.' By the end of the day Mannock had claimed two and the squadron a total of five. It was the beginning of one of the fastest accumulations of victories on the Western Front. By 7 May they had removed 18 enemy aircraft, and just over a month after arriving that number had risen to 33.[69]

Sixty miles due south, Major Keith Park arrived to take over 48 Squadron. His first few days with the unit were filled with hasty relocations to avoid being overrun by the Spring Offensive. Park retreated westward until he was able to base 48 Squadron outside Amiens in the rolling countryside at Bertangles — 48 Squadron's home for much of 1918. Catching his breath, Park was able to assess the force he now commanded. In an unusual move he had been given command of a squadron in which he had previously served as a junior officer.[70]

He was the only surviving airman from his original 1917 posting to the squadron. Casualties and transfers had removed all the pilots and observers he had started his fighting career with. For their part, his men were well versed in their commander's prodigious efforts the previous year as an airman and flight leader. Although the squadron's chief duties were reconnaissance, between them Park and his observers had 16 aerial credits by the time he took command of the unit — seven more than Caldwell. At the end of 1917 the man from Thames was New Zealand's leading airman in victories over the battlefield. Caldwell would overhaul this flying the SE5a in 1918, but Park would retain his position as 48 Squadron's most fruitful pilot to the war's end.

Unlike Caldwell, Park was not particularly close to his men; he maintained a civil distance between himself and those he commanded, in part because by nature he was not particularly outgoing. 'He was a fine upstanding man who wasn't very gregarious,' said one of his officers, Frank Ransley, 'nonetheless he was very pleasant to speak to.'[71] But Park did possess a wry sense of humour. On 21 April Manfred von Richthofen, the best-known airman of the war, was killed near Amiens. The German ace lay in state in a Bertangles hangar and then was buried in the village's small cemetery. There were numerous wild claims made about who had killed the celebrated Red Baron; Park later observed that 'he was the only airman or soldier on the Somme front who neither killed Richthofen nor saw him killed. It must have been dangerous up there . . . with all those aeroplanes milling about, not to mention 40,000 Australian soldiers firing away.'[72] Nonetheless, Park was respectful of his adversary and encouraged his men to view the body and attend the funeral.

Park was well regarded by his men. In his account of the squadron's exploits the South African pilot Vivian Voss noted that Park took a more active part in the life of the squadron than his predecessor, and on 'several occasions he led the patrols himself'.[73] Moreover, the tall New Zealander had a quiet charisma that meant 'we did exactly what Park wanted at all times', Ransley recalled. When he returned from leave with his fresh promotion and Military Cross and bar, Park 'was soon voted a jolly good fellow by the officers and the Ack Emmas [air mechanics] alike', wrote Voss.[74] He was well known to the mechanics for his appreciation of their work the previous year, and as the squadron's commander he had little tolerance for officers who failed to heed the mechanics' advice on how to get the best out of their machines.

Park set his squadron straight to work, not only in its usual deep reconnaissance sorties behind German lines but also in the low-level attacks so many squadrons were carrying out in April. 'Officers frequently flew six hours a day,' said Park, 'making five trips to bomb and machine gun enemy columns.'[75] Unfortunately, the Bristol was not well suited to evasive manoeuvrres at low altitudes; being caught by a triplane while engaged in ground strafing was to be avoided at all costs. Park did not like sending his men on such operations but had little choice.

Under the cover of fog the Germans made another attempt to break through on 24 April. Their target: the village of Villers-Bretonneux. Park had orders to use the Bristol Fighters as low as possible, shooting up German troops or other worthwhile targets. At 5 a.m. Park sent his men out to meet the onslaught but poor visibility forced their return to Bertangles. It was not until midday that the squadron was inserted into the battle. The sight was apocalyptic.

The fog had not dissipated but merely lifted a few hundred feet. It created a thick layer that blocked out the sun, leaving the land beneath shrouded in semi-darkness, a gloomy netherworld lit up sporadically by gun flashes. Forced to fly at 500 ft, the squadron passed over British infantry — mud-covered men clustered in blasted craters and broken trenches. Swirling vapours and mists rose from the tortured ground, periodically blinding the pilots. North of Villers-Bretonneux they turned east to meet the surging Germans. Some of the airmen spotted shells in flight as they whined past them. It was a bloody engagement.

They flew straight into withering groundfire: lines of tracer bullets rose from the ground as they dived on the enemy infantry. The pilots fired their forward guns on the advancing Germans and the observer-gunners opened up as the Bristol Fighters pulled away. As they dropped their bombs the Bristols were at their most vulnerable, and inevitably the squadron suffered losses. Three casualties were sustained in the fighting, all from groundfire. Mercifully, no one was killed, but Park was forced to send one airman to the local hospital with a nasty gunshot wound. The pilot was 'grinning and moaning alternatively' as he was carted off in pain but pleased to know he was Blighty bound.[76]

Although the Bristol Fighter could take considerable punishment, it was heavier and larger than the Camel and SE5 and, as such, it attracted considerable groundfire. At one point in the support of ground troops, 48 Squadron was reduced to only three serviceable aircraft.

The Germans were repulsed in heavy ground fighting. Five days later, on 29 April, the last great German push was shattered. The British, against great odds, had survived General Erich Ludendorff's offensive. Between 21 March and 29 April, the Germans lost over 330,000 men, while the British incurred some 300,000 casualties. The difference between the two sides was not great, but Ludendorff would be unable to make good his losses, just as the Americans began arriving in large numbers on the Western Front — 220,000 in May. As for the air effort, it had been costly. RAF 'wastage' — that is, lost or wrecked machines — ran close to 80 per cent of the 1230 machines in the field.[77] The three New Zealand squadron commanders had guided their charges through the storm, only for one to be lost in the immediate backwash of the April fighting.

On 2 May Balcombe-Brown despatched nine SE5s. The New Zealander followed his men shortly thereafter on a special mission to see the lines. The leading elements of the squadron spotted seven Pfalz and three Fokker triplanes south of Arras at 11.25 a.m. Among the Germans was Erich Löwenhardt, commander of Jasta 10. The Silesian Iron Cross (Second Class) holder was an aggressive pilot who, by the end of April, already had 17 victories; he would surpass 50 before his death in August. As the two sides clashed, Balcombe-Brown entered the fray and the two squadron leaders engaged. In the fighting the SE5s gained the upper hand, but not without loss. A Pfalz went down in flames and two more out of control, and a triplane was seen to crash. When it was over Balcombe-Brown was nowhere to be seen.[78]

Rainsford Balcombe-Brown was the highest-ranking New Zealand airman killed in active operations, and his death was a severe loss for the squadron. The unit's history recorded that he had commanded with 'great distinction'.[79] As Balcombe-Brown himself had done so many times before, his replacement had the task of putting pen to paper and writing to his mother, Eliza Balcombe-Brown, accounting for his death. Eliza was heartbroken: she had lost her youngest son in mid-1915, and her husband had died in February 1918. Now the last man in her life, Rainsford, had been taken from her. She remained a widow until her death 44 years later.

CHAPTER FIFTEEN
SEA ASSAULT
1918

From late May through to July, the Germans switched the weight of their effort south to the French front with three offensives: Blücher-Yorck, Gneisenau and Marneschutz-Reims/Friedensturm. Ludendorff's plan was to once again draw the Allied effort away from the British sectors in the north in preparation for another attempt on the Channel later in the year. The diversion of effort south should have lowered RAF losses, but in fact casualties increased considerably because British units were used to aid French initiatives and because the poor flying weather of the previous months had lifted, increasing the intensity of aviation work along the entire Western Front.

Three New Zealanders — Peter Nielsen, Roy Fitzgerald and Robin Barlow — were killed in operations during the Germans' southern offensive. Nielsen, a fair-haired, grey-eyed motor mechanic from Waitotara in the North Island, received a gunshot wound to the right leg five weeks into the Gallipoli campaign and was then laid low with tonsillitis, diphtheria and jaundice. By mid-1917 he was ready for a change from the hospital beds of Egypt, and was a fortunate recipient of a nomination by the commander of the NZEF for a temporary commission in the RFC.[1]

He arrived in France during the 1918 German offensive as an SE5a fighter pilot with Sholto Douglas's 84 Squadron. The unit was generally employed in offensive patrols, escorting bombers and balloon busting.[2] After a short series of practice flights Nielsen took off on his first sortie on Sunday, 16 June. It was a quiet affair, with a lone enemy machine seen in the distance and no movement on the roads. On 18 June at 9.45 a.m. Nielsen took off with the squadron's three flights. The formation encountered at least 15 enemy Fokker triplanes, Pfalzes and Fokker DVIIs.[3] Nielsen became embroiled with two fighters. The novice airman was well out of his depth, and on only his fourth offensive patrol and after just 13 days in France, he was killed over Villers-Bretonneux.

Thirteen days later, Wellington-born Roy Fitzgerald was with a Bristol Fighter squadron when he met his demise. Fitzgerald had been a mining engineer in Nigeria, and when war broke out he and his two siblings went to war.[4] His brother held a commission in the British Army and his sister was a nurse.

Fitzgerald was in his thirties and was noted for his powerful build and charismatic personality.

As a member of the Gloucestershire Regiment he had won a Military Cross in 1916 as part of a four-company assault: all the other officers were wounded in the action and Fitzgerald assumed command, 'consolidating defences of the captured position' and leading a party into nearby woods to establish forward posts.[5] Fitzgerald was less fortunate at Messines, where he was wounded in battle and was found unconscious by the Germans on 8 May 1917. He was taken to Karlsruhe for treatment and then sent on to a prisoner of war camp. Naturally, Fitzergald's mind turned almost immediately to escape.

Five months into his imprisonment the New Zealander had a plan. On occasions the German guards used 'Tommy' prisoners as general orderlies around their camp. Disguised in orderlies' uniforms, Fitzgerald and a co-conspirator fell in with these men and went outside of the camp on a water-collecting errand. When a sentry turned his back the pair bolted. The flummoxed guard was unable to get a shot off and the two men survived their first night on provisions they had pilfered from the camp, supplemented by apples gathered on their journey to the Dutch border.[6] Still in British attire and unable to speak German, they travelled under cover of darkness and walked 120 miles over seven nights. On the final leg of their journey they swam the Ems River.[7] On the last night, a Dutch border guard fired on them as they were about to enter the Netherlands. It was the first challenge they had encountered over their week-long escapade. At daybreak they discovered they had ventured well beyond the border, and contacted British authorities in the Netherlands. Fitzgerald was reunited with this brother and sister in London.

Although he married soon thereafter and was offered a home posting, Fitzgerald continued in service and was sent to Italy in late 1917.[8] On the Italian front the New Zealander gained notoriety for capturing Austrian soldiers. He dubbed the nightly raids 'man or rifle' missions; 'man' if they would come quietly, or 'rifle' if not. 'Captain Fitzgerald was the champion at this game of bagging Austrians,' wrote one English reporter, but 'one night the enemy, tiring of this sentry-snatching young colonial, set an ambush 200 strong to catch him. As it happened, it was Fitzgerald's turn to take a patrol of 14 men across the river [Piave] with him, and naturally they came face to face in the dark with the Austrian Committee of Public Safety.'[9] In spite of the odds, Fitzgerald returned with all his men unharmed. Not suprisingly, the Italian front was too quiet for Fitzgerald and he requested a return to the Western Front in the spring of 1918. He arrived as an RAF observer in 35 Squadron.[10]

Five weeks into his posting he was engaged in artillery observation over Coisy when he and his pilot in their Bristol Fighter were attacked by 10 enemy aircraft.[11] The injured pilot survived the action, but Fitzgerald was killed. One of his former army officers penned a few words that appeared in the New Zealand newspapers: 'Roy Fitzgerald was one of those exceptional men of iron nerve and powerful physique, who combined the great qualities of intelligent leadership, great initiative, and personal magnetism with splendid gallantry, displayed on every possible occasion. The whole regiment was devoted to him.'[12]

At the start of the Great War, India-born Robin Barlow was studying at Lincoln Agricultural College, near Christchurch. Like Nielsen, Barlow was wounded at Gallipoli in an attack on a Turkish position. His wounds were so severe that he was shipped back to England and, after a long recovery, was discharged from the NZEF.[13] He entered the RFC in the stream of colonial students that included Caldwell, Spragg and Hewett.

As an airman Barlow was again wounded, this time near the Belgian coastal town of La Panne in 1917. It was a routine artillery cooperation sortie in a two-seater Royal Aircraft Factory RE8, nicknamed the 'Harry Tate' — a solid if uninspiring biplane. The flight was marred by accurate anti-aircraft fire. Shrapnel hit the engine and Barlow was slightly injured. He and his observer were fortunate to survive an emergency sea-landing 100 yards from the shore.[14] In 1918 the 28-year-old Barlow had survived the early days of the German Spring Offensive, a period when 52 Squadron's losses had been particularly high — their RE8s were badly mauled in ill-suited ground attacks — only to be brought down on the German side of the lines on 30 July.[15] The squadron's casualty report for Barlow and his observer was depressingly spare: 'Were brought down — unknown. Machine left aerodrome at 9.45 and has not been heard of since. Reported missing. Struck off.'[16]

I n the first week of June 1918 a strategic bombing force was created: the Independent Force. Comprised of three day-bombing and two night-bombing squadrons, its task, in the words of its commander Hugh Trenchard, was to bring about the 'breakdown of the German Army in Germany, its Government, and the crippling of its sources of supply'. Although the German Zeppelins, Gothas and Riesenflugzeuge had failed to bring Britain to its knees, it was widely recognised that they had siphoned off resources to home defence. Trenchard realised that he did not have the capacity to destroy German towns, let alone cities, but he hoped that the Independent Force attacks on widely dispersed targets in Germany would compel Berlin to deploy extensive defensive measures at many 'different localities'.[17]

While he would have liked to strike militarily important targets — poison-gas, engine and aeroplane factories — they were too distant for much of his force. Only the twin-engine Handley Pages of the Independent Force had strategic-bomber range; the rest of the machines, DH4s and FE2bs, were really only light bombers of moderate endurance. Consequently, Trenchard would concentrate on targets closer at hand such as blast furnaces and railways, with a view to 'hastening the end of hostilities'. Both were easily spotted at night — a warm orange burning glow from the furnaces and thin silver railway lines — and they had the advantage of being within range of the greater part of his force. Trenchard believed that the railway lines, in particular, were very useful targets because Germany was short on rolling stock and a number of the 'main railways feeding the German Army in the West passed close to our front . . . it was hoped that these communications could be seriously interfered with, and the rolling stock and trains carrying reinforcements or reliefs or munitions destroyed'. With time the Independent Force was enlarged and the targets were broadened to include enemy airfields.

The Independent Force's night-time bombing began in June. Reggie Kingsford's 100 Squadron was one of the two night-bombing units incorporated into the newly established force. The squadron had developed a few unusual tactics to torment the German defenders. After a good drinking session there was a vigorous competition for empty long-necked crème

An FE2b light bomber
flown by Alfred
Kingsford of 100
Squadron. The bombers
were painted black for
night-flying duties and
dubbed the 'All Blacks'.

A852

de menthe bottles. On a sortie and caught in a searchlight, the men would hurl the bottles down, whereupon the fluted necks let out a long and unnerving scream that often led to the lights being quickly extinguished. Kingsford and others had also observed that the enemy night fighters used flares to alert German ground crews to light up landing lights on the airfield. With a full range of Very lights, 100 Squadron airmen would fly over an enemy base and fire off flares, tricking the Germans into lighting up the field, whereupon the formation would drop its bombs on the surprised enemy. 'We thought it was great fun!' one of Kingsford's colleagues recalled.[18]

On 25 June the 'All Blacks' had their first outing in Trenchard's new command. The quarry was Boulay airfield, a home to German Gothas and Friedrichshafens. The base was heavily defended and a treacherous target. Fifteen machines took off for their two-hour round journey.[19] Delayed by an engine malfunction, Kingsford and his observer, Sidney Bourne, fell well behind the main body. This meant the target would be easily found, but also that the defenders would be ready and waiting for them. One of the squadron described the strength of the Boulay defences:

> As about every third bullet was a tracer, and the Hun was firing dozens of guns vertically in a straight line, they looked like one of those Chinese bead curtains which glitter if one runs one's fingers across it. We used to run through this, getting a few holes in the process. Higher up the Hun used his high explosive anti-aircraft guns and 'flaming onions.' With the former, the Huns commenced to use shells which threw out a rain of phosphorus which was purple in colour. This was quite harmless for it actually bounced off our top wing but was very spectacular. If, of course, a shower had come into the cockpit it would have been a different matter! The flaming onions were very peculiar in that about a dozen or so flaming balls which looked like Roman candles came snaking up as if they were on a wire string.[20]

In other words, the airfield was lit up like a Christmas tree by the time Kingsford arrived. He and Bourne could see the hangar row. At 2000 ft they dropped two of the bombs; fires broke out beneath them. 'Bourney was elated,' wrote Kingsford, 'and as he leant over to me, I could see by the glow of the instrument lights his face was lit with a grin of satisfaction.' 'Go back and we'll give 'em the rest,' Bourne shouted to Kingsford. By the time they released two more bombs, a forest of tracer-laced machine-gun fire was surrounding their searchlight-ensnared FE2b. Kingsford could not evade the beam. In desperation he released a parachute flare. The decoy worked and he slipped out of the beam of light into darkness, dropping the remaining bombs, 'their little propellers spinning away, screeching their warning to those below'. Their large 230-lb bomb exploded among the buildings. Much lighter for getting rid of their munitions, they scuttled for home.

Within moments of departing Boulay, they spotted an airfield lit up nearby, a telltale sign of landing German machines. Kingsford dropped the revs on his FE2b and snuck up on the base, with Bourne expectantly leaning on the machine gun. 'Then, as though for our benefit, a twin-engine machine came into view, we were right above, and he was landing with the lights full on him. What a sight!'[21] The duo had no bombs left; the machine gun would have to suffice. The German bomber taxied right into the glare of the ground lighting and men scurried around the machine. Kingsford dived, and Bourne fired off a whole drum; the ants scattered and the lights went out. Instant darkness. Kingsford pulled out of the dive and wheeled west. One hundred bombs had been deposited on the Boulay airfield, without a single Independent Force loss, although the machines were torn and ripped with bullet holes and shrapnel bursts. Four of the German hangars were burnt out.

On the night of 25 July Kingsford was just about to take off when the airfield was attacked by German bombers. The New Zealander rose into the air and stalked the Germans home. He hoped to return the favour and bomb the German airfield but as soon as he appeared over the 'Bosch' base he faced a dense wall of anti-aircraft fire. It was accurate. Shrapnel pelted the FE2b, ripping through the wings and puncturing the radiator and engine. The diagnosis was not good; the 'jig was really up'.[22] Kingsford looked down in the faint hope of spying a piece of clear land on the pockmarked battlefield while Bourne released the bombs and began throwing everything overboard: 'Out went the Lewis gun, ammo drums, and even the thermos.' Incredibly the engine was still turning over, the propeller spinning. They chanced their arm for the Allied lines.

Eighteen miles deep behind the enemy's forward-most trenches and at only 2000 ft, it would be a close call. In the darkness, Kingsford spotted a lighthouse flickering its Morse signal, a beacon of hope that lifted their spirits momentarily. Then the FE2b began losing height and the engine began to fail. Battling the headwind, it was 'touch and go'. Visions of imprisonment or worse wafted through their minds as they prayed the prayer of the desperate. Bourne plaintively enquired whether they could make the lighthouse's emergency airfield. Kingsford did not reply. He knew they were close to the ground now and he peered in vain, searching the gloom for a landing site. 'Suddenly, dead ahead, there appeared a clear patch, and I headed for it . . . A forced landing at night is one of the most unpleasant things I have ever experienced.' The wheels faintly caressed the uneven ground; they would be alright. Then, with a terrible juddering, splintering crash, the FE2b struck a trench.

The violent impact flung Bourne free; he momentarily achieved unpowered flight before he made another unpleasant reacquaintance with the soil of the Western Front. Kingsford was ensnared in the rigging; the wires were a crazy spider's labyrinth holding him fast. What if the machine burst into flames? Desperate, 'panting with fear and exertion', he fought for release, struggled free and 'collapsed beside Bourne'.

Kingsford and Bourne could just make out the FE2b straddling the trench, a broken bird, feathers askew and thin bones rupturing the fabric skin. In the depths of the night they now crawled along the trench. As they felt their way blindly, Kingsford's principal concern was on which side of the lines had they fallen.[23] 'Sure enough we crawled around a corner and found ourselves face to face with the business end of the biggest revolver I have ever seen in my life,' said Kingsford. Would they be shot out of hand? From the gloom Kingsford heard a whispered enquiry: 'Qui êtes-vous?' (Who are you?) 'I was never so glad to hear French spoken in my life, and almost keeled over with relief.'[24]

Not only was flying at night a risky business but the bombs could also pose problems for the airmen when they failed to cooperate. On one raid a bomb would not release from its rack. Kingsford yelled a warning to Bourne before flinging the FE2b around in order to dislodge the limpet-like ordnance but, despite his pulling every aerobatic trick he knew, the attempt failed. They were only 20 miles shy of the squadron base and he was very reluctant to land with it still in place; the possibility that it might fall and explode on landing could not be dismissed. The observer leant over the side and shone his torch. The offending missile stared right back.

Bourne grabbed Kingsford's walking stick, which he had been using as a result of earlier rough landings and accidents. Kingsford held the machine steady while Bourne poked and prodded the thing.[25] No joy. Then Bourne took his life into his own hands and 'swung over the coaming' — the padded rim of the cockpit — and 'clung there completely outside of the aeroplane'. It was foolhardy in the extreme. In the darkness, with a 'murderous gale' of a slipstream, Bourne hung on to the coaming with one hand while the other gripped the inner strut, as he kicked away at the bomb with his boots. 'I sat spellbound throughout the entire performance,' confessed Kingsford. Bourne was nearing exhaustion when the recalcitrant bomb, tired of being booted, leapt free down into the darkness. With one final effort, Kingsford's observer pulled himself back into the cockpit and collapsed into his seat, the adrenalin burnt from his bloodstream. Kingsford sat dumbfounded, the solitary witness to a 'magnificent performance'. 'I had never seen anything like it till then, have never seen anything like it since.' The New Zealander immediately nominated Bourne for an award, but nothing came of it.

In the second week of August, Peps received a letter from Reggie. 'I feel extra happy this morning,' she jotted in her diary, 'he may be home in a fortnight and then he will get some leave. He will not have to go back to France for some time, if again.'[26] Kingsford richly deserved his home posting as an instructor at Upwood, Huntingdonshire. Over the Western Front in 1918 he had dropped 151 bombs across 142 hours' flying time, and survived numerous perilous missions and brushes with death.[27] Peps was elated, eagerly awaiting their reunion: 'I am very well, and shall now patiently await his home coming. I shall try and get a cottage for us to spend our leave in.'

Samuel Dawson was decorated with the Distinguished Flying Cross for his role in bombing the Tondern Zeppelin sheds in northern Germany, one of the war's most daring operations.

n addition to New Zealand efforts on the Western Front in 1918, a small number of New Zealanders were continuing to combat the airships and aircraft attacking Britain. Not all survived the experience. Cantabrian Frederick Livingstone was killed two weeks into the New Year. Livingstone had arrived at 33 (Home Defence) Squadron in December. Less than a month later the former theology student died in solo night-flying practice.[28] His premature death may well be attributable to a policy introduced at the beginning of 1918 for the northern FE2b-equipped squadrons. These units were to receive only 'partly trained pilots', who would receive their final 'passing out' in an active squadron. Livingstone needed to complete a 100-mile night reconnaissance flight, complete a written examination on night-flying armament and equipment, demonstrate proficiency in an aerial navigation test, and have completed 10 hours' night flying before being inserted into the squadron's strength of operational airmen.[29] His death just before midnight on 12 January suggested that he might well have benefited from more training before his posting. He was killed while attempting to land.

Wellington-born Cecil Noble-Campbell was the last New Zealander to tussle with the Zeppelins in defensive operations. A sheep farmer who had received a serious gunshot wound to the leg at Gallipoli, he persuaded authorities to let him enter the RFC in 1916.[30] He was in 38 (Home Defence) Squadron flying the venerable FE2b on the night of 12–13 April 1918. Among the five Zeppelins was the same German commander the New Zealanders had met on a number of occasions the previous year: Kuno Manger. His *L62* was a new V-class Zeppelin, 644 ft long and powered by five Mercedes-Benz engines. Just after midnight Noble-Campbell took off from Buckminster, Leicestershire, in his modified FE2b. The aeroplane no longer carried an observer-gunner, but it had a single forward-firing machine gun operated by the pilot. With only himself onboard he was able to patrol at 16,000 ft. He spotted *L62* on its return from Birmingham.[31] Noble-Campbell closed in and fired from extreme range, 500 yards. The Zeppelin was swallowed by cloud before reappearing. Noble-Campbell gave chase in the hope that Manger might drop the Zeppelin's altitude. Unbeknown to the New Zealander, another 38 Squadron pilot flying out of Stamford, William Brown, had also spotted *L62*. The two stalking pilots never saw each other and the Zeppelin reported no attacks. What happened next remains hazy.

At 1.30 a.m. both 38 Squadron machines crash-landed north of Coventry.[32] Noble-Campbell gave a report from his hospital bed a few days later in which he stated that he had been 'hit in the head, his propeller smashed and his aircraft controls damaged'.[33] Brown's sortie ended when his engine failed and he made an emergency landing, striking a hedge. He was also hospitalised. What caused Noble-Campbell's fall from the heavens was a mystery.[34] Machine-gun fire from the Zeppelin was subsequently ruled out as Manger reported that no enemy fighters were encountered and therefore no guns discharged. It is possible that anti-aircraft shrapnel struck the propeller and that debris from the blades flung back and hit him. Irrespective of the cause, the New Zealander's landing was not good. He crashed just short of a factory boundary wall, and the aircraft caught fire as he awkwardly freed himself. Manger was killed only a month later when his airship was destroyed over the North Sea.

The injuries sustained by Noble-Cambell and the losses of other New Zealanders in anti-Zeppelin operations would be avenged by fellow New Zealander Samuel Dawson in one of the most audacious offensive operations of the war. The target: the airships and their huge sheds in northern Germany.

These targets were well beyond the range of British aircraft flying from Britain or France. However, ships carrying aeroplanes as close as possible to the target would enable a seaborne attack. Initially this had been attempted by the use of floatplanes lowered from naval vessels for takeoff from the waters of the North Sea; when they returned from their mission they would be hoisted back on board. It was a risky endeavour. Ships, sailors and airmen were open to attack from enemy submarines during the lowering and later recovery of the floatplanes. Moreover, the launching and retrieval from the temperamental North Sea was the undoing of many men, machines and whole missions. Men drowned and floatplanes were reduced to matchwood and sodden fabric. Finally, the floatplanes were slow and highly vulnerable to defending aircraft and anti-aircraft fire. Although numerous efforts were made to find a workable solution, none was successful. The only alternative was to launch aircraft from the deck of a ship.[35]

The cruiser HMS *Furious* was converted into an aircraft carrier with a forward and rear flying deck. The conversion was far from ideal; the central superstructure prevented a full-length, unbroken flightdeck, as on subsequent carriers. However, it worked after a fashion. The movement of aircraft between the decks was achieved via wide gangways looping around the central structure. The afterdeck unfortunately proved entirely unsuitable for landings because the superstructure and large funnel generated turbulence that made an already tricky manoeuvre — landing on a ship at sea — downright dangerous. Very few attempts succeeded; the remainder crashed or went over the side. For the most part, operations involved taking off from the deck of the carrier on the outward flight and, on their return, ditching close to a destroyer for retrieval by hoist; *Furious* was too valuable to be risked in this time-consuming task. It was not perfect but it would enable a carrier-launched assault on the airship bases in 1918. Their target: the Zeppelin sheds at Tondern, Schleswig-Holstein.

Furious was equipped with Sopwith 1½ Strutters and 'navalised' Sopwith Camels. These latter machines were sometimes dubbed 'Ship's Camels'; they had their wings clipped by a foot in length, and the rear fuselage, running from behind the cockpit to the tail section, was detachable.[36] These modifications helped to stow the machines in the limited onboard hangar space. Samuel Dawson was trained and

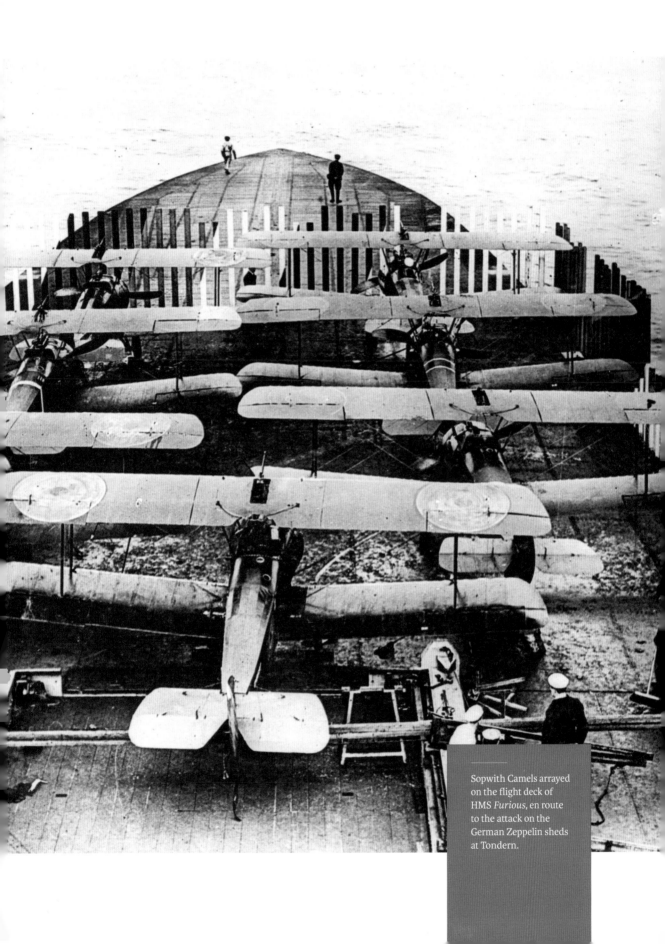

Sopwith Camels arrayed on the flight deck of HMS *Furious*, en route to the attack on the German Zeppelin sheds at Tondern.

The Toska shed at
Tondern ablaze.
Two Zeppelins were
destroyed in the raid by
the Sopwith Camels.

experienced with the Camel. In preparation for the attack he carried out practice runs at the RAF Turnhouse aerodrome, Scotland. The Tondern targets were outlined on the ground: three Zeppelin sheds — one large shed and two smaller ones. The hangars were named Toska, Tobias and Toni respectively. Toska was huge at 780 ft long and 195 ft wide, and could house two Zeppelins at a time; Tobias and Toni were 585 ft in length and 110 ft wide. In his Camel, Dawson dropped dummy bombs on the 'sheds'. The real 50-lb bombs were specially designed for the Camels and each machine carried two. The defences at Tondern were a collection of anti-aircraft guns; a flight of Albatros DIIIs had been relocated from the area because of the unsuitable nature of the aerodrome.

At the completion of the training Dawson re-embarked on *Furious* with the Camels. The raid was broken into two flights of three and four machines. Dawson was in the second flight, which meant he would arrive after the defenders' wrath had been well and truly aroused. On the return flight his most pressing concern would be locating the fleet before his Camel ran out of fuel. Taking into account the bomb load and likely weather conditions, it was estimated that the Camels had only 3.5 hours' flying time.[37] It was a very narrow margin.

After a false start the previous day the raid was slated for 19 July 1918. Standing on the carrier's foredeck, Dawson could see *Furious*'s destroyer escort and, off in the distance, a light cruiser squadron of five vessels. A further covering force was on the high seas: a battle squadron and a light cruiser squadron comprising 10 ships and additional escorting destroyers. It was an impressive naval force with hundreds of officers and thousands of sailors, collected for the sole purpose of launching a mere seven airmen, one of whom was Dawson. The young New Zealander found himself at the epicentre of the most important naval–air operation of the Great War. The target was the symbol of Germany's war of terror on England: the Kaiser's baby-killing Zeppelins. The admiralty held its breath.

Late on the evening of 18 July the Camels were pulled from their stable, herded and assembled herringbone-fashion on the deck. The armourers attached twin bombs to each Camel as *Furious* steamed undetected to within 12 miles of the Danish coast. Action stations was called at 2.30 a.m., and within half an hour they had reached the launching marker. The destroyers fell back and *Furious* turned into the wind in order to release her children. The first flight, led by Captain William Jackson, took off and swung starboard, followed by Dawson's second flight, led by Captain Bernard Smart, to port. One of

Smart's pilots suffered engine trouble and was forced to ditch, reducing his flight to three. The carrier waved off the Camels and steamed west to the rendezvous point.

Fifteen minutes into the flight, Jackson spied the Danish coast and headed south, following its outline through broken windows in the clouds below. When he saw the northern end of the Isle of Sylt he turned east, following a major road all the way to Tondern and the sleeping giants.[38] At 4.35 a.m. the first wave was over Tondern, circling to locate the targets. Woken by alarms, Horst von Buttlar-Brandenfels, commander of *L54*, could only watch horrified. 'Down they came, till they seemed to be going to ram the sheds, then one after another, they flattened out, and passed lengthwise over their targets at a height of about 40 metres, kicking loose bombs as they went.'[39] The three airmen swooped on the large Toska shed. The bombing was pinpoint: the 50-lb ordnance breached the roof and ignited the gas cells of the airships. The result was mayhem. Zeppelins *L54* and *L60* 'burst into flames and an enormous conflagration took place'. The airmen basked momentarily in the orange glow. Flames and smoke leapt and billowed to 1000 ft. The defensive batteries opened up, searching for the Camels, which were already scampering west for the coast and the recovery vessels 75 miles away.

Ten minutes later Dawson's formation arrived from the east, guided in by anti-aircraft fire. Smart saw Toska with its roof ripped open and 'emitting large volumes of dense black smoke'.[40] They entered the storm at 6000 ft and dropped low, scattering their 'eggs on the objective'. The Zeppelin base was now fully awake and mechanics and soldiers armed with rifles and machine guns were supplementing the batteries in a most 'disconcerting' manner. Smart skimmed over the vast Zeppelin field at a bare 50 ft, zigzagging his machine in order to avoid their fire.

In an attack on the airship gas plant Dawson spied Toska and 'in the middle of my dive . . . flew over it; releasing my bombs from a height of about 500 feet'.[41] The anti-aircraft fire was intense; accurate bursts picked up his Camel and tossed it around the sky. 'My machine seemed to be out of control,' he wrote in his report of the attack. Dawson's aircraft was peppered with shrapnel, a wheel was punctured, but none of the Camel's vital organs was struck. Smart's second wave hit the Tobias shed with two bombs and the balloon inside was set alight. Another bomb hit a gas wagon with no result, and the three remaining bombs failed to detonate.[42] They sped west on the heels of Jackson's flight. Dawson skimmed above the ground and hedges, avoiding the anti-aircraft fire.

In their wake they left a trail of destruction. The Zeppelins were the morning's biggest scalps. The two giant airships had made five raids on England; and, in addition to civilian losses, had played a part in the death of one New Zealander and the wounding of another in the home defence squadrons. Hubert Solomon had died in operations against a 12–13 March 1918 raid that included *L54,* and Cecil Noble-Campbell was wounded in a 12–13 April raid that included *L60* among its participants.[43] When the smoke cleared, all that remained of the Zeppelins was twisted wreckage. By some estimates the damage totalled £3 million.[44] The great Toska shed was only saved from complete destruction because the doors were open and because Zeppelins burnt slowly rather than exploding. Still, as von Buttlar-Brandenfels noted, 'Tondern, as an air station, had practically ceased to exist from that moment.'[45]

A pilot from each flight managed to locate the Royal Navy retrieval vessels, ditched their

Royal Aircraft Factory
SE5s of 85 Squadron at
Saint-Omer airfield,
21 June 1918. In spite
of its relatively late
arrival on the battlefield,
the unit was very
successful under the
leadership of Edward
'Mick' Mannock.

Camels and were hauled aboard. Of the four remaining, one airman failed to locate the ships and drowned; his body was washed ashore days later. He was the mission's only casualty.

Dawson and two other pilots were running low on fuel and were forced to make scattered landfall near Ringkjøbing, western Denmark. Having made a forced landing, Dawson found he was alone, and his thoughts turned to scavenging fuel to replenish his still flyable Camel. Unable to locate any in a local fishing village, he managed to swap his uniform for civilian clothes at a lighthouse.[46] He then walked and cycled some 20 miles to a railway station. He was captured at Esbjerg; postwar rumour had it that he had given himself away by sitting on a train pretending to read a Danish newspaper, which he was holding upside down. He was reunited with the two other pilots at an Esbjerg hotel. Though they were under guard by Danish detectives, all three were keen to escape and return to England.

By now news of the raid had spread through Denmark, and the British consul arrived at the hotel after being contacted by Dawson. When the chance presented itself, he boldly pinched a detective's hat and walked out of the hotel. With a train ticket procured by the consul he travelled to Copenhagen. After surviving three days hidden in the Danish capital, Dawson caught a boat to Sweden, where he waited for documentation before sailing to Scotland by way of Norway. It took him little more than a fortnight to return to his unit on *Furious*.

The Tondern attack was a masterful achievement, combining RAF and Royal Navy contingents. The navy was overjoyed with the results. Commander in chief of the Grand Fleet Admiral David Beatty stated it was a 'most creditable performance on the part of the Royal Air Force'.[47] *Furious's* commanding officer recommended the pilots for a decoration. Dawson received a Distinguished Flying Cross in September: 'Lieutenant Samuel Dawson (Sea Patrol) was engaged in a long distance bombing raid on an enemy aircraft station under very difficult circumstances and carried out a successful attack from a low height in face of severe enemy fire.'

Meanwhile, on the Western Front, Mick Mannock went on leave from Caldwell's 74 Squadron. On 5 July he was given command of 85 Squadron, when he arrived he found two New Zealanders among the pilots: one the very experienced ace Mac McGregor, and the other the novice Donald 'Kiwi' Inglis.

McGregor had seen limited action the previous year thanks to an injury sustained in a forced landing when the rotary engine of his Sopwith Pup failed spectacularly. One of the cylinder's connecting rods snapped and the piston removed the cylinder head. The machine jerked violently with the unbalanced engine and McGregor attempted to put it down on the pockmarked battlefield. The Pup hit a crater and overturned, and the 6 ft 3 in, 14-stone New Zealander's face smashed into the machine-gun butt. His teeth were knocked out and his upper jaw fractured; his face was cut to bits and he was bathed in his own blood. 'Well here I am in hospital,' he wrote to his parents. 'Had a crash the other day . . . I do not think the authorities sent you a cable, as I told them I did not possess any relations or next of kin. Thought perhaps you might have had enough to worry about.'[48]

It was a long and painful recovery: bone periodically worked its way through the gums,

Malcolm 'Mac'
McGregor was a
Kohimarama graduate
who became a high-
scoring fighter pilot
and flight commander
in 85 Squadron. This
serious portrait belies
his cheerful and
playful nature.

numerous stumps of broken teeth needed extraction, and false teeth had to be fitted.

It was not until the summer of 1918 that McGregor arrived back in France with his new unit, at that point commanded by the Canadian Billy Bishop. Keith Caldwell's squadron was based at an adjacent airfield and he came over to greet the new arrivals. In the mess Bishop said to Caldwell, 'Have a wild countryman of yours in the squadron — hell of a stout fellow — name's McGregor — like you to meet him.' It was a reasonable description — Mac was well known for his risk-taking and fighting abilities.

Between his injury and returning to France McGregor had a period as an instructor in England, where he grew increasingly restive. At the tail end of training officers in the art of aerial combat, he found himself in trouble with the authorities for a series of daredevil antics arising out of boredom: he had chased a train; reportedly attempted to remove a windvane from a church spire with his propeller; landed on a racecourse; and terrorised a town with a series of ever more dangerous stunting manoeuvres.[49] He later swooped over Buckingham Palace — 'a fine old place', he reckoned — much to the consternation of the London constabulary; and once flew low down the Thames. 'It was a glorious evening and there were crowds punting and rowing. We flew along a few feet above their heads, taking the bends in great style and turning back to see any extra pretty girls. Our wheels even touched the water in places.' McGregor was indifferent to sanctions, and after being 'placed on the mat' was heard to say: 'Got off with a severe reprimand, plonk!' Back with the squadron, he never failed to draw a smile. One morning, to the amusement of the squadron, he lost his false teeth and no one could understand him. He refused to fly in case he was shot down without them.

Nonetheless, McGregor had a serious side, and he kept a paternal watch over his flight members. As the fighting continued unabated, many men were struck with stress-induced maladies. Some confessed to being too nervous to hold a pen straight. Shaking hands and nervous twitches were commonplace. 'Nobody in the squadron can get a glass to his mouth with one hand after one of these decoy patrols,' wrote one of McGregor's pilots, American John Grider.[50] Sleep was fleeting and Grider and his roommate were often plagued by nightmares. 'Some nights . . . Mac has to get up and find his teeth and quiet us.' Above all, McGregor was one of the unit's most respected fighter pilots, and by the time Bishop was replaced by Mannock as the commanding officer in early July, he was an ace.

David Inglis was a quieter airman and, at only 5 ft 6 in and weighing 10 stone, he was considerably smaller than McGregor. More significantly, he lacked the latter's vast flying experience. He was not lacking in bravery, though. Unlike McGregor, Inglis came to flying from the NZEF, where he had served as a bombardier-fitter with the field artillery. At Gallipoli in 1915 he was caught in heavy fighting at Chailak Dere. At a critical juncture, three of the batteries' guns were knocked out of action by bullets and breakages. Inglis, with the aid of another man, stripped the guns and made repairs under heavy fire. It was time-consuming and exacting work, with shells bursting nearby and dirt and dust gathering above the battery. His citation for a Distinguished Conduct Medal noted the New Zealander's coolness and bravery under the most demanding of conditions.[51] Inglis was discharged from the NZEF in November 1917 for a commission in the RFC. He joined McGregor in 85 Squadron in the spring of 1918.[52]

Inglis found the squadron had its idiosyncrasies, notably its vast menagerie of animals: every officer was expected to have a pet. It had all started fairly harmlessly when the squadron was forming at Hounslow with a collection of four Chow pups that were smuggled across the Channel with the unit. Over time, though, pilots began collecting livestock and in no time they possessed 'a motley collection of assorted dogs, goats and even poultry'.[53]

McGregor had acquired his own animal on 14 June on a solo sortie hunting for Germans sneaking over the lines. He found four intruders and attacked. Though they had the odds in their favour, the quartet turned tail and ran east. McGregor had height on them and dived, pushing the SE5a to 180 mph. He pulled the trigger and, to his dismay, the Foster rail-mounted Lewis shot away one of his own propeller blades. Like a dog emerging from a river, the SE5a started to shake from nose to tail. The motor jumped from 2000 to 5000 rpm, and bit by bit the unevenly balanced propeller began disassembling the aircraft. 'Screws fell out of the fascia board, flying wires slackened, and everything that was not split-pinned came adrift.' Remembering his unpleasant engine failure of the previous year he switched off the motor, turned and glided west. He barely crossed the lines at 70 mph with 'Archie' firing off all around him. 'Plonked the old machine down without any damage to myself but plenty to bus,' he wrote. From an Allied infantry post he telephoned his commander and a car was despatched to retrieve him. When he arrived back at the base he had a nanny goat, his sole prize for the day, with him. He had 'found' it grazing roadside and had decided it should be added to the squadron's collection; it could provide milk for their cups of tea.[54]

In spite of his effort at Gallipoli, Inglis was an inexperienced airman. One of the three Americans with the unit was slightly put out when a flight commander — Spencer 'Nigger' Horn — had Inglis look over his machine. 'I hate for anybody else to fly my machine and this is the first time anyone else has touched it,' said John Grider, 'But Nigger wants Inglis to have a look at the lines and get his bearings so when one of us goes West, he will be ready to take his place. I wonder whose place it will be. He's a nice fellow, a New Zealander, and got the D.C.M.'[55]

McGregor had been up with his countryman on a number of occasions. In the middle of July they had taken to the air in order to 'secure an enemy aeroplane' for Inglis.[56] They located a two-seater, and McGregor attempted to silence the rear gunner-observer; in this way he hoped to defang the machine for Inglis to finish off. Instead he hit the pilot, who slumped forward, jamming the controls into a wide arcing circle. In spite of numerous assaults on the pilotless machine, Mac and 'Kiwi' were thwarted by the accurate and desperate machine-gun fire from the observer. And then anti-aircraft fire opened up and the two New Zealanders were forced off the wounded prey.

On 24 July McGregor was leading a patrol, with Inglis the fourth man in the flight.[57] They climbed above the squadron's other flight, which acted as a decoy. The patrol spotted eight enemy machines. McGregor almost immediately knocked one out — a Fokker DVII with its propeller stopped and out of control. Catching his breath, he scanned the heavens and saw Inglis with another Fokker on his tail. McGregor fired a good burst into the Fokker and it crashed. With that McGregor had become one of the first New Zealanders to shoot down not one but two of the Germans' most feared fighters in a single sortie. But while McGregor now

The officers of 85 Squadron show off their collection of animals. The tall Mac McGregor and a smiling Donald Inglis are second and third from left. The light-fingered airmen acquired their menagerie of pets in their travels across France.

had seven victories, Inglis was still struggling to make his first claim.[58]

The next day Inglis joined his squadron commander and the visiting 74 Squadron fighter pilot Ira Jones for tea. An Irish nurse, Sister Flanagan, joined them. The conversation turned to dispatching Germans — Jones and Mannock were engaged in a grim competition to see who could knock out the most — when Flanagan said: 'You're very casual about this dangerous game of yours, Mick. Aren't you ever afraid?'[59] Mannock turned to her and said, 'We've got a job to do, my dear and the cooler you are the more successful you'll be. And as to being frightened — I'm like any other pilot. I'm scared stiff when I see my Hun floating down in flames.' Soon after, Mannock looked at Inglis and asked, 'Have you got a Hun yet, Kiwi?'

'No sir.'

'Well, we'll go out and get one.'

The squadron commander stood up and headed off to the airfield, with the others in tow. Mannock, like McGregor, was like a lioness to the newly arrived young cubs in the squadron, taking them up on sorties to blood them. Mannock would search out a lone two-seater intruder, which he would damage, then signal to his cub to move in and finish off. Mannock took off first but Inglis discovered that his tailplane had jammed and he was unable to follow. It was two hours before Mannock returned, and Inglis ran over to the disembarking airman to splutter out his apologies and explain his absence. Mannock was distracted and vented his angst. He had failed to secure his seventy-third victory — the Germans did not want to come out to play. Then he remembered Inglis. 'Now, what was the trouble?' Inglis recounted his problems, and Mannock firmly scolded him for not checking his machine the night before, as the Englishman religiously did with his own aircraft. 'Never mind, Kiwi,' he said, 'I'll show you how it's done in the morning. Now see to your machine *and your guns* so that we can be off the ground before dawn.'

In the early morning darkness of 26 July Inglis entered the mess. He found Mannock smoking his pipe, listening to a scratched gramophone record. 'I hope we'll be able to find an early flying two-seater coming over,' he said to Inglis. As they walked over the dew-covered grass to their machines, Mannock laid out his plan to Inglis: 'Follow me closely and you'll get into a good position before we attack. Then when you get him in your sights, take careful aim and get as close as you can before you fire.' A blackbird's song broke the morning silence and Mannock took it as a good omen. As they clambered aboard the SE5s, one of the mechanics wished the ace well.

The pair circled the airfield before flying east. Periodically Mannock wiggled his wings and Inglis opened the throttle to close the gap, his eyes fixed on his commander's tail. Then at 5.30 a.m., as the two men were flying close to the 'carpet', Mannock without warning commenced climbing 'full out'. 'I knew from this he must have spotted a Hun,' said Inglis later.

It was a two-seater. Mannock rolled over and attacked, firing furiously into it. Then he pulled away and Inglis found himself staring at the damaged bird. He got in a good burst.[60] The machine blazed and plummeted earthwards. Then, in contravention of his own rules of engagement, Mannock followed the doomed machine down, 'circling round and round the falling torch'. Inglis obediently fell in behind him. Only when groundfire became insistent did he turn away, weaving the machine evasively. It was then that Mannock's SE5a dropped its nose; Inglis saw orange flame sprout from the fuselage. Machine and man fell lazily into a downward right-hand turn. The left wing lifted suddenly and the machine went straight down. The aircraft struck the soil of France and the wreckage was wreathed in black smoke and flames.

Inglis was aghast, disbelieving. He wanted to stay but heavy fire was shredding his machine. As he struggled with the controls, a well-aimed bullet punctured his fuel line; it sprayed him until he was drenched. He made Allied lines and force-landed. An infantryman rushed up to the aircraft to find Inglis bent over at the controls, crying, 'Poor old Mick. The bloody bastards have shot my major down in flames.'[61]

A telephone call to the squadron from an anti-aircraft battery, which had recognised Mannock's machine, broke the news to the unit. They were stunned. Over in 74 Squadron, Caldwell and 'Taffy' Jones took to the air in search of the wreckage in the Calonne–Lestrem area. 'It was really rather hopeless and useless,' said Caldwell. 'We couldn't hang about long as the firing was intense.' Mannock's body was never recovered.

McGregor was devastated. 'We have lost our Squadron Commander. Went down in flames after getting over 70 Huns, and so the Royal Air Force has lost the best leader of patrols, and the best Hun getter it has had. In a month he would have had over 100. However, unlike other stars, he left behind all the knowledge he had, so it is up to the fellows he taught to carry on.'[62] 'Lots of fellows turned up at No. 85 to cheer up the lads,' wrote Ira Jones. 'Among the star fighters were Mary Coningham and the Canadian, Raymond Collishaw, both of whom assisted considerably in making the evening cheerful.'[63] Major Coningham had just arrived as commander of 92 Squadron, equipped with SE5s. He listened to Caldwell deliver an unenviable after-dinner speech, assuring the men that Mannock would not have wanted them to mope. It was a valiant attempt but Caldwell was visibly 'cut-up' as well.[64]

The night before he was killed Mannock had been shooting the breeze with his good friend 'Taffy' Jones when the conversation turned grim. Jones accused Mannock of getting morbid. 'No, not morbid,' Mannock replied. 'Just a premonition, that's all. Don't forget, Taffy, when you see that tiny spark come out of my SE, it will kindle a torch to guide future air defenders of the Empire along the path of duty.'[65]

The knowledge and spirit of Mannock were not lost, and the squadron continued its work. By the end of the war it was Inglis who was leading other airmen into battle.[66]

The determined gaze
of the legendary
Mick Mannock.
His leadership was
inspirational and his
loss devastating to the
men of his unit and his
friends. He was killed
on a sortie to assist New
Zealander Donald Inglis
claim his first victory.

CHAPTER SIXTEEN

ONE HUNDRED DAYS

1918

The Spring Offensive launched with such spectacular results in March was over by July. There had been gains, but the German breakthroughs were insufficient to turn the tide of war their way. Yes, they now held territory up to the River Marne, but they had fallen short of victory. At this juncture Ferdinand Foch, the Allied supreme commander, called for a counteroperation. General Haig would plan and lead the offensive. To prevent the Germans from digging themselves in to an unassailable defensive position, Haig set the date for 8 August. Dubbed the Hundred Days Offensive, it would see out the war on 11 November.

The initial target was the old Amiens defensive line and then a push on to Ham on the Somme River. Instead of a lengthy giveaway barrage, the Anglo-French attack would be spearheaded by massed tanks supported by aircraft. British flying machines would be gathered in the rear of the Fourth Army. At dawn, bombers escorted by fighters would attack enemy airfields. After these raids, fighters would undertake extensive offensive patrols. In the late afternoon, when the Germans realised what was under way and began moving in reinforcements, Allied bombers would attack railway stations.

For these operations the RAF assembled a large force of nearly 800 aircraft; in the immediate area the Germans had 375 machines. Once the attack was launched this German force would be bolstered by the arrival of over 300 reinforcements. In reality, the Allied position was even stronger than these figures suggest, as they had large numbers of machines in reserve. The British alone had nearly 1000 additional machines spread across the RAF. Added to the 3000 French and 700 American-flown aircraft, the scales in the air had tipped irrevocably to the Allied side. Nonetheless, the Luftstreitkräfte could still inflict considerable damage on the Allied force, not least because of the ever-increasing numbers of Fokker DVIIs at the front. Many of these now sported the new 185-hp BMW engine, which could propel the Fokker to 115 mph and gave it a climb rate almost without equal in the Great War.[1]

An indication of what the New Zealanders would be up against became all too clear just five days out from the offensive, when Mac McGregor was involved in a big scrap. He was leading a flight of three near Steenwerck when intruders appeared, and they 'were much keener to scrap than usual'. Another 85 Squadron flight became embroiled in a fight and McGregor led his lads to assist. Before long there were 30 Fokkers drawn into the dogfight. They were 'everywhere', wrote McGregor to a friend in Stockbridge. 'Some neighbouring S.E.s also joined in, and we had a great old scrap for about 15 minutes. How we avoided collisions I do not know. You would get your sights on a Hun for a second and then have to pull out to avoid being rammed by another S.E. converging on the same target.'[2]

On 8 August the great Allied offensive was launched. Aside from the usual reconnaissance, bombing and artillery work, there was a heavy workload for squadrons in support of ground forces with low-level strafing and bombing. The surprise was complete, and the tanks rapidly broke through the German lines. By nightfall on the first day a yawning 15-mile gap was opened south of the Somme. Over the following three days the British infantry advanced 12 miles as the defending forces collapsed. Ludendorff ordered his forces to retreat, ceding the greater part of the territory they had acquired in the Spring Offensive.

Arthur Coningham was right into the action. The loss of Mannock had been a sobering introduction to the front line for his 92 Squadron, but he was not about to let it derail his return to combat. Three days later he shot down a two-seater. It was his first victory in the SE5a, and was an indication of the type of leadership he had to offer his men. The squadron was a diverse mix of Americans, Canadians, New Zealanders and South Africans supplementing the Home country nationals. Coningham was a lively and congenial leader; he had no airs and graces, just a ready smile and a keen helping hand. One of his subordinates was James Gascoyne, a recent reinforcement to the unit. Coningham had ferried him personally to the airfield in early August. As one of the RFC's early recruits in 1913 and three years Coningham's senior, Gascoyne had seen his fair share of officers and was highly complimentary of his new commander.

> My CO was one of the greatest men I ever met. He instilled confidence in everybody . . . He helped me in every way he could; he advised me on everything that was likely to happen in the war in the air and the whole squadron loved him. He was really a wonderful man . . . He handled the squadron beautifully because he never condemned you, but if you did anything good he always complimented it, although he knew the people who could fly and who couldn't and the people who were doing their jobs.[3]

Coningham eased the fresh arrival into the unit and the next day took him over the lines. Unbeknown to Gascoyne, his compass was faulty

When the Fokker DVII appeared over the front in the middle of 1918 it proved a formidable foe, so much so that at the Armistice it was the only aircraft Germany was required to hand over to the Allies.

and he was about to lose himself over the Western Front when Coningham appeared alongside, fetching him home. On one ill-judged landing Gascoyne ran his machine into two parked SE5s. Coningham surveyed the carnage and the chagrined pilot. 'Why couldn't you manage to hit just one?' he asked. Gascoyne replied, 'Yes, but the engines were a bit hard.' Coningham simply laughed. On another occasion Gascoyne had been wounded and had covered the damage to his helmet with a patch to disguise it. Coningham told him to remove it: 'In a few years' time you will be rather proud of that.'[4]

The squadron's main duties were two-hour patrols at between 5000 and 10,000 ft. The SE5s were ideal for attacking observation machines directing fire on Allied infantry and for engaging the obligatory German escorts. Coningham's unit often worked in close cooperation with other squadrons in the area on the patrols.

On 11 August Coningham led his men to the German Nesle airfield. Alerted to the approaching SE5s, the Fokker DVIIs were in the process of taking off. Coningham dived to meet the prey at 8000 ft. The New Zealander's method was simple: keep the upper hand by staying above the enemy. It was five British fighters against 12 Fokkers; the remaining elements of the squadron stayed at altitude, ready to intervene should more enemy aeroplanes arrive. One 'Hun' machine was shot down and another looped lazily earthward, scarring the sky with a dirty streak. The rest thought better of the fight — Coningham caught three of them scuttling away. The odds were not good, and Coningham was forced to draw on all his considerable skill and resolve. It was a nasty encounter and because of his own 'mismanagement' his machine was 'shot about badly'.[5] The self-deprecating assessment was pure Coningham. Later that day one of his flight commanders, the outstanding pilot James Robb, confirmed that Coningham's efforts had led to the demise of one enemy machine and sent another out of control.

With the departure of the Fokkers the rest of the squadron entertained themselves by vigorously strafing the aerodrome. Coningham nursed the shredded SE5a to his home airfield, where those on the ground were taken aback by the condition of his aircraft:

> His machine had been shot about in the most amazing manner. In fact, I simply cannot imagine how it held together; bullets had ripped it in scores and clusters until there was hardly an untouched portion anywhere. He accounted for two Huns, but from his own appearance and that of his machine, one might have imagined him fighting the whole German Air Force single-handed. At any rate, the state in which this skilled, daring and experienced fighter returned indicated the hottest and most desperate fighting.[6]

Coningham himself presented a ghoulish visage. He climbed down from the cockpit covered in blood. Bullets had taken a chunk out of a finger and grazed his forehead. His face was blood-smeared and his uniform red-soaked. Mercifully the wounds were superficial and he was soon cleaned and patched up — with a new SE5a.

In the second week of August Coningham's squadron was again raiding airfields. On 16 August he was involved in one of the largest and most complex aerial operations of the war: a four-squadron attack on the Haubourdin airfield, west of Lille. The squadrons, separated by 1000-ft intervals, approached the target in a swept-backwards staircase formation. The Camels of 4 Squadron AFC occupied the bottom layer because of their manoeuvrability and ground-strafing prowess; above them in turn were the SE5s of 2 Squadron AFC and Coningham's 92 Squadron, positioned there for their air-to-air combat abilities; and right at the top, at 13,000 ft, the two-man Bristol Fighters of 88 Squadron would provide the overall cover for the operation. Each squadron flew in V formation. In all, 65 machines were gathered over Reclinghem in preparation for an early-afternoon departure. In addition to Coningham, at least one other New Zealander was on hand for the attack — the Camel ace Herbert Watson. It was an impressive and destructive armada that advanced on Haubourdin: a breathtaking hammer was about to fall.

The Germans were caught completely unawares. A lone German two-seater on the same bearing spotted the looming thunderstorm behind and above. Evidently the pilot panicked and flew straight into the ground just short of the field: without a bullet fired or a bomb dropped they had their first victim. The Camels struck first, followed by the SE5s. The three squadrons dropped six phosphorus bombs and 136 explosive bombs. The defending machine guns were quickly silenced by strafing fighters. Once it became apparent that there was no threat from patrolling Germans, the Bristols descended and joined the carnage. For most of the battle the defensive and ground crews cowered in airfield trenches as 12,000 rounds raked the airfield, and many of those who made a run for the hospital were hit. Bombs ripped open three hangars, sending them and their contents up in spiralling columns of smoke. 'When I arrived 2 hangars were burning,' wrote Watson in his after-action report. 'I dropped 1/40 lb Phosphorus and 2/25 lb Cooper Bombs on what I took to be Officers' quarters in wood. My Phosphorus Bomb dropped in the centre of a group of buildings and several fires broke out.'[7] Over 30 machines were reduced to cinders and smoking engine blocks. A large building was bombed and the fuel dump went up in a burst of flames.

Not satisfied with destroying the airfield, the squadrons shot up the adjacent railway station, stopping a train and scattering milling infantry. Watson wove and bobbed his Camel between 50 and 150 ft: 'I fired 200 rounds at [a] party of mechanics running towards [the] railway. Several fell apparently hit. I then zoomed and dived on transport near a dump firing 250 rounds. One horse fell and the rest became unmanageable. Fired another 200 rounds at people on the main road.' Eager airmen spotted two fleeing staff cars and sprayed them with bullets; one overturned in a ditch and the other careened up a steep bank.[8] Coningham was relieved to count all his men and machines home with not a single loss, although Robb had been wounded in action. Watson could look back on a successful day, especially since he had shot down a Fokker biplane earlier that morning, taking his total to 13.

Two miles away, and within sight of the rising smoke from Haubourdin, lay Lomme airfield. The RAF attacked it the next day using the same units and method. As with most such endeavours, the success of the first effort would be difficult to replicate, not least because Lomme was on high alert. With a front-row seat to the diving British aircraft, the roar of bombs and the spiralling pillars of smoke at Haubourdin the previous day, the defensive crews at Lomme were wary. The only way the British could counter this was by launching the raid at the earlier hour of 7.15 a.m., a move not appreciated by many because of 'an impromptu inter-squadron binge through the Wing' the night before. Celebrating airmen were scattered hither and yon across Flanders, and Watson's 4 Squadron AFC only became aware of the scheduled follow-up raid at 4.30 a.m., less than three hours before the operation.

Search parties collected the crews, but many were not tucked under the covers until 6 a.m. 'I should say everyone had got home to his own unit,' noted the Australian Harry Cobby of 4 Squadron AFC, 'but you could almost feel the air vibrating from the number of throbbing heads in that particular portion of France that morning.'[9] Men went to sleep hoping for a 'dud' day, only to be rudely woken a short time later. Not a few batmen furnished their officers with a 'bracer' and aspirin as they struggled to pull their flying gear over pyjamas. It was only then that they were informed of their destination.

The principal ground-attack machines were once again the Camels of Watson's squadron and the SE5s of the AFC. The men were naturally confident — perhaps too confident. Explosions not only destroyed canvas hangars and assorted buildings but also rocked and tossed the Camels and SE5s; the pilots were releasing their munitions so low — 50 ft in some cases — that they were being buffeted by the blasts. The defensive machine gunners hung in bravely to their positions and let off bursts of fire, but to little effect. Pandemonium broke out across the airfield. A Jasta commander could only look on forlornly at the burning hangars and his Fokkers consigned to the flames.[10] Civilian Belgian workers plunged into waterlogged trenches; attempts to exit the trench were met with strafing fighters. A couple of German machines wanted to land in the tumult but failed in the attempt and 'crashed hopelessly'.[11] Watson deposited four 25-lb bombs on the hangars with a couple of direct hits and fired at various targets in the vicinity of the airfield. Some 17 Fokkers were destroyed.

The raids were a resounding success, and the Germans abandoned Haubourdin and Lomme to their former Belgian farmers and livestock. Coningham and Watson and the other men in the wing were jubilant: 'To be able to go and smoke your enemy out of his hide-out and then return with impunity, had a far greater moral effect upon our fellows,' said Cobby, 'than did any realisation of the actual material damage done.'[12]

The Germans, however, were not to be outdone. Numerous reprisal raids were made on British RAF airfields, though principally by night bombers. One of the most important Western Front airfields of the war — Bertangles — was attacked on 25 August. Close to Amiens, the base was heavily used and in August was home to four squadrons, including Keith Park's 48 Squadron.[13] The airfield had already been the target of two attacks in August, but these were nothing compared to what lay in store.

At 9 p.m. the centre hangar of a set of three was crowded with an expectant audience of nearly 250 men, many of them visitors from neigbouring airfields. Park used this hangar for concert and cinema events; on this night there was a full programme of entertainment planned, opening with a Rachmaninoff prelude for piano. Park was there with his pilots, including John Pugh. In the front row sat 84 Squadron's commanding officer Sholto Douglas, who had arrived for the performance with a number of his airmen. He had received his invitation from another of Park's airmen, Charles Steele.

The concert had been in progress for some time when an unholy explosion interrupted proceedings. The orderly officer rushed into the hangar and yelled above the din that he wanted the fire party. The compère pleaded for calm but was rudely shouted down by the audience, who were not about to allow the entertainment be curtailed. Then came another explosion, and then another. Douglas bolted for the cover of the grand piano. Darkness and mayhem descended on the hangar. Men fought for the exit. As they emerged into the moonlit night, they could see Gothas circling the base.

A bomb had struck the adjacent hangar, which was full of Bristol Fighters. They went up in flames. The initial loss of life was low thanks to Park: only recently, he had sandbagged the hangars to a height of four feet, and this measure had protected the seated audience from the initial explosion. The next two bombs fell on the airfield and then another hit the other flanking hangar.

The burning hangars lit up the base for the Germans and caused confusion among the milling throng, especially the visitors. They were caught between two terrible bonfires. 'This, coupled with the intense heat, caused complete panic,' recalled Park later. Like moths to a flame the remaining four Gothas attacked in turn, catching the crowd in the open. 'By then,' Douglas wrote later, 'the whole place seemed to be erupting.'[14] Some of the herd foolishly ran towards the second incoming Gotha. Two bombs hit them. Under bombing and machine-gun fire from the Gothas, Douglas and Steele ran for the trenches. Steele was hit — and would spend the remainder of the war in a hospital bed. 'The night was made hideous by the cries of the wounded and the shattering explosions of successive bombs,' recalled one of Park's airmen.[15]

Park was not immune to the stampede. 'I started to run, panic with the crowd. Everyone panicked to start with . . . It was just woosh and I started to run.' As he fled he came to his senses, realising he was running from his own unit. 'So I turned round, went back and gathered a few men . . . to pull the burning machines out of a hangar.'[16] Co-opting Australian infantry, he dragged seven machines free. The third and fourth machines dropped their bombs on the other buildings, wounding a number of Park's rescue party. Cut up and bleeding profusely, Park hauled several men from the blazing buildings; one of the flight commanders later observed that the New Zealander had 'behaved magnificently'.[17]

Surprisingly Park was not decorated for his bravery, but he made sure others were. Two were awarded the Military Medal: a private for his role in removing an aircraft from the burning hangar, and a sergeant for lifting a smouldering box of six bombs away from the airfield's armoury. A second lieutenant received a Distinguished Flying Cross for carrying wounded men away from the chaos in spite of being knocked about by the bombs himself.[18]

Casualties were high among the visitors, with six killed and 14 wounded. Two of Park's officers were killed and many were seriously wounded. A young observer, dressed in a frock and wig for his role in the concert, was taken away screaming in pain from extensive splinter wounds. Another was hospitalised with a shrapnel wound to the neck. In all, Park's men suffered 15 pilot and observer casualties.[19]

Daylight revealed the full extent of the damage to Bertangles. Park's transports had all been destroyed, five hangars had been consumed and the squadron's office and numerous huts had been reduced to kindling. Of the Bristols, nine were destroyed and two seriously damaged. Park faced one of the heaviest losses in men and machines suffered by any British squadron in the entire war.[20] That morning five airworthy Bristols took off for Boisdinghem, west of Saint-Omer. Replacement machines were delivered, but the squadron was badly bruised. 'The effect on everyone's nerves was very marked for some months later,' said Park. And it was not just the aircrew; the 'efficiency of the other ranks fell . . . September was full of uphill work.' In August, though, Park still had work to do; and incredibly, in one of the most remarkable efforts of the air war, the squadron undertook a patrol two days after its near annihilation.

The German attack demonstrated that the Luftstreitkräfte would not take assaults on its airfields lightly, and the appearance of Gothas over the Western Front was an unpleasant development. In the summer of 1918 the Gothas had been removed from strategic bombing duties against England and had been diverted to supporting the German army in France. They could carry a considerable payload, were heavily armed and were frustratingly fiendish to find in the night sky. One of the few New Zealanders who were set the daunting task of intercepting the night-flying Gothas over France was the fresh-faced Sopwith Camel pilot Trevor Bloomfield of Auckland, in 151 Squadron. He was the only New Zealander to shoot down a Gotha.

The night before this major success, Bloomfield made two attacks on large twin-engine machines between 9 and 10 p.m. He fired on the first aircraft, caught in a searchlight at 100 yards. Sparks trailed from an engine but Bloomfield got caught in the backwash of the large bomber and the Camel went into a spin. Regaining control of the machine, he attacked another intruder at 25 yards, striking the oil sump of the right-hand engine. Black oil flicked over the Camel and its pilot. Just when victory seemed certain, Bloomfield was forced to curtail the sortie when his engine began misfiring. Both assaults were inconclusive. But the next night, 25–26 September, he made sure of his victim by pressing home his assault.

> At 11.00 p.m., while over Arras at 5500 ft, I observed E.A. in beams about 1000 ft. above me, going West. I climbed up and got under his tail and saw pamphlets being thrown out through bottom trap door. I closed to about 20 yards and fired one burst of about 120 rounds. E.A. caught fire under fuselage and then the whole machine became enveloped in flames. E.A. continued level and then slowly dived vertically. He crashed between Montenescourt and Agnez, due West of Arras. E.A. blew up on the ground.[21]

It was a small victory in the bigger battle — and RAF losses were about to soar to unprecedented heights in September.

As Coningham was raiding the German airfields of Haubourdin and Lomme and as Park was gathering the remnants of his squadron, the British and French offensives cut deep into German-occupied territory. In the third week of August, Haig renewed his efforts and the German front line was in tatters. By early September the German gains of the Spring Offensive were erased. The Allies advanced on Ludendorff's last refuge: the Hindenburg Line. Although an assault proper would not take place until the very end of the month, there was a series of smaller preparatory battles to set the stage for the main event. But the intensity of the aerial war gave no indication that the Luftstreitkräfte was on its last legs. In fact, in September 1918 the RAF suffered its heaviest casualties of the war, exceeding those of Bloody April 1917 by a third, with 704 men killed, missing, wounded or prisoners of war.[22]

In spite of the large numbers of RAF men lost in September, only one New Zealander, Stuart Richardson, was killed in operations.[23] A clerk in his prewar life, Dunedin-born Richardson joined the air service at the tender age of 18. In the last week of August 1918, at the completion of his training, he was sent to the Sopwith Camels of 3 Squadron. He was eager to prove himself. 'You have to be pretty good as far as I can see to be allowed to stay in this Squadron,' he wrote to his mother not long after he arrived; 'while I have been here one chap was returned to England because he was a bit nervous.'[24]

Like all new airmen, he had a few close calls even before he could get the enemy in his sights. On one occasion during a nasty gale, he was sent up for observation duty when a combination of circumstances — including the wind, his foot slipping on the rudder and a failing engine — 'made me find myself out of control going straight for a hangar'. He turned sideways and crashed in an open space. He managed to crawl from the wreckage and enjoyed watching the ground crew, who had not seen his escape, look for him under the engine. 'Everyone else had had crashes,' he consoled himself, 'so it's high time I indulged in one.'[25]

By September he was keen to get in a scrap and spoke to the commanding officer about it; while the 'push' was on it seemed opportune. The major sent him up with an old hand: 'I showed I could fight in a scrap.'[26] One of his first sorties was protecting British kite balloons, and he was heavily 'Archied' for his trouble. 'It is a great relief when you leave the lines for home as while over them you have to follow your leader and others, keep the exactly correct position from the leader, look out for Huns and dodge anti-aircraft fire.' Coming back from the patrol the Camels dipped low above the terrain, zooming over at less than 100 ft, trees and houses skimming past. It was dark when they sighted the airfield and he nearly fouled the machine in telephone wires while avoiding another Camel that appeared 'from nowhere'.[27]

Richardson survived his first month at the front. 'I find myself quite the old hand now,' he told his family. He loved his Camel and, like the seasoned pilots, he liked his 'bus' maintained in tiptop shape. He kept the mechanics honest, 'tuning up things which they think don't matter'. In air-to-air fighting he had been in a scuffle or two, but he still hadn't claimed a victim. Nonetheless, he was now dropping bombs in low-level flights and had imbibed a healthy sense of pride in the work of the RAF.

> I've killed as many Huns in a few seconds as I would have killed in 6 months if I had been an infantryman. [Even] if you simply fly about without fighting you are being very useful because the Hun sees the formation and gets wind up and bunks. So you feel that you are really doing your bit which can only be said of some jobs in the army as far as I can see.[28]

He was, of course, still very young. He described his latest fashion purchase: a 'pair of braces of very vivid bright greeny purple with red leather fittings and golden metal parts. As, more often as not, we don't have a tunic on in our ragtime mess, the braces cheer up very gloomy surroundings.' The braces highlighted Richardson's sense of style and humour. Only days earlier, the unit had been visited by the wing's colonel, who wanted to show some nurses around the base, including the mess. The place had been cleaned up, but when the elderly colonel surveyed the mess he was concerned that the risqué pin-up pictures around the room — Art Nouveau illustrations of naked women by Raphael Kirchner — might offend his companions, a 'terribly straight laced pair of nurses'. It was too late to remove the 'art', 'so we all stood around the walls trying to cover the worst up and they kept trying to see what we were covering up'. Richardson found it all 'very funny indeed'.[29]

At 8 a.m. on 23 September Richardson was on patrol when he was seen in combat — perhaps his first real clash with an enemy machine on equal terms. The New Zealander was last seen falling from the sky. His Camel burst into flames on impact with the ground in the vicinity of Boursies. He died five days shy of his nineteenth birthday.

The other noteworthy New Zealand death in September occurred the previous day, well away from the battlefield and across the Atlantic Ocean in Indianapolis. He was not only a New Zealand aviation pioneer but also one of the world's most experienced airmen: Joe Hammond.[30] In the second half of the previous year, in an effort to boost the fledgling American air industry, London despatched the British Aviation Mission to the United States. Among the skilled technical officers and accomplished pilots was Hammond. He arrived in April 1918 and by that summer was promoting and advising on aviation matters.

In July the New Zealander attached himself to a joint American–British Liberty Bonds drive. Dubbed the 'Flying Circus' by the media, it involved a series of promotional flying shows across the American Midwest. The flying troupe was made up of American and British Empire aviators and a collection of some 18 machines painted in outlandish colours. At each new locale the circus would announce its arrival with a morning flyover, followed in the afternoon by formation flying, stunting and set-piece theatrical dogfighting.

On 22 September Hammond gave a display at a town near the Flying Circus base of operations in Indianapolis. Above a crowd of 12,000 he demonstrated the capabilities of a blue Bristol Fighter.[31] He then ferried a couple of passengers back to the state capital. Observers saw Hammond approach the airfield, then fall into a dive from 600 ft. The Bristol struck a tree and violently embedded itself nose-first into a cornfield. Hammond and one passenger were found dead by those who rushed to the scene. Whether Hammond had made an error of judgement or whether the machine had somehow failed was never fully explained. Vast crowds came out to Hammond's funeral in Indianapolis, where the New Zealander had numerous friends among the wealthy and famous. A lone airman circled overhead and descended to 100 ft to drop a wreath as the band played a dirge. A firing squad then discharged a volley in a final salute.[32]

By some reckonings Hammond had accumulated over 6000 flying hours[33] — not an impossibility given that in 1910 he was the first colonial to obtain a flying certificate and that his subsequent aviation career encompassed countless flights over the cities and farms of Britain, France, America and the dominions of Australia and New Zealand. As his biographer noted, 'Hammond was undoubtably one of the most senior and experienced aviators of his time.'[34] At his death he had 'become almost a legendary hero,' wrote the editor of *The Aeroplane*.

In addition to the loss of Richardson and Hammond there were some non-fatal casualties, including that of Herbert Hyde. From the small Central Otago settlement of Tarras, Hyde was an outspoken writer on international security matters: in 1914 he published a lengthy two-part article, 'The defence system: A proposal for its amendment'; and in 1916 a book, *Two Roads: International government or militarism; Will England lead the way?*[35] The youthful Hyde's ideas were reported in the press and discussed in internationalist circles. To eradicate war he advocated arms control and global governance via a powerful international parliament and peacekeeping force.[36] During the Great War, however, he was not about to let his idealism get in the way of hastening the end of the conflict, and he became an airman. His instructors at Manston considered him a good pilot and officer and on 7 September 1918, just as Kingsford was departing the Western Front, Hyde was posted to an Independent Force unit: 215 Squadron.[37] There, he was one of the few New Zealanders to work with one of the world's largest aircraft, the Handley Page O/400.

The three-man Handley Page had two Rolls-Royce Eagle engines and a 100-ft wingspan. Weighing over 13,000 lb, it could deliver up to 2000 lb of bombs over an eight-hour flight. It had been designed to strike the German High Seas Fleet and targets that were beyond the endurance of the single-engine machines that dominated the RAF inventory. With a range of 700 miles, it was the Independent Force's only true strategic bomber that could — unlike Kingsford's FE2s — reach deep into Germany and strike its cities. Operationally, the Handley Page reached its high point on the Western Front in the last year of the war in strategic bombing and support of ground forces. Kingsford, during his final weeks on the Western Front, worried that his own squadron might be re-equipped with the Handley Page. 'I was quite frankly not at all keen to learn to fly one of these beasts in France,' he said.[38] Like many airmen, the Nelsonian had an unfailing love affair with his own machine and was leery of any substitute, no matter how impressive. Nonetheless, the Handley Page was a fine machine and the RAF's most powerful Great War bomber.

On the morning of 16 September one of the squadron's pilots, Canadian Hugh Monaghan, was looking for a replacement gunner when he chanced on the squadron newcomer. 'Hyde was an interesting chap,' Monaghan wrote; 'an author of some importance he had written three books on world problems . . . and, as a result he had had lunch with Lloyd George.'[39] Hyde jumped at the chance of his first operation. Their objective was two bridges at Cologne — the squadron's most distant target to date. It would require an extra 90-gallon fuel tank to complete the seven-hour round trip. Hyde had not yet been kitted out, so Monaghan saw to it that he was fitted with a Sidcot suit. Known colloquially as the 'monkey suit', it was designed to combat the extreme cold at altitude in night-flying missions. He was also issued 'hip-length sheep-lined boots with thick rubber soles, fur-lined gauntlets, fur-rimmed goggles, and fur-lined helmet'.[40] Hyde was given a rundown on the machine guns, especially since a couple of them had no 'check point'; in other words, it was possible to shoot off the tail section with them. Monaghan now had his full three-man crew: pilot, observer, gunner.

At 7.35 that evening, the squadron's machines took off at two-minute intervals. It was a clear night, with a scattering of clouds skipping across the sky. Monaghan set a course due north. They were only two hours into the flight when Hyde was jolted by two ear-shattering explosions that took out the port engine: they had been hit by anti-aircraft fire over Trèves (Trier), close to the border with Luxembourg. The Handley Page staggered and yawed to the left. Monaghan eased back the throttle on the remaining engine and ordered the bombs to be jettisoned as he attempted to level off. He found some of the controls were immovable and the control wheel spun loose in his gauntlets.[41] They would not make it home. The giant lost height rapidly in the darkness. Hyde had no idea when they would strike dirt, but knew that in a machine this heavy it was going to be unpleasant, possibly terminal. The sound of ripping fabric and the breaking of wooden spars announced landfall. 'It didn't seem possible that I had survived,' said Monaghan, 'but, although pinned in the cockpit by several wires, I could breathe, move my arms and legs and felt no pain.' The observer emerged and pulled him from the encumbrances. The pair searched for Hyde: he was a 'bit roughed up but in a few minutes he was back to normal'. They surveyed the mangled bomber and discovered the reason for their miraculous escape.

> Evidently the left wings had remained down and coming in contact with the ground first had cushioned the impact. The fuselage had crashed on its side into a mass of telegraph or telephone wires and these had broken our fall. We could see two poles snapped off at their base and held in a slantwise position by unbroken wires. If we had crashed a few feet on either side we could hardly have survived. Strange the workings of fate.[42]

Of the other Handley Pages, one dropped its bombs over Cologne but, because of engine failure, was forced to land nearby in the Netherlands. Saarbrücken and Trèves were the most heavily damaged. However, the Germans were far from defenceless; they trained over 170 searchlights on the bombers and fired 16,000 shells at the intruders. Five Handley Pages were lost — the highest loss of British heavy bombers in the war. One wounded machine came down way off course near Dillingen with its bombs still in the racks; a curious onlooker set one of these off, killing eight bystanders.[43]

Monaghan and his crew were worried that German citizens would find them and seek revenge. Farmers and townspeople were known to have taken to night-bombing airmen with pitchforks and other tools that were to hand; they might well be given a savage beating or even killed. Given the treatment meted out by British civilians to downed Zeppelin and Gotha crews on occasion, the airmen expected little better. Monaghan retrieved some sardines, chocolate and a tin of cigarettes he had squirrelled away in the cockpit. The observer fired a Very light at the leaking fuel tanks. The bomber was soon ablaze. The crew lay flat on the ground some distance away just as the 1500 rounds of ammunition went off: it was a regular fireworks display with a bonfire and tracer bullets lighting up the sky. For the finale, a massive explosion. Monaghan turned to Hyde: 'And what do you think caused that?' 'The bombs,' Hyde answered. 'There were three of them still in their racks when we crashed.'

They pushed into a nearby wood and at dawn found themselves near the Moselle River, with Luxembourg on the far bank. Hyde and the observer favoured swimming the river but Monaghan, as the senior officer, would not allow it; the waterway was too wide and swift. They divested themselves of the Sidcot suits, loading them with stones and throwing them into the river before tucking into a breakfast of sardines and chocolate. Mid-afternoon, groups of searchers closed in with dogs. To the crew's relief each of the small bands was accompanied by a soldier. Trapped, they surrendered. Hyde had been with the squadron only 10 days; he saw out the final weeks of the war as a prisoner. He had ample material for another book.

Another New Zealander to work with the behemoth bombers did so in an altogether different capacity. In 1918, Raymond Goldfinch of Feilding was chosen as the lead mechanic for one of the more remarkable aeroplane deliveries in the history of the war. The Handley Page O/400's destination: Palestine and the Australian Flying Corps. This particular machine, once delivered, would be one of the largest aircraft in the Middle East and would play a crucial role in breaking the back of the Ottoman resistance at the Battle of Megiddo. The flight from England to Cairo also brought two important passengers: Brigadier General Amyas Eden Borton, commander of the Palestine Brigade; and a terrier named 'Tiny' who occupied a small, unofficial corner of the Handley Page.

Alongside Borton and the pilot, Major Archibald McLaren, Goldfinch would keep the Handley Page operational with the assistance of Nottingham carpenter and air mechanic John Francis.[44] The mechanics' biggest challenge was the twin water-cooled Rolls-Royce Eagle VIII engines, each producing a prodigious 375 hp. At Cranwell, Goldfinch spent about two weeks getting the aeroplane ready and fitting an additional fuel tank for the continent-hopping journey; this extended its capacity to 325 gallons.[45] He closely packed the fuselage with spare parts. Additional fuel and provisions would be available at a series of transit points in France, Italy, Crete and North Africa. It was a considerable undertaking and logistically demanding.

On the first leg to Paris a failing water pump forced them to land at Manston, southwest England, for repairs. Goldfinch despatched a motorcyclist for a replacement pump. In the four-day hold-up the machine was exposed to the elements and was hit with a downpour, much to Goldfinch's consternation. Eventually they took off again for Paris with Borton manning the front gun in case of 'stray Huns'.[46] He was possibly the highest-ranked air gunner of the war. The flight was a relatively short jump and the Handley Page made a half circuit of the Eiffel Tower before landing. As they did throughout the expedition, Goldfinch and Francis concluded the flight by inspecting the wings and fuselage, checking the rigging and closely examining the engines.[47]

The next day they headed south. The flight was 'uncomfortably' bumpy as they crossed the Cévennes mountains; they then descended into the intense heat of Lyon and on to the coastal town of Miramas. The airfield was vast but rough and pebbly, and they burst a tyre on

KEEP CLEAR OF THE PROPELLERS

Raymond Goldfinch (second from left) was the lead mechanic for one of the more remarkable aeroplane deliveries in the history of the war, when a Handley Page O/400 was flown from Cranwell, England, to Palestine in 1918.

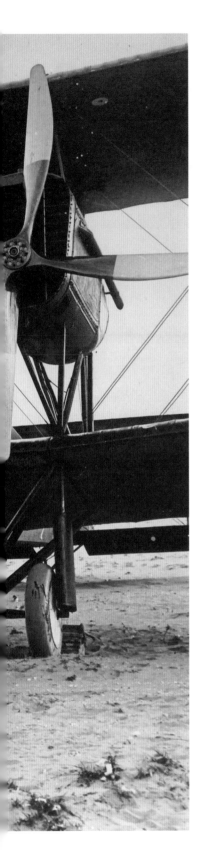

landing. In the cool of the evening Goldfinch and Francis replaced it from the onboard stores and changed the tailskid, which had lost a full three inches. One of the walnut propellers was substituted with a mahogany one.

From the coast of France they flew across the deep blue waters of the Gulf of Genoa. Italian seaplanes in the neighbourhood climbed up to look at the exotic northern European bird. The airmen took snapshots of Pisa and of the Pantheon and St Peter's Basilica in Rome. Outside the Holy City the Handley Page was jacked up and the wheels checked for alignment and ease of movement. They discovered a frayed rudder control; 'this was replaced, three valve springs to starboard engine and six new [spark] plugs to port-engine running a little hot on this journey'.[48] As on most nights, Goldfinch and Francis did not go to bed until after 11 p.m. They arose at 4 a.m. for the last European leg: Rome to Otranto in southernmost Italy.

In the morning half-light they took off and flew a leisurely circuit of Rome: the 'almost weird spectacle of the Roman Era with the adjoining Coliseum in this light will not easily be forgotten,' wrote Goldfinch. Further south they circled Naples and then Vesuvius with its crater, smoke and flames. At Otranto the mechanics undertook extensive maintenance in preparation for the most demanding section of the expedition, a six-hour, 460-mile flight to the island of Crete. Goldfinch and Francis were not about to tempt fate.

> The bus was unrigged here for the first time and we stayed for about forty hours to prepare for our longest and supreme flight. Everything in the machine was thoroughly examined, a new magneto was fitted, a dozen sparking plugs fixed and tappet clearances checked, also four new wheels were fixed as a precaution against the old ones being weakened in the tubes through the effects of the atmosphere, no chances in any respect being taken. After changing the oil in the tanks and replacing the Italian 'Benzine' with 'Shell' we had a trial run with the engines at 11.30 on the Saturday night; all being pronounced O.K. we were ready for the following morning.[49]

The Handley Page and its occupants arrived safely on Crete, and three days later embarked on another lengthy five-hour flight to North Africa followed by a couple of short hops to Cairo.

At the Egyptian capital, Goldfinch took his time before the final delivery to the AFC. Over three weeks, he overhauled the engines, which he found in good condition, and readjusted the carburettors for the warmer climate. He and Francis discovered that the fuselage bracing and the whole rigging needed adjustment; in all probability, the timber in the longerons and struts that had been soaked at Manston had shrunk as they dried out on the trip south.[50]

On 29 August they flew to Ramleh, Palestine, where Goldfinch and Francis stayed for 10 days, instructing the Australian mechanics in the intricacies and peculiarities of the Handley Page. The AFC wasted no time in putting the heavy bomber to use. Only weeks later it proved decisive in the opening stanza of the Battle of Megiddo, knocking out the Turkish army telephone junction — which meant, as the Australian historian of the AFC put it, the 'enemy commanders were blind and deaf before the battle had even really started'.[51] The last Allied offensive in the Sinai and Palestine Campaign broke through the Ottoman lines, bringing an end to Ottoman dominance in the region.

Goldfinch returned to England and was widely applauded for his efforts. The aircrew had delivered the heavy bomber in one piece and in good running order. News of the New Zealander's efforts percolated home and appeared in local papers. Goldfinch, formerly of Perry's Garage, Feilding, was awarded the Air Force Medal for his 'skill, perseverance, careful preparation, courage and initiative' over the 2592 miles and 36 hours of flight time it took to deliver the Handley Page.[52]

Alongside the efforts of Hyde and Goldfinch, a pair of fighter pilots began racking up victories in the last three months of the war. Born at opposite ends of New Zealand, both were graduates of the Kohimarama flying school. Aucklander Frederick Gordon was in Caldwell's 74 Squadron, and Invercargill-born Ronald Bannerman was in 79 Squadron.[53] Gordon joined 74 Squadron in July, and in August he made his presence known with five victories, three of which he had secured on a single day: 16 August. On the morning patrol he met two Fokker DVIIs: he sent one out of control and destroyed the other in flames. Soon after lunch, in his second sortie, he shared his third machine with an American pilot. The Rumpler two-seater with its orange nose, dark green wings and white tail was caught at 18,000 ft and attacked from above and below. It was driven down and the machine burst into flames; the pilot and observer decided to jump to their deaths rather than be burned alive.[54]

August was a good month for Bannerman, who had a law degree from Otago University and who would end the war with an almost impeccable record. Unlike Gordon, who was a relative newcomer to the Western Front, Bannerman had been with his unit since February 1918. The squadron was equipped with the latest British fighter, the Sopwith Dolphin. It was somewhat misnamed — as one commentator noted, it looked more like a midget whale than a graceful dolphin.[55] Short and squat, with a bulbous nose, it was the ugly sibling in the Sopwith stable. However, what the Dolphin lacked in looks it made up for in performance. It also boasted an unusual staggered wing arrangement. As with Coningham's first fighter, the DH5, the lower wing was well in advance of the lower one. Unlike the DH5, though, the upper wing was split so that the pilot sat elevated, with his head raised through the gap; as unconventional as this

Ronald Bannerman of 79 Squadron with his Sopwith Dolphin. Bannerman was New Zealand's most successful fighter pilot of 1918.

was, it afforded the pilot an excellent field of view. Its blimp-like nose housed a 200-hp engine, and it was armed with twin forward-firing Vickers guns. Like the Camel, the wings, guns and pilot were all gathered together hard against the engine.

While training in Scotland, Bannerman familiarised himself with the Dolphin and immediately liked it. 'Had my first flight in a Dolphin — she is a dandy bus — quite a new type of machine. She will do me to show to Fritz.' He took it up and 'fought' against the other machines in the training school's inventory and found he could 'chase hell out of every other machine in the sky'.[56] Nonetheless, Bannerman's career — and 79 Squadron in general — got off to a slow start.

The unit was hit early on by heavy casualties thanks to teething troubles with the Dolphin's engines and the low-flying duties it was given. This was followed by a period of flying almost exclusively on reconnaissance operations and bomber escort duties.[57] Moreover, the greater part of the squadron was, like Bannerman, inexperienced in aerial combat. It was not until the mechanics gained better experience with the Dolphin's engine and a new commander with a 'fine fighting record' arrived in June that their fortunes began to turn.[58] In the meantime, Bannerman had increased his solo flying time to over 200 hours by the end of July and had claimed a string of victories, although they went unconfirmed.[59]

In August, after six months over the Western Front, Bannerman began a barnstorming assault on the German air force from the squadron's Sainte-Marie-Cappel airfield. On a morning dominated by low clouds and intermittent rain, Bannerman took off with two others on an offensive patrol. Southwest of Bailleul the trio spotted an RE8 under attack from a red-tailed Fokker DVII.[60] As the German was driven off, Bannerman came under attack from another Fokker. He outmanoeuvred the enemy, closed in and fired. The machine was fatally struck; it fell and crashed into a house. He now had incontrovertible evidence of his first kill, albeit at the expense of someone's home. In his logbook he briefly noted in fountain pen the success of 4 August 1918: 'Shot down one Fokker Biplane — helped shoot down another.'[61] He was on his way. By the end of August he had shot down five aircraft and a balloon. Aside from his first kill and the balloon the rest were all two-seaters; in fact, nearly three-quarters of all Bannerman's successes in the Great War were against twin-crewed aircraft, and all were shot down at under 5000 ft.

As Gordon hit a slump in September — he destroyed only a single balloon — Bannerman hit his stride. The newly anointed ace was promoted to captain and went on to destroy seven more machines in the space of four weeks. Much of this was condensed into the week of 16–22 September, with the first day, when he was leading B Flight, his best. It was a clear, late-summer sky, and the enemy was out in number.[62] He had two successes on that day. It was also the only occasion on which he took down an enemy machine without firing a shot.

> While flying at a height of 2000 feet North of Hollebeke, I encountered a DFW or LVG [reconnaisance aircraft] apparently doing Contact Patrol at 200 feet. I dived on him and forced him to do a sharp turn. He came out of the turn into a nose dive and crashed into the ground. Shortly afterwards I saw another DFW or LVG about the same height near Hooge

shooting white lights. The enemy aircraft turned east and I fired a long burst into it at close range. The E.A. started to glide east but eventually dived into the ground and crashed. I observed a cloud of smoke issuing from the crashed E.A. on the ground.[63]

To this he added another two-seater and a Fokker DVII, making him the RAF's most successful fighter pilot for that week of the war.[64] His efforts were recognised with a Distinguished Flying Cross.

September was also Caldwell's most fruitful period of the war. On 5 September he had his famous collision with Sydney Carlin — a fun-loving Yorkshireman who had come to the RFC in 1917 with a Military Cross and a wooden leg, both acquired while holding a trench against repeated enemy infantry attacks on the Somme. He had joined Caldwell's squadron in May 1918 and was quickly dubbed 'Timbertoes' by the officers. Their clash at 8000 ft and Caldwell's coolness in the face of death only burnished the legend of the New Zealander. Flying his SE5a with a crumpled wing by standing and leaning far out to the right of the cockpit — the episode with which this book opened — he somehow balanced his machine and stopped its spin, only to jump from the doomed aircraft just before its abrupt, splintering death. Brigadier Webb-Bowen called it a heroic feat of 'self-preservation'.[65]

Unaware of Caldwell's remarkable survival, Carlin was grief-stricken and assumed the worst, as did the whole squadron. 'Timbertoes' wanted to assuage his guilt by strafing a German airfield. Some of the men knew he was asking to be killed and sabotaged his machine; it was the only way to keep him grounded.[66] Hours of gloom were broken by the news that Caldwell was miraculously alive. Carlin's turn of mood was equally remarkable, and later that evening he 'passed out' in the mess, a picture of complete happiness.

All the more astonishingly, Caldwell flew the very next day as if nothing had happened. 'Caldwell had an amazing flair for air fighting, which he treated in the most inconsequential manner,' noted Ira Jones.[67]

'Dud' weather prevented any decisive fighting until the third week of September. Around midday on 17 September, Caldwell was leading a five-strong patrol when his men became embroiled with over 20 Germans. Caldwell inserted himself into the fight when he saw an SE5a being tormented by a trio of enemy Fokker DVIIs: it was one of his officers, Frederick Hunt. Caldwell pried one of them off Hunt's back by knocking it out of the sky, but Hunt was still encumbered with the remaining pair. Caldwell closed to 50 yards and fired. His second target for the day rolled and dived away, but Caldwell was unable to follow because Hunt was still under threat from a Fokker that had height on him. When the New Zealander appeared, the German wisely dived and flattened out low and turned tail for home.

Caldwell's remaining combat of note in September occurred a week later, east of Armentières at 12,000 ft when, with three other SE5s, he dived on seven Siemens-Schuckert DIVs. The Siemens-Schuckert biplanes were built in small numbers late in the war. The initial batch entered squadrons in August, and only 125 had been produced by the end of hostilities. Not only was it faster and more agile than the excellent Fokker DVII, it also had an exceptional rate of climb: it could ascend to over 3000 ft in two minutes, 10,000 ft in six minutes and

20,000 ft in 15 minutes.[68] With a compact frame and 160-hp engine, it was a plug of muscle, simply unmatched in the Great War.

Caldwell engaged the leading machine at a right angle, nearly colliding with the plywood-skinned fuselage. They turned in towards each other, Caldwell's SE5a bearing down on the Siemens-Schuckert. Then he found himself on its tail at speed, firing at close range. Desperate, the German pulled his machine into a vertical climb to take advantage of his aircraft's climbing ability. It was too late. The enemy machine 'hung on his prop for a second and then fell over right past my wing tip'. Caldwell looked over: 'I saw the pilot leaning to the left of the cockpit with his head down on his chest.'[69]

Caldwell and Gordon added to 74 Squadron's scoreboard over the following month, culminating in their final victories on 30 October: Gordon destroyed a balloon and Caldwell a DVII.[70] They ended their campaigns on nine and 25 claims respectively. Bannerman, though, was far from finished.

In 79 Squadron, the man from Invercargill was locked in a gentlemen's tussle over who would be the top-scoring Dolphin ace of the war. The American Captain Francis Gillet was trailing the New Zealander by two victories at the end of September. In October Bannerman went on leave for three weeks and Gillet made up for lost time. By the time Bannerman returned on 22 October — the squadron was now at Reckem (Rekkem) airfield — Gillet had leapt to 16 victories, three ahead of Bannerman. In short order, the New Zealander sent a machine out of control in late October and then, in early November, he picked off three more. The final victory came on 4 November, only seven days shy of the end of the war; in all likelihood it was the last enemy machine brought down by a New Zealander. Bannerman was flying an offensive patrol near Baeygem when he located his bread-and-butter target: a two-seater at 2000 ft. He shot up the observer and the wounded machine dived and crashed into a hedge.[71] He might have pulled even with Gillet except for a freakish success on the second-to-last day of the war, when the American shot down one machine and, in quick succession, shot down another which, in turn, crashed midair into another: three Fokker DVIIs for five minutes' work.

Nonetheless Bannerman was in an élite club: he was the second highest-scoring Dolphin pilot of the war, and over the period from his first confirmed success on 4 August until his last on 4 November he was one of the highest-scoring airmen in the RAF.[72] He and Gillet accounted for about half of the squadron's victories.[73] Bannerman ended his run with 15 aircraft and a balloon against his name.[74]

A s the war entered its final days, James Sloss, a Canterbury Aviation Company graduate, appeared. The late starting date of the South Island school meant that few graduates flew operationally in the Great War; Sloss was one of only a select number to do so. As he observed in a letter to his mother on the eve of his posting to France, 'I think I must be just about the first of the Sockburn boys to go across.'[75] He joined 108 Squadron on 9 October as a pilot, flying the underpowered and unreliable two-man Airco DH9 bomber. Because of its inferior performance the DH9 was the gateway for many a young airman to enter the afterlife.

Still, Sloss did not think that he would 'see much of the war', given the Allied advances. He was wrong.

There was very little reduction in effort in the last five weeks of the Great War. On 29 September the main offensive was launched on the Hindenburg Line. A breach was made on the opening day, and within five days the Allies had broken through along a 19-mile front. The German air units still had plenty of fight left and although British air losses fell by a third, RAF casualties in October were still higher than in any other month in the war prior to July.[76] A lot of the work was carried out by the reconnaissance bomber squadrons in tracking and harassing the German retreat. Across these units two other New Zealanders joined Sloss: Leonard Isitt and Hugh Blackwell. All three were South Islanders.

Isitt had been wounded on the Somme in 1916. He then moved to the RFC, with service in a reconnaissance squadron, where he claimed a single enemy machine and long hours in artillery cooperation work. He was on home establishment duties as a flying instructor when he volunteered to return to a frontline squadron.[77] If he was hoping for something a little more exciting, he would not be disappointed. Like Sloss, he would be piloting the vulnerable DH9.

In early October, Isitt arrived at his new unit at Abscon, northern France: 98 Squadron.[78] Within days he was thrown in the deep end on a bombing and photo reconnaissance operation on the Mons railway station. Ten machines left Abscon on 9 October at 4.40 p.m, including Isitt and his observer in their DH9. It was no soft reintroduction to the Western Front for the New Zealander. On the way in and on the return they were set upon by 15 Fokkers and Pfalzes, and they experienced heavy anti-aircraft fire while they were over the target dropping their two 112-lb bombs.

This raid was followed by two more major raids for the squadron on 14 and 23 October. The latter was on the Hirson railway station; it was a costly mission. The unit attacked the target in conjunction with 107 Squadron. The formation crossed the line and dropped 24 bombs on the station, half of which were direct hits.[79] On the return flight at 10,000 ft they encountered Fokkers and Pfalz fighters. At least four of the slow and ponderous DH9s were engaged. One was shot up and its observer wounded. Another crew came down in German-held territory, destined for a prisoner of war camp. Isitt came through unscathed.

In addition to these bombing operations, Isitt was involved in demanding photo-reconnaissance flights in the last week of the war; on one occasion he and his observer exposed an exceptional 36 plates. It was not glamorous work taking photographs from a DH9, but it furnished the army with invaluable intelligence.[80]

Sloss was equally busy during the final weeks of the war: he flew no less than 26 hours with his squadron and contributed to 10 successful raids.[81] He liked his squadron, by all accounts — he felt the other airmen were 'real "dinkum" boys' — but he lamented the fact that too many of the old hands were leaving 'to go back to England for a spell of instructing',[82] which in all likelihood explains why he himself was flying operations within days of his arrival. He informed his father of his first brush with 'Archie', and on 25 October he and his colleagues had 'seven hun scouts pumping lead at us but they were afraid to come close enough to be dangerous'.[83] On 4 November he had his 'best show' to date.

Yesterday we did two bomb raids well over the lines. The first was rather an unlucky one, we were a very small formation — to a lot of archie and met a dozen huns who brought down two of our number, we got two of them. In the afternoon show we did a great bit of work right away over the objective and dropped 96 twenty lb bombs on a railway junction. There was a big lot of trucks and engines standing there 300 at least and it was grand to see it go up in flames.[84]

The Allied advance was making great gains and Sloss, when he was not flying, was able to tour the overrun German trenches. 'The huns must have cleared out of here in a great hurry because they didn't bother to destroy any of their work,' he wrote. 'It is wonderful how well they do things, to look at their trenching and buildings one would think they had been constructed for permanent use.'

In 53 Squadron, Blackwell was engaged in similar sightseeing. His unit advanced as the German tide went out. 'The war is splendid isn't it? Fritz is now right off the coast and is retreating at top speed,' he told his mother.[85] 'We have great sports these days "scrounging". The Hun has left much material behind including bombs — coloured lights — rifles — ammunition — etc.' Scrounging turned up some unusual treasures: 'We found a little kitten, probably abandoned by the Huns, and keep it up in our rooms. It is a very playful little thing and goes by the name of "Stinker".'[86] He also saw the ruinous effects of the war on the local population living on the edges of the fighting.

Near their new airfield was a Belgian farmhouse occupied by an elderly man. When the airfield was in German hands the British had raided it; they dropped bombs on the property, killing the man's wife and daughter. Now that the British 'owned' the airfield the Germans raided it; an errant bomb fell on the house and killed the old man. 'It is a most sad affair,' lamented Blackwell, 'it's not only military who suffer in this war.' As he found out in the following days, the Germans had behaved appallingly towards the Belgians, confirming the early war stories of atrocities. An elderly man who had lived under the Germans for four years recounted tales of seeing 'women, children and old men shot for no other reason than to cow the populous [sic]. Dirty swine that they are.'[87]

Like Sloss, Blackwell was heavily engaged in sorties. The squadron's RE8s were mostly deployed in contact patrols, trying to stay abreast of the infantry. On one fog-plagued patrol, he and his observer got lost seven times before they spied the troops advancing behind a creeping barrage; small, mud-covered creatures picking their way through newly ploughed-up land. He circled above at only 300 ft with shells from the barrage whistling past the RE8 and machine-gun fire raking the sky. When the soldiers reached their objective, Blackwell swung the RE8 around and headed home. Instead of landing at his airfield, the New Zealander decided to take the news directly to its final destination and, much to the amusement of the local general, landed outside the headquarters and made his report.

Blackwell came close to being killed on 30 October. He was on a photographic sortie three miles behind the lines when anti-aircraft fire almost downed the RE8. A glancing near-hit almost winded Blackwell; it ripped fabric off the fuselage and wings and loosened the framework, and it took a big bite out of the controls — only half remained. He turned to see his observer: 'his right hand was almost blown off'. The RE8 was still airborne, but barely. Blackwell nursed it home, repeating to himself, 'I must make a good landing . . . I must make a good landing.' He managed it and the observer was rushed to the hospital in an ambulance. As he surveyed his machine Blackwell marvelled that he was unbloodied, given that the RE8 had 25 holes. 'Unfortunately the bus is a write off, it quite grieves me to part with it.'

The inclement late autumn weather turned the airfield to mud, and Blackwell floundered around in it up to his ankles. 'We are all indenting for bathing costumes,' he wrote. His only solace was that the squadron was still heading east, right behind the Germans. When Turkey signed an armistice he was elated, and in the second week of November he heard that Berlin had been given an ultimatum 'to decide between peace and war, and I think he [the Kaiser] will choose the former. If he doesn't he'll live to rue the day. He will absolutely get hell.'[88] Overnight the Germans retreated again, and Blackwell was one of the first airmen to fly over liberated land. Flying lower than the trees on occasions, he was entranced by the sight of milling civilians out in the streets and countryside. 'They waved flags, handkerchiefs and even table cloths.' On a Sunday, men from the squadron drove to the town of Roubaix on the Franco-Belgian border: 'Children and grownups were wildly excited and followed us around wherever we went. I must have walked for nearly a mile with a little girl hanging on to one hand and an old man frisking around the other.'

Just before the war ended, Blackwell returned to his billet. He sat under a watery winter sun and fell into 'dreaming about distant lands' and his family: 'Quite distinctly I saw a lovely green lawn, a willow tree encircled by a rustic seat and coming through the door of "Waihui" Wee Meg, carrying cups of tea and some nut bread. Everything was nice and sunny and looking along the side of the house I saw at the windows familiar faces.' Perhaps he would be home for his birthday next year?

Sloss was of a similar mind, but imagined he might depart for Christmas; he assured his sister that when he came home in a month or so, 'I'll have plenty of yarns to tell you.'[89] On 9 November, with the war decided, Sloss was on a bombing raid on Denderleeuw, Belgium, when the flight was set upon by a dozen enemy machines. Sloss's aircraft was struck by anti-aircaft fire and he and the observer were wounded. They both survived the forced landing and received medical treatment. Sloss was admitted to a Red Cross Hospital in Boulogne with a leg wound. Initially, all went well and the wound was 'no trouble and clearing up nicely,' the hospital matron wrote to his parents.[90] She informed them that their 'son is in a small ward with 2 other patients where I hope he will be comfortable and have all he wishes for — it is always so hard for those whose homes are so far away; An anxious time for relations waiting for news. I will write again if there is anything to report, otherwise please conclude all is well.'[91]

Undoubtedly James Sloss's family — who had already lost one son to the war — would count themselves fortunate when they had received news of their younger son's improving health. By the slimmest of margins, he would survive the conflict and perhaps keep his Christmas date with his sister. But the Great War was not done with Sloss. Well before the matron's letter reached Cheviot, a telegram appeared. It was a brutal blow to his family. While he was convalescing, James had developed an acute inflammation of the throat and was unable to breathe. An emergency tracheotomy failed and the 'end came in a few minutes'.[92]

On the eve of 11 November, news spread that the end of the war was at hand. Keith Caldwell and a number of his men were dining at Mac McGregor's mess when a mechanic burst into the room, all a-fluster. He was overcome with excitement. He stood to attention in front of McGregor and blurted out, 'Oh, sir! News has come through that they are signing the Armistice tomorrow, and there will be no more war.' Either McGregor or Caldwell feigned throwing a glass at the mechanic and exclaimed, 'Out of this, you blighter, and take your dismal news with you.'[93]

Blackwell was elated. 'The war news is great isn't it? Tomorrow may be a very important day in history. Today we hear that the Kaiser has abdicated, tomorrow we hope will bring peace.'[94] At 8 a.m. the following day Blackwell flew his final sortie. Then, at the 'eleventh hour of the eleventh day of the eleventh month', the ceasefire came into effect. After four years of war he could barely believe it. The enthusiasm of the night before had given way to quiet contemplation. 'The way in which the momentous news was received was remarkable. Except for a vacant few,' he observed, 'fellows took it quietly. Chaps who had done things in the war were more or less silent. Others who had had safe jobs and ran practically no risk kicked up all the row.'[95]

That night he stayed awake for hours and penned a few words by candlelight. His strongest emotion echoed that of many New Zealand airmen: gratefulness. He had survived, through many hazards and perils. Like Caldwell, it had taken a few miracles to do so. 'I've been jolly lucky to come through,' he told his father. 'And yet I am very thankful to have been through them, but am more thankful that they are things of the past.'

James Hewett

William Wallace Cook

Hew Seton Montgomerie

Euan Dickson

Lister Briffault

John Classon Courtney

Kenneth Henry Millward

Frank Bullock-Webster

Frederick Gordon

CONCLUSION

When Henry Wigram first advanced the cause of military aviation in New Zealand in 1909, few in political power were prepared to listen. Rather, aviation's early torch-bearers were private individuals and pioneers such as Leo and Vivian Walsh and Will Scotland. Even with the gift of the monoplane *Britannia* and the abilities of pilot Joe Hammond readily to hand, the government of the day was unwilling to commit to establishing a training school, let alone a small air contingent. The novelty and undeniable costs associated with the procurement and ongoing maintenance of aircraft hobbled the development of aviation in prewar New Zealand. Nonetheless, the aeronauts sowed the seeds of flight in the minds and hearts of young New Zealanders. The part played by some 850 individuals in the Great War transcended their relatively small numbers.

During the war, New Zealand aircrew could be found flying above the hedge-enclosed farms of England, the grey waters of the North Sea, the rolling fields of northern France and Belgium, the sands of the Middle East and Mesopotamia, and the jungles of East Africa. Some were instructors and others carried out experimental and evaluative aviation work, but most were posted to operational units in the field where they were involved in every facet of the air war: Harold Butterworth gathered intelligence in reconnaissance operations; Geoffrey Callender guided shells to their targets in artillery cooperation flights; Arthur Browne kept local headquarters appraised of advancing British troops in contact sorties; William Shirtcliffe photographed enemy entrenchments and dispositions in photo reconnaissance work; Robert Munro dropped bombs on German munitions dumps in bombing raids; Percival White hunted U-boats in coastal defence duties; William Cook chased Zeppelin airships during home defence operations; Frederic Sharland strafed enemy artillery emplacements in ground attacks; Frederick Horrell protected vulnerable bombers in escort duties; Hugh Chambers struck enemy airfields in night bombing raids; and Kenneth Millward fought with enemy fighters in offensive patrols.

Among the extraordinary exploits of the New Zealanders, a few demand special attention. The antipodean mechanics were few in number, but they demonstrated that ground crew were in no way immune from danger. Sydney Anderson had a clutch of awards by the end of the war, but it was his action in a long-range operation over the North Sea for which he is best remembered. Climbing out onto the wing of a damaged seaplane flying at 5000 ft, Anderson successfully effected engine repairs in a 90-mph wind, thereby saving the crew and machine from capture. At Orfordness, England, the renowned test pilot Clive Collett became the first airman to make a parachute jump from an RFC aircraft. While this and a series of subsequent descents failed to encourage the development and provision of parachutes for deployment in the field, Collett's work demonstrated what might have been possible had there been the will to promote parachutes for practical frontline use.

In British home defence, New Zealanders gained a fine reputation battling the 'baby-killer' Zeppelins, but it was Alfred de Bathe Brandon who became the nation's best-known airman in this role: his two famous attacks on Zeppelins briefly made him a household name across the British Empire. New Zealanders also acquitted themselves well in offensive operations against the great airships — in particular Samuel Dawson, who, in the first successful aircraft carrier-delivered strike in history, struck the huge Tondern Zeppelin sheds on the German–Danish border.

To these can be added men who excelled in air-to-air combat. Fifteen New Zealand airmen achieved 'ace' status. Thomas Culling was the first, early in the summer of 1917. By the end of that year he had been joined by seven others: Harold Beamish, Keith Caldwell, Clive Collett, Arthur Coningham, Forster Maynard, Keith Park and Alan Scott. Their ranks swelled in 1918 with the addition of Ronald Bannerman, Euan Dickson, Herbert Drewitt, Frederick Gordon, Malcolm McGregor, Carrick Paul and Herbert Watson. In total, antipodean high-scorers were credited with over 170 victories between them. All but one, Carrick Paul, served on the Western Front. The Thames-born Paul reached his fifth and final victory in Palestine in August 1918 flying Bristol Fighters with 1 Squadron AFC. Tragically, he died on his homeward journey from war; he accidentally fell overboard, and by the time the vessel had come about he was nowhere to be seen.

Among these luminaries, Caldwell, Park and Bannerman shone brightest. Caldwell was by general reckoning the nation's most successful single-seater fighter pilot, with 25 claims, and Park its most effective two-seater fighter pilot, with 20.[1] Bannerman's 16 victories were striking for having only one 'out of control' entry — that is, the enemy aircraft was seen plummeting to earth but there was no confirmation that it had been 'destroyed'.[2] Low cloud, the demands of aerial combat and the fact they were commonly operating on the German side of the lines precluded verification on many occasions. Moreover, skilled German pilots were adroit at faking a 'death plunge' only to pull out at the last moment. Bannerman's 'destroyed' record was unmatched by any other New Zealand ace.

Honourable mentions must go to the trio of Collett, Coningham and Dickson. Collett's 11 victories in his Sopwith Camel were accumulated in a mere seven weeks on the Western Front, and only the fact that he was wounded prevented him adding to this number. Coningham, for his part, did not have the advantage of flying a first-rate fighter like the Camel or Royal Air Factory SE5a when he began his rise in the rankings. In 1917 he was saddled with the less-favoured Airco DH5. In spite of this limitation, Coningham collected 10 victories, making him the most successful DH5 pilot of the war.

Air Vice-Marshal Sir Keith Park, in the cockpit wearing goggles, commanded the RAF in the defence of Malta in the Second World War. Thames-born Park was famous for his leadership in the Battle of Britain. A good deal of his success was attributable to what he learnt in the Great War.

Keith Caldwell and his
wife Dorothy. During the
interwar years, Caldwell
worked their Mangere
farm near Auckland and
played an important
role in keeping military
aviation alive.

Euan Dickson flew two-seater bombers from April 1917 to August 1918. He was officially recognised not only for his bombing prowess in over 175 missions but also because, incredibly, he and his observers claimed 14 enemy machines.[3]

Close to a dozen New Zealanders went on to become squadron commanders in the Great War.[4] Hugh Reilly was the first Zealand-born airman to see action in France in 1914, and he also played a leading role in the work of Mesopotamia Flight and 30 Squadron as their commanding officer in 1915. Given the inadequate aircraft, the climatic and topographical challenges, the ravages of malaria and dysentery, and the poor and stretched support available for the unit, it is remarkable what he and his men were able to achieve. Reilly's capture proved costly: the greater part of those taken into captivity at Kut died at the hands of their indifferent and sometimes cruel Turkish guards. Few airmen before or since could claim to have had as great an impact on the course of a single campaign as the Hawke's Bay native.

The best known of the commanders during the war was undoubtedly Caldwell. The tall Aucklander took the reins of the famous 74 Squadron in 1918. He was a fine pilot and, as evidenced by his frequent appearances in the memoirs of Great War airmen, was widely respected by his fellow fighter pilots on the Western Front. He began his flying career with the Walsh brothers at Kohimarama and ended the war with an enviable reputation as a fighter pilot and commander. Rainsford Balcombe-Brown led an equally prestigious unit: 56 Squadron. During his tenure it was one of the Western Front's highest-scoring and most feared fighting formations. He was the only New Zealand squadron commander killed in operations. Park was one of the few men to be given command of a squadron in which he had served in lower ranks; his revival of the squadron after its near annihilation in a 1918 bombing raid was a model of resolute leadership.

A handful of the dominion's squadron commanders rose to even higher office during the war. Scott and Brandon both had stints in senior leadership positions as lieutenant colonels. After running 60 Squadron, Scott was made Officer Commanding, Eleventh (Army) Wing.[5] He also had a period leading the Central Flying School. His sterling war service and postwar political connections — he worked as air secretary to Winston Churchill — marked him out as a future chief of air staff.[6] Sadly, he died in 1922 from double pneumonia acquired on a skiing holiday in St Moritz. In home defence, the 'Zeppelin hunter' Brandon was plucked from directing 50 Squadron in 1918 to temporary command of Fifty-Third (Home Defence) Wing, whose three squadrons protected Britain from enemy airships and long-range bombers.

In the same year, Cuthbert Maclean rose to the highest office held by a New Zealand airman, commanding an air brigade on the Western Front. His rise had been meteoric by any standards. The former Christian missionary entered the RFC as a lieutenant in 1915 and by early 1916 he was leading a flight. Within six months he was commanding a Bristol Fighter squadron. In the summer of 1917 he was given the Thirteenth (Army) Wing and, in March 1918, Tenth (Army) Wing.[7] In that same month the 'Fighting Parson' was temporarily elevated to command I Brigade, a position usually occupied by a brigadier general. For a few days he oversaw a sizeable force comprised of three wings incorporating 11 squadrons, some 250 aircraft and a large number of balloons.[8]

The only antipodean to oversee more personnel was Harriet Simeon — one of fewer than half a dozen New Zealand women in the WRAF. In 1915 Simeon was rejected for war service by the New Zealand authorities, and she paid her own way to England. She was 42 years old when she accepted a lowly position on a night shift in a munitions canteen. By November 1918 she was the highest-ranked New Zealand woman in the WRAF — a deputy assistant commander — with thousands of women in her care.

These considerable successes were tempered by New Zealand casualties: 79 airmen lost their lives during the Great War. The rate at which they died from all causes highlights the increasing intensity of the air war and the growing number of New Zealanders entering the conflict: none in 1914, two in 1915, 13 in 1916, 35 in 1917 and 29 in 1918.[9] Of these deaths, over 40 per cent were on the Western Front and close to 35 per cent occurred in Britain. The greater part of those killed on the Western Front were operational losses and all but one in Britain were training fatalities. Hubert Solomon's fatal Zeppelin interception flight in April 1917 was the sole operational death in home defence duties. Poignantly, the last wartime death of a New Zealander happened on the last day of the war: 24-year-old Allan Macdonald of the Awatere Valley in Marlborough was killed when his machine stalled in a climbing turn and crashed to the ground.[10]

The remaining deaths were scattered across other theatres of the war, including the Middle East and Mesopotamia, where William Burn was killed in 1915 — the first of New Zealand's airmen to lose his life. Joe Hammond's 1918 death in exhibition flying in the United States was a tragic loss. Hammond had helped inspire a generation of young men and his legacy was evident in their Great War achievements.

The Armistice did not bring an end to losses — some New Zealanders were killed in training and non-aviation-related accidents in the immediate wake of the war. Wellington-born James Kitto was taken by the great 1918–20 flu pandemic. Five days after the end of the war, the 37-year-old serving with the AFC was admitted 'seriously ill' to a military hospital, where he succumbed to 'influenza-pneumonia' 20 days later.[11]

Two of the more unusual and tragic losses after the signing of the Armistice were those of Samuel Dawson and Arthur Skinner. Dawson was killed in the Russian Civil War of 1918–20. While awaiting repatriation in Britain in early 1919, he was re-posted and found himself with HMS *Vindictive* in the Gulf of Finland as part of a multinational expedition supporting the White forces against the Bolshevik Red Army. He was not the only New Zealander to be found fighting in Russia; the opportunity to continue flying and fighting drew in Gordon Pettigrew, Arthur Skinner and Roderick Carr. In the second week of September — 10 months after the Great War ended — Dawson was flying a Sopwith 1½ Strutter against Bolshevik elements at Kronstadt, 19 miles west of St Petersburg, when he was shot down by anti-aircraft fire. He failed to return. His parents and siblings were devastated.[12]

Unlike Dawson, Skinner — the former prisoner of war — completed his Russian adventure in perfect health. He settled in Christchurch, where he married Kathleen Banks. Seven years after it ended, the Great War revisited Skinner: on Christmas Eve 1925, he suffered a series of seizures. Three weeks later he was operated on, but the procedure failed and he died the following day. The shrapnel fragment the Germans had failed to extract in September 1917 had finally succeeded in its deadly purpose eight years later.[13]

Other New Zealanders were imprisoned during the Great War. Nearly 30 airmen were captured or interned.[14] In Mesopotamia, Reilly was the first New Zealand airman taken captive, and he remained a prisoner until war's end. Most of the New Zealanders survived the rigours of imprisonment — but not all. After months of deprivation in the siege of Kut and a hellish journey of more than 1000 miles to imprisonment in Anatolia, mechanic Francis Adams finally succumbed to his ill treatment at the hands of the Turks.

It was on the Western Front, however, that most of the airmen were captured. Hugh Trenchard's persistent offensive strategy invariably increased the chances of being brought down on the German side of the lines as the result of engine malfunction, damage sustained in air fighting or from anti-aircraft fire. In 1916 former mountaineer and explorer James Dennistoun's wounds proved fatal and after his third operation in captivity he died, leaving his grief-stricken pilot and cousin Herbert Russell to write the fateful letter to Dennistoun's parents. Russell himself suffered extensive burns. He was released before the end of the war in a prisoner exchange in Switzerland. More fortunate airmen were interned after coming down over the neutral Netherlands. Donald Harkness saw out the war in remarkably genteel conditions in the Netherlands and was even granted 'leave' to visit his family in New Zealand for a short period.[15]

The New Zealanders in the Russian Civil War highlighted the fact that some Great War airmen were keen to pursue postwar military aviation careers. This would be no easy feat in interwar Britain. Peace provoked a rapid deflation of the RAF: within two years, the 300,000-strong air force was reduced to a mere 30,000. This greatly reduced the prospects for New Zealanders there — something that would change only when war clouds again gathered over Europe in the late 1930s. Nor were the immediate prospects any better in New Zealand.

In early 1919, as the airmen were disembarking in the dominion, the government sought advice from Britain on how to fashion New Zealand's air defence. Lieutenant Colonel Arthur Vere Bettington of the Air Ministry was despatched to New Zealand, and when he arrived in March the famous Brandon was attached to his staff.[16] During Bettington's visit, two Bristol Fighters and a pair of de Havilland DH4s were unpacked in New Zealand — a loan from Britain calculated to spur on antipodean aviation.[17] Bettington, in his report, argued that air power was 'a new and distinct striking force' and that, in the advent of a conflict in the Pacific — where Japan was thought to pose the greatest threat — New Zealand would be vulnerable to aircraft carrier-borne machines. He advised New Zealand to establish a seven-squadron independent air service. Further inducement appeared when London offered to gift a substantial number of its surplus wartime aircraft to its colonial empire; New Zealand was allotted 100. These machines, combined with the returning airmen, meant New Zealand had an almost ready-made air force. It was the opportunity presented by *Britannia* and Hammond in 1914 multiplied hundredfold.

However, the aviation proposal was simply too ambitious, and Wellington's parliamentarians and officials were wary of committing to a force that Bettington himself estimated would drain £300,000 annually over eight years from the government's coffers.[18] Wellington dithered for six months before accepting a third of the allotted RAF machines, by which time the best machines had been dispersed to other dominions and colonies. In the end Bettington's recommendations slipped into obscurity and many of the 33 machines that arrived were loaned to private commercial initiatives.

The government's sop to the military aviation enthusiasts was the creation of an Air Board in 1920. Only its secretary, Captain Thomas Wilkes, had flown in the Great War. The board 'recommended the establishment of a skeleton air force with bases around the country that could be expanded in wartime'.[19] The authorities were uninterested; they reasoned that in the unlikely event of a war close at hand, civilian aviation resources could be quickly converted to military purposes. To this end the government subsidised 'refresher' courses for the returned airmen at the two flying schools.[20]

With only a modicum of government support, the New Zealand Flying School and the Canterbury Aviation Company struggled in the postwar era. A swift decline in student numbers and a failure to find new avenues of income drove Kohimarama and Sockburn to financial collapse in 1923.[21] The New Zealand Flying School shut its doors in October and the government bought the assets of the Walsh brothers' aviation business. Kohimarama had furnished the Great War with some of New Zealand's very best airmen, but Leo and Vivian Walsh, after a dozen years battling for greater recognition and support, now turned their backs on aviation to pursue maritime interests.[22] A frustrated Henry Wigram offered the government £10,000 towards the purchase of the Sockburn enterprise. Wellington accepted, and the land and assets of the company changed hands. In recognition of Wigram's aviation advocacy and generosity, the station was renamed after him. In a final act of desecration, the unwanted Walsh brothers' aircraft were piled up on the beachfront and set alight; 'the funeral pyre of early New Zealand civil aviation' appropriately overseen by government officials.[23]

The closure of both companies finally forced Wellington's hand, and the New Zealand Permanent Air Force (NZPAF) was established in 1923. It was a part of the army rather than an independent service; a truly independent air arm, the Royal New Zealand Air Force (RNZAF), was still 14 years away. The NZPAF was initially incredibly small with only two officers — Captains Wilkes (Staff Officer, Air Services, Wellington) and Leonard Isitt (Officer Commanding Wigram) — and two airmen. These personnel were outnumbered by the 15 aircraft based at Wigram. Alongside this, a 'territorial' air branch was established: the New Zealand Air Force (NZAF), presided over by Keith Caldwell. This was a volunteer organisation that continued the refresher work of the now defunct flying schools.

The failure of Kohimarama and Sockburn and the diminutive size of the NZPAF confirmed

Air Vice-Marshal Arthur Coningham, Air Officer Commanding Western Desert (left) with General Bernard Montgomery in Egypt in 1942. Coningham revolutionised the use of air power in tactical air operations.

for the returning airmen that a career in military or civil aviation would be difficult to sustain. Most of them slipped back into their prewar careers. Ronald Bannerman married and re-entered the legal profession as a solicitor in Dunedin before establishing a legal partnership in Gore. Reggie and Peps Kingsford settled in Nelson, where they ran a successful photographic studio. Children followed soon after: their first son, Peter, was born in 1920. Some of the men discovered that the early years of peace were difficult to negotiate. Mac McGregor found it hard to adjust to civilian life. He initially worked on his father's farm and then bought his own dairy farm in the Waikato.[24] Farming life with its daily routine and isolation was far removed from the excitement and drama of 85 Squadron over the Western Front. McGregor filled the gap with motorcycle racing, and the territorial NZAF gave him a way to pursue his love of flying.

Initially about 50 men were reunited at the NZAF-run refresher courses. They were relaxed gatherings where the wartime pilots renewed friendships and got a little flying in. But work commitments, the cost of getting to Wigram and the difficulty of maintaining the machines donated by Britain led to a slow decline in attendance in the following years. This was offset by the gradual growth of the NZPAF, the eventual establishment of the RNZAF and the proliferation of aero clubs across the country. The airmen of the Great War were instrumental in maintaining this interwar air presence in New Zealand, and a number of senior positions in the RNZAF would be filled from their ranks when the world was once again at war.[25]

The experience and expertise acquired by the Great War airmen in 1914–18 proved invaluable in the Second World War. In New Zealand, Leonard Isitt as RNZAF chief of staff presided over 40,000 personnel, and a number of others, including Blackwell and Bannerman, commanded domestic air stations. Caldwell occupied a number of posts in New Zealand, then in India and England, and finished the war as an air commodore.

Outside of the RNZAF, half a dozen veterans of the Great War attained a very high rank in the RAF in the interwar years and during the Second World War. Three of them ended their careers as air vice-marshals: Cuthbert Maclean, Forster Maynard and Herbert Russell. At his retirement in 1940, Maclean was commanding 2 Group of Bomber Command; Maynard saw out the Second World War presiding over Coastal Command's 19 Group; and Russell was overseeing the administration of Flying Training Command in the early Cold War of 1949 when he retired.

Another two were promoted to air marshal. After commanding a squadron to considerable fame in Russia, Feilding-born Roderick Carr briefly stepped away from the RAF.[26] In 1927, following his three-year absence, Carr set the world record for non-stop long-distance flying in a Hawker Horsley bomber; the 3419-mile, 35-hour flight from England to India was marred only on its last stretch by a forced landing in the Strait of Hormuz. Unfortunately, as a bedraggled Carr and his navigator were extricating themselves from the blue waters off the coast of Persia, the long-distance flyer Charles Lindbergh was closing in on Paris after crossing the Atlantic Ocean. Carr's record was broken only hours after he had achieved it; Lindbergh eclipsed it by a mere 200 miles. During the Second World War Carr orchestrated the retreat of RAF units in the face of the 1940 German invasion of France, and he was the war's longest-serving commander of a bomber group.

Arthur Coningham rose to considerable fame as the commander of the Western Desert Air Force. He was knighted for his role in the great 1942 victory in the Second Battle of El Alamein. Then, in 1944, he oversaw one of the largest air armadas in the history of warfare: the tactical air forces at Normandy — a huge force numbering close to 100 squadrons. When the war ended he looked to have a bright future, but on 29 January 1948 Coningham disappeared en route to Bermuda; the airliner in which he was a passenger was lost short of its destination. His reputation was such that he featured on the front page of the *New York Times* two days later.[27]

Keith Park's star soared the highest. The Thames-born airman excelled between the wars and gained a number of prestigious postings before serving as Hugh Dowding's deputy in the RAF's Fighter Command; together they prepared the air defence of Britain. In April 1940, he was promoted to air vice-marshal and given Fighter Command's 11 Group. Charged with protecting London and southeast England, 11 Group was the frontline defence against the German Luftwaffe in the Battle of Britain. Drawing on all his Great War and interwar expertise, Park gave Adolf Hitler his first bloody nose of the war and ensured Britain would not be invaded. Lord Tedder, head of the RAF, later declared of Park: 'If ever any one man won the Battle of Britain, he did. I don't believe it is realised how much that one man, with his leadership, his calm judgement and his skill, did to save not only this country, but the world.'[28] The New Zealander went on to ensure the survival of the strategically important Mediterranean island of Malta in 1942–43. He then became air commander, South East Asia Command in early 1945, and his last promotion was to air chief marshal. Park had joined the air service in 1916 as a pilot and, 30 years later, ended his military career with the second-highest rank in the RAF.

The Second World War was not without personal losses for the Great War airmen. A number of their sons had entered the conflict with the RAF and RNZAF. Just as their own parents had fretted over their absence in the earlier war, now it was their turn to worry. Some of their fears were realised: at least four airmen lost sons in the Second World War air services, one of these in operations: 22-year-old Peter Kingsford was killed in a bombing raid on Tobruk in July 1942.[29] Peter had been working in his father's studio when war broke out.

I n the 1950s there was a changing of the guard as the Second World War veterans rose through the ranks; as Lord Tedder told Park at the end of his RAF career, 'the young must have their turn'.[30] The Great War men relinquished their commands and marched into old age and retirement. In 1960, to keep their Great War adventures alive, Isitt, Caldwell and Bannerman were instrumental in forming the New Zealand 1914–1918 Airmen's Association.[31] The annual meetings allowed the men to remember comrades lost, reflect wistfully on their favourite Great War 'bus', recount tales of close calls, and catch up on the comings and goings of their respective families, in particular the arrival of grandchildren. The gatherings, initially numbering as high as 200 attendees, were reported in local papers: readers were transported to another age when aviation was in its infancy and flying machines were constructed of wood,

fabric and wire; where men in small open-cockpit biplanes attacked menacing Zeppelins, bombed and strafed the 'Hun' and tangled with the Red Baron's Flying Circus.

As the years advanced, ill health and the passing of its members thinned out the Association. Keith 'Grid' Caldwell was there to the end. Over his flying career he had been the recipient of numerous accolades and awards — Military Cross, Distinguished Flying Cross and Bar, Belgian Croix de Guerre, CBE — and had miraculously cheated death on more than one occasion, but at 85 years of age on 28 November 1980 he passed away. When friend and English ace William Fry was asked his opinion of 'Grid', he uttered one word: 'Fearless.'[32]

The 1970 reunion of the New Zealand 1914–18 Airmen's Association. Seated in the front row sixth from left is Leonard Isitt. Standing in the middle row fifth from right is William Angus. Standing in the back row seventh, eleventh and fifteenth from left are Alfred Kingsford, Ronald Bannerman and Keith Caldwell, respectively.

ROLL OF HONOUR
AND MAPS

NEW ZEALAND AIRMEN WHO DIED IN THE FIRST WORLD WAR

Name	Rank	Squadron	Age	Memorial/Grave	Manner of Death	Date of Death
Abbott, Victor Stephen Henry	Second Lieutenant	7 Reserve Squadron, RFC	23	Upavon	Aircraft accident	15/09/1916
Adams, Francis Luke	Air Mechanic	30 Squadron, RFC	23	Baghdad	Died while POW	29/04/1916
Aimer, George Edmund Vernon	Second Lieutenant	11 Reserve Squadron, RFC	30	Ruislip	Aircraft accident	Aug–Nov 1916
Alderton, Trevor Dudley Hall	Second Lieutenant	26 Training Squadron, RAF	24	Narborough	Aircraft accident	16/06/1918
Allan, John Alexander Macdonald	Captain	2 School of Special Flying, RAF	23	Redcar	Aircraft accident	20/05/1918
Allen, Thomas Meredith	Cadet	9 Reserve Squadron, RFC	23	Ashtead, Surrey	Aircraft accident	27/04/1917
Anketell, Charles Edward	Second Lieutenant	206 Squadron, RAF	20	Longuenesse	Operational	11/05/1918
Arden, John Henry Morris	Lieutenant Colonel	3 Cadet Wing, RAF	43	Alexandria	Self-inflicted wounds	22/07/1918
Balcombe-Brown, Rainsford	Major	56 Squadron, RAF	23	Carnoy	Operational	2/05/1918
Barlow, Robin Tudor	Captain	52 Squadron, RAF	27	Ovillers-La Boisselle	Operational	30/07/1918
Barnes, David John	Second Lieutenant	13 Reserve Squadron, RFC	22	Dover	Aircraft accident	24/04/1917
Brain, Norman Leslie	Air Mechanic 1st Class	11 Squadron, RFC	24	Special Memorial Villers Station Cemetery	Operational	22/10/1916
Brett, Leslie Henry	Flight Sub-Lieutenant	F(?) Squadron, RNAS	24	Mudros	Aircraft accident	22/07/1917
Buchanan, William Archibald	Lieutenant	1 Reserve Squadron, RFC	21	Tidworth	Aircraft accident	7/06/1916
Bullock-Webster, Frank	Lieutenant	23 Training Squadron, RFC	31	Ypres	Operational	20/09/1917
Burn, William Wallace Allison	Lieutenant	Mesopotamia Flight, Indian Flying Corps/RFC	24	Basra Memorial	Operational	30/07/1915
Burton, Ernest Wilfred	Lieutenant	36 Training Squadron, RAF	25	Montrose	Aircraft accident	4/04/1918
Butterworth, Harold Winstone	Lieutenant	18 Squadron, RFC	21	Souchez	Operational	16/07/1916
Castle, Edward Errington	Lieutenant	46 Training Squadron, RFC	33	Catterick	Aircraft accident	12/08/1917
Cato, Geoffrey Walter Gavin Maidens	Second Lieutenant	6 Squadron, RFC	21	Lijssenthoek	Operational	6/11/1917

Clarke, Nathaniel Fuhrmann	Second Lieutenant	13 Training Squadron, RFC	31	Sutton Coldfield	Dover to Farnborough, Accident	1/06/1917
Coates, William Henry	Lieutenant	32 Squadron, RFC	29	Arras Memorial	Operational	22/07/1917
Cock, John Herbert	Second Lieutenant	60 Squadron, RFC	23	Beaumont	Operational	14/04/1917
Collett, Clive Franklyn	Captain	Armament Experimental Station, RFC	31	Edinburgh	Aircraft accident	23/12/1917
Cook, Alfred Burton	Captain	57 Squadron, RFC	21	Longuenesse	Operational	20/11/1917
Cooper, Herbert Ambrose	Captain	11 Squadron, RFC	32	Aubigny	Aircraft accident	21/06/1916
Courtney, John Classon	Lieutenant	4 Squadron, AFC	24	Arras & Australian Villers-Bretonneux memorials	Operational	4/04/1918
Couturier, Claude	Sergeant Pilot	Escadrille MF2, Aviation Militaire	38	Vauquois	Operational	1/09/1915
Culling, Thomas Grey	Flight Lieutenant	1 (Naval) Squadron, RNAS	21	Arras Memorial	Operational	8/06/1917
Dawson, Harold William	Second Lieutenant	19 Squadron, RFC	21	Bailleul	Operational	4/10/1917
Dennistoun, James Robert	Lieutenant	23 Squadron, RFC	33	Niederzwehren	Operational	9/08/1916
Fidler, Carrel Watt	Lieutenant	32 Kite Balloon Section, RFC	30	Trois-Arbres	Operational (ground duty)	19/05/1917
Fitzgerald, Roy James	Lieutenant	35 Squadron, RAF	27	Vignacourt	Operational	1/07/1918
Fitzherbert, Wyndham Waterhouse	Captain	55 Squadron, RFC	25	Arras Memorial	Operational	7/07/1917
Foubister, John Leask	Second Lieutenant	40 Training Squadron, RFC	28	Beddington	Aircraft accident	8/10/1917
Gardener, Charles Eric	Second Lieutenant	5 Squadron, RFC, RAF	19	Vis-en-Artois	Operational	2/09/1918
George, Leslie	Lieutenant	Artillery and Infantry Co-operation School, RAF	25	Hursley	Aircraft accident	12/05/1918
Gordon, Albert William	Second Lieutenant	32 Squadron, RFC	29	Étaples, France	Operational	12/08/1917
Greenwell, Arthur Robert	Flight Sub-Lieutenant	Cranwell, RNAS	20	Cranwell	Aircraft accident	20/10/1916
Hammond, Joseph Joel	Captain	British Air Mission, RAF	32	Indianapolis	En route	22/09/1918

Hinton, Francis Athol	Second Lieutenant	51 Training Depot Station, RAF	29	Shotwick	Aircraft accident	9/11/1918
Homer, Charles William	Second Lieutenant	25 Training Squadron, RFC	23	Euston, Suffolk	Aircraft accident	27/10/1917
Hyslop, Ninian Steele	Second Lieutenant	63 Squadron, RFC	31	Basra	Aircraft accident	30/10/1917
Johnstone, Godfrey Gleeson	Second Lieutenant	22 Squadron, RFC	22	Merville	Operational	30/01/1918
Johnstone, Melville	Captain	27 Squadron, RFC	29	Longuenesse	Operational	16/07/1917
Livingstone, Frederick James	Second Lieutenant	33 Squadron, RFC	25	Gainsborough	Aircraft accident	12/01/1918
Macdonald, Allan William	Second Lieutenant	1 Training Depot Squadron, RAF	24	Stamford	Aircraft accident	11/11/1918
Mahoney, Brian Gerald	Second Lieutenant	189 (Night) Training Squadron, RAF	29	Kensington, London	Aircraft accident	3/09/1918
Masters, George	Second Lieutenant	11 Squadron, RFC	26	Arras Memorial	Operational	3/04/1917
Matheson, Harry MacKay	Second Lieutenant	67 (Australian) Squadron, RFC	30	Gaza	Exposure	24/12/1917
McGill, Charles Percy	Mechanic	New Zealand Flying School	18	Auckland	Workshop accident	23/06/1917
McKenzie, William Seaforth	Lieutenant	101 Squadron, RFC	21	Hazebrouck	Operational	26/01/1918
Millward, Kenneth Henry	Flight Sub-Lieutenant	1 (Naval) Squadron, RNAS	20	Pont-du-Hem	Operational	7/07/1917
Mitchell, William George	Second Lieutenant	School of Instruction, RFC	34	Beddington	Aircraft accident	23/03/1918
Myhill, Alfred William	Air Mechanic 2nd Class	3 Stores Depot, RFC	33	Portsmouth	Natural causes	4/12/1917
Neill, Lyonel Clare Fyans	Air Mechanic 3rd Class	RFC	23	At sea	Natural causes	30/10/1917
Nicol, Hector	Lieutenant	HQ, 33rd Wing, RAF	32	Stratford-sub-Castle	Motor vehicle accident	15/10/1918
Nielsen, Peter	Lieutenant	84 Squadron, RAF	32	Heath Cemetery, Harbonnières & Arras Memorial	Operational	18/06/1918
Parsons, Forrest Gale	Second Lieutenant	7 Squadron, RFC	34	Arras Memorial	Operational	26/10/1916
Pilkington, Stanley Howard	Second Lieutenant	66 Training Squadron, RFC	28	Brookwood in Woking	Aircraft accident	24/10/1917
Powell, George Aubyn	Second Lieutenant	25 Reserve Squadron, RFC	27	Bishop's Hatfield	Motor vehicle accident	7/12/1916
Reeves, Fabian Pember	Flight Lieutenant	6 (Naval) Squadron, RNAS	21	Arras Memorial	Operational	6/06/1917
Reid, John Laurie	Second Lieutenant	22 Squadron, RFC	22	Couin	Operational	16/07/1916

Richards, Henry Stokes	Second Lieutenant	1 (Observers) School of Aerial Gunnery, RAF	24	Shorncliffe	Aircraft accident	1/08/1918
Richardson, Stuart Herbert	Second Lieutenant	3 Squadron, RAF	18	Sains-les-Marquion	Operational	23/09/1918
Russell, Francis Gerald	Second Lieutenant	21 Squadron, RFC	28	Flers	Operational	28/01/1917
Russell, Lawrence Dobrée	Second Lieutenant	7 Squadron, RFC	18	Heilly	Operational	15/09/1916
Sharland, Frederic James	Second Lieutenant	23 Squadron, RFC	34	Arras Memorial	Operational	24/10/1917
Sloss, James Duncan	Second Lieutenant	108 Squadron, RAF	21	Terlincthun	Operational	23/11/1918
Solomon, Hubert Philip	Second Lieutenant	33 Squadron, RFC	34	Gainsborough	Operational	19/10/1917
Spence, Daniel George	Cadet	Had yet to formally enrol in RAF	20	At sea	Natural causes	3/09/1918
Spragg, Wesley Neal	Lieutenant	School of Armament, RFC	23	Cairo	Aircraft accident	1/01/1918
Steele, Thomas Lancaster	Second Lieutenant	111 Squadron, RAF	27	Jerusalem Memorial	Operational	10/04/1918
Talbot, Arthur Sydney	Lieutenant	198 Depot Squadron, RFC	27	Rochford	Aircraft accident	27/09/1917
Talbot, William Caithness	Second Lieutenant	Central Flying School, RAF	25	Upavon	Aircraft accident	20/07/1918
Vavasour, Rudolph Dunstan	Captain	1 Reserve Squadron, RFC	23	Fulham, London	Natural causes	16/01/1917
Veale, Allan Adolphus	Second Lieutenant	19 Squadron, RFC	24	Bailleul, France	Aircraft accident	22/01/1918
Waud, Philip Courtenay	Air Mechanic 1st Class	55 Kite Balloon Section, RFC	18/19	Chatby Memorial, Alexandria	Operational	31/12/1917
White, Melville Arthur	Second Lieutenant	24 Squadron, RFC	24	Jeancourt	Operational	23/04/1917

Adapted with permission from Errol Martyn, *For Your Tomorrow: A record of New Zealanders who have died while serving with the RNZAF and Allied Air Services since 1915*, vols 1–3 (Christchurch: Volplane Press, 1998, 1999 and 2008).

WESTERN FRONT 1914–16

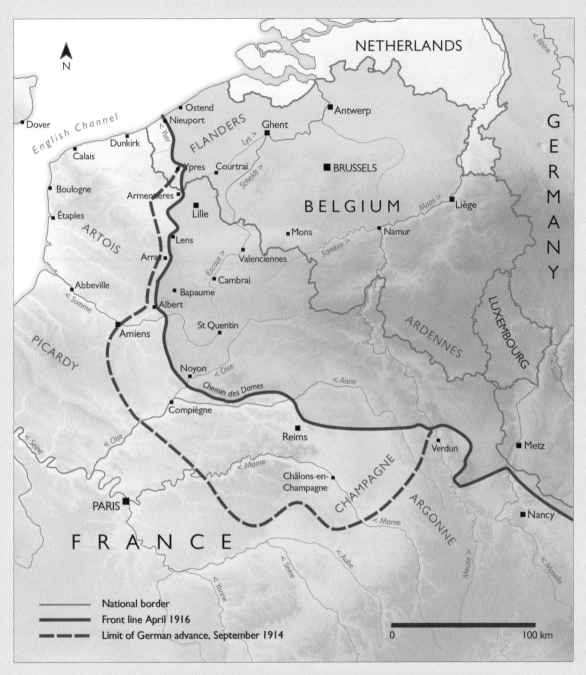

Above The German advance into France in August 1914 was finally halted in the second week of September on the Marne, only 43 miles short of Paris. The ensuing 'race to the sea' created a long line of fortified trenches which terminated at the northern French coastline. In the early months of the conflict, aircraft were something of an unknown quantity in warfare, but by 1916 they had firmly established themselves as vital components in the great arm wrestle on the Western Front: in reconnaissance, contact patrols, artillery cooperation, photography, bombing and aerial combat work.

GALLIPOLI

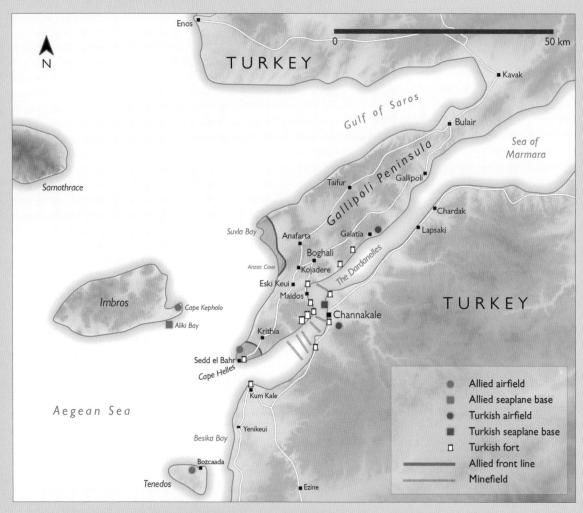

Enos

TURKEY

Gulf of Saros

Kavak

Bulair

Sea of Marmara

Gallipoli Peninsula

Samothrace

Taifur

Gallipoli

Suvla Bay

Anafarta

Galatia

Chardak

Boghali

Lapsaki

Anzac Cove

Kojadere

Eski Keui

Maidos

The Dardanelles

TURKEY

Imbros

Cape Kephalo

Channakale

Aliki Bay

Krithia

Sedd el Bahr

Cape Helles

Kum Kale

Aegean Sea

Yenikeui

Besika Bay

Bozcaada

Tenedos

Ezine

0   50 km

	Allied airfield
	Allied seaplane base
	Turkish airfield
	Turkish seaplane base
	Turkish fort
	Allied front line
	Minefield

Above While New Zealand troops endured the increasing deprivations and horrors of Anzac Cove in 1915, many airmen lived away from the front lines in relative comfort on the islands of Imbros and Tenedos. From here their aeroplanes conducted bombing and reconnaissance flights across the Gallipoli Peninsula, attacking enemy positions and gathering intelligence on Turkish dispositions and movements. Some NZEF soldiers who saw these aircraft criss-crossing the peninsula were inspired to seek a place in the flying service, but only a few succeeded.

Opposite Britain had a strategic interest in the Persian Gulf and Mesopotamia (modern-day Iraq) before war was declared with the Ottoman Empire: oil refineries in the region supplied the British Navy. By November 1914 British and Indian troops had taken Basra, and in the following year pushed north up the Tigris towards Baghdad. Though few in number, the aircraft at the disposal of British Forces were able to reconnoitre vast tracts of the region, much of which had yet to be mapped. The challenging climate, the prevalence of disease and roaming bands of Arab tribesmen were unrelenting threats to the health and wellbeing of the airmen.

MESOPOTAMIA

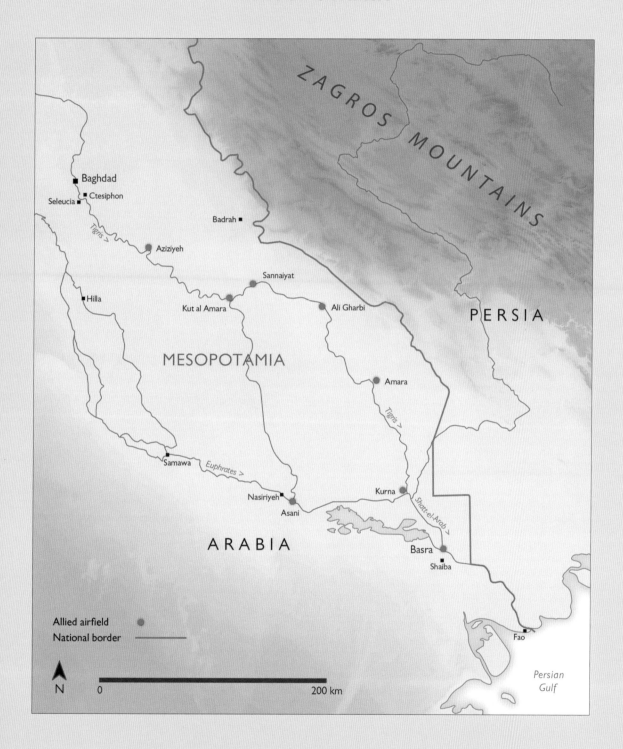

ZAGROS MOUNTAINS

Baghdad

Seleucia • Ctesiphon

Badrah ■

Tigris >

Aziziyeh

Sannaiyat

Hilla

Kut al Amara

Ali Gharbi

PERSIA

MESOPOTAMIA

Amara

Tigris >

Samawa

Euphrates >

Kurna

Nasiriyeh
Asani

Shatt-el-Arab >

ARABIA

Basra
Shaiba

Allied airfield
National border

N

0   200 km

Fao

*Persian
Gulf*

HOME DEFENCE AND THE NORTH SEA

Allied airfield /seaplane station •
German airfield •
RNAS air patrol grid ———
National border ———
Front line 1918 ———

RNAS Spider Web

N

Burgh Castle   Great Yarmouth

Covehithe

Orfordness

Martlesham Heath

ESSEX   Ipswich
Harwich   Felixstowe

Hertford   Little Wigborough
London   North   Goldhanger
Colney   Weald   Woodham
    Bassett   Mortimer
Woodford   Stow Maries
Hendon   Hainault Farm   Rochford
    Sutton's Farm   Southend
LONDON
Northolt   Ft. Victoria
Joyce Green   Eastchurch   Westgate   Margate
Croydon   Farningham   Manston   Ramsgate
Kenley   Biggin Hill   Detling   Canterbury   Bekesbourne
    Throwley
    Harrietsham   Wye   Walmer
Chiddingstone   Ashford   Hythe   Dover
Causeway   Lympne   Folkstone

KENT
ENGLAND

Telscombe
Cliffs

NORTH SEA

English Channel

NETHERLANDS

Zeebrugge
Nieuwmunster   Houtave
Ostend   Bruges
Mariakerke   Ghistelles
Nieuport   Antwerp
Leffrinckhoucke   Furnes   Mariakerke   Oostakker
Dunkirk   Frontier   St.Denis   Ghent
    Brag Dunes   Thielt   Westrem   Melle-Gontrode
Petit   St Pol   Handschoote   Schelde-
Synthe   Coudekerque   Windeke
Calais   Yser
    Abeele   Thielt
Clairmarais   Droglandt   Ypres
    St Marie   Menin   BRUSSELS
Boisdinghem   Cappel   Bailleul
Boulogne   St Omer   Armentières   BELGIUM
Drionville   Serny   Liettres
Reclinghem   Estrée   Lomme
    Blanche   Auchel   Haubourdin
Etaples   Bruay
FRANCE

0   100 km

Above The Home Defence units were established to combat German bombing of England's towns and cities and the enemy submarines that threatened shipping. The high-flying Zeppelins and heavy bombers, often operating under cover of darkness, were difficult to locate and dangerous to engage. A patrol grid resembling a spider web was established in an area of the North Sea known for its intense submarine traffic. Anti-submarine patrols by British seaplanes and airships were extremely demanding.

Opposite By early 1918 the vast losses in human life of the previous years had resulted in only modest territorial gains, and victory for either side seemed as elusive as ever. The Germans launched a massive Spring Offensive in a final push to win the war before the full impact of America's entry into the conflict could be felt. From their vast network of airfields, men of the British air service took off to meet the onslaught.

WESTERN FRONT 1918

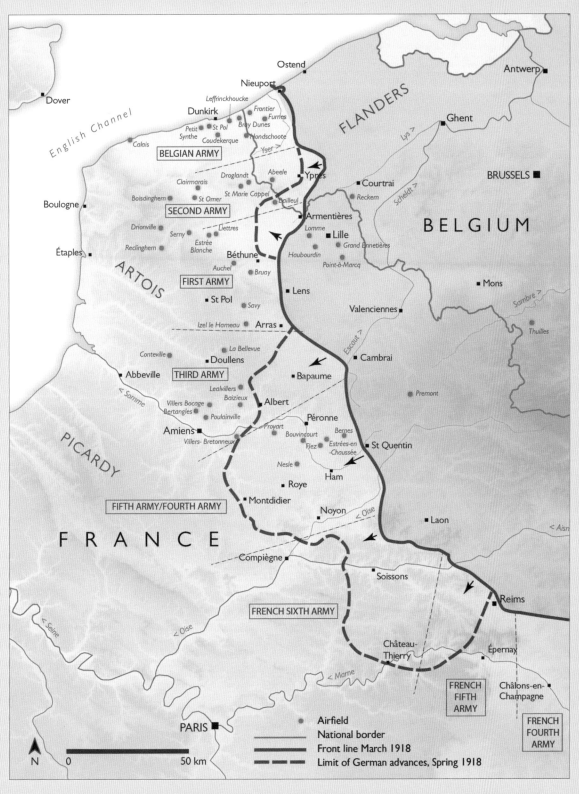

English Channel

Dover

Ostend
Nieuport
Leffrinckhoucke
Dunkirk
Frontier
Furnes
Petit St Pol   Bray Dunes
Synthe   Coudekerque   Hondschoote
Calais

FLANDERS

Antwerp

Ghent

Lys >

BELGIAN ARMY

Yser >

Droglandt   Abeele
Clairmarais   Ypres
Boisdinghem   St Omer   St Marie Cappel
Bailleul
SECOND ARMY
Drionville   Liettres
Serny   Armentières
Reclinghem   Estrée   Lomme
Blanche   Lille
Béthune   Haubourdin
FIRST ARMY   Auchel   Bruay

Boulogne

Étaples

ARTOIS

St Pol   Savy
Lens

Izel le Hameau   Arras

Conteville   La Bellevue
Doullens
Abbeville   THIRD ARMY
Lealvillers
Villers Bocage   Baizieux
Bertangles   Poulainville
Amiens   Albert
Villers- Bretonneux

PICARDY

FRANCE

FIFTH ARMY/FOURTH ARMY
Montdidier
Roye
Nesle   Ham
Proyart   Bernes
Bouvincourt   Estrées-en
Flez   -Chaussée
Péronne   St Quentin
Bapaume
Premont
Cambrai

Escaut >

< Somme

Courtrai
Reckem
Grand Ennetières
Point-à-Marcq

BRUSSELS

BELGIUM

Mons

Valenciennes

Thuilles
Sambre >

Noyon   < Oise
Compiègne

FRENCH SIXTH ARMY

< Seine   < Oise

Laon   < Aisn

Soissons

Reims

Château-
Thierry   Épernay

< Marne

FRENCH
FIFTH
ARMY

Châlons-en-
Champagne

FRENCH
FOURTH
ARMY

PARIS

N   0   50 km

- Airfield
- National border
- Front line March 1918
- Limit of German advances, Spring 1918

NOTES

ABBREVIATIONS

AFMNZ	Air Force Museum of New Zealand
AJHR	*Appendix to the Journals of the House of Representatives*
ANZ	Archives New Zealand
ATL	Alexander Turnbull Library
AWM	Australian War Memorial
AWMM	Auckland War Memorial Museum
CM	Canterbury Museum
IWM	Imperial War Museum
MOTAT	Museum of Transport and Technology
NAA	National Archives of Australia
NZPD	*New Zealand Parliamentary Debates*
RAFM	Royal Air Force Museum, Hendon
TNA	The National Archives, London

INTRODUCTION

1   The best chapter devoted to the subject is Errol Martyn, *Swift to the Sky: New Zealand's military aviation history* (Auckland: Penguin Viking, 2010), pp. 24–55. For recent contributions see Ian McGibbon, *New Zealand's Western Front Campaign* (Auckland: Bateman, 2016), pp. 238–49; Adam Claasen, 'From Artilleryman to Airman: Keith Park' in *Experience of a Lifetime: People, personalities and leaders in the First World War*, John Crawford, David Littlewood & James Watson (eds) (Auckland: Massey University Press, 2016), pp. 166–82; Simon Moody, 'Kiwis Rising: New Zealanders and the war in the air', in *Experience of a Lifetime*, pp. 194–219.

2   A. R. Kingsford, *Night Raiders of the Air: Being the experiences of a night flying pilot, who raided Hunland on many dark nights during the War* (London: Greenhill, 1988; first published 1930). The only other published work by a participant in the war was Alan Scott's short history of 60 Squadron: A. J. Scott, *Sixty Squadron*, R.A.F. 1916–1919 (London: Greenhill, 1990; first published 1920).

3   Larry R. Hill, *An Aviation Bibliography for New Zealand* (Auckland: Larry R. Hill, 2009), pp. 88–176.

4   G. H. Cunningham, *Mac's Memoirs: The flying life of Squadron-Leader McGregor* (Dunedin: Reed, 1937), pp. 23–72; Vincent Orange, *Park: The biography of Air Chief Marshal Sir Keith Park GCB, KBE, MC, DFC, DCL* (London: Grub Street, 2001), pp. 6–37; Vincent Orange, *Coningham: A biography of Air Marshal Sir Arthur Coningham KCB, KBE, DSO, MC, DFC, AFC* (London: Methuen, 1990), pp. 12–32.

5   Among these are an excellent series of short magazine articles by Paul Sortehaug on prominent aces; for example, 'Clive Franklyn Collett', *Pacific Wings* 81, no. 8 (2013), pp. 48–53 and 'Major Arthur Coningham', *Pacific Wings* 81, no. 10 (2013), pp. 50–5. An abridged version of Sutcliffe's MA thesis on Ronald Bannerman was published by Aviation Historical Society of New Zealand: Devon Sutcliffe, with Errol Martyn, 'Bannerman of Gore', *Aviation Historical Society of New Zealand Journal* 48, no. 2 (December 2005), pp. 28–48; 'Sustained Effort: The life of Sir Leonard Isitt' (PhD thesis, Massey University, 2011).

6   The most recent additions to this genre are publications looking at Donald Harkness and the Montgomerie brothers, Seton and Oswald, and their remarkable mother Annie: Bruce W. Harkness, Jeffery T. Harkness, Timothy D. Harkness, Christopher W. Harkness & Donald E. Harkness, *A World*

War 1 Adventure: The life and times of RNAS Bomber Pilot Donald E. Harkness (Bloomington, Indiana: AuthorHouse, 2014); Susanna Montgomerie Norris with Anna Rogers, *Annie's War: A New Zealand woman and her family in England, 1916–19* (Dunedin: Otago University Press, 2014).

7   Errol W. Martyn, *For Your Tomorrow: A record of New Zealanders who have died while serving with the RNZAF and Allied Air Services since 1915, vol. 1: Fates 1915–1942* (Christchurch: Volplane, 1998), and V*ol. 3: Biographies & Appendices* (Christchurch: Volplane, 2008).

8   Trevor Henshaw, *The Sky Their Battlefield II: Air fighting and air casualties of the Great War* (High Barnet, Hertfordshire: Fetubi, 2014).

9   These parameters were adapted from Martyn, *For Your Tomorrow, vol. 1*, p. 15.

10   *Press*, 27 December 1911.

11   Matthew Wright, *Kiwi Air Power* (Auckland: Reed, 1998), p. 12; Ross Ewing & Ross Macpherson, *The History of New Zealand Aviation* (Auckland: Heinemann, 1986), p. 55.

12   Errol Martyn to author, 25 May and 21 July 2017. Cf. Ian McGibbon (ed.), *The Oxford Companion to New Zealand Military History* (Auckland: Oxford University Press, 2000), p. 7.

13   Christopher Shores, Norman Franks & Russell Guest, *Above the Trenches: A complete record of the fighter units of the British Empire air forces, 1915–1920* (London: Grub Street, 1990).

CHAPTER ONE: THE PIONEERS

1   One of the first iterations of this oft-told story appeared in 1926 in the book *War Birds,* based on the diaries of 74 Squadron airman John Grinder and then retold in slightly different form in 1954 in *Tiger Squadron* by Ira Jones. Both authors have Caldwell either entirely out of the cockpit or with one leg in the cockpit and another on the wing when he got his machine under control at 8000 ft. This suggests he flew the plane in this manner all the way down before his crash. Caldwell categorically dismissed this idea in a letter published in 1980. I have tried to stay true to Caldwell's corrections of the 'embellished' story. Caldwell's letter does not preclude his climbing out onto the wing just before he leapt. See: John Grinder, *War Birds: Diary of an unknown aviator* (Sydney: Cornstalk, 1928), pp. 204–5; Ira Jones, *Tiger Squadron: The Story of 74 Squadron, R.A.F., in two world wars* (London: A. H. Allen, 1954), p. 167; cf. Ira Jones, *An Air Fighter's Scrapbook* (London: Greenhill, 1990, first published 1938), pp. 76–7; Marvin L. Skelton, *Callahan: The last war bird* (Manhattan, KS: Air Force Historical Foundation, 1980), pp. 95–9.

1A   Henry F. Wigram, *Canterbury (N.Z.) Aviation Company: The first hundred pilots* (Christchurch: Canterbury [N.Z.] Aviation Company, 1918), pp. 1–2; Margaret McClure, *Fighting Spirit: 75 years of the RNZAF* (Auckland: Random House, 2012), p. 18.

2   *Evening Post*, 20 September 1909.

3   Errol Martyn, *Swift to the Sky: New Zealand's military aviation history* (Auckland: Penguin Viking, 2010), p. 15.

4   *Waihi Daily Telegraph*, 22 May 1909.

5   *Wairarapa Age*, 23 January 1909.

6   Henry Wigram, *NZPD*, vol. 146, 1909, pp. 14–15.

7   Martyn, *Swift to the Sky*, pp. 16–17.

8   George Richardson's report on coastal defence, ANZ AAYS 8652 AD19 10/68/1.

9   Ibid.

10   *AJHR*, section H.19, 1912.

11   William Wallace Alison Burn, Army General Staff, ANZ AABK 7291 W5573/5. Burn replaced Arthur Henry Piper of Oamaru. Piper's aviation career was cut short because of 'adverse reports on him professionally and generally'. See Arthur Henry Piper, Military Personnel file, ANZ AABK 18805 W5550/27 0093174; Errol Martyn, *A Passion for Flight: New Zealand aviation before the Great War, vol. 3: The Joe Hammond story and military beginnings 1910–1914* (Christchurch: Volplane, 2013), pp. 115–18.

12 Christopher Draper, *The Mad Major: The autobiography of Major Christopher Draper DSC* (Letchworth, Herts: Air Review, 1962), p. 36.

13 Martyn, *A Passion for Flight: vol. 3*, p. 118.

14 *Evening Post*, 1 July 1913.

15 Martyn, *A Passion for Flight, vol. 3*, p. 125.

16 Ibid., p. 14; Ross Ewing & Ross Macpherson, *The History of New Zealand Aviation* (Auckland: Heinemann, 1986), p. 44.

17 *Blue and White: The Magazine of St Patrick's College*, Wellington, vol. IX, no. 1 (1918), p.7.

18 Martyn, *A Passion for Flight, vol. 3*, pp. 16–17.

19 Ibid., p. 17.

20 Michael Molkentin, *Australia and the War in the Air* (Melbourne: Oxford University Press, 2014), p. 7.

21 *Western Australian*, 4 January 1911.

22 *Argus*, 4 March 1911.

23 *Riverine Herald* (NSW), 3 March 1911.

24 *Goulburn Evening Post* (NSW), 6 May 1911.

25 Molkentin, *Australia and the War in the Air*, p. 7.

26 *Sun*, 3 May 1911.

27 *Sydney Morning Herald*, 4 May 1911.

28 *Clarence and Richmond Examiner*, 4 May 1911.

29 *The Age*, 4 May 1911.

30 Australian papers were periodically raising concern over the advances being made in other countries: *Daily Advertiser*, 24 June 1911; Martyn, *A Passion for Flight, vol. 3*, pp. 50–51.

31 *Riverine Herald*, 6 March 1911.

32 Martyn, *A Passion for Flight, vol. 3*, p. 56.

33 *Otago Daily Times*, 6 September 1913.

34 *Evening Post*, 19 November 1913.

35 Errol Martyn, *A Passion for Flight, vol. 1: Ideas, first flight attempts and the aeronauts 1868–1909* (Christchurch: Volplane, 2012), p. 11.

36 The much cited 31 March 1903 heavier-than-air flight for Richard Pearse is unsupported by the evidence. For the best examination of the 'Pearse 1903 myth' see Martyn, *A Passion for Flight, vol. 1*, pp. 151–6. Cf. Ewing & Macpherson, *The History of New Zealand Aviation*, pp. 40–3.

37 Martyn, *A Passion for Flight, vol. 1*, p. 127.

38 Leo White, *Wingspread: The pioneering of aviation in New Zealand* (Auckland: Unity, 1941), p. 23.

39 David Mulgan, *The Kiwi's First Wings: The story of the Walsh Brothers and the New Zealand Flying School, 1910–24* (Wellington: Wingford, 1960), p. 19.

40 White, *Wingspread*, p. 23.

41 Mulgan, *The Kiwi's First Wings*, pp. 24–5.

42 *New Zealand Herald*, 10 August 1911. Unfortunately popular histories of early aviation in New Zealand have uncritically followed Mulgan's incorrect dating of this event to 5 February; see Mulgan, *The Kiwi's First Wings*, p. 21. Contemporary newspaper accounts support 9 February 1911.

CHAPTER TWO: FLYING FEVER

1 *New Zealand Herald*, 21 April 1913.

2 *Auckland Star*, 21 April 1913.

3   *Dominion*, 21 April 1913.

4   *Sun*, 6 March 1914.

5   *Auckland Star*, 23 April 1913; *New Zealand Herald*, 24 April 1913.

6   *Dominion*, 26 April 1913.

7   *Dominion*, 6 June 1913.

8   *Evening Post*, 19 November 1913.

9   *Star*, 18 November 1913.

10 *Dominion*, 17 November 1913.

11 Errol Martyn, *A Passion for Flight: New Zealand aviation before the Great War, vol. 2: Aero clubs, aeroplanes, aviators and aeronauts 1910–1914* (Christchurch: Volplane, 2012), pp. 75–82, 99–124.

12 Ibid., pp. 99–100.

13 Ibid., pp. 116–17.

14 *Dominion*, 17 November 1913.

15 The date of his appointment is unknown but it appears that he was under some kind of contract by 11 December 1913 at the latest; see Errol Martyn, *A Passion for Flight, vol 3: The Joe Hammond Story and Military Beginnings 1910–1914* (Christchurch: Volplane, 2013), p. 130.

16 *Dominion*, 15 November 1913.

17 *Star*, 18 November 1913.

18 *Observer*, 31 January 1914.

19 *Evening Post*, 22 January 1914.

20 *New Zealand Herald*, 22 January 1914.

21 James Scotland to R. Heaton Rhodes (Acting Minister of Defence), 24 April 1913. ANZ AD19 34/106/9; James William Humphreys Scotland, Personnel File, ANZ AABK 18805 W5674/15 42521.

22 Letter: R. Heaton Rhodes (Acting Minister of Defence) to James Scotland 5 May 1913, ANZ AD19 34/106/9.

23 *Mataura Ensign*, 21 February 1914.

24 E. F. Harvie, *Venture the Far Horizon: The pioneer long-distance flights in New Zealand* (Wellington: Whitcombe & Tombs, 1966), p. 37.

25 Ibid., p. 37.

26 Ibid., pp. 41–2.

27 *Timaru Herald*, 5 March 1914.

28 *Timaru Herald*, 7 March 1914.

29 *Otago Daily Times*, 9 March 1914.

30 *Sun*, 16 March 1914; *Press*, 14 March 1914.

31 *Sun*, 14 March 1914; Martyn, *A Passion for Flight, vol. 2*, p. 275.

32 Harvie, *Venture the Far Horizon*, pp. 55–6.

33 *Sun*, 14 March 1914.

34 *Marlborough Express*, 17 March 1914.

35 Harvie, *Venture the Far Horizon*, p. 58.

36 *Evening Post*, 23 March 1914; Martyn, *A Passion for Flight, vol. 2*, p. 276.

37 *Evening Post*, 26 March 1914.

38 Martyn, *A Passion for Flight, vol. 2*, p. 280.

39 *Evening Post*, 26 March 1914.

40 *Colonist*, 26 March 1914.

41   Harvie, *Venture the Far Horizon*, p. 63.

42   *Dominion*, 27 March 1914.

43   *Dominion*, 28 March 1914.

44   *Dominion*, 27 March 1914.

45   Harvie, *Venture the Far Horizon*, p. 65.

46   *Hawera and Normanby Star*, 7 March 1914.

47   *Timaru Herald*, 14 March 1914.

48   *Sun*, 6 March 1914.

49   *Sun*, 3 July 1914.

50   Francis Athol Hinton, Application for Employment, New Zealand Defence Force (Aviation). ANZ AD19 34/106/10.

51   Clifford Clapcott Barclay, Application for Employment, New Zealand Defence Force (Aviation). ANZ AD19 30/95/302.

52   Raymond Curtis, Application for Employment, New Zealand Defence Force (Aviation). ANZ AD19 30/95/306.

53   Peter Thomas Hayward, Application for Employment, New Zealand Defence Force (Aviation). ANZ AD19 34/106/18.

54   Francis Hammond, Application for Employment, New Zealand Defence Force (Aviation). ANZ AD19 29/95/24/8.

55   Frank Ernest Cowlin, Application for Employment, New Zealand Defence Force (Aviation). ANZ AD19 31/95/325.

56   Cf. *Star*, 4 February 1914.

57   The claim that *Britannia* was grounded because of Hammond taking a woman on a flight ahead of prominent exhibition organisers is unlikely: see Martyn, *A Passion for Flight, vol. 3*, pp. 139–40.

58   *Lyttelton Times*, 26 January 1914.

59   Martyn, *A Passion for Flight, vol. 3*, p. 141.

60   *AJHR*, section H.19, 1914; Martyn, *A Passion for Flight, vol. 3*, pp. 111–12.

61   *Evening Star*, 23 June 1914.

62   *Otago Daily Times*, 15 April 1914.

CHAPTER THREE: LUCKY DEVILS

1   *Dominion*, 26 September 1914.

2   *Star*, 28 September 1914.

3   Errol Martyn, *A Passion for Flight: New Zealand aviation before the Great War, vol 3: The Joe Hammond Story and Military Beginnings 1910–1914* (Christchurch: Volplane, 2013), p. 167.

4   Joseph Joel Hammond, Service Record, TNA WO 339/40931.

5   Martyn, *A Passion for Flight, vol. 3*, p. 151.

6   Hugh Lambert Reilly, Liddle Collection, University of Leeds LIDDLE/WW1/AIR 259.

7   British Library, India Office Collection, 173/23, IoR/L/MIL/7/7718, in Martyn, *A Passion for Flight, vol. 3*, p. 157.

8   http://1914-1918.invisionzone.com/forums/index.php?showtopic=169994. Retrieved 20 January 2016.

9   Nigel Steel & Peter Hart, *Tumult in the Clouds: The British experience of the war in the air, 1914–1918* (London: Hodder & Stoughton, 1997), p. 27.

10   Ibid., pp. 27–8.

11 John Yoxall, 'No 4 Squadron RAF: The history of one of our most famous units', *Flight*, 23 February 1950, p. 256.

12 Walter Raleigh, *The War in the Air, vol. 1* (Oxford: Clarendon, 1922), p. 307.

13 Errol Martyn, *Swift to the Sky: New Zealand's military aviation history* (Auckland: Penguin Viking, 2010), p. 29; 'History of No 4 Squadron', http://www.rafjever.org/4squadhistory1.htm. Retrieved 19 January 2016.

14 Raleigh, *War in the Air*, pp. 294–5.

15 K. P. A. Atkinson, Diary, 17 September 1914. Private Collection, http://1914-1918.invisionzone.com/forums/index.php?showtopic=169994. Retrieved 20 January 2016.

16 Martyn, *Swift to the Sky*, p. 29.

17 K. P. A. Atkinson, Diary, 17 September 1914. Private Collection, http://1914-1918.invisionzone.com/forums/index.php?showtopic=169994. Retrieved 20 January 2016.

18 Director of Equipment and Stores to Quartermaster General, Headquarters, 14 October 1914. Correspondence regarding Aeroplane *Britannia*, ANZ AALJ W639 483/3.

19 Glyn Harper, *Johnny Enzed: The New Zealand soldier in the First World War, 1914–1918* (Auckland: Exisle, 2016), p. 94.

20 Ibid.

21 Ibid.

22 Ibid., p. 95.

23 Melville Arthur White to Family, 20 October 1914, ATL MSY-7036.

24 Christopher Pugsley, *Gallipoli: The New Zealand story* (Wellington: Reed, 1998), pp. 63–4.

25 Robert Sloss to James Sloss, 30 Sept 1915, AFMNZ.

26 Robert Sloss to James Sloss, 20 October 1915, AFMNZ.

27 Melville Arthur White to Family, 20 October 1914. ATL MSY-7036.

28 Pugsley, *Gallipoli*, p. 67.

29 Melville Arthur White to Family, 22 November 1914. ATL MSY-7036.

30 Ronald Burns Bannerman, Photographic Collection, AFMNZ.

31 Melville Arthur White to Family, 22 December 1914, ATL MSY-7036.

32 Harper, *Johnny Enzed*, p. 103.

33 Melville Arthur White to Family, 27 October 1914, ATL MSY-7036.

34 Melville Arthur White to Family, 22 November 1914, ATL MSY-7036.

35 Arthur Skinner, Diary, 2 December 1914, AFMNZ.

36 Air Historical Branch, 30 Squadron History, p. 1, TNA AIR 1/691/21/20/30.

37 Ibid., p. 5.

38 Ibid.; John F. Hamilton, *Flat Out: The story of 30 Squadron, Royal Air Force* (Tunbridge Wells, Kent: Air-Britain publication, 2002), p. 12.

39 Air Historical Branch, 30 Squadron History, p. 6, TNA AIR 1/691/21/20/30.

40 A. C. Temperley, Narrative of Fighting on Canal, 3 February 1915. ANZ ACID 17625 ZMR 2/1/12.

41 Cecil Malthus, *Anzac: A retrospect*, p. 26, quoted in Harper, *Johnny Enzed*, p. 164.

42 Hamilton, *Flat Out*, p. 14

43 Arthur Hirst Skinner, Diary, 7 February 1915. AFMNZ.

44 Hamilton, *Flat Out*, p. 12.

45 Air Historical Branch, 30 Squadron History, p. 6, TNA AIR 1/691/21/20/30.

46 Ibid., p. 7; Martyn, *Swift to the Sky*, p. 30.

CHAPTER FOUR: ABOVE THE FRAY

1   Melville White to Brethren, 21 July 1915, ATL MSY-7036.

2   Arthur Hirst Skinner, Diary, 25 April 1915, AFMNZ.

3   Melville White, 21 August 1915, ATL MSY-7036.

4   Arthur Hirst Skinner, Diary, 25 April 1915, AFMNZ.

5   *Press*, 15 June 1915.

6   Mills to Mother, 26 May 1915, Gallipoli, MOTAT 14/004/041.

7   Damien Fenton, *New Zealand and the First World War, 1914–1919* (Auckland: Penguin, 2015), p. 21.

8   *Cambridge Edition*, 23 April 1990.

9   Melville White to Brethren, ATL MSY-7036, 21 July 1915.

10   Ibid.

11   Henry Peter Rasmussen, Tape 236, Transcript, Liddle Collection, University of Leeds LIDDLE/WW1/ ANZAC/NZ/REC/55.

12   Ibid.

12A Melville White to Brethren, 18 January 1916, ATL MSY-7036.

13   Ibid.

14   Hugh Dolan, *Gallipoli Air War: The unknown story of the fight for the skies over Gallipoli* (Sydney: Macmillan, 2013), pp. 370–1.

15   Ibid., p. 383.

16   Melville White to Brethren, 4 October 1915, ATL MSY-7036.

17   Captain David Ferguson, *The History of the Canterbury Regiment, NZEF 1914–1919* (Auckland: Whitcombe & Tombs, 1921), p. 52.

18   Charles Rumney Samson, *Fights and Flights* (Nashville: Battery Press, 1930), p. 224.

19   William Melville Angus, Personnel File, ANZ WW11 610771, AABK 18805 W5937 8/0361042.

20   *Evening Star*, 23 August 1919; Samson, *Fights and Flights*, p. 224.

21   Samson, *Fights and Flights*, p. 280.

22   Donald Clappen, Sound Recording, IWM Reels 3 & 4. SR 9, in Nigel Steel & Peter Hart, *Tumult in the Clouds: The British experience of the war in the air, 1914–1918* (London: Hodder & Stoughton, 1997), pp. 77–8.

23   James Dennistoun, n.d., James Dennistoun Collection, CM.

24   Devon Sutcliffe, 'Sustained effort: The life of Sir Leonard Isitt' (PhD thesis, Massey University, 2011), p. 39.

25   Keith Park, Tape 240, Transcript, Liddle Collection, University of Leeds, LIDDLE/WW1/AIR/234.

26   G. H. Cunningham, *Mac's Memoirs: The flying life of Squadron-Leader McGregor* (Dunedin: Reed, 1937), p. 23.

27   William Coates to Mother and Sisters, 6 September 1915, Coates Collection, Ruatuna, Matakohe.

28   Denis Winter, *The First of the Few: Fighter pilots of the First World War* (Harmondsworth: Penguin, 1983), p. 20.

29   Ibid., pp. 25–6.

30   Coates to Mother and Sisters, 6 September 1915, Coates Collection, Ruatuna, Matakohe.

31   *New Zealand Herald*, 12 January 1918.

32   In Memory WNS, Dedication of Monument in Kaitarakihi (Memorial Park), Auckland, ATL Scrapbook relating to early British military aviation (II), Brent Mackrell, fl 2012: papers relating to military history, MSZ-1581.

33 Eric Croll, 'Engines in One Man's Life', unpublished memoir, n.d., AFMNZ, p. 13.

34 Bruce W. Harkness, Jeffery T. Harkness, Timothy D. Harkness, Christopher W. Harkness & Donald E. Harkness, *A World War 1 Adventure: The life and times of RNAS Bomber Pilot Donald E. Harkness* (Bloomington, Indiana: AuthorHouse, 2014), p. 2.

35 Ibid., p. 4.

36 *Lawn Tennis and Badminton*, 6 October 1910, p. 601, quoted in Len Richardson & Shelley Richardson, *Anthony Wilding: A sporting life* (Christchurch: Canterbury University Press, 2005), p. 258.

37 Anthony Wilding, *On and Off the Court* (New York: Doubleday, Page & Co., 1918), pp. 199–201.

38 Anthony Wilding to Julia Wilding, 3 October 1910. ARC1989.124.263, CM; Anthony Wilding to Julia Wilding, 7 October 1910. ARC1989.124.264.

39 Julia Wilding, Diary, 15 November 1910, CM.

40 Anthony Wilding to Julia Wilding, 22 October 1914. CM ARC1989.124.315.

41 Anthony Wilding to Julia Wilding, 16 October 1914. CM ARC1989.124.314.

42 Anthony Wilding to Julia Wilding, 19 November 1914. CM ARC1989.124.317.

43 Richardson & Richardson, *Anthony Wilding*, p. 359.

44 Anthony Wilding to Julia Wilding, 18 January 1915. CM ARC1989.124.320.

45 Rhodes-Moorhouse's birth surname was simply Moorhouse, but in order to inherit his fortune he had to change his surname to Rhodes-Moorhouse, which he did in 1913.

46 *New Zealand Truth*, 30 March 1907; *Colonist*, 25 March 1907; *Press*, 15 May 1907.

47 *Press*, 11 May 1907.

48 *Press*, 15 May 1907.

49 *Wanganui Chronicle*, 14 May and 14 August 1907. Rhodes-Moorhouse's reckless tendencies were further highlighted when he caused the death of a man on 18 October 1912 while speeding on an English country road. He was found guilty but received only a £20 fine. *Evening Post*, 17 December 1912.

50 Sholto Douglas, *Years of Combat: The first volume of the autobiography of Sholto Douglas, Marshal of the Royal Air Force Lord Douglas of Kirtleside, G.C.B., M.C., D.F.C.* (London: Collins, 1963), p. 81.

51 *Press*, 14 September 1912.

52 Douglas, *Years of Combat*, p. 81.

53 Ibid.

54 *London Gazette*, 21 May 1915.

55 Douglas, *Years of Combat*, p. 82.

56 Robin to Allen, 28 July 1915, ANZ Allen 1 7 D1/23.

57 *Wanganui Herald*, 10 September 1909; Hector McKenzie to C. M. Duthie, 9 May 1937. Walsh Memorial Library, MOTAT, quoted in Errol Martyn, *A Passion for Flight: New Zealand aviation before the Great War, vol. 1: Ideas, First Flight Attempts and the Aeronauts 1868–1909 (Christchurch: Volplane, 2012)*, p. 146.

58 Martyn, *A Passion for Flight, vol. 3*: T*he Joe Hammond story and military beginnings 1910–1914* (Christchurch: Volplane, 2013), p. 248.

59 *Rangitikei Advocate*, 25 September 1913.

60 *Wanganui Chronicle*, 27 September 1913.

61 General Staff, Wellington Military District to Chief of the General Staff, Wellington, 10 June 1915. Seaforth McKenzie, Personnel File, ANZ AABK 18805 W5568/48 0136025.

62 Seaforth McKenzie to Assistant Infantry Instructor, Featherston Military Camp, 9 May 1916. Seaforth McKenzie Personnel File, ANZ AABK 18805 W5568/48 0136025.

63 Chief of the General Staff to Camp Commandant, Featherston, 16 May 1916. Seaforth McKenzie Base

Records, AABK 18805 W5568/48 0136025, TNA.

64   Thomas Mackenzie to Godley, 3 July 1915, ANZ WA 9/5 Box 1, Item 2b.

65   Godley to Mackenzie, 5 July 1915, ANZ WA 9/5 Box 1, Item 2b.

66   Mackenzie to Godley, 7 February 1916, ANZ WA 9/5 Box 1, Item 2b.

67   Godley to Mackenzie, 3 March 1916, ANZ WA 9/5 Box 1, Item 2b.

68   Mackenzie to Godley, 10 October 1915, ANZ WA 9/5 Box 1, Item 2b.

69   Mackenzie to the Prime Minister, 3 December 1915, ANZ WA 9/5 Box 1, Item 2b; Mackenzie to Godley, 7 February 1916, ANZ WA 9/5 Box 1, Item 2b.

70   Card/Pamphlet: General Birdwood, Christmas 1915, Charles Mills Collection, MOTAT 14/004/019.

71   Charles Mills, 18 July 1915, Charles Mills Collection, MOTAT 14/004/019.

72   Dawson to Charles Mills, 8 December 1915. Charles Mills Collection, MOTAT 14/004/005 (3).

73   William Coates to Eleanor Coates, 28 November 1916, Coates Collection, Ruatuna, Matakohe.

74   NZEF Orders 15 January 1918, 480: Nominations for Commissions in the Royal Flying Corps, Errol Martyn Collection.

75   NZEF Orders 7 September 1916, 141: Applications for Commissions in the RFC. Correspondence: War Office to Officer in Charge of Records, NZEF, to 5 February 1916, Errol Martyn Collection.

76   Mackenzie to Godley, 7 February 1916, WA 9/5 Box 1, Item 2b, ANZ.

77   William Coates, Personnel File, ANZ AABK 18805 W5568/18 0135347; Charles Mills, Personnel File, ANZ AABK 18805 W5549/28 0081220.

78   *Colonist*, 10 November 1917; Ninian Steele Hyslop, Military Personnel File, ANZ AABK 18805 W5541/43 0058711.

79   *New Zealand Herald*, 29 May 1917.

80   Trevor White, unpublished manuscript, 8 March 1976, AFMNZ.

81   Arthur Coningham, Personnel File, ANZ AABK 188805 W5530/90 0027424; Vincent Orange, *Coningham: A biography of Air Marshal Sir Arthur Coningham, KCB, KBE, DSO, MC, DFC, AFC* (London: Methuen, 1990), p. 4.

82   Paul Sortehaug, 'Major Coningham', in *Wings*, p. 50; Robert Heaton Livingstone, Personnel File, ANZ AABK 18805 W5948/32 0360898; Alan Leslie Macfarlane, Personnel File, ANZ AABK 18805 W5948/34 0359686.

83   *Christchurch Star*, 8 May 1962.

84   *Press*, 27 August 1915.

85   Devon Sutcliffe, 'Sustained effort: The life of Sir Leonard Isitt' (PhD thesis, Massey University, 2011), p. 39.

86   Leonard Monk Isitt, Personnel File, ANZ AABK 18805 W5541/48 0059279.

87   *London Gazette*, no. 29308, 9514.

88   Vincent Orange, *Park: The biography of Air Chief Marshal Sir Keith Park GCB, KBE, MC, DFC, DCL* (London: Grub Street, 2001) p. 12.

89   Ibid.

90   Keith Park, Service Record, TNA WO 339/41919.

91   Orange, *Park*, p. 15.

92   Ibid.

CHAPTER FIVE: DUST AND DYSENTERY

1   Flight Commander, Mesopotamia, War Diary, 3 June 1915, TNA AIR 1/2263/209/61/1.

2   Francis Luke Adams, Service Record, NAA B2455; Robert Stanley Brewster, Personnel File, ANZ AABK

222525 W57121 BR 37/58; Laurie Pitcher, Personnel File, ANZ AABK 22525 W5712 1 BR 37/75.

3   E. F. Harvie, *Venture the Far Horizon: The pioneer long-distance flights in New Zealand* (Wellington: Whitcombe & Tombs, 1966), p. 72.

4   Scotland arrived later than the other New Zealanders on 5 September for flying duty. Deputy Assistant Director, Aviation Diary, 5 August 1915, AWM 45 43/1.

5   *Star*, 23 May 1918; Francis Luke Adams, Service Record, NAA B2455.

6   Robert Stanley Brewster, New Zealand, Electoral Rolls, 1853–1881; Robert Stanley Brewster, Personnel File, Records, ANZ AABK 222525 W57121 BR 37/58.

7   Laurence Pitcher, Base Records, ANZ AABK 22525 W5712 1 BR 37/75.

8   T. W. White, *Guests of the Unspeakable: An Australian's escape from Turkey in the First World War* (Crows Nest, NSW: Little Hill, 1990), p. 21.

9   Flight Commander, Mesopotamia, War Diary, 3 June 1915, TNA AIR 1/2263/209/61/1.

10   Deputy Assistant Director, Aviation Diary, 13 October 1915. AWM 45 43/1.

11   General Sir Fenton Aylmer's comments on a draft of Jones, *The War in the Air, Vol. V*, 6 July 1932, TNA AIR/674/21/6/87 in Michael Molkentin, *Australia and the War in the Air* (Melbourne: Oxford University Press, 2014), pp. 93, 259 fn. 118.

12   *Sun*, 11 November 1915.

13   *Sun*, 11 November 1915.

14   White, *Guests of the Unspeakable*, pp. 19–20.

15   *Wairarapa Daily Times*, 21 January 1916.

16   White, *Guests of the Unspeakable*, p. 20.

17   *Dominion*, 30 March 1916.

18   *Horowhenua Chronicle*, 22 December 1915.

19   *Sun*, 11 November 1915.

20   White, *Guests of the Unspeakable*, p. 17.

21   Deputy Assistant Director, Aviation Diary, 25 May 1915, AWM 45 43/1; J. Hamlin, *Flat Out: The story of 30 Squadron Royal Air Force* (Tunbridge Wells, Kent: Air-Britain, 2002), p. 16.

22   F. M. Cutlack, *Official History of Australia in the War of 1914–1918: Volume VIII Australian Flying Corps in the western and eastern theatres of war* (Sydney: Angus and Robertson, 1940), p. 9.

23   J. Bryant Haigh, 'The Mesopotamia Half Flight (The Genesis of the Royal and Royal New Zealand Air Forces)', *Military Historical Society* 95, vol. XXIV (February 1974), p. 129.

24   Deputy Assistant Director, Aviation Diary, 31 May 1915, AWM 45 43/1.

25   GOC 6th (Poona) Division to GOC IEF D, 11 June 1915, TNA WO95/5112, in Molkentin, *Australia and the War in the Air*, p. 81; Michael Molkentin, *Fire in the Sky: The Australian Flying Corps in the First World War* (Crows Nest, NSW: Allen & Unwin, 2012), pp. 11–23.

26   Hamlin, *Flat Out*, p. 16.

27   Flight Commander, Mesopotamia, War Diary, 14 June 1915, TNA AIR1/2263/209/61/1.

28   Flight Commander, Mesopotamia, War Diary, 10 June 1915, TNA AIR1/2263/209/61/1.

29   Deputy Assistant Director, Aviation Diary, 5–6 June 1915, AWM 45 43/1; Flight Commander, Mesopotamia, War Diary, 10 June 19, in Molkentin, *Australia and the War in the Air*, p. 83.

30   Deputy Assistant Director, Aviation Diary, 13 June 1915, AWM 45 43/1.

31   Flight Commander, Mesopotamia, War Diary, 22–24 June 1915, TNA AIR1/2263/209/61/1.

32   White, *Guests of the Unspeakable*, p. 88.

33   Francis Yeats-Brown, *Caught by the Turks* (London: Edward Arnold, 1919), p. 8.

34 White, *Guests of the Unspeakable,* p. 88.

35 *Sun*, 11 November 1917.

36 Molkentin, *Australia and the War in the Air*, p. 85.

37 Flight Commander, Mesopotamia, War Diary, 22 July 1915, TNA AIR1/2263.

38 Deputy Assistant Director, Aviation Diary, 30 July 1915, AWM 45 43/1; Map 12/D/9, 21 July 1915, TNA WO95/5142; GOC IEF D to Indian CGS, 20 August 1915, TNA WO106/892, in Molkentin, *Australia and the War in the Air*, p. 84; Deputy Assistant Director, Aviation Diary, 18 July 1915, AWM 45 43/1; Extract from report on aviation in Mesopotamia, TNA AIR1/504/16/3/23.

39 Molkentin, *Australia and the War in the Air*, p. 85.

40 Deputy Assistant Director, Aviation Diary, 31 July 1915, AWM 45 43/1.

41 War Diary of Flight Commander (Mesopotamia), 30 July 1915, TNA AIR1/2263.

42 Telegram to General Staff Intelligence, 9 August 1915, AWM 45 43/1.

43 Deputy Assistant Director, Aviation Diary, 2 August 1915, AWM 45 43/1.

44 Deputy Assistant Director, Aviation Diary, 3 August 1915, AWM 45 43/1.

45 Note by the Inspector General of Communications, 20 August 1915, TNA WO158/685, in Molkentin, *Australia and the War in the Air*, p. 84; DAD Aviation Diary, 9 August 1915, AWM 45 43/1.

46 Telegram to General Staff Intelligence, 9 August 1915, AWM 45 43/1.

47 War Diary of Flight Commander (Mesopotamia), 5 September 1915, TNA AIR1/2263.

48 Flight Commander, Mesopotamia, War Diary, 8 October 1915, TNA AIR1/2263.

49 Molkentin, *Australia and the War in the Air*, p. 86.

50 *Dominion*, 30 March 1916.

51 Deputy Assistant Director, Aviation Diary, 13 October 1915, AWM 45 43/1.

52 Deputy Assistant Director, Aviation Diary, 27 November 1915, AWM 45 43/1; *Dominion*, 30 March 1916.

53 *Feilding Star*, 14 January 1916.

54 Deputy Assistant Director, Aviation Diary, 5 August & 19 September 1915, AWM 45 43/1.

55 Sir Charles V. F. (Major-General) Townshend, *My Campaign in Mesopotamia* (London: Thornton Butterworth, 1920), pp. 100–12.

56 6th Division war diary, 16 September 1915 in Molkentin, *Australia and the War in the Air*, p. 86; Townshend, pp. 110–12.

57 Deputy Assistant Director, Aviation Diary, 3 October 1915, AWM 45 43/1.

58 6th Division War Diary, 3 October 1915, TNA WO95/5112 in Molkentin, *Australia and the War in the Air*, p. 89; cf. Deputy Assistant Director, Aviation Diary, 5 October 1915, AWM 45 43/1.

58A Molkentin, *Australia and the War in the Air*, p. 89.

59 Townshend, pp. 124–5; Paul Davis, *Ends and Means: The British Mesopotamian Campaign and Royal Commission* (Cranbury, NJ: Associated University Presses, 1994), p. 115.

60 Molkentin, *Australia and the War in the Air*, p. 89.

61 Reconnaissance Report No. 57, 6 October 1915, TNA AIR/504/16/3/23; Reconnaissance Report No. 94, 1 November 1915, TNA AIR/504/16/3/23; Molkentin, *Australia and the War in the Air*, p. 90.

62 Reconnaissance Report No. 57, 6 October 1915, TNA AIR/504/16/3/23.

63 Staff Bimbashi Muhammad Amin, 'The battle of Suliman Pak', February 1915, pp. 51–2, TNA CAB44/33, in Molkentin, *Australia and the War in the Air*, p. 91; Deputy Assistant Director, Aviation Diary, 21 October 1915, AWM 45 43/1.

64 H. A. Jones, *War in the Air: Being the story of the part played in the Great War by the Royal Air Force, vol. 5* (London: Imperial War Musueum, 1935), p. 264.

65 Ibid.

66 Ibid.

67 Paul Knight, *The British Army in Mesopotamia, 1914–1918* (London: McFarland, 2013), p. 63.

68 Ibid., p. 72.

69 Ibid.

70 Ibid.

71 William Henry Minter Candy, Diary, 18 March 1916, RAFM DC 73/48.

72 Thomas White, Diary 29 August 1916, p. 79, AWM RCDIG0001333.

73 Knight, *The British Army in Mesopotamia, 1914–1918*, p. 75.

74 Ibid.

75 Report on Aviation in Mesopotamia, May 1915–June 1916, p. 22, TNA AIR 1/504/16/3/23; Jones, *War in the Air, vol. 5*, pp. 279–80.

76 Deputy Assistant Director, Aviation Diary, 29 April 1916, AWM 45 43/1.

77 *Horowhenua Chronicle*, 30 October 1917.

78 William Henry Minter Candy, Diary, 7 May 1916, RAFM, DC 73/48.

79 White, *Guests of the Unspeakable*, p. 174.

80 Francis Yeats-Brown, *The Lives of a Bengal Lancer* (London: Viking, 1930), p. 197.

81 Ibid., p. 198.

82 White, *Guests of the Unspeakable*, p. 174.

83 White, *Guests of the Unspeakable*, pp. 174–5.

84 Francis Luke Adams Snr to Major J. M. Lean, 20 March 1918. Francis Luke Adams, Service Record, NAA B2455.

85 Francis Luke Adams Snr to Officer in Charge, Base Records, 5 February 1919. Francis Luke Adams, Service Record, NAA B2455.

86 *Dominion*, 30 March 1916.

CHAPTER SIX: AIRMEN FOR THE EMPIRE

1 Leo White, *Wingspread: The pioneering of aviation in New Zealand* (Auckland: Unity, 1941), p. 43.

2 E. F. Harvie, *George Bolt: Pioneer aviator* (Wellington: Reed, 1974), p. 18; David Mulgan, *The Kiwi's First Wings: The story of the Walsh Brothers and the New Zealand Flying School 1910–1924* (Wellington: Wingfield, 1960), p. 31.

3 *New Zealand Yachtsman*, 9 January 1915.

4 Mulgan, *The Kiwi's First Wings*, p. 41.

5 Malcolm Charles McGregor, Personnel File, ANZ AABK 18805 W6026/3 0668552; G. H. Cunningham, *Mac's Memoirs: The flying life of Squadron-Leader McGregor* (Dunedin: Reed, 1937), p. 23.

6 *Dominion*, 21 February 1916.

7 War Office to Minister of Defence, Wellington, 22 April 1916, Candidates for Commissions in Royal Flying Corps, 5 February 1917, ANZ ACHK 8604 G1 218 1917/903.

8 Ibid.

9 Appendix A: Special Standard of Fitness for the Royal Flying Corps, in Candidates for Commissions in Royal Flying Corps, 5 February 1917, ANZ ACHK 8604 G1 218 1917/903.

10 Regulations governing appointments to the Royal Flying Corps of Candidates nominated by the Government of New Zealand under the terms of War Office telegram No. 5352, 22 April 1916, in Candidates for Commissions in Royal Flying Corps, 5 February 1917, ANZ ACHK 8604 G1 218 1917/903.

11   *Dominion*, 21 February 1916.

12   Hugh Blackwell to Mother, 2 March 1916, in E. H. Poole (ed.), *Letters Home: A collection of letters written by Henry Hugh Blackwell, 1916–1919, during the training for and service in the Royal Flying Corps* (Christchurch: E. H. & H. M. Poole, 1999), AFMNZ.

13   Allen to Wigram, 8 May 1917, in Formation of School of Aviation: Canterbury, 1916–1917, ANZ AALJ W639 483 3 b D 35/85.

14   Harvie, *George Bolt*, p. 23.

15   *Dominion*, 21 February 1916.

16   Margaret McClure, *Fighting Spirit: 75 Years of the RNZAF* (Auckland: Random House, 2012), p. 21.

17   *Manawatu Times*, 14 December 1917.

18   White, *Wingspread*, p. 44.

19   Cunningham, *Mac's Memoirs*, p. 23.

20   Ronald Bannerman, Logbook, AFMNZ.

21   Mulgan, *The Kiwi's First Wings*, p. 64; Errol Martyn to Author, 17 March 2017.

22   Blackwell to Mother, 2 March 1916, in Poole, *Letters Home*, pp. 4–5.

23   Errol Martyn to Author, 17 March 2017.

24   L. M. Noble, *Sir Henry Wigram: Pioneer of New Zealand aviation* (Auckland: Whitcombe & Tombs, 1952), pp. 18–19.

25   Ibid., p. 20.

26   Henry F. Wigram, *Canterbury (N.Z.) Aviation Company: The first hundred pilots* (Christchurch: Canterbury [N.Z.] Aviation Company, 1918), p. 1.

27   *Southland Times*, 26 April 1916.

28   *Star*, 26 August 1916; Extracts from the Prospectus of the Canterbury (New Zealand) Company Limited, in Formation of School of Aviation: Canterbury, 1916–1917, ANZ AALJ W639 483 3/b D 35/85.

29   Wigram, *Canterbury (N.Z.) Aviation Company*, p. 3; 'Henry Wigram and the Canterbury Aviation Company', in *RNZAF News Special*, 15 September 1995, p. 4.

30   *Lyttelton Times*, 24 April 1917, quoted in 'Henry Wigram and the Canterbury Aviation Company', in *RNZAF News Special*, 15 September 1995, p. 4.

31   Extracts from the Prospectus of the Canterbury (New Zealand Company Limited), in Formation of School of Aviation: Canterbury, 1916–1917.

32   Wigram to Allen, 28 August 1916, in Formation of School of Aviation: Canterbury, 1916–1917, ANZ AALJ W639 483 3 b D 35/85; Noble, p. 29.

33   Allen to Wigram, 30 August 1916, in Formation of School of Aviation: Canterbury, 1916–1917.

34   James William Humphrys Scotland, ANZ AABK 18805 W5674/15 425421.

35   Wigram to Allen, 17 November 1916, in Formation of School of Aviation: Canterbury, 1916–1917.

36   Wigram to Mackenzie, 20 November 1916, in Formation of School of Aviation: Canterbury, 1916–1917.

37   *Press*, 3 May 1917.

38   Wigram, *Canterbury (N.Z.) Aviation Company*, p. 3; Scott to Wigram, 21 January 1917, in Formation of School of Aviation: Canterbury, 1916–1917.

39   Promotional Pamphlet: The Canterbury Aviation Company's Flying School, 1 October 1917, in School of Aviation: Canterbury, 1917–1918, ANZ AALJ W639 483 4/a D35/85/1.

40   Ibid.

41   Ibid.

42   Edwyn Wilding, Diary, 19 June 1917, AFMNZ.

43 Sloss to Sister, 4 October 1917, AFMNZ.

44 Ross Brodie, Diary, 19 August 1917, AFMNZ.

45 Edwyn Wilding, Diary, 1 & 10 July 1917, AFMNZ.

46 Edwyn Wilding, Diary, 2–4 July 1917, AFMNZ.

47 Edwyn Wilding, Diary, 17 July 1917, AFMNZ.

48 Chief General Staff to Secretary Canterbury (N.Z.) Aviation Co. Ltd, 8 August 1917, in Formation of School of Aviation: Canterbury, 1916–1917.

49 *Press*, 25 August 1917.

50 Edwyn Wilding, Diary, 24 August 1917, AFMNZ.

51 *Press*, 25 August 1917.

52 Notice of Appeal by Reservist called up for Service by Lot, 16 May 1917, Ross Brodie, Personnel file, ANZ AABK 18805 W5937/39 0360152.

53 Determination of Military Service Board, 4 September 1917, Ross Brodie, Personnel File, ANZ AABK 18805 W5937/39 0360152.

54 Ross Brodie, Personnel File, ANZ AABK 18805 W5937/39 0360152 ANZ; Ross Brodie, Diary, 20 July 2017, AFMNZ.

55 Ross Brodie, Diary, 5 September 2017, AFMNZ.

56 *Star*, 15 September 1917.

57 Ibid.

58 *New Zealand Motor and Cycle Journal*, 26 August 1918, p. 111.

59 Errol W. Martyn, *Swift to the Sky: New Zealand's military aviation history* (Auckland: Penguin Viking, 2010), p. 52.

60 Errol Martyn to Author, 17 March 2017; cf. Wigram, *Canterbury (N.Z.) Aviation Company*, pp. 9–10.

61 Errol Martyn to Author, 17 March 2017.

62 Edwyn Wilding, Service Record, TNA AIR 79/994/110903.

63 Edwyn Wilding, Diary, 11 November 1918, AFMNZ.

64 *Northern Advocate*, 12 January 1918.

65 Mulgan, *The Kiwi's First Wings*, p. 44.

66 Sleeman to District Headquarters, NZ Military Forces Dunedin, 23 April 1918, in Canterbury School of Aviation, 1917–1918, ANZ AALJ W639 483 Box 4/a D 35/85/1.

67 Waiting List 5 July 1918: Canterbury (NZ) Aviation Co. Ltd. Pupils waiting list, in Canterbury School of Aviation, 1917–1918, ANZ AALJ W639 483 Box 4/a D 35/85/1.

68 Coningham to Officer in Charge, Pay Duties, RFC, 4 October 1916, TNA WO 399/67882.

69 *Wanganui Herald*, 29 January 1916.

70 Gibbon to Wigram, 2 April 1918, Canterbury School of Aviation, 1917–1918, ANZ AALJ W639 483 Box 4/a D 35/85/1.

71 Sloss to Sisters, January 1918, AFMNZ.

72 Sloss to Mother, 10 January 1918, AFMNZ.

73 Sloss to Mother, February 1918, AFMNZ.

74 Blackwell to unknown, 26 May 1917, AFMNZ.

75 Bruce W. Harkness, Jeffery T. Harkness, Timothy D. Harkness, Christopher W. Harkness & Donald E. Harkness, *A World War 1 Adventure: The life and times of RNAS Bomber Pilot Donald E. Harkness* (Bloomington, Ind.: AuthorHouse, 2014), pp. 7–8.

76 Ibid., p. 9.

77 Susanna Montgomerie Norris with Anna Rogers, *Annie's War: A New Zealand woman and her family in England, 1916–19* (Dunedin: Otago University Press, 2014), p. 15.

78 Harkness et al., *A World War 1 Adventure*, pp. 18–19.

79 Ibid., p. 20.

80 Harold Butterworth, Diary, 28 May 1915, AWMM.

81 Harold Butterworth, Diary, 23 May 1915, AWMM.

82 Norris & Rogers, *Annie's War*, pp. 16–17.

83 Ibid., p. 17.

84 Ibid., p. 18.

85 Ross Brodie, Diary, 17 November 1917, AFMNZ.

86 Harold Butterworth, Diary, 22 May 1915, AWMM.

87 Harold Butterworth, Diary, 31 May 1915, AWMM.

88 Christ's College Register for 1918, page 94, from a letter by Old Boy Edmund W. ('Cocky') Reeves, Errol Martin Collection.

89 Sloss to Alex Sloss, n.d., AFMNZ.

90 Blackwell to Mother, 23 June 1917, AFMNZ.

CHAPTER SEVEN: BASHED INTO SHAPE

1 Hugh Blackwell to Mother, 8 July 1917, in E. H. Poole (ed.), *Letters Home: A collection of letters written by Henry Hugh Blackwell, 1916–1919, during the training for and service in the Royal Flying Corps* (Christchurch: E. H. & H. M. Poole, 1999), AFMNZ.

2 Hugh Blackwell to Mother, 8 July 1917, AFMNZ.

3 G. H. Cunningham, *Mac's Memoirs: The flying life of Squadron-Leader McGregor* (Dunedin: Reed, 1937), pp. 25–26.

4 Hugh Blackwell, Diary, 9–14 July 1917, AFMNZ.

5 Hugh Blackwell, Diary, 14 July 1917, AFMNZ.

6 Hugh Blackwell to Mother, 22 July 1917, AFMNZ.

7 http://www.theaerodrome.com/forum/showthread.php?t=23225&garpg=3, retrieved 20 June 2017.

8 Melville White, Letter to 'Brethren', 5 April 1917.

9 Hugh Blackwell to Mother, 22 July 1917, AFMNZ.

10 Ross Brodie, Diary, 8 February–31 July 1918, AFMNZ.

11 Edwyn Wilding, Diary, 16 March 1918, AFMNZ.

12 Edwyn Wilding, Diary, 19 March 1918, AFMNZ.

13 Ross Brodie, Diary, 30 April 1918, AFMNZ; Wilding Diary 1918, AFMNZ.

14 Edwyn Wilding, Diary, 29 March 1918, AFMNZ.

15 Edwyn Wilding, Diary, 13 May 1918, AFMNZ.

16 Edwyn Wilding, Diary, 10 June 1918, AFMNZ.

17 Ross Brodie, Diary, 14 April 1918, AFMNZ.

18 Ross Brodie, Diary, 20 April 1918, AFMNZ.

19 Ross Brodie, Diary, 10 July 1918, AFMNZ.

20 Melville White to Brethren, 5 April 1917, ATL MSY-7036.

21 Ross Brodie, Diary, 5 May 1918, AFMNZ.

22 Ross Brodie, Diary, 26 May, 9 June 1918, AFMNZ.

23   Ross Brodie, Diary, 24 June 1918, AFMNZ.

24   Ross Brodie, Diary, 3 July 1918, AFMNZ.

25   Ross Brodie, Diary, 29 June 1918, AFMNZ.

26   Bruce W. Harkness, Jeffery T. Harkness, Timothy D. Harkness, Christopher W. Harkness & Donald
     E. Harkness, *A World War 1 Adventure: The life and times of RNAS Bomber Pilot Donald E. Harkness*
     (Bloomington, Ind.: AuthorHouse, 2014), p. 61.

27   Harold Butterworth, Diary, 23, 31 October 1915, 1 January 1916, AWMM MS996.

28   Harkness et al., *A World War 1 Adventure*, pp. 44–8.

29   *Tatler*, 12 September 1917.

30   Ronald Bannerman, Diary, 10 October 1917, AFMNZ.

31   Edwyn Wilding, Diary, 31 January 1918, AFMNZ.

32   Jim Steinmeyer, *The Glorious Deception: The double life of William Robinson, aka Chun Ling Soo the
     'Marvelous Chinese Conjurer'* (New York: Carrol & Graf, 2006), p. 16.

33   I. M. Philpott, *The Birth of the Royal Air Force: An encyclopedia of British air power before and during the
     Great War 1914 to 1918* (Barnsley, South Yorkshire: Pen & Sword, 2013), p. 210.

34   Harold Butterworth, 6 January 1916, AWMM MS996.

35   Harold Butterworth, 7 January 1916, AWMM MS996.

36   James Dinneen, Brent Mackrell, Scrapbooks relating to early British and New Zealand military aviation, I
     and III, ATL MSZ-1583.

37   Errol Martyn, 12 September 1982, Michael Dinneen, Brent Mackrell, Scrapbooks relating to early British
     and New Zealand military aviation, I and III, ATL MSZ-1583.

38   *New Zealand Herald*, 14 October 1929.

39   Lister Briffault, Service Record, TNA ADM273; Errol Martyn to Author, 30 September 2016.

40   *Flight*, 27 August 1915, p. 630.

41   Harkness et al., *A World War 1 Adventure*, p. 151.

42   Auckland Grammar School, *Chronicle*, vol. 6, no. 2 (1918), p. 13; Errol Martyn, *For Your Tomorrow: A
     record of New Zealanders who have died while serving with the RNZAF and Allied air services since 1915,
     vol. 1: Fates 1915–1942* (Christchurch: Volplane, 1998), p. 48; Errol Martyn, *For Your Tomorrow, vol. 3:
     Biographies & Appendices* (Christchurch: Volplane, 2008), p. 60; Trevor Dudley Hall Alderton, Service
     Record, AIR 76/4/86 TNA.

43   Albert Ball, quoted in Ian Mackersey, *No More Empty Chairs: The short and heroic lives of the young
     aviators who fought and died in the First World War* (London: Weidenfeld & Nicolson, 2012), p. 71.

44   C. Bilney, Sound Recording, IWM SR 2, Reel 5, in Nigel Steel & Peter Hart, *Tumult in the Clouds: The
     British experience of the war in the air, 1914–1918* (London: Hodder & Stoughton, 1997), p. 84.

45   Ira 'Taffy' Jones, *Tiger Squadron: The story of 74 Squadron, R.A.F., in Two World Wars* (London: A. H.
     Allen, 1954), p. 57.

46   *Evening Post*, 23 May 1917.

47   Alfred de Bathe Brandon, Service Record, TNA WO 339/55993; Alfred de Bathe Brandon, Logbook,
     AFMNZ.

48   Alfred de Bathe Brandon, unpublished memoir, n.d., p. 3. Errol Martyn Collection.

49   Harkness et al., *A World War 1 Adventure*, pp. 144–5.

50   Ibid., p. 146.

51   Ibid., p. 81.

52   Chris Hobson, *Airmen Died in the Great War 1914–1918: The Roll of Honour of the British and
     Commonwealth Air Services of the First World War* (Suffolk: J. B. Hayward & Son, 1995), p. 416.

Unfortunately, many writers have repeated Dennis Winter's outdated research, which wrongly states that 'more pilots died training than were killed by the enemy'. See Dennis Winter, *The First of the Few: Fighter pilots of the First World War* (London: Penguin, 1982), p. 36; cf. http://1914-1918.invisionzone. com/forums/index.php?/topic/240115-rfcrnasraf-training-deaths-100-years-on/#comment-2410887, retrieved 7 April 2017.

53   *Evening Post*, 21 August 1916.

54   Ibid.

55   *New Zealand Herald*, 28 September 1916; Martyn, *For Your Tomorrow, vol. 3*, p. 40.

56   *Evening Post*, 21 October 916.

57   *New Zealand Herald*, 26 October 1916; *New Zealand Herald*, 17 June 1916; George Greenwell, Personnel File, ANZ AABK 18805 W5539/51 0047573.

58   *New Zealand Herald*, 12 May 1916.

59   Nicholas Greenwell, Personnel File, ANZ AABK 7291 W5614/71 D. 2/6020; *New Zealand Herald*, 17 June 1916.

60   Eric Croll, 'Engines in One Man's Life', unpublished memoir, n.d., AFMNZ, pp. 18–19.

61   Melville White to Brethren, 5 April 1917, ATL MSY-7036.

62   Ronald Bannerman, Diary, 2 October 1917, AFMNZ.

63   Henry Peter Rasmussen, Tape 259, Transcript, Liddle Collection, University of Leeds, LIDDLE/WW1/ANZAC/NZ/REC/55.

64   Ibid.

65   Jack Poole, *Undiscovered Ends* (London: Cassell, 1957), pp. 35–6.

66   Ibid., p. 36.

67   Alfred de Bathe Brandon, unpublished memoir, n.d., p. 2, Errol Martyn Collection.

68   Ibid., p. 4; Errol Martyn, *A Passion for Flight: New Zealand aviation before the Great War, vol. 3: The Joe Hammond story and military beginnings 1910–1914* (Christchurch: Volplane, 2013), p. 169.

69   *Blue and White: The magazine of St Patrick's College, Wellington*, vol. X, no. 1 (1919), p. 37.

70   Hugh Blackwell, Diary, 26 August 1917, AFMNZ.

71   Mackersey, *No More Empty Chairs*, p. 311.

72   Keith Caldwell, Logbook, AFMNZ; Francis William Crawford, Logbook, AFMNZ.

73   John Martin, 6 July 1918, ATL MS-Papers 1912; John Martin, Personnel Records, ANZ AABK 18805 W5549 0078505.

74   Ronald Bannerman, Logbook, 15 October 1917–5 February 1918, AFMNZ.

75   Cunningham, *Mac's Memoirs*, p. 28.

76   *Evening Star*, 28 December 1917.

77   Ronald Bannerman, Diary, 12 December 1917, AFMNZ.

78   Ronald Bannerman, Diary, 3 February 1918, AFMNZ.

79   Ronald Bannerman, Diary, 7 October 1917, AFMNZ.

80   Ross Brodie, Diary, 30 September 1918, AFMNZ.

81   Ross Brodie, Diary, 1 October 1918, AFMNZ.

CHAPTER EIGHT: DEATH FROM ABOVE

1   Alfred de Bathe Brandon, Service Record, TNA WO 339/55993.

2   Christopher Cole & E. F. Cheesman, *The Air Defence of Britain 1914–1918* (London: Putnam, 1984), p. 24.

3   James Boulton (ed.), *The Selected Letters of D. H. Lawrence* (Cambridge, UK: Cambridge University Press,

2000), p. 106.

4   Susanna Montgomerie Norris with Anna Rogers, *Annie's War: A New Zealand woman and her family in England, 1916–19* (Dunedin: Otago University Press, 2014), pp. 30–1.

5   Ibid., pp. 113–14.

6   Hugh Blackwell, Diary, 8 July 1917, in E. H. Poole (ed.), *Letters Home: A collection of letters written by Henry Hugh Blackwell, 1916–1919, during the training for and service in the Royal Flying Corps* (Christchurch: E. H. & H. M. Poole, 1999), AFMNZ.

7   Ross Brodie, Diary, 28 January 1918, AFMNZ.

8   *Wairarapa Daily Times*, 12 February 1916.

9   *Mataura Ensign*, 4 May 1915.

10   Nigel Steel & Peter Hart, *Tumult in the Clouds: The British experience of the war in the air, 1914–1918* (London: Hodder & Stoughton, 1997), p. 144.

11   Alfred de Bathe Brandon, Logbook, 29 February, 1 March 1916, AFMNZ.

12   Information obtained from the crew of the Zeppelin *L15*, examined at Chatham on April 1st, 2nd and 3rd, 1916, TNA AIR/2599.

13   Ibid.

14   Full report on the information obtained from the crew of the *L15*, April–May 1916, TNA, AIR 1/2596-2620; Rigid Airship Committee Meeting. Reports received relative to Zeppelin No. 15, TNA AIR1/2566.

15   *NZ Truth*, 28 July 1927.

16   Cole & Cheesman, *The Air Defence of Britain*, p. 105.

17   Alfred de Bathe Brandon, unpublished memoirs, p. 5, Errol Martyn Collection.

18   Information obtained from the crew of the Zeppelin *L15*, examined at Chatham on April 1st, 2nd and 3rd, 1916, TNA AIR/2599.

19   Raymond Laurence Rimell, *Zeppelin! A battle for air supremacy in World War 1* (London: HarperCollins, 1984), pp. 1–2.

20   Full report on the information obtained from the crew of the *L15*, April–May 1916, TNA AIR 1/2596-2620.

21   Information obtained from the crew of the Zeppelin *L15*, examined at Chatham on April 1st, 2nd and 3rd, 1916, TNA AIR/2599.

22   Full report on the information obtained from the crew of the *L15*, April–May 1916, TNA AIR 1/2596-2620.

23   Information obtained from the crew of the Zeppelin *L15*, examined at Chatham on April 1st, 2nd and 3rd, 1916, TNA AIR/2599.

24   Brandon, unpublished memoir, p. 7, Errol Martyn Collection; D. Robinson, *The Zeppelin in Combat: A history of the German Naval Airship Division, 1912–1918* (London: Foulis, 1963), pp. 135–6.

25   Brandon, unpublished memoir, p. 7, Errol Martyn Collection.

26   Brandon Logbook, 31 March 1916, AFMNZ.

27   Information obtained from the crew of the Zeppelin *L15*, examined at Chatham on April 1st, 2nd and 3rd, 1916, TNA AIR/2599.

28   Rimell, *Zeppelin!*, p. 5.

29   Salvage of Zeppelin 'L15', 13 July 1916–29 June 1916, TNA, AIR 1/645/17/122/305; 'Zeppelin Raids', March–April 1916, TNA 1/645/17/122/305.

30   Information obtained from the crew of the Zeppelin L15, examined at Chatham on April 1st, 2nd and 3rd, 1916, AIR/2599, TNA. In the final report this was changed to 'The aeroplane may have obtained a hit, but the crew do not believe this to be the case', though the same report confessed that 'The entire story is rather confused and nothing more accurate could be obtained from the crew' with regards to the attack by Brandon and Ridley. Full report on the information obtained from the crew of the *L15*, April–May

1916, TNA 1/2596-2620.

31   *Daily Sketch*, 3 April 1916, AFMNZ.

32   *Northern Advocate*, 31 May 1916; *Free Lance*, 7 April 1916; *Dominion*, 4 April 1916.

33   *Free Lance*, 7 April 1916.

34   *Press*, 22 May 1916.

35   Alfred de Bathe Brandon, Logbook, AFMNZ; *Sun*, 17 May 1916.

36   Trevor Henshaw, *The Sky Their Battlefield II: Air fighting and air casualties of the Great War* (High Barnet, Herts: Fetubi, 2014), p. 28.

37   Michael Gordon, Diary, 11 October 1917, Michael S. C. Gordon Collection.

38   Dennis Winter, *The First of the Few: Fighter pilots of the First World War* (Harmondsworth, Middlesex: Penguin, 1983), pp. 58-59.

38A   Gordon, Diary.

39   A. J. Scott, *Sixty Squadron, RFC 1916–1919* (London: Greenhill, 1990), p. 24.

40   A. R. Kingsford, *Night Raiders of the Air: Being the experiences of a night flying pilot, who raided Hunland on many dark nights during the War* (London: Greenhill, 1988), p. 96.

41   Hugh Blackwell, 22 May 1918, AFMNZ.

42   Kingsford, *Night Raiders of the Air*, p. 96.

43   Ian Mackersey, *No More Empty Chairs: The short and heroic lives of the young aviators who fought and died in the First World War* (London: Weidenfeld & Nicolson, 2012), p. 194.

44   Kingsford, *Night Raiders of the Air*, p. 94.

45   Mackersey, *No More Empty Chairs*, p. 183.

46   *Evening Post*, 4 June 1917.

47   Confidential Reports on Officers, 60 Squadron, December 1916 to April 1918, TNA AIR 1/555/204/79/75; Roy Champion Kean, Service Record, TNA AIR 76/269/14.

48   Collett to Claude Collett, 21 March 1916, Brent Mackrell, Scrapbooks relating to early British and New Zealand military aviation, I and III, ATL MSZ-1583.

49   Squadron Record Book, 18 Squadron, March 1918, TNA AIR 1/1374/204/23/14; Squadron Record Book, 18 Squadron, April 1916, TNA AIR 1/374204/23/15; J. W. Best, 'C. F. Collett, 1886–1917', *Aviation Historical Society of New Zealand Journal*, vol. 43, no. 2 (December 2000), p. 36. This latter article was researched by Errol Martyn: Errol Martyn to Author, 20 March 2017.

50   Best, 'C. F. Collett', p. 36; Squadron Record Book, 18 Squadron, March 1918, TNA AIR 1/374/204/23/5; Squadron Record Book, 18 Squadron, April 1916, TNA AIR 1/374204/23/5.

51   *Grey River Argus*, 16 November 1915.

52   *Wanganui Herald*, 19 October 1916; *Poverty Bay Herald*, 3 March 1915.

53   Air Historical Branch, 25 Squadron History, TNA AIR 1/690/21/20/25.

54   Ibid., p. 7.

55   Ibid., p. 10.

56   Cuthbert Maclean, Combat Report, 22 June 1916, TNA AIR 1/1221/204/5/2634; Air Historical Branch, 25 Squadron History, p. 17, TNA AIR 1/690/21/20/25.

57   Air Historical Branch, 25 Squadron History, p. 17, TNA AIR 1/690/21/20/25.

58   Rainsford Balcombe-Brown, Service Record, TNA WO 339/31372.

59   *Otago Daily Times*, 19 September 1916.

60   Errol Martyn, *For Your Tomorrow: A record of New Zealanders who have died while serving with the RNZAF and Allied air services since 1915, vol. 3: Biographies & Appendices* (Christchurch: Volplane, 2008),

p. 141; Herbert Ambrose Cooper, Service Record, TNA AIR 79/19/1389.

61   Air Historical Branch, 11 Squadron History, p. 4, TNA AIR 1/688/21/20/11; A. J. Insall, *Observer: Memoirs of the R.F.C. 1915–1918* (London: William Kimber, 1970), p. 60.

62   Insall, *Observer*, pp. 58, 125.

63   Ibid., pp. 112–13.

64   *New Zealand Herald*, 15 November 1916.

65   *Poverty Bay Herald*, 27 June 1916.

66   *New Zealand Herald*, 15 November 1916.

67   *Evening Post*, 22 July 1916.

68   *Otago Daily Times*, 19 September 1916.

69   Air Historical Branch, 25 Squadron History, p. 17, TNA AIR 1/690/21/20/25.

70   Rainsford Balcombe-Brown, Combat Report, 3 July 1916, TNA AIR 1/1339/204/17/81.

71   *Evening Post*, 22 July 1916.

72   Herbert Bainbridge Russell, Brent Mackrell, Scrapbooks relating to early British and New Zealand military aviation, II, ATL MSZ-1581.

73   *Timaru Herald*, 19 March 2012; http://www.stuff.co.nz/timaru-herald/features/6598626/Great-heights-in-life-of-adventure, retrieved 14 August 2015.

74   Joseph Beaglehole had served as a Milford Track labourer and guide over the summers of 1907–08 to 1912–13. Tim Beaglehole, *A life of J. C. Beaglehole: New Zealand scholar* (Wellington: Victoria University Press, 2006), p. 39.

75   James Dennistoun to 'Dear G.', 20 March 1911, CM, Dennistoun Collection.

76   Ibid.

77   *Press*, 27 October 2014. http://www.stuff.co.nz/the-press/news/10665516/The-magnificent-Mitre-Peak, retrieved 14 August 2015.

78   *Manawatu Standard*, 4 April 1912.

79   James Dennistoun, Diary, 6 June 1916, CM, Dennistoun Collection; Russell to George Dennistoun, 15 July 1918, CM, Dennistoun Collection.

80   Herbert Russell to George Dennistoun, 15 July 1918, CM, Dennistoun Collection.

81   Ibid.

82   Ibid.

83   Eidaw to Emily Dennistoun, 27 June 1916, CM, Dennistoun Collection.

84   Herbert Russell to Mother, 5 July 1916, CM, Dennistoun Collection.

85   Herbert Russell to George Dennistoun, 15 July 1918, CM, Dennistoun Collection.

86   Herbert Russell to Mother, 9 August 1918, CM, Dennistoun Collection.

87   Herbert Russell to Aunt Emily, 9 August 1918, CM, Dennistoun Collection.; James Dennistoun, ANZ AABK 22525 W5614/94 B.R. 37/17.

88   Herbert Russell to Mother, 9 August 1918, CM, Dennistoun Collection.

CHAPTER NINE: FIRE IN THE SKY

1   Leo Walmsley, 'An Airman's Experiences in East Africa', *Blackwood's Magazine*, vol. 206 (New York: Leonard Scott, 1919), p. 645.

2   Charles Joseph Hathaway, Service Record, TNA AIR 79/135/10796.

3   Air Historical Branch, 26 (South African) Squadron History, p. 2, TNA AIR 1/690/21/20/23.

4   H. A. Jones, *War in the Air: Being the story of the part played in the Great War by the Royal Air Force, vol.*

3 (London: Imperial War Museum, 1931), p. 24.

5   Ibid., pp. 21–22.

6   Walmsley, 'An Airman's Experiences in East Africa', p. 633.

7   Ibid., p. 634.

8   Ibid.

9   Vincent Ferris Toulmin, Diary, 17 September–11 October 1917, John V. Douglas Collection.

10 Jones, *War in the Air, vol. 3*, p. 643.

11 Geoffrey Norris, *The Royal Flying Corps* (London: Frederick Muller, 1965), pp. 124–5.

12 Jones, *War in the Air, vol. 3*, p. 56.

13 Vincent Ferris Toulmin, Diary, 27 August 1917, John V. Douglas Collection; John Douglas to Author, 10 April 2017; Errol Martyn to Author, 20 March 2017.

14 Norris, *The Royal Flying Corps*, pp. 123–4.

15 Trevor Henshaw, *The Sky Their Battlefield II: Air fighting and air casualties of the Great War* (High Barnet, Herts: Fetubi, 2014), p. 300.

16 Walmsley, 'An Airman's Experiences in East Africa', p. 800.

17 Ibid., p. 651.

18 Ibid.

19 Leo Walmsley, 'An Airman's Experiences in East Africa', *Blackwood's Magazine*, vol. 207 (New York: Leonard Scott, 1920), p. 60.

20 Ibid.

21 Jones, *War in the Air, vol. 3*, p. 57, n. 1.

22 Charles James Hathaway, Service Record, TNA AIR 79/135/10796; Director of Base Records to Director of Movements and Quartering, 13 May 1918, Charles James Hathaway, Personnel File, ANZ AABK 22525 W5712/1 BR 37/1343.

23 *New Zealand Herald*, 25 September 1917.

24 Vincent Ferris Toulmin, Diary, 20 December 1917, John V. Douglas Collection.

25 Jones, *War in the Air*, pp. 427–73.

26 Errol Martyn, *For Your Tomorrow: A record of New Zealanders who have died while serving with the RNZAF and Allied air services since 1915, vol. 1: Fates 1915–1942* (Christchurch: Volplane, 1998), p. 36.

27 18 Squadron, Squadron Record Book, 7–15 July 1916, TNA AIR 1/1374/204/23/7; Martyn, *For Your Tomorrow, vol. 1*, p. 36.

28 18 Squadron, Squadron Record Book, 16 July 1916, TNA AIR 1/1374/204/23/7; Martyn, *For Your Tomorrow, vol. 1*, p. 36.

29 John Helias Finnie McEwen, Repatriated Officer Prisoner of War Report, TNA AIR/1207/204/5/2619.

30 Carmichael to Butterworth, 18 July 1916, AWMM MS996.

31 Air Historical Branch, 7 Squadron History, TNA AIR 1/166/15/146/1.

31A *The Wanganui Collegian*, No. 103, April 1917, p. 5.

31B *The Wanganui Collegian*, No. 102, December 1916, p. 11.

31C *The Wanganui Collegian*, No. 103, April 1917, p. 6.

32 Collett to Brother, 21 March 1916, Brent Mackrell, Scrapbooks relating to early British and New Zealand military aviation, I and III, ATL MSZ-1583.

33 Keith Caldwell, Logbook, AFMNZ.

34 Keith Caldwell, Logbook, 18 September 1917, AFMNZ.

35 Keith Caldwell, Logbook, 18 September 1916, AFMNZ.

36   *Northern Advocate*, 12 January 1918; TNA AIR 1/845/204/5/374; Geoffrey Gordon Callender, Combat Report, 20 October 1916, TNA AIR 1/911/204/5/835.

37   Christopher Cole & E. F. Cheesman, *The Air Defence of Britain 1914–1918* (London: Putnam, 1984), pp. 70–1.

38   Bruce W. Harkness, Jeffery T. Harkness, Timothy D. Harkness, Christopher W. Harkness & Donald E. Harkness, *A World War 1 Adventure: The life and times of RNAS Bomber Pilot Donald E. Harkness* (Bloomington, Ind.: AuthorHouse, 2014), p. 74.

39   Ibid., pp. 74–5.

40   Air Historical Branch, 5/205 Squadron History, TNA AIR 1/695/21/20/205.

41   Harkness et al., *A World War 1 Adventure*, pp. 303–4.

42   Ibid., p. 305.

43   Ibid., p. 321.

44   Cole & Cheesman, *The Air Defence of Britain*, p. 163.

45   Alfred de Bathe Brandon, Logbook, AFMNZ.

46   Cole & Cheesman, *The Air Defence of Britain*, p. 152.

47   D. Robinson, *The Zeppelin in Combat: A history of the German Naval Airship Division, 1912–1918* (London: Foulis, 1963), p. 136; Air Historical Branch, Reports on the Destruction of German Airships During the War, IWM 44990.

48   Information obtained from the crew of the German airship *L33* examined in Colchester and in London on various dates between the 24th September and the 5th October, 1916, TNA AIR 1/2599.

49   Cole & Cheesman, *The Air Defence of Britain*, p. 169.

50   Alfred de Bathe Brandon, unpublished memoir, p. 11, Errol Martyn Collection.

51   Ibid.

52   Information obtained from the crew of the German airship *L33* examined in Colchester and in London on various dates between the 24th September and the 5th October, 1916, TNA AIR 1/2597; Cole & Cheesman, *The Air Defence of Britain*, p. 170.

53   Jones, *War in the Air, vol. 3*, pp. 226–7.

54   *Wanganui Chronicle*, 10 October 1916.

55   Robinson, *The Zeppelin in Combat*, p. 189.

56   Air Historical Branch, 11 Squadron History, TNA AIR 1/688/21/2011.

57   Martyn, *For Your Tomorrow, vol. 1*, p. 40.

58   Forrest Gale Parsons, Personnel File, ANZ AABK 18805 W5515/44 SA3010.

59   Air Historical Branch, 7 Squadron History, TNA AIR 1/687/21/20/7.

60   Henshaw, *The Sky Their Battlefield II*, p. 59.

61   *Hastings Standard*, 11 December 1916; Martyn, *For Your Tomorrow, vol. 1*, p. 41.

62   *Blue and White: The Magazine of St Patrick's College, Wellington*, vol. X, no. 1 (1919), p. 38.

63   Ibid.

64   F. D. Holden, 'Experimental Squadron RFC Orfordness 1916–1919,' *Cross and Cockade*, vol. 8, no. 2 (1977), pp. 49–61; J. W. Best, 'C. F. Collett, 1886–1917', *Aviation Historical Society of New Zealand*, vol. 43, no. 2 (2000), pp. 38–9.

65   Martin Collett to Author, 9 September 2016.

66   Collett to Margaret Cummings, 12 June 1916, Martin Collett Collection.

67   Collett to Margaret Cummings, n.d., Martin Collett Collection.

68   Collett to Margaret Cummings, 30 June 1916, Martin Collett Collection.

69   Collett to Margaret Cummings, 22 June 1916, Martin Collett Collection.

70   Collett to Margaret Cummings, 12 June 1916, Martin Collett Collection.

71   Collett to Margaret Cummings, 22 June 1916, Martin Collett Collection.

72   Collett, photograph album, AFMNZ.

73   Leonard Bridgman, *The Clouds Remember: The aeroplanes of World War I* (London: Arms & Armour, 1972), pp. 34–5.

74   Quoted in Best, 'C. F. Collett', p. 39.

75   Ian Mackersey, *No More Empty Chairs: The short and heroic lives of the young aviators who fought and died in the First World War* (London: Weidenfeld & Nicolson, 2012), p. 293.

76   Ibid., p. 294.

77   'McScotch', *Fighter Pilot* (London: Greenhill, 1985), p. 88.

78   Ira 'Taffy' Jones, *Tiger Squadron: The story of 74 Squadron, R.A.F., in two World Wars* (London: A. H. Allen, 1954), p. 84.

79   *New Zealand Motor & Cycle Journal*, September 1910, quoted in Errol Martyn, *A Passion for Flight: New Zealand aviation before the Great War, vol. 2: Aeroclubs, aeroplanes, aviators and aeronauts 1910–1914* (Christchurch: Volplane, 2013), p. 129.

80   Mackersey, *No More Empty Chairs*, p. 295.

81   Report of experiments carried out at Orfordness, January 21st 1917 [*sic*], TNA AIR 1/1121/204/5/2073.

82   Arthur Gould Lee, *No Parachute* (London: Grub Street, 2013), pp. 226–33; Mackersey, *No More Empty Chairs*, pp. 293–300.

83   Joan Burkett (née Cumming) to Family, 19 July 2004, Martin Collett Collection.

CHAPTER TEN: BLOODY APRIL

1   Peter Grey & Owen Thetford, *German Aircraft of the First World War* (London: Putnam, 1962), p. 148.

2   H. A. Jones, *War in the Air: Being the story of the part played in the Great War by the Royal Air Force, vol. 2* (London: Imperial War Museum, 1928), pp. 472–5.

3   Maurice Baring, *Flying Corps Headquarters: 1914–1918* (London: William Heinemann, 1930), p. 200.

4   Roderick Norman Loudan Munro, Service Record, TNA AIR 79/193/17178.

5   Alan Morris, *Bloody April* (London: Jarrolds, 1967), pp. 102–3.

6   Terrence J. Finnegan, *Shooting the Front: Allied aerial reconnaissance in the First World War* (Stroud, Gloucestershire: Spellmount, 2014), p. 86.

7   A. J. Insall, *Observer: Memoirs of the R.F.C. 1915–1918* (London: William Kimber, 1970), p. 155–6.

8   Ibid., p. 155.

9   Finnegan, *Shooting the Front*, p. 75.

10   Ibid., pp. 74–5.

11   Air Historical Branch, 25 Squadron History, p. 27, TNA AIR 1/690/21/20/25.

12   *Manawatu Times*, 17 May 1917; William Stanley Shirtcliffe, Combat Report, 29 January 1917, TNA AIR 1/1221/204/5/2634.

13   William Shirtcliffe, Combat Report, 29 January 1917, TNA AIR 1/1221/204/5/2634.

14   *Manawatu Times*, 17 May 1917.

15   Roderick Munro, Combat Report, 25 Squadron, 17 January, 4 March 1917, TNA AIR 1/1221/204/5/2634; Air Historical Branch, 25 Squadron History, TNA AIR 1/690/21/20/25.

16   Roderick Munro, Logbook, 17 September 1916 to 16 March 1917, AFMNZ; 21 January, 4 March 1917, TNA AIR 1/1221/204/5/2634.

17 The Combat Report says that Munro was 'wounded to his side' but his own logbook states, 'Was wounded in two places in R. leg. by bullets.' Combat Report, Roderick Munro, 25 Squadron, 17 January, 4 March 1917, AIR 1/1221/204/5/2634 TNA; Roderick Munro, Logbook, 4 March 1917, AFMNZ. For the actual losses see Trevor Henshaw, *The Sky Their Battlefield II: Air fighting and air casualties of the Great War* (High Barnet, Herts: Fetubi, 2014), p. 72.

18 Errol Martyn, *Swift to the Sky: New Zealand's military aviation history* (Auckland: Penguin Viking, 2010), p. 51.

19 Sholto Douglas, *Years of Combat: The first volume of the autobiography of Sholto Douglas, Marshal of the Royal Air Force Lord Douglas of Kirtleside, G.C.B., M.C., D.F.C.* (London: Collins, 1963), p. 163.

20 Ibid.

21 Air Historical Branch, 43 Squadron History, p. 6, TNA AIR 1/692/21/20/43; Douglas, *Years of Combat*, p. 163.

22 Officers' Record Book, 60 Squadron, TNA AIR 1/1553/204/79/56.

23 Eustace Grenfell, Combat Report, 11 December 1916, TNA AIR 1/1225/204/5/2634; A. J. Scott, *Sixty Squadron RAF: A history of the squadron, 1916–1919* (London: Greenhill, 1990), pp. 31–2.

24 Lindsey Spence Weedon, Combat Report, 11 December 1916, TNA AIR 1/1225/204/5/2634.

25 Keith Caldwell, Combat Report, 11 December 1916, TNA AIR 1/1225/204/5/2634.

26 Air Historical Branch, 60 Squadron History, TNA AIR 1/173/15/180/1.

27 Ian Mackersey, *No More Empty Chairs: The short and heroic lives of the young aviators who fought and died in the First World War* (London: Weidenfeld & Nicolson, 2012), p. 207.

28 Alan Scott, Combat Report, 31 March 1917, TNA AIR 1/1225/204/5/2634.

29 Air Historical Branch, 11 Squadron History, p. iii, TNA AIR 1/166/15/150/1.

30 Air Historical Branch, 11 Squadron History, pp. 9–10, TNA AIR 1/688/21/20/11.

31 Air Historical Branch, 11 Squadron History, p. iii, TNA AIR 1/166/15/150/1.

32 George Masters, Base Record, ANZ AABK 18805/W5549/5/0078973; Air Historical Branch, 11 Squadron History, ANZ AIR 1/688/21/20/11.

33 Wayne McDonald, *Honours and Awards to the New Zealand Expeditionary Force in the Great War 1914–1918* (Hamilton: Richard Stowers, 2013), p. 173.

34 George Masters, Diary, 27 January 1915, Lyndsay Brock Collection.

35 Ibid.

36 Lyndsay Brock to Author, 9 August 2016; George Masters, Personnel file, ANZ AABK 18805/W5549/5/0078973.

37 Military Aeronautics Directorate, Air Board, to New Zealand High Commissioner, 1 August 1917, ANZ AABK 18805 W5674/10 425297; Missing Officers of 60 Squadron RFC, December 1916 to September 1917, TNA AIR 1/1552/204/79/50; Errol Martyn, *For Your Tomorrow: A record of New Zealanders who have died while serving with the RNZAF and Allied air services since 1915, vol. 1: Fates 1915–1942* (Christchurch: Volplane, 1998), p. 41.

38 Air Historical Branch, 11 Squadron History, p. 3, TNA AIR 1/688/21/20/11.

39 Emphasis in the original. George Masters, 1915, Lyndsay Brock Collection.

40 Henshaw, *The Sky Their Battlefield II*, p. 75.

41 Ibid., p. 69.

42 Ibid., p. 79.

43 Thanks to the poor in-the-field conditions, Caldwell had been plagued with scabies for three months. Keith Caldwell, Service Record, TNA WO 339/57844.

44 *Nelson Evening Mail*, 16 November 1916.

45   Scott in his history of 60 Squadron has six machines of 'A' Flight, but the surviving combat report details only five. Scott, *Sixty Squadron*, p. 44; cf. Graham Young, Combat Report, 14 April 1914, TNA AIR 1/1225/204/5/2634.

46   Graham Young, Combat Report, 14 April 1914, TNA AIR 1/1225/204/5/2634.

47   Scott, *Sixty Squadron*, pp. 44–5.

48   Missing Officers of 60 Squadron RFC, December 1916 to September 1917, TNA AIR 1/1552/204/79/50.

49   Officers Record Book, 60 Squadron, TNA AIR 1/1553/204/79/56; Missing Officers of 60 Squadron RFC, December 1916 to September 1917, TNA AIR 1/1552/204/79/50; John Herbert Cock, Report on casualties to personnel and machines (when flying), 14 April 1917, TNA AIR 1/1551/204/79/49.

50   Scott, *Sixty Squadron*, p. 45; G. A. H. Pidcock, Combat Report, 16 April 1917, TNA AIR 1/1225/204/5/2634.

51   Scott, *Sixty Squadron*, pp. 45–6.

52   E. P. Chennells, Capt. RAMC, MO, 3rd Brigade, RFC, 26 May 1917. Confidential Reports on Officers December 1916–April 1918, TNA AIR 1/1555/204/79/75.

53   Alan Scott to Headquarters, 13th Wing, 19 May 1917. Confidential Reports on Officers December 1916–April 1918, TNA AIR 1/1555/204/79/75.

54   Alan Scott to Headquarters, 13th Wing, 27 April 1917. Confidential Reports on Officers December 1916–April 1918, TNA AIR 1/1555/204/79/75.

55   Scott, *Sixty Squadron*, pp. 45–6.

56   Alan Scott, Combat Report, 22 April 1917, TNA AIR 1/1225/204/5/2634; Lieutenant Colonel, Commanding 13th Wing, RFC, n.d., TNA AIR 1/1225/204/5/2634.

57   Air Historical Branch, 24 Squadron History, p. 19, TNA AIR 1/690/21/20/24.

58   Ibid.

59   *A Messenger from Mars* (1903) was New Zealand's first fiction film. It was the basis for a 1913 British feature-length adaptation. The New Zealand film was in turn based on a play of the same name; see *Southland Times*, 22 January 1903. It adapted Charles Dickens' *A Christmas Carol*, exposing the selfishness of humankind; see *Free Lance*, 31 January 1903.

60   Emphasis in original. Melville White to family, 5 April 1917, ATL MSY-7036.

61   Melville White to his sister, 20 April 1917, ATL MSY-7036.

62   Ibid.

63   Captain Read & W. T. Hall, 23 April 1917, Squadron Record Book, 24 Squadron March–July 1917, TNA AIR 1/171/15/160/11; Henshaw, *The Sky Their Battlefield II*, p. 82; Norman L. R. Franks, Frank W. Bailey & Russell Guest, *Above the Lines: A complete record of the fighter aces of the German Air Service, Naval Air Service and Flanders Marine Corps, 1914–1918* (London: Grub Street, 1993), p. 203.

64   Squadron Commander to White family, 25 May 1917, ATL MSY-7036.

65   Melville White to Family, 5 April 1917, ATL MSY-7036.

66   Paul Sortehaug, 'Flight Lieutenant Thomas Grey Culling', *Pacific Wings* 81, no. 12 (December 2013–January 2014, p. 50.

67   The 'Detached Squadron' became 1 Squadron in December 1916.

68   1 (Naval) Squadron, Squadron Record Book, 3 April 1917, TNA AIR 1/1502/204/40/10; 1 (Naval) Squadron, Squadron Record Book, 8, 13, 14, 19, 30 April 1917, TNA AIR 1/1502/204/40/10.

69   Adrian Hellwig, *Australian Hawk Over the Western Front: A biography of Major R. S. Dallas DSO, DSC, C de G avec Palme* (London: Grub Street, 2006), p. 118.

70   Ibid., pp. 60, 118.

71   Kenneth Millward, Logbook, 30 February 1917, AFMNZ.

72   Thomas Culling, Combat Report, 6 April 1917, TNA AIR 1/1216/204/5/2634; 1 (Naval) Squadron, Squadron

Record Book, 6 April 1917, TNA AIR 1/1502/204/40/10.

73 John Anthony Carr, Service Record, TNA AIR 76/77/159; Deborah Quilter to Author, 25 July 2016.

74 1 (Naval) Squadron, Squadron Record Book, 1–30 April 1917, TNA AIR 1/1502/204/40/10; *London Gazette Supplement*, 1 October 1915.

75 Roderic Dallas, Thomas Culling, John Carr, Combat Report, 22 April 1917, TNA AIR 1/1216/204/5/2634; Chas Bowyer, *Royal Flying Corps Communiqués, 1917–1918* (London: Grub Street, 1988), pp. 41–2.

76 Sortehaug, 'Flight Lieutenant Thomas Grey Culling', p. 54.

77 H. A. Jones, *War in the Air: Being the story of the part played in the Great War by the Royal Air Force, vol. 3* (London: Imperial War Museum, 1931), p. 358.

78 Roderic Dallas, Thomas Culling, E. Anthony, D. Ramsey, Combat Report, 23 April 1917, TNA AIR 1/1216/204/5/2634.

79 *Supplement to the London Gazette*, 22 June 1917; *Auckland Star*, 22 May 1917.

80 T. Gerrard, Forster Maynard, B. C. Ridley, Minifie, Rowley, Ellis, Combat Report: 29 April 1917, TNA AIR 1/1216/204/5/2634.

81 Forster Maynard, Combat Report, 29 April 1917, TNA AIR 1/1216/204/5/2634.

82 1 (Naval) Squadron, Record Book, 30 April 1917, TNA AIR 1/1502/204/40/12; Roderic Dallas, Thomas Culling, E. Anthony, D. Ramsey, Combat Report, 30 April 1917, TNA AIR 1/1216/204/5/2634.

83 1 (Naval) Squadron, Squadron Record Book, 30 April 1917, TNA AIR 1/1502/204/40/12.

84 Roderic Dallas, B. C. Clayton, Thomas Culling, B. C. Ridley, D. Ramsey, Combat Report, 5 May 1917, TNA AIR 1/1216/204/5/2634.

85 Thomas Culling, Combat Report, 19 April 1917, TNA AIR 1/1216/204/5/2634; Kenneth Millward, Combat Report, 19 April 1917, TNA AIR 1/1216/204/5/2634; 1 (Naval) Squadron, Record Book, 5 May 1917, TNA AIR 1/1502/204/40/10.

CHAPTER ELEVEN: THE SUPREME SACRIFICE

1 *Feilding Star*, 8 September 1915.

2 *Manawatu Standard*, 8 September 1915.

3 *Dominion*, 24 September 1915.

4 Percival Stafford White, Diary, 26 October 1918, AFMNZ.

5 Percival Stafford White, Diary, 18 October 1918, AFMNZ.

6 *Oxford Dictionary of National Biography*, http://www.oxforddnb.com/view/article/74578, retrieved 8 June 2016.

7 *Manawatu Standard*, 8 September 1915.

8 Cyril Spear, Diary, 31 May 1917, Nelson Provincial Museum.

9 Goderic Hodges, *Memoirs of an Old Balloonatic* (London: William Kimber, 1972), p. 135.

10 Ibid., pp. 137–8.

11 Ibid., pp. 146; *Northern Advocate*, 10 August 1917.

12 Hodges, *Memoirs of an Old Balloonatic*, pp. 136–7.

13 Terrence J. Finnegan, *Shooting the Front: Allied aerial reconnaissance in the First World War* (Stroud, Gloucestershire: Spellmount, 2014), p. 90.

14 Fabian Pember Reeves, Service Record, TNA AIR 76/420/188.

15 *Evening Post*, 27 November 1917.

16 Keith Sinclair, *William Pember Reeves: New Zealand Fabian* (Oxford: Clarendon Press, 1965), p. 332.

17 Ibid.

18   1 (Naval) Squadron, Squadron Record Book, 30 May 1917, TNA AIR 1/1502/204/40/10.

19   Kenneth Millward, Logbook, 8 June 1917, AFMNZ; 1 (Naval) Squadron, Record Book, 8 June 1917, TNA AIR 1/1502/204/40/10.

20   *Hawera and Normanby Star*, 4 October 1917.

21   Ibid.

22   Cyril Saunderson Spear, Diary, 5 July 1917, Nelson Provincial Museum. It seems likely that the event described in the *Hawera and Normanby Star* is the same event, but they both mention a New Zealander and it was a triplane. Moreover, Millward's squadron was flying out of Bailleul (Millward, Logbook, 1 June 1917, AFMNZ). If that is the case, Millward's display before his countrymen occurred only two days before his death.

23   Kenneth Millward, Logbook, AFMNZ; 1 (Naval) Squadron, Squadron Record Book, 7 July 1917, TNA AIR 1/1502/204/40/10; Simon Moody to Author, 11 May 2017.

24   Karl Bodenschatz (trans. Jan Hayzlett), *Hunting with Richthofen: The Bodenschatz Diaries: Sixteen months of battle with JG Freiherr von Richthofen No. 1* (London: Grub Street, 1996), pp. 14–15.

25   Hans Schroder (trans. Claud W. Sykes), *An Airman Remembers* (London: John Hamilton, 1937), pp. 231–2.

26   1 (Naval) Squadron, Squadron Record Book, 7 July 1917, TNA AIR 1/1502/204/40/12; *Evening Post*, 16 July 1917.

27   *Wanganui Chronicle*, 29 September 1917.

28   Raymond H. Fredette, *The First Battle of Britain 1917/18* (London: Cassell, 1966), p. 65.

29   Air Historical Branch, 66 Squadron History, TNA AIR 1/694/21/20/66; Christopher Cole & E. F. Cheesman, *The Air Defence of Britain 1914–1918* (London: Putnam, 1984), pp. 255–9; Jon Sutherland & Diane Canwell, *Battle of Britain 1917: The first heavy bomber raids on England* (Barnsley, South Yorkshire: Pen and Sword Aviation, 2006), pp. 70–2.

30   Air Historical Branch, 66 Squadron History, TNA AIR 1/694/21/20/66.

31   4 March 1917; http://navymuseum.co.nz/worldwar1/people/flight-lieutenant-harold-beamish/, retrieved 17 August 2017.

32   Harold Beamish, Logbook, 16 February, 2 and 23 April, 3 July 1917; Harold Beamish Combat Report, 0630, 23 April 1917, TNA AIR 1/1216/204/5/2634/3.

33   Paul Sortehaug, 'Captain Harold Francis Beamish', *Pacific Wings* 80, no. 9 (2012), p. 50.

34   Ralf Leinburger, *Fighter: Technology, facts, history* (London: Parragon, 2008), p. 30.

35   Sortehaug, 'Captain Harold Francis Beamish', p. 50.

36   *Time Magazine*, 14 August 1944.

37   *Marlborough Express*, 5 November 1903.

38   Paul Sortehaug, 'Major Arthur Coningham', *Pacific Wings* 81, no. 10 (2013), pp. 50–1.

39   *New Zealand Herald*, 27 October 1917.

40   Summary of Work, 12 July 1917, 5th Brigade, War Diary, July 1917, TNA AIR 1/2220/209/40/9.

41   Summary of Work, 20 July 1917, 5th Brigade, War Diary, July 1917, TNA AIR 1/2220/209/40/9; Chaz Bowyer, *Royal Flying Corps Communiqués, 1917–1918* (London: Grub Street, 1998), pp. 84–5.

42   Summary of Work, 27 July 1917, 5th Brigade, War Diary, July 1917, TNA AIR 1/2220/209/40/9.

43   *New Zealand Herald*, 27 October 1917.

44   Summary of Work, 31 July 1917, 5th Brigade, War Diary, July 1917, TNA AIR 1/2220/209/40/9.

45   Ibid.

46   Albert William Gordon, Service Record, TNA WO 339/100266.

47   *Thames Star*, 12 August 1918; http://www.nzhistory.net.nz/media/photo/albert-gordon, retrieved 23 August 2017.

48   William Coates to Eleanor Coates, 16 July 1917, Coates Collection, Ruatuna, Matakohe.

49   William Coates to Eleanor Coates, 2 July 1917, Coates Collection, Ruatuna, Matakohe; William Coates to Eleanor 16 July 1917, Coates Collection, Ruatuna, Matakohe.

50   William Coates to Eleanor Coates, 2 July 1917, Coates Collection, Ruatuna, Matakohe.

51   Air Historical Branch, 32 Squadron History, TNA AIR 1/691/21/20/32.

52   *New Zealand Herald*, 19 April 1915; Mary Fordyce Strachan Hovey (née Milne), ANZ AABK 18805 W5568/52 0136120.

53   Gordon Coates to Eleanor Coates, 27 July 1917, Coates Collection, Ruatuna, Matakohe.

54   Gordon Coates to Eleanor Coates, 4 June 1917, Coates Collection, Ruatuna, Matakohe.

55   William Coates to Eleanor Coates, 16 July 1917, Coates Collection, Ruatuna, Matakohe.

56   32 Squadron, Squadron Diary, 13 July 1917, TNA AIR 1/1494/205/38/4; 5th Brigade 21 July to 22 July Summary of Work, 5th Brigade, War Diary, July 1917, TNA AIR 1/2220/209/40/9.

57   Director of Base Records to Eleanor Coates, 24 May 1918, Coates Collection, Ruatuna, Matakohe.

58   Mary Hovey to Eleanor Coates, 13 September 2017, Coates Collection, Ruatuna, Matakohe.

59   Sister to Eleanor Coates, 29 July 1917, Coates Collection, Ruatuna, Matakohe.

60   Gordon Coates to Eleanor Coates, 20 August 1917, Coates Collection, Ruatuna, Matakohe; Michael Bassett, *Coates of Kaipara* (Auckland: Auckland University Press, 1995), p. 50.

61   Vincent Orange, *Coningham: A biography of Air Marshal Sir Arthur Coningham KCB, KBE, DSO, MS, DFC, AFC* (London: Methuen, 1990), p. 23.

62   32 Squadron, Squadron Diary, 22 July 1917, TNA AIR 1/1494/205/38/4; 32 Squadron Diary, 25 July 1917, TNA AIR 1/494/205/38/4.

63   Air Historical Branch, 55 Squadron History, p. 8, TNA AIR 1/693/21/20/55.

64   *North Otago Times*, 9 September 1916.

65   High Commissioner to Prime Minister, New Zealand, 27 July 1917, Melville Johnstone, Personnel File, ANZ AABK 22525 W5712/1 BR 37/1208.

66   *Hastings Standard*, 30 July 1917.

67   *Manawatu Standard*, 28 July 1917.

68   Reports on Casualties to Personnel and Machines, 22 Squadron, 30 January 1918, TNA AIR 1/1522/204/67/21.

69   Henshaw, *The Sky Their Battlefield II*, p. 117.

70   Arthur Hirst Skinner, Logbook, 21 August–15 September 1917.

71   *New Zealand Herald*, 18 January 1926.

CHAPTER TWELVE: A BIGGER ENDEAVOUR

1   Park's flying logbook for the Great War is missing, although we do have his logbook from 1939. This covers his Second World War flights and shows that he was one of the few Allied airmen of high rank still capable of flying a modern fighter. The only information carried forward from his first logbook is the number of hours he had accrued in the Great War and interwar years: 800 (Keith Park, Logbook, AFMNZ). With regards to Park's hours at the end of training and as an instructor, see Vincent Orange, *Park: The biography of Air Chief Marshal Sir Keith Park GCB, KBE, MC, DFC, DCL* (London: Grub Street, 2001), p. 17; cf. Keith Caldwell, Logbook, AFMNZ; Roger Oswald Montgomerie, Logbook, John Montgomerie Collection; Errol Martyn, *Swift to the Sky: New Zealand's military aviation history* (Auckland: Penguin Viking, 2010), pp. 49–50.

2   Keith Park, 'Experiences in the War, 1914–1918,' p. 8, TNA AIR 10/973.

3   Ibid.

4   J. Guttman, *Bristol F2 Fighter Aces of World War 1* (Oxford: Osprey, 2007), p. 14.

5   *Flight*, 4 October 1917, p. 1021; *London Gazette* (Supplement), 15 February 1918, no. 30530, p. 2163. On 15 September 1917, Noss was killed as observer-gunner for another 48 Squadron pilot. Air Historical Branch, 48 Squadron History, TNA AIR 1/692/21/20/48.

6   J. W. Best, 'C. F. Collett, 1886–1917', *Aviation Historical Society of New Zealand* 43, no. 2 (2000), p. 40.

7   Sir Gordon Taylor, *Sopwith Scout 7309* (London: Cassell, 1968), p. 270.

8   Frederick James Horrell, Combat Report, 27 July 1917, Errol Martyn Collection.

9   Clive Collett, Logbook, 27 July 1917, AFMNZ; Clive Collett, Combat Report, 27 July 1917, TNA AIR 1/1226/204/5/2634.

10 Peter Grey & Owen Thetford, *German Aircraft of the First World War* (London: Putnam, 1962), pp. 49–52.

11 John Rawlings, *Fighter Squadrons of the RAF and Their Aircraft* (London: Macdonald, 1969).

12 Clive Collett, Logbook, 9 September 1917, AFMNZ; Clive Collett, Combat Report, 9 September 1917, TNA AIR 1/1226/204/5/2634.

13 Paul Sortehaug, 'Clive Franklyn Collett', *Pacific Wings* 81, no. 8 (2013), p. 52.

14 Dennis Hylands, 'Max Ritter von Muller', *Cross and Cockade* 10, no. 2 (1979), p. 72; Sortehaug, 'Clive Franklyn Collett', p. 52; Other suggestions include ace Ludwig Hanstein, Jasta 35: see Christopher Shores, Norman Franks & Russell Guest, *Above the Trenches: A complete record of the fighter aces and units of the British Empire air forces, 1915–1920* (London: Grub Street, 1990), p. 114 and Best, 'C. F. Collett, 1886–1917', p. 41; Henshaw notes claims could be made for airmen from Jastas 4, 26 and 35: see Trevor Henshaw, *The Sky Their Battlefield II: Air fighting and air casualties of the Great War* (High Barnet, Herts: Fetubi, 2014), p. 115.

15 Norman Franks, *Albatros Aces of World War I* (Oxford: Osprey, 2000), pp. 56–7.

16 James McCudden, *Flying Fury* (Folkestone: Bailey Brothers & Swinfen, 1973), pp. 215–16.

17 Keith Park, Combat Report, 9 September 1917, TNA AIR1/1223/204/5/2634.

18 14th Wing, Summary of Work, 14 September 1917, TNA AIR 1/1567/204/80/53. Orange has mistakenly placed these victories on 15 September 1917: see Christopher Shores' introduction to Orange, *Park*; see also Shores et al., *Above the Trenches*, pp. 296–7.

19 Keith Park, Combat Report, 14 September 1917, TNA AIR1/1223/204/5/2634.

20 Keith Park, 'Experiences in the War, 1914–1918', p. 11, TNA AIR 10/973.

21 Air Historical Branch, 48 Squadron History, TNA AIR 1/692/21/20/48.

22 Chaz Bowyer, *Royal Flying Corps Communiqués, 1917–1918* (London: Grub Street, 1998), pp. 127–8; 14th Wing, Summary of Work, September 1917, TNA AIR 1/1567/204/80/53.

23 Orange, *Park*, pp. 24–5.

24 *Press*, 23 October 1917.

25 Ibid.

26 A. R. Kingsford, *Night Raiders of the Air: Being the experiences of a night flying pilot, who raided Hunland on many dark nights during the War* (London: Greenhill, 1988), p. 74.

27 Ibid., pp. 75–6.

28 Arthur Reginald Kingsford, Logbook, 21–22 August 1917, Allan Kendrick Collection.

29 Air Historical Branch, 33 Squadron History, p. 19, TNA AIR 1/691/21/20/33; *Poverty Bay Herald*, 25 October 1917. Initial reports say Solomon was in pursuit of *L42* but Cole and Cheesman state it was most likely *L41*. See Christopher Cole & E. F. Cheesman, *The Air Defence of Britain 1914–1918* (London: Putnam, 1984), p. 286.

30 Ibid., p. 287.

31 Bill Ruxton, 'Night Bird: Recollections of a Kiwi in France. An interview with Major [*sic*.] A. R. Kingsford,'

14–18 Journal (1987), p. 59.

32   Kingsford, *Night Raiders of the Air*, p. 77.

33   Ibid.; Alfred Kingsford, Logbook, 18 October 1917, Allan Kendrick Collection.

34   Ruxton, 'Night Bird', p. 59.

35   Kingsford, *Night Raiders of the Air*, p. 82.

36   Cole & Cheesman, *The Air Defence of Britain*, p. 330.

37   *North Otago Times*, 12 December 1917.

38   High Commissioner to Prime Minister, 13 October 1917, Base Records, ANZ AABK 22525 W5712/1 BR 37/1468.

39   Cole & Cheesman, *The Air Defence of Britain*, pp. 344, 350.

40   *Hawera and Normanby Star*, 8 November 1917.

41   Appendix B: Chronological Table of Air Raids and R.F.C. Action Taken, in Air Historical Branch, 6th Brigade History, TNA AIR 1/687/21/20/6.

42   *Dominion*, 27 December 1917; Air Historical Branch, History of 6th Brigade RAF, 1914–1918, TNA AIR 1/687/21/20/6; Air Historical Branch, 33 (Home Defence) Squadron, p. 31, TNA AIR 1/20/20/33.

43   Cole & Cheesman, *The Air Defence of Britain*, p. 350; Errol Martyn, *For Your Tomorrow: A record of New Zealanders who have died while serving with the RNZAF and Allied air services since 1915, vol. 1: Fates 1915–1942* (Christchurch: Volplane, 1998), p. 45; Kingsford, *Night Raiders of the Air*, p. 85.

44   *Press*, 26 December 1917.

45   Henshaw, *The Sky Their Battlefield II*, p. 117.

46   Frederick James Horrell, Personnel File, ANZ AABK 18805 W5541/23 0056768; Officers Reporting Book, 56 Squadron, TNA AIR 1/1905/204/229/8.

47   Fredrick James Horrell, Officers' Invaliding Board, 11 February 1918, Service Record, TNA WO 339/102463; Fredrick James Horrell, Combat Reports, TNA AIR 1/1223/204/5/2634.

48   Frederick James Horrell, Combat Report, 14 September 1917, TNA AIR 1/1223/204/5/2634; Field Returns, 56 Squadron, 14 September 1917, TNA AIR 1/1905/204/229/6.

49   Frederick James Horrell, Medical Board Report, 18 October 1917, TNA WO 339/102463; Frederick James Horrell, Service Record, TNA AIR 76/238.

50   Frederick Horrell to Director General Aeronautics, 20 November 1917, TNA WO 339/102463. Elsewhere he states his last flight was on 1 October 1917: see Officers' Invaliding Board, 11 February 1918, Service Record, TNA WO 339/102463.

51   Frederick James Horrell, Medical Board Report, 9 February 1917, Service Record, TNA WO 339/102463.

52   Frederick James Horrell, Medical Board Report, 13 April 1918, Service Record, TNA WO 339/102463.

53   'McScotch', *Fighter Pilot* (London: Greenhill, 1985), p. 124.

53A   Ibid., p. 182

54   Gordon Thomson Pettigrew, Service Record, TNA WO 339/64640. This file also mistakenly holds the records of another man, G. T. R. Pettigrew.

54A   Charles, Kingsley Mills, Personnel File, ANZ WWI 13/94 N/N-Army.

55   Air Historical Branch, 23 Squadron History, p. 30, TNA AIR 1/690/21/20/23.

56   Air Historical Branch, 23 Squadron History, p. 34, TNA AIR 1/690/21/20/23.

57   Frank Bullock-Webster, Combat Report, 15 August 1917, TNA AIR 1/1221/204/5/2634.

58   Air Historical Branch, 23 Squadron History, pp. 32–40, TNA AIR 1/690/21/20/23.

59   Chief of General Staff to Director of Recruiting, 17 January 1918, ANZ AABK 22525 W5712/1 BR 37/1601; *Evening Star*, 15 January 1917.

60 *Auckland Star*, 13 January 1917; *Waikato Times*, 5 November 1917.

61 Herbert Drewitt, Service Record, TNA AIR 76/141/58; Frederic James Sharland, Service Record, TNA AIR 76/455/127.

62 G. H. Cunningham, *Mac's Memoirs: The flying life of Squadron-Leader McGregor* (Dunedin: Reed, 1937), p. 69.

63 *Star*, 28 November 1917.

64 Herbert Drewitt, James Hewett, Frederic Sharland, Combat Report, 18 October 1917, Errol Martyn Collection.

65 Ibid.

66 Martyn, *For Your Tomorrow, vol. 1*, p. 45; *Taranaki Daily News*, 19 November 1917.

67 *New Zealand Herald*, 26 December 1917.

68 Air Historical Branch, 23 Squadron History, p. 41, TNA AIR 1/690/21/20/23.

69 *London Gazette*, 22 June 1918.

70 Herbert Drewitt, Combat Report, 27 October 1917, TNA AIR 1/1221/204/5/2634.

71 Herbert Drewitt, Combat Report, 17 October 1917, TNA AIR 1/1221/204/5/2634.

72 Herbert Drewitt, Combat Report, 23 March 1918, TNA AIR 1/1221/204/5/2634.

73 Herbert Drewitt, Combat Report, 16 March 1918, TNA AIR 1/1221/204/5/2634.

74 Henshaw, *The Sky Their Battlefield II*, p. 130.

75 *Cambridge Edition*, 23 April 1990.

76 Arthur Albert Browne, Personnel File, ANZ AABK 18805 W5530 9/0019373; Air Historical Branch, 8 Squadron History, TNA AIR 1/688/21/20/8.

77 H. A. Jones, *War in the Air: Being the story of the part played in the Great War by the Royal Air Force, vol. 3* (London: Imperial War Museum, 1934), pp. 236–7.

78 Henshaw, *The Sky Their Battlefield II*, p. 133.

79 Jones, *War in the Air, vol. 3*, p. 252.

80 Arthur Browne, Combat Report, 30 November 1917, Errol Martyn Collection.

81 3 Brigade Recommendations, 5 December 1917, TNA AIR 1/1515/204/58/50; HQ RFC, Casualty Report, 30 November 1917, TNA AIR 1/852/204/5/396.

82 Clive Collett, Casualty Card, 7 January 1918, Martin Collett Collection.

83 Shores et al., *Above the Trenches*, pp. 268, 264, 318–19.

84 Clive Collett to Peggy Reid, n.d., Martin Collett Collection.

85 Martin Collett to Author, 8 September 2016; Letter: Joan Burkett (née Cumming) to Family, 19 July 2004, Martin Collett Collection.

86 Joan Burkett (née Cumming) to Family, 19 July 2004, Martin Collett Collection.

CHAPTER THIRTEEN: THE 'GREATEST SHOW EVER SEEN'

1 Trevor Henshaw, *The Sky Their Battlefield II: Air fighting and air casualties of the Great War* (High Barnet, Herts: Fetubi, 2014), p. 139.

2 Peter Grey & Owen Thetford, *German Aircraft of the First World War* (London: Putnam, 1962), p. 107.

3 Henshaw, *The Sky Their Battlefield II*, p. 139.

4 Air Historical Branch, 100 Squadron History, p. 12, TNA AIR 1/694/21/20/100.

5 Ibid., p. 6.

6 Ibid., p. 3.

7 Hugh Chambers, Logbook, AFMNZ; Hugh Chambers, Service Record, TNA AIR 79/730.

8   Alfred Kingsford, Diary, 21 January 1918, Allan Kendrick Collection.

9   Charlotte Kingsford, Diary, 2 January 1918, Allan Kendrick Collection.

10   Charlotte Kingsford, Diary, 13 January 1918, Allan Kendrick Collection.

11   Alfred Kingsford, Diary, 15 January 1918, Allan Kendrick Collection.

12   Alfred Kingsford, Diary, 16 January 1917, Allen Kendrick Collection.

13   Alfred Kingsford, Diary, 17 January 1918, Allan Kendrick Collection.

14   Charlotte Kingsford, 29 January 1918, Allan Kendrick Collection.

15   Bill Ruxton, 'Night Bird: Recollections of a Kiwi in France. An interview with Major [*sic*] A. R. Kingsford',
     14–18 Journal (1987), p. 65; Charlotte Kingsford, Diary, 27 February 1918, Allan Kendrick Collection.

16   A. R. Kingsford, *Night Raiders of the Air: Being the experiences of a night flying pilot, who raided Hunland
     on many dark nights during the War* (London: Greenhill, 1988), p. 97.

17   Air Historical Branch, 100 Squadron History, p. 13, TNA AIR 1/694/21/20/100.

18   Kingsford, *Night Raiders of the Air*, pp. 102–6.

18A Ibid., pp. 105–6.

19   Ibid., p. 107; Alfred Kingsford, Diary, 9 February 1918, Allan Kendrick Collection; Alfred Kingsford,
     Logbook, 9 February 1918, Allan Kendrick Collection.

20   Air Historical Branch, 101 Squadron History, TNA AIR 1/176/15/200/1.

21   Operation Orders, 101 Squadron, 26 January 1918, TNA AIR 1/1733/204/130/9.

22   Joe Bamford, *Surviving the Skies: A night bomber pilot in the Great War* (Staplehurst, Kent: Spellmount,
     2012).

23   Squadron Record Book, 101 Squadron, 25–26 January 1918, TNA AIR 1/1732/204/130/4.

24   Errol Martyn, *For Your Tomorrow: A record of New Zealanders who have died while serving with the
     RNZAF and Allied air services since 1915, vol. 1: Fates 1915–1942* (Christchurch: Volplane, 1998), p. 47;
     Operation Record Book, 101 Squadron, 25–26 January 1918, TNA AIR 1/1732/204/130/4.

25   *Press*, 26 December 1919; Thomas Nicoll, Service Record, TNA AIR 79/208/19061.

26   Squadron Record Book, 100 Squadron, 26–27 February 1918, TNA AIR 1/863/204/5/490.

27   Ruxton, 'Night Bird', p. 69.

28   *New Zealand Herald*, 8 April 1919.

29   Grisham to Secretary of the Treasury, 6 December 1921, Thomas Nicoll, Personnel File, ANZ AABK 22525
     W5712/1 BR 37/1286; Thomas Nicoll, Award Recommendation, TNA AIR 1/1031/204/5/1433.

30   *Mataura Ensign*, 23 August 1918.

31   *Evening Post*, 5 April 1919.

32   *Poverty Bay Herald*, 17 June 1918.

33   *Flight*, 27 August 1915, p. 630.

34   Errol Martyn, *Swift to the Sky: New Zealand's military aviation history* (Auckland: Penguin Viking, 2010),
     p. 51; *Flight*, 31 July 1919, p. 1018; Lister Briffault, Military Medal Citation, TNA AIR 1/1580/204/81/53.

35   *Colonist*, 17 July 1918.

36   Sydney Francis Anderson, Service Record, TNA ADM 188/585/12676; Sydney Francis Anderson, Service
     Record, TNA AIR 79/1912/212676; Sydney Francis Anderson, Service Record, TNA AIR 76/8/58.

37   T. H. Hallam [pseudonym: P.I.X.], *The Spider Web: The romance of a flying boat war flight* (Edinburgh:
     Blackwood, 1919), p. 94.

38   Ibid., p. 93.

39   Ibid., p. 102.

40   *Evening Post*, 12 October 1918.

41   Hallam, *The Spider Web*, p. 196.

42   Officially 'The Board of Trade Medal for Saving Life at Sea'.

43   *Evening Star*, 21 November 1918.

44   Hallam, *The Spider Web*, p. 226.

45   *Evening Post*, 19 June 1918.

46   *Flight*, 2 May 1918, p. 469; *London Gazette*, 26 April 1918.

47   Peter Chapman, 'Bomber Ace: Captain Euan Dickson', *Cross and Cockade* 27, no. 4 (1996), p. 177.

48   C. P. O. Bartlett, *Bomber Pilot, 1916–1918* (Shepperton, Surrey: Ian Allan, 1974), pp. 105–6.

49   *Flight*, 26 September 1918, p. 1076; Euan Dickson, Logbook, 19 December 1917, AFMNZ; Peter Chapman, 'Bomber Ace: Captain Euan Dickson', *Cross and Cockade* 27, no. 4 (1996), 181.

50   Euan Dickson, Combat Report, 8 December 1917, TNA AIR 1/2007/204/304/5.

51   Martyn, *Swift to the Sky*, pp. 38–9; Christopher Shores, Norman Franks & Russell Guest, *Above the Trenches: A complete record of the fighter aces and units of the British Empire air forces, 1915–1920* (London: Grub Street 1990), p. 140.

52   Henshaw, *The Sky Their Battlefield II*, p. 142.

53   Euan Dickson, Logbook, 6 March 1918, AFMNZ.

54   5 Naval Squadron and 205 Squadron, Squadron Record Book, 16 March 1918, TNA AIR 1/2009/204/304/10.

55   Euan Dickson, Logbook, 16 March 1918, AFMNZ.

56   S. J. Goble to Officer Commanding, 22 Wing, 17 March 1918, in Air Historical Branch, 205 Squadron History, TNA AIR 1/695/21/20/205; Euan Dickson, Combat Report, 16 March 1918, TNA AIR 1/1217/204/2634.

57   Chaz Bowyer, *Royal Flying Corps Communiqués, 1917–1918* (London: Grub Street, 1998), p. 232.

58   Euan Dickson, Logbook, 16 March 1917, AFMNZ; Bartlett, *Bomber Pilot*, p. 143.

59   Bartlett, *Bomber Pilot*, p. 142.

60   Euan Dickson, Logbook, 18 March 1918, AFMNZ.

61   Bartlett, *Bomber Pilot*, p. 143.

62   Charlotte Kingsford, Diary, 22 March 1918, Allan Kendrick Collection.

63   Charlotte Kingsford, Diary, 24 March 1918, Allan Kendrick Collection.

64   Alfred Kingsford, 20–26 March 1918, Allan Kendrick Collection.

65   Charlotte Kingsford, Diary, 30 March 1918, Allan Kendrick Collection.

66   Charlotte Kingsford, Diary, 2, 11 and 16 April 1918, Allan Kendrick Collection.

CHAPTER FOURTEEN: SPRING OFFENSIVE

1   C. P. O. Bartlett, *Bomber Pilot, 1916–1918* (Shepperton, Surrey: Ian Allan, 1974), p. 145.

2   Trevor Henshaw, *The Sky Their Battlefield II: Air fighting and air casualties of the Great War* (High Barnet, Herts: Fetubi, 2014), p. 146.

3   Field Returns, 56 Squadron, 3 November 1917, TNA AIR 1/1905/204/229/6.

4   https://osphistory.org/2015/06/28/remembering-the-balcombe-brown-brothers-100-years-on/, retrieved 28 November 2016.

5   Alex Revell, *High in the Empty Blue: The history of 56 Squadron, RFC, RAF, 1916–1919* (Mountain View, CA: Flying Machine Press, 1995), pp. 221, 296.

6   Balcombe-Brown, Combat Report, 1 April 1918, TNA AIR 1/1913/204/229/21.

7   Ibid.

8   Dulcie S. Caller to Balcombe-Brown, 17 December 1917, Confidential Reports, 56 Squadron, TNA AIR 1/1515/204/58/56.

9   Caroline Rhys-Davids to Balcombe-Brown, 2 March 1918, Confidential Reports, 56 Squadron, TNA AIR 1/1515/204/58/56; Alex Revell, *Brief Glory: The life of Arthur Rhys Davids, DSO, MC* (Barnsley, South Yorkshire: Pen & Sword, 2010), pp. 200–2.

10   *Press*, 10 July 1915.

11   J. Cowan to Balcombe-Brown, 13 November 1917, Confidential Reports, 56 Squadron, TNA AIR 1/1515/204/58/56.

12   G. Cawson to Balcombe-Brown, 10 December 1917, Confidential Reports, 56 Squadron, TNA AIR 1/1515/204/58/56.

13   Lucy H. Lilly to Balcombe-Brown, 21 April 1918, Confidential Reports, 56 Squadron, TNA AIR 1/1515/204/58/56.

14   Revell, *High in the Empty Blue*, p. 274.

15   A. Mealing to Balcombe-Brown, 1 April 1918, Confidential Reports, 56 Squadron, TNA AIR 1/1515/204/58/56.

16   Revell, *High in the Empty Blue*, p. 274; Christopher Shores, Norman Franks & Russell Guest, *Above the Trenches: A complete record of the fighter aces and units of the British Empire air forces, 1915–1920* (London: Grub Street, 1990), p. 278.

17   Unnamed to Balcombe-Brown, 10 December 1917, Confidential Reports, 56 Squadron, TNA AIR 1/1515/204/58/56.

18   Dulcie S. Caller to Balcombe-Brown, 17 December 1917, Confidential Reports, 56 Squadron, TNA AIR 1/1515/204/58/56.

19   Correspondence on kit and inventories of kit: casualty officers, 56 Squadron, TNA AIR 1/1908/204/229/10.

20   Henshaw, *The Sky Their Battlefield II*, p. 161.

21   Beryl E. Escott, *Women in Air Force Blue: The story of women in the Royal Air Force from 1918 to the present day* (Wellingborough, Northamptonshire: Patrick Stephens, 1989), pp. 45–6.

22   *Evening Post*, 28 February 1920; Madeline Ranken, Certificate of Discharge on Demobilisation, TNA AIR 80/199/7.

23   Ibid.

24   George Ernest Simeon, Personnel File, ANZ AABK 18805 W5958/38 0359976.

25   Harriet Simeon, Personnel File, ANZ AABK 22525 W5714 9/BR 37/3726.

26   *Dominion*, 18 February 1920.

27   Ibid.

28   Harriet Simeon, Personnel File, ANZ AABK 22525 W5714 9/BR 37/3726; *Dominion*, 18 February 1920.

29   John Yoxall, 'No. 2 Squadron', *Flight*, 9 June 1949.

30   Susanna Montgomerie Norris with Anna Rogers, *Annie's War: A New Zealand woman and her family in England, 1916–19.* (Dunedin: Otago University Press, 2014), p. 156.

31   Ibid., p. 163.

32   Ibid., p. 158.

33   10th Wing, 1st Brigade, 4.00 pm 8 April to 4.00 pm 9 April, 1st Brigade Summaries of Work, April 1918, TNA AIR 1/1465/204/36/76.

34   Hew Montgomerie, Diary, 9 April 1918, Susanna Montgomerie Norris Collection.

35   Hew Montgomerie, Diary, 10 April 1918, Susanna Montgomerie Norris Collection.

36   Hew Montgomerie, Diary, 12 April 1918, Susanna Montgomerie Norris Collection; 1st Brigade Summaries

of Work, April 1918, TNA AIR 1/1465/204/36/76.

37   Norris & Rogers, *Annie's War*, p. 164.

38   Hew Montgomerie, Diary, 14 April 1918, Susanna Montgomerie Norris Collection; 10th Wing, 1st
     Brigade, 4.00 pm 14 April to 4.00 pm 15 April, 1st Brigade Summaries of Work, April 1918, TNA AIR
     1/1465/204/36/76.

39   10th Wing, 1st Brigade, 4.00 pm 14 April to 4.00 pm 15 April, 1st Brigade Summaries of Work, April 1918,
     TNA AIR 1/1465/204/36/76.

40   Henshaw, *The Sky Their Battlefield II*, p. 166; 10th Wing, 1st Brigade, 4.00 pm 14 April to 4.00 pm 15 April,
     1st Brigade Summaries of Work, April 1918, TNA AIR 1/1465/204/36/76; 10th Wing, 1st Brigade, 4.00 pm
     15 April to 4.00 pm 16 April, 1st Brigade Summaries of Work, April 1918, TNA AIR 1/1465/204/36/76.

41   Henshaw, *The Sky Their Battlefield II*, p. 161.

42   Michael Molkentin, *Australia and the War in the Air* (South Melbourne: Oxford University Press, 2014),
     p. 166.

43   4 AFC Squadron, War Diary, 23 March 1918, TNA AIR 1/2253/209/57/9.

44   Herbert Gillis Watson, Service Record, NAA B2455.

45   4 AFC Squadron, War Diary, 7 April 1918, TNA AIR 1/2253/209/57/9; John Classon Courtney, Service
     Record, NAA B2455; A. H. Cobby, *High Adventure* (Melbourne: Robertson & Mullens, 1942), pp. 88–9.

46   Molkentin, *Australia and the War in the Air*, p. 167.

47   Herbert Watson, Combat Report, 19 April 1918, TNA AIR 1/1217/204/5/2634.

48   *Australian Dictionary of Biography*, 'Cobby, Arthur Henry (1894–1955)', http://adb.anu.edu.au/biography/
     cobby-arthur-henry-5700, retreived 21 November 2016.

49   4 AFC Squadron, War Diary, 18 June 1918, TNA AIR 1/2254/209/57/11.

50   Herbert Gillis Watson, Combat Report, 17 June 1918, TNA AIR 1/1217/204/5/2634.

51   Arthur Henry Cobby, Combat Report, 17 June 1917, TNA AIR 1/1217/204/5/2634.

52   Bill Ruxton, 'Night Bird: Recollections of a Kiwi in France. An interview with Major [*sic*] A. R. Kingsford',
     14–18 Journal (1987), p. 71; Alfred Kingsford, Logbook, 20 April 1918, Allan Kendrick Collection.

53   Air Historical Branch, 5 (Naval) Squadron History, TNA AIR 1/695/21/20/205.

54   Air Historical Branch, 10 Squadron History, p. 6, TNA AIR 1/688/21/20/10.

55   Ira 'Taffy' Jones, *Tiger Squadron: The story of 74 Squadron, R.A.F., in Two World Wars* (London: A. H.
     Allen, 1954), p. 71.

56   Air Historical Branch, 27 Squadron History, p. 14, TNA AIR 1/690/21/20/27; Errol Martyn, *A Passion
     for Flight: New Zealand aviation before the Great War, vol. 3: The Joe Hammond story and military
     beginnings 1910–1914* (Christchurch: Volplane, 2013), p. 162.

57   Jones, *Tiger Squadron*, p. 64.

58   Frederick Oughton (ed.), *The Personal Diary of 'Mick' Mannock, V.C., D.S.O., M.C. (1 bar)* (London:
     Oakfield Press, 1966), pp. 185.

59   Spencer Bertram Horn, notes regarding 60 Squadron, AC86/77/4/3, RAFM.

60   Jones, *Tiger Squadron*, p. 70.

61   L. A. Richardson, *Pilot's Log: The log, diary, letters and verse of Lt. Leonard A. Richardson, Royal Flying
     Corps 1917–1918* (St Catherines, Ontario: Paul Heron, 1998), p. 144.

62   Jones, *Tiger Squadron*, p. 69.

63   Richardson, *Pilot's Log*, p. 204.

64   Oughton, *The Personal Diary of 'Mick' Mannock*, pp. 182–3.

65   Ibid., p. 183.

66   Ibid., p. 187.

67 Ibid., pp. 188–90.

68 Ibid., p. 186.

69 Richardson, *Pilot's Log*, pp. 165, 170.

70 Vincent Orange, *Park: The biography of Air Chief Marshal Sir Keith Park GCB, KBE, MC, DFC, DCL* (London: Grub Street, 2001), p. 27.

71 Frank Cecil Ransley, Transcript, Liddle Collection, University of Leeds, LIDDLE/WW1/AIR256.

72 Orange, *Park*, p. 28.

73 Roger Vee, *Flying Minnows: Memoirs of a World War One fighter pilot, from training in Canada to the Front Line, 1917–1918* (London: Arms & Armour, 1977), p. 178.

74 Ibid.

75 Keith Park, 'Experiences in the War, 1914–1918', p. 12, Liddle Collection, University of Leeds, LIDDLE/WW1/AIR/234.

76 Vee, *Flying Minnows*, pp. 186–7.

77 Ralph Barker, *A Brief History of the Royal Flying Corps in World War I* (London: Robertson, 2002), p. 470.

78 Field Returns, 56 Squadron, 5 May 1918, TNA AIR 1/1905/204/229/6; Revell, *High in the Empty Blue*, pp. 292–3; Norman L. R. Franks, Frank W. Bailey & Russell Guest, *Above the Lines: A complete record of the fighter aces of the German Air Service, Naval Air Service and Flanders Marine Corps 1914–1918* (London: Grubb Street, 1993), pp. 158–60.

79 Air Historical Branch, 56 Squadron History, p. 22, TNA AIR 1/693/21/20/56.

CHAPTER FIFTEEN: SEA ASSAULT

1 Peter Nielsen, Personnel File, ANZ AABK 18805 W5549/82 0086660.

2 Air Historical Branch, 84 Squadron History, p. 19, TNA AIR 1/694/21/20/84.

3 84 Squadron, Squadron Record Book, 18 June 1918, TNA AIR 1/1795/204/155/3.

4 *Feilding Star*, 11 February 1918.

5 *London Gazette*, 20 October 1916; *Flight*, 15 August 1918, p. 920.

6 *New Zealand Herald*, 8 January 1918.

7 Roy James Fitzgerald, Service Record, TNA WO 161/96.

8 *Evening Post*, 25 July 1918.

9 *Free Lance*, 25 July 1918.

10 *Poverty Bay Herald*, 31 July 1918; 35 Squadron, Squadron Record Book, TNA AIR 1/1400/204/27/19.

11 35 Squadron, Squadron Record Book, 2 July 1918, TNA AIR 1/1400/204/27/19.

12 *Evening Post*, 16 October 1918.

13 Robin Tudor Barlow, Personnel Record, ANZ AABK 18805 W 5520 51/0011565; *Flight*, 14 November 1918, p. 1298; Robin Tudor Barlow, Service Record, TNA WO 339/58730; *Press*, 1 June 1916.

14 Robin Tudor Barlow, Casualty Reports, 34 Squadron, 1–15 August 1917, TNA AIR 1/850/204/5/389.

15 Errol Martyn, *For Your Tomorrow: A record of New Zealanders who have died while serving with the RNZAF and Allied air services since 1915, vol. 3: Biographies & Appendices* (Christchurch: Volplane, 2008), p. 49.

16 Robin Tudor Barlow, Casualty Reports, 52 Squadron, 31 July 1918, TNA AIR 1/850/204/5/389.

17 H. A. Jones, *War in the Air: Being the story of the part played in the Great War by the Royal Air Force, vol. 6* (London: Imperial War Museum, 1935), pp. 135–7.

18 Marvin L. Skelton, 'The Long Plod Home: Lt Roy Shillinglaw recalls 100 Squadron', *Cross and Cockade* 16, no. 3 (1979), p. 119.

19   Alfred Kingsford, Logbook, 25 June 1918, Allan Kendrick Collection.

20   Skelton, 'The Long Plod Home', p. 119.

21   A. R. Kingsford, *Night Raiders of the Air: Being the experiences of a night flying pilot, who raided Hunland on many dark nights during the War* (London: Greenhill, 1988), p. 164.

22   Bill Ruxton, 'Night Bird: Recollections of a Kiwi in France. An interview with Major [*sic*] A. R. Kingsford', *14–18 Journal* (1987), p. 74; Alfred Kingsford, Logbook, 25 July 1918, Allan Kendrick Collection.

23   Alfred Kingsford, Diary, 15 May to 10 August 1918, Allan Kendrick Collection.

24   Ruxton, 'Night Bird', p. 75.

25   Ibid., p. 76.

26   Charlotte Kingsford, Diary, 17 August 1918, Allan Kendrick Collection.

27   Alfred Kingsford, Logbook, Allan Kendrick Collection.

28   Martyn, *For Your Tomorrow, vol. 3*, p. 46.

29   Air Historical Branch, 33 (Home Defence) Squadron History, p. 27, TNA AIR 1/691/17/21/20/33; Frederick Livingstone, Service Record, TNA WO 339/110719.

30   Cecil Henry Noble Campbell, Base Records, ANZ AABK 18805 W5922/56 1.

31   Jones, *War in the Air*, p. 126.

32   Christopher Cole & E. F. Cheesman, *The Air Defence of Britain 1914–1918* (London: Putnam, 1984), pp. 412–13.

33   Ibid.

34   Cole & Cheesman, ibid., p. 412–13, offer a number of theories but are unable to definitively attribute the cause of Noble-Campbell's injuries and damage sustained by his machine. Cf. Robinson, *The Zeppelin in Combat: A history of the German Naval Airship Division, 1912–1918* (London: Foulis, 1963), p. 309 and Jones, *War in the Air, vol. 5*, p. 126.

35   Dick Cronin, 'Tondern: Prelude, climax and aftermath', *Cross and Cockade* 25, no. 2 (1994), p. 59.

36   R. D. Layman, '*Furious* and the Tondern Raid', *Warship International* 10, no. 4 (1973), p. 380.

37   Report on Attack on Zeppelin Sheds at Tondern by Aeroplanes flown from HMS *Furious*, 19 July 1918, TNA AIR 1/344/15/226/287.

38   W. F. Dickson, RAF, After Action Report, 19 July 1918, Bombing of Tondern on 19 July 1918, TNA AIR 1/455/15/312/44; Intelligence summary of Tondern and district, TNA AIR 1/639/17/122/190.

39   *Wanganui Chronicle*, 3 March 1919.

40   Bernard Smart, After Action Report, 19 July 1918, Bombing of Tondern on 19 July 1918, TNA AIR 1/455/15/312/44.

41   Samuel Dawson, After Action Report, 7 August 1918, Reports on the Destruction of German Airships During the War, IWM (0)44990.

42   Layman, '*Furious* and the Tondern Raid', p. 382; Bombing of Tondern on 19 July 1918, TNA AIR 1/455/15/312/44.

43   Cole & Cheesman, *The Air Defence of Britain*, pp. 350, 412.

44   Stuart Leslie, 'Extracts from the Diary kept by Corporal John Tiplady', *Cross and Cockade* 23, no. 1 (1992), p. 39.

45   *Wanganui Chronicle*, 3 March 1919.

46   *Evening Post*, 13 December 1918.

47   Report of attack on Zeppelin sheds at Tondern by aeroplanes from H.M.S. *Furious*, TNA AIR 1/344/15/226/287.

48   G. H. Cunningham, *Mac's Memoirs: The flying life of Squadron-Leader McGregor* (Dunedin: Reed, 1937), p. 43.

49 Ibid., pp. 47, 49.

50 Elliot White Springs, *War Birds: Diary of an unknown aviator* (Sydney: Cornstalk, 1928), pp. 228–229.

51 *London Gazzette*, 26 November 1915.

52 Donald Clyde Inglis, Service Record, TNA AIR 76/249/40; Donald Clyde Inglis, Personnel File, ANZ AABK 18805 W5541 44/0058859.

53 Cunningham, *Mac's Memoirs*, p. 57.

54 Ibid.

55 Springs, *War Birds*, p. 140.

56 Cunningham, *Mac's Memoirs*, pp. 57–8.

57 Malcolm McGregor, Combat Report, 24 July 1918, TNA AIR 1/1227/204/5/2634.

58 In *Mac's Memoirs* (pp. 61–2) Cunningham put McGregor on 12 victories, but Shores et al. has only seven: Christopher Shores, Norman Franks & Russell Guest, *Above the Trenches: A complete record of the fighter aces and units of the British Empire air forces, 1915–1920* (London: Grub Street, 1990), p. 275.

59 Frederick Oughton (ed.), *The Personal Diary of 'Mick' Mannock, V.C., D.S.O., M.C. (1 bar)* (London: Oakfield Press, 1966), pp. 197–8.

60 Donald Inglis, Combat Report, 26 July 1918, TNA AIR 1/1227/204/5/2634; *Sun*, 6 October 1919.

61 Donald Inglis, 'Mannock's Last Flight', *Popular Flying*, July 1938, p. 188; Oughton, *The Personal Diary of 'Mick' Mannock*, p. 200.

62 Cunningham, *Mac's Memoirs*, p. 63.

63 Ira Jones, *King of the Air Fighters: Biography of Major 'Mick' Mannock, V.C., D.S.O., M.C., D.F.C., M.M.* (London: Nicholson & Watson, 1935), p. 251.

64 Ibid., p. 252.

65 Oughton, *The Personal Diary of 'Mick' Mannock*, p. 198.

66 Donald Inglis, Combat Report, 9 October 1918, TNA AIR 1/1227/204/5/2634.

CHAPTER SIXTEEN: ONE HUNDRED DAYS

1 Trevor Henshaw, *The Sky Their Battlefield II: Air fighting and air casualties of the Great War* (High Barnet, Herts: Fetubi, 2014), p. 196.

2 G. H. Cunningham, *Mac's Memoirs: The flying life of Squadron-Leader McGregor* (Dunedin: Reed, 1937), pp. 64–5; Malcolm McGregor, Combat Report, 3 August 1918, TNA AIR 1/227/204/5/2634.

3 J. V. Gascoyne, 'Experiences of an RFC pilot', Sound Recording Transcription, p. 24, IWM, 00016/04; Vincent Orange, *Coningham: A biography of Air Marshal Sir Arthur Coningham KCB, KBE, DSO, MC, DFC, AFC* (London: Methuen, 1990), p. 26.

4 J. V. Gascoyne, 'Experiences of an RFC pilot', p. 25.

5 Arthur Coningham, Combat Report, 11 August 1918, TNA AIR 1/1227/204/5/2634.

6 L. A. Strange, *Recollections of an Airman* (London: Hamilton, 1933), p. 192.

7 4 AFC Squadron, War Diary, 16 August 1918, TNA AIR 1/2254/209/57/13.

8 Christopher Cole, *Royal Air Force Communiqués 1918* (London: Tom Donovan, 1990), pp. 162–4.

9 A. H. Cobby, *High Adventure* (Melbourne: Robertson & Mullens, 1942), p. 167.

10 Orange, *Coningham*, p. 29; Micheal Molkentin, *Fire in the Sky: The Australian Flying Corps in the First World War* (Crows Nest, NSW: Allen & Unwin, 2012), p. 300.

11 4 AFC Squadron, War Diary, 17 August 1918, TNA AIR 1/2254/209/57/13.

12 Cobby, *High Adventure*, p. 167.

13 Mike O'Conner, *Airfields and Airmen: Somme* (Barnsley, South Yorkshire: Pen and Sword, 2002), p. 72.

14 Sholto Douglas, *Years of Combat: The first volume of the autobiography of Sholto Douglas, Marshal of the Royal Air Force Lord Douglas of Kirtleside, G.C.B., M.C., D.F.C.* (London: Collins, 1963), pp. 300–1.

15 Edward Griffith quoted in Vivian Voss, *Flying Minnows: Memoirs of a World War One fighting pilot, from training in Canada to the Front Line, 1917–1918* (London: Arms & Armour, 1977), p. 229; Park's pseudonym is 'Major Sparks'. A Canadian officer in 48 Squadron described the attack in his hometown newspaper the following year: *Hatford Courant*, 8 June 1919, p. 14.

16 Keith Rodney Park, Liddle Collection, University of Leeds, LIDDLE/WW1/AIR/234.

17 Edward Griffith quoted in Voss, *Flying Minnows*, p. 229.

18 Orange, *Park*, p. 32.

19 Keith Park, 'Experiences in the Air, 1914–1918', unpublished essay, p. 17, TNA AIR 10/973; Orange, *Park*, p. 33.

20 Henshaw, *The Sky Their Battlefield II*, p. 209.

21 Trevor Read Bloomfield, Combat Report, TNA AIR 1/1227/204/5/2634.

22 Henshaw, *The Sky Their Battlefield II*, p. 347; cf. Norman Franks, Russell Guest, and Frank Bailey, *Bloody April . . . Black September: An exciting and detailed analysis of the two deadliest months in the air in World War One*, (London: Grub Street, 1995), pp. 110–11, 245–6.

23 Stuart Herbert Richardson, Service Record, TNA AIR 79/903/99995.

24 Stuart Richardson to Family, n.d. 1918, AFMNZ.

25 Stuart Richardson to Family, n.d. 1918, AFMNZ. The crash occurred on 8 September, see Errol Martyn, *For Your Tomorrow: A record of New Zealanders who have died while serving with the RNZAF and Allied air services since 1915, vol. 3: Biographies & Appendices* (Christchurch: Volplane, 2008), p. 410.

26 Stuart Richardson to Family, 5 September 1918, AFMNZ.

27 Stuart Richardson to Family, 15 September 1918, AFMNZ.

28 Stuart Richardson to Family, 21 September 1918, AFMNZ.

29 Stuart Richardson to Family, 11 September 1918, AFMNZ.

30 Martyn, *A Passion for Flight, vol. 3*, pp. 167–82.

31 Ibid., 179–80.

32 Ibid., p. 182.

33 Ibid.

34 Ibid.

35 *Otago Witness*, 19 July and 5 August 1914; Herbert Hyde, *Two Roads: International government or militarism; will England lead the way?* (London: King, 1916).

36 Warren F. Kuehl (ed.), *Biographical Dictionary of Internationalists* (Westport, Conn.: Greenwood Press, 1983), p. 375; *Otago Daily Times*, 5 December 1951. Hyde's proposals were considered and discussed at the League of Nations in 1924 and United Nations in 1958, see *Otago Daily Times*, 19 November 1959.

37 Herbert Ernest Hyde, Confidential Report, TNA AMD 273/10/57; Herbert Ernest Hyde, Service Record, TNA AIR 76/248/10.

38 Bill Ruxton, 'Night Bird: Recollections of a Kiwi in France. An interview with Major [*sic.*] A. R. Kingsford', *14–18 Journal* (1987), p. 76.

39 Hugh B. Monaghan, *The Big Bombers of World War I: A Canadian's journal* (Burlington, Ontario: Ray Gentle/Communications Ltd, 1975), p. 99; Chaz Bowyer, *Handley Page Bombers of the First World War* (Bourne End: Aston Publications, 1992), pp. 181–2; Rob Langham, *Bloody Paralyser: The giant Handley Page bombers of the First World War* (Croydon: Fonthill, 2016), pp. 133–9.

40 Monaghan, *The Big Bombers of World War I*, p. 99.

41 Ibid., p. 100.

42 Ibid.

43 H. A. Jones, *War in the Air: Being the story of the part played in the Great War by the Royal Air Force*, vol. 6 (London: Imperial War Museum, 1935), p. 148; Henshaw, *The Sky Their Battlefield II*, p. 221.

44 John Alfred Francis, Service Record, TNA AIR 79/2024/224802.

45 Raymond George Goldfinch, Diary, 24 July 1918, Brent Mackrell, Scrapbooks relating to early British and New Zealand military aviation, II, ATL MSZ-1581.

46 Raymond George Goldfinch, Diary, 28 July 1918, Brent Mackrell, Scrapbooks relating to early British and New Zealand military aviation, II, ATL MSZ-1581.

47 Ibid.

48 Raymond George Goldfinch, Diary, 1 August 1918, Brent Mackrell, Scrapbooks relating to early British and New Zealand military aviation, II, ATL MSZ-1581.

49 Raymond George Goldfinch, Diary, 2 August 1918, Brent Mackrell, Scrapbooks relating to early British and New Zealand military aviation, II, ATL MSZ-1581.

50 Raymond George Goldfinch, Diary, 8 August 1918, Brent Mackrell, Scrapbooks relating to early British and New Zealand military aviation, II, ATL MSZ-1581.

51 Michael Molkentin, *Fire in the Sky: The Australian Flying Corps in the First World War* (Crows Nest, NSW: Allen & Unwin, 2012).

52 *Dominion*, 23 December 1918; *Feilding Star*, 21 December 1918; Bowyer, *Handley Page Bombers of the First World War*, p. 39.

53 Frederick Stanley Gordon, Personnel File, ANZ AABK 18805 W5539 35/0045992; Devon Sutcliffe with Errol Martyn, 'Bannerman of Gore', *Aviation Historical Society of New Zealand Journal*, vol. 48, no. 2 (December 2005), pp. 28–48; Paul Sortehaug, 'Captain Ronald Burns Bannerman', *Wings*, vol. 80, no. 2 (May 2012), pp. 45–9.

54 Frederick Gordon, Combat Report, 16 September 1918, TNA AIR 1/1226/204/5/2634.

55 Wayne R. Braby, 'Nothing Can Stop Us: A short history of 79 Squadron RFC/RAF', *Cross and Cockade* (Summer 1964), pp. 168–75.

56 Ronald Bannerman, Diary, 11, 12 January 1918, AFMNZ.

57 William Fry, *Air of Battle* (London: Kimber, 1974), p. 173.

58 Ibid., p. 174; Air Historical Branch, 79 Squadron History, TNA AIR 1/176/15/187/1.

59 Ronald Bannerman, Logbook, 24 July 1918, AFMNZ.

60 Ronald Bannerman, Combat Report, 4 August 1918, TNA AIR 1/1829/204/202/22.

61 Ronald Bannerman, Logbook, 4 August 1918, AFMNZ.

62 79 Squadron, Operation Orders, 16 September 1918, TNA AIR 1/1904/204/228/5.

63 Ronald Bannerman, Combat Report, 16 September 1918, TNA AIR 1/1226/204/5/2634.

64 Christopher Cole & E. F. Cheesman, *The Air Defence of Britain 1914–1918* (London: Putnam, 1984), p. 194.

65 Ira 'Taffy' Jones, *Tiger Squadron: The story of 74 Squadron, R.A.F., in Two World Wars* (London: A. H. Allen, 1954), p. 167.

66 Ira Jones, *An Air Fighter's Scrapbook* (London: Nicholson & Watson, 1938), p. 78.

67 Ibid.

68 Peter Grey & Owen Thetford, *German Aircraft of the First World War* (London: Putnam, 1962), p. 215.

69 Keith Caldwell, Combat Report, 24 September 1918, TNA AIR 1/1226/204/5/2634.

70 Frederick Gordon, Combat Report, 30 October 1918, TNA AIR 1/1829/204/202/23; Keith Caldwell, Logbook, 30 October 1918, AFMNZ.

71 Ronald Bannerman, Combat Report, 4 November 1918, TNA AIR 1/1226/204/5/2634.

72 Devon Sutcliffe, 'Bannerman of Gore', p. 44.

73   List of Enemy aircraft driven down and destroyed, 22 March to 9 November 1918, TNA AIR 1/1904/204/228/5.

74   Ibid.

75   James Sloss to Mother, 4 October 1918, AFMNZ.

76   Henshaw, *The Sky Their Battlefield II*, p. 231.

77   Devon Sutcliffe, 'Sustained Effort: The Life of Sir Leonard Isitt' (PhD thesis, Massey University, 2011), p. 12.

78   Air Historical Branch, 98 Squadron History, TNA AIR 1/694/21/20/98; Daily Routine Orders, 3 October 1918, 98 Squadron, 15 September 1918–8 March 1919, TNA AIR 1/1952/204/259/4; Weekly Field Returns, April 1918–March 1919, 98 Squadron, TNA AIR 1/1955/204/259/19.

79   98 Squadron, Squadron Record Book, 23 October 1918, TNA AIR 1/1954/204/259/11.

80   Miscellaneous correspondence and reports, 98 Squadron, TNA AIR 1/1954/204/289/12.

81   Air Historical Branch, 108 Squadron History, TNA AIR 1/694/21/20/108.

82   James Sloss to Sister, 2 November 1918, AFMNZ.

83   James Sloss to Father, 25 October 1918, AFMNZ.

84   James Sloss to Jess, 5 November 1918, AFMNZ.

85   Blackwell to Family, 21 October 1918, in E. H. Poole (ed.), *Letters Home: A collection of letters written by Henry Hugh Blackwell, 1916–1919, during the training for and service in the Royal Flying Corps* (Christchurch: E. H. & H. M. Poole, 1999), AFMNZ.

86   Blackwell to Family, 31 October 1918, AFMNZ.

87   Blackwell to Family, 6–9 November 1918, AFMNZ.

88   Blackwell to Family, 6–9 November 1918, AFMNZ.

89   James Sloss to Nell, 2 November 1918, AFMNZ.

90   M. Ashlie Thomas, Matron to Sloss Family, 23 November 1918, AFMNZ.

91   M. Ashlie Thomas, Matron to Sloss Family, 18 November 1918, AFMNZ.

92   M. Ashlie Thomas, Matron to Sloss Family, 23 November 1918, AFMNZ.

93   G. H. Cunningham, *Mac's Memoirs: The flying life of Squadron-Leader McGregor* (Dunedin: Reed, 1937), p. 69.

94   Blackwell to Molly, 10 November 1918, p. 117, AFMNZ.

95   Blackwell to Father, 12 November 1918, p. 188, AFMNZ.

CONCLUSION

1   Keith Caldwell, Logbook, AFMNZ; Christopher Shores, Norman Franks & Russell Guest, *Above the Trenches: A complete record of the fighter aces and units of the British Empire Air Forces, 1915–1920* (London: Grub Street, 1990), pp. 94–5; cf. Paul Sortehaug, 'Major Keith Logan Caldwell', *Pacific Wings* 80, no. 12 (December 2012–January 2013), p. 53.

2   Ronald Bannerman, Logbook, AFMNZ; Devon Sutcliffe with Errol Martyn, 'Bannerman of Gore', *Aviation Historical Society of New Zealand Journal* 48, no. 2 (December 2005), p. 48; Paul Sortehaug, 'Captain Ronald Burns Bannerman', *Pacific Wings* 80, no. 5 (May 2012), p. 49; Shores et al., *Above the Trenches*, p. 62.

3   Errol Martyn, *Swift to the Sky: New Zealand's military aviation history* (Auckland: Penguin Viking, 2010), pp. 38–9; Shores et al., *Above the Trenches*, p. 140.

4   Martyn, *Swift to the Sky*, p. 51.

5   H. A. Jones, *War in the Air: Being the story of the part played in the Great War by the Royal Air Force, vol. 4* (London: Imperial War Museum, 1934), p. 415.

6   A. J. Scott, *Sixty Squadron R.A.F. 1916–1919* (London: Greenhill, 1990), pp. ix–x.

7   Jones, *War in the Air, vol. 4*, pp. 416, 447.

8   Ibid., p. 447.

9   Errol Martyn, *For Your Tomorrow: A record of New Zealanders who have died while serving with the RNZAF and Allied air services since 1915, vol. 1: Fates 1915–1942* (Christchurch: Volplane, 1998), pp. 38–51.

10   *Sun*, 19 November 1918.

11   Francis Kitto, Roll of Honour Card, AWM 145; Francis Kitto, Personnel File, NAA B2455.

12   *Dominion*, 17 September 1920.

13   *New Zealand Herald*, 18 January 1926.

14   Martyn, *Swift to the Sky*, pp. 54–5.

15   *Evening Post*, 28 November 1917.

16   *New Zealand Herald*, 26 March, 17 April 1919; *Evening Post*, 20 March 1919; J. M. S. Ross, *Royal New Zealand Air Force: Official history of New Zealand in the Second World War 1939–1945* (Wellington: War History Branch, Department of Internal Affairs, 1955), p. 7.

17   *Evening Post*, 2 September 1919.

18   Margaret McClure, *Fighting Spirit: 75 years of the RNZAF* (Auckland: Random House, 2012), p. 28; Ross, *Royal New Zealand Air Force*, p. 12.

19   McClure, *Fighting Spirit*, p. 29.

20   Ibid.

21   Ibid.

22   Ross Ewing & Ross Macpherson, *The History of New Zealand Aviation* (Auckland: Heinemann, 1986), p. 75.

23   Ibid.

24   G. H. Cunningham, *Mac's Memoirs: The flying life of Squadron-Leader McGregor* (Dunedin: Reed, 1937), p. 75.

25   Simon Moody, 'Kiwis Rising: New Zealanders and the war in the air', in John Crawford, David Littlewood & James Watson (eds), *Experience of a Lifetime: People, personalities and leaders in the First World War* (Auckland: Massey University Press, 2016), p. 210.

26   Charles Roderick Carr, Personnel File, TNA AIR 76/77/137.

27   Sortehaug, 'Major Arthur Coningham', p. 55.

28   Vincent Orange, *Park: The biography of Air Chief Marshal Sir Keith Park GCB, KBE, MC, DFC, DCL* (London: Grub Street, 2001), p. 143.

29   Martyn, *For Your Tomorrow, vol. 1*, p. 223; Errol Martyn, *For Your Tomorrow, vol. 3: Biographies & Appendices* (Christchurch: Volplane, 2008), p. 286; Errol Martyn to Author, 3 June 2017.

30   Moody, 'Kiwis Rising', pp. 209–10; Orange, *Park*, p. 240.

31   Moody, 'Kiwis Rising', p. 210.

32   Alex Revell, '"Grid" Caldwell', *Aeroplane* (December 2016), p. 49.

SELECT BIBLIOGRAPHY

Bamford, Joe. *Surviving the Skies: A night bomber pilot in the Great War*. Staplehurst, Kent: Spellmount, 2012.

Baring, Maurice. *Flying Corps Headquarters: 1914–1918*. London: William Heinemann, 1930.

Barker, Ralph. *A Brief History of the Royal Flying Corps in World War I*. London: Robertson, 2002.

Bartlett, C. P. O. *Bomber Pilot, 1916–1918*. Shepperton, Surrey: Ian Allan, 1974.

Bassett, Michael. *Coates of Kaipara*. Auckland: Auckland University Press, 1995.

Best, J. W. 'C. F. Collett, 1886–1917'. *Aviation Historical Society of New Zealand Journal* 43, no. 2 (December 2000), pp. 34–43.

Bowyer, Chaz. *Handley Page Bombers of the First World War*. Bourne End: Aston Publications, 1992.

—— *Royal Flying Corps Communiqués, 1917–1918*. London: Grub Street, 1988.

Chapman, Peter. 'Bomber Ace: Captain Euan Dickson'. *Cross and Cockade* 27, no. 4 (Winter 1996), pp. 177–93.

Claasen, Adam. 'From Artilleryman to Airman: Keith Park'. In *Experience of a Lifetime: People, personalities and leaders in the First World War*, edited by John Crawford, David Littlewood & James Watson, pp. 166–82. Auckland: Massey University Press, 2016.

Cobby, A. H. *High Adventure*. Melbourne: Robertson & Mullens, 1942.

Cole, Christopher. *Royal Air Force Communiqués 1918*. London: Tom Donovan, 1990.

Cole, Christopher & E. F. Cheesman. *The Air Defence of Britain 1914–1918*. London: Putnam, 1984.

Cronin, Dick. 'Tondern: Prelude, climax and aftermath'. *Cross and Cockade* 25, no. 2 (1994), pp. 57–68.

Crowley, Patrick. *Kut 1916: Courage and failure in Iraq*. New York: The History Press, 2009.

Cunningham, G. H. *Mac's Memoirs: The flying life of Squadron-Leader McGregor*. Dunedin: Reed, 1937.

Cutlack, F. M. *Official History of Australia in the War of 1914–1918: Volume VIII Australian Flying Corps in the western and eastern theatres of war*. Sydney: Angus and Robertson, 1940.

Davis, Paul. *Ends and Means: The British Mesopotamian Campaign and Royal Commission*. Cranbury, NJ: Associated University Presses, 1994.

Dolan, Hugh. *Gallipoli Air War: The unknown story of the fight for the skies over Gallipoli*. Sydney: Macmillan, 2013.

Douglas, Sholto. *Years of Combat: The first volume of the autobiography of Sholto Douglas, Marshal of the Royal Air Force Lord Douglas of Kirtleside, G.C.B., M.C., D.F.C.* London, Collins: 1963.

Draper, Christopher. *The Mad Major*. Letchworth, Herts: Air Review, 1962.

Escott, Beryl E. *Women in Air Force Blue: The story of women in the Royal Air Force from 1918 to the present day*. Wellingborough, Northamptonshire: Patrick Stephens, 1989.

Ewing, Ross & Ross Macpherson. *The History of New Zealand Aviation*. Auckland: Heinemann, 1986.

Fenton, Damien. *New Zealand and the First World War, 1914–1919*. Auckland: Penguin, 2015.

Finnegan, Terrence J. *Shooting the War: Allied aerial reconnaissance in the First World War*. Port Stroud, Gloucestershire: Spellmount, 2014.

Franks, Norman, Frank W. Bailey & Russell Guest. *Above the Lines: A complete record of the fighter aces of the German Air Service, Naval Air Service and Flanders Marine Corps, 1914–1918*. London: Grub Street, 1993.

Franks, Norman, Russell Guest & Frank Bailey. *Bloody April . . . Black September: An exciting and detailed analysis of the two deadliest months in the air in World War One*. London: Grub Street, 1995.

Franks, Norman & Andy Saunders. *Mannock: The life and death of Major Edward Mannock VC, DSO, MC, RAF*. London: Grub Street, 2008.

Fredette, Raymond H. *The First Battle of Britain 1917/18*. London: Cassell, 1966.

Grey, Peter & Owen Thetford. *German Aircraft of the First World War*. London: Putnam, 1962.

Grider, John MacGavock. *War Birds: Diary of an unknown aviator*. Sydney: Cornstalk, 1928.

Grinnell-Milne, Duncan. *Wind in the Wires*. London: Grub Street, 2014.

Hallam, D. H. *The Spider's Web: The romance of a flying-boat war flight*. Edinburgh: Blackwood, 1919.

Hamilton, John F. *Flat Out: The story of 30 Squadron, Royal Air Force*. Tunbridge Wells, Kent: Air-Britain, 2002.

Harkness, Bruce W., Jeffrey T. Harkness, Timothy D. Harkness, Christopher W. Harkness & Donald E. Harkness. *A World War I Adventure: The life and times of RNAS Bomber Pilot Donald E. Harkness*. Bloomington, Ind.: AuthorHouse, 2014.

Harper, Glyn. *Johnny Enzed: The New Zealand soldier in the First World War, 1914–1918*. Auckland: Exisle, 2016.

Hart, Peter. *Bloody April: Slaughter in the skies over Arras, 1917*. London: Cassell, 2006.

—— *Somme Success: The Royal Flying Corps and the Battle of the Somme, 1916*. Barnsley, South Yorkshire: Pen and Sword, 2001.

Harvie, E. F. *George Bolt: Pioneer aviator*. Wellington: Reed, 1974.

—— *Venture the Far Horizon: The pioneer long-distance flights in New Zealand*. Wellington: Whitcombe & Tombs, 1966.

Hellwig, Adrian. *Australian Hawk Over the Western Front: A biography of Major R S Dallas DSO, DSC, C de G avec Palme*. London: Grub Street, 2006.

Henshaw, Trevor. *The Sky Their Battlefield II: Air fighting and air casualties of the Great War*. High Barnet, Herts: Fetubi, 2014.

Hodges, Goderic. *Memoirs of an Old Balloonatic*. London: William Kimber, 1972.

Holden, F. D. 'Experimental Squadron RFC Orfordness 1916–1919'. *Cross and Cockade* 8, no. 2 (1977), pp. 49–61.

Insall, A. J. *Observer: Memoirs of the R.F.C. 1915–1918*. London: William Kimber, 1970.

Jefford, C. G. *Observers and Navigators and Other Non-pilot Aircrew in the RFC, RNAS and RAF*. London: Grub Street, 2014.

Jones, H. A. *War in the Air: Being the story of the part played in the Great War by the Royal Air Force, vols 2–6*. Oxford: The Clarendon Press, 1928, 1931, 1934, 1935, 1937.

Jones, Ira. *An Air Fighter's Scrapbook*. London: Nicholson & Watson, 1938.

—— *King of the Air Fighters: Biography of Major 'Mick' Mannock, V.C., D.S.O., M.C.* (London: Nicholson & Watson, 1935).

—— *Tiger Squadron: The story of 74 Squadron, R.A.F. in two World Wars*. London: W. H. Allen, 1954.

Kennett, Lee. *The First Air War 1914–1918*. New York: The Free Press, 1991.

Kingsford, A. R. *Night Raiders of the Air: Being the experiences of a night flying pilot, who raided Hunland on many dark nights during the war*. London: Greenhill, 1988.

Lee, Arthur Gould. *No Parachute*. London: Grub Street, 2013.

Mackersey, Ian. *No More Empty Chairs: The short and heroic lives of the aviators who fought and died in the First World War*. London: Weidenfeld & Nicolson, 2012.

Martyn, Errol. *A Passion for Flight: New Zealand aviation before the Great War, vol. 1: Ideas, first flight attempts and the aeronauts 1868–1909*. Christchurch: Volplane, 2012.

—— *A Passion for Flight: New Zealand aviation before the Great War, vol. 2: Aeroclubs, aeroplanes, aviators and aeronauts 1910–1914*. Christchurch: Volplane, 2013.

—— *A Passion for Flight: New Zealand aviation before the Great War, vol. 3, The Joe Hammond story and military beginnings 1910–1914*. Christchurch: Volplane, 2013.

—— *For Your Tomorrow: A record of New Zealanders who have died while serving with the RNZAF and Allied* air services since 1915, vol. 1: Fates 1915–1942. Christchurch: Volplane, 1998.

—— For Your Tomorrow: A record of New Zealanders who have died while serving with the RNZAF and Allied air services since 1915, vol. 3: Biographies & Appendices. Christchurch: Volplane, 2008.

—— Swift to the Sky: New Zealand's military aviation history. Auckland: Penguin Viking, 2010.

McClure, Margaret. Fighting Spirit: 75 years of the RNZAF. Auckland: Random House, 2012.

McCudden, James. Flying Fury: Five years in the Royal Flying Corps. Folkestone: Bailey Brothers & Swinfen, 1973.

McGibbon, Ian, ed. The Oxford Companion to New Zealand Military History. Auckland: Oxford University Press, 2000.

—— New Zealand's Western Front Campaign. Auckland: Bateman, 2016.

'McScotch'. Fighter Pilot. London: Greenhill, 1985.

Molkentin, Michael. Australia and the War in the Air. Melbourne: Oxford University Press, 2014.

—— Fire in the Sky: The Australian Flying Corps in the First World War. Sydney: Allen & Unwin, 2012.

Monaghan, Hugh B. The Big Bombers of World War 1: A Canadian's journal. Burlington, Ontario: Ray Gentle/ Communications Ltd, 1975.

Moody, Simon. 'Kiwis Rising: New Zealanders and the war in the air'. In Experience of a Lifetime: People, personalities and leaders in the First World War, edited by John Crawford, David Littlewood & James Watson, pp. 194–210. Auckland: Massey University Press, 2016.

Morris, Alan. Bloody April. London: Jarrolds Publishers, 1967.

Mulgan, David. The Kiwi's First Wings: The story of the Walsh Brothers and the New Zealand Flying School, 1910–24. Wellington: Wingfield, 1960.

Noble, L. M. Sir Henry Wigram: Pioneer of New Zealand aviation. Christchurch: Whitcombe & Tombs, 1952.

Norris, Geoffrey. The Royal Flying Corps. London: Frederick Muller, 1965.

Norris, Susanna Montgomerie with Anna Rogers. Annie's War: A New Zealand woman and her family in England 1916–1919. Dunedin: Otago University Press, 2014.

O'Connor, Mike. Airfields and Airmen: Somme. Barnsley, South Yorkshire: Pen and Sword, 2002.

Orange, Vincent. Park: The Biography of Air Chief Marshal Sir Keith Park GCB, KBE, MC, DFC, DCL. London: Grub Street, 2001.

—— Coningham: A biography of Air Marshal Arthur Coningham KCB, KBE, DSO, MC, DFC, AFC. London: Methuen, 1990.

Oughton, Frederick, ed. The Personal Diary of 'Mick' Mannock, V.C., D.S.O., M.C. (1 bar). London: Oakfield Press, 1966.

Philpott, Ian. The Birth of the Royal Air Force. Barnsley, South Yorkshire: Pen and Sword, 2013.

Poole, E. H., ed. Letters Home: A collection of letters written by Henry Hugh Blackwell, 1916–1919, during the training for and service in the Royal Flying Corps. Christchurch: E. H. & H. M. Poole, 1999.

Poole, Jack. Undiscovered Ends. London: Cassell, 1957.

Pugsley, Christopher. Gallipoli: The New Zealand story. Wellington: Reed, 1998.

Raleigh, Walter. War in the Air: Being the story of the part played in the Great War by the Royal Air Force, vol. 1. Oxford: Clarendon, 1922.

Rawlings, John. Fighter Squadrons of the RAF and Their Aircraft. London: Macdonald, 1969.

Revell, Alex. Brief Glory: The life of Arthur Rhys Davids, DSO, MC. Barnsley, South Yorkshire: Pen and Sword, 2010.

—— High in the Empty Blue: The history of 56 Squadron RFC, RAF 1916–1919. Mountain View, CA: Flying Machines Press, 1995.

Richardson, L. A. Pilot's Log: The log, diary, letters and verse of Lt. Leonard A. Richardson, Royal Flying Corps

1917–1918. St Catherines, Ontario: Paul Heron, 1998.

Richardson, Len & Shelley Richardson. *Anthony Wilding: A sporting life*. Christchurch: Canterbury University Press, 2005.

Ruxton, Bill. 'Night Bird: Recollections of a Kiwi in France. An interview with Major [*sic*] A. R. Kingsford'. *14–18 Journal* (1987), pp. 56–79.

Samson, Charles Rumney. *Flight and Flights: Memoir of the Royal Naval Air Service in World War I*. Nashville: Battery Press, 1930.

Scott, A. J. *Sixty Squadron, R.A.F. 1916–1919*. London: Greenhill, 1990.

Shores, Christopher, Norman Franks & Russell Guest. *Above the Trenches: A complete record of the fighter aces and units of the British Empire Air Forces, 1915–1920*. London: Grub Street, 1990.

Sortehaug, Paul. 'Captain Harold Francis Beamish'. *Pacific Wings* 80, no. 9 (September 2012), pp. 48–52.

—— 'Captain Ronald Burns Bannerman'. *Pacific Wings* 80, no. 2 (May 2012), pp. 46–9.

—— 'Flight Lieutenant Thomas Grey Culling'. *Pacific Wings* 81, no. 12 (December 2013–January 2014), pp. 50–5.

—— 'Major Arthur Coningham'. *Pacific Wings* 81, no. 10 (October 2013), pp. 50–5.

Steel, Nigel & Peter Hart. *Tumult in the Clouds: The British experience of the war in the air, 1914–1918*. London: Hodder & Stoughton, 1997.

Sutcliffe, Devon. 'Sustained effort: The life of Sir Leonard Isitt'. PhD thesis, Massey University, 2011.

Sutcliffe, Devon with Errol Martyn. 'Bannerman of Gore'. *Aviation Historical Society of New Zealand Journal* 48, no. 2 (December 2005), pp. 28–48.

Sutherland, Jonathan & Dianne Canwell. *Battle of Britain 1917: The first heavy bomber raids of England*. Barnsley, South Yorkshire: Pen and Sword Aviation, 2006.

Vaughan, David K., ed. *Letters from a War Bird: The World War I correspondence of Elliot White Springs*. Columbia, SC: University of South Carolina Press, 2012.

Voss, Vivian. *Flying Minnows: Memoirs of a World War One fighting pilot, from training in Canada to the Front Line, 1917–1918*. London: Arms & Armour, 1977.

Walmsley, Leo. *Flying and Sport in East Africa*. Edinburgh: Blackwood & Sons, 1920.

White, Leo. *Wingspread: The pioneering of aviation in New Zealand*. Auckland: Unity, 1941.

White, T. W. *Guest of the Unspeakable: An Australian's escape from Turkey in the First World War*. Sydney: Little Hill, 1990.

Winter, Denis. *The First of the Few: Fighter pilots of the First World War*. Harmondsworth: Penguin, 1983.

Yeats-Brown, Francis. *Caught by the Turks*. London: Edward Arnold, 1919.

—— *The Lives of a Bengal Lancer*. London: Viking Press, 1930.

ACKNOWLEDGEMENTS

This book is part of the First World War Centenary History Programme developed by the Ministry for Culture and Heritage, Massey University and the New Zealand Defence Force. Thank you to those who had the foresight to create such a series and for allowing me to contribute to this with an air war volume. My efforts have been overseen and considerably inspired by Glyn Harper, a co-chair on the Centenary History project. Glyn is a great colleague, and a fine scholar. He ensured that I was able to carry out sufficient research in New Zealand and overseas and that I had the space to write up the work. This is my second book project in which I have had the good fortune to work with Glyn. The project's administrator, Tessa Lyons, made sure all ran smoothly on the research front and fielded a lot of my inane questions.

Nicola Legat, publisher at Massey University Press, immediately saw the potential of a book on the Great War air power and from our earliest meeting has been nothing but encouraging. That the finished product looks so good is a credit to Nicola and her team, including Anna Bowbyes and Hellena Stanley-Hunt and the book's editor, Gillian Tewsley. Without them the book would not have crossed the line in such robust and stylish shape.

This book was only possible with support from my academic institution, Massey University. Kerry Taylor, Head of the School of Humanities, generously freed up time and resources to allow me to research and write. The university library purchased relevant materials, and librarians — in particular Jane Leighton — hunted hard-to-find books and journal articles from the four corners of the earth. General staff at the Palmerston North and Albany campuses — Tina Sheehan, Sharon Cox, Mary-Lou Dickson and Marissa Penfold — aided me in administrative matters.

This book owes a considerable debt to a collection of people working in the field of general military history and, in particular, Great War aviation. Principal among these are Errol Martyn, Simon Moody and John Crawford. Errol is one of New Zealand's leading researchers on aviation matters and has published numerous volumes on local pioneering aeronauts and New Zealand's rich military aviation history. Without his invaluable publications my task would have been significantly more arduous. Moreover, on numerous occasions he furnished me with advice, information and materials that pointed me in the right direction, corrected misapprehensions and filled in gaps. I look forward to his upcoming multi-volume biographical work dedicated to New Zealand's Great War personnel.

Simon Moody is Research Officer with the Air Force Museum of New Zealand. The museum, directed by Thérèse Angelo, has the friendliest and most accessible archive in the country. I pestered Simon with more emails than I would care to admit and I was a grateful recipient of his extensive knowledge on aviation matters and the museum's collection of flying logbooks, diaries and letters. John Crawford is the New Zealand Defence Force Historian and assisted me at Archives New Zealand: he offered good counsel on where relevant materials were held and also answered important questions relating to New Zealand's involvement in the Great War. All three, along with Glyn Harper, reviewed my final draft and their advice has made for a better piece of work. Of course, any omissions and errors are mine.

In Australia, historian Malcolm Molkentin was extremely helpful. Malcolm has published two highly regarded books on Australia's involvement in the air war, and he helpfully served as a sounding board for my own efforts. He supplied me with documents, including many on the Mesopotamian campaign and the Australian Flying Corps on the Western Front, and answered a number of oddball questions. In England, Trevor Henshaw provided important information on New Zealand casualties and general material on the air war.

Staff at the following archives were very cooperative: Air Force Museum of New Zealand, Christchurch; Canterbury Museum, Christchurch; Archives New Zealand, Wellington; Alexander Turnbull Library, Wellington; Museum of Transport and Technology, Auckland; Auckland War Memorial Museum; Royal Air Force Museum, Hendon; The National Archives, Kew; Imperial War Museum, London; and the Brotherton Library, University of Leeds. Special mention must be made of Matthew O'Sullivan, Keeper of Photographs at the Air Force Museum of New Zealand. Matthew kept feeding me logbooks as they were digitised and furnished many of the photographs for this publication. He and Simon were great hosts during my sojourns to Wigram.

In the latter stage of the project, research assistant Rebecca Johns provided invaluable assistance in tracking down errant airmen's details, compiling databases and collecting and collating images for the book. This was immensely helpful while I finalised the text.

A number of people generously gave me access to their family papers or personal collections, including Sir Peter Jackson, Martin Collett, John Douglas, Charles Michael Gordon, Allan Kendrick, John Montgomerie, Susanna Montgomerie Norris, Wendy Pettigrew, Deborah Quilter and Devon Sutcliffe. Their enthusiasm for the subject was infectious. Others who assisted were, in no particular order: Trevor Richards, Paul Sortehaug, Ross Mahoney, Alex Revell, Ray Vann, Colin and Barbara Huston, Nick Setteducato, Katherine Moody, Damien Fenton, Ian Cadwallader, Jane Orphan, Christine Clement, Mark Brewer, Bee Dawson, Sarah Murray, Sarah Johnston, Meg Tasker, Herb Farrant, Ann McDonald, Peter Chapman, Allan Rudge, Lyndsay Brock, Lesley Courtney, Allan Davidson, Gail Romano, Mary Stevens, Michael Wynd, Ann McDonald, Larry Hill, Lynda Seaton, Peter Millward, Anna Rogers, Ewan Burnet, Jim Hall, Andy Kemo, Elizabeth Cox, Alan Weeks, Guy Revell, Dave Homewood, Frank Sharp, Brett Butterworth, Kees Kort, Bruce Harkness, and members of the Great War Forum (http://1914-1918.invisionzone.com/forums/index.php). My apologies if I have missed anyone.

Finally, on many occasions the gathering of materials from the archives for this book was a family affair. My wife Sandra is an excellent research assistant, and she and two of our sons, Nathanael and Isaac, hunted down scores of documents and made thousands of photographic copies. Their efforts meant I was able to gather far more material than I could ever have assembled alone in the time constraints of the project. Another son, Josiah, critiqued my first draft; that he did this during the latter stages of his wife April's pregnancy demonstrates a dedication beyond the call of duty.

This volume in the Centenary History series would not have been possible without generous donations to the Massey University Foundation. The Governance Group of the Centenary History Programme would like to acknowledge and thank: New Zealand Defence Force; Air New Zealand; Hawker Pacific; Safe Air; Kaman Aerospace Group; CAE Australia Limited.

IMAGE CREDITS

INTRODUCTION

p. 11 AFMNZ, ALB942099009.

CHAPTER ONE

pp. 12–13 Smithsonian National Air and Space Museum, NASM 2008-3762; pp. 16–17 Sueddeutsche Zeitung Photo/Alamy Stock Photo; pp. 20–21 courtesy of J. M. Grech; p. 25 courtesy of Philip Jarrett; p. 29 AWM, P00588.003; pp. 30–31 Fairfax Corporation; p. 33 AWMM, PH-NEG-A168; pp. 34–35 ATL, MNZ-2066-1/4-F.

CHAPTER TWO

pp. 36–37 ATL, 1/2-001629-G; pp. 42–43 AFMNZ, MUS000181; p. 47 (above) AFMNZ, MUS0603312, (below) Sir George Grey Special Collections, Auckland Libraries, AWNS-19140205-42-1.

CHAPTER THREE

pp. 54–55 Leeds University, Liddle/WW1/AIR/259; p. 58 National Army Museum of New Zealand, 1993.1223; p. 63 (above) Kees Kort Collection, (below) IWM, Q 58422; p. 65 Leeds University, Liddle/WW1/AIR/259; pp. 68–69 National Army Museum of New Zealand, 1993.1223.

CHAPTER FOUR

pp. 74–75 National Army Museum of New Zealand, 1992.776; p. 83 courtesy of Philip Jarrett; p. 88 AFMNZ, 1986-238.2; pp. 94–95 AFMNZ, MUS06066; p.97 Royal Aero Club Trust, except for: second, top row, courtesy of John V. Douglas; first, middle row, courtesy of Bee Dawson.

CHAPTER FIVE

pp. 98–99 AWM, A04131; pp. 104–05 IWM, Q 67101; p. 107 IWM, Q 25218; p. 108 (above) Leeds University, Liddle/WW1/AIR/259, (below) AWM, A02253; p. 113 Royal Aero Club Trust; p.117 (above) Ray Vann/Mike O'Connor Collection, (below) Ray Vann/Mike O'Connor Collection.

CHAPTER SIX

pp. 122–23 AWMM, PH-1976-6-19; p. 127 (above) AFMNZ, ALB8319526001, (below) AFMNZ, ALB8319526021; p. 129 ATL, 1/4-123885-F; p. 130 (above) AFMNZ, ALB8319526034, (below) AFMNZ, ALB8319526057; pp. 134–35 AFMNZ, MUS951255; pp. 136–37 AFMNZ, MUS010026; p. 140 AFMNZ, MUS03051; p. 147 Royal Aero Club Trust, except for: first, second row, courtesy of A. L. Crotty; second, third row, Sir George Grey Special Collections, Auckland Libraries, AWNS-19160629-39-1; third, third row, Unknown photographer [1918], Eric Paton Archive, 04/071/021, MOTAT.

CHAPTER SEVEN

pp. 150–51 AWM, P00394.004; p. 157 AFMNZ, ALB8319111047; p. 159 World History Archive/Alamy Stock Photo; pp. 162–163 AWM, DAAV00080; pp. 166–67 IWM, Q 96076; p 173 (above) AFMNZ, ALB8319526321, (below) AFMNZ, Bannerman 294.

CHAPTER EIGHT

pp. 174–75 Brett Butterworth Collection; p. 179 AWM, A03991; p. 185 Everett Collection Historical/Alamy Stock Photo; p. 187 AFMNZ, MUS060696; pp. 190–91 San Diego Air & Space Museum Archive, 01 00080005; p. 194 (above) AFMNZ, ALB933603038, (below) AWMM, PH-ALB-552-lP3; p. 196 (above) courtesy of Sir Peter Jackson, (below) Alamy Stock Photo; p. 201 IWM, Q 69650.

CHAPTER NINE

p. 204–05 AWM, B03576; p. 213 AWMM, C05115; p. 214 Bruce Harkness Collection; p. 217 IWM, Q 53183; pp. 222–23 IWM, Q 70185; p. 228 (above) AWM, E04646, (below) George Metcalf Archival Collection, Canadian War Museum 19920085-023; p. 231 AFMNZ, ALB933601184, ALB933601185, ALB933601188, ALB933601192.

CHAPTER TEN

pp. 232–33 IWM, Q 44803; pp. 236–37 IWM, Q 42284; p. 241 (above) AWM, J02258, (below) IWM, Q 54443; p. 243 RAF Leeming; p. 244 Royal Aero Club Trust, except for: first, first row, courtesy of Charles Michael Gordon Collection; third, first row, AWMM, C33709; second, second row, C. K. Mills Collection, 14/004/124, MOTAT; p. 247 L. & K. Brown; p. 248 courtesy of Sir Peter Jackson; p. 253 (above) courtesy of Sir Peter Jackson, (below) IWM, Q 27633; p. 257 AWMM, C18182.

CHAPTER ELEVEN

pp. 260–61 Brett Butterworth Collection; p. 265 IWM, E (AUS) 1175; pp. 268–69 courtesy of Sir Peter Jackson; p. 271 (above) AWMM, C35042, (below) Brett Butterworth Collection; pp. 272–73 IWM, Q 108846; p. 275 (above) AFMNZ, ALB942099016, (below) AFMNZ, ALB942099018; p. 279 (above) AWM, H12364, (below) Coates Collection, Ruatuna, Matakohe; p. 280 (above) courtesy of Sir Peter Jackson, (below) *Coningham*, Vincent Orange, Methuen.

CHAPTER TWELVE

pp. 286–87 AC Brett Butterworth Collection; p. 291 (above) AFMNZ, MUS150042, (below) AFMNZ, MUS1700419; p. 293 (above) courtesy of Mr Clive E. Collett, (below) AWM, E03874; p. 296 AFMNZ, MUS9510021; p. 303 C. K. Mills Collection, 14/004/325, MOTAT; p. 309 (above) courtesy of Sir Peter Jackson, (below) Brett Butterworth Collection; p. 313 AFMNZ, ALB933603116; p. 315 Martin Collett Collection.

CHAPTER THIRTEEN

pp. 316–17 AFMNZ, ALB80465S036; p. 323 courtesy of Margaret Kingsford & PROW; pp. 328–29 courtesy of Sir Peter Jackson.

CHAPTER FOURTEEN

pp. 334–35 IWM, Q 12186; p. 341 *High in the Empty Blue*, Alex Revell, Flying Machine Press; p. 344 AWMM, PH-1987-2-1; pp. 348–49 National Army Museum of New Zealand, 1990.1710; p. 352 Richard Stowers Collection; p. 355 (above) AFMNZ, MUS150041, (below) AWM, E02496; pp. 356–57 IWM, Q 10923.

CHAPTER FIFTEEN

pp. 360–61 IWM, Q 96524; pp. 366–67 courtesy of Sir Peter Jackson; p. 370 Allan Kendrick Collection; pp. 372–73 IWM, Q 20627; pp. 374–75 IWM, Q 47941; p. 377 IWM, Q 12051; p. 379 K. & M. McGregor Collection; pp. 382–83 IWM, Q 12049; p. 385 IWM, Q 73408.

CHAPTER SIXTEEN

pp. 386–87 AFMNZ, Coningham 92 Squadron; pp. 390–91 courtesy of Sir Peter Jackson; pp. 402–03 TNA; p. 405 AFMNZ, MUS040932; p. 413 Royal Aero Club Trust, except for: third, second row, AWM, P03974.001; first, third row, AWMM, C35042; second, third row AWMM, C33676.

CONCLUSION

p. 417 AWM, MED1478; p. 418 Richard Stowers Collection; p. 423 AWM, MED0824; pp. 426–27 AFMNZ, ALB862456255.

INDEX

**Page numbers in bold
indicate illustrations**

A

Abbott, Victor Stephen Henry 166,
429

Above the Trenches 9

Adams, Francis Luke 101–2, 118–21,
147, 421, 429

Adams, Francis, senior 121

Aerial League of the British Empire,
New Zealand branch 42, 44

Aéro-Club de France 24

Aero Club of New Zealand 350

aerobatics 148, 170–2, 255, 270, 354,
380, 398

The Aeroplane 399

AFC *see* Australian Flying Corps

Africa 207–10

Aimer, George Edmund Vernon **147**,
165–6, 429

Air Battalion, Aeroplane Section 21

Air Board 421

Air Force Museum of New Zealand 8

Air Ministry 342

air supply operations 119

aircraft

  Airco DH2 254

  Airco DH5 277–8, **279**, 415

  Airco DH6 **166–7**

  Airco DH9 408–9

  Albatros DIII 235–6, 240, **241**,
248, **248**, 252–3, 255–6, 270, 276,
280, 289

  Albatros DV 276, 294, 312, 319–20

  Armstrong Whitworth FK8 'Big
Ack' 311–2, 346

  Armstrong Whitworth FK10 227

  Avro 504 164–5, 170–1, 195

  balloons **174–5**, 195, 197–8, 229,
263–6, **265**

  Blériot aircraft 19, 22–4, 31, 39–42,
44–5, 52, 134

  Blue Bird 45–51, **47**

  Breguet Bre.4 218

  Bristol aircraft **204–5**

  Bristol Boxkites 24–31, **25**, **29**,
30–1

  Bristol Fighter 227, 289–90, **291**,
349

Bristol Scout **63**, **150–1**, 171

Britannia 22–3, **42–3**, 42–5, 52–3,
59, 64

Caudron 45–51, **47**, 59, **100**, 102,
111–2, 128, **130**, 132–4, **136–7**, 137,
141, 169, 218

Curtiss seaplanes **122–3**, 132, 327

Farman aircraft 207–8

Farman biplanes 71–2, **83**

Farman Shorthorn & Longhorn
102, **104–5**, 106, 109, 111–2,
162–3, 164, 171

Felixstowe flying boats 327, **328–9**

Fokker DrI 307–8, **309**, 319–20

Fokker DVII 320, 389, **390–1**

Fokker Eindecker **190–1**, 190–2,
199–200, 236

Friedrichshafen 308

gliders 32, 42, 161

Gotha GIV **272–3**, 273

Halberstadt Scout 236, 240

Hamilton Aero Manufacturing
Company plane 90–1

Handley Page O/400 **334–5**, 365,
399–404, **402–3**

Howard Wright biplane 32

L13 216

L15 182–6, **185**, 216, 221–2

L32 222

L33 220–2, **222–3**

L41 299, 301

L54 376

L55 301

L60 376

L62 371

Manurewa 32, **33**, **34**, 35

Martinsyde aircraft 165, 166

Martinsyde G100 'Elephant' 114,
117, 285

Nieuport 16 195–7, **196**, 210

Nieuport Scout 236, 245, 250

Pfalz 119, 319

Royal Aircraft Factory BE2 **54–5**,
89, 102, **166–7**, 166–8

Royal Aircraft Factory BE2c 180–3,
185, 207–8, 230, **231**, 236, **253**,
260–1

Royal Aircraft Factory DH2 236

Royal Aircraft Factory DH4 330–1,
365

Royal Aircraft Factory DH5 404

Royal Aircraft Factory FB2b 210,
300

Royal Aircraft Factory FE2 193,
195, 199, **201**, 224, 227, 236,
240–2, 245, 299

Royal Aircraft Factory FE2b 321,
365, **366–7**

Royal Aircraft Factory RE8 9,
204–5, 365

Royal Aircraft Factory SE5a 15,
171, 289, **377**, **382–3**

Roland 195

seaplanes **123–4**, 125–33, 141,
180, 372

Siemens-Schuckert D.IV 407–8

Sopwith 1½ Strutter 9, **217**, 218–9,
236, 372, 420

Sopwith Camel 255, 274–6, **275**,
289, **293**, 294, 305, 347, **360–1**,
371–2, **372–3**, 375–6, 397

Sopwith Dolphin 171, 320, 404–6,
405

Sopwith Pup 171, 240, 273–4, 278,
293

Sopwith Scout 370

Sopwith Triplane 'Tripe' **253**, 255,
270, 307

Spad SVII 171, 305, **309**

SSZ 64 264

Submarine Scout (SS) class
airships 264, **268–9**

Taube 62, **63**

Vickers FB5 'Gunbus' 190–2, **194**

White Wings 138

Wright Flyer 24, 32

Zeppelin airships **16–7**, 177–84,
179, **185**, 216–24, **214**, **223**, 273,
276, 298–300, 301, 371–2, 375–6,
416

aircraft carriers 372, 376

airfields & stations *see also*
Experimental Stations

1st Area Depot 345

Asani 111

Auchel 189

Baizieux 338

Basra Aircraft Park **100**, 106, 109

Bertangles 355, **356–7**, 357, 394–6

Biggin Hill 343

Boulay 367–8
Bray-Dunes 290, 297
Bruay 304
Duxford **167**
Épinoy 258
Estrée-Blanche 292, 314
Filescamp 245
Gontrode 325
Gosport 170
Hainault Farm 180–1
Haubourdin 393
Hendon 22, 134
Hesdigneul-les-Béthune 346
Joyce Green 183
Kut 118
Lomme 393–4
Manston 273
Martlesham Heath 312
Mons-en-Chaussée 311
Mourmelon-le-Grand 86
Nesle 382
Ochey 322
Ramegnies-Chin 285
Reckem (Rekkem) 408
Royal Naval Air Station Eastchurch
258
Royal Naval Air Station Felixstowe
274
Rumbeke 306
Saint-Denis 220
Sainte-Marie-Cappel 406
Scheldewindeke 325
Sockburn 133–42
Saint-Omer 188, **377**, **382–3**
Tondern 372, **374–5**, 375–8
Wigram 8, 133–42
Alderton, Trevor Dudley Hall **147**,
164, 429
All Blacks see 100 Squadron
Allan, John Alexander McDonald
429
Allen, James 22, 53, 133, 281
Allen, Thomas Meredith 429
American–British Liberty Bonds
drive 398
Anderson, Sydney 327–30, 415–6
Angus, William 42, 81–2, **83**, 84–5,
426–7
Anketell, Charles Edward 429
Antill, John 28, **30–1**
ANZAC 77–81
Arden, John Henry Morris 429
armaments 181, 183, 192–3, **196**, 197,
221, 225, 227

see also specific aircraft; training;
bombs
anti-aircraft guns 180–1, 184, 197,
212, 215, 219, 222, **271**, 276, 367–8
Constantinesco synchronised gun
system 227
Davis gun 225
Foster Gun Mounting **196**, 197
German 320
Lewis machine gun 153–4, 193,
196, 197, 199, 225, 245, 278, 289,
338
Maxim machine gun 153
Parabellum machine gun 308
Robey-Peters Gun-Carrier. 225
rockets & darts 181, 183, 195–8,
196
Vickers machine gun 192, 289,
330, 406
Auckland 32–42, 44, 125, **127**, 128
Auckland Flying School see New
Zealand Flying School
Australian and New Zealand Army
Corps 77–81
Australian Army 102
Australian Federal Government 51
Australian Flying Corps 102, 401
2 Squadron 393–4
4 Squadron 347–8, **355**, 393–4
Half Flight 101

B

Baghdad 115–8
Balcombe-Brown, Rainsford 195,
198, 337–40, **341**, 350, 359, 419, 429
Ball, Albert 195, 338
Banks, Kathleen 421
Bannerman, Ronald 7, 70, 132,
142, 158–60, 168, 171–2, **173**, 320,
404–7, **405**, 408, 416, 424, 425,
426–7
Barclay, Clifford 52
Barlow, Robin Tudor 363–5, 429
Barnes, David John 429
Barton, Charles 141, **244**
Basra 102–3
Bassett, Cyril 311
Battle of Megiddo 401, 404
Beaglehole, Joseph 199
Beamish, Harold 'Kiwi' **11**, 274–6,
275, 289, 416
Beatty, David 378
Beebe Balloon Company 229
BEF 60–4

Begbie, Hamilton 229
Below, Fritz von 238
Bettington, Arthur Vere 421–2
Binnie, Alan 250
Birdwood, William 92
Bishop, Billy 245, 251–2, 351, 380
Blackwell, Henry Hugh 'Hugh'
143–4, **147**, 149, 178, 189, 409–12,
424
training 131–2, 153–4, 170
Blayney, Charles 170, 224
Blenkiron, Alfred 230–40
Blériot, Louis **12–3**, 19
blimps see aircraft, balloons
Blomfield, Richard 338, **341**
Bloomfield, Trevor 396
Böcker, Alois 221–2
Bolshevik Red Army 420
Bolt, George 42, **129**, 131
bombing raids 62, 81, 89, 218,
273–6, 321, 324–6, 330–1 see
also Independent Force; specific
aircraft; specific airmen; specific
squadrons
bombs 73, 153, 163, 181, 183, 199–
200, 209, 239 see also armaments
Borton, Amyas Eden 401
Bourne, Sydney 367–9
Brackenbury 251
Brain, Norman Leslie 224, 429
Brandon, Alfred de Bathe 164–5,
169–71, **187**, 350, 421
attacks on Zeppelins 177, 180–6,
185, 216, 220–3, 298, 416, 419
Breithaupt, Joachim 182–4
Brett, Leslie Henry 429
Brewster, Robert 103, 119
Brewster, Stanley 101–2, 114
Briffault, Lister 161, 326–7, **413**
Briffault, Robert 326–7
Bristol and Colonial Aeroplane
Company 24–30 see also aircraft,
Bristol
British Army 96, 363
British Expeditionary Force 60–4
British Nursing Service 343
Brodie, Ross **97**, 137–8, 141, 148,
154–6, 172, 178
Brown, William 371
Browne, Arthur 'Brownie' 79, 311–2,
415
Buchanan, William Archibald 429
'Buffalo Bill' Cody's Wild West show
25

Bullock-Webster, Frank 305–7, **413**, 429

Burn, Robert 112

Burn, William Wallace Allison **20–1**, 100–1, 106, 109–10, 112, **113**, 420, 429

training 21–2, 53, 59–60

Burton, Ernest Wilfred 429

Butterworth, Harold Winstone 145–6, 148–9, 158, 160–1, 189–93, **194**, 211, 415, 429

Buttlar-Brandenfels, Horst von 376

C

Cairnes, Thomas 284

Caldwell, Keith 'Grid' 15–6, 215, 245, 249, 350–7, **352**, 380, 384, 407–8, 412, 416, **418**, **426–7**

leadership 229, 419, 421, 424–6

training 128, 131, 142, 171

Callender, Geoffrey **97**, 128, 142, 215–6, 415

Calthrop, Everard 230

cameras & photography 112, 238–9, 245–6, 249–50, 409 *see also* reconnaissance

Canal Defence Force 72–3

Canning, John 212

Canterbury (NZ) Aero Club 42, 82

Canterbury (NZ) Aviation Company 133–42, **134–5**, **136–7**, 421

Canterbury Battalion 72–3

Carlin, Sydney 'Timbertoes' 407

Carr, Charles Roderick 'Roderick' **147**, 169, 263–4, 420, 424–5

Carr, John 'Jack' 255–6

Castle, Edward Errington 429

Cato, Geoffrey Walter Gavin Maidens 429

Central Flying School **20–1**, 22, **54–5**, 60

Chambers, Hugh 321–2, 415

Chaytor, Edward 93

Christchurch 46, 48–9, 51–2 *see also* Canterbury

Christchurch Star 139

Chu Chin Chow 158–60, **159**

Churchill, Winston 242

Clarke, Nathaniel Fuhrmann 430

Coates, Eleanor 282–4

Coates, Gordon 84–5, 282–4

Coates, William Henry 84–5, 92–3, **280**, 281–4, 430

Cobby, Harry 348, 394

Cock, John Herbert 249–50, 430

Collett, Clive Franklyn 'Jack' 171, 188–93, **194**, 212, 289–95, **293**, 314, 416, 430

testing 224–7, 230, **231**, 312–4, **313**

Collett, Ralph 218–20

Collishaw, Raymond 384

Coningham, Arthur 'Mary' 7, 82, 277–81, **279**, 294, 384, **386–7**, 390–4, 416, **423**, 425

training 142

wounds 94–6, 284–5

Constantinesco, George 227

Cook, Alfred Burton 430

Cook, William Wallace 142, 301, **413**, 415

Cooper, Herbert Ambrose 195–7, 430

Courtney, John Classon 347, **413**, 430

Couturier, Claude 430

Cowlin, Frank 52

crashes *see also* fire; specific airmen

in training 91, 161–70, 172, **173**, 242

pre-war 41, 50, 230

wartime 15, 110–1, 181–2, 209, 211, 215, 225, **228**, **241**, 245, **293**, **303**

Crawford, Francis 171

Crogg, Cecil 85

Crogg, Eric 85–6

Croll, Eric 168, 172

Ctesiphon **106–7**

Culling, Thomas Grey 254–9, **257**, 267, 269, 273, 416, 430

Culling, Thomas Shepherd 254

Cumming, Margaret 226, 230

Cumming, Marion Renée Collett 314, **315**

Cunningham, G. H. 7

Curtis, Raymond 52

Curtiss Flying School 148

Curtiss, Glenn 125

D

Daily Express 19

Daily Sketch 186

Dallas, Roderic 255–9, 269–70

darts *see* armaments

Dawson, Harold William 307, 430

Dawson, Samuel **370**, 371–2, 375–8, 416, 420

Dennistoun, James Robert 82, 195, 198–203, **244**, 421, 430

Deutsche Luftstreitkräfte *see* Luftstreitkräfte

Dewitt, Herbert 142

Dexter, Reuben 125

Dickson, Euan 330–4, 337, **413**, 416, 419

Dinneen, James 161

dogfights *see* specific aircraft; specific airmen; specific battles; specific places

Dolan, Henry 354

Dominion 50, 131

Douglas, Sholto 89–90, 242, 363, 394–5

Dowding, Hugh **20–1**, 22, 425

Draper, Christopher 22

Drewitt, Herbert **97**, **173**, 306, 308–10, 416

E

Eastbourne Flying School, Sussex 31

Edwardes-Evans, Huw 324–5

Egypt 64, 71–3, 84–5, **157**, **423** *see also* Middle East

training 93–4, 154–5, 168, 304

Eidau, Lili 202

engines

Anzani engine 48, 51, 125

Bentley rotary 276

BMW 389

Gnome 26, 44, 165, 192

Maybach HSLu 182

Mercedes 236

Rolls-Royce 134, 264, 289, 327, 330, 399, 401

Evening Post 31–2, 42

Experimental Stations 61, 188, 224–7, 230, 312 *see also* airfields & stations; test flying

F

Farman planes *see* aircraft, Farman

Ferrie, Robert 227

Festner, Sebastian **236–7**

Fidler, Carrel Watt 263–6, 430

Fighting Parson *see* Maclean, Cuthbert

fire, on aircraft 221–2, 225, 229, 250, 326, 331, 371, 396 *see also* crashes; specific aircraft

First Battle of the Marne 64

Fitzgerald, Roy James 363–4, 430

Fitzherbert, Wyndham Waterhouse 285, 430

Flanagan, Sister 383
Flanders offensive *see* Ypres
floatplanes & flying boats *see*
    aircraft, seaplanes
Flying Circus 235, 398
Foch, Ferdinand 347, 389
For Your Tomorrow 7
Foster, Ralph 197
Foubister, John Leask 430
Fourth Army 252, 389
Francis, John 401–4
Franks, Norman 9
French Army 354
French, John 61
Fry, William 426

G

Gallipoli 73–82, **74–5**
Gardener, Charles Eric 430
Garland, Edgar **147**, 164, 273
Gascoyne, James 390–2
Geelong **30–1**
George, Leslie 430
German Air Force *see*
    Luftstreitkräfte
Gibbon, Colonel 91
Gillet, Francis 408
Godley, Alexander 21, 53, 90, 91–3
Goldfinch, Raymond 401–4, **402–3**
Gordon, Albert William **244**, 278,
    281, 284, 430
Gordon, Frederick 404, 406, 408,
    416
Gordon, Joseph 28
Gordon, Michael 188, **244**
Gore **47**
Gorringe, George 109–11
Gosport System 170
Gosport tubes 170
Greenwell, Arthur Robert 166–8,
    430
Greenwell, George 168
Greenwell, Nicholas 168
Grenfell, Eustace 245
Grider, John 380, 381
Guardian Angel, parachutes 230,
    314
Guest, Russell 9

H

Haig, Douglas 310, 350, 354, 389,
    396–7
Hamel, Gustav 22–3, 89
Hamilton, Ian 53

Hammes, Karl 295
Hammond, Ethelwyn **25**, 26
Hammond, Francis 52
Hammond, Joseph (Joe)
    pre-war 23–31, **25**, **29**, **30–1**, **42–3**,
        42–5, 51–3
    wartime 59, 61, 169–70, 224–5,
        398–9, 415, 420, 430
Harkness, Donald 86, 144–5, 158,
    161–3, 165, **217**, 216–20, 421
Hathaway, Charles 207–10
Hawker, Herbert 154
Hayward, Peter 52
Henri Farman planes *see* aircraft,
    Farman
Henshaw, Trevor 7, 337
Hewett, James 307–10, **413**
Hill, Cecil **134–5**, 134–41, 164, 169
Hinton, Francis Athol 431
Hodges, Goderic 266
Holden, Albert 93
Homer, Charles William 431
Horn, Spencer 'Nigger' 381
Horrell, Frederick 292, 294, 302–4,
    415
Hovey, Mary 282–4
Hundred Days Offensive 389–412
Hunt, Frederick 407
Hyde, Herbert 399–401
Hyslop, Ninian Steele 93, 431

I

Imperial Air Fleet Committee 22
Imperial Air Service *see*
    Luftstreitkräfte
Imperial Army 92
Independent Force 365–9, 399 *see*
    also bombing raids
Indian Army 60, 351
    Flight 101
Indian Central Flying School 60
Industrial, Agricultural and Mining
    Exhibition 44
Inglis, Donald 'Kiwi' 378, 380–4,
    382–3
Insall, Algernon 197
Isitt, Leonard 7, **94–5**, 96, 409, 421,
    424–5, **426–7**

J

Jackson, William 375–6
Johnstone, Godfrey Gleeson 285,
    431
Johnstone, Harold 285

Johnstone, Melville 285, 431
Jones, Cedric 292–4
Jones, Ira 'Taffy' 164, 351, 353, 383–4

K

Kean, Roy 190
Kingsford, Alfred 'Reggie' 7, 189,
    298–300, 321–4, **323**, 333, 348,
    365–9, 399, 424, **426–7**
Kingsford, Peter 425
Kitchener, Lord 119
Kitto, James 420
Kut al Amara **108**, 109, 114–5, 118–21

L

Lawrence, D. H. 177–8
Lawrence, T. E. 119
Le Prieur rockets *see* armaments
Lee, Maurice 351
Lester, Charles & Alfred **33**, 35
Lettow-Vorbeck, Paul von 207
Lindbergh, Charles 424
Livingstone, Frederick James
    369–71, 431
Livingstone, Robert 94–6
Lockhead, William 52
London Times 314
Lovell, Robert 325–6
Löwenhardt, Erich 359
Ludendorff, Erich 359, 363, 390
Luftstreitkräfte 224, 235–6, 249, 311,
    319–20, 337, 389, 396–7 *see also*
    aircraft; specific airmen
    Geschwader 289
    Jagdgeschwaders 'JG' 235, 289,
        319–20
    Jagdstaffeln 'Jastas' 235–8, 250,
        252, 270, 278, **280**
Lyttelton Times 133

M

Macdonald, Allan William 420, 431
Macfarlane, Leslie 94–6
Mackenzie, Thomas 91–3
Mackie, John 134, 138
Maclean, Cuthbert 193–5, 242,
    245–7, **247**, 350, 419–20, 424
Mahoney, Brian Gerald 431
Malone, W. G. 81
Malthus, Cecil 72–3
Manger, Kuno 299, 301, 371
Mannock, Edward 'Mick' 229, 305,
    351, 353–7, 378, 383–4, **385**
Māori recruitment 139–41

Marne, First Battle of the 64
Martin, John 171
Martyn, Errol 7, 432
Massey, William 22, 84
Masters, George 238, 246, 249, 431
Masters, Lester 246
Matheson, Harry MacKay 431
Mathy, Heinrich 216
Maurice Farman planes *see* aircraft, Farman
Maxwell, John 73
Maybery, Richard 292, 314
Maynard, Forster 255, 258, 267, 416, 424
McCudden, James 292, 295, 312, 314, 338
McEwen, John 211
McGill, Charles Percy 431
McGregor, Malcolm 'Mac' 7, 84, 126, **127**, 306–7, 378–84, **379**, **382–3**, 389–90, 412, 416, 424
training 132, 142, 153, 171–2
McKenzie, Hector 90
McKenzie, William Seaforth 90–1, 325–6, 431
McLaren, Archibald 401
McLennan, Esme 45
Mealing, Maurice 338–42
Mediterranean Expeditionary Force 77–81
Megiddo, Battle of 401, 404
Melbourne 26–7
Mesopotamia Flight 101–14, **104–5**
Messines 263, 267–73 *see also* Western Front
Merz, George **108**, 112
Middle East 71–82, **100**, 100–21, 154–6, 401 *see also* specific places
Mills, Charles 79, 92–3, **244**, 305
Millward, Kenneth Henry 255, 258–9, 267, 269–73, **271**, **413**, 415, 431
Milne, John 297–8
Mitchell, William George 431
Monoghan, Hugh 399–401
Montgomerie family 145–8, 178, 345–6
Montgomerie, Hew Seton 'Seton' 345–7, **413**
Montgomerie, Oswald 147
Montgomery, Bernard **423**
Müller, Max Ritter von 248, **248**, 295
Munich **16–7**

Munro, Roderick 'Robert' 238, 240–2, **244**, 415
Murray, Keith 350–1
Musgrave, Christopher 277
Myhill, Alfred William 431

N

Napier 41
Neill, Lyonel Clare Fyans 431
Nethersole, Michael 314
New York Times 425
New Zealand 1914–1918 Airmen's Association 425–6, **426–7**
New Zealand Air Force 421, 424
New Zealand Army 21
New Zealand Defence Force 42, 44
air force development 1908–1914 21–3, 51–3
air force development 1914–1918 57–9, 126, 128, 142
air force development post-war 421–2, 424
naval development 1914–1918 57–9
New Zealand Expeditionary Force 57–9, 90–2, 131, 142
in transit **58**, 64–71, **68–9**, 143–6
New Zealand Flying School 125–33, **127**, **130**, 141–2, 215–6, 421
New Zealand Herald 35, 40, 45, 51, 161, 210
New Zealand Motor & Cycle Journal 229
New Zealand Permanent Air Force 421, 424
New Zealand Pioneer (Maori) Battalion 246
New Zealand Volunteers 304
Nicol, Hector 431
Nicoll, Thomas 326
Nielsen, Peter 363, 431
night flying 85, 180–4, 211, 216–7, 220–1, 297–300, 320–2, 365–8, 371
Nivelle Offensive 238, 246, 250, 263
Nixon, John 106, 109–10, 114–5
Noble-Campbell, Cecil 371, 376
Noss, Arthur 292
NZEF *see* New Zealand Expeditionary Force

O

observation *see* reconnaissance
observation balloons *see* aircraft
Operation Georgette 346–50

Operation Michael 319–21, 337–42, 347, **348–9**
Orange, Vincent 7, 298
Orr, Eric 154–5
Otago Daily Times 53, 198

P

parachutes 227–31, **231**
Paris, Dorothy 'Dol' **291**, 298, **418**
Park, Keith 7, 82, 96, 171, 227, 289–98, **290**, **296**, 394–6, 416, **417**
leadership 350, 355–8, 419, 425
Parsons, Forrest Gale 224, 431
Passchendaele *see* Ypres
Paul, Carrick 416
Payne, Godfrey 269–70
Pearce, George 28
Pearse, Richard 32
Pepperdine, Charlotte 'Peps' 321–2, **323**, 333
Perth 26
Petre, Henry 101, **108**, 109–10, 114
Pettigrew, Gordon **244**, 303–5, 420
photography *see* cameras & photography
Pitcher, Laurence 'Laurie' 101–2, 103, 114, 119–20
Pomeroy, John 181
Poole, John 169
Porter, Wilson 339–42
Powell, George Aubyn 224, 431
Powley, Alfred **33**, 35
Press 139, 186
Pugh, John 394

R

RAF *see* Royal Air Force
Ranken, Madeline 343
Rankin darts *see* armaments
Ransley, Frank 357
Rasmussen, Henry 80, 168–9
reconnaissance 61–4, 72–3, 193, 195, 224, **232–3**, 238–40, 263–6 *see also* cameras & photography
Mesopotamia 101, 106, 109, 114–6
recreation & tourism 154–60
recruitment 81–6, 90–4, 128–30 *see also*; Royal Air Force; Royal Flying Corps; Royal Naval Air Service
Māori 139–41
Reeves, Edmund **97**, 149
Reeves, Fabian Pember 267, 273, 432
Reeves, William Pember & Maud 267

Reid, John Laurie 211, 432
Reid, Peggy 226, 230, 314
Reilly, Alice 64, **65**
Reilly, Hugh **54–5**, 59–60, 62–4, **65**,
    71–3, 419, 421
    Mesopotamia 101–2, 106, 109,
    110–7, 120
RFC *see* Royal Flying Corps
Rhodes, Mary Ann 87
Rhodes-Moorhouse, Linda (Morritt)
    89–90
Rhodes-Moorhouse, William
    87–90, **88**, 139
Rhys-Davids, Arthur 292, 314,
    339–40
Rhys-Davids, Caroline 339–40
Rich, Gordon 149
Richards, Henry Stokes 432
Richards, Leonard 353
Richardson, George 21
Richardson, Stuart Herbert 397–8,
    432
Richthofen, Lothar von **236–7**
Richthofen, Manfred von 235–6,
    236–7, 280, 289, 307, 332–3,
    356–7, 357–8
Ridley, Claude 183
RNAS *see* Royal Naval Air Service
Robb, James 392–3
Roberts, E. G. 'Robie' 299
Robin, Alfred 23
Robinson, Leefe 221–2
Robinson, William 160
Robson, Herbert **127**
Rolls, Charles 230
Ross 251
Rowell, Robin 230
Royal Aero Club 24, 128
Royal Air Force 84, 320, 342, 389,
    421 *see also* recruitment; specific
    aircraft; specific airmen; specific
    squadrons
Royal Aircraft Factory 21–2, 60 *see
    also* aircraft, Royal Aircraft Factory
Royal Army Medical Corps 251, 326
Royal Flying Corps 59, 60–2, 72–3,
    84–5 *see also* recruitment; specific
    aircraft; specific airmen; specific
    squadrons
Royal Flying Corps & RAF units
    1 Brigade 419
    1 Squadron 195, **204–5**
    3 Squadron 397
    4 Squadron 60, 62

6 Training Squadron 171
7 Squadron 211
8 Kite Balloon Section 85
8 Squadron 215, 311–2
10 Squadron 350
11 Squadron 197, 224, 245
18 Squadron 188–90, 193
19 Squadron 292, 307
23 Squadron 305–8
24 Squadron 252
25 Squadron 193, 240
26 (South African) Squadron
    207–10
27 Squadron 285, 351
30 Squadron 71–2, 114–21
32 Squadron 277, 281–2
33 (Home Defence) Squadron 298,
    371
38 (Home Defence) Squadron 371
39 (Home Defence) Squadron 221
41 Squadron 327
48 Squadron 227, 249, 290–2,
    295–7, 355–9, 394–6
50 (Home Defence) Squadron
    350, 419
53 Squadron 410
54 Squadron 332–3
56 Squadron 292, 302–4, 337–8,
    419
59 Squadron 249
60 Squadron 189, 242–5, 249–52
65 Squadron 305
66 Squadron 273–4, 292
70 Squadron 292–5
74 Squadron 351–4, 404, 419
75 (Home Defence) Squadron 301
79 Squadron 404, 406
84 Squadron 332–3, 363
85 Squadron 332, **377**, 378, 380–1,
    382–3, 384, 389–90
92 Squadron **386–7**, 390–3
94 Squadron 384
98 Squadron 409
100 Squadron 321–5, 326, 348–50,
    365–7
101 Squadron 321, 325–6
108 Squadron 408
151 Squadron 396
205 Squadron 342
208 Squadron 346
215 Squadron 399
Eleventh (Army) Wing 419
Independent Force 365–9, 399
Tenth (Army) Wing 419

Thirteenth (Army) Wing 419
Royal Marines 87
Royal Naval Air Service 61,
    81–2, 84, 87, 90, 180, 255 *see
    also* recruitment; specific
    aircraft; specific airmen; specific
    squadrons
Royal Naval Air Service units
    1 (Naval) Squadron 255–9, 267–70
    3 (Naval) Squadron 274–6
    5 (Naval) Squadron 218, 330–4, 337
    6 (Naval) Squadron 267
Royal New Zealand Air Force 421,
    424
Russell, Andres 93
Russell, Francis Gerald 211, 213,
    215, 432
Russell, Herbert **147**, 195, 198–203,
    211, 421, 424
Russell, Lawrence Dobrée 211–2,
    213, 215, 432

S

Saalfeld, Baron von 193
Samson, Charles 'Sammy' 82, 87
Sanchez-Besa flying school 24
Saw, Ralph 331
Schäfer, Karl Emil **236–7**
Schlieffen Plan 60–1
Schneider, Kurt 252
School of Military Aeronautics
    153–4
Scotland, James 'Will'
    Mesopotamia 101–3, 106, 111–2,
    114
    pre-war 45–51, **47**, 51
    wartime 59, 121, 125, 133, 415
Scott, Alan 'Jack' 242–5, **243**,
    249–52, 350, 352, 416, 419
Scott, Robert Falcon 199
Scott, Walter 332–3
Second Army 263
Sharland, Frederic James **127**, **244**,
    306, 308, 415, 432
Shepherd, Arthur 224
ships
    aircraft carriers 372, 376
    Arawa 64, 148
    Athenic **58**, 64–6, **68–9**
    Hampshire 71
    HMS *Ark Royal* 82
    HMS *Furious* **360–1**, 372, **372–3**,
    375–8
    HMS *New Zealand* 19, 59

HMS *Powerful* 28
HMS *Queen Elizabeth* 77
HMS *Vindictive* 420
Karamea 146
Lusitania 148
Maunganui 66
Mokoia 149
Paparoa 144
Remuera 145
SS *Limerick* 188
Terra Nova 199
Waitemata 66
Ship's Camels *see* aircraft, Sopwith Camel
Shirtcliffe, William 238–40, 415
Shores, Christopher 9
Simeon, George 343
Simeon, Harriet 343–5, **344**, 420
Skinner, Arthur 71–3, 78, **97**, 285, 420–1
Skinner, Jack 66
The Sky Their Battlefield II 7
Sleeman, James 138
Sloss, James Duncan 137, 143, **147**, 149, 408–9, 411–2, 432
Sloss, Robert 66–7
Smart, Bernard 375–6
Smith-Barry, Robert 170–2, 320
Smuts, Jan 342
Sockburn *see* airfields; Canterbury (NZ) Aviation Company
Solomon, Hubert Philip **244**, 298–9, 301–2, 376, 420, 432
Somme 82, 96, 186, 188, 193, 195, 210–6, 224, 245 *see also* Western Front
Sopwith Aviation Company 9, 52, 255 *see also* aircraft, Sopwith
South Island 45–9
Spear, Cyril 264
Spence, Daniel George 432
Spragg, Wesley Neal 85, **97**, 432
Stedman, Ralph 273–4, 292
Steele, Charles 395
Steele, Mary 277
Steele, Thomas Lancaster 432
Stone, Arthur 'Wizard' **36–7**, 38–42, 51
stunt flying *see* aerobatics
submarine warfare 148–9
Sun 28, 46, 51
Sutherland, Donald 199
Sutherland, Ernest Taniwha 139–41, **140**, 148
Sydney 27–8

T
Talbot, Arthur Sydney 432
Talbot, William Caithness 432
Tayler, St Cyprian 283–4
test flying 35, 181, 193, 195, 215, 338
   see also Experimental Stations
Thames Star 281
theatre *see* recreation & tourism
Third Army 338
Toulmin, Vincent **97**, 207, 209–10
tourism *see* recreation & tourism
Townshend, Charles 106, 109, 114–9
training *see also* specific aircraft; specific airmen; specific schools
   pre-war 21–3, 31, 45, 51–2, 60
   wartime 125–42, 153–4, 160–72, 290–2, 320, 371
Trenchard, Hugh **20–1**, 22, 186–8, 210–1, 236–8, 249, 365–7, 421
Two Roads: International government or militarism; Will England lead the way? 399

U
Udet, Ernst 236
Umbers, Clarence 78–9, 172

V
Vavasour, Rudolph Dunstan 432
Veale, Allan Adolphus 432
Voss, Vivian 358
Voss, Werner 307

W
Waihi Daily Telegraph 18
Wairarapa Age 18
Wairarapa Daily Times 103
Wakefield, Charles 178, 184
Walsh, Leo & Vivian 32, **33**, **34**, 35, **122–3**, 125–33, 141–2, 164, 215–6, 415, 421
Walsh, Veronica & Doreen 32
Wanganui Chronicle 90–1
The War of the Worlds 16, 18
War Office 52, 59–60, 93, 128–30, 139
Ward, Joseph 22–3, 32
Warneford, Reginald 255
Warnock, John 273–4, 292
Warnock, Owen **97**
Watson, Herbert 347–8, **355**, 393–4, 416
Waud, Philip Courtenay 432
weapons *see* armaments

Wellington 49–50
Wells, George 278, 281
Wells, H. G. 16–7
Western Front 9, 81–2, 87, 126, 186–90, 199–200, **228**, 235–8, **286–7**, 310–4, 319–21, 331–2, 409–10 *see also* specific offensives; specific places
White, Melville Arthur 66–71, 77–81, 154, 168, 252–4, 432
White, Percival 263–5, 268, 415
White, Thomas 102, 106, **108**, 109–11, 114, 120–1
White, Trevor 'Tiny' 93–4
Wigram Aerodrome *see* airfields, Wigram; Canterbury (NZ) Aviation Company
Wigram, Henry 16, 18–20, 42, 59, 132–4, **134–5**, 138, 415, 421
Wilding, Anthony 86–7
Wilding, Edwyn 87, **97**, 137–8, 141–2, 154–5, 160
Wilkes, Thomas 421
Wilson, Alexander 73
Wolff, Kurt 236, **236–7**, 270, 278
Women's Royal Air Force (WRAF) 342–5
Woods, James 154

Y
Yeats-Brown, Francis 111, 120
Ypres 89, 235, 263, 289–97, 302–10
   see also Western Front

ABOUT THE FIRST WORLD WAR CENTENARY HISTORY PROGRAMME

Massey University, the Ministry for Culture and Heritage (MCH), the New Zealand Defence Force and the Royal New Zealand Returned and Services' Association have joined forces to produce a series of authoritative print histories on New Zealand and the First World War. Scholarly yet accessible to broad audiences, the works in this series draw on an extensive range of primary sources held in New Zealand, Britain and elsewhere, and contain high-quality maps and illustrations. Together they form the first complete and detailed account of New Zealand's First World War experience.

These print histories will be complemented by digital resources published through the www.firstworldwar.govt.nz website, part of the Ministry for Culture and Heritage's NZHistory.net.nz site. The programme's historians are also contributing to other centenary activities, including major international conferences, museum and art exhibitions, television documentaries, heritage trails and commemorative events in New Zealand and overseas.

The Centenary History Programme Governance Group is co-chaired by Gerald Hensley and Massey University Assistant Vice-Chancellor Research, Academic and Enterprise Giselle Byrnes. The group includes MCH Chief Historian Neill Atkinson, Defence Force Historian John Crawford, Massey University Professor of War Studies Glyn Harper, and other representatives of the four agencies.

More information about the Centenary History series can be found at: http://ww100.govt.nz/first-world-war-centenary-print-histories.

This volume of the Centenary History would not have been possible without generous donations to the Massey University Foundations for this purpose. The Governance Group of the Centenary History Programme would like to acknowledge and thank the following organisations for their generosity:

The New Zealand Defence Force

Air New Zealand

Hawker Pacific

Safe Air

Kaman Aerospace Group

CAE Australia Limited

The Governance Group would also like to acknowledge the support provided by the Air Force Museum Wigram in bringing this book to publication.

MASSEY
UNIVERSITY
PRESS

First published in 2017 by Massey University Press
Private Bag 102904, North Shore Mail Centre Auckland 0745, New Zealand
www.masseypress.ac.nz

Text copyright © Adam Claasen, 2017
Images copyright © as credited, 2017

Design by Kate Barraclough
Cover photographs: Imperial War Museum Q 44803 (front top), Air Force Museum of
New Zealand Coningham 92 Squadron (front bottom) and Imperial War Museum Q
12051 (back cover).
Maps: Geographx
Endpaper illustrations: from *Airplanes of the World 1490 to 1962*, by Douglas Rolfe and
Alexis Dawydoff (New York: Simon and Schuster, 1962).

A catalogue record for this book is available from the National Library of New Zealand

Printed and bound in China by Everbest

ISBN: 978-0-9941407-8-4